UNIVERSITY LIBRARY
W. S. U. - STEVENS POINT

PRINCIPLES OF ECONOMICS

PRINCIPLES OF ECONOMICS

DANIEL B. SUITS

PROFESSOR OF ECONOMICS

UNIVERSITY OF MICHIGAN

HARPER & ROW, PUBLISHERS

NEW YORK, EVANSTON, AND LONDON

Cover photographs are from:

American Airlines / 8
Michel Craig / 1
Free Lance Photographers Guild / 2
Emily Harste / 1
International Business Machines / 1
Lockheed Aircraft Corporation / 1
United Nations / 2
United States Department of Agriculture / 2

PRINCIPLES OF ECONOMICS

Copyright © 1970 by Daniel B. Suits

Printed in the United States of America. All rights reserved. No part of this book may be used or reproduced in any manner whatsoever without written permission except in the case of brief quotations embodied in critical articles and review. For information address Harper & Row, Publishers, Inc., 49 East 33rd Street, New York, N.Y. 10016.

LIBRARY OF CONGRESS CATALOG CARD NUMBER: 74–108411

HB
171.5
.S93
c.3

To Adelaide

182805

PREFACE

Work on this book began six years ago when, after working primarily with graduate students for a number of years, I resumed teaching the economic principles course at The University of Michigan. There were two important reasons for returning to the teaching of beginners. The first was the recognition that this is probably the most important job an economist can do. It is in the beginning course, after all, that we reach the largest number of students. If we hope to help future legislators, executives, businessmen, labor leaders, and citizens at large make better social decisions, this is where we must do the job. Even the one student in fifteen or twenty who goes on to major in economics gets his first (and frequently his last!) overall view of the economic system as a functioning social structure in a beginning class in economic principles.

At the same time, I came increasingly to feel that we could improve courses at the beginning level. A student usually comes to the principles course with a strong interest in the subject matter—he knows that economics not only touches the intimate concerns of his daily life, but provides useful insights into the society around him and into the dynamics of history itself. Yet many students initially view the subject of economics as "too theoretical," "impractical," "abstract," or, in the most recent voicing of the same complaint, "not relevant."

Listening to such expressions, I came to believe that a great part of the difficulty lay in the way we were presenting the material. We were supplying students with powerful theoretical tools, but we were rarely demonstrating their power. We taught students how to manipulate economic theory for its own sake, but we rarely showed them how to apply it in accounting for observed social behavior. In short, we were showing them the abstractions, but not what it was that we were abstracting from.

My hope was to improve the effectiveness of the course by emphasizing the role of economic theory as a useful contribution to our understanding of social behavior. It should be possible, I thought, to bring "theory" and "practice" into close unity. My first attempts to accomplish this involved nothing more ambitious than the preparation of mimeographed supplements and case studies to illustrate applications of the theory already presented in other texts. But I soon found that studying these applications not only strengthened and deepened students' understanding of economic principles, often clarifying theoretical points that had been confusing, but it actually made economic theory itself easier for them to understand. It became evident that, when the theory was developed in connection with the reality it was supposed to explain, it not only became more solid and real to the student, it became technically more sophisticated and easier to teach all at the same time. Moreover, the end result was a set of economic principles immediately recognizable in the unfolding events described daily in the news media. Students' reception to these ideas, and their enthusiastic involvement in the resulting principles course, eventually led to the preparation of this book.

The book covers the syllabus of the standard principles course, in this case organized with macroeconomics in the first half and microeconomics in the second. Its contribution is not meant to be in the choice of topics covered, but in the way in which economic theory is developed. The reader can best judge the result himself, but it may be worthwhile to say a few words about the book's general organization and structure. Following a brief introduction, Part One opens with a straightforward chapter on the national accounts. After the concepts of production and the gross national product have been developed, they are put to work in a discussion of poor nations and their behavior. This leads naturally to the idea of opportunity cost, and the classical roles of specialization and capital formation emerge in connection with problems of economic development. Although the discussion of business enterprise is relegated to the microeconomics section of many texts, it is included here along with the material on economic development to emphasize the relationship of institutional structure to economic performance. Part One concludes with a rapid survey of recent U.S. economic history, not only as an interesting and important topic in its own right, but to bring together the elements of the Part and to serve as a lead-in to the material that follows.

Part Two is motivated by the twin problems of unemployment and inflation. The multiplier is developed through the use of a simple flow chart that emphasizes the dynamics of income changes rather than the determination of the static equilibrium level. The result is a simple but realistic view of economic fluctuations that I have found is easier for students to grasp than the usual presentation, and that also builds foundations for subsequent analysis and forecasting. Student preparation of an economic forecast for the coming year is a standard feature of my course. Applications of this kind not only present convincing evidence that the theory really works, they also foster a realistic appreciation of the limitations of economic analysis.

The microeconomic material begins in Part Three with an analysis of demand curves and the role of demand in allocation. Prices set by business firms are treated in a separate chapter, and it is here that what is probably the largest departure from the traditional presentation occurs. By emphasizing the importance of pricing margins and markups within a context of realistic costs, price theory emerges not only as a believable set of principles, but in terms that lend themselves directly to empirical demonstration. The behavior of markups becomes an important element of the industrial behavior examined in subsequent chapters, and the vital topic of environmental pollution is treated as a special aspect of industrial behavior.

Part Four concludes the book with the analysis of income distribution, first in terms of functional shares. The emphasis here is on factor costs and on their important role in the allocation of economic resources. Analysis of income distribution on a family basis leads naturally to the discussion of poverty in America. The final chapter serves to review generally some of the theoretical concepts, to place economics among other sciences of human behavior, and to lead the student toward the more intensive study of economics in later courses.

The book as a whole has been kept comparatively short to provide ample opportunity for the use of supplementary materials. I regularly have students read the current Economic Report of the President as a supplement to Part Two and employ a variety of materials to augment other Parts, selected according to the areas that appear to be most interesting at the time. A wide assortment of excellent materials is now available for this purpose, many of which are included as suggested further reading in the Study Guide designed to accompany this text.

Quite literally thousands of people participated in the preparation of this book. I am indebted to my many colleagues in the economics department at The University of Michigan for their sympathetic interest in the work. Particular thanks are given to Professors W. H. Locke Anderson, Morris Bornstein, Harvey Brazer, George Johnson, Saul Hymans, Harold Levinson, Shorey Peterson, Harold Shapiro, Frederick Scherer, Warren Smith, Wayne Snyder, and Robert Stern, each of whom gave generously of his advice and criticism or provided me with material from his field of specialty. In other schools, Professors Robert F. Adams, Robert B. Fabian, Frank A. Farnsworth, Max E. Fletcher, Stanley Lebergott, Milton Nadworny, and James A. Stephenson read most of the first draft of the manuscript, and their many suggestions greatly improved the final version. Thanks are also due the many young economists who taught with me as the book evolved and whose advice and feedback were invaluable. Most helpful were: Dennis Appleyard, Gerald Auten, Richard Barfield, Peter Barth, Michael Bass, Richard Billsborrow, Irwin Blackstone, Rafford Boddy, Barry Bosworth, Bruce Cameron, John Chang, Francis Connor, Dave Denny, Larry Dildine, John Edgren, Gail Ellis, Dawn Elvis, Eric Fredland, Deborah Freedman, William Freithaler, Bruce Gensemer, Paul Gernant, Alan Ginsberg, Steven Gold, John Hambor, William Hewett, Thomas Hutcheson, Anna James, Gregory Jump, Sonders Kelman, David Lane, Jane Lane, Fred Leonard, Ewen McCann, Craig Morgan, Richard Morganstern, Howard Myers, Seamus O'Cleire-acain, Ann Putallaz, David Rapport, Sandra Rice, Charles Roehrig, Elizabeth Rothman, Leonard Sahling, Larry Sawers, Joseph Schulman, Marvin Snowbarger, Douglas Stewart, Fred Surls, Larry Thompson, E. Lane Vanderslice, Wayne Vroman, Howard Wachtel, William Wares, David Zinn, and Michael Zweig.

I also thank the three thousand students who read, argued about, added to, corrected, and otherwise helped to shape the final version of this book. The services of Vivian Choi, Shirley Ann Hoffer, and Patricia Ramsey were invaluable in carefully and speedily typing the many versions of the manuscript. Finally, of course, thanks to my wife Adelaide for her patience and tolerant understanding through the entire process.

DANIEL B. SUITS

CONTENTS

CHAPTER 1

What Is Economics?

Economics involves the study of topics like wealth and poverty, money and banks, incomes, taxes, prosperity and depression, big business and labor unions, and hundreds of other matters that intimately affect the way we live. Economic forces surround our daily lives, influencing how easy or how hard it is to get a job, how much we can earn in our chosen occupations, and how much our paychecks will buy after we receive them. Economic factors are major concerns in governments' decisions about how much to spend and for what purposes, and how much to raise in taxes and who should be taxed as well as in their evaluations of the consequences of war, peace, and disarmament. Urban slums, job discrimination, unequal educational opportunities, and civil rights have important economic consequences for all of us, for both those who are discriminated against and those who are not. At a still more global level, economic factors are involved in birth, health, death, population growth, and the dynamics of history. In fact, probably without exception, each topic in this book not only touches somewhere on your own personal life but is also important to some current economic problem of government or social policy and is, at the same time, involved in the long-range concerns of human history.

PRODUCTION

The common thread that runs through all of these topics, binding them together into a coherent body of study, is that, one way or another, each deals with the way society produces and uses goods and services. Practically nothing that we eat, wear, or use comes to us directly from nature. A loaf of bread is the end result of a long series of operations that begins with planting and harvesting grain and proceeds through milling, baking, and shipping to the point at which the housewife can pick the loaf off the grocer's shelf. The driver filling his tank at a service station is taking the final step in a long chain of activities: drilling oil wells, moving petroleum in ships and pipelines, chemical treatment, refining, and storage. The same is generally true of all goods.

The process of bridging the gap between the original resources of nature and the needs of the final consumer is *production*. Production includes any activity that makes goods and services available to people. It is not restricted to work on tangible physical commodities, but encompasses services as well. Doctors, lawyers, teachers, and barbers are productive, as are actors, musicians, entertainers, and others who perform services for our benefit. It is particularly worth noting that the services of wholesalers, retailers, bankers, and similar "middlemen" are an important part of the productive process. After all, it is not enough simply to manufacture the product. Before it can be used it must be made available to the family that wants to buy it, a job that requires the services of store clerks, managers, transportation workers, and many others.

Production as a Social Process

Converting raw natural resources into usable goods and getting them where they are wanted is an almost unbelievably complicated process. Even in the simplest case, it involves the coordinated efforts of hundreds of different people. To take a specific example, consider the number of people who, in one way or another, contributed to getting this book into your hands. In the first instance, the book probably came to you from a store, or from somebody who got it from a store. The purchase directly involved a clerk and possibly a cashier, while behind the scenes were a manager, perhaps other clerks, and probably a banker to handle the money. Beyond this,

however, the sale involved the carpenters, masons, architects, and laborers who constructed the store building, using tools and machinery produced by still other workers to assemble glass, cement, masonry, wood, paper, and other materials produced by still other workers.

The book probably arrived at the store in a truck manufactured by automobile workers from steel, glass, plastics, aluminum, and other materials. The workers used machines made in other industries by still other workers. The truck burned gasoline which came originally from an oil well and was shipped across country in a pipeline (that had to be built, maintained, and operated by somebody) to a refinery where other workers used other equipment to convert it into fuel.

Millions of people are already involved with your book and we have only reached the printer! The book itself took shape on paper produced from wood pulp derived from timber, in ink produced from chemicals obtained from wells, mines, and farms. It was printed on presses manufactured in another industry using machines manufactured in still another industry where still other machines were employed. Each of these machines required steel, glass, rubber, and other materials as well as fuel, raw materials, and services to function, and all involved shipping over railroads, highways, and waterways using still more fuel. Nor should we forget the army of typists, filing clerks, office workers, bankers, insurance men, and others involved at each stage, nor the workers at the utilities responsible for the power, light, water, heat, telephone, and other services, not to mention the workers that strung the power lines, laid the pipes, and produced the materials from which they were made.

There is no need to go further, for the process has no end. The contribution of each worker, anywhere along the line, requires the services of many more. The use of a machine at any point in the process is only possible because the machine was produced at an earlier time using machines produced still earlier, back and back in an intricate tangle that extends, quite literally, to the stone axes and flint chips of the cave dweller. In short, if we could really identify all the people whose efforts went into this one book, we should probably include a substantial fraction of the people who ever produced anything during the entire history of mankind.

The Circular Flow of the Economy

This intricate tangle of human relationships is not a gigantic mob scene, but orderly human behavior, controlled and directed toward specific ends. The social process may be too lengthy and too complex to trace back or even to describe, but it *did* pro-

duce this book and get it into your hands.

The network of institutions that controls production and consumption by the members of a society is called an *economic system*, or an *economy*. We have already seen that an economic system is much too complicated to be described realistically, but Figure 1 is a useful, if highly schematic, representation of the activity of an economic system like ours. The figure represents 2 sets of social institutions. People organized into families and households are located at the right, while farms, mines, factories, and other producing units organized as business firms appear at the left. Productive activity is represented by the black curve as a clockwise flow around the figure. The lower branch of the flow represents the action of households in supplying business firms with the labor of their mem-

FIGURE 1 THE ECONOMIC CIRCULAR FLOW

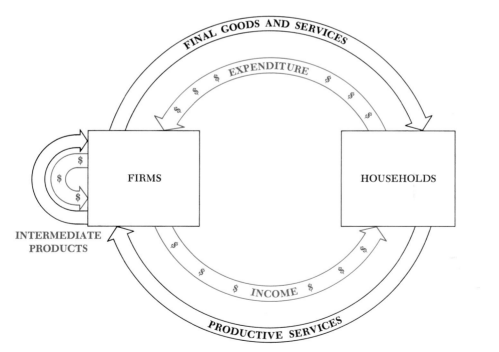

bers and the services of the land and other property they own. The business firms hire these productive services and organize them to turn out products desired by the households. The productive process also involves a complex flow of materials and products among different business firms, as represented by the separate black clockwise flow at the extreme left of the figure. The resulting products are then supplied by the producer firms to households for their use, as represented by the flow back to the households on the upper branch of the black curve.

Accompanying each movement of goods or productive services there is an equal and opposite flow of money, represented by the blue curve as a counterclockwise flow around the figure. On the lower branch, households receive income in the form of wages, salaries, rent, interest, and profit for the services contributed by their members and the property they own. This money income, in turn, permits them to buy the things they need, providing a money flow of spending equal and opposite to the flow of real goods on the upper branch. In addition, money circulates among business firms in payment for intermediate materials and supplies as represented at the far left.

ECONOMIC RELATIONSHIPS

This circular flow of economic activity ties together firms and households in such a fashion that a change in the behavior of any group alters the circumstances of the others and leads them to change their behavior in turn. For example, when manufacturers discover how to make more shoes with the same amount of labor, their efforts to sell the expanded output lead them to reduce prices, thus inducing households to buy more shoes. But the influence of the change does not end there. To turn out more shoes, shoe manufacturers need more

leather, and their increased buying pushes up leather prices. The higher cost of leather makes briefcases, luggage, and other such articles more expensive and leads households to buy fewer than before, perhaps purchasing items made from plastic or other materials instead. At the same time, the higher price of leather may induce producers to turn out more leather, perhaps importing hides for the purpose or making it profitable for small local meat packers to save and ship hides that would otherwise have been discarded.

Each step in the adjustment process defines an *economic relationship* involving two or more *variables,* or measured aspects of economic phenomena. There was, in the first place, a relationship between the amount of labor needed and the price of shoes. A second relationship connected the price of shoes to the number of pairs that households bought. A third involved the price of leather and the amount of leather going into briefcases and luggage, while still another connected leather production to leather prices.

Study of Relationships in Economics and in Laboratory Science

Economics involves the study of these relationships and the way they fit together in a system that transmits to other parts the consequences of a change in one of its parts.

In terms of the final object to be attained the study of economics is like physics, chemistry, or any other science. Where a chemist is concerned with molecular structure and its effect on the behavior of compounds, an economist may be concerned with market structure and its effect on the behavior of industries. The chemist may be interested in altering molecular structure by chemical action to obtain a compound with certain desirable properties, while the economist might be interested in altering market structure by legislative action to induce certain desirable characteristics in industrial behavior. Each attempts to observe and measure certain relationships to gain better understanding of and control over the world in which we live.

Beyond this, however, any close resemblance between laboratory and social science ends. The great power of sciences like physics and chemistry is their ability to explore relationships by experimenting in a controlled laboratory environment from which all variations in extraneous factors have been excluded, but which permits the variables under study to be freely manipulated. A scientist who wants to explore the effect of light on a chemical reaction can perform his experiment over and over with compounds of the same purity, maintained at the same temperature in a laboratory environment in which light intensity can be varied and controlled to suit his purpose and which is free of outside influences.

The economist is not so fortunate. He cannot cut off a piece of the economic system and bring it into a convenient laboratory. He must deal with the whole in all its vast complexity or with nothing. There is no way to put a family in a test tube, inject a little extra income under controlled conditions and observe the reaction. Nor can the stock market be put in a box shielded from other economic events to see how it responds when profit expectations are raised and lowered under controlled conditions.

In place of the highly controlled observations of the physicist or chemist, the economist must depend on extremely imperfect observations made under a wide range of circumstances. The best he can do is to find principles that hold on the average, or as a tendency, or for a large proportion of cases. This is why carefully stated economic relationships abound with terms like "on the average," "tends to," "generally," and "other things being equal."

Depicting Economic Relationships

The nature of an economic relationship is most conveniently represented by a simple graph or chart. Although most students are already familiar with graphical representation, the properties of economic relationships are worth special consideration. As a convenient example, let us explore the relationship between the amount of income a family receives as one variable and the amount its members spend on recreation as another. The idea behind the relationship is that people with higher incomes take more time for recreation, take up more expensive sports, buy better equipment, and consequently tend to spend more. Note the use of the term "tend to"; we know that not all people with higher incomes spend more on recreation. Some do and some do not, since each of us lives his own life in his own way. At the same time, if we consider numbers of families, we should expect that the *average* expenditure on recreation among those with higher incomes would exceed the *average* expenditure of those with lower incomes.

This is borne out by the results of interviews with 10 families chosen to represent different income levels. The income and recreation expenditure reported by each family is recorded in Table 1. A glance down the table reveals the expected ten-

TABLE 1   INCOME AND ANNUAL
RECREATION EXPENDITURES
OF 10 FAMILIES, 1961

FAMILY NUMBER	INCOME	RECREATION EXPENDITURE
1	$1,500	$200
2	2,000	140
3	2,750	160
4	3,500	240
5	4,500	160
6	5,500	260
7	6,500	260
8	7,500	380
9	8,500	340
10	9,500	460

dency. Taken as a group, the families in the lowest income brackets spent much less than the average spent by the families with the highest incomes. Of course, when we compare individual families, we find that higher income was not always accompanied by higher recreation outlay. For example, the $200 spent by family number 1 exceeded even the spending by family number 5 despite the considerable difference in their incomes, and other cases of this kind can be observed throughout the table.

This same relationship can be represented graphically as in Figure 2, in which each point represents the income and recreation spending of one of the families. Income is represented by the distance the point lies to the right, measured along the horizontal axis. Families with low incomes correspond to points close to the origin at the left, while high-income families correspond to points farther out to the right. The number of dollars the family spent for recreation is represented by the height of the point measured along the vertical axis. Families with low expenditure are represented by points near the bottom of the figure, while those with high expenditures correspond to points located higher up. Each dot in Figure 2 represents the family with the corresponding number in Table 1. Family number 4, as shown, is represented by the dot corresponding to $3,500 on the income scale and $240 on the spending scale. Family number 9 is represented by the dot corresponding to $8,500 of income and $340 of recreational spending, and so on.

Once all the points have been located on the chart, the economic relationship is represented by a smooth curve drawn through the midst of the points. The line does not exactly correspond to any one family, but represents the *tendency* of recreational spending to vary with family income. If income were the only cause of differences in spending, all the dots would lie on the smooth curve, and we would have the same kind of exact relationship

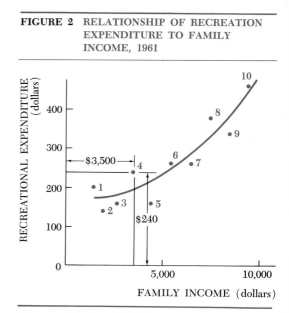

FIGURE 2   RELATIONSHIP OF RECREATION EXPENDITURE TO FAMILY INCOME, 1961

SOURCE: Data from Table 1.

that a physicist or chemist might obtain in a laboratory. But each of our dots represents a real family. In addition to its income, its behavior depends on the number, age, and state of health of its members, the region of the country they live in, their attitudes and habits, and so on. For this reason, the dots do not lie on a smooth curve, but scatter around it under the varying influence of all these other factors.

Interpreting Economic Relationships

The smooth curve of Figure 2 represents the way rising income *contributes to* higher spending on recreation but in the case of individual families, this contribution is often offset by other influences. For example, if we compare a family with a 35-year-old husband to a higher-income family in which the head is 55 years old, we are likely to find the older family spending less on recreation than the younger, despite its higher income. The difference in income might be more than offset by the difference in age, since older people tend to spend less on recreation than younger people do. Another expression of the same idea is that the smooth curve shows the effect of family income on recreation outlays, *other things being equal.* That is, given 2 families exactly alike except in income, the family with the higher income would spend more on recreation. Naturally, in comparing any real families these "other things" stubbornly refuse to remain "equal," with the resulting departure of observed behavior from the smooth relationship.

The precise way that income differences contribute to differences in spending is described by the location and shape of the curve. The height of the curve at each income level represents the amount we would expect families at that income level to spend on the average. The curve slopes upward (that is, it is higher at the right-hand end than it is at the left) to represent the tendency of families with higher incomes to spend more for recreation than families with lower incomes. The steepness of the curve indicates how much recreational spending tends to rise as income increases. The flat segment at the left indicates that, among low-income families, a rise in income tends to be accompanied by little or no increase in outlays for recreation. This is entirely reasonable, since low-income families have many more urgent uses for any extra income they earn. At higher incomes, the family has already satisfied most of its needs and can devote a larger percentage of any income increase to fun, with the resulting increase in the steepness of the curve as it moves into the higher levels of income at the right.

Charts like Figure 2 appear throughout this book, although frequently, in order to focus attention on the theory rather than the data, we will omit the scatter of points and merely present the final relationship as a smooth curve. These curves are powerful tools for exploring and understanding how our economic system operates, for predict-ing what to expect under different circumstances, and for prescribing government policies to improve economic performance. But we must always remember that these relationships represent only "tendencies" that hold "on the average," indicating the contribution of only one factor to a final result that also depends on other things.

Problems in Estimating Economic Relationships with Charts and Graphs

In order to make the discussion as clear as possible, we chose an example of data that were particularly well behaved. Other factors varied enough to show that they were present, but not enough to interfere with the measurement we were trying to make. However, not all cases are so neat. In general, the more the behavior of individual families is influenced by "other things," the less representative they become of the relationship under study. Since variation in "other things" scatter the dots away from the smooth curve, it is evident that if they vary enough, the observed data will correspond to a formless "blob" of points that gives no clue at all to the shape or location of the desired curve. The measurement of economic relationships under these circumstances becomes more difficult, and involves careful analysis of large quantities of data with the aid of powerful statistical techniques. The examination of statistical procedures in economic research can be safely left to more advanced study, but it is important that the student understand at the very outset that observed behavior is the result of the simultaneous influence of many factors and is frequently at odds with what would be predicted "other things being equal." This does not mean that economics is wrong, only that the world is complicated.

When physics and chemistry are brought out of the laboratory, they often exhibit the same phenomenon. A penny and a feather that fall at the same rate when "other things" like air resistance are kept "equal" in a laboratory vacuum, behave quite differently when dropped in the everyday world of air and wind currents. The remarkable difference in their observed behavior does not violate the laws of gravity, but merely represents the way "other things" assert themselves in a real situation.

THE STRUCTURE OF ECONOMICS

As the circular flow of Figure 1 indicates, economic activity involves a complete system that closes back on itself. There is no point at which it is more natural or more logical to begin than any other. No matter where we start or which way we go, we must ultimately come back to the starting point. Moreover, since each part is connected to all the others, each step along the way not only leads into new territory and new relationships, but deepens and enriches our understanding of what has gone before.

For the purposes of study, economics is divided into two very broad branches. One branch, called *macroeconomics* (from the Greek prefix *macro* meaning "large"), involves the study of economic relationships from the standpoint of their effects on the total size of the overall flow of goods and services. The other branch, called *microeconomics* (from the prefix *micro* meaning "small") involves the study of relationships from the standpoint of their effect on the behavior of individual firms and families, particularly how the total output is divided among different kinds of goods and services on the one hand, and how total income is divided among families and households on the other.

Since the economic system is a functioning whole, it would be a mistake to view this grand division as anything more than an expositional convenience. Economic relationships have both macroeconomic and microeconomic implications and our understanding of them is incomplete until we have acquired a grasp of both. Neither division has any logical priority over the other; some students prefer to start their study with the main emphasis on the more global aspects of the field, and some prefer to begin with microeconomics. The choice here has been to devote the first half of the book to the economic system viewed primarily from the macroeconomic standpoint and to follow this by the study of microeconomics in the second half. This arrangement is not essential, however, and with a little rearrangement of chapters, the two halves can be interchanged.

THE STRUCTURE OF THE BOOK

Each half of the book is divided into 2 subdivisions, forming 4 main parts in all, each addressed to an important set of questions about the economic system and its behavior. Part One, "Rich Nations and Poor Nations," introduces some of the important aspects of economic organization by exploring the question of why some nations have so much more productive power than others. What sets limits to the ability of people in some nations to provide for themselves? Why, for example, can the United States with less than half the population turn out a total volume of goods and services 15 times that of India? Or, to look at the problem in another way, what makes the productive power of the United States grow so rapidly that we can turn out 10 times as much for each person alive today than we could 100 years ago? In seeking some insight into these questions we not only discover important elements in our own economic system but begin to understand some of the severe problems now besetting the emerging nations of

Africa and the underdeveloped countries of Asia and South America. In addition, the analysis of the powerful dynamics of economic growth not only points up what is involved in the formulation of effective policies of economic aid, but enriches the understanding of our own economic history.

Part Two "Prosperity and Depression," recognizes that total output does not always live up to productive potential. Sometimes output is so far below capacity that factories stand idle and many men and women ready, willing, and able to work are left unemployed. At other times, society demands a greater total stream of goods and services than the existing labor force and productive equipment can turn out. Unable to meet the demand placed on it, the economy responds with rapidly rising prices. In a recent 7-year span, the U.S. economic system went from a situation in 1961 in which nearly 7 percent of all potential workers were unemployed and prices moved sluggishly, to one in 1968 of severe labor shortage with prices rising 4 percent per year. We must understand what these events mean, and how they are related to the demands that society imposes on its productive resources. We shall explore why this aggregate demand varies and how we can organize our knowledge to forecast economic trouble before it occurs. Most important, we shall explore the problems of using government spending, tax rates, and monetary policy as tools to control the system in an effort to head off economic problems or to minimize their impact.

Part Three, "Prices and Markets," shifts away from the macroeconomic emphasis of the first two parts to examine how the total stream of output is divided up into quantities of individual goods. The kinds of goods and services we produce and use has changed dramatically during our history, and smaller shifts occur almost continually. Between 1955 and 1965, for example, the U.S. clothing industry doubled the total number of pairs of bluejeans turned out

yearly while the number of overcoats and topcoats declined 50 percent. Over the same period the number of airline passengers doubled, while intercity bus travel declined by a third, and the number of rail passengers was cut in half. Such shifts represent the responses of business firms to changes in the buying habits of their customers and the responses of consumer households to changes in prices and in the availability of different kinds of goods. Their analysis involves the important relationship between costs and prices and between prices and consumer buying. We shall find that these relationships are not the same for all commodities and all industries, and we shall explore how industrial behavior is affected by the structure of markets and by differences in competitive conditions. At this point we shall also examine the important role of international trade, and how payments are made among people of different nations. In addition, we shall see how the competitive behavior on which we rely to provide us with better products at lower cost is a major cause of the rising problem of environmental pollution.

Finally, Part Four, "The Distribution of Income," examines how the total stream of income is divided up among different people. We shall try to find out why one worker gets paid more than another, and we shall explore the relationship between rates of pay and the number of workers in different occupations, and the important connection between labor productivity and the buying power of workers' wages. We shall investigate why natural resources earn the rents they do, the effects of different interest rates, and where profits come from. Taking all factors together, we shall examine the striking differences in the incomes of different families and try to find out why we have poverty and starvation in the richest country in the world.

It is essential to remember, however, that the parts outlined are only convenient divisions for study. Each is intricately involved with what has gone before and with what is to come later. Many of the relationships discussed in the early parts reappear later to be explored more fully from another point of view, and once the circuit of the economy has been completed, we return to our starting place to conclude with an overview of the economy as one among a number of systems of social control.

ECONOMICS IN THE NEWS

The student of economics is surrounded by his subject matter. Although he cannot perform delicately controlled laboratory experiments in economics, the daily newspaper, radio, and television newscast, the weekly news magazine, and many specialized media bring the economic world directly to him. Taxes are debated; welfare payments are altered. Wide swings occur on the stock exchange; a crisis develops in the dollar, the pound, the franc, or the mark. Government budgets are furiously debated in Congress, and a state has a fiscal crisis and is unable to pay its bills. Interest rates rise and people are unable to finance new houses. Farmers protest low prices while housewives complain about the cost of food.

The world of daily events is the only laboratory the economist has, and the student who keeps up with the unfolding of economic news increases his understanding not only of the events around him, but of economic principles themselves. These principles are not something to learn in abstraction, or to memorize and forget, but are to be used actively by the citizen in understanding how his society works and how it might be made to work better. The examples and problems included in any book are necessarily those from yesterday's experience. But the study of economics is designed to help with the problems of today. It must be left to the reader to bring the science up to date as he goes along.

SUMMARY

The *production* and *consumption* of goods is a social process involving the coordinated activities of millions of different individuals. Viewed as a whole, the process appears as a *circular flow* in which households provide labor and property to business firms in exchange for incomes which are then spent for goods and services to meet household needs.

An *economic system* consists of the social institutions and relationships by which this activity is coordinated. A change in conditions at one point in the circular flow or in the behavior of any one group of people transmits effects throughout the entire system and alters the behavior of other groups of people. *Economics* is the study of the institutional arrangements and *relationships* by which these influences are transmitted from one part of society to another, of how these social relationships fit together into a system, of how the system coordinates behavior, and of the problems that result.

In the study of these relationships, the economist can neither control the experimental environment nor design families, business firms, or markets to suit his purposes. He must accept the individuality of people and the full complexity of the system. Although his descriptions of economic relationships represent only average behavior and depict only general tendencies to be expected when "other things" are "equal," when combined into a system they provide powerful tools with which to explore economic behavior, to probe economic problems, and to analyse proposed solutions.

PART
ONE
Rich Nations and Poor Nations

There are vast differences in material living standards in the world today. The quantity of goods and services annually enjoyed by the average American, for example, is about 100 times greater than that available to people in some of the emerging nations of Africa. Historically, similar differences can be found in the growth of individual societies. We are all familiar with the contrast between the lot of the average British worker of today and his position in the London of Dickens. Data also show that the average material living standard in modern America is 7 times greater than it was 100 years ago.

These differences involve not only the availability of goods and services, but many other qualities of life. Whether viewed in the cross-section of modern nations or historically, rising output per capita is found associated with smaller families, lower death rates, and longer average life. Rising material standards tend to be accompanied by rising urbanization and declining agriculture, and by increasing education and literacy.

Part One is devoted to the extent and causes of these vast differences. Chapter 2, "Production, Income, Expenditure, and Wealth," sets the scene by dealing with the measurement of output and income and with the relationships between them. In Chapter 3, "Determinants of Productive Capacity," these measures are applied to the exploration of differences in productive capacity in different nations. Productive capacity is carefully defined, together with the limitations it imposes not only on the volume of output, but on the kinds of goods that can be produced. Some of the causes of international differences in productive capacity are examined, but the most significant feature, differences in the productivity of labor, is pursued in Chapter 4, "Productivity and Economic Growth," where productivity differences are related to the ratio of population to land, and to· the specialization of labor and the use of capital equipment. It is shown that rising productivity is part of a coherent economic growth process that involves many interrelated changes that reenforce each other. Chapter 5, "The Organization of the Business Firm," is devoted to the business firm as a basic unit of production, and shows the important connection between types of business organization and methods of production. Part One concludes with Chapter 6, "A Century of U.S. Economic Growth," in which the concepts and principles developed in the preceding chapters are applied to the American economy as a case study.

CHAPTER 2
Production, Income, Expenditure, and Wealth

The most important characteristic of the overall economic performance of any society is the size and composition of the circular flow of economic activity, which involves the total production, income, expenditure, and changes in wealth of the households, business enterprises, and governments of which it is composed. These aspects of economic activity are interesting in their own right, but in addition, some understanding of their size, how they are measured, and how they are related to each other is fundamental for everything that follows.

PRODUCTION

Gross National Product

The total production of the U.S. economy during any given year is a vast outpouring of an almost endless list of goods and services. Imagine an immense catalog listing them all: 200,000 tractors, 2 million kitchen ranges, 3 billion pounds of salad oil, 600 million pairs of shoes. In another section of the catalog, we would find dental service provided by 90,000 dentists, lectures by 150,000 college professors, and 3 million retail clerks waiting on customers.

Since we would need one of these catalogs to describe the output of each nation during each year, it would be exceedingly difficult to compare the output of one country with another, or to study the growth of output over time. We need some kind of summary measurement of the total quantity of output as a whole without reference to the particular kinds of things turned out in any given case. In one sense this great outpouring of goods and services defies measurement because there is no way to add up things in different units to get a meaningful total. How can you add together loaves of bread, pairs of shoes, gallons of gasoline, and number of visits to the doctor?

In another sense, however, all economic goods and services share a common unit of quantity—the "dollar's worth." While we cannot add 5 billion loaves of bread to 600 million pairs of shoes to get any recognizable total, once we take account of prices there is no difficulty at all in adding $1 billion worth of bread to $6 billion worth of shoes to get a total output of goods worth $7 billion. The *gross national product* (GNP) is the total value of all final goods and services produced in a nation during a year's time.

The gross national product is the most important single measure of the way an economic system is functioning, and much of the analysis in the remainder of this book will deal with the size, composition, and variation of the U.S. gross national product, and with comparisons between the GNP of the U.S. and those of other nations. For this reason it is important to examine the concept quite carefully at the outset.

1. Gross national product is a way to *measure* the output of goods and services. Because these goods and services have only dollar units in common, the measurement is made in dollar terms, and expressed as a dollar total. But GNP is not money. It is an outpouring of goods and services. The money figure should never obscure the underlying flow of physical commodities and actual services.

This point was emphasized by earlier economists who referred to dollar measurements as forming a "veil of money" in front of the things being measured and warned students to "strip away the money veil" so they could see the reality beneath. Whenever you see the words "gross national product," "GNP," or any related terms, strip away the veil of money and think of the physical products and services themselves.

2. The gross national product is the value of all *final* goods and services. But not all products are final products. Most goods pass through a number of intermedi-

ate stages before they are ready for use in their final form, and it is necessary to avoid double counting the value of these intermediate products in the gross national product. For instance, shoes are made from leather, and the cost of the leather is included in the price of the shoes. If we added the value of the leather to the value of the shoes, we would obviously count it twice. If the values of wheat, flour, and bread were all added together, the wheat would be counted 3 times—once as wheat, once as flour, and again as bread—and the flour would be counted twice.

To avoid this kind of duplication, the GNP includes the value of final products only. This counts each contribution to the flow of output once and only once, at the point at which it becomes available for use in its final form.

3. Although the gross national product measures quantities of goods and services in dollar units, not all goods and services are sold in the marketplace. Those that are not must have dollar values placed on them in some other way. The most important example is goods and services provided by government to the public at large. Police and fire protection, grade-school education, and use of the streets are not sold to the user for a price, but are provided for everybody without direct payment. Of course the services are paid for by taxes, but unlike prices, taxes are paid without regard for the use of any particular service. In the absence of market prices, government services are included in the gross national product at their cost of production. The "value" of police protection, for example, is measured by the wages paid to policemen.

4. Some important final products are excluded entirely from the GNP. The work of a woman who cleans somebody else's house, cooks, washes the dishes, and raises the children for a wage is counted in the GNP. When she does the same thing for her own family, it is not.

In the modern U.S. economy, in which most products and services pass through the marketplace, the exclusion of purely domestic chores is a relatively minor problem. But in less-developed countries, home production of food and clothing sometimes amounts to a substantial omission. Even in the U.S., historical comparisons must be made with care. To some extent, the apparent growth of our GNP during the last century merely represents the rise of commercial dairying, butchering, canning, brewing, soap making, spinning, weaving, sewing, and other activities that used to be done by the housewife at home where it was not counted as part of the gross national product.

There is one important exception to the treatment of domestic production. A house renders the same shelter to a family whether they own it themselves or rent it from somebody else. For this reason the rental value of all owner-occupied dwellings is included as a final service in the U.S. gross national product along with the rental value of actually rented houses.

5. The gross national product measures the *rate* at which final goods and services flow off the production lines of the nation and always has a time dimension. It must be in dollars *per quarter*, or *per year*, or *per day*, and the measurement is not complete unless the time unit is either stated or clearly understood. The time unit normally used with the GNP is the year, and unless specifically noted to the contrary, GNP figures always imply production flows measured at annual rates. For example, the U.S. GNP during the 3-month period January, February, and March, 1969 was estimated at $908 billion. This was not the actual value of goods turned out during the quarter, but represented the *annual rate* at which goods were becoming available. Thus, if that same rate of production were continued for an entire year, the total outflow would amount to $908 billion.

Even though GNP is always stated in billions of dollars per year, the flow of GNP changes from quarter to quarter, or from month to month, just as the speed of an automobile can change from minute to minute while the speedometer reads miles per hour.

6. Most of what we know about the gross national product of the United States comes from the Office of Business Economics in the U.S. Department of Commerce. Each quarter the Office of Business Economics compiles a careful estimate of the GNP, based on sales figures reported by business firms, data on the number of houses under construction, government wage payments, and other sources of information. In addition to the overall total, the Department of Commerce provides breakdowns of GNP by type of final product, by type of purchaser, and by the industry of production. The distribution of gross national income originating in production is also shown, together with details of a number of important aspects of output and income.

This body of interrelated estimates is the *National Income and Product Accounts* and is regularly published in the *Survey of Current Business*, a monthly publication of the Department of Commerce. Annual revisions and more detailed compilation are published annually, usually in the July issue. Because of their importance, quarterly GNP figures released by the Office of Business Economics are widely republished in the financial and business press, in weekly news magazines, and often in the daily newspapers.

Size of the U.S. GNP Because of the dynamic growth of the American economic system, any discussion of the size of the gross national product is rapidly out of date. The Department of Commerce estimate for 1969 exceeded $930 billion per year, and at present rates of growth, U.S. GNP should pass the trillion-dollar mark before the end of 1970. The nature of this growth can be seen in Table 1 and in the historical record shown by the blue line in Figure 1. From a level of just over $100 billion in 1929, the gross national product

TABLE 1 U.S. GROSS NATIONAL PRODUCT AND IMPLICIT GNP DEFLATOR, 1929-1968

YEAR	GNP (IN BILLIONS)	GNP IN 1958 PRICES (IN BILLIONS)	GNP IMPLICIT PRICE DEFLATOR 1958=100
1929	$103.1	$203.6	50.6
1930	90.4	183.5	49.3
1931	75.8	169.3	44.8
1932	58.0	144.2	40.2
1933	55.6	141.5	39.3
1934	65.1	154.3	42.2
1935	72.2	169.5	42.6
1936	82.5	193.0	42.7
1937	90.4	203.2	44.5
1938	84.7	192.9	43.9
1939	90.5	209.4	43.2
1940	99.7	227.2	43.9
1941	124.5	263.7	47.2
1942	157.9	297.8	53.0
1943	191.6	337.1	56.8
1944	210.1	361.3	58.2
1945	211.9	355.2	59.7
1946	208.5	312.6	66.7
1947	231.3	309.9	74.6
1948	257.6	323.7	79.6
1949	256.5	324.1	79.1
1950	284.8	355.3	80.2
1951	328.4	383.4	85.6
1952	345.5	395.1	87.5
1953	364.6	412.8	88.3
1954	364.8	407.0	89.6
1955	398.0	438.0	90.9
1956	419.2	446.1	94.0
1957	441.1	452.5	97.5
1958	447.3	447.3	100.0
1959	483.7	475.9	101.6
1960	503.7	487.7	103.3
1961	520.1	497.2	104.6
1962	560.3	529.8	105.8
1963	590.5	551.0	107.2
1964	632.4	581.1	108.8
1965	684.9	617.8	110.9
1966	747.6	657.1	113.8
1967	789.7	673.1	117.3
1968	865.7	707.6	122.3

SOURCE: *Survey of Current Business,* July, 1969.

FIGURE 1 U.S. GROSS NATIONAL PRODUCT, 1929-1968

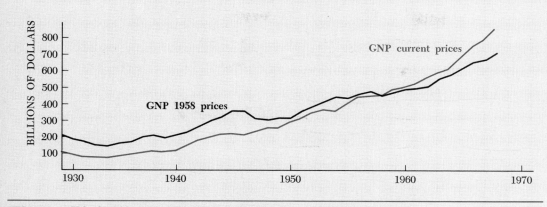

GNP current prices

GNP 1958 prices

FIGURE 2 U.S. GROSS AND NET NATIONAL PRODUCT, 1929-1968

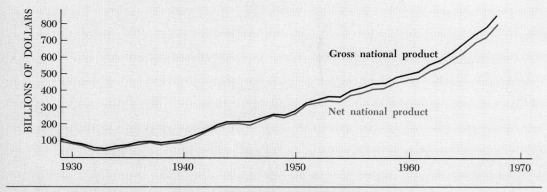

Gross national product

Net national product

FIGURE 3 IMPLICIT DEFLATOR FOR THE U.S. GNP, 1929-1969 (1958 = 100)

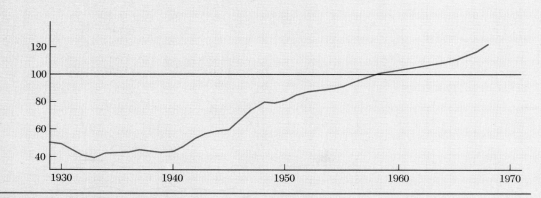

SOURCES FOR FIGURES 1–3: U.S. Department of Commerce, *The National Income and Product Accounts of the United States, 1929–1965*. Later figures from *Survey of Current Business,* July, 1969.

grew to $865 in 1968, but the growth has not been uniform. The decline in GNP from its 1929 level clearly marks the Great Depression of the 1930s. Output rose rapidly during World War II, and then leveled off. Since then, the course has been sharply upward with only brief interruptions in 1954, 1958, and 1960, the last so slight it hardly shows in the graph.

Composition of the GNP For analytical purposes, final products are divided into 4 broad classes. *Durable goods* are products like furniture and machinery that are not consumed immediately after they are produced, but which gradually wear out as they render service over a long period of years. *Nondurable goods* are physical commodities that either are used up shortly after they are produced—food, for example —or wear out in a relatively short time, like clothing. Services, as the name implies, are unstorable final products like air travel, electrical energy, and live symphony concerts that are consumed at the instant of production. *Structures* consist of houses, factories, dams, highways, and similar products that are permanently constructed in fixed locations.

The composition of the gross national product during 1968 is shown in Table 2. About one-fifth of all final products were durable goods. About half of these were automobiles and other durables delivered to households. About a third consisted of machinery and equipment delivered to businesses, and most of the remainder was fire trucks, aircraft, and defense hardware delivered to governments.

The term *net exports* that appears in the table is worth special note. Some of the durable goods delivered in the United States were produced abroad (cameras and radios), others were produced in this country, but involved foreign parts or materials (imported iron ore). In either case, the value of the final product exceeded the amount of production that actually oc-

TABLE 2   COMPOSITION OF U.S. GNP, 1968

	BILLIONS OF DOLLARS	PERCENT OF TOTAL
Gross national product	$865.7	100.0
Durable goods	176.7	20.4
Delivered to:		
Households	83.3	
Businesses	59.5	
Governments	28.1	
Net exports	0.4	
Added to business inventories	5.3	
Nondurable goods	254.4	29.4
Delivered to:		
Households	230.6	
Governments	21.6	
Net exports	0.2	
Added to business inventories	2.0	
Services	347.5	40.1
Rendered for:		
Households	222.8	
Governments	122.9	
Net exports	1.9	
Structures	87.1	10.1
Residential structures	30.2	
Business structures	29.3	
Government structures	27.6	

SOURCE: *Survey of Current Business,* July, 1969.

curred in the U.S. Since we are trying to measure the gross *national* product, imports must be deducted from total deliveries. At the same time, however, American goods which were produced here but exported to other countries, were not included among the goods delivered to U.S. households, businesses, or governments. *Net exports* measures the value of the goods produced in the U.S. but delivered to other countries less the value of goods produced abroad and imported into the U.S.

Some durable goods produced in a given year are not delivered to anybody, but are added to the stocks of goods on dealers' shelves, in warehouses, and on showroom floors. The value of these goods is recorded as *additions to business inventories.* In years when production exceeds deliveries, as in 1968, the addition to business inventories is positive. When more is delivered than is produced, inventory is depleted and addition to business inventories is negative.

Of the total output during 1968, 30 percent consisted of nondurable goods, mostly food, clothing, and other nondurables delivered to households. Governments are relatively small users of nondurable goods, requiring mostly food for armed services and institutions, uniforms, and gasoline. Note that no nondurable goods were reported as delivered to businesses. This is because chemicals, cotton, paper, and other nondurables that businesses use are not final products but only intermediate commodities to be used up or transformed into final products for delivery to somebody else. These intermediate products have already been counted as part of some other final product, and to include them again would be double counting.

Services composed 40 percent of all final products. Of these, two-thirds consisted of barber and beauty shop services, telephone service, medical care, public transportation, and other services rendered for households. Most of the services rendered for government consisted of work done by government employees. Note again that although businesses purchase large volumes of services such as telephone, power, and transportation, these are not final products, but are intermediate services used up in the production of other products.

About 10 percent of total output was structures. This figure was divided about equally among new houses and apartment buildings, new factories and other nonresidential construction, and construction for government, including highways.

Net National Product Production of goods and services requires the use of buildings, machinery, and other equipment that were part of the gross national product of earlier years. Since these wear out or *depreciate* with age and use, some of the machinery and structures produced in any given year represent replacement of those used up, rather than a net addition to the production facilities of the community.

When a *capital consumption allowance* for wear and tear on productive facilities and structures is deducted from the gross national product, the result is the *net national product*, the total value of the flow of goods and services net of those needed for replacement. The net national product measures the total output of goods and services that the community can freely dispose of while still retaining its productive equipment intact. A community can, of course, consume more than its net national product, but only at the expense of postponing renewal of equipment that is wearing out. If this practice is continued over an extended period, the economic capacity of the society is reduced.

The historical relationship of gross to net national product is shown in Figure 2.

Gross National Product at Constant Prices

One problem that arises when production is measured in monetary terms is that the rise and fall of prices alters the dollar value of the GNP quite independently of the rate of real output. The dollar, in other words, is a "rubber yardstick" for economic measurement, and one must be careful not to confuse a stretching of the yardstick with a change in the size of what is measured.

To keep the yardstick the same size, the value of all final products must be measured, not by their changing, day-to-day market prices, but rather in terms of fixed prices. For this purpose, prices of some convenient year are chosen—1958 is now used in the U.S.—and these are used to evaluate output, year after year. For example, when a certain kind of shoes sold for $10 in 1958, 1.5 million pairs constituted

$15 million worth of final product in the 1958 GNP. In 1960, when the output of the shoes rose to 2 million, their price fell to $7. Despite the substantial increase in the number of pairs turned out, measured by current prices they represented output worth only $7 × 2 million, or $14 million, $1 million less than before. When the 1960 price tags are removed from the shoes and replaced with 1958 prices, 1960 shoe production *valued at 1958 prices* becomes $10 × 2 million, or $20 million.

To measure the gross national product without the distortion of price changes, this same technique is applied to all final products. Instead of their values being added in prices current at the time, the current price tag is removed from each item and replaced with the price the item had during the base year. The result is called the *gross national product at constant prices*, or, when 1958 prices are used for the purpose, the *GNP at 1958 prices*. Since the same constant prices are used year after year, any changes observed in GNP at constant prices must reflect changes in the quantity or composition of final output rather than price fluctuations.

The gross national product at 1958 prices was given in Table 1, and plotted as the black line in Figure 1. Comparison of the black line with the blue line of GNP at current prices shows the effect of price changes. Since prices were rising during most of this period, the GNP of the years prior to 1958 was greater at the higher 1958 prices than at the low prices that were current at the time. By the same token, GNP of more recent years was lower at the 1958 prices than at the high current prices.

There are several points at which the line indicating GNP at 1958 prices shows important movements in real output that escape detection when current prices are used. In particular, note that the decline in real output from the wartime peak in 1944 to 1946 is completely disguised in the current price series by the rapid price in-

creases of that period. The recessions of 1954 and 1958, also obscured by price increases, show clearly as dips in GNP at 1958 prices.

Measurement of the Price Level Since the figures for GNP at current and at constant prices represent the identical batch of final products valued at 2 different sets of prices, comparison tells us how prices have changed. If the same batch of goods that is worth $130 at today's prices could have been bought for $100 in 1958, prices today on the average must be 130 percent of their 1958 level.

A *price index* is the ratio of the value of a batch of goods and services at current prices to the value of the identical items at the constant prices of a fixed year. It expresses the average price level of the current year as a percent of prices in the fixed year. Therefore, when the GNP at current prices is divided by the value of the same goods at 1958 prices, the result shows average prices as a percent of their 1958 level. For example, since the 1968 output of final goods and services was worth $865.7 billion at the prices current in that year, but worth only $707.6 billion when 1958 price tags were used, the 1968 price index was 865.7/707.6, or 122.3. That is, the average price of all final goods and services in 1968 was 22.3 percent higher than in 1958.

One of the important uses of a price index is to adjust money figures for the varying purchasing power of the dollar. For example, since prices had risen, an outlay of $100 in 1968 would buy less than it would have bought in 1958. To calculate the buying power of $100, divide by the price index. Thus $100 in 1968 would buy a quantity of goods worth $100/1.223, or $81.77 at 1958 prices. This adjustment for buying power is called "deflating," and the price index used is called a *deflator*. After they have been deflated, dollar figures are said to be expressed in *dollars of constant purchasing power,* or merely in *constant dollars.* When the price index used is based on 1958 prices, the result is said to be expressed in "1958 dollars." The $100 in 1968 would thus represent $81.77 in 1958 dollars.

Since the GNP price index is implicit in the way the GNP is measured, it is referred to as the *implicit deflator* for the GNP. The history of the implicit GNP deflator was included in Table 1 and is plotted in Figure 3. Although prices declined during the 1930s, the general course has been upward, with the most rapid increases occurring during and following World War II.

Measurement of Production by Value Added

The final goods and services that emerge from the production process are the result of a series of operations or stages, and for many purposes it is important to measure how much production occurs at each stage. Since final output is measured by its value, it is natural to measure the amount of production at any stage by the *value added* to the product at that stage. This is the difference between the value of the output of that stage of production and the value of all intermediate products purchased as inputs at that stage.

One example, the value added at different stages of the production of bread, is schematically represented in Figure 4. The process begins with the production of $30 worth of wheat by a farmer. This wheat then becomes an intermediate product used as an input by the flour mill, where workers and machinery grind it into flour worth $40. Since the value of the flour contains the value of the wheat within it, the milling process has added $40—30, or $10 to the value of the product.

The $40 worth of flour becomes, in turn, an intermediate product used by the bakery, where bakers and ovens turn it into $90 worth of bread, adding $90—40, or $50

FIGURE 4   BREAD PRODUCTION FROM FARM TO TABLE

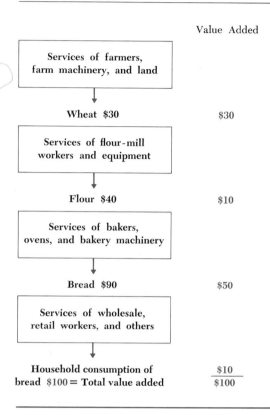

in value. The bread then becomes an intermediate product acquired by a retailer who sells the final product to consumers for $100, adding another $100 − 90, or $10 in the process. Looking back over the route from farm to table, we see that the product grows in value at each stage of production as workers and equipment push it closer and closer to its final form. The $100 value of the final product is exactly the total of the value added at all the stages along the way.

The bread example is oversimplified in one respect. Most production involves not one but many intermediate products as inputs, and yields not one but a number of different products as outputs. In addition to flour, bakers purchase such intermediate products as sugar, milk, and paper wrappers, and in addition to bread they produce rolls, cakes, cookies, and other final products. Nevertheless, the value added by the productive activity of the baking industry is easily calculated from its sales and cost records by subtracting the total value of all intermediate products purchased from the total value of all products sold or added to inventory. A more realistic picture of the value added by the baking industry, based on data from the Census of Manufactures, is given in Table 3.

Table 4 shows the 1968 value added by U.S. industrial groups, as estimated by the

TABLE 3   VALUE ADDED BY THE BREAD AND RELATED PRODUCTS INDUSTRY

	QUANTITY (MIL OF LBS, EXCEPT AS NOTED)	VALUE (MIL OF $)
Intermediate products purchased as inputs:		
Wheat flour and mixes	10,018	$ 635
Sugar	1,296	128
Shortening and lard	600	78
Margarine	40	7
Other fats and oils	156	29
Dried milk	233	33
Frozen and liquid eggs	178	45
Wrappers	—	254
Other ingredients	—	464
Fuel oil	1.7 mil bbl	7
Gas	24.9 bil cu ft	15
Electricity	1.2 bil KWH	20
Other purchased inputs	—	381
Total Input		$2,100
Output products:		
Bread and rolls	13,733	$2,497
Sweet yeast goods	863	330
Soft cakes	1,138	438
Pies	714	206
Pastries	—	51
Doughnuts	369	141
Other products	—	837
Total Output		$4,500
Value Added		$2,400

SOURCE: *Census of Manufactures,* 1963.

TABLE 4   VALUE ADDED BY MAJOR U.S. INDUSTRIAL GROUPS, 1968

INDUSTRY	VALUE ADDED BIL OF $	% OF TOTAL
Agriculture, forestry, and fisheries	$ 27.2	3.1
Mining	14.2	1.6
Contract construction	39.5	4.6
Manufacturing	246.4	28.5
Transportation	34.6	4.0
Communication	19.0	2.2
Electricity, gas, and sanitation services	20.0	2.3
Wholesale and retail trade	142.2	16.4
Finance, insurance, and real estate	117.1	13.5
Other services	95.3	11.0
Government and goverment enterprises[a]	108.0	12.5
Rest of the world	4.7	0.5
Gross national product	865.7	100.0

[a] Since government services are valued at cost, value added by government operations is equal to wages and salaries paid to government workers.

SOURCE: *Survey of Current Business,* July, 1969.

U.S. Department of Commerce. Of the total GNP of $865.7 billion, only about a third was contributed by agriculture, mining, construction, and manufacturing. Almost two-thirds of the total value added represented services rendered directly to governments and households, and the services of transportation, communication, trade, banking, and other "middleman" activities.

Value added represents an attempt to measure the productive activity taking place in a given firm or industry. The activity itself consists of jobs done by workers and operations performed by different kinds of machines and equipment. The activity is measured in dollar terms because these are the only units that performances on different kinds of jobs have in common, but we should remind ourselves that value added is not money. When you consider value added figures, strip aside the money veil to see machines running and men at work in factories and stores.

INCOME

Claims to Output

When goods are produced, claims to the use of these goods are produced at the same time. The worker who adds value by doing his job receives wages that enable him to buy a share of any final products he wants. The investor who loans money for the operation receives an interest payment as his share. The government cuts out a share for itself in the form of tax collections, and so on. In fact, every penny of value added becomes a claim against total output. The total value of all claims against output is *gross income* and this is exactly equal to the total value added by productive activity.

Contractual and Residual Claims There is, of course, nothing really surprising about this equality. Wages, rents, interest, some taxes, and similar claims against total output represent *contractual claims*. Workers agree to perform their jobs in return for wages specified in advance. Landowners lease or rent at agreed prices, and so on. The owners of businesses agree to pay these contractual claims out of the value added by the firm's operations in exchange for the right to the *residual claim,* which is the amount left after all contractual claims are paid. That is, any value added that is not due by contract to anybody else is automatically part of the owners' claim. Since the machinery and buildings used by the firm belong to the owners, their residual claim is not all clear gain. Depreciation must be deducted to allow for capital consumption in order to determine the net residual. Any owners' residual claim remaining after allowance for depreciation represents *profit*.

Distribution of Claims Within the Firm
The distribution of claims is probably most easily understood if we first look at the distribution of the value added by the productive activity of a single business firm. As shown in Table 5, operations of the United States Steel Corporation during 1964 resulted in value added of $2.7 billion. Almost two-thirds of this value accrued to employees as compensation for work performed, and a small share went as contractual interest to people who had loaned money to the corporation.

Federal, state, and local governments claimed $110 million in the form of indirect business taxes. These property, sales, and excise taxes must be paid whether the business is profitable or not, and hence constitute contractual claims by governments.

TABLE 5 PRODUCTION AND CLAIMS AGAINST OUTPUT, U.S. STEEL CORPORATION, 1964
(billions of dollars)

PRODUCTION		CLAIMS AGAINST OUTPUT	
Value of output	$4.13	Compensation of employees	$1.80
		Indirect business taxes	0.11
Less: intermediate products purchased		Interest	0.03
from other firms	1.40	Residual shares:	
		Depreciation	0.34
		Corporate profits	0.46
Value Added	$2.73		$2.73

SOURCE: Compiled from data in United States Steel Corporation, *Sixty-third Annual Report,* New York, 1964.

After paying contractual claims, the residual share amounted to almost 30 percent of the total. After allowing $340 million for wear and tear on buildings and equipment, a profit of $460 million was left. Of course, this was only the initial distribution of claims to value added. As we shall see in a moment, further claims asserted by governments in the form of taxes on corporate profits and personal income, and adjustments in the form of transfer payments must be taken into account in the final distribution.

Distribution of Claims Within an Industry

The distribution of the $2,400 million value added by the bread industry in 1965 was approximately as shown in Table 6. Of this figure, 70 percent was paid out in contractual claims, mostly as wages and salaries to people employed by the industry, with small amounts paid as interest, rent, and indirect business taxes. There remained 30.5 percent as a residual. After deduction of $262 million to allow for depreciation, $500 million was left as profit.

TABLE 6   DISTRIBUTION OF VALUE
ADDED, BREAD AND RELATED
PRODUCTS INDUSTRY, 1965

	MILLIONS OF DOLLARS	PERCENT OF TOTAL
Value added	$2,400	100.0
Contractual claims:	$1,638	69.5
Employee compensation	$1,300	56.0
Indirect business taxes	200	8.0
Interest	60	2.4
Rent	78	3.1
Residual claims:	$ 762	30.5
Depreciation	$ 262	10.5
Incomes of unincorporated owners	250	10.0
Corporate profits	250	10.0

SOURCE: Value added net of wages and salaries allocated according to data in U.S. Treasury Department, *Statistics of Income: Business Tax Returns, 1963.*

Gross National Income

The total of all claims against the gross national product is called the *gross national income.* The equality between production and claims against output that holds for the individual firm or industry also holds for the entire economy: Gross national income is equal to gross national product.

The distribution of claims against the 1968 U.S. gross national product is shown in Table 7 and Figure 5. Nearly 60 percent of gross national income consisted of wages, salaries, and other employee compensation. Interest and rent amounted to only about 3 percent each; 9 percent was claimed by government as indirect business taxes. Among the residual claims, capital consumption allowances came to 8.5 percent of GNP. Earnings of business proprietors (including farmers) and professionals like doctors and lawyers amounted to 7.4 percent, while the remainder was corporate profits.

Note that when the claims were all added up, the total gross national income slightly exceeded the gross national product as estimated by adding up the value of final products. Since different sources of data are employed in the 2 estimates, some disagreement in results is unavoidable and this difference, the *statistical discrepancy,* is recorded as shown.

The identity of income and output is an elementary point, but it has profound implications. In the first place, once the money veil is stripped aside, it is clear that money payments represent merely claims to the flow of real goods and services. Real income consists of the goods and services themselves, not of the money claims. Societies with high incomes are rich because they are productive. Societies with low incomes are poor because they are unproductive. To a limited extent, the real income of one person or group can be raised by reducing the claims of another, but the only

TABLE 7 U.S. GROSS NATIONAL INCOME AND ITS COMPONENTS, 1968

	BILLIONS OF DOLLARS	PERCENT OF TOTAL
Contractional claims		
Compensation of employees	$516.2	59.6
Rental income	21.2	2.4
Net interest	28.0	3.2
Indirect business taxes	77.9	9.0
Residual claims		
Capital consumption allowances	$ 73.3	8.5
Income of proprietors and professionals	63.8	7.4
Corporate profits	87.9	10.2
Statistical discrepancy	—2.5	—0.3
Gross national product	$865.7	100.0

FIGURE 5 COMPONENTS OF U.S. GROSS NATIONAL INCOME, 1968

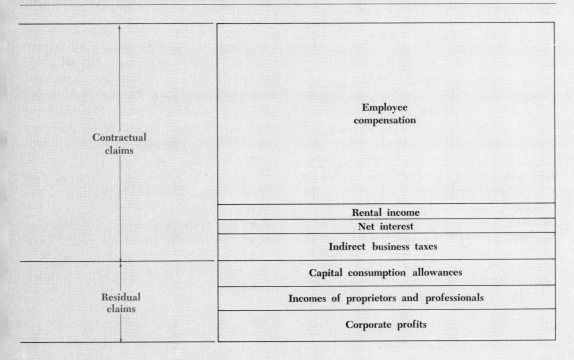

SOURCES: *Survey of Current Business,* July, 1969.

source of higher total income is greater real output.

In the second place, in an economic system like ours, the residual nature of profits make them a powerful incentive for firms to increase the efficiency of their operations and to improve their products. The business firm that can combine labor and materials to produce more output or a more desirable product increases the difference between value added and its contractual payments. The resulting high profits reward the owners for increased efficiency. The business firm that uses labor and materials wastefully or inefficiently, or that turns out inferior goods, earns low profits and, unless it mends its ways, may be driven out of business by losses.

The Structure of Income

An analysis of the distribution of income must take into account the fact that a given dollar of income sometimes passes through several different hands before it reaches a final recipient who can spend it. For example, when corporate profits are passed on to individual business owners as dividends, the owners are required to turn over a share of them to the government in the form of income taxes. Or as another example, social security contributions deducted from the paycheck of an employed worker are transferred by the government to a retired worker as a social security pension.

National Income   The distribution and redistribution of gross national income is shown in Table 8. *National income* is the total compensation paid for the services of labor and productive property employed in turning out the gross national product. It includes all receipts of wages and salaries, rents, interest, incomes of proprietors and professionals, and corporate profits before

any of these are subdivided with the government by payment of personal taxes or taxes on corporate income.

The difference between national income and the total value of the gross national product consists of 4 types of claims against output that do not correspond to income payments for currently supplied productive services.

1. *Depreciation* or *capital consumption allowances,* as we have already seen, are not income, but represent compensation of owners for the value of property worn out in the process of production.

2. *Indirect business taxes* are legal claims asserted in the form of sales taxes and similar charges to divert revenue to the government. They are not accompanied by any corresponding productive service, but merely raise the market prices of final products above the cost of production.

3. *Subsidies less surpluses of government enterprises* are, in a sense, the opposite of indirect business taxes. When a government enterprise like the post office sells its services to the public at a loss, payments for the services of mail carriers and others exceed value added. Therefore, the subsidy needed to cover the loss must be added to the value of the output to arrive at national income.

4. *Business transfer payments* consist of pensions, sick pay, and similar payments made by business firms to employees who were not on the job. Also included are such items as prizes paid to customers who win advertising games and contests, scholarships, donations, and similar contributions unconnected with current production.

As shown in Table 8, these 4 items involve almost 20 percent of the total gross national income.

Personal Income   The total of all income received by people as individuals, whether in compensation for services performed or as transfer income, is *personal income.* Personal income differs from national income in 2 important ways. On one hand, although national income is the total amount paid out for the labor and property employed in current production, not all these payments reach individuals. On the other hand, some individuals receive payments unconnected with service currently rendered.

Only about a quarter of corporate profits earned during a given year are actually paid out as personal income to the individual owners of the firm. Nearly half of corporate profits are collected directly by the government via the corporate profits tax, while roughly half of what remains after taxes is retained by the corporation to be invested in the business. Only the part paid out in the form of *dividends* becomes part of the owners' personal income. In the compilation of Table 8, all corporate profit has been subtracted from national income, and only the part paid out in dividends has been added back as part of personal income.

A wage earner's paycheck does not represent the entire amount by which he is compensated for his labor. For one thing, his employer makes a contribution on his behalf directly into his social security account. In addition to the employer's contribution, an equal amount is deducted from each worker's paycheck and contributed to his social security account, making personal income smaller than national income by the contributions for social insurance of employer and employee combined.

As the other side of social insurance contributions, some people receive personal income in the form of social security pensions, unemployment insurance, welfare, and similar payments. To distinguish them from compensation for services currently rendered, payments of this kind are called *government transfer payments to persons,* and are added as shown in Table 8. Business transfer payments to persons, de-

ducted earlier because they were not part of national income, are also added back at this point. Interest received by individual holders of government bonds is a similar transfer of income and is also included in the table.

Disposable Personal Income Before people are free to spend their personal income they must first pay their taxes. What remains of personal income after personal taxes have been deducted is *disposable personal income,* the annual income that people can freely dispose of as they choose.

Of the original gross national income, about 70 percent finds its way to households as disposable personal income. The remaining 30 percent consists of depreciation, corporate profits retained in the firm, and government tax revenue remaining after transfers, subsidies, and government interest have been paid.

The historical relationship of disposable income to gross national product, shown in Figure 6, indicates that disposable personal income tends to be more stable than GNP. The gap between them narrows when GNP falls, and widens when it rises. One reason for this is that as output declines, taxes decline, deducting less from GNP and personal income, while unemployment compensation and other transfers rise, supplementing personal income. Another reason is that corporations tend to maintain dividend payments even when their profits decline. This shows clearly in the narrowing difference between GNP and disposable income at the bottom of the depression of the 1930s. Total dividend payments were $4 billion in 1931, although all corporations together had earned a total of only $2 billion in profits. In 1932, although total profits were negative (−$1.3 billion), dividends of $2.5 billion were paid. The widening difference between GNP and disposable personal income after 1941 was due to the imposition of wartime tax rates.

TABLE 8 RELATION OF U.S. G.N.P. TO U.S. DISPOSABLE PERSONAL INCOME, 1968

	BILLIONS OF DOLLARS
Gross national product	$865.7
less:	
Capital consumption allowances	73.3
equals:	
Net national product	$792.4
less:	
Indirect business taxes	$ 77.9
Business transfer payments	3.4
(Statistical discrepancy)	(−2.5)
plus:	
Subsidies less surpluses of government enterprises	0.8
equals:	
National income	$714.4
less:	
Corporate profits	$ 87.9
Contribution for social insurance	47.0
plus:	
Government transfer payments to persons	55.8
Interest paid by governments	26.1
Dividends	23.1
Business transfer payments	3.4
equals:	
Personal income	$687.9
less:	
Personal taxes	$ 97.9
equals:	
Disposable personal income	$590.0

FIGURE 6 RELATION OF U.S. G.N.P. TO U.S. DISPOSABLE PERSONAL INCOME, 1929-1968

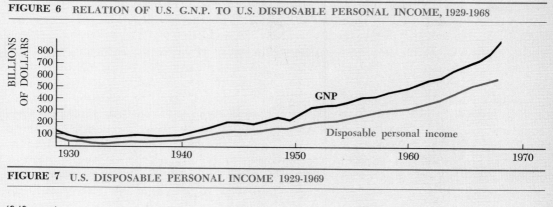

FIGURE 7 U.S. DISPOSABLE PERSONAL INCOME 1929-1969

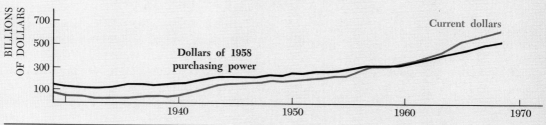

TABLE 9 U.S. DISPOSABLE PERSONAL INCOME, 1929-1968 (billions of dollars)

YEAR	PERSONAL INCOME	LESS: PERSONAL TAX AND NONTAX PAYMENTS	EQUALS: DISPOSABLE PERSONAL INCOME	DISPOSABLE PERSONAL INCOME, IN 1958 PRICES
1929	$ 85.9	$ 2.6	$ 83.3	$150.6
1930	77.0	2.5	74.5	139.0
1931	65.9	1.9	64.0	133.7
1932	50.2	1.5	48.7	115.1
1933	47.0	1.5	45.5	112.2
1934	54.0	1.6	52.4	120.4
1935	60.4	1.9	58.5	131.8
1936	68.6	2.3	66.3	148.4
1937	74.1	2.9	71.2	153.1
1938	68.3	2.9	65.5	143.6
1939	72.8	2.4	70.3	155.9
1940	78.3	2.6	75.7	166.3
1941	96.0	3.3	92.7	190.3
1942	122.9	6.0	116.9	213.4
1943	151.3	17.8	133.5	222.8
1944	165.3	18.9	146.3	231.6
1945	171.1	20.9	150.2	229.7
1946	178.7	18.7	160.0	227.0
1947	191.3	21.4	169.8	218.0
1948	210.3	21.1	189.1	229.8
1949	207.2	18.6	188.6	230.8
1950	227.6	20.7	206.9	249.6
1951	255.6	29.0	226.6	255.7
1952	272.5	34.1	238.3	263.3
1953	288.2	35.6	252.6	275.4
1954	290.1	32.7	257.4	278.3
1955	310.9	35.5	275.3	296.7
1956	333.0	39.8	293.2	309.3
1957	351.1	42.6	308.5	315.8
1958	361.2	42.3	318.8	318.8
1959	383.5	46.2	337.3	333.0
1960	401.0	50.9	350.0	340.2
1961	416.8	52.4	364.4	350.7
1962	442.6	57.4	385.3	367.3
1963	465.5	60.9	404.6	381.3
1964	497.5	59.4	438.1	407.9
1965	538.9	65.7	473.2	435.0
1966	586.8	75.3	511.6	459.2
1967	628.8	82.5	546.3	478.0
1968	687.9	97.9	590.0	497.6

SOURCES FOR TABLES 8, 9 AND FIGURES 6, 7: U.S. Department of Commerce, *The National Income and Product Accounts of the United States, 1929–1965*. Later data from *Survey of Current Business*, July, 1969.

Money Income and Real Income

Income is distributed in paychecks and other money receipts. Again, however, it is important to strip away the money veil and reveal the reality beneath. *Real income* consists not of money, but of claims to goods and services. The important thing is not the number of dollars people receive, but the *purchasing power* of these dollars, the amount of goods the dollars can buy. The power of a dollar to buy goods depends on prices. When gasoline was $.20 a gallon, a dollar had the power to buy 1/.20, or 5 gallons. When the price went to $.30 the purchasing power of a dollar fell to 1/.30, or 3.33 gallons.

A given number of dollars can command fewer real goods and services when the average price level is high than when it is low. Therefore, in order to show changes in buying power, money income must be adjusted for changes in the price level. This is accomplished by deflating money income by the implicit deflator for personal consumption expenditure, a price index similar to that for the gross national product as a whole, except that it applies only to goods and services intended for personal consumption. As an example of how this deflation works, consider the change in disposable personal income from 1953 to 1966. During this period, disposable personal income rose from $252 billion to $509 billion. In other words, the number of dollars available for consumers to spend annually had almost exactly doubled. At the same time, however, the implicit deflator for personal consumption goods (1958 = 100) had risen from 91.7 in 1953 to 111.5 in 1966. Expressed in dollars of constant 1958 purchasing power, real disposable personal income in 1953 was $252/.917, or $275 billion. That is, although in 1953 people had a total of only $252 billion to dispose of, low prices gave this amount a purchasing power equivalent to $275 billion at 1958 prices. Because of the higher prices in 1966, the $509 billion of income was the equivalent in buying power of only $509/1.117, or $455 billion at 1958 prices.

These adjustments reveal that although dollar income had doubled over the period, rising prices reduced the real gain in personal disposable income to about 65 percent. The history of money and real disposable personal income is shown in Table 9, and charted in Figure 7. The difference between the two concepts is especially clear in the period 1943–1947, when the number of dollars received as disposable income increased more slowly than prices. After adjusting for rising prices, we can see that, despite higher money income, the real buying power of disposable personal income actually declined and was lower in 1947 than it had been 5 years earlier.

EXPENDITURE

Gross National Expenditure

People, business firms, and governments use their claims against GNP to purchase the products they need. If we include business spending for additions to inventory along with other purchases, it is clear that the *gross national expenditure* by all groups combined must exactly equal the gross national product. This follows because all goods produced belong initially to the producing firm. If they are not bought by anybody else, they are automatically added to business inventory.

The components of the 1968 gross national product viewed as gross national expenditure are shown in Table 10. Of the $865.7 billion total spent by all groups in the nation, $536.6 billion, or over 60 percent of the total, represented *personal consumption expenditure*. This corresponds to the value of durable goods, nondurable goods, and services shown earlier as delivered to households (Table 2). Nearly 15 percent of the total GNP, or $126.3 billion, represented *gross private domestic investment*. This consisted of business expenditures for new plants and equipment, investment by landlords and households in new residential construction, and business inventory buying.

Net exports of goods and services represent expenditures in the U.S. by residents of other nations less the amounts spent abroad by Americans. The remaining expenditure of $200.3 billion, almost 25 percent of the GNP, consisted of the purchase of goods and services by federal, state, and local governments.

Like the gross national product as a whole, the value of the goods acquired by each group can be expressed either in terms of current prices to correspond to actual current dollar outlay, or at constant prices to correspond to the deflated values of the outlay.

Expenditure by Individuals and Groups

Although gross national expenditure by all groups combined adds up exactly to gross national income, expenditures by individuals or groups rarely correspond precisely to their particular income shares.

Personal Consumption Expenditure   Some households spend in excess of their disposable income, financing the additional spending by money withdrawn from the bank, by the sale of property or investments, or by consumer installment credit. Other households spend less than their incomes, putting the difference in the bank, using it to pay off installment debts or other loans, or investing it in new housing, business securities, or other assets.

The personal consumption expenditure of all households is compared with disposable personal income in Figure 8. The gap between the two curves shows the general

disposition of households as a group to spend less on personal consumption items than they receive in income, although the years 1932 and 1933 at the depths of the Depression represented an exception. The unusual widening of the gap between income and expenditure that occurred between 1941 and 1944 is particularly interesting. These were, of course, the years of World War II, when most consumption goods were rationed. With limited amounts available for purchase, households were compelled to save their incomes whether they wanted to or not.

Business Investment Expenditure   Some individual business firms invest more than their share of gross national income, financing the difference by withdrawing money from bank accounts, by borrowing, or by issuing new securities to the public. Other firms invest less than their share of receipts, using the difference to build up bank balances, pay off debts, or issue credit to their customers. As a whole, the business community typically spends more on gross private domestic investment than it receives in depreciation allowances and retained earnings, and must continually seek additional funds from banks and individual investors. According to the historical record depicted in Figure 9, the only exceptions to this rule were observed during the Depression of the 1930s, and during the years of World War II when investment goods, like consumer goods, were rationed.

Government Purchases of Goods and Services   Unlike households, which typically spend less on consumption goods than they receive, and businesses, which generally spend more on investment goods than they receive, governments exhibit no typical historical pattern, except during wartime, when government spending rises more rapidly than net tax receipts. This is clearly seen in Figure 10—during World War II, during the Korean War of early 1950s, and

TABLE 10 U.S. G.N.P. AS GROSS NATIONAL EXPENDITURE IN CURRENT AND CONSTANT DOLLARS, 1968 (billions of dollars)

	CURRENT PRICES	1958 PRICES
Gross national product or expenditure	$865.7	$707.6
Personal consumption expenditure	536.6	452.6
Durable goods	83.3	80.7
Automobiles and parts	37.0	36.1
Furniture and household equipment	34.2	33.3
Other durable goods	12.1	11.3
Nondurable goods	230.6	196.9
Food and beverages	115.0	98.4
Clothing and shoes	46.3	37.9
Gasoline and oil	19.1	16.9
Other nondurable goods	50.1	43.8
Services	222.8	175.0
Housing	77.4	66.7
Household operation	31.2	26.9
Transportation	16.1	12.6
Other services	98.1	68.7
Gross private domestic investment	126.3	105.7
Nonresidential	88.8	75.8
Structures	29.3	22.7
Producers' durable equipment	59.3	53.2
Residential structures	30.2	23.3
Increase in business inventories	7.3	6.6
Net exports of goods and services	2.5	0.9
Exports	50.6	45.6
Imports	48.1	44.7
Government purchases of goods and services	200.3	148.4
Federal	99.5	78.9
Defense	78.0	n.a.
Nondefense	21.5	n.a.
State and local	100.7	69.5

FIGURE 8 U.S. HOUSEHOLD RECEIPTS AND EXPENDITURES, 1929-1968

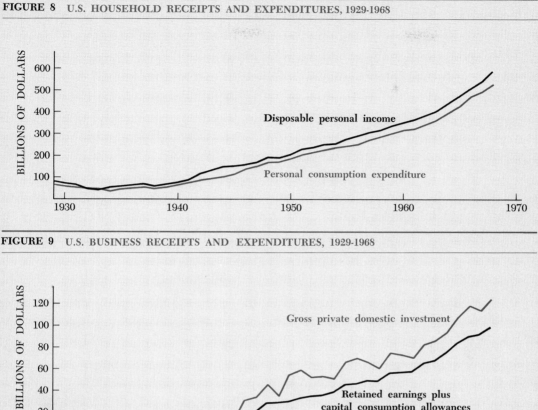

Disposable personal income

Personal consumption expenditure

FIGURE 9 U.S. BUSINESS RECEIPTS AND EXPENDITURES, 1929-1968

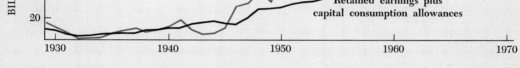

Gross private domestic investment

Retained earnings plus
capital consumption allowances

FIGURE 10 U.S. GOVERNMENT RECEIPTS AND EXPENDITURES, 1929-1968

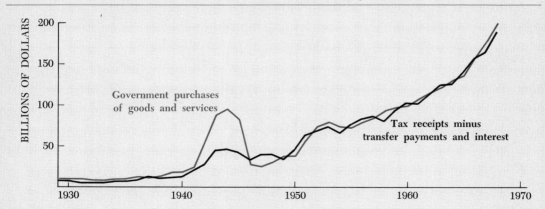

Government purchases
of goods and services

Tax receipts minus
transfer payments and interest

SOURCES FOR TABLE 10 AND FIGURES 8–10: U.S. Department of Commerce, *The National Income and Product Accounts of the United States, 1929–1965*. Later figures from *Survey of Current Business,* July, 1969.

again with the onset of the war in Vietnam in the late 1960s. As we shall see later on, the ebb and flow of government spending and tax receipts exercise an important influence over the size of the gross national product at any particular time.

WEALTH

Production and Income vs. Wealth

In concluding this chapter it is useful to note an important distinction between production and income on the one hand and *wealth* on the other. Although the distinction is obvious enough, failure to make it is a frequent source of confusion in thinking about economic matters. As we have seen, production and income measure the *rate* at which goods and services are turned out *over a period of time.* In contrast, *wealth* consists of the total quantity of goods in existence and ready for use *at a given moment of time.* The *production* of houses is the rate at which new houses are being built, say 1,500,000 per year. Our *wealth* contains the entire 60 million or so dwellings in existence on a given date. New automobile *production* is roughly 9 million new cars per year. Our *wealth* contains the entire 90 million or so cars on the road today.

Real wealth consists of 2 different classes of goods: (1) Natural resources like ore beds, farm land, and construction sites are part of our *natural wealth;* (2) Machinery, buildings, and equipment, together with inventories of raw materials and finished products are *produced wealth* or *capital goods.* Capital goods, in turn, consist of *consumers' capital* in the form of automobiles, appliances, furniture, and the like, owned by households; *producers' capital,* consisting of the total stock of goods owned by business firms in the form of buildings, productive equipment, and in-

ventory; and *government capital,* which consists of fire trucks, school buildings, highways, sewers, dams, and other structures and equipment owned by society as a whole through its various governments.

Real Wealth and Money

Since the total stock of wealth consists of many different things, it must be measured in dollars, but it is again of utmost importance to strip off the money veil and see that *real wealth* consists of the actual goods themselves. It is especially important to distinguish real wealth from *rights to* or *claims against* wealth. Factory buildings and machinery are real wealth. The stocks and bonds of the company that owns the factory are *property rights* or *claims to wealth.* They represent title to real wealth, much as a claim check represents a hat in a check room.

The claim most often confused with real wealth is money. Indeed, most people probably think of wealth as a pile of money. Yet as real wealth, money is only so much paper or metal. A penny contains only a fraction of a penny's worth of copper, and the paper in a $20 bill is worth even less. Coins and currency are valuable to the owner, not because they are real wealth, but because they represent claims that can be used to buy real wealth from somebody else. When a man burns a $20 bill, he loses his right to buy goods, and is personally poorer. But the total real wealth of society is undiminished. There is just as much land and machinery as before.

Investment

The process of adding to the total stock of capital goods is called *investment.* As we have seen, *gross investment* is the total value of all new structures, equipment, and additional inventory produced during the year. It is called "gross" investment because some of the items represent replacement of older equipment rather than additions to the total amount of equipment available. *Net investment* is the value of the net addition to the stock of capital goods, and is measured by what remains after capital consumption allowances have been deducted from gross investment.

Investment has a two-fold relationship to production. In the first place, structures and equipment added to wealth must first be produced, and hence are part of production during the year the investment is made. Secondly, when the additional capital equipment is used in subsequent years, it increases the total volume of goods and services produced. These interrelated aspects of investment have important consequences that we will examine later.

SUMMARY

The most important single index of the performance of an economy is its *gross national product* (GNP), the total annual outflow of all final goods and services. Because different goods and services are in unlike physical units, their total must be measured in dollar terms, but the GNP consists of real goods and services, not money. Unless care is taken, however, the use of dollar values may cause the confusion of changes in the real output of goods and services with mere price variations. The *gross national product in constant prices* is the flow of final products as measured by the application of fixed price tags in place of day-to-day market prices. Comparison of the current market value of output with its value at constant prices also gives us an index of movements in the average price level.

Production by any particular firm or industry is measured by *value added,* which is the difference between the total value of the output of the firm or industry and the cost of the intermediate products used up in the production process. The total value added by all individual producers in the nation equals the gross national product.

Every dollar of value added accrues to somebody as an income claim against production. The total of these claims is *gross national income,* another view of the gross national product. Gross national income is distributed to the households and institutions of society in the form of money payments. *Disposable personal income* is the income that people as individuals are free to spend as they choose. The remainder of gross national income consists of taxes paid to federal, state, and local governments, and a residual share retained by business firms and reinvested in production.

All final goods and services produced are either piled up in business inventories or delivered to buyers in exchange for money expenditure. *Gross national expenditure,* including business expenditure for increased inventory, necessarily equals gross national product.

Unlike *production* and *income,* which represent flows of new goods becoming available during a period of time, *wealth* represents the stock of old and new goods on hand at a particular moment. An important type of wealth is *capital goods* in the form of buildings, machinery, and other durable equipment. These are products saved out of the stream of output and invested for use in future production.

CHAPTER 3

Determinates
of Productive Capacity

The best single measure of the ability of an economic system to provide for the material welfare of its members is its potential gross national product per capita—the ratio of potential GNP to population. It is by no means a perfect measure, however. Output can either be devoted to important needs or wasted on trivial satisfactions, and the mere total quantity of goods available to people is no indication of how well off they are. Moreover, a given average can represent widely different ways of distributing the same total output among the members of society, and unless income is divided so that everybody gets an equitable share, most of the benefits from production will be enjoyed by a favored few. Nevertheless, unless a society has sufficient productive capacity to begin with, most of its members will be ill-fed, ill-clothed, ill-housed, and ill-educated regardless of how carefully production is limited to essentials and how evenly income is parceled out to households. In this chapter the great in-equalities in the material living standards of different nations are first explored. This discussion is followed by a careful consideration of the nature of productive capacity and of the limitations it imposes not only on the total output available, but on the kinds of goods and services that can be produced. The chapter concludes with an examination of why the productive capacity of some nations is so much greater than that of others.

THE DISTRIBUTION
OF WORLD OUTPUT

Estimated GNP per capita for most of the nations of the world is tabulated in Table A at the end of this chapter. All estimates are expressed in U.S. prices for comparability. The gap between the material welfare enjoyed by the average American and that of the majority of the world's population is almost beyond belief. The $3,310 per capita of the U.S. economy is 50 percent greater than those of Canada and Sweden, the countries ranking next, and 100 times that of the nations at the bottom of the list. Half of the world's people live in countries where the average GNP per person is $100 or less per year.

How unequally the world's productive power is distributed can be seen in Table 1, which shows the percentage of gross world output turned out by corresponding percentages of world population, accumulated from poorest to richest. According to the table, the poorest 10 percent of the world's people produces no more than 1 percent of total world output! The poorest 20 percent turns out little more than 2 percent, while even the poorest 80 percent is responsible for less than a third of the world's goods and services.

The distribution of world output is presented graphically in Figure 1. The world's population is arranged along the horizontal axis from the poorest people at the left, to the richest at the right, and the accumulated percentage of gross world product produced by the corresponding percentage

FIGURE 1   LORENZ CURVE OF DISTRIBUTION OF GROSS WORLD PRODUCT

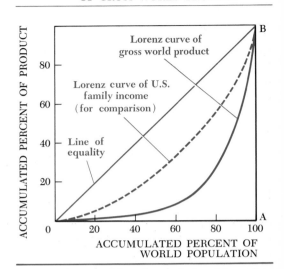

SOURCE: Gross world product calculated from data of Table A. Distribution of U.S. family income from U.S. Bureau of the Census, *Consumer Income,* Current Population Reports Series P-60 No. 43, September, 1964.

of the total population is plotted vertically. The result, called a *Lorenz curve,* shows the degree of inequality in the distribution of productive power. If output were equally distributed, the Lorenz curve would follow the diagonal line *OB,* which would indicate that 10 percent of the world's population turned out 10 percent of the gross world product, 20 percent of the population turned out 20 percent of gross world product, and so on. Since, in fact, the poorest 10 percent of the world's people produces less than 10 percent of the world's output, the Lorenz curve is pushed below the diagonal, and the more unequally productive power is distributed, the farther the curve departs from the diagonal. If productive power were so unequally distributed that the most productive 1 percent of the world's population turned out all the

TABLE 1   PERCENTAGE OF TOTAL WORLD OUTPUT BY TOTAL WORLD POPULATION
(accumulated from poorest to richest)

PERCENT OF WORLD POPULATION	PRODUCES	PERCENT OF WORLD OUTPUT
Poorest 10 percent		1
20		2
30		3
40		4
50		6
60		8
70		15
80		28
90		52
100		100

SOURCE: Calculated from data of Appendix A.

gross world product, and the remaining 99 percent of the people produced nothing, the Lorenz curve would roughly correspond to the axis lines *OAB*.

The Lorenz curve of Figure 1 indicates that the poorest third of the world's population produces less than 4 percent of gross world product, and the poorest 50 percent produces less than 7 percent. At the upper end, the most productive 10 percent of the world's population produces half of the gross world product. The United States, with only 6 percent of the world's population, produces 36 percent of the total output of the world.

To give some basis for comparison, a dotted line has been added to Figure 1, representing the Lorenz curve of the distribution of family income within the United States alone. Although there are obviously great differences in income between city slums and suburban estates, it can be seen from the chart that the degree of inequality this represents is only about half that of the world as a whole.

Perhaps one of the most important things an American student should learn in the study of economics is how unrepresentative of the world his own situation is. Americans generally not only have plenty to eat and to wear, but take for granted the diversion of output from necessities to the production of luxury automobiles, television sets, and professional sports. Where the poorest half of the world lives, hunger is endemic and famine is frequent, while Americans use valuable resources to produce foods that are guaranteed to be free of calories. The $100 per-capita income a year shown in Table 2 leaves little to spare for doctors, education, or newspapers. In our rich society, old clothes, empty cans and bottles, old newspapers, and even used furniture pose serious problems of waste disposal. In a poor country, such things are carefully preserved resources. Old clothes are worn until they can no longer hang

together, and the rags are saved for patches. Old tin cans become cups, buckets, or a source of raw material for light metal products. Bottles are carefully preserved for reuse, and yesterday's newspaper (if any) becomes today's wrapping paper and tomorrow's fuel.

GNP per capita as a Measure of Economic Performance

A rough economic profile of rich and poor countries is given in Table 2. To compile this table, the countries in Table A were grouped by GNP per capita, and averages were calculated from the data available for each group. Averages are at best only roughly representative, and since some data were available for only a few of the countries in each group, these averages are doubtless less representative than most. But crude as they are, they exhibit strongly systematic behavior in relation to GNP per capita.

Life and Death   The life and death implications of productive power are shown in Figure 2. Life expectancy at age 20—the number of additional years of life the average 20-year-old can look forward to—is plotted on the right-hand scale, and GNP per capita is plotted horizontally. The average for each group of nations is represented by a black dot in the figure, and the upward trend of life expectancy in the richer countries is represented by the black curve, drawn freehand through the midst of the points. In the more productive areas, 20-year-olds can look forward to an average of 54 more years of life, compared to only 37 years in the least productive areas, a gain of 17 years of life. Moreover, the chances of reaching age 20 are better where material output is higher. As shown by the blue dots in Figure 2, plotted on the left-hand vertical axis, infant mortality—death

TABLE 2 ECONOMIC PROFILES OF POOR AND RICH COUNTRIES

GNP PER CAPITA	NO. OF COUNTRIES	GNP PER CAPITA	GROSS INVESTMENT PERCENT OF GNP	AGRICULTURAL PRODUCTION PERCENT OF GNP
Under $100	12	$ 72	15.3	48
100 - 199	14	154	16.1	37
200 - 299	18	244	16.2	33
300 - 499	12	400	18.6	29
500 - 999	14	691	23.7	22
1,000-1,699	12	1,391	26.9	18
1,700 or more	11	2,090	25.5	8

SOURCE: Computed from data in Appendix Table A.

FIGURE 2 GNP PER CAPITA AND HEALTH: LIFE EXPECTANCY AT AGE 20 AND INFANT MORTALITY PER 1,000 BIRTHS

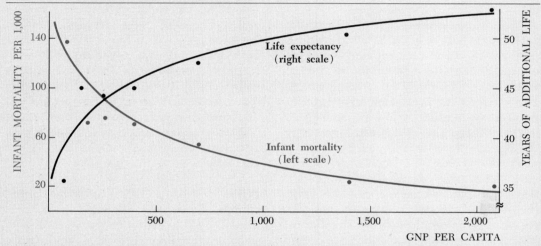

FIGURE 3 GNP PER CAPITA AND LITERACY: COPIES OF DAILY NEWSPAPERS PER 1,000 PEOPLE AND PERCENT OF POPULATION OVER AGE 15 ILLITERATE

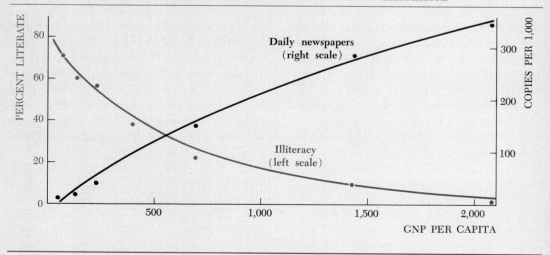

TABLE 2 (*Continued*)

GROWTH RATE OF REAL GNP PER CAPITA 1960-1964 % PER YEAR	POPULATION GROWTH % PER YEAR	HEALTH			STEEL CONSUMPTION PER CAPITA
		PERSONS PER PHYSICIAN	INFANT MORTALITY PER 1,000 BIRTHS	LIFE EXPECTANCY AT AGE 20 YEARS	
1.4	2.3	14,900	129	36	11
2.0	2.7	10,700	67	45	16
2.0	2.9	4,100	74	44	37
3.8	1.9	3,100	72	45	55
4.3	1.6	1,200	53	47	146
4.5	1.3	800	26	51	339
3.8	1.3	788	21	53	414

FIGURE 4   GNP PER CAPITA AND COMPOSITION OF OUTPUT: PERCENT OF GNP IN AGRICULTURE AND PER CAPITA STEEL CONSUMPTION

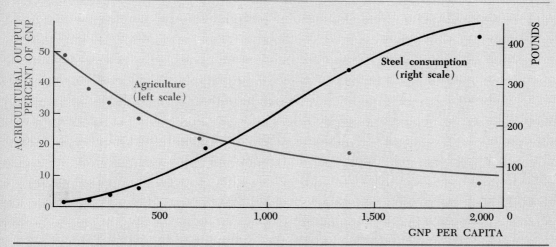

FIGURE 5   GNP PER CAPITA AND ECONOMIC GROWTH: ANNUAL GROWTH OF PER CAPITA GNP AND POPULATION

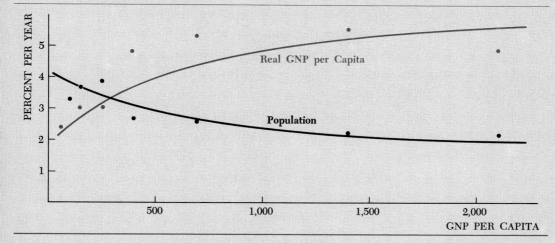

during the first year of life—takes 129 of every 1,000 babies born in the least productive areas, but only 20 per 1,000 in the most productive areas.

Quality of Life   Higher GNP per capita means not only more life, it means a superior quality of life. The black line of Figure 3 shows the relative availability of a simple amenity like a daily newspaper in countries with a high output per capita. The colored line shows that over 70 percent of the adult population in the least productive areas is unable to read or write, compared to only 2 percent in productive countries. In addition, as total productive power grows, the composition of output changes. The colored line of Figure 4 shows the decline of agricultural output as GNP per capita rises. The high proportion of total output devoted to agriculture in the least productive areas reflects the struggle of poor people to turn out enough to eat. More productive countries devote a smaller proportion of total output to food, and more to automobiles, refrigerators, machinery, and other steel products.

Economic Growth and Investment in the Future   Perhaps the most dramatic difference between rich and poor nations is illustrated by the data of Figure 5. The larger the output per capita is in the first place, the faster it grows. Not only are the less productive nations poorer to begin with, but their productive capacity grows more slowly than that of their rich neighbors. At the same time, population grows most rapidly in the least productive areas. The result of these 2 factors is that the gap between the economic position of the few most productive people and that of the mass of less productive people, great to begin with, is steadily widening with the passage of time. This implies that the Lorenz curve of Figure 1 is being pushed farther and farther away from the diagonal in the direction of greater inequality.

PRODUCTIVE CAPACITY AS AN INFLUENCE ON ECONOMIC PERFORMANCE

The most important reason poor countries have poor economic performance is that fewer alternatives are open to them than are available to rich countries. Economic performance is severely limited by available productive capacity, and low productive power not only restricts output as a whole, but narrowly limits the kinds of products that a nation can include in its GNP. This limitation of alternatives explains not only the low living standards in poor countries, but also such characteristics as the predominance of food in the composition of output and even the slow growth rate of GNP.

The Production-Possibilities Curve

The alternatives available to a nation with a given productive capacity are represented by its *production-possibilities curve*. Although it is difficult to depict the bewildering variety of products available to even a primitive society, we can get a good idea of the limitations by considering a nation's production of 2 classes of goods. In Figure 6, total output has been divided simply into "food," measured on the vertical axis, and "other goods," measured horizontally. The black curve *ABCDE* is the nation's production-possibilities curve, and represents the alternative combinations of "food" and "other goods" that the country could turn out on a normally sustained basis by using all labor, land, and capital equipment available. For example, the nation could produce a GNP whose composition is represented by point *B*, consisting of 700 units of food and 300 units of other goods. Or, if people preferred more other goods, the nation could produce a GNP composed of 500 units of other goods, but only 400 units of food, corresponding to point *C*.

The production-possibilities curve represents the normal limits to a nation's GNP, but nations do not always produce up to this limit. During a severe recession, for example, GNP might correspond to a point like X, which represents a situation in which unemployed labor and equipment are available to increase the output of both products simultaneously. Note, however, that when the nation is using the entire productive capacity available to it, any increase in the output of one product necessarily means a reduction in the output of the other. The nation could not, for example, sustain a GNP composed of 600 units of food and 800 units of other goods, as represented by point Y.[1] There is, of course, nothing mysterious about this limitation. Workers and productive equipment can be used on only one job at a time, and if there are no unemployed workers or idle equipment available, the production of any one thing can be stepped up only by diverting labor and productive facilities from other products.

---

[1] The production-possibilities curve does not represent a rigidly fixed limit to what a nation can turn out, but it does establish the maximum that can be produced on a *normally sustained* basis. The limits of the curve can be exceeded for short periods of time by inducing people to work longer hours and to skip vacations. Production can be further expanded by taking students out of school and putting them to work, or by bringing retired workers back to the job.

At the peak of World War II all belligerents were producing well beyond the limits of capacity. In 1944, for example, American manufacturing workers averaged 45 hours a week instead of the normal 40. In addition, housewives, retired workers, and students were put to work in industry and drafted into the military, increasing the number of workers to 10 percent above normal. As a result of these adjustments, U.S. wartime output exceeded peacetime capacity by more than 20 percent. However, this rate could not have been sustained, and could not have been reached in the first place without the psychology produced by the war, the military draft, and a number of emergency government measures.

The Slope of the Production-Possibilities Curve The relationship between the gain in the output of one product and the lost production of another is represented by the slope of the production-possibilities curve. At the upper end of the curve in Figure 6 where productive facilities are heavily concentrated on the production of food the slope is flat, indicating that substantial gains in the output of other goods could be obtained at the cost of only a small reduction in food output. For example, point A represents a GNP consisting of 800 units of food and only 100 units of other goods. By taking land and manpower out of agriculture and setting them to work on other jobs, the nation could expand the output of other goods to 300 units while cutting food output only to 700 units, as represented by point B. The shift in composition would increase the output of other goods by 200 units at a cost of only one-half unit of food per unit of other goods produced. As more men, land, and machinery are taken from agriculture and put into industry, however, the production-possibilities curve becomes increasingly steep, showing that more and more food must be sacrificed per unit gain in output of other goods. For example, when the nation is producing the GNP represented at point C, it obtains 400 units of food and 500 units of other goods. Further shifts of land and manpower out of agriculture to expand the production of other goods to 600 units, as represented at point D, would result in a further drop of food production to 200 units. The gain of 100 units of other goods would be obtained at a cost of 2 units of food per unit of other goods produced.

This rising cost of other goods in terms of lost food production follows from the fact that a nation's manpower, land, and equipment are not homogeneous, but vary widely in quality. When output is concentrated in food production, many infertile acres must be brought into cultivation and many workers who are not particularly skilled as farmers must be put to work growing crops. Since much agriculturally unproductive land is ideal for industrial locations, and since many people who are unskilled as farmers are highly skilled industrial workers, their transfer to industrial production provides a substantial boost to the output of other goods while costing little in terms of lost food output. At the other extreme, a heavy concentration of production on other goods would require the use of highly fertile farm land for out-of-the-way industrial sites, and the transfer of highly skilled farmers into industrial jobs for which they had no special qualifications. As a result, there would be a relatively small gain in the output of other goods, but the loss of food production would be substantial.

Opportunity Cost

What has been represented in terms of "food" and "other goods" in Figure 6 holds true of all goods and services. All products are rivals for a nation's limited productive capacity, and an increase in the output of any one involves a reduction in the output of one or more others. The *opportunity cost* of each product is the sacrificed opportunity to use the capacity involved in its production for any other purpose. Opportunity cost represents the only real economic cost, the final restriction on society that prevents it from having everything it might want. Since productive capacity is limited, we must choose the things we want from among the alternatives available, and the choice to have one product is likewise the choice not to have something else. If we want more clothes, we can produce them, but only if less food, gasoline, or other products are turned out, and the real cost of the clothing is the sacrificed opportunity to produce these other things.

Cost versus Finance   Nothing can be produced without incurring an opportunity

cost. The mere fact that an item exists is evidence that labor and materials went into its production that might have been used in some other way. It also follows that somebody somewhere in the community necessarily bears the cost by being deprived of the chance to have the alternative goods. *Finance* consists of the arrangements whereby it is decided which members of society are to bear the burden of the costs of particular items. When a family buys a new car, for example, the answer to the question of who sacrifices the products that could have been produced instead of that car depends on how the purchase is financed. A family that uses its own money and pays cash assumes the burden of the cost itself, for in spending its money for the new car, it automatically deprives itself of the use of the money to buy anything else. When the new car is financed by a loan, however, the family acquires the use of the car without depriving itself of anything else. The sacrifice is assumed on their behalf by the lender, who deprives himself of the right to use his money for any other purpose. Later on, of course, the family will deprive itself of the use of some of its income and repay the loan, thus restoring the ability of the lender to have whatever other products he wants.

Although the costs of most goods and services are assumed by their purchasers, there are other important methods of financing. The costs of goods and services for government use are generally financed by taxation (although sometimes borrowing is also used). Taxation deprives the taxpayers of a portion of their income and forces them to forego alternative products. Moreover, once the money veil is stripped aside, it is clear that military conscription is actually a special way of financing manpower for the armed services whereby the main share of the cost burden is forced onto the draftee. The drafted soldier is, of course, partly compensated, but the existence of the draft is, in itself, evidence that

FIGURE 6   A PRODUCTION-POSSIBILITIES CURVE

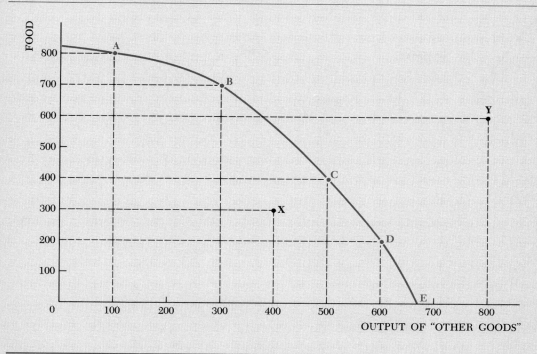

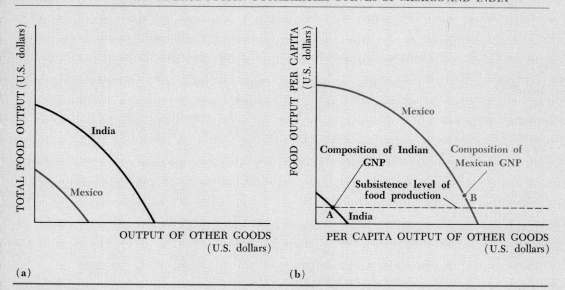

(a)

(b)

SOURCE: Table 2.

the compensation covers something less than the full cost.[2]

Financing does not alter cost, nor does it even "pay" the cost of an item, but merely determines *who* pays. The real cost of an item consists of the sacrifice of the products that could have been produced instead, and these products are sacrificed whether the buyer pays with his own or with borrowed funds. Indeed, the cost is the same if he receives the item as a gift or even if he steals it, although in one case the giver voluntarily assumes the burden of the cost himself, and in the other it is illegally forced by the thief onto somebody else. In order to understand the world's economic problems, it is vital to understand the real nature of cost and finance. Whenever you come across the word "cost," try to strip away the veil of money and find the sacrificed opportunity to have other things; try to see all money payments as ways of dividing the burden of this sacrifice among the members of society.

Opportunity Cost and Economic Behavior

Since a nation with a larger productive

[2] The distinction between cost and financing is the essence of the discussion of whether the United States can "afford" a volunteer army. Some people protest that the added tax "cost" of the arrangement would be too high for the nation to "afford," but the tax bill is not the cost of the army. The cost consists of the alternative products sacrificed because men are in the army rather than on the job, or because they have been taken from school and their entry into the work force is postponed. Under conscription, the fact that the cost is imposed on the draftee does not make it any smaller, nor does it become larger when the taxpayer assumes the burden. What taxpayers object to is not the *cost* of a volunteer army, but the fact that the burden of the cost would be shifted to them.

Having said this, however, it is important to add that there is also a distinction between what a nation can afford to do and what it ought to do. The question of how the armed forces should be financed is less an economic question than a political and social question involving the propriety and even the political safety of maintaining a large standing army whose ranks are filled by professionals.

capacity can turn out more of all kinds of goods, its production-possibilities curve lies farther to the right than that of a nation with smaller capacity. In the comparison of the curves of India and Mexico in part (a) of Figure 7, the production-possibilities curve for India, whose productive capacity is well over $40 billion per year, lies far to the right of that of Mexico with a capacity of no more than $20 billion. India could approximately double any output of food and other goods that Mexico could turn out.

For most purposes of comparing opportunity costs, however, it is more important to represent production-possibilities curves on a *per capita* basis. That is, the curves are drawn so that the coordinates of each point represent the per capita output of the respective products. A comparison of the per capita production-possibilities curves of India and Mexico is shown in part (b) of Figure 7. Since Indian GNP must feed and clothe more than 10 times the Mexican population, Mexico has a vastly greater productive capacity than India on a per capital basis.

We can now see how great disparities in productive capacity help account for some of the observed differences in the economic behavior of rich and poor countries. In Figure 4, for example, we saw how nations with a larger GNP per capita tend to devote a smaller proportion of GNP to agricultural production, and this is certainly the case with India and Mexico. The composition of Indian GNP corresponds to point A in Figure 7, indicating that almost half of Indian output consists of agricultural products. In contrast, less than 20 percent of Mexican GNP consists of food, as represented by point B. The reason for the great difference in the composition of output is that the real cost of nonfood products consists of the sacrificed opportunity to produce food. India cannot use much of its productive capacity for non-food purposes without reducing per capita food production below the level required for survival (represented by the level of the dashed line). The real cost of automobiles, for example, would be a further reduction of an already inadequate diet. In contrast, while Mexicans tend to eat more than people in India, they prefer not to sacrifice other, more desirable things in order to continue the expansion of food output. Average Mexican agricultural output per capita is well over the subsistence level, but it still occupies a small fraction of total output.

Later we shall see how opportunity cost helps to account for many other important aspects of economic behavior, and how it is an important element in the dynamics of economic growth.

SOURCES OF INEQUALITY IN PRODUCTIVE CAPACITY

The productive capacity of a nation at a given time depends on 2 classes of factors. The first class involves those things that influence the total number of manhours of labor annually available for work. These include the size, age distribution, sex composition, and rate of growth of population, as well as the customs, laws, and other institutions that affect who works and who does not and the number of hours each worker devotes to the job. The second class of factors are those of a more technical sort that determine the productivity of an average hour's work. This class includes the health, education, and skill of the work force, the quantity and quality of natural resources available, the state of technical knowledge, and the quantity and types of capital equipment on hand.

The Capacity Equation

The relationship among the determinants of productive capacity is easily summarized in a simple formula. Let the maximum GNP a nation can produce on a normally sustained basis be GNP*, and let L designate the number of people ready, willing, and able to work, while h represents the average number of hours normally worked per person. Accordingly, hL is the total number of manhours annually available for productive work, and where π represents average output per manhour, it then follows that GNP* $= \pi hL$.

As an example of the application of the formula, 78 million people in the United States were ready, willing, and able to work in 1965, and normal hours averaged 1,900 per year. This made a total of 1,900 × 78 million, or about 147 billion manhours available for turning out goods and services. The average output per manhour during that year was estimated to have been about $4.52 at 1958 prices, so the 1965 productive capacity of the United States was given by GNP* $= \$4.52 \times 1,900 \times 78$ million, or about $670 billion (1958 prices).

For purposes of comparison among countries, of course, we are less concerned with total productive capacity than we are with GNP per capita. Accordingly, we are interested in the ratio of productive capacity to N, the total number of people in the population. The relationship is obtained by dividing both sides of the GNP formula by N, to obtain GNP*$/N = \pi h(L/N)$.

This formula expresses potential output per person as the product of output per manhour, average hours normally worked per year, and the fraction of the population ready, willing, and able to work. In the case of the United States in 1965, for example, population was 194 million. Therefore, L/N was 78/194, or .40. Using the earlier values for output per manhour and hours, the formula gives 1965 U.S. productive capacity per person as GNP*$/N = \$4.52 \times 1900 \times .40$, or about $3,500.

The term GNP*$/N$ sets the normal limit to per capita GNP, but during a given year a nation can produce either less or more than this figure. During recession periods, production falls below capacity, as many potential workers are unemployed or work short hours. On the other hand, as we have noted, GNP per capita can be driven above capacity for short emergency periods by recruiting housewives, students, and others who would not normally be available for work, and by getting people to work longer than normal hours.

The formula for productive capacity provides a useful framework within which to analyse international differences in output per person, or to study the nature of economic growth within any one nation, by centering the analysis on 3 elements: L/N, the proportion of the population ready, willing, and able to work; h, the average number of hours available per year, and π, the average output per manhour.

The remainder of this chapter deals with the labor force and hours of work, while the analysis of productivity is sufficiently important to take up the entire next chapter. It should be emphasized, however, that the individual elements of the formula are not independent, but influence each other in important ways. In many respects the relationships of the elements to each other are more important and more interesting than the determinants of the elements themselves.

Ratio of Labor Force to Population

The *labor force* consists of all the people in the nation who are ready, willing, and able to work. Thus the symbol L/N in the productive capacity formula represents the ratio of labor force to total population. This ratio depends on 3 separate factors: the *age distribution* of the population, the customary *working age*, and the *labor force participation rate*, the fraction of adults who are in the labor force. The ratio of labor force to total population is equal to the adult fraction of the population multiplied by the labor force participation rate. In the U.S., for example, about 69 percent of the population is aged 15 or older. Of these, about 56.5 percent are in the labor force. This makes the ratio of labor force to total population equal to .69 × .565, or 39 percent.

The Influence of the Age Distribution of the Population

The proportion of adults in any population depends partly on how fast the population is growing. A rapidly growing population in which families are large, means large numbers of children per adult and a correspondingly low ratio of adults to total population. This, in turn, tends to hold down GNP per capita, since the output of a few adults must support the entire community. There is, of course, no clearly defined age at which a person automatically becomes a potentially productive member of society, but for purposes of international comparison it is convenient to use the percentage of population aged 15 or over. The ratio of persons 15 or over to total population varies widely among the nations of the world. The lowest ratios are found in Costa Rica, Nicaragua, and the U.A.R., where just over half the total population is 15 or older. The highest ratios are found in Luxembourg, Sweden, and West Germany, where they reach nearly 80 percent.

These wide differences are related to the rate of population growth, as shown in Table 3. Among the 10 countries with the highest proportion of adult population, growth rates below 1 percent predominate. Among the 10 countries with the lowest proportion of adult population, most have population growth rates in excess of 3 percent per year, and in Costa Rica the growth rate exceeds 4 percent.

The wide differences in age distribution make an important contribution to the observed difference in GNP per capita. If the percent of adults in the population were the only difference between countries, with

TABLE 3 RAPID POPULATION GROWTH CONTRIBUTES TO LOW GNP PER PERSON

NATION	POPULATION GROWTH (PERCENT PER YEAR)	PERCENTAGE OF POPULATION AGE 15 OR OLDER
Ten nations with the greatest percentage of population 15 or over:		
Luxembourg	0.9	78.5
Sweden	0.6	78.0
West Germany	1.3	78.2
Belgium	0.6	76.5
Switzerland	2.1	75.6
France	1.3	75.5
Denmark	0.7	75.0
Hungary	0.8	74.0
Greece	0.7	73.4
Ten nations with the smallest percentage of population 15 or over:		
Jordan	3.1	54.7
Ecuador	3.1	54.5
Pakistan	2.1	54.0
Tunisia	2.0	53.5
Syria	3.2	53.6
Philippines	3.3	52.0
Honduras	3.3	52.0
U.A.R.	2.7	51.8
Nicaragua	3.1	51.6
Costa Rica	4.3	50.0

SOURCE: United Nations, *Demographic Yearbook, 1964,* New York, 1965.

productivity and all other factors the same, a nation like Luxembourg with 78.5 percent of the population 15 or older would have a per capita GNP 50 percent greater than that of a nation like Costa Rica in which adults make up only 50 percent of the population.

Population Growth and Economic Dynamics

The relationship between population growth and productive capacity works both ways. As we have just seen, high birth rates contribute to a low proportion of adults in the population and hold down material standards of living. At the same time, however, low standards of living contribute to high birth rates. The result is a cycle in which poverty feeds on itself: Poor people have high birth rates, and high birth rates keep people poor. A society caught in such a cycle is "locked in" its poverty. Its standard of living will rise if the birth rate falls, but to get the birth rate down requires a rise in the standard of living!

Once a society can somehow break this lock, however, rising living standards contribute to lower birth rates and slower population growth. A rising fraction of adults in the population adds further to the increasing living standard, reenforcing the decline in the birth rate, and rising material welfare feeds on itself.

The Influence of Working Age

Another important determinant of the ratio of labor force to population is the minimum working age, which varies widely from one society to another. In the United States, 16 is the normal minimum job-holding age, but according to a recent survey, almost 10 percent of U.S. children aged 14 were in the labor force, at least as part-time workers of some kind. In Iraq, on the other hand, nearly 60 percent of the children between 5 and 14 were counted in the labor force.

Accurate comparisons of the extent of child labor in different nations are impossible. In many of the richest countries, the proportions are so small that data are not collected, and among the very poorest countries, estimates, if they exist at all, are crude. Moreover, the kinds of children's activities that are counted as employment differ widely from place to place. Nevertheless, we can get some idea of the nature of the variation from Table 4. As one might expect, the highest rates of child labor are found in the poorest of the reporting countries. In a country where labor productivity is low to begin with, everybody has to pitch in to turn out enough to go around. Children either work or they starve. Where

TABLE 4   LABOR FORCE PARTICIPATION OF CHILDREN IN SELECTED COUNTRIES

	GNP PER CAPITA	PERCENT IN LABOR FORCE	AGE
Poorer countries:			
Iraq	279	58.0	5–14
Thailand	109	45.5	11–14
Taiwan	342	36.9	12–14
Sudan	101	32.2	5–14
Pakistan	84	31.5	10–14
India	91	29.3	10–14
Ecuador	211	27.0	12–14
Portugal	372	21.8	10–14
Iran	230	19.7	10–14
Richer countries:			
Switzerland	2,170	0.3	10–14
Sweden	2,300	0.8	10–14
Malta	425	2.4	10–14
Netherlands	1,380	2.6	10–14
Belgium	1,640	3.0	10–14
Spain	870	7.6	10–14

SOURCE: United Nations, *Demographic Yearbook, 1964,* New York, 1965.

labor productivity is high enough so that an adequate standard of living can be attained without their help, children are released from labor and sent to school. That is, as productivity grows and living standards rise, people rarely take the entire gain in the form of greater material output. Some of it is used to relieve the economic burden on children by raising the customary working age.

Child Labor and Economic Dynamics
This relationship between rising productivity and reduced child labor is another dynamic element in economic growth. Education is one of the important determinants of labor productivity. A modern, complex economy could not function without a corps of highly skilled technicians, and extensive investment in education is an important aspect of any program of eco-

nomic development. There are, however, serious opportunity costs involved in education. Not only must some of the few already educated people be withdrawn from other activities to teach, but large numbers of young people must be withdrawn from the labor force to go to school. The goods and services that students could otherwise produce represent a substantial part of the real cost of education, and where labor productivity is very low, society cannot afford much of it.

The older and stronger children become, the greater the output that must be sacrificed to keep them in school, and therefore education in low-income societies must be restricted largely to the very young. Since in agricultural economies child labor is most needed in summer, the opportunity cost of education is further reduced by restricting the school year to the less productive winter months, a practice carried over into modern educational schedules. Even so, the sacrifice of the output of child labor is a serious loss to an economy already near the bare subsistence level, thus low productivity means the use of child labor. Child labor means poor education. Poor education means low productivity, completing another dynamic cycle in which poverty feeds on itself. Once a society can somehow make a start that raises productivity above the danger level, the labor of children can be spared for education, resulting in further productivity gains from a better-educated labor force. The higher productivity makes it possible to release even more children for even more years of school, and a cycle of self-sustaining growth is under way.

The Influence of Differences in Labor Force Participation Rates   Not all adults are part of the economically active population, the labor force. To be a member of the labor force, a person must not only be of working age, but must be ready, willing, and able to work on a job whose output is counted as part of the GNP. The *labor force participation rate* of any group of adults is the percentage of adults who are members of the labor force.

The labor force participation rates of men of prime working age—say 25 to 65—are uniformly high in all nations. There are always a certain number of sick, injured, or retired workers, and others who are not economically active for one reason or another, but well over 90 percent of men in these age brackets are ready, willing, and able to work. Differences in male labor force participation occur primarily among the youngest and the oldest age groups. The U.S. labor force shown in Figure 8 includes over 96 percent of men age 25 to 34, but only 43 percent of men under age 20. Most of the difference lies in the large numbers of young men in high school and college. Labor force participation rates decline again among older men as sickness and injury take their toll, and, more important in a productive society like ours, as workers retire.

The principal reason that labor force

FIGURE 8   U.S. LABOR FORCE PARTICIPATION RATES BY AGE AND SEX

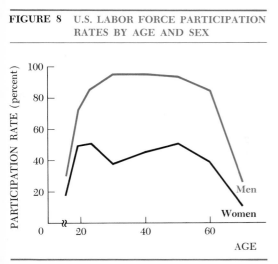

SOURCE: *Statistical Abstract of the United States, 1965.*

participation among men is lowest in the richer European and North American nations is that young men stay in school longer while older workers retire at younger ages than they do in other parts of the world.

The biological and social role of women as mothers and housewives not only makes their labor force participation rates lower than those of men the same age, but gives a distinctive pattern to the variation among age groups. Labor force participation rates reach nearly 50 percent for American women age 20 to 24, but drop to 37 percent for ages 25 to 35, and then rise steadily to over 50 percent in the age bracket 45 to 54 years before declining again. The dip in labor force participation is, of course, associated with the appearance of children, and the more children a woman has, the longer she tends to remain at home. The more rapidly the population is expanding, therefore, the deeper and wider this dip becomes. Thus population growth has a second depressing influence on output per capita. At the same time that it reduces the proportion of adults in the population, it also reduces the proportion of adults who can enter the labor force. The greatest international differences in the labor force participation rates of women, however, arise out of religious and cultural differences. As shown in Table 5, the lowest female labor force participation rates are found in Islamic countries, where they normally average less than 10 percent. The contrast between Pakistan and India is especially striking in this regard. Rates in Spanish- and Portuguese-speaking countries, while double those of Islam, are well below those of the rest of the world.

The women with the highest labor force participation rates are those in the Eastern European Communist countries and those in the emerging nations of Africa. High rates of job holding by women make an important contribution to per capita output

TABLE 5 LABOR FORCE PARTICIPATION RATES, SELECTED COUNTRIES

| | PARTICIPATION RATE | | |
	TOTAL	MEN	WOMEN
Selected Islamic nations:			
Morocco	47.1	87.2	8.8
U.A.R.	46.5	89.0	5.2
Iran	52.1	93.4	9.4
Iraq	45.3	89.1	2.9
Pakistan	55.0	90.7	14.6
For comparison:			
India	67.3	90.2	42.9
Selected Spanish- and Portugese-speaking nations:			
Spain	51.6	89.0	17.7
Costa Rica	53.8	90.8	15.7
El Salvador	54.2	92.4	19.2
Argentina	53.5	83.4	24.0
Mexico	55.3	92.4	19.7
Portugal	51.5	91.0	17.0
Brazil	54.3	92.0	16.5
Selected West European and North American nations:			
France	56.4	78.6	36.2
West Germany	60.5	83.3	41.1
Sweden	55.4	78.6	32.7
U.K.	59.5	86.0	35.3
Canada	54.0	78.1	29.7
U.S.	56.3	78.9	35.1
Selected Eastern European nations:			
Bulgaria	74.9	87.9	62.2
Poland	69.9	82.9	58.4
U.S.S.R.	68.2	83.0	57.0
Romania	80.9	92.6	70.2
Selected emerging African nations:			
Congo	81.7	84.0	79.8
Ghana	73.0	89.1	56.6
Niger	95.8	97.3	94.4

SOURCES: United Nations, *Demographic Yearbook, 1964,* New York, 1965. Figures for U.S.S.R. calculated from data in U.S. Joint Publications Research Service, translator and publisher, *The National Economy in the U.S.S.R. in 1960* (Statistical Yearbook), Washington, D.C., 1962. Brazil calculated from data in United Nations, *Demographic Yearbook, 1955.*

in the U.S.S.R. and other Communist countries. Due to heavy military losses during World War II, women constitute 57.5 per-

cent of the Soviet population of working age. If female labor force participation rates were the same in the U.S.S.R. as they are in the U.S., the labor force and output per capita of the U.S.S.R. would be 20 percent below the levels actually observed.

International Differences in Hours of Work

The number of hours worked per year depends on the length of the typical work week and the total number of weeks worked, adjusted for holidays, vacations, and so on. A 12-hour, sunrise-to-sunset schedule 6 days a week would result in a 72-hour work week, or 3,744 hours per year. Even in agriculture, however, seasonal variations in work schedules would hold the total work year somewhat below this, and the number of part-time workers employed during planting and harvest periods would reduce the average still further. As productive power rises, moreover, people prefer to take part of the gain in increased leisure rather than in more material goods. This means shorter work days, fewer days per week, and more holidays and vacations. A century ago, full-time workers in the U.S. put in an average of 66 hours per week in 6 11-hour days.[3] Today, the U.S. workday is typically 8 hours instead of 11, a 5-day week is uniform, holidays like Thanksgiving, Labor Day, and Memorial Day have been added to the calendar (together with the provision that when the holiday falls on a Sunday, the following Monday is taken off), and at least 2 weeks' vacation with pay is the privilege of most workers.

The tendency for average hours to decline as productive capacity rises can also

[3] U.S. Bureau of the Census, *Historical Statistics of the United States, Colonial Times to 1957,* Washington, D.C., 1960.

be seen in the international comparisons of Table 6 and Figure 9.

The Interdependence of Manhours and Productivity

When the average number of hours per worker is multiplied by the ratio of labor force to population, the result is the potential number of manhours annually available per person in the nation. Clearly, if the productivity of labor is about the same in 2 countries, GNP per capita will tend to differ with the per capita manhours available. A good example is provided by comparison of GNP per capita in West Germany with that in Israel. According to Table 6, West German workers averaged 44.7 hours per week on a full-time basis, compared to only slightly more than 40 in Israel. In addition, the West German labor force involved 47.7 percent of the population compared to only

FIGURE 9   AS PEOPLE GET RICHER, THEY TEND TO WORK SHORTER HOURS

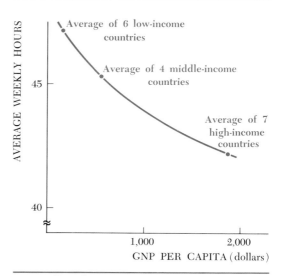

SOURCE: Data from Table 5.

34.5 percent in Israel. Ignoring any differences in the proportion of part-time workers in the 2 nations, we can estimate that about 55 percent more manhours were annually available to the average West German than to the average Israeli, and on this basis alone we could expect GNP per capita to be about 55 percent higher in West Germany. The result is in very close agreement with the GNP per capita figures of $1,860 for West Germany and $1,180 for Israel given in Table A.

But when the 55 percent difference between West Germany and Israel is laid against the observed fact that GNP per capita in the richest country of the world is about 100 times that in the poorest, it becomes clear that the principal cause of the inequality in world living standards is not the number of manhours available, but the productivity of those hours. Even at the extremes, the highest ratio of labor force to population is no more than double the lowest, and the longest hours per year are

TABLE 6   AVERAGE WEEKLY WORKING HOURS

COUNTRY	HOURS PER WEEK	GNP PER CAPITA
Algeria	46.0	$ 206
U.A.R.	48.0	110
U.S.	40.1	3,210
Haiti	45.2	86
Mexico	45.3	443
Peru	47.2	238
Cyprus	44.0	623
Israel	40.7	1,204
Japan	45.5	813
Malaysia	49.0	272
Philippines	48.1	237
Belgium	41.3	1,565
France	45.9	1,614
West Germany	44.7	1,651
Ireland	44.6	2,146
Malta	46.8	414
U.K.	47.6	1,561
New Zealand	39.1	1,877

SOURCE: International Labor Office, *Yearbook of Labor Statistics, 1964.*

no more than double the shortest. At a maximum, then, the 2 elements combined could contribute no more than a factor of 4 to international differences in living standards.

As a matter of fact, however, the influence is more often the other way, for productivity, labor force, and hours are closely interrelated. Heavy labor force participation and long hours are, as we have seen, ways in which poor nations partially compensate for low productivity. For example, as a rough estimate, the output per man-hour of American workers is about 100 times greater than that of workers in the African nation of Niger, yet the U.S. GNP per capita of $3,310 is only 40 times the $82 per capita produced in Niger. Part of the difference is made up by maintaining 55 percent of the Niger population in the labor force compared to only about 40 percent in the U.S. The remainder is made up by working longer hours.

In the next chapter we turn to an examination of the causes of the great differences in labor productivity and a more detailed analysis of the relationship between productivity and the other elements of the equation.

SUMMARY

The distribution of productive capacity among the nations of the world is highly unequal. Output per person in the United States is roughly 100 times what it is in the poorest parts of the world. Compared to an average GNP per capita of over $3,000 in the United States, more than half the world lives in countries in which the average is no more than $100. The most productive tenth of the world's people turns out almost half of the world's goods and services.

The great disparities in productive power are mirrored in the way people live. In poor nations, more babies die at birth and adults live fewer years; few people can read, and few amenities are available. Output is concentrated on food and essentials. Most ironically, poor nations have higher birth rates than rich nations, and because their incomes grow more slowly, economic disparities increase as time passes.

Productive capacity imposes limitations on the combinations of goods and services that a society can produce. A *production-possibilities* curve is a representation of this limitation showing the different combinations of output a nation can produce on a normally sustained basis with the manpower, natural resources, and equipment available to it. Along the production-possibilities curve, all products are rivals for the limited productive capacity. The *opportunity cost* of any one product is the sacrificed opportunity to produce something else with the same labor and resources. Opportunity cost is the only *true economic cost* and represents the ultimate limitation on any nation to have everything it might want. People can have more of anything they choose, but only at the cost of sacrificed opportunity to have something else.

In contrast to cost, *finance* involves the arrangements (usually but not necessarily monetary) for assigning the sacrifice of opportunity to particular members of society. In most cases, production is financed by purchase, an arrangement by which the buyer voluntarily deprives himself of the chance to have other things. The burden of cost can also be assigned by borrowing, taxation or donations, or through such institutions as conscription. The concepts of opportunity cost and finance are fundamental to all economic analysis and will recur throughout the rest of this study.

International inequality of output and income arises from inequality of productive capacity. The many sources of inequality are conveniently summarized in a capacity equation: $GNP^* = \pi h L$, or on a per capita basis, $GNP^*/N = \pi h(L/N)$, where GNP^* stands for the maximum GNP a nation can produce on a normally sustained basis, π is the productivity of labor, h is the average number of hours worked per person, L is the labor force, and N is total population. The formula permits the systematic analysis of economic inequality in terms of three elements:

1. The ratio of labor force to population (L/N), which depends on the age distribution of the population, on the typical working age, and on labor force participation rates as these are affected by custom, population growth, and labor productivity itself.

2. Average hours worked per year (h), which are influenced by law, custom, and productivity.

3. Average output per manhour of labor (π), which depends on technical factors to be examined in the next chapter.

Although the elements in the equation can be analysed separately, they are actually closely interdependent. In particular, poor nations tend to compensate for low productivity by employing a larger percentage of the population and by working longer hours.

TABLE A SELECTED ECONOMIC DATA FOR 93 COUNTRIES

COUNTRY	1964 PER CAPITA GNP (U.S. $)	CAPITAL FORMATION % OF GNP	1960–1964 GROWTH RATE OF REAL PER CAPITA GNP	POPU-LATION (MILLIONS)	LIFE EXPECT-ANCY AT AGE 20 YEARS	ANNUAL RATE OF POPULATION GROWTH % PER YEAR	INFANT MOR-TALITY PER 1,000 BIRTHS	AGRI-CULTURE % OF GNP
Malawi	35	15	−1.1	3.9	n.a.	3.1	n.a.	47
Nigeria	57	n.a.	2.5	56.4	n.a.	2.0	68	65
Tanzania	62	12	1.3	10.3	n.a.	1.9	n.a.	57
Burma	66	18	2.3	24.2	n.a.	2.0	n.a.	33
Congo	66	18	2.9	15.3	36	2.0	180	28
Haiti	73	n.a.	0.4	4.6	34	2.3	n.a.	n.a.
Uganda	76	14	−1.3	7.4	n.a.	2.0	n.a.	61
Kenya	84	n.a.	n.a.	9.1	33	2.9	n.a.	42
South Korea	84	15	3.2	27.6	45	2.9	n.a.	51
Pakistan	84	n.a.	3.1	100.8	n.a.	2.1	n.a.	49
China Mainland	90	n.a.	n.a.	690.0	n.a.	1.5	n.a.	48
India	91	n.a.	0.7	471.6	33	2.3	139	47
South Vietnam	100	11	0.1	15.7	n.a.	3.3	29	33
Sudan	101	15	2.0	13.2	n.a.	2.8	n.a.	51
Thailand	109	21	2.4	29.7	43	3.0	38	34
U.A.R.	110	n.a.	2.1	24.7	46	2.7	119	58
Cambodia	117	18	2.3	6.2	38	2.7	n.a.	41
Bolivia	153	16	3.4	3.7	47	1.4	n.a.	24
Philippines	154	17	0.8	31.3	46	3.3	73	33
Ceylon	166	13	−0.4	11.0	50	2.6	53	46
Tunisia	181	24	3.3	4.6	n.a.	2.0	n.a.	21
Morocco	189	11	0.6	12.9	n.a.	2.8	149	32
Jordan	191	18	n.a.	1.8	n.a.	3.1	48	62
Zambia	193	14	0.5	3.6	n.a.	2.9	n.a.	11
Syria	195	n.a.	8.2	5.2	n.a.	3.2	26	37
Paraguay	196	n.a.	1.0	2.0	n.a.	2.6	n.a.	37
Brazil	200	18	1.5	78.8	43	3.1	n.a.	28
Colombia	204	20	2.0	14.7	n.a.	3.2	83	32
Libya	210	n.a.	n.a.	1.6	n.a.	3.6	n.a.	25
Ecuador	211	20	0.8	4.9	47	3.1	90	36
Lebanon	221	n.a.	n.a.	1.9	n.a.	2.4	n.a.	58
Honduras	225	14	0.7	2.1	n.a.	3.3	45	45
Iran	230	13	0.2	22.9	n.a.	2.5	n.a.	24
S. Rhodesia	233	15	0.3	4.1	n.a.	3.3	n.a.	21
Peru	237	24	3.2	11.3	39	3.0	84	22
Dominican Republic	254	9	n.a.	3.5	n.a.	3.5	80	n.a.
El Salvador	254	10	n.a.	2.8	45	3.3	n.a.	32
Ghana	254	18	n.a.	7.5	n.a.	2.7	82	n.a.
Turkey	261	13	1.6	30.7	n.a.	2.8	165	38
Cuba	273	18	n.a.	7.4	n.a.	2.1	n.a.	n.a.
Guyana	279	17	n.a.	0.6	n.a.	2.8	48	26
Iraq	279	14	n.a.	7.0	n.a.	1.7	21	16
Malaysia	282	19	2.8	7.8	n.a.	3.1	57	31
Nicaragua	295	17	4.8	1.6	n.a.	3.1	55	65
Algeria	336	26	7.7	10.4	n.a.	0.9	70	21
Taiwan	342	19	3.6	12.1	40	1.6	24	27
Guatemala	370	16	2.8	4.3	38	3.3	95	28

TABLE A   SELECTED ECONOMIC DATA FOR 93 COUNTRIES *(Continued)*

COUNTRY	1964 PER CAPITA GNP (U.S. $)	CAPITAL FORMATION % OF GNP	1960–1964 GROWTH RATE OF REAL PER CAPITA GNP	POPU-LATION (MILLIONS)	LIFE EXPECT-ANCY AT AGE 20 YEARS	ANNUAL RATE OF POPULATION GROWTH % PER YEAR	INFANT MOR-TALITY PER 1,000 BIRTHS	AGRI-CULTURE % OF GNP
Portugal	372	15	5.3	9.1	52	0.7	65	23
Gabon	390	n.a.	n.a.	0.5	n.a.	1.6	229	n.a.
Barbados	396	22	n.a.	0.2	43	1.0	40	26
Costa Rica	402	15	n.a.	1.4	48	4.3	86	32
Panama	414	17	2.2	1.2	50	2.8	44	62
Malta	425	25	n.a.	0.3	n.a.	0.1	35	7
Jamaica	445	20	7.2	1.6	46	1.7	37	61
Uruguay	450	14	−1.3	2.7	n.a.	1.4	n.a.	15
Mexico	460	16	3.0	39.6	39	3.2	65	18
Chile	545	14	1.0	8.5	45	2.5	114	10
Cyprus	545	13	2.0	0.6	n.a.	0.8	29	18
Greece	565	16	2.8	8.5	45	0.7	36	28
Poland	600	34	5.6	31.3	51	1.3	42	33
Trinidad and Tobago	600	31	6.8	0.9	47	3.1	42	62
Union of South Africa	600	22	3.5	17.5	38	2.4	115	9
Argentina	620	n.a.	0.3	22.0	47	1.6	60	19
Bulgaria	625	32	7.9	8.1	45	0.9	65	n.a.
Yugoslavia	635	44	7.2	19.3	49	1.1	72	28
Japan	725	39	9.7	96.9	51	1.0	19	13
Ireland	850	21	3.8	2.8	n.a.	1.9	25	22
Spain	870	24	3.5	31.3	50	0.8	37	21
Venezuela	923	20	1.5	8.4	n.a.	3.4	49	8
Italy	970	22	5.0	51.1	53	0.7	36	15
Puerto Rico	1000	29	5.9	2.6	47	2.0	42	8
Austria	1175	30	2.6	7.2	51	0.5	29	10
Israel	1180	33	6.5	2.5	53	3.6	27	10
Hungary	1210	28	5.6	10.1	51	0.4	39	21
Czechoslovakia	1230	n.a.	5.3	14.1	52	0.7	25	14
U.S.S.R.	1350	25	7.5	228.0	n.a.	1.6	28	20
Netherlands	1380	28	3.1	12.1	55	1.4	14	9
Luxembourg	1582	26	2.7	0.2	50	0.9	29	61
Finland	1590	29	4.4	4.6	50	0.8	17	19
Belgium	1640	21	4.6	9.4	51	0.6	24	7
United Kingdom	1670	19	2.6	54.2	53	0.7	20	4
Iceland	1690	27	3.7	0.2	52	1.9	18	n.a.
Norway	1710	29	4.6	3.7	55	0.8	17	9
E. Germany	1800	n.a.	n.a.	16.0	53	−0.2	25	11
France	1830	23	3.8	48.4	51	1.3	22	8
W. Germany	1860	27	3.5	56.1	52	1.3	24	5
Denmark	1880	24	4.1	4.7	54	0.7	19	12
New Zealand	1900	24	1.8	2.6	53	2.2	20	n.a.
Australia	1910	30	2.6	11.1	52	2.1	19	13
Switzerland	2170	31	3.1	5.9	52	2.1	19	n.a.
Sweden	2300	25	4.7	19.3	54	0.6	12	n.a.
Canada	2320	24	3.2	19.3	52	2.0	25	6
U.S.	3310	18	2.7	192.1	52	1.6	25	3

SOURCE: Data adapted from *United Nations Statistical Yearbook, 1965.*

CHAPTER 4
Productivity
and Economic Growth

The 2 basic elements in productive capacity are the quantity of manpower available for work and the productivity of that manpower on the job. Taken as separate determinants of living standards, productivity is by far the more important, for although a larger number of manhours per person might make output per capita in one nation as much as 4 times that in another, productivity is often responsible for differences as large as 100 times or more. Moreover, the elements are not independent. On one hand, the proportion of the population in the labor force and the typical number of hours worked depend partly on labor productivity, since poor nations compensate for low output per manhour by employing more manhours. On the other hand, the rate of growth of productivity is encouraged by reduction in the quantity of manpower applied to current production, for it is necessary to keep young people out of the labor force to educate them for skilled occupations. This chapter is devoted to an examination of the causes of the great disparities in labor productivity and to further exploration of the important interaction of productivity with population and manpower in the dynamics of economic growth.

THE FACTORS
OF PRODUCTION

Production occurs when land and other natural resources are combined by human effort working in combination with capital equipment to turn out goods and services. In economic terminology, all types of natural resources are often lumped into a single category and called "land"; all mental, physical, or other human productive effort is classed together as "labor"; while all structures, equipment, and other capital goods are referred to as "capital."[1] Land, labor, and capital are the three *factors of production,* the basic ingredients of the production process. The productivity of labor in a nation depends on the quality of the factors of production available to it, on the proportions among them, and on the way in which they are combined on the job.

Natural Resources The productivity of labor depends on the quality of natural resources. It takes fewer manhours per bushel to grow wheat on fertile Kansas prairie loam than on the dry stony hillsides of a Greek island. The same amount of labor can turn out more steel where rich iron, coal, and limestone deposits lie close together than when poor ores, thin coal seams, and scanty quarries lie far apart. The benign climate and favorable environment of Polynesia permits a comfortable and leisurely life with minimum effort, even using primitive technology, while life in the Arctic is a constant battle for food and warmth. An extreme example of the effect of high-quality resources is Kuwait, on the Persian Gulf, where thanks to rich

oil deposits, minimum effort yields the highest GNP per capita in the world.

Labor The productivity of labor depends on the strength, health, skill, and training of the workers themselves. Strong healthy workers turn out products better and faster than those who are weak and sick. In regions to which debilitating diseases are endemic, workers are slow, easily tired, and unable to sustain productive effort. To quote the World Health Organization, "Programmes for social improvement set great store by village development, but if the villager is periodically on his back with chills and fever and has chronic anemia, such schemes have little prospect of success. Similarly, emphasis on agricultural improvement—better seeds and farming methods—is of little purpose if the peasant, because of malaria, can hardly drag himself into the fields at planting time; for him the learning of new methods is only an added burden."[2]

Another important factor in the quality of the labor force is its level of education. Jobs that require understanding written instructions or following written plans or schedules require workers who can read, and skilled technical jobs demand high proficiency in reading. Illiterate workers must be trained without the advantages of written instruction and cannot even take notes on what they hear. Illiterate farmers are closed off from new equipment or chemical fertilizers until their use can be explained orally and repeated often enough for them to learn. Many jobs in a modern technical economy require a college education. Unless enough highly educated people are available, less productive methods must be used.

[1] Like many other economic terms, the word "capital" has several different meanings that must be carefully distinguished. As a factor of production, "capital"—sometimes called "real capital" for emphasis—refers to the collection of structures, machinery, equipment, and inventory stocks in existence at a given time. In another usage "capital" designates a sum of money accumulated for the purpose of financing the acquisition of capital goods. In this sense, a business firm raises capital (money) to finance the purchase of additional real capital (machinery and equipment).

The term "capitalism" is a third usage, and designates an economic system like that of the United States in which productive equipment is predominantly owned by privately organized business firms financed by privately raised funds. *Capitalism* in this sense is distinguished from *socialism,* an economic system in which productive equipment is predominantly owned by government enterprises financed by government funds.

[2] World Health Organization, *Malaria Eradication: A Plea for Health,* Geneva, 1958. As quoted in Robin Barlow, *The Economic Effects of Malaria Eradication,* School of Public Health, The University of Michigan, 1968, p. 7.

Capital Goods Capital goods are items of produced wealth that cannot be directly consumed themselves, but greatly increase the productivity of labor when applied to further production. These goods include the entire range of durable equipment from hammers, saws, and other simple tools to jet aircraft, electronic computers, and nuclear reactors.

Capital goods are so much a part of everyday life that their nature and use need hardly be explained. Modern capital equipment permits us to use power to perform operations faster and more accurately than could be done by hand and to do things that simply could not be done any other way. In addition to machinery and equipment, capital goods include the social *infrastructure*, that is, capital goods in the form of roads, highways, and other facilities that are essential for the operation of the rest of the economic system.

Primitive man discovered that he could increase his productivity by using rocks shaped to his fist and flint chips as knives and axes. He soon learned the merits of the lever, the boat, the fish net, and other primitive capital. Modern precision tools and power equipment are a heritage from past production that has slowly evolved over the entire span of human existence. Today's capital goods were produced with the aid of older tools and equipment. These, in turn, were the products of still older and less refined equipment, and so on back in an unbroken chain. If all the equipment in the world were suddenly destroyed, we would have to rebuild from the most primitive level.

A special form of capital consists of the inventories of raw materials and finished goods held by producers at various points along the production line. Probably the first inventories were grain stored after harvest to be consumed as needed. This replaced seasonal "feast or famine" with a secure year-round food supply. Stockpiles of materials also form buffers between successive stages of processing, permitting each to operate at its own pace without running out of materials when it temporarily operates faster than the supplier stage, and without needing to speed up when it temporarily falls behind the demands of its own customers. Production as we know it would be impossible if everything were made to order. Imagine how long it would take to get a new suit if nothing happened *anywhere* along the line until you ordered it!

THE RATIO OF LABOR TO LAND

In addition to the quality of land, labor, and capital, average output per manhour depends on the proportions among these factors. Even if all natural resources were of uniform quality, and all workers were equally skilled and equipped with tools of the same caliber, the productivity of labor would depend on the size of the population to be supported with the given natural resources.

A larger population means more people to be fed, clothed, and housed. Although the population itself provides the extra manpower to produce the additional output, there are no more natural resources than before. Existing resources must be worked harder, and this fact tends to lower output per manhour.

Output per manhour is highest when natural resources can be used lavishly to conserve labor time. Carpenters can build much faster when they can waste wood. An odd-size piece or one cut by mistake is simply thrown aside. When more houses must be built from the same lumber pile, boards must be carefully sorted to get the most out of each; when mistakes are made, the piece must be fitted in somewhere else. The same principle can be seen in the kinds of products nations produce and the methods they use. Nations with relatively sparce populations like those of the U.S. and

Canada grow wheat for cereal because it can be grown extensively on vast acreages of land with little labor effort. In contrast, the densely crowded countries of Asia depend on rice which, with intensive care and hand cultivation, gives much higher food yield per acre, although at great labor cost.

Since resources vary in quality, growth in population also lowers productivity by requiring the use of lower-grade resources. A small population can confine itself to the most fertile fields and to the richest mines, but a large population must supplement them by bringing into use poorer fields and thinner ore veins that are harder to work and yield output of lower quality. A small population can use resources close at hand. A large population must go farther afield, devoting more labor to transportation and materials handling.

Specialization of Production

If its only effect were to bring lower-quality natural resources into use and to intensify the use of better-quality resources, a larger population would automatically mean lower labor productivity. Fortunately, however, a larger population also permits the employment of more highly specialized methods of production, with the result that the question of whether productivity rises or falls as population grows depends on which of the effects is stronger in any given case.

Specialization means that individuals, groups, or regions produce only a portion of the products they use. In a completely unspecialized society, each household would provide all the products for its own needs by hunting and gathering, or by subsistence agriculture. In a specialized society, in contrast, one man is a doctor, another a shoemaker; one store sells men's clothing, another sells books; one region manufactures automobiles, another grows corn. In modern mass-production indus-tries, jobs are extremely specialized. Each worker on a production line performs only a single limited task—twisting a particular bolt, or inspecting a single part as it goes by. Such specialization saves the time spent in changing tools or shifting jobs. A single worker who used 3 tools for 3 different tasks might spend as much time putting down, picking up, and adjusting his tools as he did applying them to the job. Giving 3 different workers 1 tool each enables them to work faster.

Specialization raises labor productivity in several other ways. In the first place, not everyone is equally suited to all jobs. Some are stronger than others, some have greater dexterity, keener eyesight, or greater intelligence. If each one had to do the jobs at which he was poor as well as the jobs at which he excelled, average productivity would be low. When each one does the job at which he is best, average productivity is higher. Obviously the same thing holds for regions, and output is greater when each region specializes in the things it produces best.

Many jobs are technically so complex that they require a long investment in training. If people could not be given specialized education for such work, it would not be performed at all, or it would be done on an ineffective, primitive level. Once trained and working, a specialist becomes increasingly skilled in the requirements of his job, and by continuous experience with a narrow range of similar problems learns how to diagnose and deal with them. This is an important aspect of the productivity of a medical, legal, engineering, or other professional specialist.

Specialization involves more than simply dividing existing production processes more finely; it is often an important aspect of changes in technique. For example, the shift on the part of American manufacturing firms from producing their own steam, water, or animal power to purchased electricity represented specialization of power production in electrical utilities. That is, the introduction of electricity to some extent represented a shift of the jobs that used to be performed in manufacturing firms by engineers, firemen, and other steam-plant employees to more highly specialized workers employed in electrical utilities. A more recent example of a similar kind is the increased reliance on precooked frozen items among restaurants that once did their own cooking.

Finally, it is important to note that the result of increased specialization is not all clear gain, but necessarily brings with it a greater need for exchange of products among different members of the community. The smaller the proportion of total product each group of the society supplies for itself, the greater the proportion of productive activity that must be devoted to trade, and the larger the fraction of the work force engaged in commerce, transportation, banking, communications, and similar services. The increased absorption of productive resources by these middleman occupations must be taken into account in evaluating the gains from greater specialization.

Population Density as a Limit to Specialization Given known production techniques, specialization is limited by the number of people to be served. A man can be a specialist only when there is enough call for his services to keep him fully occupied. An isolated community of 10 or 15 families could hardly have a full-time doctor, lawyer, or clergyman. Within industry, the degree to which production of a product can be specialized depends on the number of units to be made. If only a few typewriters were produced each year, they would be handcrafted because an elaborate typewriter production line would stand idle most of the time.

The need to keep specialized workers and equipment fully occupied is often described by the statement that "specialization is limited by the extent of the market." Since the "extent" of the market is partly a

matter of population density, specialization can be carried further in large, dense metropolitan centers than in outlying regions. The kinds of stores found in towns of different sizes is an interesting example of this fact. Since everybody needs daily groceries, even a very small hamlet will have some kind of grocery store. Because clothing is more durable and is bought less frequently, a slightly larger town is needed to support a clothing store. Still fewer people buy musical instruments in any given year; these stores must draw customers from a town of some size. The average populations served by various kinds of retail stores is shown in Table 1. The average grocery store serves only a few more than 500 people, while it takes about 60,000 people to keep a bookstore in business. If you want to specialize in selling religious goods, you need an average market of nearly 150,000 people.

TABLE 1   SPECIALIZATION IS LIMITED BY THE MARKET: AVERAGE POPULATION SERVED BY RETAIL STORES

Average U.S. population served	by a store that specializes in:
147,835	Religious goods
122,987	Luggage and leather goods
96,321	Typewriters
60,363	Books
40,885	Cameras and photographic supplies
34,246	Musical instruments
23,623	Children's and infants' wear
15,000	Movie houses
9,082	Flowers (florist shops)
3,097	Drugs and sundries (drug stores)
1,800	Haircuts (barber shops)
1,250	Hair care, etc. (beauty shops)
849	Gasoline (filling stations)
758	Meals (restaurants and eating places)
503	Groceries

SOURCE: Calculations from data in U.S. Bureau of Census, *Census of Business*, 1958.

Transportation and Communication as Limits to Specialization In addition to population density, specialization depends on the ease with which goods can be transported and the facility with which people can communicate. A good system of roads, railroads, and telephones encourages specialization. Where roads are poor, or where people are cut off from one another by political or cultural differences, less specialization can occur. One of the great sources of American productivity is our long history of a continental trading area, well equipped with cheap communications and devoid of any cultural or political hindrance to interstate commerce. One of the serious barriers to higher European productivity has been the region's long history of political and cultural fragmentation into small market areas. The European Common Market is an attempt to extend the European market to permit greater specialization.

Technical Limits to Specialization Even when the market is large enough, there is ultimately an end to the gains from increased specialization. In any kind of production a level is finally reached beyond which further expansion of markets no longer permits any useful subdivision of operations. At this point, productivity gains from specialization reach their maximum, and any further increases in output are achieved by duplicating existing operations rather than by making them more highly specialized.

The Principle of Diminishing Returns

The actual relationship between population and productivity represents the difference between the 2 opposing forces of intensive resource use and specialization. At one extreme, despite abundant high-quality resources, labor productivity may be low in a country whose population is too small to permit effective specialization of produc-

tion. Under these circumstances, a larger population permits more productivity gain from increased specialization than would be lost from intensified resource use, and labor productivity tends to rise with population. As population grows increasingly dense, however, smaller and smaller gains are made due to increased specialization, while problems of resource availability intensify. When the point is reached at which further gains from specialization of operations are completely offset by rising resource limitations, labor productivity has reached its maximum, and it thereafter declines as the intensification of resource use detracts more from productivity than can be gained from further specialization.

The total relationship of productivity to population for a given quality of labor force and given technical knowledge is shown in Figure 1. Population is measured on the horizontal axis. The productivity corresponding to the resource use and specialization permitted by that population is plotted vertically. The black curve shows how output per manhour tends to change with population. A small population need exploit only the highest-grade resources, but it must do so with minimum specialization. The resulting low productivity is represented by the low level of the curve at the left of the figure. As population grows, resources are worked more intensively, and lower-grade land and ore beds must be brought into use. But labor productivity rises because the gains from increased specialization outweigh the depressing influence of more intensive resource use. The rising segment of the curve is called the *stage of increasing returns to population growth.*

Population growth continues in the stage of increasing returns until some maximum output per manhour is reached at population N_o. When the number of people exceeds N_o, the productivity loss from further intensification of resource exploitation and from the need to bring inferior resources into production overbalances the

FIGURE 1   RELATIONSHIP OF LABOR PRODUCTIVITY TO POPULATION:
THE PRINCIPLE OF DIMINISHING RETURNS

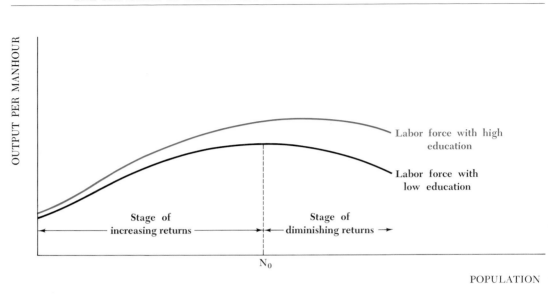

gains from increased specialization, and output per manhour declines. This is called the *stage of diminishing returns*. The population N_0 at which productivity is a maximum is called the *point of diminishing returns*.

Productivity and Population Policy It is clear from Figure 1 that low productivity can result from either too few or too many people, and national population policies vary accordingly. Countries in the stage of increasing returns, like Australia, Brazil, and Canada, and like the United States of an earlier day, actively recruit immigrants from other areas. Immigration adds to native population growth and raises productivity that much faster.[3] Countries like

[3] Immigration, of course, makes special additional contributions to productivity. Since most immigrants are young adults of prime working age, immigration raises the percentage of adults in the population. Moreover, when trained workers can be attracted, the society gains the skills of the newly arrived workers without paying the opportunity cost of their education.

modern India, Greece, and much of Southeast Asia, and like Ireland in an earlier period, that are far into the stage of diminishing returns, must depend on emigration to supplement birth control and other population limitations if productivity is to be maintained above a starvation level.

Shifts in the Productivity Curve The general level of the curve in Figure 1 depends on the quality of resources available, the quality of the labor force, the level of technical knowledge, and the capital available per worker. Improvement in these basic factors is represented by raising the entire level of the curve. For example, the black curve in Figure 1 might represent a society with low average education, while the blue curve represents a better-educated labor force. The comparison of the 2 curves indicates thaat a better-educated labor force of a given size is more productive than one with poorer education. Moreover, the blue curve reaches its maximum productivity at a larger population, corresponding to the fact that increased education expands the limits of productivity gains—for example by preparing students for specialized professions—and raises the point of diminishing returns to population growth.

CAPITAL AND PRODUCTIVITY

Since the capital available to a society consists of its accumulated inheritance from past economic activity, the quantity and quality of the different types of structures and equipment available are as fixed on any given date as the resources with which the society is endowed by nature. Unlike natural resources, however, capital goods are man-made products and the types, quantities, and qualities that will be available in the future depend on the composition of output today. As something given from the past but variable in the future, capital goods are a key element not only in the determination of the level of productivity at a given time, but in the dynamics of its growth.

The Use of Capital Goods as "Roundabout" Production

The use of capital equipment is often called a "roundabout" method of production. Instead of trying to produce directly with labor and materials, we first turn out tools and machines, and then use these together with other resources to turn out the desired end product. Since production is a very complex process, it is difficult to illustrate realistically, but a highly schematic comparison of 3 different ways to organize shoe production is shown in Figure 2. In unspecialized method A, each worker performs all the operations involved in making the complete shoe, working entirely by hand methods. In method B, the same tools are employed, but different workers have been assigned to specialized jobs. In roundabout method C, one group of specialized workers produces shoes with the aid of machinery supplied by the other workers. Once the machines are produced, of course, they continue to render service for a number of years, but the workers in the machinery industry are engaged in turning out replacements for the equipment that wears out each year, and thus their labor is properly a part of the cost of shoe production. Even when the labor of the machine workers is counted, however, output per manhour is highest when the roundabout method is employed.

Careful consideration of the long-run structure of production reveals that, once in use, machinery is merely a special kind of specialization. Since the ultimate product is shoes, shoe machinery is really an intermediate product used as an input by the industry, and producers of shoe machinery are just as much a part of shoe production as are cattle ranchers, leather tanners, or other specialized workers.

Although this is an elementary and rather obvious point, failure to understand it has been at the base of much economic misunderstanding. Abstracted from the physical forms involved, the introduction of machinery represents a *reorganization of labor*. Relatively less labor is applied in direct production, and relatively more is employed indirectly in the production of capital goods. This process is sometimes referred to as the "substitution" of capital in place of labor, but it actually represents the substitution of labor and resources in one industry—machinery production—in place of labor and resources employed in another, such as shoe production.

The Opportunity Cost of Capital Goods

There is, however, an important difference between the roundabout process of using capital equipment and other methods of specialization. Machines must be produced *before* they can be used. Therefore, before more capital can be employed to increase

FIGURE 2   THREE METHODS OF MAKING SHOES

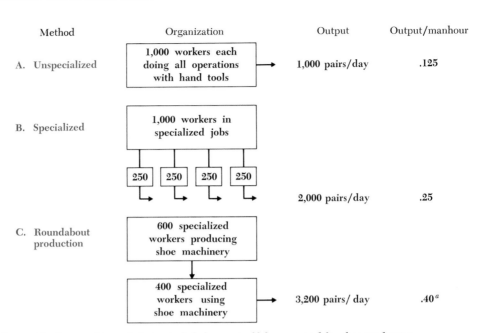

Method	Organization	Output	Output/manhour
A. Unspecialized	1,000 workers each doing all operations with hand tools	1,000 pairs/day	.125
B. Specialized	1,000 workers in specialized jobs — 250 250 250 250	2,000 pairs/day	.25
C. Roundabout production	600 specialized workers producing shoe machinery; 400 specialized workers using shoe machinery	3,200 pairs/ day	.40[a]

[a] Employment in shoe machinery industry included as part of labor required for shoe production.

the output of consumer goods, extra labor and resources must first be diverted from consumer goods into the machinery industry. In other words, the opportunity cost of adding to the stock of capital for use tomorrow is the sacrifice of consumer goods for use today.

As a simple illustration of the opportunity cost of adding to the capital in the shoe industry, suppose that 600 men employed in the machinery industry can turn out 1 set of shoe machines per year. In addition, suppose that, once produced, each set of machines requires 80 men to operate it, and lasts for 5 years before it needs replacement. The transition from hand to machine methods under these conditions is shown in Table 2. In years 1 and 2, 1,000 workers using hand methods produce a total of 500,000 pairs of shoes per year. The process of capital accumulation begins in year 3 with the shift of 600 workers to the machinery industry to pro-

duce 1 set of machines. During this year, the remaining 400 workers, still using hand methods, turn out only 200,000 pairs of shoes. The need to divert labor and resources to investment goods has reduced the output of consumer goods by 300,000.

In year 4, while the 600 workers are making a second set of machines, the first set goes into operation, and 80 workers are put to work using machine methods. This raises total shoe output to 320,000 pairs, but output is still below the original level. In year 5, as the third set of machines is produced, 160 workers using the 2 existing sets raise output to 440,000 pairs. In year 6, the employment of 3 sets of machines restores output to slightly above the original level. As sets 4 and 5 come into use in years 6 and 7, shoe output reaches 800,000, 20 percent above initial yearly output.

At this point the transition is completed, and shoe production has been entirely shifted over to machine methods. From

TABLE 2   THE OPPORTUNITY COST OF INVESTMENT

| YEAR | SHOE MACHINERY INDUSTRY | | SHOE INDUSTRY | | | | | |
| | EMPLOY-MENT | OUTPUT | MACHINE METHODS | | | HAND METHODS | | TOTAL |
			MACHINES	WORKERS	OUTPUT	WORKERS	OUTPUT	
1	—	—	—	—	—	1,000	500,000	500,000
2	—	—	—	—	—	1,000	500,000	500,000
3	600	1	—	—	—	400	200,000	200,000
4	600	1	1	80	160,000	320	160,000	320,000
5	600	1	2	160	320,000	240	120,000	440,000
6	600	1	3	240	480,000	160	80,000	560,000
7	600	1	4	320	640,000	80	40,000	680,000
8	600	1	5	400	800,000	—	—	800,000
9	600	1	5	400	800,000	—	—	800,000
10	600	1	5	400	800,000	—	—	800,000

here on, the new set of machines produced each year by the 600 machinery workers merely replaces an old set wearing out. Where formerly 500,000 pairs of shoes were produced annually by 1,000 workers all performing hand operations in the shoe industry, the same 1,000 workers now turn out 800,000 pairs per year. Of course, the organization of production has been altered. Of the workers 600 are now employed making shoe machines, while the remaining 400 use the machines. Nevertheless, the reorganization merely represents a better way for 1,000 men to specialize in turning out shoes.

The opportunity cost of the transition has been substantial. Before the higher levels of shoe output were reached, shoe production actually declined below its original level, and the total output of years 3, 4, and 5 was only 960,000 pairs compared to 1,500,000 pairs that would have been turned out at the initial rate of 500,000 pairs a year. In other words, the cost of the investment was the sacrificed opportunity to turn out 540,000 pairs of shoes—more than a year's output at the old rate.

The Cost of Investment Shown by the Production-Possibilities Curve The cost of new investment is represented more gen-

erally in Figure 3, where the black production-possibilities curve *ABCD* shows the division of GNP into consumer goods (measured horizontally) and investment goods (measured vertically). Although society could choose to produce any combination of consumer goods and capital equipment on the curve, the choice it makes today will influence the productivity of labor tomorrow, and hence the location of tomorrow's production-possibilities curve.

For one thing, since existing plant and equipment depreciate, a certain minimum annual investment in replacements is necessary to keep productivity from falling.

FIGURE 3   THE OPPORTUNITY COST OF CAPITAL ACCUMULATION

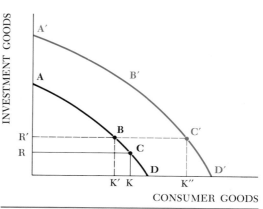

These replacement requirements are represented in the figure by the production of R units of capital goods. Thus society can afford a maximum of K units per year of consumer goods—corresponding to a composition of output represented by point C—while still maintaining its productive facilities intact. However, this choice would represent consumption of the entire net national product, and would leave nothing for expansion of capacity. If future productive capacity is to be increased, the current output of new plant and equipment must exceed replacement. If society chose a composition of GNP corresponding to point B, for example, current output of consumer goods would be cut from K to K', but the production of R' units of equipment would result in an increase in future productive capacity to the level represented by the blue curve $A'B'C'D'$. The transition to the new production-possibilities curve would be complete when the stock of capital reached the point at which the annual output of R' new units was just sufficient to replace old equipment as it wears out. The new production-possibilities curve would permit a maximum output of K'' units of consumer goods per year, corresponding to a composition of GNP represented by point C', but the cost of the investment would have entailed the sacrifice of $K - K'$ units of consumption during the period of the transition.

THE DYNAMICS OF ECONOMIC GROWTH

Growing productivity is not an isolated fortuitous phenomenon, but a coherent process during which the quantity, quality, and proportions of productive factors change to yield higher output per person. In many nations it is difficult to get started, but once under way, economic growth feeds on itself and becomes increasingly easy to maintain.

Although investment is a key element in the growth process, the dynamics of population growth, psychology, and economic institutions also play important roles.

The Dynamics of Investment

The opportunity cost of capital accumulation is one of the most serious initial barriers to starting economic growth. It is one of the ironies of life that people who are ill-fed and poorly clothed to begin with, and who thus have the greatest need for higher productivity, are the very ones who can least afford the further cuts in living standards that are the cost of investment, while those who are already well off can easily pay for further growth.

In fact, once capital accumulation and economic growth are well established, rich nations no longer pay for investment through any actual reduction of living standards. They merely use a portion of each addition to productive capacity to turn out still more investment rather than using it all for extra consumption. The operation of the process is illustrated in Figure 4. The black line OM denotes the gross investment needed merely to maintain the corresponding level of productive capacity. For example, to maintain a capacity represented by the production-possibilities curve $A_1B_1C_1D_1$ would require gross investment of R_1 units of capital goods to replace depreciation of existing plant and equipment, as indicated at Point C_1. To maintain capacity $A_2B_2C_2D_2$ would require annual gross investment indicated at C_2, and so on.

Now a society whose productive capacity is $A_1B_1C_1D_1$ can obtain maximum current consumption of K_1 by selecting a composition of GNP corresponding to point C_1. To raise its productive capacity, however, it must be able to cut consumption below this maximum level, say to K_1', permitting investment to rise to R_1'. The OM line indicates that continued annual in-

FIGURE 4 THE DYNAMICS OF INVESTMENT

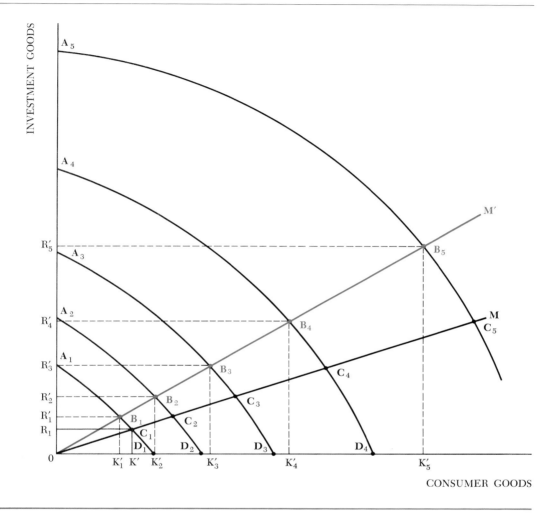

vestment of R_1' units of capital goods will ultimately raise the production-possibilities curve to $A_2B_2C_2D_2$ and no further, but if society uses a part of its increased productive capacity to raise the output of capital equipment above R_1', investment and consumption will continue to grow simultaneously. For example, suppose the society chooses not merely to raise investment to R_1', but to establish permanently a composition of GNP that devotes a greater proportion of output to investment than is required for replacement. This choice might

correspond to the blue line OM'. That is, when productive capacity reaches A_2B_2-C_2D_2, society selects the composition of GNP corresponding to B_2, yielding not only more consumer goods than formerly but also investment for continued economic growth. When capacity reaches $A_3B_3C_3D_3$, consumption will have risen to K_3', but investment of R_3' generates even greater economic growth, and so on. Under these circumstances, the path of GNP in successive years would be represented by the points B_1, B_2, B_3, and so on as shown in

Figure 4. Not only do consumption and investment grow simultaneously, but they grow by increasing amounts each year.

Them That Has, Gits! The mutually reinforcing growth of investment and productive capacity can be clearly observed in the data of Table A at the end of Chapter 3. Figure 5 shows the response of investment to productivity. Countries were divided into 7 groups and average percent of GNP invested was plotted against average GNP per capita for each group as a point. The curve drawn through the midst of the points indicates the strong tendency for richer nations to invest both more resources and a larger fraction of GNP than poor nations do.

The other side of the process is shown in Figure 6, which indicates the response of real growth in GNP per capita to the frac-

FIGURE 6   RELATIONSHIP OF GROWTH OF
REAL GNP PER CAPITA TO PERCENT
OF GNP INVESTED

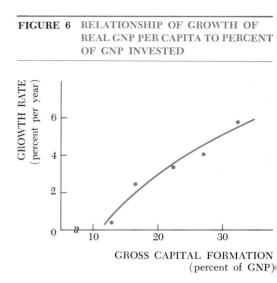

GROSS CAPITAL FORMATION
(percent of GNP)

SOURCE: Calculated from data from Table A of Chapter 3.

tion of GNP invested. Countries for which both investment and rate-of-growth data are available in Table A have been grouped by percent of GNP invested, and the average rate of growth of real GNP per capita has been calculated for each group and plotted. The strong tendency for investment to force up growth rates is revealed not only by the strong upward trend to the curve drawn through the points, but by the behavior of individual nations in each group. The 12 countries that invested less than 15 percent of GNP averaged less than one-half of 1 percent per year growth in GNP per capita. Only 1 member of this group (Cyprus) had a growth rate as high as 2 percent, while in 3 (Uganda, Ceylon, and Uruguay) real GNP per capita actually declined during the period. In contrast, among the 9 nations that invested 30 percent of GNP or more, the average growth rate was nearly 6 percent per annum. Only 1 member of the high-investment group (Australia) had a growth rate as low as 2.6 percent, while two-thirds of the group grew faster than 5 percent. The highest growth rate of

FIGURE 5   GNP PER CAPITA AND PERCENT OF
GNP DEVOTED TO GROSS CAPITAL
FORMATION

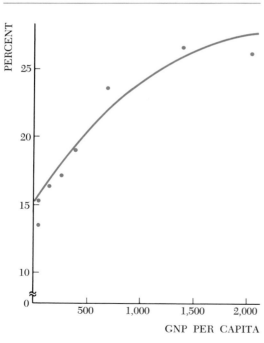

GNP PER CAPITA

SOURCE: Calculated from data from Table A of Chapter 3.

9.7 percent per year was found in Japan, where investment amounted to almost 40 percent of GNP!

The relationship depicted suggests that a nation must devote a minimum of 10 to 12 percent of its GNP to gross capital expenditure, merely to prevent productivity from declining. As larger fractions are invested, the growth rate accelerates accordingly. The result is the ironic phenomenon we saw earlier in Figure 5 of Chapter 3. The richer people are to begin with, the more of their total output they can afford to devote to capital goods, and the more rapidly their productivity rises. Unfair as it may seem, the conclusion is inescapable that the first dynamic law of economic growth is "Them that has, gits!"

Foreign Trade and Foreign Aid   A given nation often lacks the industrial facilities to produce the equipment it needs, but the problem of capital accumulation is much the same when equipment is purchased abroad. Foreign purchase requires the nation to export enough of its current production to finance the cost of the new equipment. Thus, whether a nation shifts resources directly into the production of capital goods, or whether it buys its equipment abroad, it nevertheless must pay the opportunity cost of capital by sacrificing consumption goods during the period of accumulation.

Since underdeveloped nations are heavily agricultural, they must often depend on the export of sugar, coffee, tea, cocoa, oil seeds, or other crops to finance investment. This leaves them in a doubly precarious position. On the one hand, crops are subject to growing conditions, and a bad monsoon or an unusual insect problem not only may leave no investable surplus, but may require that precious reserves of foreign currency be used to finance food imports rather than to buy new capital equipment. On the other hand, prices received for raw material exports depend on economic conditions in the

developed nations and an economic recession in Europe or North America can completely dislocate the development process in the poorest parts of the world where growth is most needed.

During the last 25 years the industrial nations of the world, individually and through such agencies as the World Bank, have undertaken programs of loans to developing countries to permit them to finance economic development. Although interest and repayment are tailored to the long-run development prospects for the country, they can create serious financial problems for poor countries, and industrial nations, particularly the United States, have made extensive outright grants for economic development. Although many people think of these grants as some kind of international "charity program" for taking care of the immediate needs of poor foreigners, this is not the case. Foreign economic aid programs are not "relief" but are intended to help poor nations finance the initial cost of beginning economic development. It is hoped that, once the high initial cost is financed, these countries can get in an expanding cycle of economic growth, and be able to continue on their own.

*The Repressive Force
of Population Growth*

Population enters into economic growth in 3 ways: through its age composition, its size, and its rate of growth. In Chapter 3 we dealt with the importance of age composition as an influence on the ratio of labor force to total population, and in the first part of this chapter we examined the effect of population size in the principle of diminishing returns. But the rate of growth of population has a double effect on productivity gains which is quite independent of those of size and age composition.

First of all, a rapidly growing population maintains continual pressure on the economic system to turn out consumer goods rather than to invest. It is hard for a country with a rapidly growing population to get on a growth path like *OM'* in Figure 4, because as fast as additional productive capacity becomes available, it is met by more mouths clamoring to be fed. Indeed, instead of raising per capita output, the nation may find itself chasing its own population growth on an economic treadmill like Alice in *Through the Looking Glass,* running as fast as possible just to stay in the same place.

Not only does population growth leave less output available for investment, but it alters the kinds of capital goods produced. In particular, a rapidly growing population must put more of its investable resources into new housing, leaving a smaller fraction to produce plants and equipment. In addition, population growth actually decreases the effectiveness of whatever new productive equipment does become available. In order to raise labor productivity, gross investment must result in an increase in the amount of capital *per worker*. If capital accumulation merely provides enough capital goods to equip new members of the labor force with the same tools and machinery the old workers had, nothing will happen to the productivity of labor. If productivity is to be raised, capital must be accumulated faster than workers are added to the labor force. It follows that among nations that devote the same percentage of GNP to capital formation, GNP per capita will grow most slowly where population growth is fastest.

The repressive force of rapid population growth is so strong that the long-run economic effects of many social improvements —especially those affecting public health— sometimes turn out to be the opposite of what might at first be expected. Here is a startling illustration: Careful estimates of the consequences of the eradication of malaria from Ceylon in 1947 suggest that the 1970 GNP per capita of that country will fall 2 percent *below* what it would have been if the disease had not been eradicated.[4] When the calculations were further projected, it was estimated that by 1977 GNP per capita in Ceylon will be 13 percent below the figure that would otherwise have been reached! These results follow from the fact that although the eradication of malaria added to the number of hours of work annually available per person, and gave an initial boost to the productivity of labor, it also raised the population growth rate from 1.9 percent per year to 2.7 percent per year, and the rapid population growth more than offset the other gains.[5]

The retarding influence of population growth is an important cause of differences in the rates of growth of real per capita output in different nations, as can be seen by comparing data from Table A of Chapter 3 for different countries that invested the same fraction of GNP. For example, in Jamaica and Venezuela, although each devoted 20 percent of total output to investment, real per capita GNP grew 5 times faster in Jamaica, partly because Jamaican population was growing only half as fast as Venezuelan population. As another example, although New Zealand and Belgium both invested 24 percent of GNP, a population growing 3 times faster in New Zealand helped hold its growth of GNP per capita to less than half that of Belgium.

Individual instances can be deceptive, but the general tendency of population growth to retard economic development is

[4] Robin Barlow, *op. cit.*

[5] As Professor Barlow is careful to point out, we are dealing here only with the *economic* effects of the program. Even if part of the opportunity cost of malaria eradication is fewer material goods per person, it may still be worth the price. In any case, malaria is not the only way to hold population in check. According to Professor Barlow, if eradication in 1947 had been accompanied by a program of birth control effective enough to have reduced birth rates by 40 percent within 10 years, 1970 GNP per capita would have been almost 50 percent higher.

FIGURE 7   POPULATION GROWTH AND
GROWTH OF REAL GNP PER CAPITA
(16 countries investing 20 to 24 percent of
GNP)

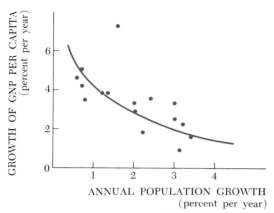

ANNUAL POPULATION GROWTH
(percent per year)

SOURCE: Table A of Chapter 3.

shown in Figure 7 where growth rate of per capita GNP is plotted vertically against annual population growth on the horizontal axis. Each point on the chart represents 1 of the 16 countries listed in Table A of Chapter 3 as investing 20 to 24 percent of its GNP. With the proportion invested roughly the same, the retarding influence of population growth is clearly indicated by the downward slope of the curve drawn through the scatter of points.

Psychological Factors in Economic Development

Since economic development is the result of human actions, it depends on deliberate choices that people make about the way they want to live and what they want to do with their material goods. For this reason, economic development depends on beliefs, attitudes, and other psychological factors. But like other elements in economic growth, social psychology interacts with the development process. It adds to the difficulty of getting it under way in an underdeveloped

area, but contributes to it and reenforces it once it is well started.

In a static society it is taken for granted that total output is fixed and that if one person gets more, somebody else is going to get less. Anyone trying to better his own position is likely to be treated with suspicion and open hostility. The personal viewpoint encourages protecting what one already has, not striving for something better. This view is reenforced by the risks involved in development, for there is no guarantee that a new idea, even a good one, will pay off for the first man who tries it. Any new venture contains a risk of failure that must be run, and this risk may appear overwhelming to people with little to spare. The values of nondeveloping societies tend to denigrate effort. Striving after gain is "coarse," "crude," or even "evil." Inherited aristocratic family status is "noble," denial of material things is "holy," and society venerates the status quo, engendering attitudes that increase the probability of a poor society's staying poor.

A developing nation tends to encourage an opposite set of attitudes. It is taken for granted that output and living standards will rise. It is possible for one man to gain while others gain, or at least while nobody else loses. Improvement in personal condition is seen as the reward for hard work and self-discipline and as open to all. Failure is viewed as personal inadequacy, the results of not venturing enough, of not trying hard enough. Hard work, investment, rising income, and increasing wealth come to be looked on almost as ends in themselves and carry high status among the materialistic values of society, while aristocratic family pride is labeled "snobbish." The attitudes engendered by economic development contribute to the pressure for further growth.

Growth and Economic Institutions

In this chapter we have examined the technical side of economic growth, but we must also recognize that technical factors do not operate alone. Although the cost of investment in terms of consumer goods sacrificed is a purely technical matter, whether a given society will make the sacrifice or not depends partly on how the cost is to be financed. Many societies with enough productive capacity to provide a generous margin over current consumption needs are unable to marshal the surplus to finance investment. In some of these countries investable income flows to oil sheiks or absentee landlords to be spent on sophisticated living or invested in already developed countries. Other countries divert much of their investable income to the military. For many years colonialism operated to siphon investable income out of colonies for use at home, and a depression is one way of wasting investable capacity by leaving it unemployed.

Unless a nation has a system of institutions through which investment can be financed, economic growth is slow, if not impossible. A variety of institutions are available, however. A check of Table A of

Chapter 3 quickly reveals that several of the Eastern European countries invest greater proportions of GNP than their more prosperous western neighbors do. One reason lies in the power of the state planners to finance investment through state control over incomes. Households have no say in the matter; the sacrifice of consumer goods is simply imposed by holding down their disposable incomes.

Centrally planned investment financed by taxation also plays a role in many emerging nations, as does finance by foreign loans and development grants. Even in the United States, as we shall see later, the government exercises broad indirect control over the fraction of GNP devoted to investment. But in the first instance, American investment is financed largely by voluntary sacrifices of individuals and groups who save part of their current receipts. These individual savings are amassed and invested by business firms, and it is to the organization of these firms and their role in the investment process that we turn next.

SUMMARY

The greatest differences in the productive capacity of various nations arise from differences in the productivity of labor, measured as the average amount of real output produced per hour of labor on the job. Differences in productivity are analysed in terms of the quantity and qualities of the 3 *factors of production—land, labor,* and *capital*—and in terms of the proportions among them and the way they are combined in production.

The ratio of population to land affects labor productivity in 2 opposite ways. On the one hand, when more people must be fed and clothed with the same natural resources, inferior resources must be brought into use, and better-quality resources must be used more intensively. This intensification of resource use tends to lower labor productivity. On the other hand, the more extensive market provided by a larger population permits greater *specialization* of labor, which tends to increase labor productivity.

The actual behavior of productivity results from the difference between the 2 opposing tendencies, which gives rise to the *principle of diminishing returns*. Productivity is low when population density is too low to permit specialized production, but when population grows too large, the need to intensify resource use tends to lower productivity more than it is raised by specialization. As a result, nations can be poor either because they are underpopulated or because they are overpopulated and population policies vary accordingly.

An important key element in the productivity of labor is the extent to which production is carried on by the use of *capital goods* in the form of structures, equipment, and stocks of inventory inherited from the past. Viewed in the long run, the use of capital goods represents a *"roundabout"* method of production. It is a very special kind of specialization in which part of the labor force is removed from the production of goods and services for current consumption, and set to work making machinery and equipment for other workers to use in the future. Changes in the quantity of capital used in production really represent a *reorganization of labor* in which workers and resources are shifted into the capital goods industry instead of being directly employed for the production of consumer goods. Unlike other methods of specialization, however, increased use of capital goods involves opportunity cost because current consumption must be held in check to release resources for the production of machinery and equipment. As a result, the cost of greater output of consumer goods tomorrow is less consumption today.

Economic growth is a coherent process of change in which a high level of investment is sustained, productivity grows, and fundamental shifts occur in birth rates, education, personal psychology, and economic institutions as well as many other aspects of life. Powerful forces work against economic growth in poor countries and tend to keep them poor, but once economic growth is started, it becomes increasingly self-reenforcing. In contrast to poor nations, rich nations are surrounded by powerful dynamic forces that tend to keep them growing even richer.

Investment is an important part of the dynamics of economic growth. Because of its high initial opportunity cost, the least investment occurs in poor countries where it is most needed, while rich countries reinvest a portion of each year's gain to maintain simultaneous growth in both investment and consumption. Nations unable to produce the particular types of equipment they need must finance investment by exports. Exporting does not alter the cost of investment, but the problems of financing in foreign markets puts developing nations at a further disadvantage. Foreign aid programs are designed to help poor countries get started by providing loans and grants for investment financing.

Rapid population growth, characteristic of poor countries, adds to the difficulties of economic development. Where the number of people is rising, opportunity costs of investment are higher, and the effectiveness of any investment made is lower.

Customs, habits, and personal attitudes are important aspects of growth dynamics. Poor people tend to place high priorities on the status quo, on security, and on noneconomic rewards, but people in rapidly developing countries tend to replace these attitudes by others that emphasize material goods, economic accomplishment, and risk-taking. In addition to technical and psychological factors, economic growth depends on social institutions, particularly those relating to economic incentives and to the financing of investment.

CHAPTER 5

The Organization of the Business Firm

The basic unit of planning and control over production is the *enterprise*. All modern economic societies have such control units, but there are wide differences in the ways they are organized. Indeed, the organization of enterprise is one of the characteristics distinguishing different types of economic systems. In a socialist economy like the U.S.S.R., most production is centrally planned, controlled, and financed. Thus the Soviet economic system is characterized by centralized enterprise and actually functions much like a single giant consolidated firm. Although socialist production is subdivided into managerial units frequently referred to as "enterprises," these smaller units have minimum responsibility for planning and control and function more like branches or divisions of an enterprise than like individual business firms.

In contrast, an economic system like that of the United States is characterized by *private enterprise*. That is, control and financing of most production is vested in independent, privately organized enterprises. This chapter is devoted to the institutional organization of these private enterprises as *business firms*. We will examine different types of firms, and we will see how the modern corporation has emerged to meet the needs of mass production techniques for which huge amounts of capital must be privately assembled under central control, and how the increasing complexity of corporate organization has required government regulation.

Without going into the problems of accounting, we will examine the statements that summarize the financial position and operations of a business firm, and we will conclude the chapter with an examination of the giant corporation.

THE ROLE OF ENTERPRISE IN PRODUCTION

In order for production to occur, somebody must decide what products are to be produced. Someone must take the initiative in bringing men, machines, and materials together; assign jobs; and organize and direct the operations. The important function of initiating and organizing production is called *enterprise,* and people who perform this function are called *entrepreneurs* or *enterprisers.* Skillful, energetic, and imaginative enterprisers are the most valuable of all our productive resources. Without them, resources and labor represent only unrealized possibilities. The more enterprisers there are, and the easier it is for them to assemble effective combinations of workers and equipment, the more rapidly productivity rises. In an economic system like ours, enterprisers organize *business firms* to carry out their plans. The easier it is to set up and operate a business firm, the more effectively enterprisers can mobilize resources and apply them to production.

The Element of Risk

Of course, not every new idea is a good one. Sometimes expensive equipment and labor are assembled to make something that few people want. Sometimes the enterpriser is less effective as a manager than he thought he would be. Sometimes a better idea, a superior product, or a cheaper process is developed a little later. In each of these cases, the enterpriser has made a mistake. The labor, materials, and equipment assembled by the firm actually have produced something *less* valuable than they could have in some other employment. Instead of raising social productivity, the enterpriser has actually lowered it.

Before it commits resources to new uses society must protect itself from the consequences of such mistakes by making sure that enterprisers balance the gains possible from successful organization against the losses that will accompany failure. This is done by requiring the enterpriser to finance part of the investment with his own money and to receive, as his reward, only the residual of the value added by the operation, after all other claims have been paid. If he is successful in taking labor, equipment, and materials from less valuable jobs and using them to produce a more valuable product, the profit resulting from the difference in value is his. If he is unsuccessful, and puts valuable resources to a less valuable use, the loss is also his. His investment acts as a buffer to the rest of society, protecting it from his mistake.

THE SOLE PROPRIETORSHIP

The simplest type of firm is the *sole proprietorship.* This is a firm owned by a single person. All the firm's decisions are centered in him, all profit from the firm is his, and he is personally liable for all the firm's debts. In a sole proprietorship there is no legal distinction between the personality and possessions of the owner and those of the firm. In fact the owner *is* the firm and is personally responsible for everything the firm does.

There are several advantages to the sole proprietorship. It is legally simple and easy to establish. Moreover, the identification of the owner with the business provides a powerful incentive for efficient operation, and encourages careful weighing of the risks involved in the undertaking. Any profit the firm makes accrues directly to the owner, but he is also personally liable for losses. Not only can he lose all he has invested in the firm directly, but if this is not enough to cover the firm's debts, he can be sued personally for the balance.

Limitations to the Size of Proprietorships

Its simplicity makes the proprietorship especially well adapted to small-scale business. However, there are severe limitations to its size. First, the proprietorship can grow no larger than the wealth of a single person will permit. In an age of large-scale operations that often require expensive, specialized equipment, few people can accumulate enough capital to finance efficient production.

Of course, the proprietor can supplement his own wealth by borrowing from other people, but even this technique is limited by his resources. The reason is, of course, the ever-present risk of losses. A firm that loses can still repay its debts as long as the loss is no larger than the owner's own investment in the business, for the owner's share of the total wealth of the firm, the *owner's equity*, provides a cushion to protect the creditors. When a $1 million firm is financed by $750,000 invested by the owner and $250,000 borrowed from creditors, the owner's equity is $750,000. If the firm has to be liquidated, the assets can lose this much value and creditors will still receive 100 cents on the dollar. If the owner's equity were only $250,000 and $750,000 were borrowed, however, any loss in asset value exceeding $250,000 would involve losses to creditors.

A second limitation to the size of a sole proprietorship is the difficulty of changing ownership. Investment in a personal business is necessarily a long-term proposition. To get out for any reason—perhaps to follow a more profitable venture in another line—requires sale of the physical assets of the business to a new owner, which is a slow process. The owner must find another man who combines the ability to run the business with the desire to enter it, and who has the money to buy out the owner's equity. The classified sections of any metropolitan newspaper contain advertisements of "business opportunities," representing the attempts of proprietors to sell their stores, shops, or small plants. It may take months to find the right man, and if the owner is in a hurry to sell out, he may have to sacrifice a substantial part of the value of the firm.

The difficulties involved in selling a sole proprietorship mean that this type of business tends to tie down those with the greatest talent for business organization. It takes more enterprising talent and organizing skill to start a successful business than it does to keep one going after it has been set up. Economic growth will be most rapid when those with the greatest initiative and talent can specialize in setting up new firms to exploit new opportunities. This is impossible if, once the firm is established, the organizer cannot sell it to somebody else to run, and move on to new fields. This fact becomes a serious limitation to an economic system that depends on private enterprise to get things done in the best way.

THE PARTNERSHIP

A logical way to increase the capital available to a firm is to increase the number of owners. A *partnership* is composed of several owners who pool their resources together to form the firm. The partners agree among themselves about how much capital each is to contribute, what role each will play in the management, and how much each will share in the profits.

Limitations to the Size of Partnerships

The partnership contract legally defines the duties and the responsibilities of the partners to each other. As far as the public is concerned, however, each of the partners has the legal status of a sole proprietor.

Each partner can sign contracts for the firm, can buy or sell goods or assets belonging to the firm, can borrow or lend on the firm's behalf, and can commit the firm just as a sole proprietor could. Such a commitment is legally binding on the firm and on all the other partners as owners of the firm, whether they agree to it or not. Moreover, each partner is fully liable for all the firm's debts, just as if he were the sole owner. If the firm fails, leaving assets inadequate to cover its debts, creditors can sue any partner individually to collect the balance due. The legal responsibility of partners for each other's acts necessarily confines partnerships to small groups of people with complete confidence in one another. For this reason partnerships rarely grow large enough to apply modern production methods.

Changing ownership of a partnership is even more of a problem than it is for a sole proprietorship. Since partnerships are formed by a legal contract among the owners, the withdrawal of any partner from the firm requires that the business be completely reorganized. Either the assets must be broken up and sold, or else another person must be found who is not only ready and able to buy the departing partner's equity, but who is also acceptable to, and trusted by the remaining partners.

A partnership is automatically terminated by the death of a partner, and must be reorganized as a new firm. It is the practice for each member of the firm to carry life insurance in favor of his partners so they can buy his equity from his estate in the event of his death.

THE CORPORATION

The corporation is a legal form of enterprise designed to take advantage of large-scale production methods by pooling the wealth of many people into a single enter-prise, while at the same time maintaining centralized control over, and responsibility for operations. Unlike partnerships, which are established by private agreement among the partners, a corporation can be established only by charter from the state. Indeed, in the U.S. a century ago corporate charters were issued only by special act of the state legislature. In those days, most farming, manufacturing, and commercial businesses were small enough to be carried on as proprietorships and partnerships. The corporation was looked upon as a very special form of business organization largely restricted to enterprises like canal and railroad companies, for which huge agglomerations of wealth were essential. With the development of mass production technology and the attendant increase in the amount of capital needed for efficient operation, the economic advantages of the corporate form of organization grew rapidly, and today corporate charters are issued routinely by state bureaus.

Organization of the Corporation

Stockholders The corporate charter establishes the corporation as a legal entity distinct and separate from its owners. The corporation is said to be a "legal person." That is, the firm itself is legally treated like a person and can make contracts in its own name and can sue and be sued like a real person. The ownership of the corporation is divided into a specified number of shares of *common stock*, each share representing equal participation in the affairs of the firm. The owners of the company, called *common shareholders* or *common stockholders*, receive certificates of common stock or shares in proportion to their participation in the firm. A man who invests 10 percent of the total capital receives 10 percent of the common shares. Each share entitles its holder to participate in the earnings of the firm in common with other shares. For example, when there are 100,000 shares, each share is entitled to one hundred-thousandth of any earnings. Also, each share entitles the owner to one vote in the annual stockholders' meeting.

By pooling together the individual contributions of a large number of stockholders —often hundreds or thousands—a corporation can accumulate immense amounts of capital. It is free of the size limitations of the proprietorship and the partnership and can grow as large as the most efficient production technique requires.

Directors and Management   In a partnership, any individual partner can transact business for the firm. With thousands of shareholders, however, such an arrangement would lead to immediate chaos and a breakdown of operations. Instead, control of the corporation is centralized in a *board of directors,* elected at the annual stockholders' meeting, each share of stock having one vote. The board of directors acts on behalf of the stockholders to set corporate policy, to make major decisions, and to hire *management* to carry on the day-to-day operations of the firm.

Profits and Dividends   The profits from the operation of the firm accrue to the equity of the stockholders, and are distributed by the board of directors. The board decides how much of the profit is to be paid out to shareholders as dividends. The remainder of the profits constitutes *retained earnings* and is reinvested in the firm, thereby increasing the stockholders' equity.

Limited Liability of Stockholders   In a partnership, all agreements entered into or debts contracted by the firm are personally binding on all the partners. Since the shareholder has given up all immediate control over the corporation, however, he must be protected in some degree from liability for its actions. This is done by defining a limit to the liability of the individual stockholder.

Agreements and debts contracted by the directors and management are binding on the corporation, but not on the shareholders personally. If the corporation cannot fulfill its contracts or pay its debts, it can be sued like a person and, like a person, its property can be taken in payment. The stockholder can lose all he has invested in the company, but he has no personal liability beyond this. As an individual, he is in no way responsible for the debts of the company. This aspect of corporate organization is called *limited liability.*

Transferable Ownership   Individual shareholders can transfer their shares of corporate ownership merely by selling their stock to somebody else. Organized stock exchanges (see the Appendix to this chapter) permit the transfer of the stocks of many corporations in a matter of hours. This easy transferability permits many investors who would hesitate to tie up their wealth in a proprietorship or partnership to participate in corporate ownership.

Fixed Income Securities

Preferred Stock   As owners of the firm, common stockholders stand to make good profits when the firm is successful, but will sustain losses when business is poor. Some investors prefer to give up the chance at a high return in exchange for greater security in the event of low earnings or losses. One way to tap capital held by such people is to offer them preferred stock. *Preferred stock* is, like common stock, a share in the ownership of the company, but instead of equal participation in the profits, preferred shares carry fixed annual dividends that must be paid before dividends can be declared on common stock. There are many different types of preferred stock, but most are *cumulative.* That is, if the fixed preferred dividends are not paid in a given year, they accumulate, and all arrears must be paid before any dividends can be declared on common stock.

In exchange for this preferred dividend position, preferred stockholders forego the chance of participating in greater profits. Since preferred stock usually does not vote, preferred stockholders also give up any participation in management. Nevertheless, they are still owners. They have no claim on the firm beyond its assets and earnings, and even though they are preferred owners in the event of liquidation, they must wait, like other owners, until all creditors are paid off. If any ownership equity remains after the creditors are paid, the preferred stockholders are entitled to recover their equity before the common stockholders.

Bonds   In addition to the various classes of ownership, some corporations borrow money for long periods by issuing *bonds.* Bondholders are not owners, but creditors of the firm. Bonds are corporate I.O.U.'s that promise to pay a specified annual rate of interest and to repay the borrowed principal on a specified date. Bond interest and principal are contractual claims against the firm and must be paid whether the firm makes profits or not. If payments are not made on time, the bondholders can sue the firm to collect.

The use of bonds makes it possible for a firm to borrow large amounts of money from a number of small creditors by breaking up the debt into small units, just as issuing stock breaks up the ownership equity. Certain kinds of firms, most notably public utilities, raise more of their capital by bonds than by stocks.

Leverage   When part of a firm's capital is raised through preferred stocks and bonds, fluctuations in total earnings have a magnified effect on the income of common stockholders. This phenomenon, called "leverage," arises because preferred stocks and bonds are fixed income securities. Leverage is best illustrated by example. Suppose a corporation's ownership equity

of $10 million consists entirely of 100,000 shares of common stock. Since there are no fixed income securities, earnings per common share vary exactly in proportion to total earnings. Total earnings of $500,000 would be $5.00 per share. If total earnings doubled to $1 million, earnings per common share would likewise double to $10. If earnings shrank 80 percent from $500,000 to $100,000, earnings per common share would likewise decline 80 percent from $5 to $1.

Now suppose, however, the same corporate ownership consists of $5 million of 5 percent preferred stock and $5 million divided into 50,000 shares of common stock. Regardless of total earnings, the preferred stock is entitled to dividends of .05 × $5 million, or $250,000. This fixed income gives leverage to the common stock. Thus, when total earnings are $500,000, preferred stockholders receive $250,000, leaving $250,000, or $5 per share of common stock, just as before. But when total earnings double to $1 million, the leverage provided by the fixed income securities triples the earnings per common stock share. Preferred stockholders still get only their $250,000, leaving earnings of $750,000, or $15 per share, to the common stock. Unfortunately, leverage also works when earnings decline. Should total earnings fall to $100,000, preferred stockholders would still be entitled to their fixed $250,000. This would leave common stockholders a loss of $150,000, or $3 per share, despite the positive total earnings made by the company.

Corporate Finance

When a corporation is established by a small group of investors, the owners merely contribute cash or property to the newly chartered company in exchange for shares of stock. When funds are to be raised from a large number of people, however, this informal arrangement will no longer suffice. The people founding or *promoting* the corporation do not know who the would-be shareholders are. Nor can the prospective buyer of only a few shares of stock afford to spend time and money hunting for a company in which to invest.

Investment Banks   Bringing would-be investor and investment opportunity together is the job of a specialized financial institution called an "investment bank." *Investment banks* are what might be called "retailers" of corporate securities. They take blocks of stocks or bonds from the corporation "at wholesale" and break them up into smaller holdings to sell "at retail" to the final owner. The investment bank collects a commission for performing this service.

The same procedure is followed when an existing corporation issues new shares to increase its capital by expanding its ownership. Advertisements by investment banks announcing the availability of new issues of securities are often seen in the financial pages of newspapers.

The Securities and Exchange Commission The buyer of a security invests his wealth to become one of the owners of the firm. Yet he is often remote from the actual operation of the company, and may lack the information necessary to make a sound judgment concerning the investment. Frequently all he knows about the company and its prospects is what the management or the investment banker tells him. Since these have special interests in encouraging him to buy the stock, he needs some assurance that he is being told everything he needs to know.

Making sure that prospective stockholders are fully informed is one of the duties of the *Securities and Exchange Commission* (SEC), a federal agency established by the Securities Exchange Act of 1934. Before a corporation can offer a new issue of securities for sale to the public, it must file a registration statement and a prospectus with the Commission. The registration statement must disclose such

matters as "the names of the persons who participate in the management or control of the . . . business; the security holdings and remuneration of such persons; the general character of the business, its capital structure, past history and earnings; underwriters' commissions; payments to promoters made within 2 years or intended to be made; the interests of directors, officers, and principal stockholders in material transactions; pending or threatening legal proceedings; . . . the purpose to which the proceeds of the offering are to be applied; and . . . financial statements certified by independent accountants."[1] The prospectus is part of the registration statement and embodies the more important of the required disclosures.

The SEC staff examines the registration statement and prospectus for accuracy and completeness. Unless it is found to be misleading, inaccurate, or incomplete, the registration becomes effective, and the security can be offered for sale. No securities can be sold, however, or even offered for sale, until a copy of the prospectus, containing the most important of the disclosures in the registration statement, has been placed in the hands of the prospective buyer. This is why advertisements of new securities always say: "This advertisement is neither an offer to sell, nor a solicitation of an offer to buy any of these securities. The offering is made only by the Prospectus." In other words, it is illegal to sell, or even to try to sell, securities to anybody without first putting in his hands the prospectus containing the information he needs to reach an intelligent decision.

Of course, the buyer need not read the prospectus. What he does with the information is up to him. Further, it must be emphasized that SEC approval of the registration statement and prospectus does *not* constitute endorsement of the security as a good investment. It means merely that, in

---

[1] Securities and Exchange Commission, *Thirty-first Annual Report, 1965,* Washington, D.C., 1966, p. 23.

the opinion of the Commission, all the information an investor needs to decide *for himself* has been disclosed to him. For example, the Commission recently found a registration statement false and misleading because it failed to disclose that "large sums had been transferred from . . . [the corporation] to its controlling stockholder and chief executive officer for use in his own business ventures. . . ."[2] Note that it was not the transfer of funds that caused rejection of the registration, but the failure to disclose the transfer. If an investor, properly informed of the questionable transfer of funds, should still want to buy stock, he would be free to do so, but the securities cannot be offered to him until he is so informed.

Another registration statement was disapproved as seriously deficient because, among other things, "a suggestion that significant improvements in efficiency could be effected by a program to be financed out of . . . future earnings was highly misleading since the prospectus failed to point out that such improvements would have required a massive program of capital investment that had not even been formulated. . . ."[3] In other words, the promoters were trying to sell the security on the basis of unfounded optimism. The registration was withheld, not because the optimism was unfounded, but because the lack of foundation was not acknowledged in the prospectus.

Concentration of Control

In addition to their leverage effect on earnings, bonds and preferred stocks facilitate concentration of control over the firm.

Absolute control over a corporation is guaranteed by ownership of one more than half the voting shares. If the capital of the

[2] *Ibid.*, p. 30.
[3] *Ibid.*, p. 32.

company is $10 million, represented by 100,000 shares of common stock, absolute control requires ownership of 50,001 shares, an investment of $5,000,100. If, however, half the firm's capital is provided by bonds and preferred stock, neither of which are entitled to vote, absolute control can be exercised by ownership of only 25,001 shares of common stock, requiring an investment of only $2,500,100.

In fact corporate control is often exercised by people without a majority control. When ownership of common stock is widely dispersed over thousands of people, each holding only a few shares, their participation in running the company is limited to sending in proxy votes to be cast on their behalf by a representative of the controlling management group. In such a case, a concentrated minority block of shares can exercise control.

Problems Created by Minority Control   In most cases the minority in control of a corporation manages the company in the interest of all the shareholders and performs the proper role of owner-enterpriser in raising productivity. As owners, the controlling group receives part of the profit from their activity and all other stockholders share in it.

At the same time, unless special checks are placed on their behavior, a minority control group is in a strong position to exploit the corporation for its own personal advantage. Among an endless list of abuses, such groups have been known to vote themselves extravagant salaries and unwarranted bonuses, to provide themselves with lavish expense accounts, to have the corporation furnish them with houses, cars, and even yachts. They have been known to have the company purchase materials, supplies, and equipment at high prices from other companies that they themselves have set up for this specific purpose. They have even borrowed money from the company, free of interest and on inadequate security, to buy land that was immediately resold to the company at double or triple what they paid for it, and to charge the company a brokerage fee on the transaction, in the bargain!

Members of a minority control group are likewise in a position to benefit from dealing in the stock of their company. They have been known to withhold news of oil strikes, discoveries, or new inventions that will enhance the earnings prospects of the company until after they themselves buy up the stock. When the news is released, they can unload the stock at the higher price. On the other hand, they have also concealed bad news that would lower the value of their shares until they could unload them on an unsuspecting public. They have even been known to manufacture fake "news" to raise or lower the market value of corporate stocks to their own advantage.

Protection of Stockholders   The protection of the stockholder from abuses of a controlling minority is a second function of the Securities and Exchange Commission. As in the case of new securities, the Commission first ensures that the stockholder is provided with the information he needs to reach wise decisions, and secondly, sees that he is given an opportunity to act on the information if he wants to.

The law requires every director and officer of a corporation whose shares are publicly traded, and any person who owns 10 percent or more of the securities of the corporation to disclose his ownership in the company and to report any changes in this ownership. These reports are available for public inspection and are often reproduced in the financial press.

Other provisions of the law apply to the solicitation of proxies and to proxy voting procedures. Before the days of the Securities and Exchange Commission, stockholders were often poorly informed about matters to be voted on. The stockholder was asked to send a blank proxy to an appointed representative of the management, who would cast the votes for the management's slate of candidates for the board of directors and vote in favor of all the management's proposals for company policy.

The law now provides that any solicitation of proxies must disclose "pertinent information . . . to enable holders of securities to act intelligently on the matters involved." Copies of proposed proxy material must be filed with the Commission prior to solicitation and must be approved by the Commission as meeting the disclosure requirements before it can be sent out to stockholders. Moreover, the proxy must permit the stockholder to specify how he votes on each issue. He is no longer merely offered a "blank check" to sign.

EVALUATING PERFORMANCE OF THE FIRM

The Balance Sheet

The complex organization of a modern firm makes it important to keep systematic records of the claims of different classes of people against it. The accounting instrument employed for this purpose is called a *balance sheet,* or a *statement of financial position.* On the left side of the sheet are listed all the wealth and all the claims to wealth owned by the firm, together with the value of each. These are the firm's *assets.* As in Table 1, assets are usually classified and listed in order of their *liquidity,* that is, by the ease with which they can be converted into money. Cash and bank accounts, the most liquid assets, are listed at the top, with accounts receivable (bills due from customers and others), which are somewhat less liquid next, and land and buildings that take time and trouble to sell listed last.

On the right side of the balance sheet are listed all the claims against the firm's assets. *Liabilities* are debts owed to people

TABLE 1   KIRKWOOD STEEL CORPORATION: STATEMENT OF FINANCIAL POSITION, JUNE 30, 1968

ASSETS		LIABILITIES	
Cash	$ 268,000	Notes and accounts payable	$ 453,000
Marketable securities	496,000	Accrued taxes payable	351,000
Accounts receivable	345,000	Bonded debt	516,000
Inventory	690,000	Total liabilities	$1,320,000
Current assets	$1,799,000		
		OWNERSHIP EQUITY	
Plant and equipment		Preferred stock (5000 shares	
(original cost)	5,867,000	5 percent cumulative)	$ 500,000
Less: accumulated depreciation	3,098,000	Common stock (54,000 shares)	900,000
		Retained earnings	1,848,000
Total assets	$4,568,000	Total	$4,568,000

outside the firm. They are listed first and usually listed according to their permanence. *Current liabilities,* which are least permanent, include bills and accounts payable to individuals and to other firms, amounts owed to banks on short-term notes, payroll due to workers, and other debts due or coming due in the immediate future. Outstanding bonds are a longer-term liability.

The residual, or *balance,* left over after subtracting all liabilities from the total value of assets, is the *ownership equity.* Where there are different classes of owners, the preferred stock equity is distinguished from that of the common stockholders. Moreover, it is customary to separate the common stockholders' equity into the amount originally contributed to the firm in exchange for common stock and the amount accumulated from past earnings.

The statement is called a "balance sheet" because the total of the claims must exactly equal, or balance, the total of the assets. There is, of course, nothing mysterious about this. It simply means that whatever part of the value of the assets is not owed to somebody else is automatically part of the owners' equity.

Accounting for Changes in Financial Position   The balance sheet summarizes the

firm's financial position at a given moment of time, and it necessarily changes from moment to moment to reflect the changes in that position as the firm does business. If we think of the firm's ever-changing financial position as recorded on movie film the balance sheet is a stop-action shot printed from one of the frames.

Since balance sheets remain in balance at all times, every transaction influences a firm's financial position in 2 ways. An increase in an asset is balanced either by an increase in a liability, by the reduction of another asset, or by some combination of these. Likewise, the reduction of an asset is balanced by the reduction of a liability, the increase in another asset, or some combination of these. For example, when a firm buys additional inventory on credit, the increase in inventory (an asset) is balanced by the increase in accounts payable (a current liability). When the firm pays the bill with cash, the reduction in its cash (an asset) is balanced by the reduction in accounts payable (a liability). When customers pay their bills, the increase in cash (an asset) is balanced by the reduction in accounts receivable (another asset).

If a transaction is not balanced in any other way, it is automatically balanced by a change in owners' equity. For example, when $1 million of finished goods, carried in inventory at cost, is sold for $1,100,000, the $1,100,000 increase in accounts receivable (an asset) is balanced by a reduction of $1 million in inventory (another asset), and by an increase of $100,000 in owners' equity. When $50,000 is paid out in dividends, the reduction in cash is balanced by a reduction in owners' equity. Ownership equity is also affected when the firm increases its capital. When a corporation issues new shares of common stock, the rise in cash assets is balanced by the increased ownership equity.

The Income Statement

As the balance sheet summarizes the financial position of the firm on a given date, so the income statement summarizes the firm's productive operations during a given period of time, usually a fiscal year. The *income statement* is a systematic summary of revenues and costs, organized to enable owners to see how the firm has operated.

While accountants differ in the exact arrangement of items and in the amount of detail given, the essence of the income statement is to show the year's total receipts, total costs, and profit. The statement also shows the allocation of profit between dividends and retained earnings, and the distribution of the dividends among the different classes of shareholders.

The hypothetical income statement in Table 2 covers the operations of the Kirkwood Steel Corporation during the fiscal year ending June 30, 1968. As shown, total revenue from products sold was $4,480,000. To produce these products, the firm paid $1,864,000 in wages and other employment-related costs. In addition, $1,625,000 of materials were used up—$1,497,000 purchased from other firms during the year, and $128,000 drawn out of inventory; $325,000 was allowed for wear and tear on buildings and equipment, $31,000 was paid

TABLE 2   THE KIRKWOOD STEEL CORPORATION INCOME STATEMENT
Covering operations for the fiscal year July 1, 1967–June 30, 1968 (hypothetical data)

Products sold	$4,480,000
Costs:	
Materials and supplies	
Products and services bought	$1,497,000
Net withdrawal from inventory	128,000
Employment costs	
Wages and salaries paid	1,630,000
Social security, pension contributions, and other employee benefits	234,000
Allowance for depreciation	325,000
Interest on debt	31,000
State, local, and misc. taxes	110,000
Total cost	$3,955,000
Profits before corporate income tax	$ 525,000
Estimated U.S. corporate income tax liability	210,000
Profits after taxes	$ 315,000
Dividends declared	
On preferred stock	$ 25,000
On common stock	125,000
Retained earnings	$ 165,000

out in interest, while $110,000 was paid in property, excise, and other indirect business taxes.

When the total costs of $3,955,000 were deducted from total sales revenue, the remainder was a profit of $525,000. Almost half of this profit, an estimated $210,000, was owed to the federal government as corporate profits tax. Of the earnings of $315,000 remaining after taxes, $25,000 was paid as dividends to preferred stockholders, $125,000 was distributed in dividends to common stockholders, and $165,000 was retained and reinvested in the company.

The income statement involves the same view of output and income that we applied earlier to the measurement of production. In fact, as shown in Table 3, the income statement can be reorganized to show the value added by the firm's operations and

TABLE 3   CONTRIBUTION OF THE KIRKWOOD STEEL CORPORATION TO GROSS NATIONAL PRODUCT AND INCOME, FISCAL 1968 (hypothetical data)

Sales	$4,480,000
Plus: net increase (less net decrease) in inventory	128,000
Less: intermediate products purchased	1,497,000
Value added (contribution to GNP)	**$2,855,000**
Less: capital consumption allowance	325,000
Contribution to net national product	2,530,000
Less: indirect business taxes	110,000
Contribution to national income	2,420,000
Less: corporate profits	525,000
Plus: dividends	150,000
Contribution to personal income	**$2,045,000**
Employee compensation $1,864,000	
Interest 31,000	
Dividends 150,000	

the distribution of this value among the different participants in production.

THE IMPORTANCE OF THE CORPORATION

The Number of Corporations

Data on the number and size of U.S. firms are presented in Table 4. In terms of numbers, corporations represent a small minority of U.S. business firms. In fact, 80 percent of the 11 million business firms now active in the U.S. are sole proprietorships, and another 8 percent are partnerships. Proprietorships are especially numerous in the farming, retailing, and service industries where there are many family-sized firms. Even in mining and manufacturing, however, there are more sole proprietorships and partnerships than corporations.

The Size of Corporations

However, when we look at size and economic importance rather than numbers, we find that the 12 percent of all firms that are corporations receive nearly 80 percent of total sales revenue. Even in retail trade, where many small stores are operated by their proprietors, corporations do 50 percent more business than partnerships and proprietorships combined. The biggest contrast between numbers and sales appears in transportation and public utilities. While 84 percent of the firms in this industry are sole proprietorships and partnerships, these are mostly owner-operated taxis and trucks. Corporate truck and bus lines, railroads, airlines, and telephone, gas, and power utilities sell more than 90 percent of the total output. Only in agriculture is the total volume of corporate sales relatively small. Even so, while only 1 percent of agricultural firms are incorporated, these corporations account for 14 percent of the value of agricultural products sold.

Differences in the type of business organization that predominates in different industries are in keeping with the requirements of efficient production. Sole proprietorships predominate where technology permits economical operation with no more capital than a single enterpriser can command, corporate organization is found where the scale of production requires the combined capital of many people.

Giant Corporations

Of course, not all corporations are large. Many small stores, garages, and family manufacturing businesses are incorporated. Indeed, figures compiled from corporate income tax returns suggest that almost 95 percent of all corporations have assets less than $1 million. The few largest corporations, on the other hand, are very large indeed. As shown in Figure 1, the 5 percent

TABLE 4   COMPARISON OF NUMBER AND SIZE OF DIFFERENT TYPES OF FIRMS IN DIFFERENT INDUSTRIES

INDUSTRY		SOLE PROPRIETORSHIPS	PARTNERSHIPS	CORPORATIONS	ALL FIRMS
Agriculture, forestry, fishing	Percent of firms	96	3	1	100
	Percent of total industry sales	74	12	14	100
	Sales per firm	$ 8,800	$ 37,000	$ 270,000	$ 11,000
Mining	Percent of firms	55	23	22	100
	Percent of total industry sales	7	6	87	100
	Sales per firm	$28,000	$128,000	$ 530,000	$ 216,000
Construction	Percent of firms	82	7	11	100
	Percent of total industry sales	25	11	64	100
	Sales per firm	$23,000	$120,000	$ 440,000	$ 75,000
Manufacturing	Percent of firms	44	11	45	100
	Percent of total industry sales	2	2	96	100
	Sales per firm	$37,000	$155,000	$2,180,000	$1,000,000
Transportation and public utilities	Percent of firms	80	4	16	100
	Percent of total industry sales	6	1	93	100
	Sales per firm	$15,000	$ 58,000	$1,200,000	$ 210,000
Wholesale trade	Percent of firms	65	8	27	100
	Percent of total industry sales	10	7	83	100
	Sales per firm	$53,000	$300,000	$1,100,000	$ 350,000
Retail trade	Percent of firms	76	11	13	100
	Percent of total industry sales	29	10	61	100
	Sales per firm	$45,000	$100,000	$ 590,000	$ 120,000
Finance, insurance, real estate	Percent of firms	44	21	34	100
	Percent of total industry sales	9	9	82	100
	Sales per firm	$11,000	$ 22,000	$ 130,000	$ 53,000
Services	Percent of firms	87	7	6	100
	Percent of total industry sales	42	16	42	100
	Sales per firm	$12,000	$ 62,000	$ 170,000	$ 38,000
All industries	Percent of firms	76	11	13	100
	Percent of total industry sales	29	10	61	100
	Sales per firm	$45,000	$100,000	$ 590,000	$ 120,000

SOURCE: Adapted from Treasury Department, Internal Revenue Service, *Statistics of Income, 1962, U.S. Business Tax Returns.*

FIGURE 1   ALMOST 90 PERCENT OF ALL CORPORATE ASSETS ARE OWNED BY ONLY
5 PERCENT OF THE FIRMS

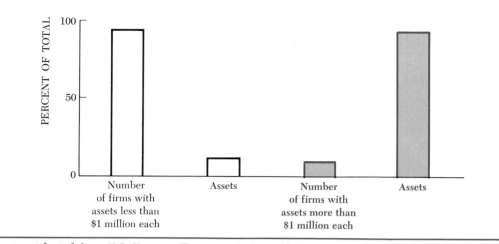

SOURCE: Adapted from U.S. Treasury Department, Internal Revenue Service, *Statistics of Income, 1962, Corporate Income Tax Returns.*

with assets over $1 million owned almost 90 percent of total corporate assets. In 1962, only 638 corporations out of the 1,268,042 filing income tax returns—five one-hundredths of 1 percent—reported assets of $2.5 billion or more, but these few firms owned almost 50 percent of all corporate assets. The value added by the operations of one firm, the General Motors Corporation, the largest industrial employer in the country, is more than $10 billion per year. This is something over 1 percent of the total U.S. GNP, and represents a contribution to total output equivalent to about one-quarter of the real GNP of India!

The size of these giant firms produces a number of serious problems, not all of which are resolved. It is clear that large firms are needed to take full advantage of modern capitalistic mass production methods. But it should be equally clear that existing firms greatly exceed any size that can reasonably be justified on the grounds of productive efficiency alone.

Size of Firm Versus Size of Plant   In evaluating giant firms, it is necessary to dis-

tinguish carefully between the size of the firm and the size of the individual physical factories, plants, or establishments that the firm owns and operates. Efficient production requires individual plants large enough to use expensive specialized equipment and to employ specialized workers. This means that firms must be large enough to own and operate these large plants. Once the firm is operating the most economical plant, however, there is no increase in engineering efficiency when the firm grows large enough to own and operate several plants, all equally efficient.

For example, fruit can be canned in a plant costing less than $100,000 (or, for that matter, in an ordinary household kitchen). With hand labor and simple equipment, however, the cost per can is very high. A larger cannery, operating on a production-line basis with automatic cooking, canning, and conveying equipment may require an investment of $1 million, but the production cost per can is a fraction of what it is in the smaller plant. If the output can be sold, a $1 million corporation with one big plant is more economical than 10 $100,000 corporations, each operating a small, inefficient plant. But a $10 million corporation, operating 10 efficient plants, achieves no greater production economy than 10 $1 million corporations operating only one plant each.

The force of this point is increased when we realize that giant corporations not only operate many plants, but usually operate plants in many different industries. Thus an "automobile" company not only has many plants producing automobiles, it also has plants producing trucks, locomotives, refrigerators, air-conditioning equipment, radios, television sets, and electrical generating equipment. The world's largest "steel" company is also, among other things, one of the world's largest cement producers. A large "food processing" firm also makes electric irons and other household appliances.

Specialized Management If engineering efficiency and production-line economy were all that mattered, much could be said for a public policy designed to put severe limits to corporate size. But there is more to productivity than engineering. To return to the example of the fruit cannery, the assembly of raw materials requires specialized knowledge of different kinds of fruit and their canning properties. Moreover, somebody must keep track of crops in different areas and know when and where to buy, and in what amounts. Somebody must keep in constant touch with the many markets for canned fruit to decide how much output will be needed and where it will go. If these decisions are not properly made, the engineering efficiency of the plant can be more than offset by marketing losses. To can a poor quality of fruit, or a kind that few people really want, or to pack it in cans of the wrong size or of poor design, or to can too much or too little, is just as wasteful of resources as operating a plant that is too small to be efficient. Careful attention to such details is the function . of specialized management; but the elaborate division of labor necessary for most effective use of management ability requires a workload large enough to keep managers employed at their specialities. A company large enough to operate only 1 plant of the most economical size is often too small to specialize its management effectively. Full-time staffs devoted exclusively to production, marketing, purchasing, personnel, finance, and accounting can be kept busy only as adjuncts to a large productive operation which is spread over many plants.

Even more important is the great advantage of providing as wide a field as possible for the skill, imagination, and initiative of enterprisers. Steady rise in productivity and improvement of quality are the results of conscious human effort. Somebody must perceive the advantages of each specific change in a method or product, decide to adopt it, and be able to put the decision into effect. People with the combination of ability, imagination, energy, discipline, and drive required for effective enterprise are probably our scarcest economic resource. It takes a large firm to give full employment to the talents of such people.

Other Reasons for Large Firms Beyond productive efficiency and enterprise, however, there are other reasons why firms grow large. In many cases, growth feeds on itself. The larger a firm becomes, the easier it is to grow still larger by trading on its reputation. Reputation is especially important when prospective buyers are unable to experiment. For example, a firm offering standardized nationwide service seldom does a better job in any given place than the best local firms, but many travelers prefer to patronize filling stations, stores, motels, or restaurants bearing familiar names and reliable reputations, rather than risk disappointment by an unknown firm. Durable goods, like washing machines and television sets, that are purchased infrequently, provide another example. The unknown product may be superior, but the cost and inconvenience of a thorough quality comparison is too high for many

consumers, and they prefer to buy a familiar brand. For a similar reason, it is
easier for an established firm with a good
reputation to bring out a new product than
it is for a new and unknown firm, even
when the new product is completely unrelated to the old ones.

Some large firm grow merely because it
is easier for customers to get service for
products that are widely used and familiar
to mechanics and maintenance men. Once
a firm gets an edge on its competitors, this
very fact makes it easier to expand still
more. Another special advantage of size is
that a large firm can employ nationwide
advertising in radio, television, and other
media at costs that would be prohibitive
for a firm with a small local market.

A large successful firm is also in an
advantageous position when raising capital
for still further expansion. For not only do
its own retained earnings provide a flow
of cash for investment, but when funds are
to be raised outside, an established firm
enjoys the advantage of many people preferring to buy new securities in a company
whose reputation and performance are familiar, rather than invest in a new and un-
tried venture. Also, borrowing is facilitated
when bankers and other lenders already
know the company.

Problems Created by Giant Firms Many
of the causes of growth represent a kind of
economic "survival of the fittest." The most
productive firms thrive and grow. The
wasteful firms die. The result is often economic gain, but not all the consequences
of size are good. A large company can
sometimes take advantage of its powerful
market position to exploit others. For example, intermediate products bought by a
large firm often represent the entire output
of several small producers, and the ability
of the big firm to withdraw its business
from any one of the smaller ones can be
used to extract lower prices, faster delivery,
or other concessions that are unavailable to
other firms. Such concessions enable the
large firm to prosper and to grow still
larger, not because it is more productive
than its competitors, but because of its
power over suppliers.

Sometimes one firm, or a few large firms
together, gain so large a share of the total
market for their products that they hold
monopoly power. Having no important
competitors, they can manipulate the price
and quality of output to their own advantage. We will return to this problem in
Chapter 19 when we study the nature of
monopoly and the laws designed to hold it
in check.

SUMMARY

In a *private enterprise* economic system, control over most production
is vested in privately organized enterprises or *business firms*. There are
3 common types of business firms in the United States: the sole
proprietorship, the partnership, and the corporation. There is an element of risk in running an enterprise because of the opportunity cost of
the labor, materials, and equipment that must be assembled before it
can be known whether the venture will result in products more valuable than the alternatives that have been sacrificed. Society tries to
protect itself against ill-conceived schemes by requiring that owners
maintain an *equity* in the business by financing part of the investment

with their own resources. The need to maintain this equity limits the size of different types of firms.

Most American firms are *sole proprietorships,* which are firms with a single owner and in which there is no distinction between the personality of the owner and that of the firm. Since the size of a sole proprietorship is limited by the wealth of the owner, and since transfer of ownership presents difficulties, this form of business organization is poorly adapted to the needs of modern mass production technology.

Partnerships permit several individuals to finance production by pooling their wealth. Although pooling permits somewhat larger firms, size is limited by the responsibility of each partner for all the affairs of the firm, and by additional difficulties in the transfer of ownership.

The *corporation* is the form of business organization best suited to private financing of large quantities of capital. Unlike proprietorships or partnerships, a corporation is created by legal charter, and is endowed with a legal life and personality of its own, entirely distinct from its owners as individuals. The owners of the corporation are its *stockholders,* who vest control of the firm's affairs in an elected board of directors. As individuals, stockholders have neither control over, nor responsibility for the actions of the company, making it possible for large numbers of individuals to pool their wealth to finance investment. Moreover, since ownership is easily transferred from one individual to another, corporations can be financed without a permanent commitment of resources by the individual investor. Finance is further facilitated by tapping a variety of investor preferences through the use of *preferred stock* and *bonds.* Preferred stockholders and bondholders exchange the chance at large gains for smaller but more secure fixed incomes. Common stockholders are willing to make such a trade in order to obtain *leverage.*

Corporate securities are sold to the public through *investment banks,* and to make sure that potential investors receive all necessary information about the securities they are offered, security sales are regulated by the *Securities and Exchange Commission.* Where corporate ownership is widely spread over a very large number of small stockholders, a consolidated minority can elect the board of directors and control the affairs of the firm. Since such minorities are in a position to exploit the rest of the stockholders, protection must be provided by SEC regulation of proxy voting, and by enforced disclosure of the stockholding interests of "insiders."

The economic performance of firms is evaluated by their accounts. The *balance sheet* shows the firm's financial position on a given date, listing the firm's *assets,* the *liabilities* against those assets, and the residual *ownership equity.* The *income statement* represents the firm's operations over a period of time and accounts for the value added by the firm's operations and its distribution among the participants in production.

Only a minority of business firms in the U.S. are organized as corporations. However, the corporation is by far the most important kind of firm in terms of sales and assets. As would be expected, corporations are most prevalent in industries in which mass production technology requires large amounts of capital under central control. But the largest corporations are far larger than the size needed for engineering efficiency. A more important cause of large corporations is the need to specialize management. In addition, however, many firms grow larger than necessary because of marketing or financial advantages that are unrelated to economic performance. In some industries, excessively large firms are associated with predatory behavior, monopoly, and other consequences that we will examine in later chapters.

APPENDIX   THE STOCK MARKET

A stock market consists of brokers, dealers, and organized exchanges whose function is to facilitate the transfer of securities from one private owner to another. The corporation itself is not a party to transactions in its securities on the stock market, nor are stock markets places where corporations raise capital. The function of the stock market is, rather, to provide the easy transferability of ownership that characterizes the corporate form of business organization.

There are two distinct types of stock market: Securities that are less frequently traded are generally bought and sold through the facilities of the *over-the-counter market,* while the *organized stock exchange* is set up for the purchase and sale of a selected list of securities that are usually traded in large daily volume.

The Over-the-Counter Market

Once a stock or bond has been issued, its owner is entitled to sell it to anybody else, at any time, at any price that can be agreed on. The transaction can be completed privately, but most people enlist the services of a specialized middleman. An *over-the-counter* dealer plays essentially the same role in the securities market that a used

car dealer does in the used car market: He buys securities from individual owners for resale to others at slightly higher prices, getting his commission from the difference between the buying and the selling prices. Since over-the-counter dealers are organized into a National Association of Security Dealers, there is a nationwide competitive market. Quotations of security prices being paid (bid) and charged (asked) by dealers are published in the daily financial pages.

Organized Stock Exchanges

As in any other part of the economic system, greater specialization in securities trading is possible in more extensive markets. Securities that are bought and sold in large volume every day are traded through highly organized special markets called *organized stock exchanges.* An organized stock exchange is an institution with a limited membership, whose members are permitted to trade securities with each other. Since only members are permitted to conduct business on the exchange, others who want to buy or sell in this way must employ members to act on their behalf.

Trading among members of each exchange is restricted to a special list of securities, and the stocks and bonds of corporations not listed on the exchange cannot be bought or sold there. Each exchange has established rules governing which securities can be listed for trading. Among other requirements, securities are listed only if they are traded in sufficient volume to make it worthwhile. In addition, before a security can be listed, it must have been outstanding long enough to have "seasoned." Securities of young companies, for example, are not listed. Moreover, the listed corporation must agree to file certain reports with the exchange and with the SEC.

There is an organized stock exchange in almost every major U.S. city, but most of these are small and limit their lists largely to the securities of local firms. The securities of most large, nationally known corporations are traded on the 2 large New York exchanges, the New York Stock Exchange and the American Stock Exchange.

How Stock Is Traded

A typical transaction is represented schematically in Figure 2. Mr. Brown in Boston has some money to invest and has decided to buy 100 shares of common stock of the Kirkwood Steel Company. The stock has been selling at about $50 a share, a price Mr. Brown considers satisfactory in view of the prospects for the company. Of course, Mr. Brown has no idea who wants to sell the stock, or where to find him. He merely instructs his local broker to buy 100 shares of Kirkwood Steel at $50.

The broker in Boston is not a member of the stock exchange where Kirkwood Steel is listed, but he has an arrangement with a member firm to transact business on his behalf. The broker therefore transmits the purchase order by phone or teletype to his correspondent member firm in New York. This firm phones the order to its representative on the trading floor of the exchange, who goes to the post where steel stocks are traded and announces an offer to buy 100 shares of Kirkwood Steel at $50.

In the meantime, Mr. Smith in St. Louis decides to sell 100 shares of Kirkwood Steel and places an order with his broker to sell the stock at the market price. The order is transmitted by the St. Louis broker to his correspondent member firm in New York and from there to a representative on the trading floor. When the representative of the seller goes to the steel post on the floor and hears Mr. Brown's bid, he accepts on behalf of Mr. Smith, and the transaction is complete. Stockbrokers and exchange members charge established commissions for their services as intermediaries.

Speculation

In our example, Brown's buy order and Smith's sell order arrived at the trading post at the same time. But what happens when an offer to sell finds no buyer at the post, or when an offer to buy finds no seller? There are 2 ways an order to buy or sell can be placed. By the first, the broker can be ordered to deal at a specified price. This is what Mr. Brown did when he instructed his broker to buy at $50. The other way to place an order is "at the market"; that is, to have the broker buy or sell at whatever price is being paid on the market at the time. This is the way Mr. Smith placed his order to sell.

Clearly an order to buy or sell at at specified price cannot be executed unless somebody else is also willing to trade at that price. Anybody can place an order to buy at $50 even when the going price is $55 or higher, but he will not buy any stock. Of course, if the price later goes down, his order will be executed unless he has cancelled it in the meantime. By the same token, one can place an order to sell his shares at $60, even when the going price is $50, but the order will simply stand on

FIGURE 2 A TYPICAL STOCK EXCHANGE TRANSACTION

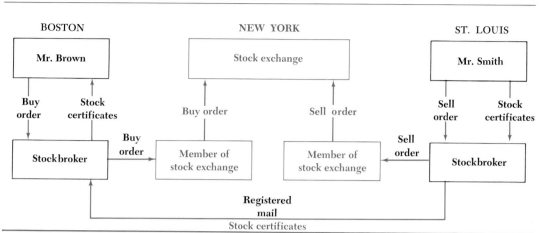

the books unexecuted until somebody is willing to pay the specified price.

But what happens when an order to sell "at the market" is not matched by somebody else's order to buy? For example, suppose Mr. Smith's order to sell 100 shares of Kirkwood Steel arrived at the post, but there were no matching buy order from Mr. Brown. Among the members of the exchange there are some who specialize in steel stocks, keeping close track of the values of the shares. The specialist knows that although there is no buyer for the stock at the moment, one will appear in the next few minutes, hours, or days. Moreover, knowledge of stock values leads the specialist to believe that when a buyer does arrive, he will be willing to pay, say, $50 for the shares.

If the specialist can buy Mr. Smith's stock at $49 and resell it a few hours later at $50, he will make a comfortable profit on the transaction. This act of buying something at one time and reselling it later in the same market is called *speculation*. A speculator is a middleman who stands between a person wanting to sell at one time and a person wanting to buy at a different time. The effect of speculation is to link up buyers and sellers from different *times,* just

as wholesaling and retailing link up buyers and sellers in different *places.* Like a retailer, the speculator earns his income by buying at a low price and reselling at a higher price.

Naturally, the less the speculator has to pay for the stock the more he can make on the resale. If he expects to resell the security at $50, why should he pay $48 or $49? Why not offer $40 or $30 or even less? The answer is, of course, that there are many speculators competing for the shares. A speculator who offered to pay only $30 would be immediately outbid by a competitor who could pay, say, $35 and still make a sizable profit. The latter would be outbid by still other speculators, until the price offered to Mr. Smith was only enough below the expected resale price of $50 to cover costs and leave the speculator a normal operating profit.

Buying on Margin Competition among speculators is increased by the institution of *margin buying.* A speculator who buys on margin does not pay the full purchase price, but only a specified percentage called the *margin.* The remainder of the price is financed by a bank loan using the stock as security. On a 60 percent margin, the speculator buying at $50 puts up .60 × $50, or $30 of his own money for each share bought and borrows the remainder from a bank.[4] A speculator with $600,000 could purchase only 12,000 shares at $50 if he had to buy the stock outright, but on 60 percent margin his $600,000 can buy 20,000 shares.

Bank loans extended to finance margin purchases are, of course, very secure. If, contrary to expectation, the stock should go down, the price reduction merely eats into the speculator's equity in the stock. The bank calls for more margin, asking the speculator to put up enough additional cash to restore the margin to its original percentage of the price. For example, when Kirkwood Steel is bought at $50 on 60 percent margin, the speculator's equity is $30, and the bank puts up $20. If the security goes down to $45, the loss in value is deducted from the speculator's equity, cutting it to $25. Since the speculator is required to maintain his equity at 60 percent of the market value of the security, he must put up another $2 in margin to bring his equity up to .60 × $45, or $27. If he is unable or unwilling to supply the additional margin, the bank sells the securities at the market to recover its loan and returns any remaining funds to the speculator.

Short Sales Speculators play a similar role in filling buy orders when there are no sellers on hand at the moment. The practice that makes this possible is the *short sale*. In this type of transaction, the speculator, who does not own any of the stock himself, arranges with his broker to borrow the required number of shares from another owner. The speculator sells the borrowed stock in the expectation that it will later go down in price, permitting him to buy it

[4] The regulation of margin requirements is one of the duties of the Federal Reserve Board, the principal agency in the regulation of U.S. banks.

back for less than he got for it and to pocket the difference as a speculative gain. During the time the borrowed shares are outstanding, the proceeds from their sale are kept on deposit with the lender of the shares. In addition, the speculator is required to deposit margin to guarantee that the shares can be replaced even if—contrary to his expectation—their price should rise rather than fall.

As an example of a short sale, suppose a speculator, believing a stock to be overpriced at $50 and expecting it soon to go down, decided to sell short 100 shares. He would first deposit margin of $30 per share with his broker, who would then borrow 100 shares of the stock from one of his other clients. The shares would be sold at $50 and the proceeds deposited in the former owner's account along with the margin. In place of the securities, the lender of the shares now has $8,000 in his account: $5,000 from the sale of the shares and $3,000 margin. If, contrary to the speculator's hope, the stock goes up instead of down, he would have to add more margin to protect the lender of the shares, and if he were unable or unwilling to do this, the broker would buy the securities back and replace them, returning any remaining portion of the margin to the speculator.

If the speculator were right, however, and the stock went down to $40, he would order his broker to buy back the shares and close out the account at a profit. The shares, originally sold for $5,000 would be replaced for $4,000, leaving the speculator with $1,000 less fees and commissions as speculative gain.

Reading the Financial Page

When a transaction is completed on the floor of the stock exchange, the name of the stock, the number of shares traded, and the price are reported on the stock ticker to brokerage houses all over the country. At the end of the day, a summary of all the transactions in each listed security is carried in the stock market report of the daily newspaper. An excerpt from the trading reported on the New York Stock Exchange during a typical day is shown in Figure 3. Stocks are listed in alphabetical order. In front of the name of each corporation is noted the highest and lowest price at which the stock was sold at any time during the past 12 months. The dividend paid during the past year is noted directly after the name of the stock. For example, Abbott Laboratories is the second stock listed in the clipping. The preceding high price for the security had been 75½. The lowest price had been 64¾. The stock had paid a dividend of $1.10 a share.

The summary of the day's transactions is then given. The total number of shares traded is indicated—in hundreds of shares because securities are usually bought and sold in blocks of 100. The price at which the security *opened* is shown. This is the price at which the first sale of the day occurred. This price is followed by the day's

high and *low*—the highest and lowest prices paid during the day. The *closing* price is the price on the day's last sale of the stock. The *net change* is the difference between the closing price of the day and the closing price of the preceding day.[5] On the day shown, 3,400 shares of Abbott Laboratories had been traded. The first sale of the day had been at 71⅜, and during the day prices paid for the stock ranged from a high of 72 to a low of 71. The last sale of the day was at 72, 1⅛ higher than the close of the preceding day.

Stock Averages In addition to the prices of individual securities, financial pages usually publish various indexes representing movements in the average prices of all shares taken together. One of the oldest of these is the Dow-Jones Index. Other averages are compiled by Standard and Poor, *The New York Times,* and other publications. Because the time, effort, and expense of calculating complete averages used to be prohibitive, each of these indexes reflects the price movements of only a specified small example of stocks. For example, the Dow-Jones Industrial Average shows the average price movements of the stocks of 30 selected industrial firms. Since high-speed electronic computers have become available, however, the New York Stock Exchange now produces a daily average that takes account of the prices of all listed securities.

Determination of Stock Prices

We now come to the important question of how security prices are determined. To begin with, remember that a share of stock represents a claim against the future earn-

FIGURE 3 NEW YORK STOCK EXCHANGE TRANSACTIONS

1969 High. Low.	Stocks and Div. In Dollars.	Sls. 100s.	First.	High.	Low.	Last.	Net Chge.
		A–B–C–D					
35⅞ 28½	Abacus .49f	82	34	34⅞	33⅝	34½ − ¼
75½ 64¾	Abbtlab 1.10	34	71⅜	72	71	72 +1⅛
66¼ 48	ACF Ind 2.40	34	49⅜	49⅞	49⅛	49⅛ − ¾
30⅞ 26¾	AcmeCl 1.40a	14	26⅝	26⅝	26½	26½ − ¼
51 41¾	Acme Mkt 2b	75	50¼	50¼	48¾	49 − ⅝
20¾ 17⅝	Adam E 1.41g	60	18⅛	18⅛	18⅛	18⅛ − ¼
22⅜ 17	Ad Millis .20	39	19	19⅜	18⅛	18⅛ − ⅞
76⅞ 65¼	Address 1.40	83	4⅛	74⅛	73	73⅛ −1⅜
20⅜ 15	Admiral	293	20⅝	21	20⅛	20⅛ − ¼
65¼ 46⅞	Aetna Lif 1.40	139	49¼	51⅝	49¼	50¾ +1⅛
21¼ 16¼	Aguirre Co	23	19⅞	19⅞	19⅞	19⅞ + ⅜
46⅞ 40¾	Air Prod .20b	16	42¾	43¼	42¾	43¼ ......
34⅛ 27¼	Air Redtn 1.50	106	28¼	28⅜	27⅞	27⅞ − ⅛
18¾ 12⅝	AJ Industries	253	13	13⅞	13	13⅝ + ½
45 35⅝	AlbertoC .32	x137	44½	46	44½	45½ +1⅛
31⅝ 26¼	Alcan Alu 1.10	318				
28⅜ 18¼	Alleg Co					
62⅛ 50						

SOURCE: *The New York Times,* April 25, 1969.

[5] By long-standing custom—probably going back to colonial days of Spanish pieces-of-eight—stock prices are quoted in units of one-eighth of a dollar. This unit is called a *bit;* hence the slang designation for 25 cents.

ings of the corporation, and the value of the stock derives from the expected size of the earnings. Anything that doubles the earnings outlook of the company tends to double the price of its stock. This is why stock prices rise when good economic news improves the outlook for profits and fall when the news is bad.

Given the outlook for earnings, the value of a share of stock depends on what *rate of return* people insist on getting from their investment. A man who insists on a return of 20 percent will pay no more than $5 for a share of stock he expects to earn $1 a year because 20 percent of $5 is $1. Of course, he would be delighted to buy the stock for $4 if he could, since the prospective $1 earning would constitute a return of 25 percent on his investment, but he would refuse to buy at $6 because the $1 earnings would amount to a return of only 16.7 percent per year, a figure below the minimum rate of return he requires.

The minimum acceptable rate of return depends on 3 things. First of all, since people buying stock are investing funds that might otherwise be loaned at interest, the minimum return they will accept on stock tends to rise and fall with interest rates. The higher interest rates are, the higher the minimum return that investors insist on and, hence, the lower the prices they are willing to pay for securities with given expected earnings.

A second important determinant of the minimum return is the degree of risk. Nothing is guaranteed about future earnings, and there is always a risk that investments will not work out. The earnings of some companies are looked upon as very secure. These are the so-called "blue chip" stocks and, because of their security, investors are willing to accept lower rates of return on them. Other companies are highly speculative, and while great earnings may materialize, there is a substantial risk of losses. Buyers of such shares generally demand a *risk premium* in the form of a higher re-

turn. Prices of such stocks are low in relation to the high (but uncertain) earning prospects of the company. A third determinant of the minimum return is the investor's own personal outlook, his attitudes and whims, his financial position, and his alternative investment opportunities.

Schematic Representation of Price Determination[6] Since each investor has his own opinion both about the prospective earnings of a company and about the minimum return acceptable on an investment, opinions about the value of any given stock generally vary greatly. At one extreme, investors who are the most optimistic about earnings prospects and those who are willing to accept the lowest return will put high values on the stock. They will be willing to buy it even at high prices and consider it a great bargain at low prices. At the other extreme, investors with the most pessimistic outlook for the company and those who insist on high returns will place a low value on the stock. They will buy it only at very low prices; they will be unwilling to buy at high prices, and if they already own the shares would rather sell and take the money.

This spread of opinion can be represented by the curve *DD* in Figure 4. Each point on the curve represents the number of shares—measured horizontally—that investors would be willing to invest in, provided they could buy them for the corresponding price—measured vertically. The left end of the curve is high to indicate that few investors would want the stock at very high prices. According to the figure, the most optimistic investors would want only about 10,000 shares if they traded for $100 per share. The curve slopes downward to the right to show that more and more investors would be interested at lower prices. At $28 even very pessimistic inves-

[6] Price determination by supply and demand, of which this is a special case, will be studied in detail in Chapter 16.

FIGURE 4 HOW STOCK PRICES ARE
DETERMINED

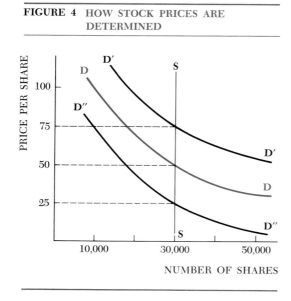

NUMBER OF SHARES

tors would be willing to buy the stock and hang onto it, and more than 50,000 shares would be wanted at this price.

A curve like *DD* is called a *demand curve,* or simply the *demand* for the stock. The *supply curve,* or the *supply* of the stock, is represented by the line *SS.* Since the shares are already issued and in the hands of investors, the number outstanding is constant regardless of the price. For this reason *SS* is a vertical line, showing the same number of shares at all prices. In Figure 4 the supply curve *SS* indicates that 30,000 shares of the stock are outstanding.

Now we can see the forces at work on the price of the stock. Suppose the price were momentarily $28. At this price investors would want to hold about 50,000 shares, 20,000 more than the 30,000 shares in existence. Competition among buyers for the available shares would quickly drive the price upward. On the other hand, suppose the price were momentarily $100. At this price investors—who already own 30,000 shares—want to keep only 10,000. The resulting flood of sell orders would quickly drive the price down.

Somewhere between the 2 extremes is a price at which the security can be traded without upward or downward price pressure. The desire of investors to hold 30,000 shares at this price balances the 30,000 shares available, and there is no net force on the price one way or the other. This price is the *equilibrium price* and is represented by the height of the intersection of the demand and supply curves. The equilibrium price in Figure 4 is $50.

At the equilibrium price people like Smith sell stock to raise money, and people like Brown buy stock as a way to invest their savings, but orders to buy and sell arrive in equal volume and exert no net pressure on the price. Of course, transactions do not necessarily occur exactly at the equilibrium price. Specific prices may be slightly above or slightly below equilibrium, as speculators match buy and sell orders arriving on the market at different times. In other words, the equilibrium price is a central point around which the prices actually paid for the stock oscillate from transaction to transaction.

Changes in Equilibrium Price When the earnings outlook for the company improves, investors revise their evaluation of the stock. Those who used to think it was a good buy even at $100, now may look on it as worth $130. Those who used to think it was not worth more than $25 may now be willing to pay $50.

This revision of values is represented in Figure 4 by an upward shift of the demand curve to a new position, indicated by the black curve, *D'D'.* The figure shows clearly what happens. Because of the improved outlook, investors want to increase their ownership of shares. The market is flooded with buy orders, and competition for the limited supply drives the price upward toward its new equilibrium of $75.

Bad news, bringing a downward revision of the expected earnings would have just the opposite result. People formerly willing to pay $100 might now look on the stock as worth no more than $60. Those who would formerly have considered buying it at $20 would now think it worth no more than perhaps $5. This reassessment of the outlook would be represented by a downward shift of the demand curve DD to a new position, say $D''D''$, and would be accompanied by a corresponding reduction in the equilibrium price.

Speculation and Prices Judgment about the equilibrium price and its movement guides the speculator in his transactions. He tries to buy at prices below equilibrium and to sell at prices above it. When demand rises, he tries to be the first to buy so that he can get the stock cheap for later resale at the new high price. When demand falls, he wants to unload or to sell short and buy back at the new low price.

In trying to anticipate price movements, however, speculators sometimes have an unstabilizing effect on security prices. Suppose, for example, that a stock is selling near its equilibrium, but that—entirely without any factual basis—speculators get the idea that the stock is underpriced and is going to rise. This belief might lead them to rush to buy the shares in the expectation of making a gain when the price rise materializes. Moreover, when their buying pushes the price up, the speculators may take the effect of their own actions as "proof" that they are right! This encourages them to buy even more, driving the price up still faster and attracting other speculators to the game. Although the flurry can push the stock far above any equilibrium level based on actual earnings prospects, such levels cannot last. Sooner or later the price rise begins to slow down, and this trend is taken as a signal that it is time for the speculators to sell out and take their profits. As soon as they try to do so, however, they learn that they have few people to sell to other than each other, and a mad scramble ensues to get out while prices collapse.

Regulation of Stock Exchange Trading

Before the days of SEC regulation of stock exchanges, unscrupulous traders could sometimes profit from the eagerness of amateur speculators to get something for nothing. A group would pool their funds and acquire a large block of stock, buying slowly and quietly to avoid raising prices. When the pool had accumulated all the shares it needed, it was ready to operate. An appearance of great activity could be created by having pool members place large buy orders with one broker and sell orders almost as large with another. When reported on the ticker, the large transactions would attract attention, and since the pool steadily bought more than it sold, the price would start to rise. The rising price would attract amateurs, whose purchases added to the pace of sales and to the rate of price increase.

Pool members often added fuel to the fire by circulating "hot tips" on the "prospects" of the stock, sometimes even bribing financial columnists, consultants, brokers, and others to publish the tips as reliable news. The get-rich-quick psychology being what it is, the most effective tip for this purpose was often merely to leak the news that the price was being artificially raised by a pool! As the tempo of purchases grew, however, the pool would reverse its strategy and began to sell more shares each day than it bought, unloading at a gain—first slowly and carefully, and then as its block of stocks was reduced, faster and faster to halt the rise and reverse it. Finally, the members of the pool would make large short sales to reap a second gain as the price collapsed.

Since the Securities Exchange Act of

1934, this kind of operation has been illegal. "The Exchange Act describes and prohibits certain forms of manipulative activity in any security registered on a national exchange. The prohibited activities include wash sales and matched orders effected for the purpose of creating a false impression of trading in . . . any such security; a series of transactions in which the price of such security is raised or depressed, or in which actual or apparent trading is created for the purpose of inducing sales or purchases of such securities by others; circulation by a broker, dealer, seller, or buyer, or by a person who receives consideration from a broker, dealer, seller, or buyer of information concerning market operation conducted for a rise or decline in the price of such security; and the making of any false or misleading statement of material information by a broker, dealer, seller, or buyer of such security for the purpose of inducing sales or purchases."[7]

To enforce the provisions of the law, the SEC maintains a market surveillance staff that monitors the ticker on major national exchanges and that follows daily summaries of trading on regional exchanges. In the event of suspicious activity, the commission can require brokers, dealers, and exchange members to open their accounts and to show what orders have been placed and by whom. When evidence is found of illegal activity, the SEC can initiate appropriate legal action.

[7] Securities and Exchange Commission, *Thirty-first Annual Report, 1965*, pp. 51–52.

CHAPTER 6

A Century of
U.S. Economic Growth

By the standards of most people in the world even today, the United States of a century ago was already a wealthy nation. The average U.S. GNP for the decade 1869–1878 has been estimated at $21.8 billion (at 1958 prices), or about $500 per person. This is enough to place a modern nation well out of the poorer class of societies, in a position comparable to that of modern Mexico or Greece. Yet during the past 100 years, U.S. output per person has grown more than sevenfold to reach over $3,500. The path of this growth has not been smooth, and the general upward movement has occasionally been interrupted by periods of reduced output, yet over the 100 years it has represented an average growth rate of over 2 percent per year compounded, as shown by the smooth red curve of Figure 1. At this rate of increase the real buying power of a typical family income has doubled every 35 years.[1]

On the average, in other words, the material standard of living of each succeeding generation has been double that of its parents.[2]

As shown by the key indicators given in Table 1, growth in material output was accompanied by widespread changes in the nature of American life. Families moved from farm to city, and the population became better educated. Occupations changed, while a new technology provided products and services unheard of 100 years ago.

The story of this rapid evolution is fascinating in its own right, but there is a special reason to consider it at this partic-

[1] See the appendix to this chapter for a discussion of the uses of percentage growth rates and a

simple way to estimate how often doubling occurs at any given rate.

[2] Or, to reverse the roles, each generation of parents has had occasion to remark to their offspring that "When we were your age, we didn't *have* all these things." Along with its other results, economic growth automatically contributes to the generation gap.

FIGURE 1   GROWTH OF REAL PER CAPITA GNP IN THE U.S., 1870-1970

SOURCE: Years 1874–1965 from U.S. Department of Commerce, *Long-Term Economic Growth, 1860–1965.* More recent figures from appropriate issues of *Survey of Current Business.*

ular point. Society is the only economic laboratory available, and the past 100 years of U.S. history provide an important case study by which to test the concepts and principles developed in the 5 preceding chapters. The results not only provide a summary of the material in Part One of our study, but form a living outline of the material to follow.

It is convenient to organize the study of American economic growth around the elements of the equation for productive capacity. It will be recalled that the equation expresses potential GNP per capita (GNP^*/N) as the product of the fraction of the population normally found in the labor force (L/N), the average annual number of hours worked per person on the job (h), and the average productivity of labor (π). That is,

$$\frac{GNP}{N} = \pi h \frac{L}{N}$$

The growth of U.S. productive capacity as estimated from this equation is shown in Table 2 together with its underlying elements. The fraction of the population aged 14 or older rose from 64.5 percent of the 1870 population to 73 percent in 1970. Labor force data for 1870 are unavailable, but in 1890 the fraction of the adult population ready, willing, and able to work was

TABLE 1   GROWTH OF THE U.S. ECONOMY 1870–1970

YEAR	GNP BILLIONS OF 1958 $	POPU-LATION (MILLIONS)	REAL GNP PER CAP. (1958 $)	AGRI-CULTURAL OUTPUT % OF GNP	URBAN POPU-LATION, % OF TOTAL	HIGH SCHOOL GRADUATES, % OF POPU-LATION 17 YEARS OLD
1870	n.a.	39.9	n.a.	n.a.	26	2.0
1875	21.8*a*	45.1	500*a*	39	n.a.	n.a.
1880	31.2*a*	49.2	640*a*	n.a.	28	2.5
1885	40.8*a*	55.3	750*a*	30	n.a.	n.a.
1890	51.0	63.1	815	26	35	3.5
1895	58.4	69.6	880	24	n.a.	n.a.
1900	75.5	76.1	985	23	41	6.4
1905	95.0	83.8	1,123	20	n.a.	n.a.
1910	120.1	92.4	1,300	17	45	8.8
1915	124.5	100.5	1,238	19	n.a.	n.a.
1920	140.0	106.5	1,315	14	51	16.8
1925	179.4	115.8	1,549	12	n.a.	n.a.
1930	183.5	123.2	1,490	11	56	29.0
1935	169.5	127.4	1,331	12	n.a.	n.a.
1940	227.2	132.1	1,720	10	56	50.8
1945	355.2	139.9	2,538	8	n.a.	n.a.
1950	355.3	151.7	2,342	7	64	59.0
1955	438.0	165.3	2,650	5	n.a.	n.a.
1960	487.7	180.7	2,699	5	70	65.1
1965	614.4	194.6	3,158	4	n.a.	n.a.
1970		207*b*				

a Decade averages.
b Census projection.
c Includes both government and private investment.

SOURCES: GNP, population, GNP per capita, and agricultural output as percent of GNP are adapted from U.S. Department of Commerce, *Long-Term Economic Growth, 1860–1965.* Other figures from *Historical Statistics of the United States.*

53.9 percent, which grew to 57 percent by 1970. The combined effect of these tendencies raised the proportion of total population belonging to the labor force, but the number of hours in the standard work year declined more than proportionately. As a result, the annual number of manhours of work normally available per person in the population declined over the period. At the same time, however, the average productivity of each hour worked rose so rapidly that capacity real output per capita grew despite the shrinking number of manhours worked.

Our analysis of American economic growth will follow the structure of the equation and its elements. We will first examine the causes of the downward trend in the number of manhours of labor available per person in the population. This discussion then will be followed by an analysis of rising productivity in terms of the changing quantity and quality of natural resources, labor, and capital equipment, and of the influence of evolving technology. The contribution of American institutions and government will next be examined, and the chapter will conclude with a discussion of some of the costs of economic growth.

TABLE 2 ESTIMATED GNP PER CAPITA AT CAPACITY OUTPUT UNITED STATES, 1870–1970

YEAR	POPULATION 14 OR OLDER[a] (PERCENT)	NORMAL LABOR FORCE PARTICIPATION RATE[a] (PERCENT)	POTENTIAL HOURS PER YEAR (NUMBER)	OUTPUT PER MANHOUR AT HIGH EMPLOYMENT (1958 DOLLARS)	ESTIMATED GNP PER CAPITA AT CAPACITY OUTPUT (1958 DOLLARS)
1870	64.5	n.a.	n.a.	n.a.	$ 627[b]
1880	64.1	n.a.	n.a.	n.a.	755[b]
1890	67.3	53.9	2,789	.90	910
1895	67.7	54.6	2,764	.99	1,011
1900	67.7	55.4	2,766	1.05	1,089
1905	69.0	56.4	2,749	1.13	1,209
1910	70.7	57.3	2,700	1.36	1,488
1915	70.1	57.1	2,678	1.41	1,511
1920	71.2	56.0	2,630	1.50	1,573
1925	71.0	55.4	2,573	1.65	1,670
1930	72.7	55.0	2,518	1.89	1,903
1935	74.7	55.6	2,429	2.05	2,117
1940	76.9	56.2	2,286	2.30	2,272
1945	77.0	57.0	2,206	2.34	2,265
1950	74.6	58.4	2,138	2.77	2,580
1955	71.5	59.1	2,086	3.53	3,116
1960	69.6	58.4	2,060	3.84	3,215
1965	70.1	57.4	2,003	4.27	3,441
1970	73.0	57.0	1,950	4.60	3,730

[a] For historical comparability, 14 years has been taken as the minimum working age throughout the period. Official U.S. labor force data are now compiled for persons aged 16 or older, and participation rates derived from them are higher than those shown here.
[b] Calculated by backward extension of growth trend.

SOURCES: All basic data except 1970 and population figures for years before 1900 were obtained from U.S. Department of Commerce, *Long-Term Economic Growth 1860–1965*, Washington, D.C., 1966. Data for 1970 are projections. Population percentages before 1900 were estimated from Census data on the number of people aged 15 or older. Normal labor force participation rates were obtained by smoothing actual rates as estimated by Stanley Lebergott. Potential hours per year are those compiled by James Knowles, except 1905 and earlier which are estimates of actual hours prepared by John W. Kendrick. Output per manhour was estimated by first interpolating the productivity of private workers between years of minimum unemployment, and then adjusting the series to allow for the difference in productivity between private and government workers. GNP per capita at capacity output was then calculated as the product of the first 4 columns.

THE CHANGING QUANTITY OF LABOR

The quantity of labor available to support each person in the population depends on the age distribution of the population, the labor force participation rate among people old enough to work, and the average length of the work year.

The Changing Age Distribution of the U.S. Population The steady rise in the proportion of Americans old enough to work resulted primarily from the reduction in birth rates shown in Figure 2. In 1870, 40 children were born per 1,000 of population, but by 1968 the birth rate had declined to 17.3 per 1,000. Where there had been 814 children under 5 alive per 1,000 women of

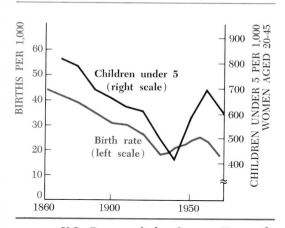

FIGURE 2   U.S. BIRTH RATE AND NUMBER
                        OF CHILDREN ALIVE, 1860-1960

SOURCE: U.S. Bureau of the Census, *Historical Statistics of the United States, Colonial Times to 1957*, Washington, D.C., 1960. Later data from *Statistical Abstract of the United States, 1969.*

child-bearing age in 1870, there are now fewer than 700. A more dramatic view of the change in child-bearing is obtained by considering the number of children borne by a woman during her entire lifetime. Women who had been 16 to 20 years old in 1870 were past child-bearing age by 1910. Looking back over their families, the Census of 1910 reported that among these women, those who had married had borne an *average* of 5.2 children. In fact, a third of them were found to have borne 7 or more, and almost 15 percent had had 10 or more offspring! By contrast, women born in the years 1910–1914, old enough to have completed their families by the time of the Census of 1960, were reported to have borne an average of only 2.4 children. Only 5.3 percent had borne 7 or more, and only 1.5 percent had had as many as 10.

The change in birth rate was not an independent phenomenon, but part of a recognizable pattern of interdependent developments. As a consequence of rising farm productivity, only 4 percent of present-day U.S. GNP originates on farms, com-

pared to nearly 50 percent a century ago, and the accompanying migration from farm to city has had profound consequences for the birth rate. On farms, particularly in a day when unmechanized cultivation depended on manual labor, children were important contributors to family output. But city children could no longer make substantial contributions to family income, and larger city families meant a lower standard of living for each member. At the same time, city life and educational improvement opened new economic and cultural interests outside the family circle, and fewer women remained content to devote themselves exclusively to a large family of children.

Even short-run economic events sometimes influence birth rates and alter the age distribution of the population. The temporary peak reached in 1940, when 77 percent of population was 14 or older, was a consequence of the Depression of the 1930s when many couples postponed having children. By 1960, however, the ratio had fallen below 70 percent as a consequence of the post-Depression adjustment and of the "baby boom" that followed World War II.

Rising Labor Force Participation We have little information about how many adult men and women normally participated in production as members of the labor force a century ago, but by 1890 the normal labor force included about 53.9 percent of the population aged 14 or older. By 1970, normal labor force participation had grown to 57 percent. This increase was the net difference between reduced participation by men and increased participation by women. As shown in Figure 3, between 1890 and 1960, labor force participation by men of all ages declined, but the decline was most noticeable among the youngest and oldest groups. The diminished job holding by men under 25 was, of course, associated with the steady rise in the pro-

FIGURE 3   PERCENT OF ADULT MEN AND
WOMEN IN THE U.S. LABOR
FORCE, 1890 AND 1960

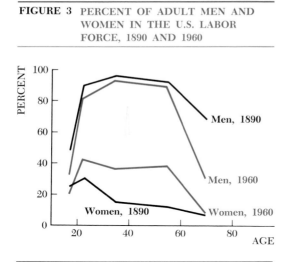

SOURCE: Adapted from data in *Historical Statistics of the United States.*

portion of young people attending high school and college, while reduced labor force participation of men over 60 was connected with earlier retirement.

In contrast to men, more women work today than formerly. Unless she is either under 25 or over 60, the chance that a modern woman will be found in the labor force is 2 to 4 times that of her counterpart in 1890. This trend is related to the general social emancipation of women that accompanied rising income and increased urbanization, but it is most particularly connected with lower birth rates, smaller families, and the greater proportion of children in school. The causation works both ways, however, for the falling birth rate was, itself, partly a manifestation of the preference of modern women for jobs. Labor force participation by women was further stimulated by increased accumulation of household capital in the form of washers, dryers, vacuum cleaners, and other implements to lighten household chores, combined with the increasing transfer of clothing manufacture, food prepara-

tion, and other household functions from the home to the factory.

Since the increased entrance of women into the labor force exceeded the rate at which labor force participation by men declined, the fraction of the adult population ready, willing, and able to work tended to grow, and combined with the rising adult fraction of the population, it raised the ratio of labor force to total U.S. population from slightly more than one-third in 1890 to very nearly one-half by 1965, a growth of about one-fourth of 1 percent per year, compounded.

Fewer Hours per Worker   Table 2 also shows the average annual number of hours of work normally available per worker, given the composition of output, customary work habits, laws, union rules, and other institutional factors. Typical full-time industrial workers in 1870 put in 10 and one-half hours a day in a 6-day week. With no vacations and few holidays, their work year probably exceeded 3,200 hours. Farmers, who made up more than half of the labor force at that time, worked even longer hours. Of course, even on farms not everybody worked full time; therefore, the average work year doubtless contained fewer than 3,000 hours. No reliable average figures are available for 1870, but the average work year in 1890 has been estimated at 2,789 hours.

In the 100 years since 1870, hours of work have been reduced by almost half. As shown in Table 3, the 40-hour week has become typical for industrial workers. Although some still put in 60 hours a week or more, and although 60 hours was characteristic of more than a third of farm workers, the overall average during a typical work week was only a fraction over 40 hours. Even this difference understates the change over the century, for of the 77 million workers employed in May, 1969, nearly 3 million did not work at all during the week

TABLE 3   DISTRIBUTION OF HOURS WORKED, SURVEY WEEK OF MAY, 1969

| HOURS PER WEEK | THOUSANDS OF WORKERS ON THE JOB IN | | |
	ALL INDUS-TRIES	NON-AGRICUL-TURAL INDUSTRY	AGRI-CUL-TURE
Total at work	74,463	70,639	3,825
1–4 hours	681	630	51
5–14	3,443	3,215	228
15–29	7,871	7,167	704
30–34	3,789	3,608	181
35–39	5,004	4,835	170
40	30,360	29,999	361
41–48	9,557	9,252	305
49–59	7,004	6,595	409
60 hours and over	6,754	5,338	1,417
Average hours worked	40.2	39.7	48.5

	THOUSANDS OF PERSONS WITH A JOB, BUT NOT AT WORK, BY REASON GIVEN
Vacation	933
Illness	1,120
Bad weather	50
Industrial dispute	121
All other reasons	576
Total	2,801

SOURCE: *Employment and Earnings*, June, 1969.

shown. These people were not unemployed, but were workers with jobs who, for one reason or another, did not work that particular week. Over the course of the year more than half of these workers would be people on vacation, but May is not yet the height of the vacation season, and vacations accounted for only about a third of the employed workers who were not on the job. The remainder were temporarily unable to work because of sickness, weather, industrial disputes, or other causes. When account is taken of these workers with 0 hours, the overall average work week dropped to 38.7 hours. At this rate, the 1969 work year would have averaged about 2,015 hours per worker.

There are a number of reasons for the downward trend in hours over the 100-year period. In part, shorter hours resulted merely from the changing composition of employment that accompanied migration of labor from the farm to the city. Industry characteristically had shorter hours. Likewise, the rising importance of women in the labor force contributed to shortening hours because women are more likely than men to want only part-time employment. For example, almost a quarter of the women at work in May, 1969 were in voluntary part-time jobs, compared to fewer than 8 percent of the men.

Part of the shortening of hours took the form of reduced work weeks in all occupations, as standard factory hours declined from 63 hours per week in 1870 to 40 hours. But an important contribution was also made by increasing the number of workers eligible for vacations. Where vacations for plant workers were almost unheard of a century ago, almost all workers in modern industrial plants are entitled to a week's vacation with pay after 1 year's employment, and to 2 weeks after no more than 5 years on the job. Over three-quarters of all plant workers with 10 years' seniority are entitled to 3 weeks with pay.

Still further reduction in the work year has been achieved by adding holidays to the calendar. From 1960 to 1966, the average number of paid holidays rose from 6.9 to 7.3 per year, and in 1966, 70 percent of industrial plant workers got 7 or more paid holidays.

The downward trend in number of hours worked per year was an important expression of the desire of most people to use part of their growing productivity to provide greater leisure rather than more material goods, but a variety of institutional devices were required to make this desire effective. Although to some extent shorter hours, longer vacations, and more holidays were used by business firms as competitive devices to attract and keep loyal, high-caliber workers, collective bargaining was probably a more important element in the decline in number of hours worked. Hours, holidays, and vacations have been consistent targets for collective bargaining. Part of the reason lies in the fact that shorter hours help spread available jobs among more union members, a particularly important point during severe depressions. But in addition, unions seemed to have an almost mystical belief in the efficacy of shorter hours in improving the economic position of the worker. As an old slogan had it, "If you work by the piece or work by the day, to shorten the hours increases the pay." Most of this mystique has disappeared from modern collective bargaining, however, and the issue of hours is more likely to be settled in terms of the desirability of additional leisure compared to additional material income for the worker.

During the last 50 years, hours of labor have been subject to important legislation. The most important was the Fair Labor Standards Act of 1938 which legally required most employers to pay time-and-a-half for hours in excess of 40 a week. This added to the economic pressure for shorter hours.

On the other hand, not all workers place the same premium on leisure, and some persist in working longer hours, often by "moonlighting"; that is, by taking extra work at night or during vacations. A study conducted in 1966 indicated that nearly 5 percent of all employed workers held 2 or more jobs. Some of the industrial workers reported as working 60 hours or more a week in Table 2 were workers reporting time spent on more than one job. Despite the offsetting effect of overtime and multiple job holding, however, the normal hours potentially available per worker declined from about 2,789 in 1890 to 1,950 by the year 1970, an average rate of reduction of about four-tenths of 1 percent per year, compounded over the period.

Less Labor Effort per Person   Multiplying the average number of hours in the work year by the normal fraction of the population in the labor force, we find the yearly number of manhours available per person in the population. According to the data of Table 2, this figure decreased from about 1,010 manhours per person in 1890 to 770 in 1970.

This decline is in keeping with our earlier discovery that poor nations partially compensate for low productivity by exerting greater labor effort per person. Reduction of labor effort is a natural response to the changed opportunity cost of leisure that occurs as productivity rises. As people increase their productive power, they generally prefer to sacrifice some of the extra output that becomes available to them in exchange for greater enjoyment of leisure.

RISING PRODUCTIVITY OF AMERICAN LABOR

In the United States as elsewhere, the major factor in rising material welfare has been the increase in output per manhour of

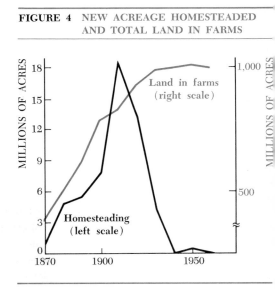

FIGURE 4   NEW ACREAGE HOMESTEADED AND TOTAL LAND IN FARMS

SOURCE: *Historical Statistics of the United States.*

labor. In fact, since somewhat fewer hours per capita are available now than 100 years ago, our vastly increased living standard must be the consequence of a more than proportional rise in productivity. This is borne out by the estimates of Table 2 which show output per manhour, measured in 1958 prices, growing from $.90 in 1890 to $4.60 in 1970, an average growth of 2.04 percent per year, compounded.

As we know, labor productivity depends on the quality of available natural resources, the number and quality of people in the labor force, the degree of specialization of labor, the amount of capital used, and the level of scientific and technical knowledge. These elements are interdependent in complex ways. To understand U.S. economic growth, we must examine the change that has taken place in each of these elements over the last 100 years.

Quantity and Quality of Natural Resources

Despite the rapid population expansion, the early part of the past 100 years was

FIGURE 6 U.S. CONSUMPTION OF IRON ORE

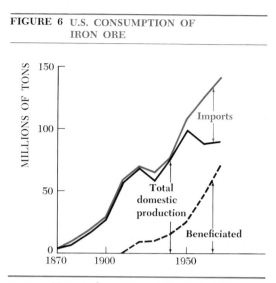

SOURCE: *Historical Statistics of the United States.*

marked by expansion of the quantity and improvement in the quality of natural resources available for use. As the population moved westward, new land was brought into farms by homesteading and in other ways, as shown in Figure 4. Cattle raising and farming developed in the West. The iron and copper mines of Lake Superior, and the chemical resurces of Michigan were tapped. Petroleum and natural gas were developed in Texas, Oklahoma, and California. The rich timber resources of the Great Lake States and the South were exploited.

In more recent years, however, the expansion of natural resources has been slowed, and problems of intensified use have arisen. Most high-quality land has already been brought into use. Timber near the market has been cut, and the lumber industry has been pushed toward the Pacific, a trend clearly visible in Figure 5, while Figure 6 shows how the rising requirements of an expanding steel industry have exhausted easily accessible ores and have driven mining farther afield. As shown in Figure 6, iron ore is now imported from

FIGURE 5 LUMBER PRODUCTION, CENTRAL AND LAKE STATES, AND SOUTH COMPARED TO WEST COAST

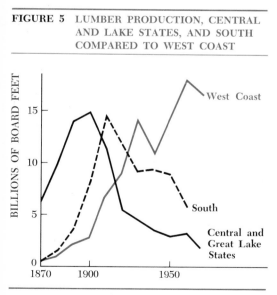

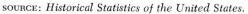

SOURCE: *Historical Statistics of the United States.*

FIGURE 7   U.S. LIFE EXPECTATION AND
            DEATH RATE OF 20-YEAR-OLDS

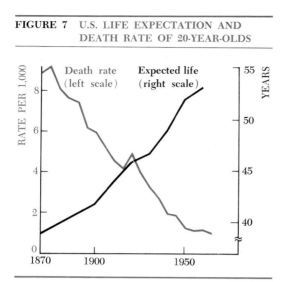

SOURCE: *Historical Statistics of the United States.*

abroad, and domestic ores of inferior quality are now *beneficiated,* or processed at
the mine to raise their quality to usable
levels. Oil wells are now often more than a
mile deep, and increasingly it is necessary
to drill in ocean beds.

Improvements in the Labor Force

Health   Over the past 100 years, the
health of the American people has improved dramatically, as shown in Figures
7 and 8. In 1870, nearly 1 percent of all
men and women aged 20 died each year
and among those who survived the average
expectation was only 40 more years of life.
The death rate among 20-year-olds today
is below 1 in 1,000, and their average life
expectancy is 53 additional years. Diseases
like diphtheria and typhoid which are rare
causes of death in modern America used to
kill 100 people per 100,000 annually. The
death rate from tuberculosis has been cut
from 343 to 6 per 100,000.

The falling incidence of disease contributed to healthier, happier, larger, and

stronger workers who performed better on
the job and who lost fewer days to sickness.
Reduction of illness also helped release
housewives and others from care of the sick
for other productive labor. The longer life
expectation of adults resulted in the average worker contributing more years on the
job after he had received his education and
acquired mature working experience. The
improved health of the population was an
important result, not only of the reduction
in disease, but of rising material living
standards in the form of better diet, better
clothing and housing, more and better education, and improved water supplies and
sewer systems. Additional contributions to
general health were made by the disappearance of child labor, improved safety
and working conditions, and shorter hours
and longer vacations, all of which were
themselves permitted by rising productivity.

Education   The second important source
of improvement in the caliber of the labor
force was increasing education. Barely more
than half of the children between the ages
of 5 and 17 were enrolled in public schools

FIGURE 8   U.S. DEATH RATES FROM
            SPECIFIED DISEASES

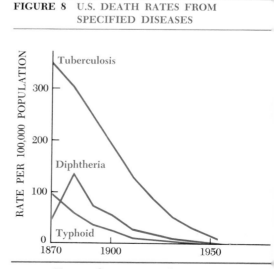

SOURCE: *Historical Statistics of the United States.*

100 years ago. By 1965 public school enrollment had grown to include 83 percent of school-age children, and when private schools are taken into account, enrollment was very nearly 100 percent. At the same time, the average number of days attended during the school year more than doubled from 78 in 1870 to 160 today. This increase was partly due to the lengthening of the average school year from 132 days in 1870 to 178 days, as shown in Figure 9, but it was also the result of the fact that young people were healthier and were relieved of the need to contribute to the family income.

The combined effect of greater enrollment and more days of school attendance was to triple the average number of pupil-days of schooling per child of school age. At the same time, increasing numbers of better-trained teachers raised the average quality of the education offered. Even after adjusting for rising prices, the real daily public school outlay per pupil increased sixfold between 1890 and 1960 as shown in Figure 10. If, as seems likely, the annual rate of increase was much the same during the rest of the period, we can assume that the real outlay per pupil-day has increased

FIGURE 9   PERCENT OF U.S. POPULATION AGES 5 TO 17 ENROLLED IN PUBLIC SCHOOL AND AVERAGE LENGTH OF SCHOOL YEAR

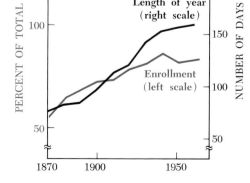

SOURCE: *Historical Statistics of the United States.*

FIGURE 10   U.S. CURRENT EXPENDITURE PER PUBLIC SCHOOL PUPIL PER DAY AT 1947-1949 PRICES

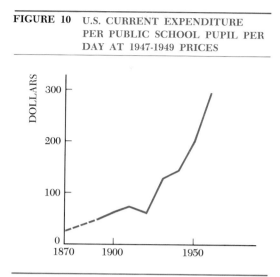

SOURCE: *Historical Statistics of the United States.*

approximately thirteenfold in the past 100 years.

The higher level of education has added greatly to the productivity of people at work. Almost any productive job requires at least the ability to read and write, but in 1870 1 American out of every 5 was illiterate, compared to only 1 in 50 today. Probably more important, the increase in the number and quality of educated workers permitted the steady shift of production away from hand methods to greater dependence on capital equipment whose design, construction, maintenance, and operation required more highly trained technical people. As shown in Figure 11, an important consequence of increased education was a rapid rise in professional and other white-collar occupations.

There is, of course, no sure method to measure the contribution of increased education to labor productivity. For one thing, a considerable part of education is aimed at the enrichment of life rather than at increased output. The data in Table 4, however, show how much harder it is for men with little schooling to find jobs in modern industry. Among the men who reported to

FIGURE 11   U.S. OCCUPATIONAL
                     DISTRIBUTION OF JOBS

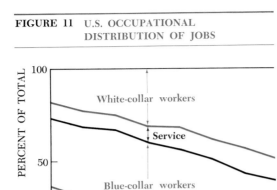

SOURCE: *Historical Statistics of the United States.*

the Census of 1960, the unemployment rate
was 7.6 percent for those who had attended
school less than 5 years, but only .8 percent
for college graduates. Among those who
succeeded in getting work, moreover, there

TABLE 4   UNEMPLOYMENT RATES AND
                   MEDIAN INCOME OF MEN 25
                   YEARS OLD AND OLDER, BY
                   YEARS OF SCHOOL
                   COMPLETED

SCHOOLING	UNEMPLOYMENT RATE	MEDIAN INCOME OF THOSE WITH INCOME
No. of school years completed	8.3	$1,439
Elementary:		
1–4 years	7.6	1,844
5–7 years	6.8	3,062
8 years	5.4	3,885
High school:		
1–3 years	4.7	4,847
4 years or more	2.7	5,437
College:		
1–3 years	1.2	5,980
4 years or more	0.8	7,646

SOURCE: *United States Census of Population,
1960.*

were wide differences in income. The median income of those with the least education was below $1,500 in 1960, while that
of college graduates was above $7,500.

Greater Specialization of Jobs

Not only has the U.S. labor force vastly
improved in quality over the past century,
but its activity has become much more
highly specialized. Increased specialization
was permitted by the growth of population and by the rapid rise in transportation
and communication facilities that bound
the nation into a single, continent-wide market. In May, 1869, when Leland Stanford
drove the golden spike to mark the comple-
tion of the first coast-to-coast rail line,
there were only 50,000 miles of railroad in
operation. New lines were constructed to
form a network covering the entire conti-
nent, involving nearly 430,000 miles of railroad at its peak in 1930. Development of
the automobile and motor truck further
increased the size of the market as the
mileage of surfaced road grew from 150,-
000 in 1900 to 2,557,000 by 1960. Most recently, the introduction and expansion of
air travel has speeded up the movement
of goods and people even more, and the
market has been further expanded by rapid
communication. The telephone, not even in
existence in 1870, now interconnects virtually every home and business in the country, while radio and television bring the
showroom into the living room.

Within industrial plants, operations became highly specialized by the introduction
of mass production technology, which divided complex processes among highly
specialized workers and employed production-line methods by which material being
worked on is moved from worker to worker,
each performing a single simple operation.
In the economy at large, increased specialization meant more and more effort devoted
to the transportation and exchange of goods

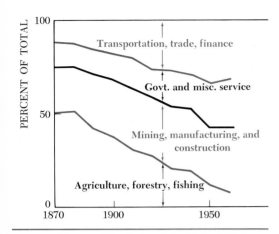

FIGURE 12   U.S. INDUSTRIAL DISTRIBUTION OF GAINFUL WORKERS

SOURCE: *Historical Statistics of the United States.*

as opposed to their manufacture. The result, shown in Figure 12, has been an increasing proportion of workers employed in trade, transportation, finance, advertising, and related jobs.

Growth of Capital

The last 100 years was also a period of rapid capital accumulation. During most of the period, about 20 percent of gross national product was devoted to investment in new equipment and structures, and by 1970 the value of the total stock of producer capital in use was about 30 times larger than it had been 100 years earlier. Of course, not all of this additional capital contributed to higher productivity. Some of it was needed merely to provide machinery and equipment for the growing number of workers in the labor force. Nevertheless, the average amount of capital per worker rose substantially. When measured in constant dollars of 1954 purchasing power, for example, the value of capital shown on the balance sheets of U.S. manufacturing firms rose from $1,930 per worker in 1879 to

$9,000 per worker in 1960. This represented an average growth of nearly 2 percent per year in the amount of equipment available to the average manufacturing employee.

Capital accumulation was hardly an independent force. It was intricately entangled with all the other elements contributing to rising productivity. New transportation and communications technology could expand markets only when implemented through massive capital investment in railroads, rolling stock, highways, trucks, telegraph and telephone lines, and other installations. In addition, equipment was required for coal mines, refineries, cement plants, steel mills, and other facilities to supply and service the new communications system. By 1948, the automobile industry, which did not even exist in 1870, accounted for nearly 6 percent of all manufacturing capital. As another example, capital was doubly connected with education. The rising output of educational service could not have occurred without the underlying investment in school buildings, libraries, laboratories, and such support industries as book publishing. Nor, on the other hand, could the better-educated workers have been more productive without the technical equipment to make their education effective.

Changes in the Types of Capital Goods in Use   The introduction of new technology did not always require a net addition to the amount of capital goods on hand, for to some extent its needs could be met by altering the composition of the existing stock of equipment rather than by adding to its total. To change the kind of equipment in use, labor and other resources already employed in the capital goods industry were withdrawn from the production of older types of equipment and put to work turning out the new types. As old equipment wore out, "replacements" arrived in the new form, altering the composition of capital accordingly.

FIGURE 13   TECHNICAL CHANGE ALTERS THE KIND OF CAPITAL IN USE

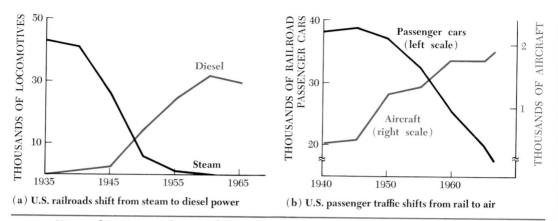

(a) U.S. railroads shift from steam to diesel power   (b) U.S. passenger traffic shifts from rail to air

SOURCE: *Historical Statistics of the United States.*

One good example of a change in capital composition occurred in connection with the shift of American railroads from steam to diesel power, as shown in Figure 13(a). Beginning about 1935, as steam locomotives were retired, they were replaced by diesels; thus virtually the entire stock of locomotives was changed over within 20 years. While there may have been some net addition to the total capital invested in railroad traction power during the process, it was small compared to the size of the shift that had been accomplished.

In some cases, old equipment in 1 industry was replaced by new equipment in another. For example, as travelers began to go by air instead of by train, railroads permitted coaches and other passenger cars to deteriorate. As the coaches were retired, their "replacements" appeared in the form of aircraft operated by scheduled airlines, as shown in Figure 13(b).

Development of New Products

True productivity is measured not only by the physical quantity of goods that a given number of workers can turn out, but by the usefulness of the goods themselves. Thus the discovery and introduction of new materials and products over the past 100 years contributed as much to rising productivity as any of the other changes. It is hardly possible even to begin a list of innovations. What proportion of the contents of an ordinary house would be recognizable to somebody from a century ago? And how many of those items recognized would be made of familiar materials? Aluminum was a laboratory curiosity 100 years ago, and plastics as we know them today hardly existed before 1940. Over the past 100 years rayon replaced silk, only to give way to nylon, acrylic fibers and other synthetics that have also made important inroads into the use of cotton, wool, and leather.

The revolution in the kinds of products in use is even more apparent. Alexander Graham Bell spoke his first sentence into the telephone in 1876. Edison patented the phonograph in 1878 and produced a commercially practical incandescent lamp in 1879. In Germany, Karl Benz built the first vehicle powered by a gasoline motor in 1885, and in 1903 the Wright brothers flew their plane at Kitty Hawk.

The first motion picture, *The Great*

Train Robbery, was produced in 1903. The broadcast of regularly scheduled radio programs began in 1920, and television equipment came on the market in 1945. Computers and computer-controlled automated processes were introduced in the 1950s, and by the early 1960s the application of nuclear reactors to commercial production of electric power was underway. The 100 years that had begun in the era of hand production using steam and animal power ended with automation, computer technology, and nuclear power, and spanned the time from the driving of the golden spike, to the year men reached the moon.

The development of new products not only contributed to rising productivity, but was in turn influenced by it in several ways. In the first place, the research and development required to discover, perfect, produce, and market new products often involved high opportunity costs. Skilled engineering and technical labor had to be diverted from existing production processes before the new product could be put in production, and the success of a new venture was anything but assured. Only a society that was already highly productive could have risked the cost. In addition, many of the most successful of the new products were items that only a highly productive society could afford. Many of the developments in consumer goods, especially consumer hardware like automatic washers and dryers, television sets, and outboard motors, were luxuries beyond the grasp of people with the low incomes found in most of the world.

*Institutional Contributions
to Growing Productivity*

The past century of American economic development did not "just happen," but was the result of the deliberate choices and decisions that people made in the course of their normal lives. Although these choices were individually made, they were coordinated and made effective through economic and social institutions.

Private Enterprise The basic drive for American economic growth stemmed from the powerful incentive provided to business enterprisers by their position as receivers of the residual share of output. The production of better products or the adoption of new production methods rewarded the successful with profits, while those who were slow to recognize new possibilities suffered losses and were driven out. But profit was more than merely an incentive, for high profits flowing to successful enterprisers furnished people of demonstrated ability with additional income for financing more investment. In other words, the cycle by which economic growth feeds on itself was implemented at the level of the business firm. The man with the imagination, energy, and willingness to assume risks, who could apply his ability to obtain greater productivity, was automatically supplied with more income with which to expand the financing of his activities.

The rapid accumulation of capital was accompanied by the rise in the importance of the corporation as a form of enterprise. As modern technology required the concentration of greater and greater amounts of capital, more and more output came to be produced by incorporated firms. As Figure 14 shows, in contrast to 1880 when less than half of all manufacturing value added was produced by corporations, manufacturing today is almost entirely incorporated.

A still more important aspect of the operation of private enterprise was that, despite the huge rewards to successful enterprisers, the benefits from higher productivity were widely shared by the workers themselves. Adjusted to 1957 prices, total compensation per manhour in manufacturing rose from less than 46 cents in 1889 to $2.55 in 1963. Indeed, as shown in Figure

FIGURE 14   GROWTH IN IMPORTANCE OF
U.S. CORPORATIONS IN
MANUFACTURING

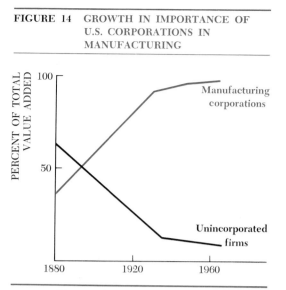

SOURCE: *Historical Statistics of the United States*
(1880 estimated).

15, there was an almost perfect parallel between rising output per manhour on the one hand and rising real compensation paid per manhour of labor on the other. This close parallel developed from the necessity of business firms to compete with one another for labor and other resources, for before a business firm could reap the residual profits from a new method of production, it had to contract for the labor and resources it needed. As more and more productive techniques were introduced, therefore, the competitive scramble for available labor tended to drive up wages, while at the same time the competition to sell the new product drove down prices. The result of rising wages and falling prices was the upward trend of real wages shown in the figure.

Land Tenure and Economic Development

In the United States we are prone to take our system of land tenure for granted, yet it had an important effect on agricultural productivity. The land policy of the U.S., best exemplified by the Homestead Laws,

was to turn new land over to those who were eager to live on it, work it, and develop it. Ownership of his land provided a powerful incentive to the farmer to invest in improvements. Moreover, the income from successful agricultural practice flowed back to the farmer, not only as a reward and incentive for increased productivity, but as a source of additional investment financing.

In some other countries, land at the disposal of the government has been granted to a landed aristocracy or otherwise consolidated into private estates to be worked by a landless peasantry for the benefit of absentee landlords. Such a system of absenteeism often produces results that are exactly the opposite of those needed for economic growth. Since any improvement of the land by the peasant simply means higher rent, he has no incentive to raise his own productivity. Extra income that

FIGURE 15   TOTAL REAL COMPENSATION
PER MANHOUR IN U.S.
MANUFACTURING COMPARED TO
REAL OUTPUT PER MANHOUR,
1890-1960

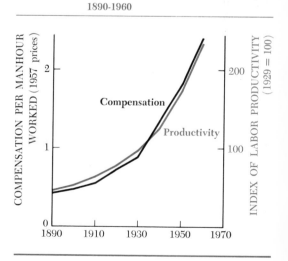

SOURCE: Compensation per manhour according to Albert Rees. Output per manhour according to John W. Kendrick. Both as published in U.S. Department of Commerce, *Long-Term Economic Growth, 1860–1965.*

comes from the land is siphoned off as rent to aristocrats, who are often more interested in their own lavish consumption than in enterprise and investment, further retarding economic growth. The system of land tenure has been called one of the most serious obstacles to economic development in Latin America, and many people look upon land reform transferring ownership of land to those who farm it as an important step toward capital accumulation and economic development.[3]

The fact that the rising productivity of farm labor was a central element in American economic development provides an important clue to the problems of growth in other parts of the world. Since society must maintain enough people on farms to feed the total population, labor can be released for industrial development only about as fast as farm productivity can be raised. In a primitive society in which each family can raise only enough food for itself, everybody lives on the land. When farm productivity doubles, each farm family can grow enough for 2, and half the population is freed to work in industry. When each farm family can grow enough food for 3, only a third of the population need stay on farms, and so on. It follows as almost a matter of simple arithmetic that the percentage of total population on farms must be inversely proportional to the productivity of farm labor.

As shown in Figure 16, the American experience of the last 100 years followed this relationship almost exactly. The black dots in the figure show the percentage of the American population on farms in each of the years indicated. The blue curve varies inversely with farm productivity. The closeness with which the dots follow the theoretical relationship is witness to the powerful

[3] See for example, Raul Prebisch, "Economic Aspects of the Alliance for Progress," in Shante S. Tangri and H. Peter Gray, eds., *Capital Accumulation and Economic Development*, Boston: Heath, 1967.

FIGURE 16 COMPARISON OF TOTAL U.S. FARM POPULATION AND FARM PRODUCTIVITY

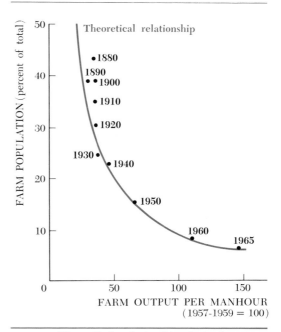

SOURCE: Theoretical relationship derived as explained in the text. Calculated from data in U.S. Department of Commerce, *Long-Term Economic Growth, 1860–1965*.

role of productivity as a force in reducing the farm population.

It follows that any nation bent on industrialization must first invest heavily in agriculture. Until farm productivity reaches a level at which a fraction of the population can feed the whole, industrialization cannot even begin. Failure to appreciate this simple and rather obvious proposition has led to the failure of several ambitious attempts to foster economic growth. People eager for higher living standards are often tempted to turn away from agriculture, the symbol of economic backwardness, and invest in steel mills, power installations, skyscrapers, and other symbols of economic progress. But a development plan that neglects agriculture has slim chances of success.

The Indian 5-Year Plan of 1956–1961 devoted only 11 percent of total development outlays to agriculture. Slow productivity growth and bad weather combined to force food imports from an expected level of slightly more than 1 million tons a year to 4 million tons. In the 5-Year Plan for 1961–1966, agricultural outlays were raised to 14 percent of the total. But this figure was still insufficient, and after a succession of poor crop years, massive foreign aid was required to prevent widespread famine. The most recent 5-Year Plan calls for still greater investment in agriculture.

The Role of Government in Raising Productivity One of the fundamental factors in the growth of the American economy has been the existence of a stable system of political institutions. Since the end of the Civil War, social unrest and major swings in political opinion have, without important exception, worked themselves out through reasonably orderly political processes without important alterations of the economic environment or the basic rules of the game. The stable social environment encouraged people to plan for, and invest in the future and to venture on careers to further their own long-run interests. In a society with an unstable government, investment in a factory is a risky business, since the next man to seize political office may take it away from you. People in such situations prefer to keep their wealth in gold, jewels, or other unproductive forms that are easily hidden and readily portable. If income is invested at all, it is likely to be invested in foreign countries, either by the direct purchase of the securities of foreign corporations or indirectly through deposits in foreign banks. The famous "numbered Swiss bank account" is an instrument by which a person with a high income can shift his wealth abroad, rather than risking it in investment at home.

In the role of government, we can see a special case of the social dynamics by which economic growth feeds on itself. Social unrest tends to be greatest where income is the lowest. Unstable institutions discourage enterprise and investment, closing the circle and locking the society in its own poverty. Stable institutions promote economic growth which adds to social stability and facilitates even faster growth.

In one important respect, the American people have been particularly lucky. Despite 5 major wars fought during the last 100 years, the amount of direct war damage to the American economy has been trivial. These wars cost heavily in American lives and in the diversion of resources to the production of war materials, and to this extent they have periodically retarded the rate of economic development. But during the entire century the U.S. did not suffer a major invasion or the destruction of cities and factories as other nations did.

In addition to the provision of a strong institutional framework, the American government has played an important direct role in stimulating economic growth. Government capital accumulated in the form of roads, highways, irrigation, and flood control systems provided the communication network needed to bind together a continent-wide market. The government contributed to this growth by offering subsidies to railroads, airlines, and shipping, and by granting the right of eminent domain to enable light and power lines, gas mains, telephone cables, and other public utilities to extend their lines over the community.

Much of the increased educational service upon which economic development depended was provided by government in the form of compulsory grade-school attendance, free public high schools, and heavily subsidized state universities. The subsidized research activities of colleges and universities contributed a steady stream of technical innovation to the economy. Government research, particularly at land-grant colleges and agricultural research stations, was probably the main contributor to new agricultural technology.

COSTS OF ECONOMIC GROWTH

Human Dislocation American economic development has not been without cost. Although the end result has been higher living standards spread widely through the community, economic development has forced readjustments in employment that have often been personal disasters to the people affected. Rising productivity "released" people from agriculture for work in industry, but what happened in human terms was that falling farm prices made it impossible for many farmers to make a living. They were not so much "released" from the farm as driven off, and the past 100 years have been one long agricultural problem. The same economic growth that produced greater material welfare also filled our cities with an uneducated rural population no longer needed on the farm, but lacking the skills and work habits needed for modern industry.

The same was true of many other adjustments. Technical change sometimes replaced a craftsman who had a lifetime investment in his skill with a worker with a few weeks' training on a machine. Sometimes, on the other hand, numbers of unskilled workers were replaced by machines produced by technical workers in other industries, or by technical changes that eliminated the need for their products. For example, the mechanization of coal mining, plus the shift of railroads from coal to petroleum and the shift of home heating to natural gas left a depressed region where the coal industry had flourished.

In a very real sense, a private enterprise system tends to impose economic development on society, forcing individuals to adjust as best they can. Moreover, until 50 years ago, little was done to protect individuals from the impact of change, or even to help them readjust. More recently, however, we have begun to recognize the responsibility of society for human dislocation and have initiated programs to mitigate its impact. These include unemployment insurance, manpower retraining and development, social security, farm price supports, and other government programs that we will study later. The rate at which labor-saving devices are introduced in industry and the fate of the workers displaced by them have also become increasingly important aspects of collective bargaining by labor unions.

Environmental Pollution A second direct cost of economic growth has been the rapid rise in air and water pollution, waste disposal problems, and other forms of environmental contamination. Air and water resources are limited. A small pioneer society can use them indiscriminately as disposal fields for refuse, since the small volume of waste materials is easily carried in suspension until it is reabsorbed into the environment. As the volume of waste materials rises, however, a point is reached at which air currents and streams are overburdened, and pollution appears, first as an aesthetic consideration, then as a real problem of health.

On the average over the past century, the amount of discharge into the environment has been growing at an annual rate of at least 3 percent per year. As an indication, during the last 30 years, daily U.S. water use has risen an average of 4.3 percent per year—nearly 3 times as fast as population (see Figure 17). Because of such technical changes as the increasing use of automobiles, trucks, and jet aircraft, the growth of air pollution has been closer to 5 percent per year.

At these rates of increase, the amount

FIGURE 17   TOTAL U.S. WATER USE, 1900-1965

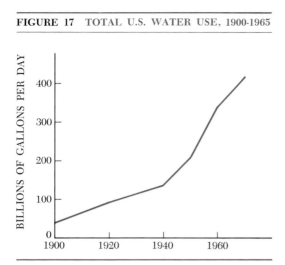

SOURCE: *Historical Statistics of the United States.*

the spurts of actual output. The 33 years from 1906 to 1939 were particularly interesting, for output per capita was very little higher at the end of the period than it had been at the beginning. Instead of steady growth, there had been a succession of business cycles of increasing violence, culminating in the Great Depression of the 1930s. This was followed by World War II, during which output exceeded calculated capacity by a substantial margin, as men and women who would normally have been in school, at home, or retired joined the armed services and entered industry. After the readjustment of the economy following the war, the course continued more smoothly upward.

of environmental pollution tends to double every 14 to 16 years. Thus the difference between a serious level of pollution and one only half as bad is only 14 to 16 years. This is one of the important reasons that pollution has appeared as a real social problem only during the last 2 decades, despite its steady growth for more than a century. It is also why it is now a critical problem that requires prompt and energetic action.

Business Cycles   A third cost of U.S. economic development has been periodic widespread unemployment. The growth of the past 100 years was anything but a smooth process. Some years were characterized by high rates of investment, rapidly rising productivity, and full use of available productive capacity, but these bursts of growth have alternated with periods of low investment, idle capacity, declining output, and the paradox of economic misery in the midst of plenty. The successive oscillations of output, called *business cycles,* could be seen in Figure 1 of this chapter, where actual GNP per capita was compared with its overall growth trend. The continual up-and-down movement of the black curve showed

ECONOMIC HISTORY AND THE STUDY OF ECONOMICS

This rapid survey of American economic development serves as a fitting conclusion to the first of the 4 parts into which we have divided the study of economics. It is important and interesting in its own right as history, but even more important to the economist, it provides a case study in which the powerful overall pressures that shape economic events can be seen in operation. We begin to get a glimpse of the way the elements of the economy fit together as a *system* in which the behavior of each influences the others and is in turn affected by them.

Each of the remaining parts of this book can be identified with an important aspect of the system of relationships revealed in history. Part Two is concerned with fluctuations in the use of existing productive capacity. It delves more deeply into the nature of unemployment and inflation, examines their causes, and discusses the major public policies that can be applied to control them. Part Three is devoted to the market mechanism that compels enterprisers to turn out products in accordance with consumer demand and that rewards them for bringing out new products and for introducing more productive methods. In Part Four we explore the distribution of income, its relationship to the transfer of labor and land from one use to another in response to consumer desires and technical innovations, the way the benefits of rising productivity are spread over the community, and why it is that in a land as rich as ours there remains such a thing as poverty.

SUMMARY

The past 100 years of American economic growth form a case study in economic development. During the period, average real income increased 7 times, doubling almost once every generation, and the growth in material output was accompanied by widespread changes in the way Americans lived. Almost half the U.S. GNP originated in agriculture 100 years ago, while today no more than 5 percent of total output comes from farms, and fewer than 4 percent of U.S. families lives on farms.

As the importance of agriculture declined and workers moved to the city, birth rates fell, leaving a larger fraction of population of working age. At the same time, rising incomes permitted children to stay in school longer and allowed older workers to retire sooner. But because the increased entrance of women into the labor force more than made up the difference, a larger fraction of the population works today than a century ago. While more people work, however, average hours are shorter and people take longer vacations and holidays, with the net result that today's living standards are enjoyed with less labor than ever before. These shorter hours and the reduction in child labor not only resulted from higher income, but helped raise income even further by contributing to a healthier, better-educated, more productive population.

Population growth together with the rise of rapid communications widened the American market and permitted further specialization of jobs, especially the introduction of mass production technology. In addition, the vast expansion in the amount of capital equipment per worker and the great improvements in the equipment in use added further to rising productivity, while countless new products revolutionized the style of living.

As productivity grew, the opportunity cost of additional capital goods steadily declined, and a high level of investment became self-sustaining. Most of the investment occurred through the agency of private enterprise, which not only provided powerful incentives for people to invest in new ideas, but rewarded the successful with an enlarged flow of income from which to finance even more investment. At the same time, however, competition for the labor and resources needed for the new methods of production spread material gains widely through the community, and the average real wage of labor rose steadily, keeping pace with productivity.

An important force contributing to U.S. development was the system of land tenure that placed most land in the hands of owners who wanted to develop and use it, provided important incentives to farmers to invest in their own farms, and rewarded the successful with income for further improvements. The rising productivity of agriculture released labor for industry and made development possible.

Although the main force of U.S. development came from private firms, the stable social and political environment maintained by the government was an important contributing element.

Economic growth was also attended by costs. There were serious costs in human suffering imposed on workers and their families who had been displaced by mechanization and technical change. Further costs were imposed in the form of environmental pollution and in periodic depressions. These costs, and what can be done to minimize them, form important topics for later study. In particular, Part Two of this book is concerned with the causes of prosperity and depression and how public policy can be applied to stabilize employment and output at high levels.

APPENDIX PERCENTAGE GROWTH RATES

Trends of growth in population, GNP, price levels, and other economic magnitudes are usually expressed by their percentage increase per year. There are several reasons for this. For one thing, percentage growth rates are often easier to remember and interpret than changes in actual magnitudes. Indeed, since many economic series—price indexes, for example—are measured in arbitrary units, expressions of their growth are meaningless in any other terms than percentages. Even when units are clearly defined, however, the real meaning of a given amount of growth often depends on how it compares with the size of the thing growing. A gain of $30 billion per year, which would be considered a disappointing performance for the modern U.S. economy with a GNP of $900 billion, would have been a fantastic increase from the 1933

level of $56 billion. An annual gain of 1 million people would be a remarkably small growth in China's population of over 600 million, but such an increase added to Ireland's population of 3 million would result in widespread starvation.

More important, percentages can be used to compare the rates of growth in entirely different areas. There is no way to compare directly the 2,221,000 growth in U.S. population with the $47.5 billion rise in personal income between September, 1965 and September, 1966. In terms of percentages, however, we can say that population grew 1.1 percent compared to an 8.6 percent rise in personal income. This statement shows immediately that personal income was growing faster than population, and that income per head was rising.

As another example, there is no direct

comparison between a 25-cent rise in wages from $2.25 to $2.50 per hour on the one hand and an increase of 3.4 points in the Consumer Price Index from 114.0 to 117.3 on the other. Expressed as percentage growth, however, the 10 percent wage increase exceeds the 3 percent price rise, showing that the buying power of an hour's work has risen.

Combinations of Growth Rates

Another useful property of percentage growth rates is the ease with which they apply to the ratio or to the product of 2 things. The growth rate of the ratio of 2 magnitudes is the growth rate of the numerator less that of the denominator. For example, per capita personal income is the ratio of personal income—growing (as we have just seen) at 8.6 percent per year—in the numerator, to population—growing at 1.1 percent per year—in the denominator. The growth rate of per capita income is, therefore, 8.6 − 1.1, or 7.5 percent per annum. Likewise, when hourly wages rise 10 percent and consumer prices rise 3 percent, the real buying power of an hour's work— the ratio of the two—rises by 10 − 3, or 7 percent.

The growth rate in the product of 2 things is the sum of their individual growth rates. For example, the total dollar value of physical output is the product of physical quantity and price. When quantity grows at 4 percent while price grows at 3 percent, the total dollar value of output grows 4 + 3, or 7 percent per year.[4]

These rules make it possible to determine the growth rate of an economic quantity like real income or output per manhour

[4] These rules are good approximations when growth rates are compounded annually or at other discrete intervals. They hold exactly for instantaneously compounded, or exponential, growth rates.

from knowledge of the growth rates of its components. They also make it possible to decompose the growth of economic quantities and to evaluate the contribution of each part to the whole. For instance, since potential GNP per capita is the product of output per manhour, average standard hours per year, and the ratio of labor force to population, its growth rate is the sum of the growth of the 3 component factors. From 1890 to 1965, U.S. labor productivity rose 2.15 percent per year, hours declined .46 percent per year, and the ratio of population to labor force increased annually at .19 percent. The 1.88 percent per year rise in capacity GNP per capita, therefore, resolves into 2.15 − .46 + .19, or 1.88 percent per year. It is clear that the predominant force in the growth of productive capacity has been labor productivity, and that reduction in hours has more than offset the rising ratio of labor force to population.

Projecting Growth at a Fixed Percentage Rate

The long run implications of growth in economic magnitudes are easily explored when growth is expressed in percentage rates. Any magnitude growing at a fixed percentage rate per year increases like an investment at compound interest. In compounding, interest is added to the principal as it is earned. Since interest is a constant percentage of the increasing principal, each successive addition is greater than before, and the principal rises faster and faster. For example, $100 invested at 10 percent compounded annually becomes $110 the first year, $121 the second, $132.10 the third, and so on. In general, each dollar invested at compound interest rate r becomes $(1 + r)^t$ dollars at the end of t years.

Values of the factor $(1 + r)^t$, already calculated for selected values of r and t, can be found in published tables of compound interest.[5] An abbreviated version appears in Table B at the end of the chapter. To illustrate the use of the table, suppose we want to project the level that productive capacity per capita in the U.S. would reach by 1980 if it grew from its 1965 level of $3,450 at a rate of 2 percent per year compounded. In the 2 percent column of the table we find that any quantity growing at that rate reaches 1.346 times its initial size at the end of 15 years. This would make the 1980 level equal to 1.346 × $3,450, or $4,644.

Calculating Growth Rates

Given figures for 2 adjacent years, an annual percentage rate of growth is easily calculated by expressing the difference as a percentage of the initial level. For example, when U.S. GNP rose from $629 billion in 1964 to $671 billion in 1965, this represented an annual growth rate of $(671 - 629)/629 = 42/629 = .076$, or 7.6 percent per year.

Since the initial level rises with each succeeding year, this procedure must be modified when applied to figures more than 1 year apart. A good approximation to growth rates can be made by expressing the average annual growth observed over the period as a percentage of the average of the initial and final magnitudes. For example, U.S. population grew from 152 million in 1950 to 194 million in 1965. This

represented an average growth of $(194 - 152)/15$, or 2.8 million per year over the 15-year period. Dividing this average growth by the average population, $(152 + 194)/2 = 173$ million, we get an estimated growth rate of $2.8/173 = 0.0162$, or 1.62 percent per annum. This procedure yields useful results when the time period is short and when growth rates are small. When the final figure is several times the initial quantity, either because the time period is long or because the growth rate is high, the method uniformly underestimates the true growth rate, and compound interest tables, logarithms, or a log-log slide rule must be employed.[6]

The "Simple-Seventy" Rule

For most everyday purposes and for quick estimation, the accuracy given by compound interest tables or logarithmic calculations is rarely required. Growth rates can be more easily interpreted in terms of the length of time that must elapse for a quantity to double in size. These doubling periods are quickly and easily estimated by the simple-seventy rule, so called because it is simple to use and is based on the number 70.

It can be shown that a quantity growing at 1 percent per annum doubles every 70 years.[7] To a very accurate approximation,

---

[5] Values of $(1 + r)^t$ for any values of r and t can be computed with the aid of logarithms. Recall that to raise any number $(1 + r)$ to the power t, its logarithm is multiplied by t. The value of $(1 + r)^t$ is the number whose logarithm corresponds to the product. For example, each dollar invested for 12 years at 5 percent compounded annually grows to 1.05^{12} dollars. To evaluate this factor, enter a table of logarithms to find log $1.05 = 0.02119$. Then log $1.05^{12} = 12 \times 0.02119$, or 0.25428. Reentering the log table, find that the number whose log is 0.25428 is 1.7959. That is, in 12 years at 5 percent compounded, each dollar initially invested grows to almost $1.80.

By substituting the exponential e^{rt} in place of $(1 + r)^t$, growth and interest rate problems can also be easily calculated on a log-log slide rule.

[6] To see what happens for long time periods, note that, according to the compound interest table, a quantity compounded for 70 years at 4 percent reaches 4 times its initial level. If we apply the method above to a quantity growing from 100 to 400 in 70 years, however, we would obtain an "estimated" growth rate of 4.29/250, or 1.71 percent per year, less than half the true rate of growth.

[7] This can be shown as follows: In t years, growth at 1 percent compound interest reaches $(1.01)^t$. Using the logarithmic formula, log $(1.01)^t = t$ log $(1.01) = t \times .00432$. It is desired to find the value of t such that $(1.01)^t = 2$. Hence, log $(1.01)^t = $ log $2 = .30103 = t \times .00432$.

Or $t = \dfrac{.30103}{.00432} = 70$, approximately.

then, the number of years required to double at any other rate r is equal to $70/r$. That is, anything growing 2 percent per annum doubles every $70/2$, or 35 years; growth at 7 percent doubles every $70/7$, or 10 years, and so on.

By reversing the simple-seventy rule, we can calculate the annual growth rate necessary to double within any specified period. A rate of $70/14$, or 5 percent is needed to double every 14 years; $70/20$, or 3.5 percent is necessary to double every 20 years, and so on.

Some "growth" rates are negative, representing a constant percentage decrease. A rate of -7 percent means that the quantity declines by 7 percent each year. The implications of negative rates can be investigated by applying the simple-seventy rule just as it is applied to positive rates. The resulting periods are those required for the quantity to decay to half its initial size. This period is often called the "half life" of the decay process. Between 1950 and 1960 the number of U.S. farmers declined 2.7 percent per year. Continued into the future, this rate cuts the farm population in half every $70/2.7$, or 26 years.

The simple-seventy rule can also be used to estimate growth rates over long time periods, when the final value is many times the initial level. For example, U.S. GNP per capita grew from $500 in 1875 to $3,158 in 1965 (both figures at 1958 prices). Since the 1965 figure was about 6 times the level of 1875, U.S. GNP per capita had doubled 2 and one-half times in 90 years, or about once every $90/2.5$, or 36 years. To double every 36 years implies a growth rate of 70/36, or 1.94 percent per year compounded. This agrees closely with the rate of 2.05 percent per year calculated by more accurate methods.

Population and Other Explosions

An important corollary of the simple-seventy rule is that all quantities growing at *any* fixed positive percentage rate double periodically. The only question is how long such doubling takes. Unless something interferes to slow it down, the quantity will outgrow any preassigned limit. In particular this means that population growth at any rate above 0 sooner or later outstrips available food resources and living space. Unless growth rates are reduced, severe population pressure will create a world crisis of starvation and war as people fight for the limited room available.

Moreover, the margin of safety is deceptive. When population doubles periodically, the difference between a population too large for the available land and a population only half that dense is only a single doubling period. The U.S. population, now growing at 1.65 percent per year, tends to double every 40 years. This means that a comfortable population can grow to crisis size in only 40 years—about half a human lifetime. As was pointed out in this chapter, the apparent suddenness of the recent emergence of air and water pollution as severe social problems is another manifestation of this phenomenon. We have now reached the point at which the danger level is in sight.

APPENDIX TABLE B COMPOUND INTEREST RATE TABLE
(Amount of 1 at compound interest)

YEAR	0.5	1.0	1.5	2.0	2.5	3.0	3.5	4.0	YEAR
1	1.00500	1.01000	1.01500	1.02006	1.02500	1.03000	1.03500	1.04000	1
2	1.01002	1.02010	1.03022	1.04946	1.05062	1.06090	1.07122	1.08160	2
3	1.01508	1.03030	1.04568	1.06121	1.07689	1.09273	1.10872	1.12486	3
4	1.02015	1.04606	1.06136	1.08243	1.10381	1.12551	1.14752	1.16986	4
5	1.02525	1.05101	1.07728	1.10408	1.13141	1.15927	1.18769	1.21665	5
6	1.03038	1.06152	1.09344	1.12616	1.15969	1.19405	1.22926	1.26532	6
7	1.03553	1.07214	1.10984	1.14869	1.18869	1.22987	1.27228	1.31593	7
8	1.04071	1.08286	1.12649	1.17166	1.21840	1.26677	1.31681	1.36857	8
9	1.04591	1.09369	1.14339	1.19509	1.24886	1.30477	1.36290	1.42331	9
10	1.05114	1.10462	1.16054	1.21899	1.28008	1.34392	1.41060	1.48024	10
11	1.05640	1.11567	1.17795	1.24337	1.31209	1.38423	1.45997	1.53945	11
12	1.06168	1.12682	1.19562	1.26824	1.34489	1.42576	1.51107	1.60103	12
13	1.06699	1.13809	1.21355	1.29361	1.37851	1.46853	1.56396	1.66507	13
14	1.07232	1.14947	1.23176	1.31948	1.41297	1.51259	1.61869	1.73168	14
15	1.07768	1.16097	1.25023	1.34587	1.44830	1.55797	1.67535	1.80094	15
16	1.08307	1.17258	1.26899	1.37279	1.48451	1.60471	1.73399	1.87298	16
17	1.08849	1.18430	1.28802	1.40024	1.52162	1.65285	1.79468	1.94790	17
18	1.09393	1.19615	1.30734	1.42825	1.55966	1.70243	1.85749	2.02582	18
19	1.09940	1.20811	1.32695	1.45681	1.59865	1.75351	1.92250	2.10685	19
20	1.10490	1.22019	1.34685	1.48595	1.63862	1.80611	1.98979	2.19112	20

APPENDIX TABLE B COMPOUND INTEREST RATE TABLE (*Continued*)
(Amount of 1 at compound interest)

YEAR	4.5	5.0	5.5	6.0	7.0	8.0	9.0	YEAR
1	1.04500	1.05000	1.05500	1.06000	1.07000	1.08000	1.09000	1
2	1.09202	1.10250	1.11302	1.12360	1.14490	1.16640	1.18810	2
3	1.14117	1.15762	1.17424	1.19102	1.22504	1.25971	1.29503	3
4	1.19252	1.21551	1.23882	1.26248	1.31080	1.36049	1.41158	4
5	1.24618	1.27628	1.30696	1.33823	1.40255	1.46933	1.53862	5
6	1.30226	1.34010	1.37884	1.41852	1.50073	1.58687	1.67710	6
7	1.36086	1.40710	1.45468	1.50363	1.60578	1.71382	1.82804	7
8	1.42210	1.47746	1.53469	1.59385	1.71819	1.85093	1.99256	8
9	1.48609	1.55133	1.61909	1.68948	1.83846	1.99900	2.17189	9
10	1.55297	1.62889	1.70814	1.79085	1.96715	2.15892	2.36736	10
11	1.62285	1.71034	1.80209	1.89830	2.10485	2.33164	2.58043	11
12	1.69588	1.79586	1.90121	2.01220	2.25219	2.51817	2.81266	12
13	1.77220	1.88565	2.00577	2.13293	2.40984	2.71962	3.06580	13
14	1.85194	1.97993	2.11609	2.26090	2.57853	2.93719	3.34173	14
15	1.93528	2.07893	2.23248	2.39656	2.75903	3.17217	3.64248	15
16	2.02237	2.18287	2.35526	2.54035	2.95216	3.42594	3.97030	16
17	2.11338	2.29202	2.48480	2.69277	3.15881	3.70002	4.32763	17
18	2.20848	2.40662	2.62147	2.85434	3.37993	3.99602	4.71712	18
19	2.30786	2.52695	2.76565	3.02560	3.61653	4.31570	5.14166	19
20	2.41171	2.65330	2.91776	3.20713	3.86968	4.66095	5.60441	20

PART
TWO
Prosperity and Depression

Achieving economic growth is only half the problem of overcoming poverty. Once high productive capacity is attained, it is necessary to use that capacity to turn out needed goods and services. People are just as poor when they use only half of the products potentially available to them as they are when their productive capacity is only half as large. The economic history of every western country contains frequent periods when total output fell far short of capacity. The result was unemployment, often severe and prolonged, with large numbers of people ready, willing, and able to work, but unable to find jobs.

Goods and services are produced in response to demand for them by private households, business firms, and governments. When the aggregate of these demands matches the productive potential of the economy, we have prosperous times. Business firms find profitable markets for their products and people who want work find jobs easily. When aggregate demand falls short of productive capacity, firms find operations less profitable. Rates of production are cut back, many who want jobs are laid off, and it takes longer for unemployed workers to find new jobs. At other times the combined spending of households, business firms, and governments has far exceeded the volume of goods and services the economy can produce, resulting in inflation.

Part Two begins with Chapter 7, "Unemployment," and Chapter 8, "The Dynamics of the Price Level," to provide an analysis of the important consequences of fluctuations in total demand. We then turn to the study of private demand and its impact on total spending in Chapter 9, "Consumer Expenditure and the Multiplier," and Chapter 10, "Investment Expenditure and the Accelerator." Different types of demand are interdependent, and spending by one person influences how much others spend. As a result, a small initial change in spending by one group has a multiplied impact on GNP. Chapter 11, "Economic Analysis and Forecasting" is devoted to calculation of the impact multiplier, and to its use in the analysis of the causes of past fluctuations in output and in the prediction of the future economic outlook.

The principal tools used by governments to stabilize output and income are government spending, taxation, and control over the money system. Chapter 12, "Government Services and Taxation," deals with the kinds of services governments perform and the nature of the taxes used to finance them. Chapter 13, "Money and Banks," is a study of the nature of money and the operation of the banking system. Chapter 14, "Public Policy for Stable Economic Growth," concludes Part Two with a demonstration of how control over government spending and taxation can be coordinated with control over the operation of the banking system to steer a stable path between the extremes of severe unemployment on the one hand and severe inflation on the other.

CHAPTER 7

Unemployment

Unemployment has been a chronic problem of the American economy. As can be seen in Figure 1, during 46 of the last 67 years, more than 4 percent of all people ready, willing, and able to work have been without jobs, and the proportion has frequently risen above 8 percent. During the Depression of the 1930s, unemployment remained above 10 percent of the labor force for 11 years in succession, and at its worst, 1 out of every 4 American workers was unable to find a job.

Even these unemployment statistics do not tell the whole story. A person is officially unemployed only if he is entirely out of work and is actively engaged in looking for work. This definition disguises the partial unemployment of many part-time workers and of workers in jobs of low productivity. Moreover, unemployment is not only a question of how many people are found unemployed at any given time, but of how long the average unemployed person remains unemployed, and of how

unemployment is distributed among occupational groups, among races, and be-

FIGURE 1   PERCENT OF U.S. LABOR FORCE UNEMPLOYED, 1900-1967

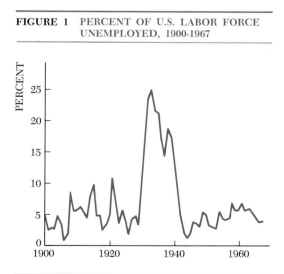

SOURCE: 1900–1950 from *Historical Statistics of the United States*. Later data from *Economic Report of the President, 1968*.

tween the sexes. This chapter is devoted to a discussion of the dimensions and causes of different types of unemployment and the public policy taken toward them.

MEASURING UNEMPLOYMENT

Most of what we know about how many people are unemployed and who they are comes from the monthly Current Population Survey conducted by the U.S. Bureau of the Census. During the week containing the 19th day of each month, a crew of interviewers visits each of a large representative sample of American households to determine the employment status of each member of the family. The interviewer finds out whether each member worked at a job the previous week, and if so, in what occupation he worked, and whether part-time or full-time. If he did not work during the week, did he apply for a job? Was he making inquiries for work, or waiting to hear the results of job interviews, or otherwise actively looking for work? If not, was he in school, on vacation, sick, retired, home taking care of the house, or what?

As a result of this interview every person 16 years of age or over is classified as one who either (1) worked during the week, (2) did not work during the week, but actively looked for work, or (3) neither worked nor looked for work. The economically active population or *labor force* consists of the first 2 categories, those who worked (the employed) plus those who did not work but actively looked for work (the unemployed). All others are classed as not belonging to the labor force.

The results of the Population Survey for March, 1969 are shown in Table 1. The *noninstitutional population* consisted of 137,143,000 people aged 16 or older who were not in prisons, mental hospitals, or similar institutions, of whom 82,770,000 were members of the labor force. Since 3,504,000 men and women were in the

TABLE 1   EMPLOYMENT STATUS OF THE POPULATION AGED 16 OR OLDER, MARCH, 1969
(figures, except percentages, are thousands of people)

	MALES	FEMALES	TOTAL
Noninstitutional population	66,063	71,081	137,143
Total labor force			
Number	52,832	29,938	82,770
Percent of population	80.0	42.1	60.4
Armed services	3,464	40	3,504
Civilian labor force	49,368	29,898	79,266
Employed	47,907	28,613	76,520
Full-time	42,974	20,804	63,778
Part-time	4,933	7,809	12,842
Voluntary	3,867	6,914	10,781
For economic reasons	1,066	895	2,051
Unemployed			
Number	1,461	1,285	2,746
Percent of civilian labor force	3.0	4.3	3.5
Not in the labor force	13,230	41,143	54,373
Keeping house	177	34,610	34,787
Going to school	4,595	4,360	8,955
Unable to work	1,463	865	2,303
Other	6,996	1,307	8,303

SOURCE: *Employment and Earnings*, April, 1969.

armed services, the remaining 79,266,000 were in the civilian labor force. During the week covered by the survey, 76,520,000 people had been employed, but some had worked only part-time including 2,051,000 who worked less than a full week for "economic" reasons. These were people who had been laid off after working only part of the week, or had been on short hours because of reduced operations in the plant, or had been able to find only part-time work.

Of the labor force, 2,746,000 members had been *unemployed*. These were the people who did not work at all during the survey week, but had actively looked for work in one way or another. To facilitate historical and other comparisons, unemployment is usually measured by the *unemployment rate*, that is, by the number of unemployed expressed as a percentage of the labor force. In March, 1969 the unemployment rate was 3.5 percent.

Finally, 54,373,000 people were keeping house, going to school, ill, or not in the labor force that week for one or more of a variety of "other" reasons, ranging from knocking off work to go fishing to spending the week on personal business. Most of these people were permanently retired. Of the men classified as not in the labor force for "other" reasons almost 75 percent were 65 or older. "Other" reasons also covers people so discouraged by prolonged unemployment that they have given up the search for a job and are no longer classed as unemployed.

Of course, many people fit more than one of the categories. In addition to carrying a full program of study, a college student might work part-time and during the particular week in question might also have gone for an interview for a better job. Is he "employed" because he worked, "unemployed" because he actively looked for a job, or "going to school" and hence "not in the labor force"? To settle such questions, labor force classifications are ranked in the order in which they appear in the table, with "employment" first, "unemployment" next, and "not in the labor force" last, and each person is placed in the highest class for which he qualifies. Our college student is classed as employed because he worked during the week. In the same way, a man who worked Monday morning but was laid off at noon is classified as employed (part-time, for economic reasons), even though he spent the rest of the week in a desperate hunt for another job. On the other hand, a student who did not work but who actively looked for work during the week is classified as unemployed, even though he was also going to school full-time.

An understanding of the technical nature of unemployment statistics helps to avoid many misconceptions about unemployment and the unemployed. It is sometimes believed, for example, that "people are unemployed because they just don't want to work" or "there are plenty of jobs if people would just take the trouble to look for them." Doubtless there are people too lazy or too discouraged by failure to look for work, but they are seldom counted among the unemployed, since only those actively looking for work are included.

Nor can unemployment be identified with the loss of a job. College graduates and other people entering the labor force are unemployed during the time they are looking for a first job, even though they have never worked. In any case, rising employment is not the same as falling unemployment. In a growing society the number of people employed must continually grow in proportion to increasing population if the number of unemployed is merely to stay constant. To *reduce* unemployment the number of jobs must grow even faster than the labor force.

Disguised Unemployment

Because of the way unemployment figures are gathered, many people are omitted who are, in a very real sense, partially or totally unemployed but whose unemployment eludes the technical definition. One such group consists of the people who were employed part-time for economic reasons. The 2.5 percent of the civilian labor force that involuntarily worked less than a full work week in March, 1969 were counted as part-time employed; their part-time *unemployment* was ignored.

A second important group consists of those who would take jobs if they were available, but who, for one reason or another, do not actively seek them. Some housewives fall into this category. A housewife is not counted as unemployed as long as she is not looking for a job, but she may take one if an attractive opening appears in the help wanted section of the local paper. A more important group consists of workers who have become so discouraged at their inability to find or to keep jobs that they give up the search. Careful surveys of slum areas reveal large numbers of workers whose unemployment is disguised in this way.

Finally, there are the workers with high potential who are employed in low productivity occupations because they are unable to get training for more skilled jobs, and the trained workers engaged in work below the level of their qualification because they are unable to find anything better. This class contains many young people working as car washers or parking lot attendants or in similar occupations. It also includes some self-employed owners of small stores and other businesses who spend much of their time waiting for a few customers, as well as farmers who try to make a living on unproductive land.

Dimensions of Unemployment

Although unemployment is commonly expressed by a single percentage or number, it is actually made up of several dimensions. It is a question not only of how many people are found unemployed on any given date, but also of how many people become unemployed at one time or another during the year and how long the average person stays unemployed. Even when the *same number* of people are found unemployed in a succession of monthly surveys, they are not all the *same people*. Some of those counted as unemployed last month will have found jobs in the meantime, or will have left the labor force and gone back to school, and their places will have been taken by others who have been laid off or who have left school to find work.

The percentage of different individuals in the labor force that experiences unemployment at one time or another during the year is the annual *incidence* of unemployment. As can be seen in Table 2, the annual incidence of unemployment is regularly 3 to 4 times the average proportion found unemployed by the monthly Survey. In 1965, for example, while an average of only 4.5 percent of the labor force was found unemployed in the Census Survey, over 16 percent of the members of the labor force became unemployed at one time or another during the year.

Another important aspect of unemployment is its *duration*. There is a vast difference between the problems faced by a worker who is laid off and called back after a week or 2 and those of a worker who remains without work for half a year or more. According to Table 2, the average number of weeks per spell of unemployment varied from 8.1 in 1965 to 10.6 in 1958, the worst year shown.

A third important dimension of unem-

TABLE 2   DIMENSIONS OF U.S. UNEMPLOYMENT

	UNEMPLOYMENT RATE, %	UNEMPLOYMENT INCIDENCE, %	AVERAGE SPELLS PER PERSON	AVERAGE WEEKS PER SPELL
1957	4.3	17.0	1.61	8.1
1958	6.8	20.6	1.61	10.6
1959	5.5	17.6	1.61	10.0
1960	5.6	20.4	1.57	8.7
1961	6.7	21.1	1.56	10.5
1962	5.5	21.1	1.59	8.5
1963	5.7	19.5	1.57	9.6
1964	5.2	18.9	1.58	9.1
1965	4.5	16.3	1.56	9.3
1966	3.8	14.7	1.53	8.7
1967	3.8	14.7	1.51	8.9

SOURCE: Calculated from data given in U.S. Department of Labor, *Statistics of Manpower, A Supplement to the Manpower Report of the President,* Washington, D.C., March, 1969.

ployment is its *frequency,* the number of spells of unemployment per unemployed person. Long periods of unemployment are not always the result of a single uninterrupted spell. For many people, unemployment is a constantly recurring problem. They suffer long durations of unemployment as a succession of spells of alternating work and idleness. Almost half of the workers who became unemployed during 1958 reported at least 2 spells of unemployment, and even in the relatively prosperous year 1965, nearly 20 percent of those who became unemployed reported 3 or more spells of unemployment.

Incidence, duration, frequency, and average unemployment rate are mathematically related. During a year in which the monthly surveys reported an average of 1 million people unemployed, the total number of people experiencing unemployment at one time or another during the year would also be 1 million only if each person stayed unemployed for the entire 52 weeks. If the average spell of unemployment lasted only 1 week, on the other hand, it would take 52 million spells spread over the year to make the surveys show an average of 1 million unemployed. Mathematically, if the incidence of unemployment is represented by n, the number of spells per person by s, and the average number of weeks per spell by d, then u, the average unemployment rate as observed by the Monthly Population Survey is given by $u = (n \cdot s \cdot d)/52$. For example, during a year when 20 percent of the labor force experienced unemployment at one time or another, when those unemployed averaged 2 spells of unemployment each, and when the average duration of a spell of unemployment was 7 weeks, the average unemployment rate as shown by the Survey would be $n = (20 \times 2 \times 7)/52$, or 5.4 percent of the labor force.

The dimensions of U.S. unemployment during recent years are shown in Table 2. Although there is a noticeable downward trend in the frequency of unemployment, it varies only slightly from year to year, and most of the differences in unemployment rates are associated with incidence and duration. There appears to be no clear rule as to which dimension is more important. The rise in the unemployment rate from 4.3 percent in 1957 to 6.8 percent in 1958 was accompanied by increases in both incidence and duration, but the decline from 6.8 percent to the 1959 level of 5.5 percent was associated with a drop in incidence with only a small change in duration. The decline in the unemployment rate from its 1961 level of 6.7 percent to 5.5 percent in 1962 resulted from shorter duration with no change in incidence, while the continued decline to the 3.8 level of 1967 was connected chiefly with lower incidence.

Unemployment rates have quite different implications depending on whether a large number of different individuals are each unemployed for a short time, or a few people are unemployed many weeks. A striking example is the comparison in Figure 2 of unemployment among workers of different ages. Unemployment rates are highest among the very young and the very old workers, and are lowest among workers of prime employment age. When the dimensions of this unemployment are examined however, it can be seen that the incidence of unemployment is highest among the youngest workers and declines steadily with age. The average length of a spell of unemployment, on the other hand, rises with age. While many young workers are unemployed during the year, their idleness is of short average duration. Unemployment strikes older workers more rarely, but it tends to be a serious problem of long duration for those whom it strikes.

The dimensions of unemployment also vary by sex and race, as shown in Table 3. Among women in the labor force, the higher unemployment rates are due about equally to higher incidence and longer duration per

FIGURE 2   DIMENSIONS OF UNEMPLOYMENT
IN U.S. BY AGE OF WORKER

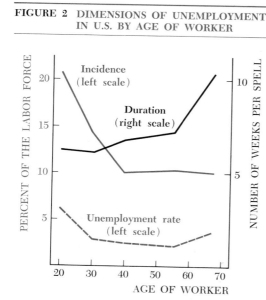

SOURCE: Calculated from data in U.S. Bureau of
Labor Statistics, *Handbook of Labor Statistics,
1967.*

spell, although the frequency of unemployment appears to be lower. The unemployment rate for Negro workers is double that
for whites, largely because of the higher
incidence of unemployment, although unemployed Negro workers also tend to ex-

perience higher frequency of repeated spells
of unemployment and longer duration per
spell.

Unemployment and Occupation

The problem of unemployment varies
widely among occupations. Low incidence
and short duration combine to hold unemployment rates down among professional
people, managers, and the self-employed.
The highest incidence and the longest duration of unemployment are found among the
less skilled blue-collar workers who are employed as operatives and common laborers.
Other occupations range in between, with
white-collar workers generally more secure
than blue-collar workers. These differences
arise partly from institutional differences.
For example, many professional employees
like teachers and civil servants are hired on
annual contracts and some even have life
tenure in their jobs. Moreover, some workers owe the security of their jobs to their
seniority and the protection this provides
through their unions.

Some highly trained workers like technicians, accountants, and engineers are protected against high unemployment because
they occupy jobs that must be performed if
the firm is to operate at all, even at reduced
rates of output. Such people keep their jobs
even when production cutbacks result in
layoffs for production workers. Some firms
also make a practice of keeping certain
skilled workers on the payroll even when
they are not really needed, rather than run
the risk of being unable to replace them
when conditions improve and their services
become essential. Unskilled workers, on
the other hand, have jobs more directly
related to the volume of output, and are
laid off when demand declines and replaced
when needed. They are often younger, less-
experienced workers without seniority or
other job protection.

The low unemployment rates among the

TABLE 3   DIMENSIONS OF
UNEMPLOYMENT BY SEX AND
RACE, 1965

	UNEMPLOYMENT RATE, %	UNEMPLOYMENT INCIDENCE, %	AVERAGE SPELLS PER PERSON	AVERAGE WEEKS PER SPELL
Men	4.0	15.1	1.87	6.7
Women	5.5	18.4	1.56	7.3
White workers	4.1	15.1	1.72	6.7
Negro workers	8.3	26.2	1.96	7.3

SOURCE: Calculated from data in U.S. Bureau of
Labor Statistics, *Handbook of Labor Statistics,
1967,* Washington, D.C., 1967.

TABLE 4 DISTRIBUTION OF EMPLOYMENT AND UNEMPLOYMENT RATES BY OCCUPATION AND RACE

OCCUPATION	PERCENTAGE DISTRIBUTION OF EMPLOYMENT		UNEMPLOYMENT RATE, %	
	WHITE	NEGRO	WHITE	NEGRO
Professional, technical and kindred workers	11.0	3.9	1.4	2.3
Farmers and farm managers	5.6	4.4	0.7	1.7
Managers, officials, proprietors, ex. farm	11.5	2.3	1.4	2.9
Clerical and kindred workers	7.1	5.0	3.2	5.6
Sales workers	7.4	1.5	2.5	5.6
Craftsmen, foremen, and kindred workers	20.5	10.2	5.2	8.3
Operatives and kindred workers	19.5	23.5	6.2	8.2
Private household workers	0.1	0.7	5.8	8.2
Service workers, ex. private household	5.2	13.7	4.9	7.1
Farm laborers and foremen	2.3	7.1	6.6	7.4
Laborers, ex. farm	5.6	19.4	12.1	14.5
Occupation not reported	4.2	8.4	7.1	11.3
All occupations	100.0	100.0	4.5	8.4

SOURCE: *1960 Census of Population.*

self-employed, particularly among farmers and farm managers, frequently involve a substantial amount of disguised unemployment.

Unemployment and Race

There are 2 reasons why unemployment rates among Negro workers are typically double those among whites. In the first place, as the Census data of Table 4 shows, inequality of job opportunities concentrates Negro workers in occupations with higher unemployment rates. Even if Negro workers were subject to exactly the same unemployment risks as white workers in the same occupation, the percentage distribution of Negro employment among the various occupations would have given them an average 1960 unemployment rate of 6.4 percent compared to 4.5 percent for whites.

In the second place, the observed difference in unemployment rate was even greater than this figure because Negro and white workers are often treated unequally. The Negro's position as "last man hired, first

man fired" leads to higher unemployment rates among Negro workers than among whites in the same occupation, and these differentials account for the remainder of the observed difference in average unemployment rates.

International Comparison of Unemployment Rates

As shown in Figure 3, unemployment in the United States is higher than in most other industrial nations. To some extent low unemployment rates abroad are the reflection of an acute sensitivity to the political implications of unemployment, and a history of energetic positive government action to hold it in check.

Most industrial nations of Western Europe have permanent manpower programs designed to match workers with available jobs and, to some extent, to match jobs to available workers. These programs generally include permanent arrangements for training adults for employment, with liberal allowances paid to the trainee. In addition,

FIGURE 3   INTERNATIONAL COMPARISON OF
UNEMPLOYMENT RATES, 1959-1966

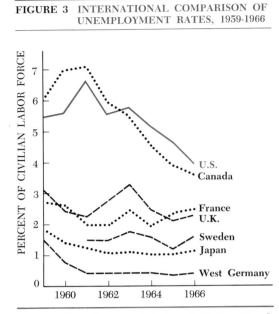

SOURCE: U.S. Bureau of Labor Statistics, *Handbook of Labor Statistics, 1967*. All rates have been adjusted to correspond to U.S. concepts.

there are nationwide placement services to keep track of the number, type, and location of job openings, as well as the number, type, and location of workers needing jobs.

Employers are often required to give advance notice of layoffs to both the worker and the local employment service so that new jobs will be waiting for the discharged workers. In Sweden, notice of a layoff must be given 60 days in advance. In the Netherlands, certain layoffs require the permission of the director of the local employment office. In West Germany, 30 to 60 days' notice must be given of a layoff exceeding a specified fraction of the firm's work force.

Travel and relocation allowances are available in one form or another to unemployed workers in the Netherlands, West Germany, Norway, and France. In Sweden, the government provides unemployed workers with travel expenses for a job interview in another location. If he gets the job, he can receive commuting expenses or a daily

allowance to enable him to live away from home until he can arrange housing for his family, and he may also receive a contribution toward his moving expenses.

European governments commonly influence the location of industry as well as that of the worker. In the United Kingdom, the Board of Trade must approve the location of large new establishments and can provide tax incentives to encourage location in certain areas. In Sweden, the National Labor Market Board has the authority to approve tax exemptions and loans to influence the location of industry. A system of loans and grants is used in West Germany for the same purpose, and in France subsidies and loans are offered to firms that will locate in areas of surplus labor, while firms trying to move into tight labor-market areas may find it impossible to obtain building permits and are also often subject to special high taxes.

Fiscal and monetary policy is also used at an early stage of declining demand to offset unemployment. The Swedish National Labor Market Board can act to step up procurement by central and local governments and can approve tax exemptions to spur investment. In the Netherlands, a special arm of the employment service initiates projects to offset cyclical unemployment.

To some extent, however, international differences in unemployment rates represent differences in working habits. American workers are highly mobile. In the United States, from 1 to 2.5 percent of all manufacturing workers quit their job *every month* to look for better opportunities. Some of these are counted among the unemployed while they are looking, and naturally make the U.S. unemployment rate higher than that of a society in which employees often stay in the same town at the same job for a lifetime.

Another important international difference is in the proportion of workers who are self-employed. There are proportionally more farmers in most other countries than are found in the U.S., and also a higher proportion of owners of small shops or stores. Since many of the self-employed are engaged in low-productivity occupations, the result is lower reported unemployment and higher disguised unemployment than are generally found in this country.

The low unemployment rates in West Germany partly reflect the practice of using imported workers. Since recovering from World War II, West German output has typically exceeded what the domestic labor force could produce. German firms make up the difference with workers from Southeastern Europe and other less industrialized areas. Since these workers are sent home when they are laid off, West Germany maintains low unemployment rates by exporting most of its unemployed workers.

In the U.S.S.R. and most other Communist countries unemployment is held to be an exclusive feature of bourgeois capitalism and hence is not recognized in official statistics. As a result of this 100 percent disguise, it is impossible to tell how these countries actually rank in unemployment. In Yugoslavia—the only Communist country reporting unemployment data—rates are about as high as those in the United States, but it seems likely that those of the U.S.S.R., Czechoslovakia, and the other more industrialized Communist countries have unemployment rates nearer those of West Germany or Sweden.

KINDS OF UNEMPLOYMENT

Any effort to reduce unemployment must recognize the variety of its causes. There are basically 3 kinds of unemployment. First, is *normal* or *frictional* unemployment, associated with the normal entrance of new workers into the job market and with the everyday movement of workers from one job to another. Second, is *structural* unem-

ployment, which arises when there are plenty of jobs open to qualified workers but when the qualifications of unemployed workers do not correspond to those sought by employers. Third is *cyclical* unemployment, which results when aggregate demand is inadequate to provide a job for everybody who wants to work.

Normal or Frictional Unemployment

Frictional unemployment is the irreducible minimum of unemployment in a free society. Wherever people can choose among occupations and are free to move from one job to another in order to better themselves, a certain number will always be found unemployed during any given week. New graduates from high school or college do not grab the first opening that comes their way, but look the field over for the best job they can find. During the time they are looking, these people are counted among the unemployed. Likewise, a worker who deliberately quits one job to look for a better one is unemployed until he finds it. Even a certain number of layoffs must be considered a normal part of life in an economy where firms must adjust their output to the dictates of consumer demand. When consumers change the pattern of their purchases, sales of some products decline while others rise. Workers laid off jobs in declining industries are unemployed until they locate new positions with expanding firms.

This normal activity involves a large number of people. Each year from 1.5 to 2 million young people, or from 2 to 2.5 percent of the labor force, are looking for their first jobs, and an equal number of people are reentering the job market after a period in school or at home. As we have seen, even larger numbers are involved in normal movement from job to job. From 1 to 2.5 percent of manufacturing workers quit their jobs every month, and about an equal number are laid off.

How much unemployment results from all this labor turnover depends on how long it takes to find work. In terms of the dimensions of unemployment, normal labor turnover creates a uniformly high *incidence* of frictional unemployment, but the unemployment *rate* depends on the average *duration* of unemployment. If everybody moved smoothly into a new job the same week he started to look, duration would be 0, and no measurable unemployment would be observed. The longer it takes experienced workers to move from one job to another, and the longer new workers must hunt before they find suitable employment, the more frictional unemployment will be observed.

Unemployment duration is shortest among workers who voluntarily quit one job to get another. Many—perhaps most—leave the old job only after the new one is lined up. Indeed, these workers are often attracted from the old job by the opportunity to get the new one. In any case, people who quit and move are often experienced, confident workers, those who have the least trouble getting jobs. The least skilled, most poorly trained workers are more vulnerable to layoff and tend to remain unemployed longer than workers who voluntarily quit. Longer periods of unemployment are likewise characteristic of new workers looking for their first jobs.

Public Policy Toward Frictional Unemployment As we have seen, the incidence of frictional unemployment is the result of the normal operation of a free economic system. Its root cause is the right of individual workers to quit, the right of new workers to take time to look for jobs that suit them, and the right of consumers to dictate which industries must expand output and which must cut back production. To the extent that it reflects the exercise of these rights, frictional unemployment is not really a social problem. Rather, it con-

tributes to higher labor productivity by encouraging workers to find the jobs in which their contribution to production is greatest.

The social problem of frictional unemployment derives not from its incidence but from its duration, and anything that helps shorten the time required for job transition reduces the burden on the unemployed worker. Until recently, however, the task of bringing worker and job smoothly together was left mainly to private employment agencies, want ads, union hiring halls, and word of mouth. The Manpower Development and Training Act of 1962 (MDTA) and its subsequent amendments have greatly expanded government responsibility for reaching unemployed workers, identifying their qualifications and needs, and locating job openings for which they are suited. The service is implemented through local Employment Service Agencies, whose original function was to administer unemployment insurance. Employment Service Agencies no longer wait for the unemployed to appear for help, but actively seek workers in need of assistance. An important new element in the program was added by the amendments of 1968 which provided for the establishment of a network of electronic data processing and telecommunications systems to aid in matching unemployed workers with job opportunities on a nationwide basis. Although the United States does not yet have a relocation program on anything like the scale of many European countries, the 1965 amendments to MDTA provided for a "demonstration" program to test the feasibility of a systematic program of relocation assistance.

It is much too early to assess the effectiveness of the new programs, or to estimate how much they may have shortened the duration of purely frictional unemployment, but they are clearly important as a belated recognition of public responsibility in this critical area.

Structural Unemployment

Many people have trouble finding work even when there is a shortage of labor and plenty of good jobs are vacant. These are people without ability, experience, skill, or training needed to qualify for the openings, or who do not meet employers' specifications in some other way. Some of them are young people coming into the labor force with education inadequate for employment in modern industry. Some are older workers whose jobs have been replaced by the appearance of new products, shifts in the kinds of things consumers buy, or technical change.

Much of today's structural unemployment is related to the rapid disappearance of jobs for unskilled labor. A few years ago any worker with a strong back could make a living by digging ditches, shoveling coal, or harvesting crops. Today this work is done by power shovels, conveyors, and mechanical harvesters. The introduction of mechanical cotton pickers in the South has resulted in large-scale unemployment of workers who have no other marketable skills. Sometimes workers are stranded by the relocation of industries and are unable to find jobs near home or to get to the places where jobs might be found. The demand for coal declined with the shift of railroads to diesel-powered locomotives, and of residential heating to natural gas. This, together with mechanization of the coal mines, has been largely responsible for high unemployment rates in Appalachia. The steady migration of industry out of central cities to suburbs and outlying areas has intensified the employment problems of people in urban slums.

The problem of structural unemployment is often intensified by discrimination of various kinds in the employment of labor. Some employers refuse to hire qualified workers because of their color, religion, sex, age, or other personal characteristics.

Some workers are barred access to jobs by the refusal of labor unions to admit them as members for many of the same reasons, and others are unable to move into communities where jobs are available.

Many workers are disadvantaged by a combination of inadequate training and discrimination. Adding geographical concentration in an area with inadequate access to such jobs as do exist creates the explosive mixture found in the slum ghettos of our cities. Surveys of neighborhoods in which severe riots have occurred show a long history of unemployment rates that are not only several times that of the national average, but often are growing worse even in the face of improvement in the rest of the nation.

Unemployment rates in selected urban areas are shown in Figure 4. The situation is much worse when disguised unemployment is taken into account. Careful studies of a number of slum areas in which explicit allowance was made for the amount of involuntary part-time work, the number of workers on jobs of low productivity, and the number of discouraged workers not counted in the labor force indicated that disguised unemployment ranged from 2 to 5 times the unemployment rates observed directly in the survey! This means that in some areas as many as half of the people in the labor force suffer some degree of unemployment all the time.[1]

Public Policy Toward Structural Unemployment

Structural unemployment is a complex problem, and a wide variety of policies have been applied or suggested to combat it. On the broadest scale, enforcement of civil rights, legislation to improve opportunities for education and training, equal employment opportunity, and related programs make important long-run contributions. These policies not only involve training people in useful skills, but, perhaps

[1] *Manpower Report of the President, 1967.*

FIGURE 4   U.S. UNEMPLOYMENT RATES IN
SELECTED URBAN AREAS,
NOVEMBER, 1966

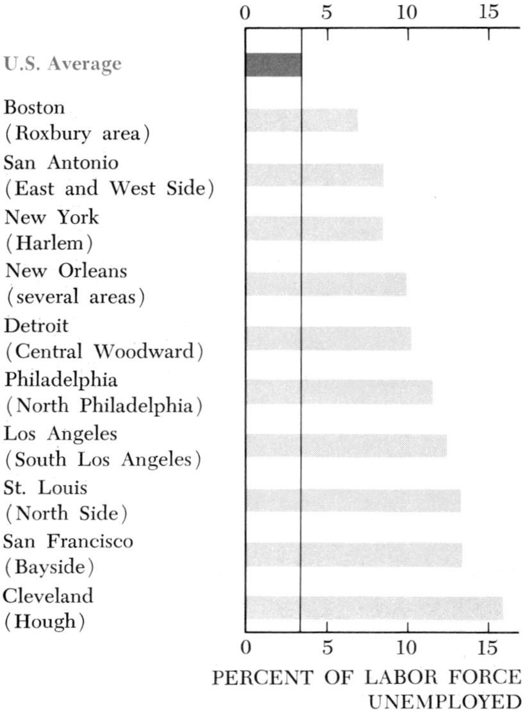

SOURCE: *Manpower Report of the President, 1967.*

more important, they contribute to the feelings of personal dignity and worth which are essential to productive lives. Area redevelopment programs are designed to relieve structural unemployment by attracting industry to depressed areas through the construction of roads, provision of credit, tax concessions, and similar policies.

A more direct attack on structural unemployment has recently been initiated under the Manpower Development and Training Act in the form of job training programs to enable workers to acquire marketable skills. MDTA programs provide both training in a formal institutional setting and on-the-job training, and furnish allowances to trainees. From its origin in 1963

through July, 1968, over 600,000 individuals had completed training courses, 90 percent of whom got jobs during the first year following training, and over three-quarters of whom were still employed when contacted a year later.

Most of those enrolled in the early years of the program received institutional training, but on-the-job training has become increasingly important, and in 1968 nearly half of those in training programs were being taught on the job. On-the-job training carried out by private firms, business associations, and labor unions under contract with the government has the advantage of training workers in a setting in which they can see an immediate return from what they learn. In one program, Job Opportunities in the Business Sector (JOBS), disadvantaged workers are hired first and trained by the employer afterward. The employer contributes his normal cost of recruitment and training, but any costs of added training, counseling, remedial education, and so on are paid by contract with the U.S. Department of Labor. By the fall of 1968, 12,000 business firms had provided employment for 84,000 workers of whom 61,000 remained on the job after their training was completed.

The JOBS program is specifically directed at disadvantaged workers. Of those enrolled up to September, 1968, 75 percent were Negro. The average educational achievement had been below the 11th grade and during the year preceding entry into the program, average duration of unemployment had been 23.7 weeks.[2]

But training programs take time to become effective. To meet critical immediate problems in our cities it has been suggested that, failing other job opportunities, the government should serve as an employer of last resort. This approach would apply the same emergency measures to structural unemployment that were applied to cyclical unemployment at the depths of the Depres-

[2] *Manpower Report of the President, 1969.*

sion in the 1930s via the Works Progress Administration and other governmental job-creation programs.

Finally, it should be recognized that the amount of structural unemployment partly depends on the number of jobs available, and hence is influenced by policies that affect the total demand for labor. Structural unemployment occurs when applicants do not meet the job requirements set by employers, but job requirements themselves are not rigidly fixed. Jobs are often upgraded merely because workers with high qualifications are available. When there are plenty of college-trained people looking for work, employers often insist on a college education, even when it has little to do with job performance. This leaves the high-school graduate "structurally" unemployed, but the structural barrier disappears when college graduates are no longer available. Younger, inexperienced workers are "structurally" unemployed when employers insist on experience, but when experienced workers are hard to find, employers are usually willing to invest in the training of inexperienced people. In the emergency mobilization during World War II, untrained workers from the rural South flocked into aircraft plants and housewives became welders and riveters. It is also worth remembering that the technical industry of West Germany meets a labor shortage by importing unskilled, often illiterate workers from underdeveloped areas 1,000 miles away.

Cyclical Unemployment

Both frictional and structural unemployment exist in an economy in which the number of job openings equals or even exceeds the number of unemployed workers. In contrast, *cyclical* unemployment is a situation in which there are fewer jobs than there are people who want to work, necessarily leaving somebody unemployed.

Cyclical unemployment results when the total production of goods and services falls short of the productive capacity of the economic system and is most easily discussed in terms of the equation of productive capacity. If demand were sufficient to keep the entire labor force working normal hours, gross national product would be GNP* $= \pi hL$. When demand sinks below capacity to a level at which only E workers can be employed at normal hours, the number of workers left unemployed (U) would be equal to $L - E$, and we would have GNP of only πhE. The amount of unused capacity would be the gap between potential and actual output, or $\pi hL - \pi hE$, which can be rewritten as $\pi h(L - E)$ or πhU. When the amount unused is expressed as a percentage of total productive capacity, we have the useful result: Unused capacity/GNP* $= \pi hU/\pi hL$, or U/L. In words, the percentage of capacity left unused is identical with U/L, the percentage of the labor force that would be left unemployed if those at work put in normal hours.

The formula measures the true amount of unemployment that results from production below capacity, but because short hours and lower productivity generally accompany low output, part of the true unemployment is disguised and does not appear in the official statistics. When output declines, workers reduced to part-time jobs are still counted as employed in the official statistics, leaving their part-time unemployment disguised. Some workers who are normally part of the labor force when jobs are plentiful become too discouraged to look for work when jobs are scarce and escape the unemployment count. Other workers accept jobs of lower productivity than their normal work and are, to that degree, effectively unemployed, but are included among those employed.

There is no theoretical reason to expect any particular relationship between the true unemployment rate as calculated from the percentage of unused productive capacity and the rate officially reported by the

FIGURE 5 GAP BETWEEN U.S. CAPACITY
AND AGGREGATE DEMAND,
1910-1967

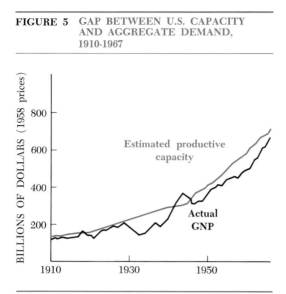

SOURCE: Estimated capacity calculated by the techniques of Table 2 of Chapter 6. GNP from *Historical Statistics of the United States*. Later data from *Survey of Current Business*, July, 1969.

Census, but the experience of the U.S. economy over the past 60 years suggests that, in peacetime at least, reported unemployment rates tend to be about half the percent of capacity left unused.

The trend of U.S. productive capacity since 1909 is plotted in Figure 5 together with actual GNP. As would be expected, except during wartime emergencies, actual output fell short of capacity by varying amounts. The correlation between underutilization of capacity and the unemployment rate is clearly shown in Figure 6, in which the percentage of total capacity left unused is compared to the official unemployment rate. The unemployment rate has been inverted (notice the scale on the right of the figure) to make its movements easier to compare with capacity utilization. The 2 lines match closely, with the official unemployment rate very close to half the percentage gap. In 1966, for example, the chart shows that aggregate demand was 7.1 below the capacity limit, while officially observed unemployment was 3.8 percent of the labor force. At the bottom of the Depression in 1933, 44 percent capacity under-utilization was accompanied by an official 25 percent unemployment rate, and so on.

The only periods that departed significantly from the normal relationship were

FIGURE 6   OBSERVED UNEMPLOYMENT RATE AND CAPACITY UNDERUTILIZATION

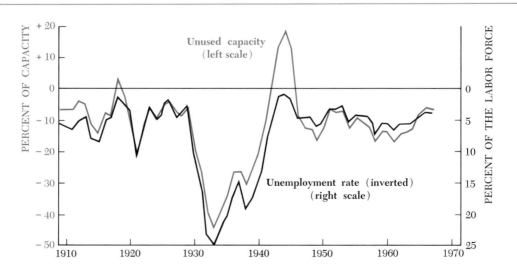

SOURCE: Calculated from data underlying Figure 5.

years of emergency production during World War I (1918) and World War II (1942–1945). Wartime mobilization of labor temporarily brought many people into the labor force who would not ordinarily be working, and everybody worked longer than customary hours. The result was cyclical overemployment, but even during these exceptional times, a small amount of unemployment, mostly frictional, could still be observed.

Public Policy Toward Cyclical Unemployment Public policy toward cyclical unemployment has 2 distinct aspects. First, *unemployment insurance* is designed to mitigate the effect of the loss of jobs on unemployed workers and their families. Second, *stabilization policy* consists of action designed to prevent cyclical unemployment from occurring.

Unemployment insurance This is a program to protect workers against complete loss of earnings in the event of unemployment. In the United States, each state has its own program and legal provisions vary widely from state to state, although most firms outside the fields of agriculture and food processing are required to pay a state unemployment tax levied on their payrolls. The average effective tax rate amounts to about 1.5 percent of all wages paid, although to encourage employment stability the tax rate is often variable among firms on the basis of unemployment experience, with the firms having the best records for sustained employment paying the lowest rates.

After a minimum period of employment to establish their eligibility, employees of firms that pay unemployment taxes are automatically covered by unemployment insurance. When a worker who is covered loses his job, he usually must wait until he has been unemployed a full week before he becomes eligible to receive benefits. When payments begin, the size of his weekly benefit check depends on his earnings while he was employed plus (in a few states) an allowance for dependents. The amounts are calculated by various formulas, but historically the average weekly benefit check has amounted to roughly one-third of the average weekly earnings of covered employees.

The number of weeks an unemployed worker can continue to draw unemployment insurance benefits during a year is limited to some maximum, usually 26 or 39 weeks. Workers unemployed over a long period or experiencing repeated spells of unemployment exhaust their benefit rights and cannot receive further insurance payments until they have rebuilt their eligibility by a new record of employment.

On the average, unemployed workers draw unemployment checks from 10 to 15 weeks, depending on economic conditions, but even in the most prosperous times, one-fifth of all claimants remain unemployed long enough to exhaust their benefit rights. For instance, during a period of serious recession such as 1958, when over 20 percent of all workers became unemployed at one time or another during the year, nearly a third of those who drew unemployment benefits remained unemployed long enough to exhaust their benefit rights.

The limitations to both the size and the duration of benefits follow from the limited purpose of unemployment insurance. It is not intended to cure the problems of unemployment, but only to sustain an unemployed worker temporarily while he looks for another job. It does not prevent hardship, but it does avert disaster.

Stabilization Policy Since cyclical unemployment results when not enough goods and services are bought to keep everybody at work, policies to prevent it are designed to stabilize total demand at a high level despite fluctuations in spending by firms and households. The tools available for this purpose are *fiscal policy,* which involves government spending and taxation, and *monetary policy,* which is concerned with the amount of money in the nation, interest rates, and the availability of credit. Before these policies can be properly understood, however, it is necessary to have a working knowledge of the relationship of unemployment to prices, and an understanding of what causes fluctuations in spending by different groups in the economy and how the expenditures of one group influence those of another.

These topics and their relationship to stabilization policy constitute the material in the remaining chapters of Part Two.

SUMMARY

In a private enterprise economic system in which income is shared among those who participate in production and the social value placed on individuals is heavily influenced by their incomes, those unable to find jobs are seriously disadvantaged. Nevertheless, unemployment has long been a chronic problem in the United States. Not only have our unemployment rates been consistently higher than those of most other industrial nations, but, except during wartime, it is rare to find fewer than 4 percent of the labor force out of work.

Unemployment rates tell only part of the story, however, for many workers suffer from *disguised unemployment* and escape the official count. Moreover, *unemployment rates* show only the proportion unemployed on a given date, rather than the *frequency* and *incidence* of unemployment among different individuals and the average *duration* that they remain unemployed. The average rate is also deceptive because the risk of unemployment is unequally distributed among members of the labor force. Unemployment is highest among laborers and production workers, and lowest among professionals and white-collar workers. Unemployment rates tend to be higher among women than among men, and are twice as high for black workers as for white.

There are 3 principal types of unemployment, and the public policy appropriate to treating an unemployment situation depends on its type. *Frictional unemployment* results from the delay experienced by new entrants into the labor force in getting jobs, and from the time lost by workers moving from job to job. The incidence of frictional unemployment is fixed by the normal amount of labor turnover, but its duration can be held to a minimum by improving the flow of information in the job market and by assisting workers who need to relocate.

Structural unemployment is a situation in which unemployed workers and vacant jobs exist simultaneously because the workers do not match the qualifications demanded by employers. Structural unemployment is especially severe among untrained residents of our central cities and has been an important factor contributing to riots and social unrest. Fair employment practice laws and civil rights in general are important parts of the attack on structural unemployment. More recently, rising government concern for the disadvantaged worker has taken the form of training programs designed to fit workers for employment in modern industry, to get jobs for them, and to encourage them to remain at work.

Cyclical unemployment results when total output falls below the capacity of the economic system. Indeed, the true unemployment rate can be defined as the percentage of total productive capacity left unused. Due to disguised unemployment, however, observed unemployment rates are only about half the true rate. Public policy toward cyclical unemployment takes the form of *unemployment insurance* to mitigate the effects of job loss on the worker and his family, and of *stabilization policy,* which attempts to prevent cyclical unemployment through regulation of government spending and taxation and by control over bank lending. We will return to a detailed discussion of stabilization policy at the end of Part Two after first establishing the important connection between unemployment and the price level and exploring fluctuations in demand among households and business firms.

CHAPTER 8

The Dynamics of the Price Level

Prices represent the terms on which commodities can be exchanged for one another. A $6 book exchanges equally for a $6 shirt. An hour's labor at $3 exchanges for 2 pounds of beefsteak at $1.50 a pound. Variation in relative prices represents the changing supply of different kinds of goods. When a new printing process makes it cheaper to publish books, the price of books tends to decline. A poor cotton crop is reflected in higher prices for cotton shirts, and so on.

In addition to the normal variation of prices in relation to each other, however, we often find the average index of all prices rising or falling. Movements in the price level are important because they alter the distribution of buying power among different groups in the community. People whose incomes are fixed can buy less as prices rise; people whose incomes grow faster than prices rise can buy more.

Like employment and unemployment, the rate of increase in price level depends on GNP. Prices rise most rapidly when total output is high and unemployment is low. This situation sometimes poses serious policy dilemmas for government, because efforts to contain rising prices tend to create unemployment, and efforts to reduce unemployment tend to speed up the rate of price increase. In an extreme case, sustained demand for more goods than the economic system can produce gives rise to hyperinflation and to a complete breakdown of the monetary system.

INDIVIDUAL PRICES AND THE PRICE LEVEL

As long as all prices remain the same relative to each other, their absolute level is of no consequence. As long as their prices are equal, a book exchanges for a shirt, whether each is priced at $6, $1,000, or 25 cents. Whether the price of his labor is $3 or $600 per hour, a worker can exchange an hour of labor for 2 pounds of beefsteak as long as the price of the beefsteak is half his hourly wage. If all prices, wages and other money contracts in the world should rise overnight by 100 times, each of us would be left exactly as he was the day before. The worker whose $3 wage rate bought 2 pounds of steak yesterday could still get the steak with the earnings of an hour's labor. He would now pay $150 a pound, but he would earn $300 per hour.

The catch is, of course, that prices do not change this way. When prices rise, some prices increase more rapidly than others, and this alters the terms on which goods can be exchanged. If the price of a book goes from $6 to $9, while the price of a shirt rises from $6 to $12, books and shirts no longer exchange equally. It takes more than 1 book to buy a shirt. If wages rise from $3 to $4 while steak goes from $1.50 to $1.75, an hour's work will buy more than 2 pounds of steak.

When prices rise, people providing services whose prices lag behind the average lose out. People whose incomes are fixed by long-run contracts are especially hard hit. Schoolteachers and civil service employees, for example, receive salaries that change only slowly. When prices rise, the quantity of goods that can be bought with the earnings of an hour of teaching or an hour's duty at the fire station declines rapidly. Elderly people retired on pensions or living off savings find their living standards pinched as their fixed money incomes buy less and less.

Rising prices tend to benefit people in debt. A farmer who borrowed $3,000 when wheat was $1 a bushel, received buying power equal to 3,000 bushels of wheat. When wheat rises to $2 a bushel, he repays the loan with the proceeds of the sale of only 1,500 bushels. A family that buys a $20,000 house with a $10,000 mortgage borrows the value of half the house. If the house is later sold for $30,000, the family repays the loan with only one-third of the proceeds of the sale. Stockholders of a corporation that must pay $100,000 interest to its bondholders keep half of the total capital earnings of $200,000. When rising product prices increase capital earnings to $300,000, stockholders keep two-thirds.

The reverse is true when prices fall. People on fixed incomes or with fixed dollar savings find that each dollar buys more than before, and their living standards rise. Creditors gain and debtors lose. The farmer who borrowed the equivalent of 3,000 bushels of wheat when it sold for $1 a bushel must sell 4,000 bushels to repay the loan when wheat sinks to 75 cents. A mortgage that originally represented half the value of a house may entail repayment of three-quarters or more of the value as the price of houses declines. Stockholders find their share of earnings shrinking as the prices of output fall.

An increase in the average level of prices is *inflation*. Falling prices are *deflation*. In these terms, inflation tends to benefit debtors and people whose incomes respond quickly to rising prices at the expense of creditors and those whose incomes are slow to change. Deflation, on the other hand, tends to benefit creditors and people whose incomes respond only slowly to falling prices at the expense of debtors and those whose incomes are more flexible.

THE U.S. PRICE LEVEL SINCE 1860

Data for wholesale prices in the United States are available before the Civil War, making it possible to trace the general movement in U.S. price levels for more than a century. In the 107-year period from 1860 to 1967 the index of wholesale prices (1957–1959 = 100) rose from 33.7 to 106.1. This amounted to a general upward, or inflationary, drift of roughly 1.1 percent per

FIGURE 1   THE U.S. PRICE LEVEL, 1860-1969

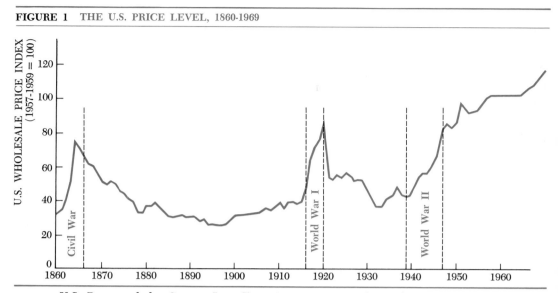

SOURCE: U.S. Bureau of the Census, *Long-Term Economic Growth*, Washington, D.C., 1966. Later data from *Survey of Current Business*.

year. However, the actual course of the price level has been anything but smooth.

When the index is plotted in Figure 1, 3 periods of rapid inflation stand out, each associated with war. Prices more than doubled during the Civil War, rising from 33.7 in 1860 to 74.7 by 1864. The Civil War was followed by steady deflation as prices fell slowly. By 1895 the index had reached 25.4, 25 percent below the pre-Civil War level. Prices began a slow climb after 1895 and by 1915 had reached 38.0, a level only slightly higher than that of 1860. A second rapid inflation occurred during World War I, with the index reaching a peak of 84.5 in 1920 but dropping sharply during the recession of 1921.

Prices remained nearly steady through the remainder of the 1920s. The Great Depression of the 1930s was accompanied by severe deflation, the price index reaching 35.6 in 1932, a level nearly back to the 1860 mark. After rising slowly from the Depression low, the price level again doubled during World War II, hitting 87.9 in 1948 after the removal of wartime price controls.

Unlike earlier wartime inflations, however, this one was not followed by a severe deflation. The price level remained almost stable through the 1950s and the early 1960s, and then began another inflationary climb in the late 1960s with the involvement in the Vietnam War.

UNEMPLOYMENT AND THE PRICE LEVEL

The history of U.S. prices reveals that price inflation tends to occur during periods when total output approaches the productive capacity of the economic system. Indeed, the greatest inflation has occurred during wartime, when output has exceeded the limits normally set by productive capacity. This fact is hardly surprising. The only way an economic system with a productive capacity of, say, $900 billion can deliver $945 billion worth of goods is to raise prices 5 percent.

As aggregate demand rises, farm prices

and the prices of basic industrial materials tend to respond first. Would-be buyers of grain, meat, cotton, metals, and other commodities try to buy more than is available on the market, and their competitive bidding for limited quantities drives prices up. Prices of finished goods tend to rise more slowly. Some producers begin to raise prices when they find demand for their products growing, but the main pressure on the prices of finished goods is rising costs.

Prices, Wages, and Labor Costs

Labor is the basic ingredient of all production, and rising labor costs exert the greatest force on the price level. Higher labor costs in finished goods industries contribute directly to the price of final products, but since labor is used in the production of all intermediate products, higher labor costs likewise mean higher costs of raw materials and semifinished products. As higher-priced materials reach each stage of fabrication, the increased labor costs are passed on, finally to emerge as higher-priced final output.

Unit labor cost is the average amount per unit of product that employers must pay to obtain the services of the labor used in production. Although the largest part of labor cost is the hourly wage rate paid to labor, wage rates must be carefully distinguished from labor cost. In the first place, wages are not the only cost of employing labor. In addition to the wages that the worker receives, employers must pay social security and unemployment taxes based on their payrolls, provide workers with workmen's compensation insurance, contribute to union pension programs, and provide supplementary unemployment benefits, vacations with pay, hospitalization insurance, and other fringe benefits. At the present time the total amount of

these supplementary employment outlays is more than a 10 percent addition to wages and salaries as such.

In the second place, rising wages and employment-related outlays do not always mean increases in the cost of producing goods. Production costs depend not only on how much must be paid to hire an hour of labor, but also on how much the worker produces once he is on the payroll. If 100 manhours hired for $3 per hour turn out 50 tons of product, the unit labor cost is $300/50, or $6 per ton. When the productivity of labor rises by 20 percent, the output of the 100 manhours will rise to 60 tons, and if the hiring cost of labor is still $3 an hour, the unit labor cost will have been cut to $300/60, or $5 per ton. If wages and supplementary costs had risen 10 percent, unit labor cost ($330/60 = $5.50 per ton) would still have been lower than before. In fact, if hiring costs rose by 20 percent to $3.60 per hour, the unit labor cost of the product would still be at its original level of $360/60, or $6 per ton.

In general, as long as the average amount employers must pay to hire an hour's labor rises no more rapidly than the annual rate of productivity increase, employers can pay the higher labor compensation and still keep the unit labor cost—and hence prices—from rising. In an economic system like ours, in which the productivity of labor rises 3 to 3.5 percent annually, prices tend to remain stable only as long as wages and supplementary employment costs rise no faster than 3 to 3.5 percent. If the price of an hour's labor rises only 2 percent per year, the unit labor cost and prices tend to fall 1 to 1.5 percent annually.

The Phillips Curve

The rate at which wage rates rise depends on how many workers are unemployed. When total demand is well below productive capacity, unemployed workers form a pool of manpower which employers can tap without raising wages. When an employee retires, or when a man quits to take a job somewhere else, employers can quickly find a qualified replacement. A help wanted ad will bring in many replies from qualified people, and the firm can take its pick. When production rates are to be raised, and plenty of additional people are ready and able to take the extra jobs, there is little occasion for firms to pay higher wages, and wage rates rise slowly, if at all. However, once production rates rise and unemployment declines, things begin to change. Good job replacements become hard to find. An experienced man who wants to quit and take a job somewhere else represents a serious loss to the firm, and wage increases are offered in an effort to convince him to stay. Help wanted ads bring in fewer replies, and many firms unable to find employees with the desired ability and experience begin to offer higher wages to attract workers from other jobs. Since these are met by counter-offers from other firms, wages begin to rise rapidly.

The power of labor unions is likewise affected by the amount of unemployment. When unemployment is widespread, unions often accept lower settlements rather than expose the membership to a strike. In any case, a strike is much less of a threat to a firm that is operating at only half its capacity, and the low profits which are associated with low operating rates only stiffen the company's resistance to union demands. The situation is reversed, however, when labor is scarce. A strike imposes severe loss of business on a firm that is working at capacity, and the high profits from the high sales rate tend to soften the employer's resistance to wage demands.

The tendency of wage rates to grow more rapidly at low levels of unemployment can be seen when both are plotted together as in Figure 2. The unemployment rate

each year is plotted on the horizontal axis, and the percentage increase in hourly earnings is plotted vertically. The observed trend of the points indicates the strong tendency for wages to increase more rapidly when unemployment is low and the labor market is tight, and less rapidly when unemployment is high.

The idealized relationship, represented by the blue curve in the figure, is called a *Phillips curve* after its discoverer, the British economist A. W. Phillips.[1] The curve has been drawn to represent the average rate of wage increase—taking one year with another—that can be expected to result from the corresponding unemployment rate. As can be seen from the individual points in the figure, during years of the same rate of unemployment, wages sometimes rise faster and sometimes more slowly, depending on the skills and training of the particular workers who happen to be unemployed at the time, the rate at which workers shift from low-paid to higher-paid industries, the timing of union contract negotiations, and similar factors. According to the curve of Figure 2, during years in which 7 percent of the labor force is unemployed, wage rates tend to rise an average of 2.5 percent per year. When unemployment is reduced to 6 percent, wages tend to rise about 3 percent per year, while unemployment of 3 percent represents a labor shortage that tends to force wages up about 6 percent per year.

Prices and the Phillips Curve The relationship of the Phillips curve to the dynamics of the price level is shown in Figure 3. The curve represents the approximate position of the Phillips curve in the U.S. economy at the present time. The horizontal

[1] A. W. Phillips, "The Relation Between Unemployment and the Rate of Change of Money Wage Rates in the United Kingdom, 1861–1957," *Economica,* November, 1958.

dotted line is drawn at a level corresponding to an increase in average hourly earnings of 3 percent per year. Since this is about the annual growth in labor productivity in the U.S., if supplementary hiring costs remain constant, prices should tend to rise when wages increase faster than this, and to fall when wage rates rise more slowly.

According to the Phillips curve, when unemployment is 6 percent of the labor force, wage rates tend to rise about 3 percent annually. Since this increase is offset by rising productivity, prices tend to remain stable. When more than 6 percent of the labor force is out of work, wages in the slack labor market rise more slowly than productivity, and prices tend to fall with declining unit labor costs. When fewer than 6 percent of the labor force is unemployed, however, competitive bidding for scarce workers tends to raise wages more rapidly than 3 percent per year, and rising unit labor costs tend to force prices upward.

This prediction is in rough agreement with U.S. experience during the decade 1958–1968 as shown in Table 1. During the 7 years 1958–1964, unemployment varied between 5.2 and 6.8 percent of the labor force. The resulting "softness" of the labor market held down the rate of wage increase, and prices rose an average of only 1.3 percent per year. That prices rose at all during this period was due largely to increases in social security taxes and other supplemental employment costs, rather than to rising wages. The rapid increases in GNP after 1964 reduced unemployment, and wage rates rose more rapidly in the tightening labor market. This situation was reflected in faster growth of the price level.

The interplay between unemployment and prices has profound implications, for it means that the government policy that cures one economic problem tends to create another. An unemployment level of 5 or 6 percent of the labor force is intolerable,

particularly when we consider who the unemployed are and the personal and social implications of unemployment. On the other hand, public policy to stimulate demand in order to provide jobs increases competition among employers and starts unit labor costs and prices rising. Moreover, prices continue to rise as long as unemployment is kept low. Prices do not rise to a new plateau and then level off. They keep right on climbing. The comparative price stability of the late 1950s and early 1960s was bought at the cost of burdensome unemployment. The low unemployment of the later 1960s was purchased at the expense of more rapid inflation.

If economic policy were limited to altering the balance between productive capacity and the total demand for output, we would be caught in a serious contradiction and forced to choose between 2 evils. Fortunately there is an alternative policy—to shift the terms of the choice.

Shifts in the Position of the Phillips Curve
The position of the Phillips curve is not rigidly fixed. The rate of increase in wages at any given level of unemployment depends on how well trained and mobile the unemployed workers are. Today one of the important reasons that labor costs rise rapidly when unemployment falls below 5 or 6 percent of the labor force is that most of the workers left unemployed at that point are the poorly educated, untrained, inexperienced workers who are isolated in urban ghettos and rural poverty areas. As these workers are trained and brought into the mainstream of employment, thus providing a large group of employable persons, the pressure on wages and prices will be reduced, and a slower rate of wage increase will tend to accompany any given level of unemployment.

A sufficient investment in training and a great enlargement of educational and employment opportunities for underprivi-

FIGURE 2 THE PHILLIPS CURVE FOR THE U.S. ECONOMY, 1953-1968

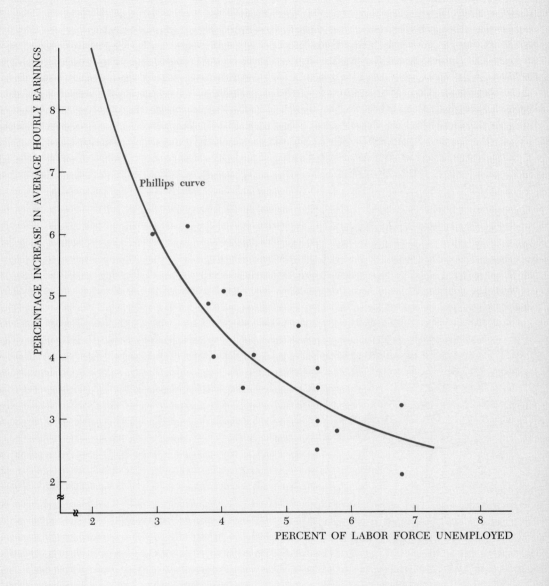

SOURCE: Adapted from data in the *Economic Report of the President, 1969*.

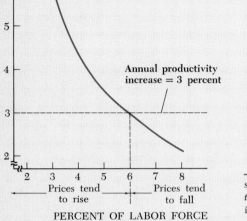

TABLE 1 U.S. UNEMPLOYMENT AND PRICE
INCREASES, 1958-1968

	PERCENT OF CIVILIAN LABOR FORCE UNEMPLOYED	PERCENTAGE INCREASE IN IMPLICIT DEFLATOR FOR PRIVATELY PRODUCED GNP
1958	6.8	1.7
1959	5.5	1.8
1960	5.5	1.3
1961	6.7	0.9
1962	5.5	0.9
1963	5.7	1.1
1964	5.2	1.3
Average 1958-1964	5.6	1.3
1965	4.5	1.4
1966	3.8	2.3
1967	3.8	3.5
1968	3.6	3.6
Average 1965-1968	4.0	2.7

SOURCE: Unemployment rates from *Economic Report of the President, 1969*. Price increases calculated from the implicit deflator of private nonfarm GNP as given in appropriate issues of *Survey of Current Business*.

FIGURE 4 SHIFTS IN THE PHILLIPS CURVE

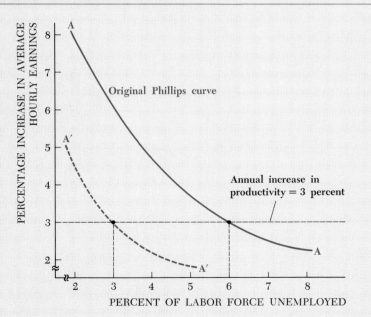

leged people may make it possible to reduce unemployment to the bare frictional level before serious price inflation occurs. With more skilled workers available, wages would rise no faster than productivity, even when unemployment had been reduced to 3 percent of the labor force. The effects of equal employment opportunity, open-housing legislation, job-training programs, and enforcement of civil rights in general not only benefit those directly concerned, but help to stabilize prices and improve the operation of the entire economic system.

The effect of such a training program is illustrated in Figure 4. The line *AA* represents the Phillips curve of the U.S. economy today. Unemployment below 5 or 6 percent of the labor force pushes wages up more rapidly than the 3 percent annual growth in private output per manhour. The curve *A'A'* represents the position of the Phillips curve after the establishment of an effective program to train unskilled workers and place them in productive jobs.

International Comparison of Phillips Curves

The effect of differences in the labor market on the position of the Phillips curve can be seen when rates of unemployment and price increase are compared among countries. The average rates of increase in consumer prices over the period 1960–1964 appear in Figure 5 together with the average percent of the labor force unemployed over the same period in a number of industrial nations. The strong tendency for prices to rise more rapidly at lower levels of unemployment is clearly reflected in the scatter of points. Some nations purchase their characteristically lower unemployment rates at the cost of more rapidly rising prices, but this cost is not uniform among countries. Fewer than 1 percent of the labor force was unemployed in West Germany, the Netherlands, and Japan, yet prices rose less than 3 percent in Germany, and almost 6 percent in Japan. Rates of inflation differed widely in Italy, Austria, and Belgium, although

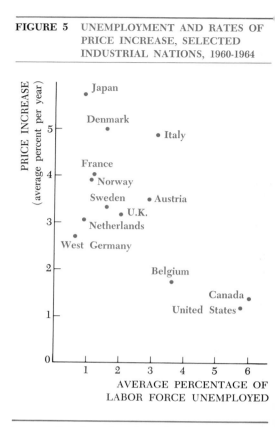

FIGURE 5   UNEMPLOYMENT AND RATES OF PRICE INCREASE, SELECTED INDUSTRIAL NATIONS, 1960-1964

SOURCE: Based on data from the Organization for Economic Cooperation and Development.

their unemployment rates differed by less than 1 percentage point.

These differences suggest that the nations lie on different Phillips curves, and the direction of the differences correspond to what would be expected. Italy, for example, has serious problems of structural unemployment associated with its underdeveloped South. Labor in Japan is notoriously immobile. The typical Japanese college graduate expects to remain for the rest of his life with the firm that gives him his first job. Where such conditions exist, the nations are on high Phillips curves. A given level of unemployment in these countries involves a more serious shortage of available labor than it would in a place like Germany or Sweden where highly mobile labor and a minimum of structural problems hold the Phillips curve to a lower level.

LIMITS TO INFLATION

When high demand for output produces very low levels of unemployment, wages rise and keep on rising as long as low unemployment continues. Wages and prices continue to rise unless and until consumers, business firms, and governments reduce their buying enough for rising unemployment to check the rate of wage increase.

At first, one might suppose that buying would be checked automatically as rising prices reduce the purchasing power of incomes. When we recall that output and income are merely different ways of looking at the same thing, however, the fallacy of this view is immediately apparent. Every dollar's worth of value added in the production of goods becomes a dollar of income to somebody. The same rising prices that cut the buying power of each dollar automatically provide enough more dollars to maintain aggregate buying power equal to the value of output.

Bank Credit as a Limit to Rising Prices

Nevertheless, there is an important connection between rising prices and aggregate demand. Demand for new house construction, business demand for inventory, plant, and equipment, and even household demand for automobiles and other durable goods purchased on time are affected by the availability of credit. Unless credit is permitted to expand to keep pace with rising prices, it becomes increasingly difficult to sustain buying. As prices rise a smaller volume of real purchases can be financed with a given number of dollars. When

houses cost $20,000 to build, $1 billion of bank credit will supply enough purchasing power to pay for 50,000 new homes. If construction costs double, the same amount of bank lending will finance only 25,000 new homes.

At the same time, rising prices of groceries, magazines, haircuts, and other consumer items force housewives to carry larger and larger amounts of hand-to-hand currency in their purses to do their daily shopping, while stores must keep larger amounts in their cash registers to make change. This means steady net withdrawal of currency from banks, and further reduction in bank reserves. Thus rising prices not only reduce the physical volume of demand that can be supported by a given number of dollars of lending, they also tend to reduce the number of dollars the banking system can lend. The result of the combination of these factors is that, unless banks are supplied with additional reserves, the scarcity of credit forces a reduction in the demand for those products that are financed by bank credit. When this has cut aggregate demand enough to induce severe unemployment, prices stop rising.

Progressive Taxation as a Check to Inflation

In the U.S. and many other industrialized countries, the existence of progressive taxes causes an important shift of buying power from households to the government as prices rise. A *progressive tax* is one by which the percentage of earnings each income receiver must pay in taxes rises with the amount of income he receives. The U.S. personal income tax is a good example of a progressive tax. Each family is allowed to exempt a certain amount of income per member and to deduct charitable contributions, interest payments, a proportion of its medical expenses, and certain other outlays from its total income in order to arrive at its taxable income. As a result of these deductions, families with the lowest money incomes have no taxable income and pay no income tax at all. Families whose earnings exceed their exemptions and deductions are taxed at a rate that depends on the level of their incomes. According to the U.S. tax schedule applicable during 1967, a family with taxable income of $1,000 paid a tax of $140, or 14 percent of its income. A family earning $4,000 paid $620, or 15.5 percent, while a family with taxable income of $200,000 turned over $110,980, or about 55.5 percent of it, to the government.

The effect of the progressive tax is to increase the percentage of their real purchasing power that families must pay to the government when prices rise. Consider the case of a family with taxable income of $20,000: Their tax liability is $4,380, or 21.9 percent of real income. If all prices and incomes double, the family income becomes $40,000. Since each dollar has half its previous purchasing power, the family's real income is unaffected by the change. But taxes are paid on the basis of the total number of dollars received, regardless of their purchasing power. The family now owes the government $12,140 in taxes, which amounts to 30.2 percent of its real purchasing power. Because of the progressive income tax, inflation has deprived the family of almost 10 percent of its real purchasing power.

As families lose real purchasing power to the government, consumer demand is reduced and production slows down. When unemployment becomes severe enough, prices stop rising and become stabilized. Of course, the power of the income tax to check inflation is effective only as long as the government holds its own purchases of real goods and service in check. If the government uses the extra purchasing power acquired from the higher tax yields to increase its own demand for goods and services, it offsets declining household demand. Such action supports the high level of employ-ment, causing the rate of price increase to continue unabated.

HYPERINFLATION

When there is a sustained aggregate demand for more output than the economic system can produce, backed up by a continually expanding money supply and unchecked by taxes, a condition known as "hyperinflation" sometimes results. During *hyperinflation* prices rise faster and faster and price levels reach astronomical heights.

Hyperinflation is invariably the result of a continued large demand for goods and services by a government that is unable or unwilling to enforce its power to tax. A government with adequate taxing power can obtain the goods and services its needs and still hold prices in check by taxing away enough purchasing power from consumers and businesses to offset its own additional demand. But a government whose demand is a substantial fraction of total output and that cannot or will not use its tax power to offset its own actions often finds itself caught in a spiral of rising prices.

The problem begins when production is at or near capacity. The government enters the marketplace like a private party and bids materials and labor away from households and business firms, but instead of using its tax power to divert purchasing power from others, it borrows from the banking system or prints money itself. When the government pays for the goods it buys, however, this new money goes to workers and employers as higher incomes. Next month when the government comes to market again, it must again compete with businesses and households, but this time the competition is keener because people have higher incomes than before. To outbid them, the government must force up wages and prices again, and must borrow or print more money than it did the first time, again adding to household incomes. The following month the government must again outbid people trying to spend their still larger incomes and, in the process, raise incomes again.

When we look carefully at what is happening, we see that in order to obtain a fixed share of total output, the government must come to market each month with enough new money to compete with businesses and consumers whose incomes are swollen by the government spending of the preceding month. Unable to curtail private demand by taxation, the government resorts to outbidding businesses and households, and in the process keeps supplying them with ever-higher incomes with which to bid next month. In effect, the government is reduced to competing against its own past actions. As surely as government spending forces up wages and prices this month by more than it did last month, it must force up wages and prices next month more than it did this month. The inflationary spiral continues faster and faster until either the government asserts its tax power or the currency is no longer acceptable and trade becomes barter.

The American Revolution was accompanied by a hyperinflation of the kind just described. Faced with the need to raise and maintain troops for the war, the Continental Congress imposed its demand for goods and services in competition with that of the rest of the colonial economy. Having no tax power, the Congress printed currency to make its purchases. As nearly as we can now estimate, the result was a rise in the price level from an index of 100 in 1775 to a peak of 13,520 in 1780.[2] This was an average annual increase in price level of roughly 173 percent per year. The money that would have lasted a family an entire year in 1775 was gone in 2 and a half days

in 1780! The notes issued as money by the Continental Congress were popularly known as "continentals" and the phrase "not worth a continental" is still part of American vocabulary.

The Hungarian Inflation of 1946

An economy whose communications and capital equipment have been damaged by war has a greatly reduced productive capacity that is especially vulnerable to the efforts of a defeated government, which has no facilities for tax collection, to maintain essential services. Probably the most astonishing of all hyperinflations occurred in Hungary following World War II.[3]

Bombing, wartime destruction, and disruption of communications had destroyed an estimated 40 percent of Hungarian productive capacity. The government that had replaced the Nazi regime not only assumed the burden of providing normal government services, but in addition had to provide for many refugees and displaced persons. Moreover, it was required to cover occupation costs and to make reparation for war damage with goods delivered to Czechoslovakia, Yugoslavia, and the U.S.S.R. Since the weak government was virtually incapable of enforcing tax collections, it had to rely on the printing press. Its effort to function without taxation resulted in hyperinflation.

The Hungarian price index that stood at 100 in August, 1939, had grown to 5,371,300 by the middle of January, 1946. This was an average growth rate of 15 percent per month during World War II. But the worst was yet to come. By the middle of June, only 6 months later, the price index stood at 19,686,163,000,000! During the last weeks of the hyperinflation, the price level doubled every day. Enough money to last

---

[2] The estimates are based on price indexes published in U.S. Bureau of the Census, *Historical Statistics of the United States, Colonial Times to 1957.* Washington, D.C., 1960.

[3] Data on the Hungarian inflation are drawn from Hungarian Commercial Bank of Pest, *Survey of the Economic Situation in Hungary,* no. 1, July, 1946, no. 2, January, 1947.

a Hungarian family a year, even at the prices of January, 1946, would not have bought a postage stamp at the prices ruling at the end of June.

The hyperinflation was financed by rapid expansion of the money supply. The note circulation of the Hungarian National Bank grew from roughly 1 billion pengö in January, 1939 to 765 billion pengö on January 1, 1946. By June, 1946 circulation exceeded 6×10^{18} (6 billion billion) pengö. One month later it reached 348×10^{36} (348 billion billion billion billion) pengö.

Such rates of inflation are, of course, intolerable. When people find prices doubling every day they soon stop accepting money. If you have a commodity to sell, it is foolish to exchange it for money that will lose most of its value before you can spend it. It is much better to wait until you can swap your goods directly for something

you can use, or can trade in turn. When workers refuse to work for money and insist on payment in goods they can use or trade, money stops functioning as a medium of exchange. Historically, governments faced with a complete collapse of the monetary system have created a new currency unit to exchange with holders of the old money. If aggregate demand is then held within the limits of productive capacity, the new currency will gain acceptance; consequently the economy will begin to function more normally.

In August, 1946 the inflated Hungarian pengö was replaced by a new unit, the florin. Taxes were raised, and the new currency was further protected by direct government control over wages and prices. Before the effectiveness of the measures could be thoroughly tested, however, the Hungarian government was overthrown.

SUMMARY

If all prices, wages, and money contracts varied in proportion, there would be no problem of *inflation*. Everybody would always receive just enough additional dollars to make up for the higher prices of the things he bought. The harm done by inflation is that not all prices and incomes change in proportion, and creditors, the retired, and other people whose incomes are slow to adjust suffer losses in purchasing power.

Since prices depend on costs, and since the basic cost of all output is labor cost, inflation occurs when wage rates rise more rapidly than labor productivity. Thus the main factor in inflation is the relationship of rising wages to unemployment as represented by the *Phillips curve*. When there is a large pool of unemployed workers, employees can easily be added as necessary with little or no increase in wages, but when only a few high-quality workers are unemployed, the competitive scramble for them keeps wages rising rapidly.

The connection between unemployment and prices poses a serious dilemma for public policy. Measures taken to eliminate cyclical unemployment result in rapid inflation, while steps to hold inflation in check put people out of work. Either way somebody is injured, and the divisive forces in modern society are aggravated. One way to resolve this contradiction is to *shift the position* of the nation's Phillips curve.

The rapidity with which wages rise at a given level of unemployment depends on the quality of the unemployed workers and on their mobility, as can be seen when Phillips curves are compared on an international basis. One of the reasons the U.S. prices rise so rapidly at a comparatively high level of unemployment is that there is still a substantial amount of structural unemployment. One way to shift the U.S. Phillips curve, therefore, is to raise the quality and mobility of the labor force.

As long as unemployment rates remain low, inflation continues. However, there are 2 important ways in which rising prices tend to create unemployment. First, certain purchases like houses, new equipment, and other durable items are heavily financed by *credit*. As prices rise, a given volume of bank credit can finance a smaller and smaller real volume of purchases, and as real purchases decline, unemployment rises. Second, the amount of real income taken away from households by *progressive taxes* rises with prices, leaving households with less real purchasing power, and the subsequent reduction in spending tends to create unemployment.

These limits are effective, however, only when bank credit is limited, and when the government refuses to spend the extra tax receipts. *Hyperinflation* occurs when governments with ineffective tax power continue to rely on bank credit or the printing press to finance a greater output than the productive capacity of the economic system can produce. Under these circumstances, price levels rise astronomically until the tax power is exercised or the currency is finally abandoned.

CHAPTER 9

Consumer Expenditure and the Multiplier

Since they constitute about two-thirds of gross national product, household purchases of consumer goods are a fitting place to begin the analysis of aggregate demand. The most important influence on how much households spend for consumer goods is how much income they receive. Although little can be said about any individual family, families on the average tend to spend about 75 cents out of each extra dollar they earn after taxes. This means that whenever production starts to rise, the additional amount households spend out of their extra incomes tends to multiply the initial rise in output. Whenever production starts to decline, the reduction in spending of households with falling incomes multiplies the initial decline. The nature and size of this multiplier effect is an important key to the analysis of economic fluctuation.

HOUSEHOLD CONSUMPTION EXPENDITURE

In the normal course of daily life, every family spends money for a wide assortment of goods. Consumer expenditure typically includes the purchase of food, clothing, utilities, house furnishings, household appliances, automobiles, medical care, recreation, and so on. As shown in Figure 1, the largest category of consumer spending, almost half the total, consists of food, clothing, gasoline, and other nondurable goods. Expenditures for housing, household operation, public transportation, and other services are almost as large. The smallest category of expenditures consists of outlays for durable goods such as automobiles, furniture, and household appliances. Although these usually make up less than 15 percent of total consumer spending, they tend to

FIGURE 1   PERSONAL CONSUMPTION
EXPENDITURES, 1950-1968

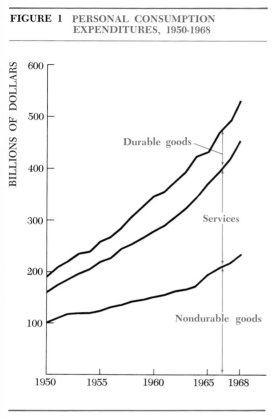

SOURCE: *Economic Report of the President, 1969.*

appear almost impossible to fit them into any kind of predictable system. Families buy a new car when they are impressed by the new styles. They have a big medical bill when illness strikes. They reduce their spending for education when their daughter graduates from college. When we look at expenditure in the aggregate, however, the problem is greatly simplified. In the first place, the *total* outlay by any family for all types of consumer goods combined is more stable than its expenditure for any single item. Purchase of a new television set may mean fewer new clothes; lower education expenses make it possible to buy new furniture, and so on. In the second place, when a large number of households are taken together, variations among individuals tend to average out. As a result, the bewildering assortment of causes underlying variations in household spending can be reduced to a handful of important factors.

CONSUMER SPENDING AND INCOME

The most important single determinant of a family's expenditure is the amount of income available for it to spend. Although there is wide variation in the amounts spent by individual families, even when they have the same income, the *average* outlay exhibits a remarkably stable relationship to disposable income, as shown in Table 1. This relationship is shown graphically in Figure 2 where disposable incomes and consumption expenditures are plotted. The height of each dot represents the average consumption outlay by all families in the corresponding income bracket. A smooth curve drawn through the dots represents the relationship of consumption expenditure to income.

show the greatest year-to-year variation in magnitude. For example, while aggregate outlays for both nondurable consumer goods and services increased every year of the period 1950–1968, total consumer purchases of durable goods declined in 1952, 1954, 1956, 1958, and 1961. One important reason for this difference in behavior is that purchases of durable goods can be postponed when necessary. If this year's model is unsuitable, or if households are a little short of cash, the old car, or television set can be made to last another year or 2.

Patterns of expenditure vary widely from family to family, and for such a bewildering number of reasons that it might

TABLE 1 AVERAGE DISPOSABLE INCOME AND CONSUMPTION EXPENDITURE BY INCOME BRACKETS, ALL URBAN FAMILIES AND INDIVIDUAL CONSUMERS, U.S., 1960

INCOME BRACKET	(1) PER-CENT OF FAMI-LIES	(2) MEAN DIS-POSABLE INCOME	(3) MEAN CON-SUMP-TION EXPEN-DITURE
Under $1,000	2.3	$ 702	$ 1,205
$ 1,000– 1,999	8.4	1,507	1,781
2,000– 2,999	10.1	2,506	2,657
3,000– 3,999	11.9	3,528	3,785
4,000– 4,999	14.0	4,523	4,555
5,000– 5,999	13.2	5,501	5,202
6,000– 7,499	16.4	6,697	6,300
7,500– 9,999	14.3	8,571	7,589
10,000–14,999	7.1	11,683	9,774
15,000 and over	2.3	21,762	14,599
Total	100.0	5,829	5,368

SOURCE: Adapted from U.S. Bureau of Labor Statistics, *Consumer Expenditures and Income, Urban United States, 1960–61,* BLS Report no. 237–8, Washington, D.C., April 1964, p.15, Table 1B.

FIGURE 2 RELATIONSHIP OF CONSUMPTION EXPENDITURE TO FAMILY DISPOSABLE INCOME, U.S., 1960

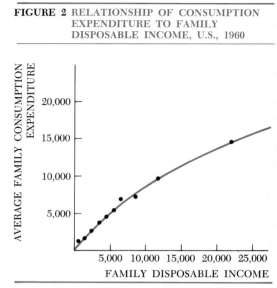

SOURCE: Data of Table 1.

The Average Propensity To Consume

The curve of Figure 2 shows the propensity of families to consume their incomes and can be characterized in 2 quite simple ways. The *average propensity to consume* is the average proportion of income spent by families in any income bracket. Calculation from Table 1 reveals that at the lowest income level the average propensity to consume is 1.75. That is, families in this bracket spend on the average 75 percent more on consumer goods than they receive as income. Many of these families consist of young people who are receiving help from their families. Others are heavily engaged in acquiring furniture, new cars, clothes, and similar items that are bought on credit.

Some are families who are temporarily in straitened circumstances and are living off accumulated savings, insurance benefits, or sale of assets. A large number consist of retired couples who are drawing down assets that they have intentionally saved for the purpose. The average propensity to consume tends to decline as income rises, falling to .67 in the highest bracket. For all families combined, the average propensity to consume is abut .92.

The average propensity to consume serves to characterize the *height* of the consumption curve at any given income. An increase in the average amount of consumption expenditure of families in any income group shows up as a rise in the average propensity to consume at that income level. This is equivalent to a rise in the height of the curve in Figure 2 at that point.

The Marginal Propensity To Consume

A second and more important characterization of the relationship of consumption to income is the typical proportion of any *increase* in income that will be spent by families in any given income bracket. This proportion is the *marginal propensity to consume.*

The marginal propensity to consume is represented by the *slope* of the smooth curve of Figure 2. To measure the marginal propensity to consume, select 2 income brackets fairly close together and note, from the curve, the consumer expenditure that corresponds to families in each. The marginal propensity to consume is the ratio of the increase in consumer expenditure to the increase in income between the 2 brackets.

As shown in Figure 3, for example, families with $5,000 disposable income tend to spend an average of $5,000 per year for consumption items, while families with $6,000 income spend $5,800. When income rises $1,000 from $5,000 to $6,000, consumer spending tends to rise $800 from $5,000 to $5,800. The marginal propensity to consume is thus $800/$1,000, or .80. Careful measurement of Figure 2 reveals a marginal propensity to consume of about .9 in the lowest income bracket. That is, low-income families tend to spend about $.90 out of each additional dollar of income

they receive. Families with higher incomes exhibit lower marginal propensities to consume. Between $6,000 and $12,000, consumer expenditure tends to rise about $.70 with each additional dollar of income. At the highest levels of income shown, the marginal propensity to consume is less than .5, since wealthier families spend only about $.50 of each additional income dollar on consumption items.

The observed decrease in the marginal propensity to consume is to be expected. Many low-income families are hard pressed to maintain a satisfactory living standard. Almost all of a pay increase is needed for necessities or other goods which have been entirely out of reach. As families rise in the income scale, however, fewer and fewer immediate needs are unmet. Families in the higher income brackets spend their additional income for finer food, better clothes, more education, and recreation. At the same time, provision for the future becomes increasingly important. Higher-income families withhold a larger share of any additional income from consumption expenditure and divert it into savings accounts, investment in business, insurance, purchase of securities, acquisition of property, and similar uses.

The marginal propensity to consume is a quantitative measure of one of the important interrelationships among different types of demand. We already know that a rise in production gives families more income to spend. The marginal propensity to consume tells us how much of their additional incomes they tend to spend on consumption items.

Marginal Propensity To Consume, All Families Combined Since the marginal propensity to consume is higher for poor than for rich families, the amount of spending that is induced by a rise in disposable income depends on who gets the money. In general, however, when national income rises, families at all levels of the income

---

FIGURE 3 CALCULATION OF THE MARGINAL PROPENSITY TO CONSUME

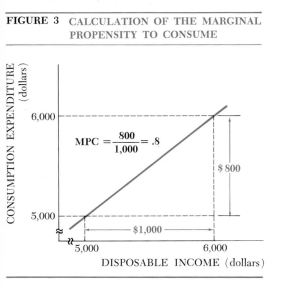

CONSUMPTION EXPENDITURE (dollars)

$$MPC = \frac{800}{1,000} = .8$$

$800

6,000

5,000

$1,000

5,000   6,000

DISPOSABLE INCOME (dollars)

scale find their incomes increasing together. The demand that provides a job for an unemployed worker also means higher wages to others already at work and higher profits for suppliers. Because of this, the total amount of additional consumption spending to be expected from a given rise in aggregate income depends on the marginal propensities of all the families in the community, rather than that of any particular group. Careful calculation from Figure 1 shows that when a rise in income is distributed over all families, as a group they spend about 75 cents out of every additional dollar. When total disposable income of all families rises by $1 billion, their total consumption expenditure tends to increase by $.75 billion. In other words, the marginal propensity to consume by all families together is about .75.

OTHER INFLUENCES ON CONSUMPTION SPENDING

Of course, household expenditure for consumption items is influenced by many things besides income. To mention only a few, some people spend more when they can buy on credit and take longer to pay. Some people are attracted by changes in style, or by the appearance of new kinds of goods for sale. Advertising sometimes induces people to buy more than they otherwise would. People who expect that prices will be lower next year or that next year's model will be better may postpone purchases that would otherwise be made.

Consumer psychology is of great importance. There appear to be times when people feel secure and optimistic about the future and are willing to spend freely. At other times they feel insecure, doubtful of the future, and disposed to postpone or cut back their buying, especially buying of big expensive items.

In view of all these factors it is hardly surprising to find that historical comparisons show only a loose relationship between changes in average family income and those in average consumption expenditure. The wide range of behavior is especially evident when the data are plotted as in Figure 4. Each point represents a year-to-year increase in income (plotted horizontally) and the attendant increase in consumption spending (plotted vertically). If spending depended only on disposable income, we would expect the points to lie exactly on the line with the slope of .75. The wide dispersion of the points around the line indicates the importance of causes that act independently of income.

From 1963 to 1964 per capita income increased $144 and consumer spending rose by $108 in almost exact agreement with the .75 estimated marginal propensity to consume, but the very next year, although disposable personal income rose almost exactly the same amount, consumer spending grew by $138 per person. The $77 growth in per capita income from 1955 to 1956 was accompanied by $46 more spending per person, but the $74 growth from 1958 to 1959 led people to spend $92 more on consumer goods.

The Annual Trend in Consumer Spending

Not only does consumer spending vary widely from year to year, but on the average there is a strong tendency for expenditures to increase more than would be expected on the basis of income increases alone. Notice the number of points above the line in Figure 4 compared to the number below. This tendency for consumers to increase expenditure annually regardless of income is known as the *trend* in consumer expenditures. It is easily measured by comparing the rise in consumer spending over a period of several years with the corresponding increase in income, as shown in Table 2.

FIGURE 4   ANNUAL INCREASES IN DISPOSABLE PERSONAL INCOME AND IN CONSUMPTION EXPENDITURE, 1950-1951 TO 1967-1968

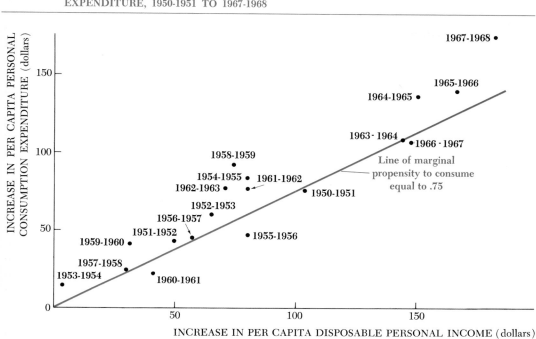

SOURCE: Calculated from data in the *Economic Report of the President, 1969.*

In the table incomes and consumption expenditures are given 10 years apart. Both 1955 and 1965 were years of comparable prosperity in which most factors acted on

TABLE 2   CALCULATION OF THE ANNUAL TREND IN CONSUMER SPENDING, 1955–1965

YEAR	DISPOSABLE PERSONAL INCOME	CONSUMPTION EXPENDITURE
1965	$472.2	$433.1
1955	275.3	254.4
Increase	196.9	178.7

Due to higher income	.75 × 196.9, or 147.7
Difference = trend increase over 10 years	31.0
Annual increase	3.1
Trend	3.1/343.8 = .009, or .9 percent per year

SOURCE: Data from *Economic Report of the President, 1969.*

consumer demand in much the same way. During the decade the total disposable income received by all U.S. households rose by $196.9 billion. Since the marginal propensity to consume is .75, we would have expected to find American families spending $147.7 billion more for consumption items in 1965 than they had 10 years earlier. In fact, however, they had increased their spending by $178.7 billion. The extra $31 billion represented an upward trend in consumer spending of about .9 of 1 percent per year. That is, over the decade, Americans increased their consumption outlays by an average of .9 of 1 percent per year more than their rising incomes would have suggested.

Several reasons have been advanced for this extra growth in spending. First is that the amount families can afford to spend depends not only on their incomes but also on their wealth, in the form of real and financial assets. As their wealth grows, families have less incentive to save to accumulate more wealth and tend to step up their consumption expenditure. This may be one reason that the United States as a whole has a noticeably lower savings rate and devotes a lower fraction of its gross national product to capital formation than many lower-income nations.

A second cause of the trend in consumption spending is population growth. Even if its income did not rise, a growing population would have to spend more on consumer goods to support its members at the same standard as before.

Probably a third important cause of the trend is that many people pay a great deal of attention to what their neighbors spend and regulate their spending less by the size of their income than by their position in the income scale. The richest people spend the smallest portion of their incomes partly because they are already on top and have won the status race. Other families spend higher proportions partly in an effort to close the gap between their living standards and those of families with incomes higher than their own. Families whose incomes rise relative to others move up in society and can assume the lower average propensity to consume of their new peers, but when all family incomes rise together, each family remains in the same relative position. Although it has a higher income than before, it must retain its high average propensity to consume just to keep its place in the spending race.

Probably a fourth contribution to the annual growth in consumer spending is made by the increasing variety of consumer products. Our estimate of the marginal propensity to consume was based on a cross-section of families and showed how spending was related to income during a given year, the products available at that time being fixed. New discoveries and inventions produce a steadily growing stream of new goods that encourages people to spend more as time passes.

Autonomous and Induced Changes in Spending

In general, changes in consumer spending can be classed under 2 headings. When the members of a family alter their purchases because the family income has increased or decreased, the result is called an *induced* change in consumer spending. Thus when a wage-earner loses a job, the reduction in income *induces* the family to trim its buying. When somebody in the family gets a job or a raise, the added income *induces* the members of the family to spend more freely than before. The marginal propensity to consume is associated only with induced changes in consumer expenditure and measures the amount of spending that a given increase or decrease in income will induce.

When family members alter their spending for any other reason, the result is called an *autonomous* change in consumption. Autonomous changes occur when members of the family are asserting their own needs, tastes, or preferences, without regard to income. A rise in spending to meet the needs of a growing family, increased buying in response to new styles, the effects of human impulses, and all other such changes in consumer outlays are classified as autonomous. Whatever its sources, the $3.1 billion trend constitutes an annual autonomous increase in consumer spending.

The relationship between induced and autonomous changes in consumption buying is shown in Figure 5. Income is plotted horizontally and consumption vertically. Line *CC* represents the relationship of induced consumption to income. The slope of the line corresponds to the tendency for consumer spending to increase $.75 for each $1 addition to income, in keeping with the marginal propensity to consume of .75. The increase in consumption expenditure

FIGURE 5 AUTONOMOUS AND INDUCED
CONSUMPTION EXPENDITURE

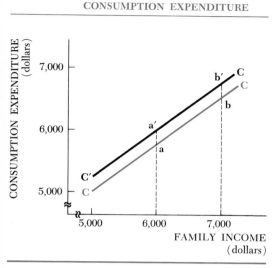

omous expenditure raises total family spending to *a'*, the increase in income induces the further increase from *a'* to *b'*.

THE PRODUCTION-SPENDING CYCLE

Figure 5 is a reasonable representation of the position of any given family, but when generalized to include the income and spending of all families taken together it becomes misleading in a very important respect. When all families are considered together, induced changes in consumer spending cannot be treated as if they were independent of autonomous changes. On the contrary, any autonomous rise in spending by one group of consumers necessarily stimulates business firms to increase production. The resulting rise in employment and incomes induces increased consumption spending by other families. For example, the rapid rise in automobile demand during 1963, 1964, and 1965 was partly an autonomous increase in new-car buying by an unusual number of families whose younger members had just reached driving age. The resulting rise in automobile production gave extra employment and higher incomes to automobile workers and suppliers, higher profits to automobile dealers, and greater dividends to stockholders of automobile firms. All these people naturally spent part of their higher incomes.

that will be induced by any given rise in disposable income is easily found by comparing 2 points on the line. Thus a rise in total disposable income from $6,000 per family to $7,000 per family, unaccompanied by any autonomous change, would induce family members to increase their spending on consumption goods by $750, from $5,350 (the height of point *a*) to $6,100 (the height of point *b*).

An autonomous change in consumption spending, on the other hand, is represented by a shift in the *CC* line itself. For example, when family members become more optimistic about the future, they often begin spending more, even given the same income. This is represented in the figure by an upward shift in the consumption line to the new position *C'C'*, indicating that the family is now spending $200 a year more on consumer items despite the fact that its income is still only $6,000.

A combination of the 2 effects is also easily represented. If a family that has undertaken a $200 autonomous increase in spending also receives a $1,000 increase in income, the resulting expenditure position is represented by the point *b'*. The auton-

These induced expenditures then caused a second increase in income. When producers of food, clothing, gasoline, and the other items bought by automobile workers and others with increased incomes found their sales rising, they responded with greater output, and still other workers and investors found themselves with greater earnings. Their families added still further to the total amount of consumer spending, which in turn meant still greater production of consumer goods, still more wages and dividends, and additional spending by still more families.

The Flowchart

The endless chain of buying-production-income-more buying that follows from an autonomous change in consumer spending can be conveniently depicted by the flowchart of Figure 6. The arrows in the figure show how changes in spending by one group induce changes in the spending of others. An original autonomous increase in demand occurs among the families at *A*. The arrow indicates that their increased buying raises the total sales of U.S. business firms at *B*. The higher sales induce the firms to schedule additional production in

their factories at *C*. To increase production more labor must be employed, adding to the taxable incomes of families at *D*. After personal tax payments are deducted and government transfer payments are added, the families are left with increased disposable personal incomes at *E*. The higher disposable incomes induce the families to increase their own buying at *F*. The induced consumption buying at *F*, however, means another addition to total sales of U.S. firms at *B*, and the cycle of buying, production, and spending starts all over again.

The Multiplier

As the process of spending and responding spreads through the community, the effect of

FIGURE 6 FLOWCHART OF THE U.S. ECONOMY

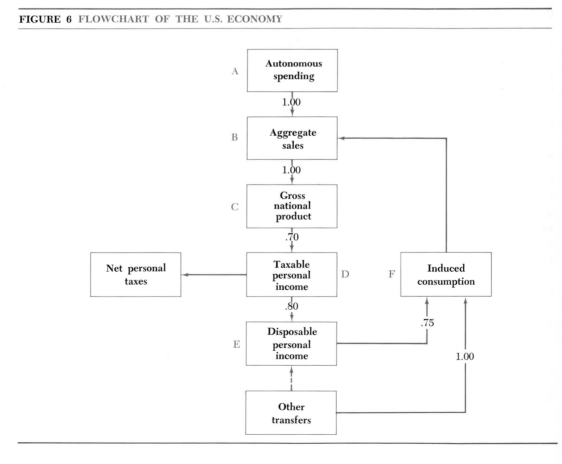

the initial autonomous increase in demand becomes multiplied. The amount of this magnification is measured by a factor appropriately called the *multiplier*. In an economic system with a multiplier of 2, an initial $1 billion autonomous rise in demand would accumulate to a total rise of 2 × $1 billion, or $2 billion, by the time its induced effects had worked their way through the community. Where the multiplier is 3.5, the same autonomous rise in demand would accumulate to 3.5 × $1 billion, or $3.5 billion, and so on.

The size of the multiplier in any economy depends on several fundamental factors: (1) the amount that firms tend to increase output per dollar of increased sales, (2) the amount of taxable personal income paid out per dollar of increased production, (3) the effective personal tax rate, and (4) the marginal propensity to consume. Firms tend to increase output in response to rising sales by amounts that very widely from one economic system to another. For one thing, the response depends on the extent to which consumers buy imported goods and the proportion of imported materials used in domestic industrial production. In a country where everything is domestically produced, a $1 addition to final sales involves production worth $1. If, on the other hand, one-third of the value of final sales is composed of imported goods and materials, a $1 addition to final sales involves only $.67 of domestic value added to $.33 of imported materials. In addition to imports, the short run response of production to sales depends on how much inventory business firms normally hold per dollar of sales. As a first approximation, to be modified later, we will neglect both imports and inventory accumulation and examine the multiplier in a situation where a $1 addition to sales induces firms to increase output by $1. This is indicated by the number (1.00) on the arrow leading from total sales to gross national product in Figure 6.

The amount of taxable personal income

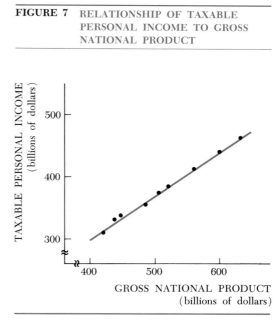

FIGURE 7   RELATIONSHIP OF TAXABLE PERSONAL INCOME TO GROSS NATIONAL PRODUCT

SOURCE: Data from the *Economic Report of the President, 1969.*

that is paid to families per dollar of additional production depends on a large number of conditions. To summarize these, we need only review the relationship between gross national product and personal disposable income. Looking back to our earlier study of the relationship between output and income, we find that the difference between production and taxable personal income depends on capital consumption allowances, indirect business taxes, corporate income taxes, and corporate savings. A direct estimate of the relationship can be made from Figure 7. Each point in the figure represents the U.S. gross national product of a given year, plotted on the horizontal scale, and taxable personal income of the same year, plotted vertically. The line is carefully drawn to represent the relationship as closely as possible. The slope of the line gives us the amount of taxable personal income paid out per additional dollar of production. Careful measurement reveals the slope of the line is 0.70. That is, when the gross national product grows by $1 billion, individuals and families receive an additional $.70 billion in earnings. This number is recorded is Figure 6 between gross national product at C and taxable personal income at D.

The relationship of personal tax liabilities to taxable income is similarly estimated in Figure 8. In making this estimate, the receipt of unemployment compensation has been treated as a deduction from tax payments. Personal tax payments constitute a transfer of purchasing power from households to the government, while unemployment benefits constitute a transfer of purchasing power from the government back to households. Since both these transfers vary with changes in production and income, their difference, called "net personal taxes" in Figure 6, is used to represent the net withdrawal of purchasing power from rising income. Calculation from Figure 8 reveals that as aggregate taxable incomes rises $1 billion, net personal taxes tend to

rise $.20 billion. This leaves $.80 billion of disposable income, and the fraction .80 is recorded in Figure 6 between taxable personal income at D and disposable personal income at E.

The final figure recorded on the flowchart is the .75 marginal propensity to consume, indicating that 75 percent of any increase in disposable personal income is spent for consumer goods. Social security pensions, medicare, and other transfer payments that do not vary with production are recorded on the flowchart as a separate addition to disposable personal income. Because the recipients of these transfers are in low-income groups and are often aged people, any increase is generally spent completely. That is, the marginal propensity to consume increases in social security and other transfers is approximately 1, and for this reason the expenditure of these transfer payments is represented by a special line on the flowchart.

FIGURE 8   RELATIONSHIP OF NET PERSONAL
TAX PAYMENTS TO TAXABLE
PERSONAL INCOME

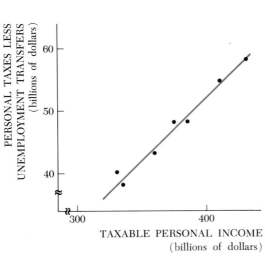

SOURCE: Plotted from data adapted from the *Economic Report of the President, 1969.*

Calculating the Multiplier

We can now estimate the multiplier simply by following successive cycles of buying-production-income-buying around the flowchart of Figure 6. We begin with the families at A buying $1 billion worth of new automobiles from the firms at B. Automobile firms order an increase of $1 billion in production at C. After the deduction of depreciation charges, business taxes, and corporate savings, families at D receive 70 percent of the value of the increased output as taxable personal income. This gives them $.70 billion more income than they had before, but 20 percent of this is taken in personal taxes, leaving them with .80 × $.70, or $.56 billion additional disposable income at E. When 75 percent of the new income is spent at F, induced consumption rises by .75 × $.56 or $.42 billion.

The number .42 is called the *respending ratio*. It indicates what proportion of the value of an initial rise in sales at the beginning of one buying-production-income-more buying cycle will emerge at the end as additional consumption expenditure. The value of the respending ratio is found by following the income flow around a complete cycle and multiplying together the factors recorded in the flowchart. In our example, the respending ratio, r, is $1 \times .70 \times .80 \times .75$, or $.42$. On the first cycle, therefore, the initial $1 billion rise in demand ultimately induces additional consumer spending of $.42 billion and brings the total rise in GNP to $1.42. Of course the process does not end there, because the $.42 billion sales of new consumer goods starts a second cycle. To produce the consumer goods, business firms must pay workers and investors $.70 \times .42$, or $.296 billion in taxable income, which will add $.8 \times \$.296$, or $.235 billion to disposable income. When the new income receivers spend the usual 75 percent, induced consumption rises by another $.75 \times \$.235$, or $.176 billion.

Here again we see the respending ratio. The $.42 billion of induced consumer spending results in a further rise of $.42 \times \$.42$, or $.176 billion in spending. Moreover, the process continues as the additional $.176 billion initiates still another cycle that ends with the contribution of still another $.42 \times \$.176$, or $.074 billion to consumer spending, and so on.

The multiplier, m, measuring the total influence of the initial autonomous rise in consumer buying is represented by the sum of an infinite series of such respending cycles:

$$m = \$1 + \$.42 + \$.176 + \$.074 + \ldots$$

The ratio of each term in the series to its predecessor is the respending ratio $.42$. In general, designating the respending ratio by r, the multiplier is approximated by the sum of an infinite geometric series:

$$m = 1 + r + r^2 + r^3 + r^4 + \ldots$$

The sum of such a series is given by the usual algebraic formula $m = 1/(1 - r)$.

Applying this formula to the calculated respending ratio $r = .42$, the multiplier is estimated as $m = 1/(1 - .42) = 1/.58$, or 1.7, approximately. By the time all of its ramifications have worked their way through the economy, the initial autonomous rise of $1 billion in spending will have resulted in a total rise in gross national product equal to $1.7 \times \$1$ billion, or $1.7 billion. The first $1 billion of this increase is the initial autonomous rise in buying, the remaining $.7 billion consists of additional consumer buying induced by the successive respending cycles.

The Relationship of Consumption to Other Components of Demand   In our example, the multiplier gave the total increase in GNP to be expected in response to an initial autonomous rise in household consumption expenditure. However, it applies equally to an initial rise in expenditure for business investment, government service, or anything else. When the rate of business investment in new plant and equipment rises by $1 billion, it starts a similar income-spending chain. Production of $1 billion of new equipment results in $700 million of additional taxable income. The $560 million remaining after taxes induces $420 million of consumer spending, hence more production, more income, more spending, and so on. When the initial $1 billion increase in annual investment expenditure has percolated through the nation, annual GNP will have risen by $1.7 billion. Of this, $1 billion is the initial increase in investment; the remaining $700 million is induced consumption expenditure.

The Multiplier in Action

The multiplier can be seen in operation by comparing the change in gross national product from one year to the next. Government spending, business investment, residential construction, and net exports should all be considered. To these we must add any increase in transfer payments and enough to allow for the trend in consumer outlays. When the multiplier is applied to this total, the resulting estimated rise in GNP can be compared with that actually observed. For example from 1965 to 1966 autonomous government spending, business investment, residential construction, and net exports grew by a total of $31.4 billion. To this should be added $3.9 billion for the consumption trend, and the $4.6 billion rise in social security and other government transfers to persons. The total $39.9 billion initial increase then implies a rise in gross national product of 1.7 × $39.9, or about $67.6 billion. This figure is only slightly larger than the observed increase of $65.0 billion.

THE MULTIPLIER AND ECONOMIC STABILITY

It follows from the formula that the larger the respending ratio, the greater the multiplier becomes. In an economy in which the respending ratio is only .25, the multiplier would be $1/(1-.25)$, or 1.33. If the respending ratio were 0.9, the multiplier would be 10. Moreover, as the respending ratio approaches 1, the multiplier grows larger without limit. This follows directly from the nature of the respending cycles. If every dollar of expenditure meant another dollar of production, if every dollar of production meant another dollar of disposable income, and if people spent every extra dollar of disposable income for consumer goods, then each successive cycle would increase consumer spending just as much as the preceding one, and the total influence of any autonomous increase in demand would be multiplied without limit.

The multiplier is a key value in understanding the problems of unemployment and inflation, and the governmental policies

intended to promote economic stability. The larger the multiplier, the more sensitive the economic system becomes to the impact of autonomous changes. If multipliers are large, a small initial change in spending in any one part of the economy will have greatly multiplied effects on all parts. A small decline in demand, for example, may set off a chain reaction that—unless somehow offset—will precipitate widespread unemployment, while a relatively small increase in buying may be multiplied into an aggregate demand exceeding the capacity of the economic system and result in rapidly rising prices.

An economic system with a low multiplier, on the other hand, tends to be relatively insensitive to autonomous changes in spending. This is fine as long as the economy is prosperous. When unemployment is low, it is likely to remain low, even in the face of a substantial initial reduction in demand. By the same token, however, when unemployment is high, it tends to remain high, despite substantial initial increases in demand.

As we will see in Chapter 14, the size of the multiplier has important implications for the size and timing of governmental policies. In a low-multiplier economy, policies designed to correct unemployment or to hold down price increases require massive changes in taxation and government spending. In an economy in which a high multiplier magnifies a small policy change into a large overall effect on demand and employment, the government must proceed much more carefully to avoid pushing the system too far in the desired direction. In this respect an economic system is something like an automobile. If the multiplier is too low, the economic "steering wheel" is hard to turn, and it is difficult to steer at all. If the multiplier is too high, the economic system responds quickly to the slightest touch and there is constant danger of oversteering. Ideally the multiplier should be somewhere between these extremes.

Before we can thoroughly evaluate the policy implications of the multiplier for the U.S. economy, however, we must look more closely at demands for other types of goods. The simple multiplier developed in this chapter is subject to a serious defect in that some of the spending we have considered autonomous is really induced by changes in income and output. Net exports, for example, depend on imports,which rise and fall with sales and production. Inventory accumulation is induced when firms respond to rising sales by increasing output more than enough to replace the goods sold in order to increase the volume of inventory stocks on hand. We will examine the nature of these induced relationships in the next chapter.

SUMMARY

Personal consumption expenditure, which makes up about two-thirds of the gross national product, depends on disposable personal income. Although spending varies widely from family to family, when large numbers are considered there is a close relationship between income bracket and average consumption expenditures. The *average propensity to consume* is the percentage of income that families in any given income bracket tend to spend on consumption items. The *marginal propensity to consume* is the fraction of any *increase* in income that families tend to spend for *additional* purchases of consumer goods as income rises.

Since poor families have many unmet needs, they tend to spend almost all of any increase in income on additional consumption, giving them a high marginal propensity to consume. Rich families that have satisfied most of their consumption needs devote more of any further increase in income to savings accounts, insurance, or business investment, giving them a low marginal propensity to consume. Taking the community as a whole, however, the marginal propensity to consume can be estimated at .75. That is, an increase in aggregate disposable personal income of $1 billion tends to be accompanied by an increase of about $.75 billion in outlays on consumer goods.

Of course, income is not the only influence on consumer spending. Household consumption outlays also depend on the age and composition of the population, and are affected by such factors as consumer expectations and attitudes. An important manifestation of these other influences is the annual *trend* of consumer spending, representing the tendency of households to increase outlays for consumption goods by about .9 of 1 percent annually, independently of income.

The distinction between the influences of income and other factors is maintained by separating each observed change in consumption expenditure into 2 components: an *autonomous change*, represented by a shift in the average propensity to consume at a given level of income, and an *induced change*, produced by a rise or fall in disposable income. Although analytically separate, autonomous and induced changes in spending are actually interdependent, because autonomous increases or decreases in spending produce corresponding changes in income, and hence in induced expenditure. The cycles of spending-production-income-responding can be represented in terms of a flowchart of the economy that permits the calculation of a *multiplier* to measure the total effect on GNP of any given initial autonomous change in spending. The multiplier is calculated from the *respending ratio* whose magnitude depends on the structure of income and on the marginal propensity to consume. The larger the respending ratio, the greater the change in consumption expenditure induced by an initial autonomous change in outlay, and the higher the multiplier.

The multiplier is related to economic stability. An economy with a low multiplier tends to be stable. It provides minimum leverage to antonomous changes that might alter GNP. By the same token, however, it also provides minimum leverage to policies designed to raise the economy out of a depression or to cool off an inflation. An economic system with a high multiplier is very sensitive to changes in conditions, and is therefore more vulnerable both to autonomous changes and to shifts in economic policy. The policy implications of the multiplier will be more thoroughly examined after the concept has been broadened to include the behavior of other types of expenditures.

CHAPTER 10

Investment Expenditure and the Accelerator

Gross investment consists of the total amount spent on construction of new dwellings, on the purchase of new plant and equipment, on the value of goods added to business inventory, and on net exports. Combined expenditure for residential construction, plant and equipment, and inventory is the total amount privately invested in the domestic economy and constitutes *gross private domestic investment*, while the excess of exports over imports constitutes American financing of *net foreign investment*. Although gross investment normally amounts to only about a quarter of what is spent on consumption, it is subject to greater year-to-year fluctuations and therefore constitutes an important source of economic instability.

In this chapter we will examine the behavior of each type of investment spending in turn. We will consider the influences that affect decisions to invest in each type of investment and how different types of investment spending are related to each other and to other types of expenditures.

RESIDENTIAL CONSTRUCTION

Investment in residential construction embraces expenditures for all types of dwellings, including individual houses, apartment buildings, and other multifamily structures. The basic determinant of the demand for new housing is population growth. During the past 15 years an average of 2,800,000 people were added to the U.S. population each year. To house this population and to replace old dwellings razed or destroyed, 1,400,000 new dwelling units were built annually, costing from $19 to $25 billion each year.

The Influence of Income on Residential Construction

Of course, population growth is not the only element underlying this demand. A family's decision to seek better housing depends partly on its income. Poor families find it necessary to crowd themselves into fewer rooms and must often settle for substandard accommodations. As family income rises, so do the family's housing requirements. More rooms are needed to provide separate bedrooms for each member of the family. Guest rooms, playrooms, and extra bathrooms are added. The style and construction of the house becomes expensive, and it is more likely to be accompanied by a multicar garage, patio, or swimming pool.

Unlike spending for immediate household consumption, however, housing demand responds only slowly to rising income. The purchase of a home involves a long-run commitment, not to be undertaken hurriedly. Families with rising incomes begin to feel dissatisfaction with their old housing, but it may take several years before dissatisfaction gives rise to action. For one thing, it takes time to overcome human inertia. For another, families must be sure that their new income status is permanent before they commit themselves to 15 or 20 years of mortgage repayment. The decline of incomes during the Great Depression of the 1930s held housing demand below the rate of population growth. Curtailment of construction during World War II added further to the housing deficit. The resulting backlog created a need and contributed to the high level of home-building immediately following the end of the war.

The Influence of Interest Rates on Residential Construction

Since the cost of a new house is 3 to 4 times the average family income, few families can afford to pay cash when they buy. It would take so long to save the necessary money that the family would get only a few years of service from the home once they had bought it. For this reason, most homes are partly financed by money borrowed on a mortgage. This enables the family to have the use of the house while it repays the debt.

Of course, in addition to repaying the principal of the loan, the family must pay interest on the outstanding balance as compensation to the lender for the use of his money. When credit is plentiful and interest rates are low, families who want new homes can borrow easily, but when credit is tight, high interest rates put home-buying out of the reach of some families. The general responsiveness of residential construction to variations in interest rates is clearly seen when the number of houses built each year is compared with the prevailing interest rate. The blue line in Figure 1 represents the number of housing units started, while the black line represents the cost of borrowing, measured by the interest rates on 3-month treasury bills. The effect of variations in credit conditions on the housing market is seen in the general tendency for

FIGURE 1   INTEREST RATES AND HOME
            BUILDING, 1950-1968

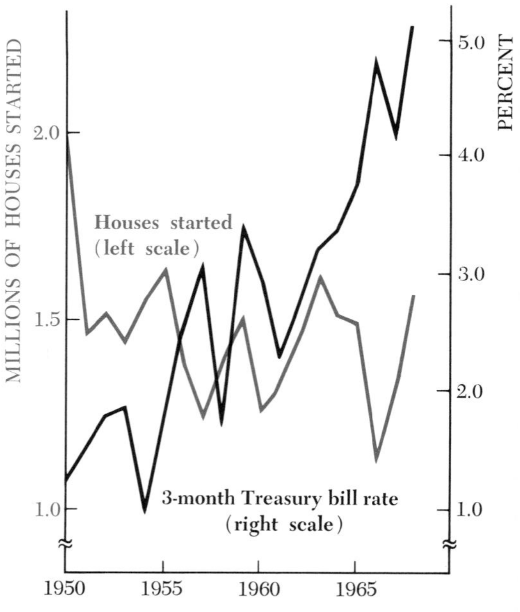

SOURCE: Data from the *Economic Report of the President, 1969.*

the 2 lines to move in opposite directions. Rising interest rates in the early 1950s reduced the number of dwelling units built from nearly 2 million during 1950 to hardly more than 1 million in 1960, although housing construction spurted somewhat when interest rates declined during the recession of 1954 and again during the recession of 1958. Construction reached another peak in 1963, but declined abruptly as interest rates rose thereafter.

The sensitivity of residential construction to interest rates has 2 important consequences. In the first place, home-buyers must compete for loanable funds with industrial and commercial borrowers. As a result, when business firms are trying to borrow money to buy new machinery and equipment, interest rates tend to rise. Since business firms investing in new plant and equipment are less sensitive to interest costs than builders and home-buyers, business is willing to borrow at rates that are too high for many buyers. As a result, rising business borrowing for new plant and equipment tends to be partly offset by a reduction in outlays for residential construction. When business investment declines, the reverse is true. As interest rates fall, builders and home-buyers come back into the market and their expenditures partly offset the reduction in business investment. The interest rate, in other words, helps to stabilize total demand in the face of variations in business expenditures for new plant and equipment (see Figure 2).

As we shall see later, however, the total amount of money available to lend is subject to control. When lending power is expanded, interest rates fall and residential construction is encouraged. When lending power is curtailed, interest rates rise and prospective home-builders are unable to borrow. Since residential construction produces the same multiplied effect on total output as any other autonomous rise in spending, the housing market is one of the most important points at which monetary

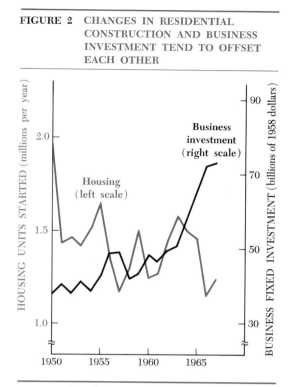

FIGURE 2 CHANGES IN RESIDENTIAL CONSTRUCTION AND BUSINESS INVESTMENT TEND TO OFFSET EACH OTHER

SOURCE: Plotted from data in the *Economic Report of the President, 1969.*

policy affects the level of aggregate demand and production.

INVESTMENT IN NEW PLANT AND EQUIPMENT

Additions to plant and equipment consist of machinery, tools, and other equipment together with the construction of industrial buildings and other permanent structures. In a private enterprise economy like ours, business firms invest in plant and equipment because they expect to make profits from the subsequent output, and the decision to acquire new facilities is reached after firms have carefully balanced the prospective gain from the use of the equipment against its cost.

Operating Rate and Investment

One of the most important factors determining the profitability of new investment in a business is the demand for the products of the firm compared to the productive capacity already available. When sales are slow and firms have equipment standing idle, it is clearly unprofitable to buy more. Indeed, a firm with enough idle machinery need not even replace machines that wear out. On the other hand, a firm whose sales are outstripping its ability to turn out goods will find new facilities a highly profitable investment. The utilization of existing equipment is usually expressed as the *operating rate,* the ratio of output to productive capacity. An operating rate of 70 percent means that the plant is turning out only 70 percent as much output as it could.

Productive capacity is defined as the amount of production a plant can turn out when it is operating most economically. That is, it is the rate of production at which the average cost per unit of product is lowest. The output of a plant is rarely confined to a rigidly fixed physical limit. When necessary, most plants can be pushed to operating rates over 100 percent by overloading equipment, working overtime, or bringing obsolete stand-by machinery into use, but the high cost of the overload can be tolerated only during temporary spurts in demand. When sales pull permanently ahead of existing capacity it is profitable for a firm to invest in additional productive capacity in order to hold costs down.

In large corporations the first step in buying new capital equipment occurs when the board of directors appropriates the necessary funds. Figure 3 shows clearly how the decisions of directors are influenced by operating rates. The black line represents the average operating rate of manufacturing firms. The blue line represents the funds appropriated each quarter to acquire new plant and equipment. The general correspondence between the major movements

FIGURE 3   RELATIONSHIP OF CAPITAL APPROPRIATIONS TO OPERATING RATES

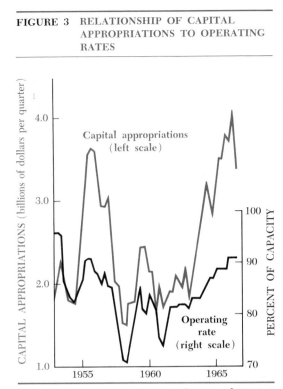

SOURCE: Average operating rate for manufacturing from *Federal Reserve Bulletin,* no. 52, November, 1966, p. 1615. Appropriations from *Investment Statistics: Quarterly Survey of Capital Appropriations* (sponsored by *Newsweek*), *Historical Statistics, 1953–1964,* National Industrial Conference Board, New York, 1967. Later data from later issues. In plotting, capital appropriations were divided by the index of manufacturing capacity to adjust for trend.

of the 2 series reflects the rise and fall of capital appropriations with operating rates.

Time Lags in Investment Outlays

The way a board of directors responds to rising sales is another example of how spending by one group of people influences spending by others, but there is an important difference between the response of a firm to higher sales and the response of a family to higher income. In the first place, a firm's investment spending responds only slowly to its need for new facilities. Before a new plant can be built, plans and specifications must be drawn up, alternative sites examined, and land acquired. Once construction has begun it may take months to complete. Machinery must be ordered before it can be delivered, and so on, adding up to a substantial delay between the time that the need for additional capacity is first recognized and the actual outlay of money on construction and equipment.

The lag between the time money is appropriated and the time it is actually spent for new construction and equipment can be seen in Figure 4. The black line, representing expenditure, lags anywhere from 2 to 6 quarters behind the appropriation of funds shown by the blue line. The lag is especially noticeable when we look at the peaks and troughs of the 2 series. Careful analysis has shown that expenditures on investment projects typically extend over 2 or more years after the funds have been formally appropriated.[1]

The Investment Accelerator

There is an even more important difference between the way a firm responds to higher sales and the way a family spends its income. When family income rises, so does family spending. Moreover, families maintain their higher level of spending as long as they continue to receive the income. When sales rise, on the other hand, although a firm's need for additional capacity induces it to purchase machinery and equipment, once capacity has been expanded sufficiently to supply the new demand, investment spending naturally falls back to the level required merely to replace equipment as it wears out. In other words, a rise in sales tends to be followed by a short spurt of investment activity. The spurt begins after firms have decided that the new level of sales is going to last long enough to justify investment in capacity, and ends when capacity has reached the desired level. The point is illustrated in Table 1. The hypothetical data represent the operations of a manufacturing firm. Column 1 shows the sales and output each year. Column 2 gives the number of machines available for operation. The most economical operating rate is assumed to be 10,000 units per year; operating beyond this rate involves overtime pay and other additional expenses that raise the average cost per

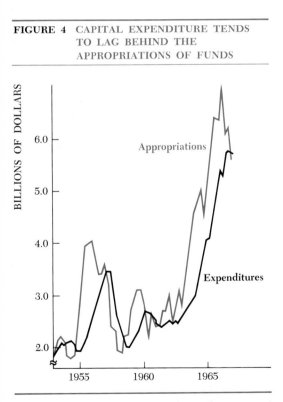

FIGURE 4 CAPITAL EXPENDITURE TENDS TO LAG BEHIND THE APPROPRIATIONS OF FUNDS

SOURCE: *Investment Statistics: Quarterly Survey of Capital Appropriations* (sponsored by *Newsweek*), *Historical Statistics, 1953–1964*, New York, National Industrial Conference Board, 1967. Later data from subsequent issues.

[1] See, for example, the excellent study by Shirley Almon, "The Distributed Lag Between Capital Appropriations and Expenditures," *Econometrica*, no. 33, January, 1965, pp. 178–196.

TABLE 1	RESPONSE OF INVESTMENT TO AN INCREASE IN SALES			
	(1)	(2)	(3)	(4) NEW MACHINES BOUGHT
		NUMBER OF MACHINES		
		IN OPERA-		(INCLUDING REPLACE-
YEAR	ANNUAL SALES	TION	NEEDED	MENTS)
1963	1,000,000	10	10	1
1964	1,300,000	10	13	1
1965	1,300,000	13	13	4
1966	1,300,000	13	13	1

unit. The number of machines the firm "needs," shown in Column 3, is the number required to meet its yearly sales at minimum cost. The difference between the number of machines needed and the number available represents an equipment deficiency that is made up by the subsequent purchase of new machines, Column 4.

According to the table, the firm was operating at capacity in 1963. The 10 machines in operation were just the number required for most economical production, the 1 new machine bought was a replacement for 1 wearing out. In 1964, when the firm's sales rose to 1,300,000, production increased correspondingly, but costs rose. Ideally, the firm needed 13 machines to operate at this level of output, but, presumably because the management was not sure whether the higher sales rate would continue, it postponed the decision to expand and bought only the normal replacement. When the new high sales rate persisted into 1965, however, the firm decided to expand, and bought 4 machines to raise capacity to match its sales. High sales continued in 1966, but since the expansion program was completed, purchase of machines dropped back to the replacement level.

Accelerators as Relationships Between Stocks and Flows of Goods Because of the short duration of spurts of investment spending, the relationship of investment outlays to changes in sales is known as an *accelerator* to distinguish it from a multiplier. The distinction between accelerators and multipliers is most easily understood in terms of the difference between *stocks* of goods and *flows* of goods. Production consists of a *flow* of goods. Raw materials enter the process at one end, move down the production line and are shipped out at the other end. Consumption is another flow. Goods move from store to household and are worn out and used up.

A flow of goods always has a *time dimension*. A firm produces 1,000 tons of steel *per week,* an oil well yields 100 barrels of oil *per day,* or the GNP is $900 billion *per year.* As a matter of fact, unless the time dimension is clearly understood, flow magnitudes are meaningless. For example, the attractiveness of a job "paying $3,000" surely depends on whether the flow of income is $3,000 per year or $3,000 per week!

Capital equipment, on the other hand, consists of *stocks* of goods. The buildings, machinery, and other equipment stay in place, so to speak, as the production of goods flows through them. Stocks have no time dimension. A firm operates 15 blast furnaces or has a fleet of 50 trucks or owns 100,000 square feet of warehouse space. Of course, capital goods must initially be produced, and the equipment now in the stock was originally part of the flow of production. In fact, stocks represent goods saved from past flows in order to increase the future flow of output.

Multipliers involve relationships between *one flow and another.* When the flow of income to households increases, they respond by increasing the flow of consumer spending. The flow of spending remains high as long as the families continue to receive a higher flow of income. In contrast, an *accelerator* involves the relationship of a *flow* of goods on the one hand to a *stock* of goods on the other. When the flow of sales rises, it induces firms to enlarge their stocks of capital equipment. Moreover, the larger stock of equipment is maintained as long as firms continue to experience higher sales. In order to add to their stocks of capital equipment, however, firms must build factories and buy newly produced equipment, which induces a temporary increase in the flow of production. When stocks of equipment have been built up to the required level, the flow of production declines, and the spurt is over.

The Effects of Technical Change on Investment

Many changes in investment spending are unrelated to output and operating rates. As we have already seen, the discovery of new products and the invention of new ways to produce old products is an important occasion for investment expenditure. Some technical changes occur on a small scale and influence only a few producers as when a beverage manufacturer switches from bottles to cans, replacing bottling machinery with new canning equipment. As another example, the adoption of a new oxygen steel process requires extensive investment in steel furnaces of the new type, but little else.

Many discoveries, however, generate investment demand on a massive scale. The invention of a practical electric light and electric motor resulted in a vast, prolonged flood of investment involving the construction of power lines, generating stations, and facilities to manufacture electrical equipment, and the virtual replacement of steam power by electrical machinery. The automobile was responsible not only for investment in automobile factories, but also for the construction of our modern network of roads, streets, and expressways, together with oil-drilling equipment, pipelines, refineries, and a filling station on every corner, not to mention motels, parking facilities, and drive-in movies. Similar stories can be

told about the investment impact of the airplane, radio, television, and many other inventions. The long-run investment implications of modern electronics, particularly as they apply to automation and the application of computer technology, are only beginning to appear.

Interest Rates and the Marginal Efficiency of Investment

Investments require large expenditures, and unless the money is available even the most promising venture dies in the planning stage. Investment funds are usually available, of course, but only at a price, and an investment project that would be profitable when money is plentiful at low interest rates may be postponed or abandoned as unprofitable when interest rates rise.

For every investment project there is a highest interest rate that a firm can afford to pay without making the project too unprofitable to undertake. This highest interest rate is the *marginal efficiency of investment* in the project. To say that the marginal efficiency of investment in a new rolling mill is 7 percent means that the owners of the firm would be eager to build the mill if they could raise the necessary funds at 4 or 5 percent, or at any interest rate up to and including 7 percent per year. But if they must pay more than 7 percent interest for the use of the funds, they will postpone the project until interest rates decline, or until improved business conditions increase the profitability of the mill and raise the marginal efficiency of investment in it.

At any given time, business firms have a variety of projects under consideration, with a wide range of marginal efficiencies. When interest rates are high, only the projects with the highest marginal efficiency of investment are undertaken, and annual business spending for new plant and equipment is correspondingly small. Lower interest rates, however, make more projects profitable, and investment spending is correspondingly greater. The relationship between investment spending and the marginal efficiency of investment is shown in Figure 5. We can imagine the combined cost of all prospective investment projects lined up in order of profitabilty along the horizontal axis, with projects becoming less profitable as we proceed to the right. The interest rate is measured vertically, and the marginal efficiency of investment corresponding to each investment project is represented by the height of the solid curve MEI. The curve is highest near the origin where the most profitable projects are located and declines toward the right in keeping with the declining marginal efficiency of investment in less profitable projects. Now, if the interest rate were at the level marked r_0, business firms would find it profitable to invest in all projects whose marginal efficiency of investment was no lower than r_0. As the figure shows, these projects would involve a total outlay of I_0 dollars per year. Investment in excess of I_0 would involve projects whose marginal

efficiency of investment was lower than the interest rate, and would not be undertaken. However, given the same marginal efficiency of investment curve together with a lower rate of interest like r_1, total investment spending could expand to I_1 dollars per year as firms undertook additional projects that would have been unprofitable at the higher interest rate.

The level of curve MEI depends on the sales outlook, on the rate at which new products and processes are appearing, and on similar factors that affect the profitability of investment projects. The dashed curve represents what happens when sales outlook improves or when a new discovery comes along to make investment more profitable. The greater prospective return from investment projects is represented by the upward shift of the marginal efficiency of investment curve to MEI'. Given this higher marginal efficiency of investment, business firms would tend to invest I'_0 at the interest rate r_0, and I'_1 at the lower r_1. Figure 5 has been considerably exaggerated to illustrate the principle, and in actual fact the response of business firms to differences in interest rates is much less marked than the curves suggest. Nevertheless, as we shall see when we discuss monetary policy and interest rates in Chapter 14, the marginal efficiency of investment plays a key role in monetary and banking policy.

FIGURE 5   THE RELATIONSHIP OF
             INVESTMENT SPENDING TO
             THE MARGINAL EFFICIENCY OF
             INVESTMENT AND THE
             INTEREST RATE

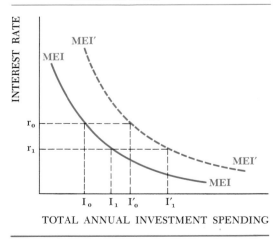

TOTAL ANNUAL INVESTMENT SPENDING

INVENTORY ACCUMULATION

In addition to their fixed plant and equipment, producers must keep certain stocks of goods on hand. Firms typically have stockpiles of fuel, raw materials, and supplies waiting to enter the production process, stocks of semifinished goods being worked on, and stocks of finished goods in warehouses and on retailers' shelves awaiting final sale. Producers maintain these stockpiles for several reasons. First, since most raw materials are delivered periodically, enough must be ordered to last from one delivery to the next. Even if production processes used raw material at a uniform rate so that the last bit was consumed just as the new shipment was received, plants would have an average inventory equal to half a shipment. For example, if 5 tons were delivered every Monday, a plant that used 1 ton per day would have an inventory of 5 tons on Monday morning, 4 on Tuesday, 3 on Wednesday, and so on, ending up Friday night with no stock at all. Taking the week as a whole, the firm would carry an average inventory of 3.5 tons.

Second, production is not generally a smooth or even a closely predictable process. Output varies from day to day, and plants must carry enough raw-material inventory to cover emergency needs when they arise. This means that inventory is drawn down to 0 only under exceptional circumstances; firms usually expect to have a comfortable margin of stock left when the new shipment arrives.

Firms keep stocks of finished goods for similar reasons. Even if the production processes were continuous and uniform, sales and deliveries are not, and firms must have finished goods available for sale when customers come in. Furthermore, many products are made in batches. When this is the case, the plant is set up for a particular type, size, or style and enough is run off to last for a reasonable period. The plant is then shifted over to the next type, and so on. The finished goods are held in inventory until sold. Again, since sales are variable and uncertain, firms are likely to keep minimum levels of finished inventory high enough to enable them to meet an unexpected spurt in demand.

The inventory of goods in process is the result of the physical fact that production takes time. In cases in which raw materials are almost instantly converted into finished goods, as in the generation of electricity, for example, there are no goods in process. In most instances, however, materials pass down assembly lines or stand around being finished. The value of product tied up in this way is the inventory of goods in process.

Inventories as Capital

Although individual items move into and out of inventory at a rapid rate, the total volume of inventory is maintained, and is as much a part of the capital of a firm as its buildings and machinery. Firms can no more produce and sell without inventory than they can without equipment. Additions to the total stockpile of goods represent investment spending just as additions to the "stockpile" of machinery do. Similarly, selling goods out of inventory to reduce the total stock represents a reduction of productive capacity just as allowing machines to wear out without replacement does.

Inventories and Production Rate

Business firms tend to keep their inventory stocks at levels proportional to their output and sales. Stocks of goods in process vary almost automatically with output. Every production line is full of materials moving through it, and the more lines are in operation, the more goods are in process at any given time. Although the connection is less mechanical, stocks of both raw materials and finished goods likewise tend to vary with production and sales. To keep firms supplied with materials between delivery dates, deliveries must be proportionally larger and the average inventory on hand during the week proportionally higher. To supply a larger demand between runs, output batches must be larger, and so on.

Of course, stocks do not depend exclusively on sales and output. In the first place, manufacturing production schedules and retail buying are keyed to expected future sales, rather than to current experience. If the expected sales fail to materialize, firms are caught with inventories that are out of line. When sales turn down, for example, firms that have based their holdings of finished goods on optimism are suddenly overstocked. When sales rise unexpectedly, inventories are too low, and firms scramble to place orders and shorten production schedules to bring stocks up to normal.

In the second place, there is a certain amount of flexibility in the inventory-sales ratio. To the extent that it is obtained by faster operations rather than by more production lines operating at a given rate, output can be increased without a correspondingly larger volume of goods in process. Likewise, when increased flows of raw materials are met by more frequent, rather than larger, deliveries, the average stock of raw materials is kept down. Stocks of finished goods are kept down when smaller batches are produced more often, and so on. Finally, as we shall see, businessmen occasionally alter their inventory holdings for speculative or other reasons unconnected with sales and production.

The recent history of the ratio of total inventory held by U.S. firms to annual aggregate final sales is shown in Figure 6. Inventories were kept between 18.1 percent and 17.0 percent of annual sales, with the average for the period shown about 17.4 percent.

Inventory Investment as an Accelerator

Firms with steady sales sooner or later build their inventory up to the required size, making further inventory buying unnecessary. This means that induced inventory investment, like the acquisition of plant and equipment, is an accelerator rather than a multiplier phenomenon. Inventory buying holds up only as long as sales keep

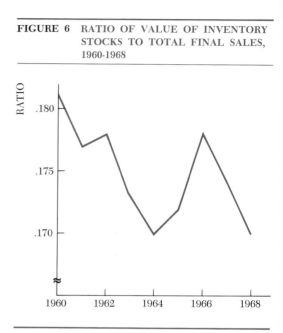

FIGURE 6   RATIO OF VALUE OF INVENTORY STOCKS TO TOTAL FINAL SALES, 1960-1968

SOURCE: Total value of inventory stock was divided by GNP less inventory investment plus imports. All data from *Economic Report of the President, 1969.*

rising. When sales stop rising and level off, inventory accumulation stops.

The accelerator effect can be seen in operation when final sales are compared with production, as in Figure 7. The difference between gross national product and sales is inventory accumulation. Inventory is accumulated whenever GNP exceeds sales. When sales exceed GNP, inventory is reduced. The figure shows how firms accumulate inventory while sales are rising, stop accumulation when sales level off, and reduce their inventory holdings when sales are falling. Notice how inventory was reduced when sales declined in 1954 and 1958.

Cost and Inventory Investment

Holding inventory involves cost. Not only must storage space be maintained, heated, and protected, but the contents must be

FIGURE 7   THE ACCELERATION EFFECT:
FINAL SALES AND GNP

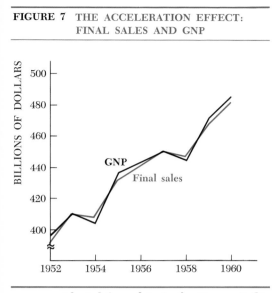

SOURCE: Adapted from data in the *Economic Report of the President, 1969.*

insured. In addition, some goods deteriorate in storage, while others may be damaged by insects and rodents. When storage costs rise, part of the value and convenience of having extra stock on hand is offset, and firms find it advisable to reduce their holdings. When storage costs decline, firms can afford the advantages of larger inventory.

An important cost of carrying inventory is the interest on the money tied up in the goods. Money invested in inventory must either be borrowed, in which case interest payments are an explicit business expense, or purchased with the firm's own funds, foregoing the interest that those funds might otherwise have earned. In either case, interest rates affect the profitabilty of inventory. Inventory investment tends to be greater when interest rates are low and to decline as interest rates rise.

The Influence of Expectations on Inventory Investment

Inventory accumulation is affected by the expected future movement of prices. A businessman who expects the price of raw materials to rise will naturally tend to buy more than he needs while prices are low. When prices are expected to come down, he is clearly advised to keep his inventory at a bare minimum and wait to rebuild it when prices are lower.

Inventories are also sometimes built up in anticipation of coming shortages of goods due to strikes and similar economic disruptions. During the 6 months or so preceding the scheduled expiration of collective bargaining agreements between the United Steel Workers and firms in the steel industry, for example, manufacturers of automobiles, cans, and other steel products usually accumulate extra steel inventory to carry them through a possible steel strike.

NET FOREIGN INVESTMENT

Net foreign investment consists of *net exports;* that is, the difference between exports sold by U.S. firms to people in other countries and imports purchased abroad by American consumers and firms.

Exports

The demand for American exports depends on income and production in other countries and on the prices of American goods compared to those of substitutes produced elsewhere. Because export demand depends so heavily on conditions outside the U.S., it can be taken as almost entirely autonomous as far as the U.S. economy is concerned, at least in the short run.

Imports

American demand for imported products, on the other hand, depends heavily on the incomes of American families. As family incomes rise, consumers eat more bananas; drink more tea, coffee, and French wine; and buy more imported sports cars, woolens, furniture, and so on. Moreover, much of the tin, nickel, copper, rubber, petroleum, and other industrial materials and components used by American firms are produced abroad, and the amounts imported automatically rise and fall with the rate of U.S. output.

The relationship of U.S. imports to the total of final purchases from American producers is shown in Figure 8. The import buying induced by rising aggregate demand is reflected in the upward slope of the line. Careful measurement of the figure reveals that Americans tend to increase their purchases from abroad about $5.3 billion for every $100 billion increase in their total purchases from U.S. firms. The points representing import buying in individual years vary around the central line, indicating that some of the variations in imports reflect such autonomous changes in demand as

changing consumer tastes, altered production techniques, and differences in prices. The fact that the points cling closely to the overall relationship, however, suggests that most of the behavior of imports is induced by changes in income and output, rather than by autonomous factors.

Imports and the Multiplier

The proportion of total spending that goes for imports and the proportion of imported materials and components required for domestic products have an important effect on the multiplier. To the extent that purchased goods and services consist of imports rather than domestic production, something less than $1 of added production can be expected from an additional dollar of spending. In the United States, $1 of expenditure involves $.053 of imports. Thus domestic business firms produce only $.947 of additional domestic output, which reduces the respending ratio and lowers the multiplier accordingly.

The U.S. economic system is so large that it meets a very large proportion of its needs by domestic production. Imports are a small part of total U.S. sales, and their effect on the multiplier is correspondingly minor. In some small nations the dependence on imported goods is so great that the multiplier is less than 1. In Greece, for example, an increase of 1 billion drachmas in business expenditure for new plant and equipment tends to raise the GNP by only .8 billion drachmas, less than the amount spent for the initial investment! The reason is that a relatively small amount of machinery and equipment is produced in Greece. Most of the initial expenditure represents equipment imported from West Germany, Britain, or the United States. Likewise, the proportion of imports and imported materials in goods bought by Greek consumers is much larger than it is in a country like the United States, making

FIGURE 8   RELATIONSHIP OF U.S. IMPORTS
TO TOTAL FINAL PURCHASES

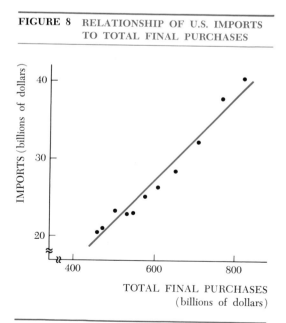

TOTAL FINAL PURCHASES
(billions of dollars)

SOURCE: Adapted from data in the *Economic Report of the President, 1969.*

the coefficient of respending smaller, and reducing the multiplier.

AUTONOMOUS AND INDUCED CHANGES IN INVESTMENT SPENDING

Like household consumption expenditure, changes in investment spending can be classed as autonomous or induced on the basis of their immediate causes. Induced changes are those that represent responses to changes in output and income that are associated with accelerator effects and with imports. Autonomous changes are those that tend to alter the volume of investment spending that occurs at a given level of output. Autonomous effects include those connected with rising and falling interest rates, changing expectations, new technology, and the like.

Induced and autonomous changes are not independent, because any autonomous variation in investment exerts a multiplier effect on total output that, in turn, operates via the accelerator to induce a further rise in investment. The induced investment contributes further to the multiplier and hence to the accelerator again, and so on in a long chain of impacts. The result is an intricate system of relationships among different types of spending that will be further developed in the next chapter.

SUMMARY

Gross investment consists of the sum of expenditures for residential construction, new plant and equipment, additions to inventory, and net exports. Although small compared to personal consumption expenditure, gross investment is subject to wider year-to-year variations and is therefore an important source of economic instability.

Residential construction is influenced in the long run by population growth and rising real income, but in the short run it is sensitive to interest rates and credit availability.

Investment in new *plant and equipment* is partly a response to technical change, but it is also induced by rising sales and production. Since time is required to construct a new plant even after the decision to build it, however, investment outlays tend to lag behind rising sales. Moreover, once the need for additional capacity has been met, further investment in plant and equipment is unnecessary. Therefore, an increase in sales tends to induce a short spurt of investment spending. Because of its special properties, the relationship between plant and equipment spending and rising sales is called an *accelerator*. Unlike multipliers, which represent relationships between one flow of goods and another, accelerators represent relationships between a stock of goods on the one hand and a flow on the other.

The *marginal efficiency of investment* in a project is the maximum interest rate at which investment in it would be profitable. Projects under consideration at any given time cover a wide range of marginal efficiencies. These can be represented by a curve of marginal efficiency of investment which indicates the importance of the interest rate as a determinant of the volume of investment spending.

Stocks of goods held in *inventory* are an important form of capital. Since business firms tend to keep the stock of inventory proportional to the flow of production and sales, changes in production tend to induce short spurts of inventory accumulation via an accelerator relationship. Inventory investment also depends on storage costs, interest rates, and business expectations.

Net foreign investment is the difference between *exports* and *imports*. The level of exports depends largely on conditions in foreign markets and on the prices and competitive position of U.S. firms. Imports are likewise sensitive to relative prices, but their volume also fluctuates with total sales and production at home. The proportion of imported goods and components in final sales has an important influence on the size of the multiplier.

Changes in investment expenditure can be separated into induced changes (associated with accelerator effects and imports) and autonomous changes (connected with interest rates, technical change, expectations, and similar factors). The systematic relationship among autonomous and induced changes in both investment spending and personal consumption will be developed in the next chapter.

CHAPTER 11

Economic Analysis and Forecasting

When any one group of people increases its spending, it induces many others to follow suit. But not all react at the same time. When demand for their products rises, business firms are quick to take advantage of increased sales potential by stepping up production. This puts income in the hands of workers, investors, and others whose families lose little time in spending it. The successive cycles of production and respending follow one another rapidly, and most of the multiplier effect of any initial rise in demand is worked out in a very short time. The acceleration effect of sales on inventory buying is also rapid. Since inventory buying requires little advance planning, firms can accumulate inventory fast enough to match rising sales and bring inventory stock into line in a short period. By the same token, however, inventory buying occurs in short-lived spurts. It tends to rise sharply when sales are increasing, but decline promptly when stocks reach the required ratio to sales.

In contrast to these rapid reactions, there is typically a long delay between the time a firm starts selling more and the time it can implement a program of capacity expansion. Moreover, once begun, investment programs often involve expenditures spread over several years before the new facilities are ready for operation. In consequence, investment spending during any given year is predominantly the result of programs initiated in response to the sales of earlier years and is rarely influenced by current sales or output. The termination of the expansion program is attended by a decline in business investment, with further downward multiplier effects, and so on.

IMPACT MULTIPLIERS

Because the different responses occur neither simultaneously nor instantaneously, the implications of a given initial change in spending depend on how long afterward the measurement is made. The ratio of the rise in GNP in the first year following the initial stimulus is the *1-year impact multiplier*. Impact multipliers can be defined to match the first quarter, the first year, or any other time period, but the 1-year impact multiplier is the easiest to estimate and the most useful to apply. Therefore, we shall restrict our attention to the 1-year period, and in what follows whenever we refer to "the" impact multiplier, it is the 1-year multiplier that is meant.

The impact multiplier is neither a pure multiplier nor a pure accelerator, but involves the *combined* effects of multiplier and accelerator acting together during the first year following an initial change in autonomous spending. Impact multipliers do not measure the full, long-run effects of initial changes, but they are practical and effective tools for analyzing the year-to-year behavior of the economic system.

Measuring the Impact Multiplier

The calculation of the impact multiplier is shown in Figure 1. At the top of the figure are recorded autonomous changes in spending for consumer goods by households; for new plant, equipment, and inventory by businesses; in the construction of residential dwellings; in the export of U.S. products abroad, and in the purchases of goods and services by governments. At any given time some of these expenditures are rising while others are declining. The net stimulus to demand is the net effect of all changes taken together.

The impact of this net stimulus is easily calculated by following it step by step around the flowchart. Since each additional dollar of demand entails $.053 of imported goods and raw materials, domestic production need rise by only $.947 to supply $1 of final sales. If, however, firms are to keep inventory up to the normal level of 17.4

percent of sales, they must increase production another $.174 for each dollar rise in annual sales. When this is included, firms must raise total output by $.947 + .174, or $1.121 for each dollar of additional demand.

Each dollar of additional production requires the services of workers, investors, and others who, by the time business taxes and depreciation are taken into account, receive about $.70 of taxable income on which they must pay 20 percent in taxes. The normal response of families is to spend 75 cents out of each $1 of any increase in disposable income, and their purchase of consumer goods represents additional induced consumption spending. Each dollar of induced consumer spending involves $.053 more imports, $.174 more inventory accumulation, and hence a further $1.121 rise in gross national product. The increased production marks the start of a second production-income-spending cycle to be followed by a third, and so on.

To calculate the respending ratio, begin with GNP and follow the cycle around to GNP again. When GNP rises by $1, taxable income rises by $.70, and disposable income grows by .80 × $.70, or $.560. This induces additional consumer spending of .75 × $.560, or $.42. Taking account of both imports and inventory accumulation, we find the induced consumer sales require additional production equal to 1.121 × $.42, or $.471. This is the respending ratio. Once production begins to rise, it sets in motion a series of respending cycles, each contributing a further addition to gross national product equal to .471 of the preceding one.

The impact multiplier is now readily calculated. A $1 stimulus causes GNP to rise by $1.121 and initiates a series of respending cycles. The first cycle contributes an additional .471 × $1.121, or $.528, the second cycle adds another .471 × $.528, or $.249, while the third contributes .471 × $.249, or $.117, and so on. Since most of these cycles occur within the year, the impact multiplier, *m*, is approximately the sum of the infinite geometric series

FIGURE 1   FLOWCHART FOR MEASURING THE IMPACT MULTIPLIER

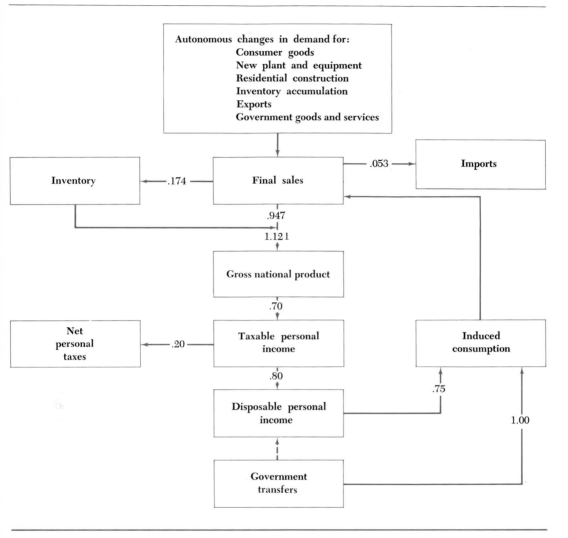

$m = 1.121 + 1.121(.471) + 1.141(.471^2) +$
$\quad 1.121(.471^3) + \ldots$
$\quad = 1.121(1 + .471 + .471^2 + .471^3 + \ldots)$
$\quad = 1.121(1/(1 - .471))$, or approximately
$\quad 2$

In other words, after all the ramifications have been worked out during the year, an initial increase of $1 in autonomous spending contributes about $2 to the annual increase in gross national product.

Simple Applications of the
Impact Multiplier

The impact multiplier is a simple but powerful tool of economic analysis, by which we can predict the change in total GNP to be expected during the year in response to any specified initial stimulus to autonomous spending. For example, an initial $3 billion rise in expenditure for residential construction touches off a series of respending cycles that tend to add 2 × $3 billion, or $6 billion to the GNP for the year. Of this increase, $3 billion would be the value of the new houses built, the remainder would consist of slightly more than $3 billion worth of goods sold to consumers and piled up in inventory, less a small increase in imports. As another example, if consumers decide that they like the new models and autonomously increase new car buying by $1.5 billion, the impact would tend to raise the total GNP by $3 billion.

The impact multiplier also works in reverse. A $2 billion reduction in business spending for new plant and equipment would represent an initial stimulus of −$2 billion. The negative stimulus would set in motion a series of successive reductions in spending that would tend to change the level of total GNP by 2 × −$2, or −$4 billion. Of this reduction, $2 billion would represent the cut in investment spending, while the remainder would represent reduced consumer spending by households whose incomes had fallen and reduction of inventory stocks by business firms whose sales had declined.

The impact multiplier can also be used to estimate the effect on total GNP of changes in the size of social security pensions, tax laws, or similar government policies. To do this, we must first estimate the initial stimulus to be expected from the policy change and then apply the impact multiplier. For example, when the social security law is altered to increase annual pensions to the aged by $2 billion, what impact will this tend to have on GNP? Since higher pensions have no effect on production until the recipients spend them, the first question is how much initial spending to expect when the aged receive their increase. Although this is impossible to answer exactly, a good approximation is to suppose that they will spend the entire increase. After all, most of the retired aged are in low-income brackets and have a high

propensity to consume; moreover, since they are already retired, they have little motivation to save for the future. On this basis, we can assume that the stimulus would initiate a series of respending cycles, the impact of which would be 2 × $1.5, or $3 billion.

HISTORICAL ANALYSIS WITH THE IMPACT MULTIPLIER

Obviously, the same technique can be employed to estimate the combined effect of any number of initial autonomous changes in spending. The individual changes are added together (with due regard to their signs), and their sum represents the resulting net stimulus to the economy. When this net stimulus is multiplied by the impact multiplier, the result is the estimated impact on GNP.

Autonomous Cause or Induced Result?

In applying this technique to historical data, care must be taken to distinguish the past changes in spending that *cause* changes in output and income from those that *result* from changes in output and income. Most year-to-year variations in household outlays for consumer goods are the induced results of changes in disposable personal income that were initiated by an autonomous change in some other type of spending. These induced changes were already included in our calculation of the multiplier, and to treat them as independent initial stimuli would count them twice.

For example, suppose that a $4 billion rise in government outlay were the only true initial autonomous rise in spending over the preceding year. It would result in a 2 × $4 billion growth in GNP, of which $4 billion would be the government outlay and the other $4 billion induced consumer spending. Now suppose that when we looked back historically, we mistakenly thought that the rise in consumer spending was an initial autonomous increase additional to the growth in government outlay. If we were to apply the impact multiplier to the rise in the 2 items combined, we would calculate an estimated rise in GNP equal to 2 × $8, or $16 billion, greatly in excess of the observed increase.

Identifiable and Unidentifiable Causes of Change

As we shall see in what follows, it is relatively easy to avoid including induced spending among the causes of economic change. However, there is an unavoidable problem: Not all sources of true initial autonomous changes in outlays can be recognized, even in retrospect. If we could always identify every individual autonomous change in spending as it occurred, we could account accurately for the variation observed in GNP each year. The sum of all the individual initial changes would be the true net economic stimulus and would multiply into the change in GNP actually experienced.

In practice, unfortunately, information about individual initial changes in spending is necessarily incomplete. For example, we have estimated that consumers increase their outlays by a trend value of .9 percent per year. Among other things, this increase in spending is due to population growth and to the appearance of new products on the market. The trend was estimated as the annual average increase over a decade, but population growth is not constant, and the rate of appearance of new products varies from year to year. As a result, during any year in which population growth is unusual, or in which an unusual number of

new products appears, consumers will increase their spending by more or less than the .9 percent trend. When the behavior of consumer spending was examined in Chapter 9, it was found that during years of nearly identical increases in disposable personal income, consumer outlays deviated widely from the magnitudes predicted by the marginal propensity to consume. These deviations can involve as much as $4 billion in consumer spending from unidentified causes.

There are many other examples of unidentifiable causes of initial changes in expenditures. Inventory buying often departs considerably from the expected amount, and observed movements in imports are often at variance with the amounts calculated on the basis of their characteristic relationship to domestic production. Such matters are not, of course, completely obscure. When easier credit permits lower down payments and allows installment buyers a longer time to pay for new cars or television sets, consumer buying tends to pick up independently of income. When imported products become cheaper, Americans are likely to react by buying more goods from abroad. The expectation of higher future prices sometimes leads businessmen to stock their inventories while goods can still be acquired cheaply.

Much of the material in the second half of this book deals with the reactions of buyers to prices and of business firms to costs. In this chapter, however, we will restrict ourselves to the analysis of movements in gross national product in terms of only those underlying stimuli that can be directly observed and identified. This kind of analysis is necessarily incomplete, and the variation in gross national product estimated only from identifiable stimuli therefore differs from that actually observed. As we shall see, however, the errors are often surprisingly small, and even in the absence of more sophisticated analysis, the method provides a powerful tool for exploring economic behavior.

Steps in Historical Analysis

Quantitative analysis of past year-to-year variations in gross national product consists of 2 steps. First, national accounts and related data are examined and all identifiable sources of economic stimulation are recorded, together with the amount of initial stimulation attributable to each. The total of these changes represents the estimated net simulus to the economic system. The second step is to multiply the estimated net stimulus by the impact multiplier to obtain the expected increase in GNP. If all economic stimuli were properly identified, and if the impact multiplier were exactly measured, the estimated increase in GNP would agree exactly with the change actually observed. The difference between the 2 figures gives us a measure of the error in the analysis for that particular year.

The method of analysis is most easily explained in terms of a specific example,

the $41.9 billion growth in U.S. GNP from its 1963 level of $590.5 billion to the $632.5 billion of 1964. The historical data are given in Table 1.

The first task in the analysis is to determine the magnitude of each identifiable source of economic stimulation.

Autonomous Increases in Consumer Spending

Table 2 provides a convenient format for the analysis. As shown, a total $9.4 billion initial autonomous rise in consumer spending could be identified, consisting of 3 parts.

1. Since personal consumption expenditure during 1963 had been $375 billion, the normal .9 of 1 percent trend in consumer outlays amounted to .009 × $375, or $3.4 billion.

2. Of the total, $1.5 billion was identified as autonomous increased receipt of government transfer payments to persons. Transfer payments had risen only $1.2 billion, but it was necessary also to subtract the reduction in unemployment compensation because this was an induced response to the rise in output and employment be-

TABLE 1   U.S. NATIONAL ACCOUNTS AND RELATED DATA, 1963–1964 (billions of dollars)

	1963	1964	INCREASE
Gross National Product	$590.5	$632.4	$41.9
Personal consumption expenditure	375.0	401.2	26.2
Gross private domestic capital expenditure	87.1	94.0	6.9
Nonresidential fixed investment	54.3	61.1	6.8
Residential construction	27.0	27.1	0.1
Increase in business inventory	5.9	5.8	−0.1
Net exports	5.9	8.5	2.6
Exports	32.3	37.1	4.8
Imports	26.4	28.6	2.2
Government purchase of goods and services	122.5	128.7	6.2
Federal	64.2	65.2	1.0
State and local	58.2	63.5	5.3
Government transfer payments to persons	$ 33.0	$ 34.2	$ 1.2
Unemployment compensation	2.9	2.6	−0.3
All other transfers to persons	30.1	31.6	1.5

SOURCE: All data from *Survey of Current Business*, July, 1967.

tween the 2 years. As shown at the bottom of Table 1, subtraction of the −$.3 billion change in unemployment compensation from the total $1.2 billion increase in government transfer payments to persons gave a net increase of $1.5 billion as recorded in Table 2.

3. Since tax rates were reduced in 1964, a third source of initial autonomous change in consumer spending could be identified. The tax bill passed by Congress and signed into law on February 16, 1964 reduced tax rates enough to lower personal tax liabilities initially by an estimated $9 billion, Two-thirds of this cut, or about $6 billion, was made effective during 1964, while the remaining third was to apply in 1965. Reduction of income tax withholding by employers made the tax cut immediately effective in restoring $6 billion in purchasing power to households. Since the marginal propensity to consume is .75, the tax cut led households to increase their spending by .75 × $6, or $4.5 billion, the amount entered in Table 2.

TABLE 2 ANALYSIS OF THE INCREASE IN GNP FROM 1963 TO 1964
(billions of dollars)

IDENTIFIABLE STIMULI		VALUES
Consumer spending		$9.4
Annual trend	$3.4	
Transfer payments	1.5	
Tax reduction	4.5	
Business investment in new plant and equipment		6.8
Residential construction		0.1
Inventory investment (allowance for termination of 1963 inventory buying)		−5.9
Exports		4.8
Government purchase of goods and services		6.2
Estimated net stimulus		$21.4
Expected increase in gross national product	2 × $21.4	$42.8
Observed increase in gross national product		41.9
Error		$ 0.9

Autonomous Increases in Investment Spending The next group of identifiable stimuli involved investment spending. Although rising sales induce business firms to invest in new facilities, the process takes so long that business investment during any particular year is largely autonomous as far as that year's sales activity is concerned. This year's investment spending is an important initial stimulus to this year's sales and output, but most of any plant and equipment that firms buy because of *this* year's sales will materialize as a stimulus to changes in GNP *next* year or even later. For this reason, the increase in business expenditure for new plant and equipment shown in Table 1 as nonresidential fixed investment can be identified as an economic stimulus and entered directly into Table 2.

A similar argument applies to residential construction. Although family income exercises a long-run influence on home-buying, year-to-year movements are dominated by credit conditions, the rate of new family formation, and other demographic phenomena, making any increase in residential construction an identifiable source of economic stimulation.

Inventory Accumulation: A Special Problem A particularly important problem of stimulus identification involves the behavior of inventory buying. In the first place, a substantial part of any observed change in inventory buying is a passive response to rising sales. As such, it has already been incorporated in the multiplier and cannot be included among the identifiable stimuli without duplication. But there is an important aspect of the change in inventory buying that is identifiable as an independent economic stimulus inherited from past inventory accumulation. If inventory investment is high one year, it tends to decline the next, as stocks of goods are brought into line with sales levels. If firms are liquidating inventory and stocks are being drawn down one year, inventory accumulation tends to rise back to 0 during the following year after firms have reduced stocks to the desired level. In other words, the rise or fall in inventory investment during any given year depends not only on how fast sales rise that year, but also on how much inventory accumulation took place the preceding year. A high rate of inventory investment one year acts to depress the economy the next.

The effect can best be shown by example. Under an initial stimulus of $10 billion, GNP tends to rise by $20 billion, of which about $3.5 billion consists of products added to inventory to bring stocks into line with the higher level of sales. If there were no further initial increases in autonomous spending during the following year, what would happen? At first, it might appear that with nothing to stimulate change, sales and production would remain unaltered from the previous year. If this were so, however, firms would find that their inventories were now adequate for the level of sales, and that further inventory buying was unnecessary. When business firms stopped buying for inventory, however, their action would have the same effect as an autonomous decline in spending from any other cause. Unless offset by other autonomous changes, the $3.5 billion reduction in inventory buying would initiate a reduction in total output of 2 × $3.5, or $7 billion.

In analyzing the behavior of output during any given year, we must include the inventory buying of the preceding year as one of the identifiable sources of stimulus to GNP. Table 1 shows that, during 1963, business firms added $5.9 billion worth of goods to their stock of inventory. In Table 2,—$5.9 billion is recorded as the identifiable economic stimulus to output associated with the termination of this buying in 1964.

Autonomous Increases in Exports and Government Outlays for Goods and Services
U.S. imports of foreign products stimulate

production and raise incomes abroad. In the long run, this improvement in foreign economic conditions is reflected back as an increased demand for U.S. exports, but during any one year sales abroad are little influenced by domestic production and income. Year-to-year movements in exports can, therefore, be identified as part of the net stimulus operating on the U.S. economy. The $4.8 billion increase shown in Table 1 was recorded in Table 2.

The final identifiable stimulus to production during 1964 was the $6.2 billion increase in goods and service purchased by federal, state, and local governments, which was transcribed directly from Table 1 to Table 2.

The Expected Increase in GNP The total of the entries in Table 2 represents an estimated identifiable net stimulus to GNP of $21.4 billion. Application of the impact multiplier reveals that the net stimulus would be expected to raise the 1964 GNP about $42.8 billion above the 1963 level. This expected increase is remarkably close to the historically observed rise of $41.9 billion, which suggests that the important sources of the rise in GNP were successfully identified and recorded in Table 2.

The fine degree of "accuracy" shown by this analysis is, however, misleading. In the first place, any realistic assessment of the national accounts reveals that the data themselves are not this accurate. The true increase in gross national product cannot be known within a $1 or $2 billion. In fact, although gross national product and gross national income are necessarily equal by definition, independent measurements of the 2 rarely agree and have been known to differ by as much as $4 billion. The statistical discrepancy between gross national product and gross national income as independently measured in 1964 was $1.3 billion.

In the second place, and more important, our analysis includes only *identifiable* sources of net stimulation. Changes in GNP initiated by such unidentifiable sources of economic stimulus as consumer psychology can easily amount to $4 billion; other unidentified stimulation in the form of speculative additions to or withdrawals from inventory, or movements in imports caused by changing consumer tastes for foreign goods or changes in the price of imports compared to domestic products can contribute further inaccuracy to the analysis.

Analysis of the Growth in GNP from 1966 to 1967

Analysis of the increase in GNP from 1966 to 1967 provides a more realistic picture of the accuracy of the method. The identifiable stimuli are entered in Table 3. Stimuli identified with consumer spending include $4.2 billion from the usual .9 percent annual

TABLE 3   ANALYSIS OF THE INCREASE IN GROSS NATIONAL PRODUCT FROM 1966 TO 1967 (billions of dollars)

IDENTIFIABLE STIMULI		VALUES
Consumer spending		$11.3
Annual trend	$4.2	
Increase in government transfer payments	7.6	
Rise in personal contribution for social insurance	−0.5	
Business investment in new plant and equipment		2.3
Residential construction		0.1
Inventory investment (allowance for termination of last year's inventory buying)		−13.4
Exports		2.4
Government purchase of goods and services		22.0
Estimated net stimulus		$24.7
Expected increase in gross national product = 2 × $24.7		$49.4
Observed increase in gross national product		42.1
Error		$ 7.3

trend and $7.6 billion from rising government transfer payments, partly offset by a $.5 billion decline in consumption in response to rising social security tax rates. The rapid rise in government spending ($22 billion), mainly due to the war in Vietnam, was heavily offset by the projected decline in inventory spending following the inventory build-up of 1966.

On the basis of the net identifiable stimulus of $24.7 billion, GNP would have been expected to grow by $49.4 billion between 1966 and 1967. The fact that this expected growth exceeded the historically observed change by $7.3 billion suggests that approximately $3.6 billion in offsetting autonomous reductions in initial spending escaped detection in the analysis.

Analysis of the Recession of 1958

Unfortunately, the economy does not inevitably rise as fast as it did in 1964 and 1967. When business firms have no immediate need for more equipment, when exports decline in response to reduced buying abroad, or when government spending declines, the negative items are sometimes enough to yield a 0 or even a negative net stimulus. Under these circumstances the GNP grows slowly or even recedes from the level reached the previous year.

The recession of 1958 is such an example and is analyzed in Table 4. The sharp $4.8 billion drop in business expenditure for new plant and equipment combined with the $3.4 billion decline in export sales and the expected $1.3 billion drop in inventory buying was almost enough to offset the positive contributions of the other factors. The estimated net stimulus of $3.9 billion yielded an expected increase of only $7.8 billion in gross national product, which came close to the observed growth of $6.2 billion.

Growth of gross national product from one year to the next is partly a matter of

TABLE 4 ANALYSIS OF THE RECESSION OF 1958 (billions of dollars)

IDENTIFIABLE STIMULI	VALUES
Consumer spending	$4.7
Annual trend	$2.5
From rising government transfer payments	2.2
Business investment in new plant and equipment	−4.8
Residential construction	0.6
Inventory investment (allowance for termination of last year's inventory buying)	−1.3
Exports	−3.4
Government purchase of goods and services	8.1
Estimated net stimulus	$3.9
Expected increase in gross national product = 2 × 3.9	$7.8
Observed increase in gross national product	6.2
Error	$1.6

FIGURE 2 ANNUAL INCREASES IN GNP, 1950-1967

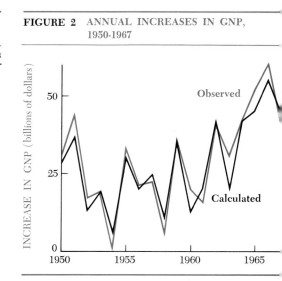

SOURCE: Observed changes from *Economic Report of the President, 1968.* Calculated changes computed by applying the impact multiplier to estimated net stimulus, as described in the text.

changing physical output and partly a matter of prices. If account is taken of rising prices, real GNP actually declined in 1958, and it was this decline that identified 1958 as a year of economic recession.

Analysis of Other Years

The analysis can be applied to any other year in the same way. The observable stimuli are compiled from published data and entered in a format like that of Table 4. Their total is the net identifiable stimulus which, when multiplied by the impact multiplier, gives the estimated increase in gross national product. The results obtained by this method for each year of the 18-year period 1950–1967 are depicted in Figure 2. The blue line shows the course of year-to-year movement in GNP as actually observed in the data. The black line represents the estimated values obtained by applying the impact multiplier to the identifiable net stimulus of each year in turn. The close correspondence of the movements is

convincing evidence of the power of the method.

ECONOMIC FORECASTING

Economic forecasting is a logical extension of the technique of historical analysis. The only difference is that in forecasting, identifiable sources of change in economic activity cannot be looked up in past data but must be projected into the future. Economic forecasting is important for many reasons. Business firms often need estimates of changes in demand on which to base production schedules or expansion plans. Predictions of coming developments in the economy are vital to government officials and legislators responsible for fiscal policy and to members of the Federal Reserve Board responsible for monetary policy. Sometimes, indeed, the most important role of an economic forecast is not to predict what *is* going to happen, but rather to point out the direction in which the economy is moving under the stimulus of existing policies. If the course is likely to lead to increasing unemployment or unnecessary inflation, policy can be altered to change the direction of the system.

The accuracy of the economic forecast depends mainly on the accuracy with which future economic stimuli are projected. If the forecast is to be useful, projections must be compiled with the greatest care and judgment. If we can project the net stimulus for the coming year, a GNP forecast can be obtained by multiplying it by the impact multiplier.

Forecasting Economic Stimuli

For purposes of projection, economic stimuli can be grouped into 4 classes. The first consists of those that tend to increase steadily year after year by approximately constant amounts. This class includes the .9 percent increase in consumer expenditure. In addition, state and local government purchases of goods and services and transfer payments to persons by state and local governments tend to rise fairly uniformly with the growth of the nation, so that their most recently observed increases can be projected forward to form the basis of a forecast.

The second class of stimuli includes those whose values are already fixed by the end of the year preceding the one to be forecast. One important member of this class is the value of last year's inventory accumulation, which can be looked up in the national income and product accounts. Another in this class is the projected initial change in consumer spending caused by changes in tax rates that have already been enacted and are scheduled to take effect during the year being forecast.

Strictly speaking, business expenditures for new plant and equipment are not fixed in advance, but business plans must be laid so far in advance that it is possible to obtain accurate forecasts by surveying the investment spending anticipated by business firms. Such a survey is conducted annually by the Office of Business Economics of the U.S. Department of Commerce in cooperation with the Securities Exchange Commission.[1] Each of a large sample of firms—including all the largest ones—is asked how much it expects to spend on new plant and equipment during the coming year. The amounts reported have proved to be reliable indicators of actual investment outlays.

The third class of stimuli contains those whose values will be determined by policy actions to be taken in the future. Proposed tax legislation, changes in social security laws, and the outlook for federal government spending for goods and services must be carefully evaluated. Here the accuracy of the forecast depends less on the economist's professional insight than on his political acumen, but he must do the best he can. A good place to start is with the proposed federal budget. The President's budget message, delivered to the Congress each January, contains estimated budgetary expenditures for the current fiscal year (ending the coming June 30) and for the coming fiscal year (beginning the coming July 1 and terminating at the end of June of the following year). Since each calendar year contains the second half of the old and the first half of the new fiscal year, a good initial approximation to government spending is obtained by averaging the amounts budgeted to the 2 fiscal years.

Federal government transfers to persons for the coming calendar year can likewise be forecast by averaging the amounts proposed in the budgets for the 2 fiscal years. Federal budgets for the current and approaching fiscal years are conveniently analyzed in the February issue of the *Survey of Current Business*.

[1] Results of the OBE-SEC survey are usually published in the March issue of the *Survey of Current Business*.

Forecasts must often be prepared while important changes in tax legislation are pending, and while it is still unclear what action, if any, the Congress will finally take. Under these circumstances forecasters sometimes make alternative forecasts, each predicated on a different tax law. Comparison of the 2 forecasts yields an estimate of the probable economic effects of the proposed alternatives and is often more useful than the forecast itself.

The final class of economic stimuli consists of those that depend on future economic circumstances. One of these is residential construction which, as we have seen earlier, depends on future housing demand as it is affected by population growth, building costs, and credit availability. The other important member of this class is exports, which depend on relative prices of U.S. and foreign goods and on economic conditions abroad. Accurate forecasting of residential construction and exports requires careful analysis of expected conditions and their probable effects on demand.

An Example: The Forecast Increase in GNP from 1966 to 1967

A forecast rise in GNP from 1966 to 1967 as compiled during the first week of April, 1967 is shown in Table 5. The projected values of the identifiable stimuli involved a net increase of $23.2 billion. Application of the impact multiplier gave a forecast rise in GNP of $46.4 billion. In retrospect it can now be observed that the GNP rose from $743.3 billion in 1966 to $785.1 billion in 1967, an increase of $41.8 billion. The forecast was in error by $4.6 billion.

Most of the information underlying the items in Table 5 was obtained from the February and March issues of the *Survey of Current Business*. The February issue usually carries the preliminary estimates of the national accounts for the preceding

TABLE 5 THE FORECAST RISE IN GNP FROM 1966 TO 1967 (billions of dollars)

IDENTIFIABLE STIMULI		PROJECTED VALUES
Consumer spending		$11.9
Annual trend	$4.2	
Increase in government transfer payments	8.2	
Scheduled rise in social security taxes	−0.5	
Business investment in new plant and equipment		2.4
Residential construction		0.0
Inventory investment (allowance for termination of last year's inventory buying)		−11.9
Exports		3.0
Government purchase of goods and services		17.8
Federal	$10.8	
State and local	7.0	
Projected net stimulus		$23.2
Forecast increase in gross national product = 2 × 23.2		$46.4
Increase in gross national product observed in retrospect		41.8
Forecasting error		$ 4.6

SOURCE: Compiled from data sources and by methods indicated in text.

year, and also an analysis of the President's proposed budget. The March issue contains the results of the OBE-SEC survey of business spending intentions. The projections in the table were arrived at as follows:

1. *Transfer payments to persons.* According to the published budgets, federal transfer payments to persons were expected to be $39.8 billion during the fiscal year ending in June, 1967, and $44.0 billion was proposed for the fiscal year to end June, 1968. The figure for the calendar year 1967 was taken to be the average of these figures, $41.9 billion to be transferred from the federal government to persons during calendar year 1967. To this was added $0.5 billion to represent the steady rise in transfers to persons by state and local governments.

2. *Social security taxes.* The 1965 amendments to the Social Security Act that established the medicare program also provided a new series of rate increases. According to this schedule, social security taxes paid by employees were to increase 5 percent on January 1, 1967. Applying this increase to the $1.2 billion personal contributions for old age and health insurance during 1966, and taking into account the .75 marginal propensity to consume, we arrive at a projected reduction of about $.5 billion in consumer spending as a partial offset to the other projected stimuli.

3. *Business expenditure for new plant and equipment.* According to the OBE-SEC survey of business spending intentions published in March, all U.S. business firms combined planned to invest $63.0 billion during 1967. Since expenditures during 1966 had been $60.6 billion, the survey indicated a planned increase of $2.4 billion.

4. *Residential construction.* The value of new houses built had declined throughout the year 1966 from an annual rate of $27 billion in the first quarter to less than $21 billion in the last. The growing backlog plus the prospect of a Federal Reserve policy of easier credit suggested that construction would recover during 1967. If the path of recovery were to be roughly the reverse of the decline, total expenditure for new houses during 1967 should equal its value in the preceding year and 0 change was projected.

5. *Inventory accumulation.* According to the national accounts as published in February, U.S. business firms had added $11.9 billion to their inventory stocks during 1966. Termination of this buying would constitute an $11.9 billion offset to other stimuli.

6. *Exports.* These were projected to grow by $3 billion, an average of the growth of the 2 preceding years.

7. *Government purchases of goods and services.* Expenditures by the federal government were projected from the proposed budgets. The $83.6 billion budgeted for the fiscal year ending June, 1967 was averaged with the $91.9 billion proposed for the fiscal year ending June, 1968. This gave an estimate of $87.7 billion for the calendar year 1967, an increase of $10.8 billion over the $76.9 billion recorded in the national accounts as spent during calendar year 1966. Purchases of goods and services by state and local governments were expected to rise $7 billion in keeping with their recent trend.

Forecasting Accuracy

The $4.6 billion error in forecasting the increase in GNP from 1966 to 1967 was remarkably small, but again, it is important to recognize that some part of this "accuracy" is purely accidental. As a matter of fact, the forecast error was smaller than the error that resulted when we analyzed the same change after it had occurred! This is because, in addition to all the other errors inherent in the analysis, forecasts are subject to errors in the projected stimuli, and in this particular case certain projection errors partly offset others.

Comparison of Tables 3 and 5 shows something of the size of these projection errors. The most serious was in projecting government spending to rise only $17.8 billion, rather than the $22.0 billion actually realized. This $4.7 billion underestimate was partly offset by an inventory figure that was off by $1.5 billion because of errors in the preliminary estimates of the national accounts, by a $0.6 billion overestimate of the stimulation provided by rising government transfers, and by a projected increase in exports that was $0.6 billion too high. As a result of these partially offsetting errors, the net stimulus as forecast was smaller than what could be identified after the fact, giving the forecast a spurious appearance of accuracy.

Econometric Models

The problems of economic forecasting are considerably simplified by using the data available in February and March of the year being forecast. To be most useful, however, forecasts must usually be available earlier than this, and many are compiled in November and December preceding the year forecast. Although the basic theory is essentially the same as that applied above, more refined methods are required to project the future values of economic stimuli, and greater care must be taken in measuring the relationships of the parts of the economic system to each other.

An *econometric model* is a method of economic analysis in which a greatly elaborated flowchart of the economic system is represented by an extensive system of statistically estimated mathematical equations. The "unknowns" in the equations are the values of GNP, consumer expenditure, employment, price levels, and the other economic phenomena that are to be forecast. The "knowns" are the projected values of government spending, transfer payments, tax policy, and other stimuli that provide the basis for the forecast.

Once the model has been compiled and the values of the "knowns" have been projected and inserted in the equations, it is a relatively simple task for an electronic computer to solve the system and print out the forecast. Since 1953 the Research Seminar in Quantitative Economics at the University of Michigan has been using an econometric model of the U.S. economy to prepare forecasts for presentation before the Conference on the Economic Outlook, held annually during November at the University of Michigan. Each of the past forecasts by the Research Seminar is represented in Figure 3 by a point with the forecast increase in real GNP plotted on the horizontal axis and the changes actually observed in retrospect plotted vertically. If forecasts were perfect, the points would all lie on the line passing through the origin with a slope of 45 degrees. Points above or below the line represent situations in which the increase in GNP exceeded or fell short of the forecast. The forecasts have captured the general direction of economic movements very well. The recessions of 1954 and 1958, represented by the 2 points in the negative quadrant, were correctly predicted, and with the exception of 3 sizable errors (the years 1955, 1959, and 1965) the predictions have been remarkably accurate.

Although the Michigan model has the longest history of published forecasts, a number of other models are now in use. An econometric model compiled in the Wharton School at the University of

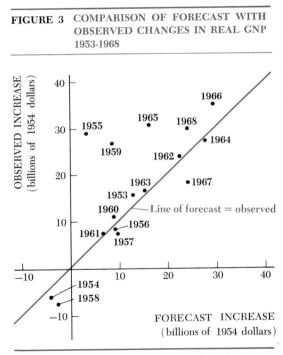

FIGURE 3   COMPARISON OF FORECAST WITH OBSERVED CHANGES IN REAL GNP 1953-1968

SOURCE: On the horizontal axis, each point represents a forecast as published at the annual Conference on the Economic Outlook, held each November preceding the years in question at The University of Michigan. The observed changes were calculated in retrospect from the national income and product accounts of the United States.

Pennsylvania has accumulated an impressive record of accurate quarterly forecasts that are widely consulted by business firms and government agencies, and another quarterly model is now in operation in the U.S. Department of Commerce. Other recent attempts to construct econometric models include one built under the joint auspices of the Federal Reserve Board and the Massachusetts Institute of Technology. Perhaps the most elaborate econometric model ever put together was compiled at the Brookings Institution under a grant from the Social Science Research Council, but it has yet to bring out a published forecast.

For many years, the government of the Netherlands has used an econometric model as an important tool of government economic policy. Econometric models have also been constructed for Canada, Japan, the United Kingdom, Belgium, Greece, and a number of other countries.

ANALYSIS, FORECASTING, AND POLICY

Economic analysis and forecasting are important tools for guiding government efforts to smooth out economic fluctuations and to foster stable economic growth. Historical analysis by means of impact multipliers provides important insights into the causes of past fluctuations, while forecasting is an important element of any program of corrective action. In fact, probably the most important aspect of any economic forecast is not that it predicts what is *actually* going to happen, but rather that it indicates what will probably happen *if* taxes, government spending, interest rates, and other elements of the economic outlook remain unchanged. When the resulting outlook is unfavorable, taxes, spending, or monetary policy can be altered to improve it. Analysis with the impact multiplier provides a guide to what kind of change is required and how much is needed.

The next 3 chapters relate to this important topic of steering the economy. Chapter 12 deals with government spending and taxation, while the monetary system is examined in Chapter 13. In Chapter 14 we will conclude Part Two of our study by showing how economic analysis and forecasting, government action, and monetary policy can be integrated into a coordinated policy to help keep the economic system on a stable path of growth at high employment and output.

SUMMARY

Since economic responses do not occur simultaneously, the amount by which effects of initial autonomous changes in spending are multiplied depends on the time period involved in the measurement. A *one-year impact multiplier* measures the amount of multiplication that occurs during the first year following the stimulus.

Once the flowchart of the economy has been carefully laid out, impact multipliers are easily calculated from the respending ratio. The impact multiplier in the United States is approximately 2.

Impact multipliers can be used to analyze the sources of historically observed changes in GNP by identifying *economic stimuli* in the form of autonomous changes in consumer spending, investment, exports, and government outlays. Since not all stimuli can be identified, however, the analysis is not perfect, although errors are generally small.

Economic forecasting employs the same procedure as historical analysis, but forecast values are substituted for identifiable historical stimuli. Although forecasts are necessarily in error, they are sufficiently accurate to be useful for policy and business planning. Accuracy can be improved by the use of more elaborate procedures like *econometric models*.

Analysis and forecasting play a key role in the formulation of policies designed to *stabilize* the economy at a high level of employment and output.

CHAPTER 12

Government Services and Taxation

It is clear from the preceding chapter that the government is an important source of economic stimulus. Changes in government spending initiate responding cycles that produce multiplied changes in output and income. Changes in tax laws and transfer payments alter household disposable incomes and cause total spending to fluctuate. Carefully applied, changes in government spending and taxation can be used to offset other economic stimuli and to increase the stability of employment, prices, and income. Carelessly used, however, the government's spending and tax power can aggravate depression or inflation. Before we can turn to a careful study of how government policy can stabilize the economy, we must first examine the services that governments perform and the tax laws by which their costs are financed.

SERVICES PROVIDED BY GOVERNMENT

Governments perform a wide variety of services. Some of these are "essentially governmental" in nature. If the government did not undertake responsibility for them, they would not be supplied at all or would be supplied in amounts inadequate to meet society's needs. At the same time, many governments provide services that could equally well be supplied to individual buyers on the private market, but which for one reason or another have come to be an accepted government function. If we are to evaluate the performance of government, it is important to examine the variety of services governments perform.

Collective Services

A *collective service* is one that (1) must be supplied to an entire group of people as a whole rather than to individuals, and (2) cannot selectively be withheld from any individual in the group. For example, maintaining safe and orderly traffic flow benefits all motorists on the street and protects all pedestrians and bystanders alike, a flood control dam necessarily protects everybody in the valley, and control of air pollution benefits the entire area affected.

By their very nature, collective services cannot be sold for prices on private markets but must be supplied to the community as a whole. The essence of a price is that it excludes individuals from the benefits of a service unless they pay. When benefits cannot be withheld from particular people, prices cannot be charged, and the service cannot be supplied by the private market. One alternative is to support the service on a volunteer contribution basis. American churches are supported in this fashion, as are educational television, noncommercial FM broadcasting, and similar collective services in some communities. Unfortunately, voluntary support is unreliable because individuals who automatically receive the benefit of the service have no direct economic incentive to contribute. Unless there is a civic-minded group willing and able to assume the cost burden, the service often cannot be provided. When collective services are essential to the safety and welfare of the community, it is better to have the government provide them on a continuing basis and to employ its tax power to finance their costs.

Service with "Spill-over" Benefits

Relatively few government services can be classified as purely collective. Many more consist of services that can be supplied in- dividually, but that have benefits that "spill over" from the individual user onto the public. Air navigation facilities increase the safety not only of airborne passengers but of residents in the houses below. Health measures like immunization and vaccination not only protect the person treated but, by lowering the incidence of the disease in the community, reduce the chance that others will contract it. Education not only benefits the student, but contributes to a better-informed society to the benefit of everybody. In addition, the benefits of highways, railroads, airports, and other transportation systems extend beyond the individual user. Expanded markets increase specialization and the use of mass production techniques and the resulting rise in productivity provides more goods at lower prices for consumers as a whole.

When the production of services with social spill-over is left to the private market, firms and households purchase them only on the basis of their own personal benefit. Some people will, therefore, refuse the service because its value to them is smaller than the value of other things they have to forego in order to pay for it. Since their acceptance of the service benefits society as a whole, however, it pays the community to *subsidize* their use of it. That is, it is to the advantage of society as a whole to finance part of the cost of the service, and lower its price to encourage use. When public benefits are sufficiently great compared to private, the service is often provided free, as in the case of elementary education and most highways. When private benefits are larger, the public finances a correspondingly smaller part of the cost, as in the case of higher education.

Subsidies are sometimes provided by voluntary private contributions, as when the patrons of a symphony orchestra, museum, or theater company make up the difference between the revenue from ticket sales and the actual cost of the service, or when private groups subsidize education by endowments or donations of scholarships or buildings. As every fund-raiser knows, however, voluntary support is unreliable, and when an important public interest is at stake, systematic government support is required.

Services with High Collection Costs

A third class of government services includes those which could be withheld from individuals and marketed on an individual basis, but for which the cost of collecting the price would be much greater than the cost of the service itself. For example, it would be physically possible to install toll gates at every city intersection to collect from each car for each block it traveled on the street, but the cost of collection, in terms of both the installation and operation of toll gates and the great inconvenience of creeping traffic would be astronomical compared to the small cost per car of using the street. It would be better, therefore, to make the service available without charge and to finance the cost through taxes.

Natural Monopolies

Many services like electricity, water, and public transportation are most economically provided by natural monopolies large enough to supply the entire market. Such services are often produced by regulated public utilities, but an alternative is government ownership. The jurisdictions of government and private enterprise overlap in this area, and the dividing line between them varies widely with time and place. Most European services such as railroads, telephone, telegraph, bus, and electric power are provided by government enterprises, and many governments operate their own airlines. In the United States, the Post

Office is a government enterprise, but most telephone, telegraph, and other communications are private. Gas utilities are private, but almost one-quarter of all U.S. electric power is sold by publicly owned utilities. Because of their intimate connection with public health, all but about 17 percent of American municipal water systems are publicly operated.

Governments also specialize in services that are deemed to be subject to some kind of "abuse." Many foreign governments retain monopoly rights to the manufacture and sale of tobacco products. In some American states, sale of alcoholic beverages is a government monopoly, and in some, the government retains monopoly rights to race-track gambling and lotteries.

GOVERNMENT SPENDING

Goods and Services Purchased by U.S. Governments

In the United States, the task of providing government services is divided among a large number of different governmental units. In addition to the federal government, there are 50 states and over 81,000 distinct county, municipal, school district, or other local governmental units. To render the many services required of them, these governments purchase goods and services that amount to 25 percent of the gross national product. Among U.S. wage and salary workers, 1 out of 5 is employed directly by federal, state, or local government.

Some idea of the relative importance of different government functions and their division among governments is given by Table 1. The total value of goods and services purchased during the year shown was divided almost equally between the federal government on the one hand and all state and local governments combined on the

TABLE 1 GOVERNMENT PURCHASES OF GOODS AND SERVICES BY FUNCTION, 1966

FUNCTION	BILLIONS OF DOLLARS			PERCENT		
	ALL GOVERN-MENTS	FEDERAL	STATE AND LOCAL	ALL GOVERN-MENTS	FEDERAL	STATE AND LOCAL
Total[a]	$154.2	$77.0	$77.2	100.0	100.0	100.0
National defense	60.9	60.5	0.4	39.5	78.6	0.5
Space research and technology	5.9	5.9	—	3.8	7.7	0.0
General government	8.0	2.1	5.9	5.1	2.7	7.6
International affairs	0.6	0.6	—	0.4	0.8	0.0
Education	34.2	0.4	33.8	22.2	0.5	43.8
Health and hospitals	7.5	1.0	6.5	4.9	1.4	8.4
Sanitation	2.0	—	2.0	1.3	0.0	2.6
Administration of social security and welfare services	3.7	1.0	2.7	2.4	1.4	3.5
Police, fire, correction	5.7	0.1	5.6	3.7	0.1	7.3
Veterans' benefits	1.5	1.5	—	1.0	1.9	0.0
Highways	12.3	0.1	12.2	8.0	0.1	15.8
Other transportation and commerce	3.1	1.4	1.7	2.0	1.8	2.2
Housing and community development	1.1	0.4	0.7	0.7	0.5	0.9
Public utilities	2.1	—	2.1	1.4	0.0	2.7
Postal service	0.1	0.1	—	0.1	0.2	0.0
Natural resources	4.5	2.3	2.2	2.9	3.0	2.8
Other	1.1[b]	−0.4[b]	1.5	0.7	−0.7[b]	1.9

[a] Details may not add to total due to rounding.
[b] Includes sale of farm surpluses as a negative expenditure for goods and services.

other. Military expenditures accounted for nearly 40 percent of the goods and services purchased by all governments combined, and absorbed over 78 percent of federal expenditures for goods and services. Among state and local purchases 2 items bulked large. Education—largely a function of local governments—involved nearly half of all state and local purchases of goods and services. Highway construction and maintenance—largely a state function—absorbed about 15 percent. As the table shows, such services as fire, police, sanitation, and hospitals are largely the province of state and local governments (as might be inferred from their nature), while international affairs and space technology are the exclusive concern of the federal government.

Growing Government Demand for Goods and Services As shown in Figure 1, total government purchases of goods and services have risen steadily over the past 20 years. Since the end of World War II, outlays by all American governments combined have grown an average of 9 percent per year, measured at current prices, and 6 percent per year in dollars of constant purchasing power. Since the demand for state and local services parallels the growth in the number and incomes of the people to be educated and protected, purchases by state and local authorities have followed a fairly smooth trend. Federal spending, however, varies with developments on the international scene, and is subject to sharp changes associated with wars and shifts in

FIGURE 1   GOVERNMENT EXPENDITURE FOR GOODS AND SERVICES, 1947-1967

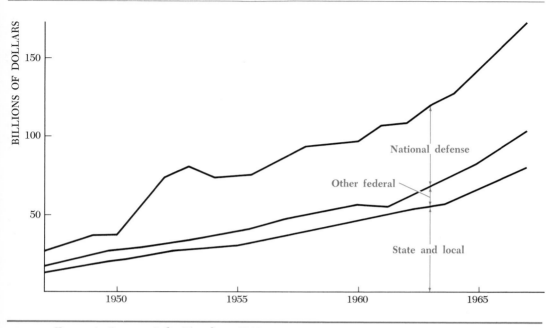

SOURCE: *Economic Report of the President, 1969.*

defense posture. The Korean War shows up in Figure 1 as a distinct bulge in defense expenditures between 1950 and 1954, while the intensification of the war in Vietnam appears in the rising curve after 1965.

Government Transfer Payments

Not all government expenditure involves purchases of goods and services for public use. An additional important governmental activity is the transfer of purchasing power from one group in the community to another in connection with social security pensions, veterans' benefits, public welfare assistance, unemployment insurance, and so on. The amount transferred is surprisingly large. The 1968 total of roughly $100 billion represented approximately a third of all government outlays, and included $30.3 billion paid out in social security

pensions as its largest element. Other large items included $7.2 billion in veterans' benefits, $5.7 billion in welfare payments, $4 billion in farm subsidies and price supports, and $13 billion interest on public debt. Other transfers took the form of government loans to farmers, to low-cost housing projects, and to community development agencies.

The Cost of Government Services

As in the case of any other product, the economic cost of government services consists of the goods and services that could otherwise be produced with the same resources. The opportunity cost of government service is illustrated in Figure 2. The curve *EBD* represents the production-possibilities curve for the U.S. economy, with output for private use plotted horizontally

FIGURE 2   THE OPPORTUNITY COST OF
GOVERNMENT SERVICE

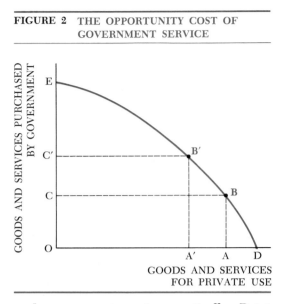

GOODS AND SERVICES PURCHASED BY GOVERNMENT

GOODS AND SERVICES
FOR PRIVATE USE

and government services vertically. Point B is typical of the composition of gross national product in recent years: 75 percent of output is delivered to satisfy private demand (OA) and 25 percent goes to government (OC). The cost of government services is the output AD that could have been produced for private businesses and households, had resources not been diverted to government use. If the composition of GNP were shifted to point B', more resources would be devoted to government, but only at the cost of further reduction in the volume of goods available for private use. Purchases of goods and services by government would rise to C', but the output of goods and services for private purchase would decline to A'.

In one respect, Figure 2 is misleading. Since productive capacity normally grows from one year to the next, part of the increase can be devoted to providing goods and services for government without any actual cutback in the output for private use. This does not alter the meaning of opportunity cost, of course, for the real question is how much of the *additional* capacity to devote to government and how much to private purposes. If more of the addition is

used for one purpose, less remains for the other.

A very special problem in the definition of the cost of government service is encountered during periods of severe unemployment. In a very real sense, the employment of workers who would otherwise be idle entails a double benefit. Not only is there more service available, but hitherto unemployed workers gain jobs. We will return to this question of government service and unemployment in Chapter 14, when we discuss stabilization policy.

Cost Versus Benefit

The proper criterion for evaluating any proposed governmental program is its desirability compared to that of the alternative products that must be sacrificed to it. If the government program serves ends that are less important than the private uses to which the resources could otherwise be put, it is wasteful. If, on the other hand, the ends served by the governmental program are of greater importance than the private output that must be sacrificed, it would be wasteful *not* to institute it. In other words, economy in government does not mean minimum government spending, but a proper balance between private and public use of resources. No government spending, however small, is "economical" if it does not produce results at least as valuable as the private products sacrificed to it. No government expenditure, however large, is wasteful if it produces results more valuable than the alternative products foregone.

As an important extension of this principle, there is no economic bias either in favor of or against government expenditures as such. Both the "collectivist" who, on principle, favors the widest extension of government and the "individualist" who, on principle, favors its narrowest limitation make the identical mistake of committing themselves to dogmatic positions regardless of cost. Purely doctrinaire views of this kind have no place in a sound appraisal of the role and function of government.

Application of the opportunity-cost criterion is perfectly consistent with the entire range of views concerning which services should be undertaken by government and how much should be devoted to them. People disagree about both the value of particular governmental programs and the value of the private wants that must be sacrificed to them. Moreover, even people who agree as to the desirability of the ends sought, often disagree about whether a given governmental program will, in fact, accomplish what is desired, or indeed whether the desirable objective can be accomplished by any governmental program at all. For this reason, ultimate decisions about the kind and amount of government service to be rendered are properly political matters, settled by political processes.

GOVERNMENT BUDGETS

The political process of deciding which services a government should render and how much should be spent on each centers around the government budget. A *budget* is a systematic array of amounts of expenditures by types of service to be rendered, together with a list of the revenue sources by which the expenditures are to be financed. Budgets are used not only by governments but also by businesses and institutions, whenever it is important to evaluate expenditure patterns and to maintain control over spending. Young married couples often prepare household budgets to help them get the most from their incomes.

The complete U.S. federal budget consists of about 1,500 pages of detailed analysis of proposed expenditures organized by type of service to be provided. The budget

for the fiscal year beginning the following July 1 is compiled by the President with the assistance of the Bureau of the Budget and presented to Congress in the annual Budget Message in January. Highly condensed summaries of the actual federal budget for fiscal year 1967, the estimated budget for fiscal year 1968, and the proposed budget for fiscal year 1969 are given in Table 2. Each budget includes a list of outlays and receipts. Budgetary outlays are divided into expenditures and net lending. Expenditures include all outlays for the purchase of goods and services, for payment of interest on the national debt, and for government transfer payments. Net lending consists of the excess of new lending over repayments on loans made to foreign governments, on loans to U.S. farmers as part of the farm price-support program, and on loans made for housing and community development.

During the fiscal year ending June 30, 1967, the federal government spent a total of $153.2 billion, and its net lending came to $5.2 billion more, making total outlays $158.5 billion. Almost half of the total, or $70 billion, was spent for the military, of which $20 billion represented the extra cost of the war in Vietnam. Outlays for health, labor, and welfare—almost $40 billion in 1967—represented the second largest expenditure in the budget. The biggest item in this category is social security pensions, which together with medicare and medical assistance make up about three-fourths of the total.

The outlay for interest on the national debt—$12.5 billion in 1967—represented the third largest item in the budget. The 3 largest expenditure categories combined involved $122 billion, or almost 80 percent of the $158 billion total outlays. Certain expenditures consist of bookkeeping transfers of funds from one government agency to another. These purely internal transactions are netted out in arriving at total expenditures.

TABLE 2   U.S. BUDGET OUTLAYS AND RECEIPTS, 1967, 1968, 1969
(Fiscal years. Billions of dollars)

	1967 ACTUAL	1968 ESTIMATE	1969 ESTIMATE
Expenditures by function:			
National defense	$70.10	$76.49	$79.79
Excluding special Vietnam	(49.96)	(51.96)	(54.01)
International affairs and finance	4.11	4.33	4.48
Excluding special Vietnam	(3.69)	(3.87)	(3.10)
Space research and technology	5.43	4.80	4.57
Agriculture and agricultural resources	3.16	4.41	4.47
Natural resources	2.11	2.41	2.48
Commerce and transportation	7.31	7.70	7.10
Housing and community development	.58	.70	1.43
Health, labor, and welfare	39.51	46.40	51.95
Education	3.60	4.16	4.36
Veterans' benefits and services	6.37	6.80	7.13
General government	2.45	2.62	14.40
Interest			
Allowances:			
Civilian and military pay increase			1.60
Contingencies		.10	.35
Undistributed intragovernmental payments:			
Government contribution for employee retirement (−)	−1.74	−1.91	−2.10
Interest received by trust funds (−)	−2.29	−2.68	−3.04
Total expenditures	153.24	169.86	182.80
Total expenditures, excluding special Vietnam	(132.68)	(144.87)	(156.53)
Net lending:			
International affairs and finance	.54	.71	.67
Agriculture and agricultural resources	1.22	.90	1.16
Housing and community development	1.71	3.26	1.36
Other	1.71	.91	.99
Total net lending	5.18	5.78	3.27
Total outlays	158.41	175.64	186.06
Total outlays, excluding special Vietnam	(137.86)	(150.65)	(159.80)
Receipts by source:			
Individual income taxes	$61.5	$67.7	$80.9
Corporation income taxes	34.0	31.3	34.3
Excise taxes	13.7	13.8	14.7
Employment taxes	27.8	29.7	34.2
Unemployment insurance	3.7	3.7	3.6
Premiums for insurance and retirement	1.9	2.0	2.3
Estate and gift taxes	3.0	3.1	3.4
Customs	1.9	2.0	2.1
Miscellaneous receipts	2.2	2.4	2.7
Total receipts	149.6	155.8	178.1

SOURCE: U.S. Bureau of the Budget, *The Budget in Brief, 1968.*

GOVERNMENT FINANCE: ASSIGNING THE COST BURDEN

As we have seen, the opportunity costs of goods and services sold on competitive markets are automatically assumed by their buyers, but since government services are not generally sold to individuals, their cost must be financed in some other way. The main purpose of taxation is to assign the opportunity cost of government to particular members of the community by systematically depriving them of purchasing power. Payment of taxes means that the taxpayer must either forego products that he might have bought with his income or find a way to increase his earnings by working more. Either way, he bears a specific share of the total opportunity cost of government.

Types of Taxes

Every tax law must define the amount, called the *tax liability,* that each individual owes the government. The law usually does this by defining a *tax base* and a *tax rate.* Tax liability is then calculated by multiplying the base by the rate. The tax base is defined by the item or activity taxed— dollars of income earned, value of real estate owned, number of cigarettes manufactured, size of automobile driven, or whatever. Tax rates indicate how a family or firm with a given tax base should calculate how much it owes the government. A wide variety of taxes is in use today. We can examine only a few of the more important types.

1. *Excises* are a broad class of taxes imposed on economic activities—usually the production or sale of merchandise. Excises are *selective* or *general* according to whether the tax base is restricted to a selected commodity (the excise on gasoline) or applies to a wide class of transactions (a general sales tax). Excises are also classified as *specific* or *ad valorem,* depending on whether the tax rate is a specified number of dollars per item taxed or a stated percentage of its value. The federal government applies a selective excise to the sale of gasoline. Since the tax rate is $.04 per gallon, this is a specific excise. The federal selective excise on the manufacture and sale of automobiles is an *ad valorem* tax, the rate being 10 percent of the wholesale price of each car. The retail sales tax employed by many state governments is a general *ad valorem* tax whose base is the total value of goods purchased at retail unless expressly exempted. Purchases of most services are excluded from the general sales tax base, and many states also exempt the purchase of food.

2. *Property taxes* take the value of specified kinds of properties as the tax base. The value is usually assigned or *assessed* for tax purposes as a designated fraction of market value.

3. A *personal income tax* is levied on a tax base defined by personal income after various exclusions, deductions, and exemptions.

4. *Payroll taxes* like those used to finance state unemployment insurance systems have as a base the wages or salaries paid to each employee up to a specified number of dollars per year, often $3,600, while the tax rate often depends on the employer's past record of employment stability.[1] Payroll taxes to finance social security are similar. As this is written the tax base consists of the first $7,800 per year of each employee's wages and salaries, and the rate is 4.8 percent. The tax must be deducted from the employee's paycheck and must be matched by an equal contribution from the employer.

5. *Corporate profits taxes* collect either

[1] See Chapter 7.

a flat or sliding percentage of corporate profits above a specified level.

As shown in Table 3, different levels of government tend to depend on different taxes. The federal government draws most of its revenue from taxes on personal and corporate income and from payroll taxes. State governments also collect substantial amounts from income and payroll taxes, but rely more heavily on selective excises and general sales taxes. Local governments derive almost half their revenue from property taxes. The direct revenues of state governments are supplemented by transfers of revenue from the federal government, while local governments receive transfers of both federal and state funds.

TABLE 3 SOURCES OF GOVERNMENTAL REVENUE IN THE UNITED STATES, 1966 (millions of dollars)

	FEDERAL	STATE	LOCAL
Taxes			
Personal income	$55,446	$4,288	$472
Corporate income	30,073	2,038	*a*
Payroll	22,595	7,128	837
Selective excises	12,874	9,170	688
Customs duties	1,767	—	—
Estate and gift taxes	3,066	808	—
Motor vehicle licenses	—	2,237	125
General sales taxes	—	7,873	1,352
Property taxes	—	834	23,836
Other taxes	869	2,132	887
Charges and misc. general revenue	14,452	5,131	8,044
Public utility revenue	—	—	5,069
Liquor store revenue	—	1,361	189
Transfers from other governments	—	12,246	17,768
Total	$141,142	$55,246	$59,268

a Small amount included in personal income tax receipts.

SOURCE: *Statistical Abstract of the United States, 1968.*

Fairness of Taxes

Our ideas about what makes a tax "fair" or "just" extend in 2 different directions. On the one hand, we feel that when certain people obtain specific benefits from government service, they should pay in proportion to the benefits received. On the other hand, we also feel that the burden of community-wide services should be shouldered according to ability to pay.

Taxation on the Benefit Principle The *benefit principle* implies that taxes should be so assigned that those who benefit most from government service pay the most taxes. This principle represents a logical extension of the idea of market price to government services. That is, when benefits to particular people can be identified, those people should be compelled to pay, just as they would in a private transaction. Since the biggest users of highways buy the most gasoline, financing highway maintenance by an excise tax on gasoline agrees with the benefit principle, as does the application of a property tax to defray the cost of fire protection.

Taxation in Proportion to Ability to Pay There are, however, obvious limitations to the benefit principle as a general basis for taxation. The benefits of some governmental services are so broadly diffused that it is impossible to measure how much accrues to any particular person. Moreover, even when they are identifiable and measurable, substantial benefits often accrue to people unable to afford them. This is most clearly the case of transfers and welfare services for the poor. Indeed, the very purpose of hot-lunch programs in schools, welfare payments to the disabled, and social welfare agencies is to provide income and services to people who could not obtain them otherwise.

An alternative to taxation on the basis of benefit received is that each taxpayer be required to contribute in proportion to his ability to pay. The more income a family receives, the lower the priority of the items it would have to sacrifice in paying taxes. Poor families who need all their income for high-priority essentials can often afford only an inadequate diet, and the cost of taxation for them would be greater hunger. Rich families, on the other hand, pay their taxes with income that might otherwise be spent to satisfy trivial whims.

It follows that people with higher incomes should pay more taxes than similarly situated people with lower income, but the important question is *how much* more? If a total of $3,000 in taxes is to be collected from 2 families, one with income of $10,000, the other with $20,000, how should the tax be apportioned? Should the low-income family pay $1,200 and the other $1,800? Should the tax be divided $1,000–$2,000, or $800–$2,200, or how?

The Need for Progressive Taxes To help analyze this problem, taxes are classified according to the ratio of tax liability to income. A *proportional tax* is one for which the ratio is the same at all levels of income. In the example above, the tax that would divide the liability $1,000–$2,000 would represent a proportional tax, because it would take 10 percent of the income of both families. Under a *regressive tax* the ratio of tax liability to income is smaller for higher than it is for lower incomes, and although families with lower incomes usually pay less total tax than those with higher incomes, the tax represents a larger fraction of their income. In the example above, the tax that would collect $1,200 from the $10,000 income and $1,800 from the $20,000 income would be a regressive tax. The liability of the low-income family would be $1,200/$10,000, or 12 percent of its income, while the higher income family would pay only $1,800/$20,000, or 9 percent.

A retail sales tax on food is regressive because the proportion of family income spent on food tends to decline as income rises. Since the average food budget is about one-third of a $3,000 family income but only about 20 percent of a $10,000 income, a 4 percent tax on food purchases takes 1.33 percent of the lower but only 0.8 percent of the higher income.

A *progressive tax* is one for which the ratio of tax liability to income rises with income. Not only do lower-income families pay less tax, but the tax liability is a smaller fraction of their income than it is for higher-income families. The $800–$2,200 division of liability would represent a progressive tax, since the liability would be $800/$10,000, or 8 percent of the lower income, but $2,200/$20,000, or 11 percent of the higher.

Since families with higher incomes have more than proportionally greater ability to pay, it is generally agreed that a **fair tax** system should be progressive, but it is not clear how steeply progressive it should be. A progressive tax that collects 10 percent of a $10,000 income must collect more than 10 percent from an income of $20,000. But should it collect 11 percent, 40 percent or how much? There is no simple answer to this question, although there is clearly an upper limit. Taxes should never be so steeply progressive that their payment leaves a higher-income family with less disposable income than a similar family that started with a lower income before taxes. Put another way, a family that manages to raise its own income must always be permitted to keep some of the additional receipts. This is not only justice, but is also an important economic incentive.

Average and Marginal Tax Rates

A useful way to examine the question of the steepness of progressive taxes is to distinguish the *average* tax rate, defined as the ratio of tax liability to income, from the *marginal* tax rate, defined as the increase in tax liability incurred when income is increased by $1. Table 4 shows representative average and marginal rates under a state income tax of 2 percent on all family income in excess of $1,200 per family member. Since the calculations are made for a family of 4, the average tax rate is 0 until income exceeds $4,800. At incomes below $4,800, the marginal rate is also 0, since an additional dollar of income would still lie below the taxable level. At exactly $4,800, the average rate is 0, but the marginal rate becomes 2 percent, since the next dollar of income would increase tax liability to $.02. The marginal tax rate remains constant as income rises, the average rate rising with it, to approach the constant marginal rate at the limit.

The federal personal income tax is a progressive tax with a rising marginal tax rate. In calculating its tax the family is first permitted to deduct a number of items from its income, including charitable contributions (in general not exceeding 30 percent of total income), a specified portion of its medical bills, interest paid on its debts, taxes paid to state and local governments, and any business expenses connected with the income receiver's job. In general, these deductions must be specifically itemized and explained on the tax return, but taxpayers are permitted to apply a standard deduction of 10 percent up to a maximum of $1,000 without itemization

or explanation. The family is then permitted to deduct an exemption of $600 for the head, his wife, and each dependent family member. What remains, called "taxable income," is the tax base. The income tax base for a family of 4 with a $6,000 income would be about $6,000 − 600 − 2,400, or $3,000.

Each tax payer's income-tax liability is determined by applying a system of rising marginal rates to his tax base. At the rates in force in 1967, shown in Table 5, the liability corresponding to a taxable income of $3,000 would be $290 plus 16 percent of all income over $2,000, making a total tax liability of $450. Payment of this much tax out of a $6,000 family income would represent an average tax rate of 450/6,000, or

TABLE 4 AVERAGE AND MARGINAL TAX RATES FOR A FAMILY OF 4 UNDER A 2 PERCENT TAX ON INCOME OVER $1,200 PER FAMILY MEMBER

FAMILY INCOME	LIABILITY	AVERAGE RATE, %	MARGINAL RATE, %
$ 3,000	$ 0	0	0
4,000	0	0	0
4,800	0	0	2
5,000	4	.080	2
10,000	104	.104	2
100,000	1,904	1.904	2

TABLE 5 1967 U.S. FEDERAL INCOME TAX SCHEDULE, MARRIED TAXPAYERS FILING JOINT RETURNS

IF TAXABLE INCOME IS OVER—	BUT NOT OVER—	INCOME TAX IS OF EXCESS OVER—
$1,000	- $2,000....$140, plus 15%	- $1,000
$2,000	- $3,000....$290, plus 16%	- $2,000
$3,000	- $4,000....$450, plus 17%	- $3,000
$4,000	- $8,000....$620, plus 19%	- $4,000
$8,000	- $12,000...$1,380, plus 22%	- $8,000
$12,000	- $16,000...$2,260, plus 25%	- $12,000
$16,000	- $20,000...$3,260, plus 28%	- $16,000
$20,000	- $24,000...$4,380, plus 32%	- $20,000
$24,000	- $28,000...$5,660, plus 36%	- $24,000
$28,000	- $32,000...$7,100, plus 39%	- $28,000
$32,000	- $36,000...$8,660, plus 42%	- $32,000
$36,000	- $40,000...$10,340, plus 45%	- $36,000
$40,000	- $44,000...$12,140, plus 48%	- $40,000
$44,000	- $52,000...$14,060, plus 50%	- $44,000
$52,000	- $64,000...$18,060, plus 53%	- $52,000
$64,000	- $76,000...$24,420, plus 55%	- $64,000
$76,000	- $88,000...$31,020, plus 58%	- $76,000
$88,000	- $100,000..$37,980, plus 60%	- $88,000
$100,000	- $120,000..$45,180, plus 62%	- $100,000
$120,000	- $140,000..$57,580, plus 64%	- $120,000
$140,000	- $160,000..$70,380, plus 66%	- $140,000
$160,000	- $180,000..$83,580, plus 68%	- $160,000
$180,000	- $200,000..$97,180, plus 69%	- $180,000
$200,000	..........$110,980, plus 70%	- $200,000

7.5 percent. The marginal tax rate would be the 16 percent indicated in the tax table.

Both marginal and average rates rise with income. For example, after deductions and exemptions, the tax base for a family of 4 with $10,000 income would be about $6,600 which, according to the table, would result in a tax liability of $1,114. This would amount to an average rate of 11.1 percent, while the marginal rate would be 19 percent shown in the table. It is important to note again, however, that although the average tax rate rises with income, the taxpayer is always allowed to keep part of any additional earnings. He does not end up with fewer dollars when rising income "throws him into a higher tax bracket." A taxpayer with taxable income of $32,000, for example, would be at the upper end of the bracket having a marginal tax rate of 39 percent and would be subject to a tax of $8,660. If his income increased by $1, he would be "thrown into the 42 percent bracket," but only the extra dollar would be taxed at the higher marginal rate. The taxpayer would still keep 58 cents out of the additional dollar and have that much more to spend.

Tax Loopholes

In one important respect the tax table seriously overstates the amount of progression in the personal income tax because the tax law distinguishes among sources of income and gives certain types of income more favorable treatment than others. Special provisions of the law, often called "tax loopholes" permit exclusion of all or part of certain kinds of incomes from the tax base, or permit the application of special accounting procedures in calculating them. These tax loopholes enable many people, particularly those in high tax brackets, to pay much lower taxes than the table would suggest. In fact, in 1967, 115 Americans with incomes exceeding $200,000 per year

paid no income tax at all! Some loophole provisions are highly technical, but 3 can be briefly mentioned:

Tax-exempt securities   Income received as interest on bonds issued by state and local governments and their agencies is exempt from the federal income tax. This feature enables state and local governments to borrow at lower rates than would otherwise be possible, but it also permits investors in high tax brackets to reduce their tax liabilities. We will explore the effect of tax-exemption on interest rates in Chapter 24.

Mineral Depletion Allowances   The law allows people engaged in the extraction of coal, iron ore, petroleum, and other minerals to apply special accounting provisions that exclude a substantial part of the income earned from mineral extraction. The most important of these is the *mineral depletion allowance*, which permits the owner of a well or mine to deduct, as a cost of operations, a substantial percentage of the market value of the minerals extracted. In 1967 the allowance varied from 5 percent for sand and gravel to 27.5 percent for petroleum and natural gas. In other words, the law permitted the owner of oil wells to set aside 27.5 percent of the gross value of extracted oil before he started to calculate the profitability of the operation for tax purposes.[2]

Capital Gains   When an investor buys securities or other property at a low price and later resells it at a high price, the difference is called a *capital gain*. Income from capital gains is given special treatment in terms of both tax base and tax rate. One-half of the capital gain on all property held longer than 6 months before resale is ex-

[2] The total amount of depletion allowable *was* restricted, however, to half of the net income the property earns when income is calculated without the depletion allowance.

empt from the tax base. The remainder is taxed at the rate that would normally apply to the taxpayer or at an average rate of 50 percent, whichever is least. In other words, the combined effect of exemption and rate limitation is to hold the average tax on capital gains to a maximum of 25 percent, regardless of their size or of the size of any other income the family may receive.

Taxes and Economic Behavior

Taxation involves more than fairness. When taxes change the earnings to be made in one industry compared to others, they provide a powerful force attracting capital into the favored industry. When excise taxes raise the prices of selected products relative to others, they drive buyers to cheaper untaxed substitutes. These powerful effects on economic behavior must be carefully considered in evaluating tax laws.

The oil depletion allowance increases the profitability of petroleum extraction compared to other industries. Investors continue to find it profitable to drill new wells long after the price of oil has fallen to levels that would be unprofitable in other industries. As a result, the tax law draws more labor and capital into petroleum extraction than could be profitably employed if oil profits were taxed like other incomes.

Economic Effects of Excise Taxes Since excise taxes tend to raise the prices of taxed compared to untaxed commodities, selective excise taxes sometimes result in widespread shifts in buying. Indeed, the very purpose of some excises is to divert buyers from the taxed commodity and induce them to purchase something else. A *protective tariff* is an excise imposed on imported commodities that have domestic substitutes. The idea behind them is to increase the use of the home-produced article by raising the price of the import. Similar excises are sometimes used internally. In one state, for example,

the sale of wine is taxed at 40 cents a gallon unless the wine is made from grapes grown within the state, in which case the tax is only 4 cents. In an earlier period, yellow margarine was subject to a special excise tax to protect the butter industry.

The Effect of Income Taxes on Work Incentives Since an income tax reduces net earnings, it tends to alter the willingness of people to work in 2 mutually offsetting ways. On the one hand, when taxes reduce the disposable income of the family, its members must increase their total earnings if they are to maintain their standard of living. To this extent, higher tax rates lead people to work more than they otherwise would. On the other hand, high marginal tax rates reduce the real reward from extra effort and lead some people to work less than they otherwise would. If you keep only 30 cents out of a dollar anyway, they argue, why not take another couple of weeks' vacation?

Obviously, both effects are at work at the same time, and their net influence on work effort varies from time to time and from family to family. However, international and historical comparisons suggest that the net effect of income taxes is to increase the supply of labor. In the poorest countries people work the longest hours and more children and old people are in the labor force. As labor grows more productive, people tend to work less, despite the higher reward each additional hour brings.

Since one way in which a family can increase its supply of labor is to have the wife take a job, job holding by married women provides another clue to the incentive effect of taxation. Table 6 shows how job holding by married American women varies with husband's income. As we can see, the greatest influence on a wife's employment is whether she has young children at home. As might be expected, a substantially smaller percentage of mothers with children under 6 work at outside jobs, compared to wives with no young children. But the greater value attached to the wife's role as mother must be compared to the greater need for income when there are more mouths to feed. In families in which the husband's income is in the highest brackets shown, job holding among mothers of young children is less than one-fifth that of wives with no children under 18. As husbands' incomes fall, however, this ratio rises and more than half the wives of husbands in the lowest income bracket are found at work. It is reasonable to suppose that this also represents the response to be expected when family take-home pay is reduced by higher taxes. Lower disposable income tends to encourage mothers to enter the labor force to supplement the family earnings.

Among wives with no young children, the relationship of employment to husbands' incomes is less well defined, but there is no clear indication that wives in higher-income families are seriously deterred from employment by the high marginal tax rates.

Tax Credits as Economic Incentives Another way in which taxation is used to alter economic behavior is by reducing tax liability as a reward for specified actions taken by the taxpayer. Such a reduction of tax lia-

bility is called a *tax credit.* As part of a program to increase employment and stimulate economic growth, an *investment tax credit* was introduced in 1962. It was designed to encourage investment by permitting firms to subtract from their corporate profits tax liabilities an amount equal to 7 percent of the value of new investment in machinery and equipment.

The effect of an investment tax credit is shown in Figure 3. The black curve MEI_0, represents the marginal efficiency of investment in equipment before the investment tax credit had been instituted. Given the interest rate, r_0, business firms would tend to invest only I_0 dollars in new equipment. After firms were permitted to deduct part of the cost of the new equipment from their tax bills, investment projects immediately became more profitable and the marginal efficiency of investment rose to the position represented by the blue curve MEI_1. Given the same interest rate, the tax credit would expand investment to I_1. The effect of the tax credit did not stop here, however, for as

FIGURE 3   THE EFFECT ON INVESTMENT OF THE 7 PERCENT INVESTMENT TAX CREDIT OF 1962

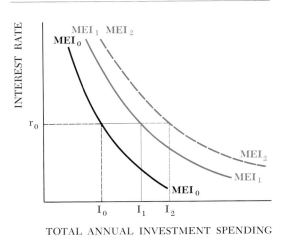

TOTAL ANNUAL INVESTMENT SPENDING

TABLE 6   PERCENT OF EMPLOYED WIVES IN RELATION TO HUSBANDS' INCOMES

	PERCENT OF WORKING WIVES IN FAMILIES WHERE THERE ARE		
HUSBAND'S INCOME	CHILDREN UNDER 6	CHILDREN 6–17 ONLY	NO CHILDREN UNDER 18
$10,000 or more	8	19	n.a.
$7,000–9,999	9	32	51
$5,000–6,999	17	38	60
$3,000–4,999	22	49	63
$2,000–2,999	24	48	64
Under $2,000	29	53	54

SOURCE: Data are for wives aged 22–40 drawn from the *Census of Population,* 1960.

the impact of the higher investment rate made itself felt on the level of total output, the improved sales outlook caused the profitability of investment to increase even further, raising the marginal efficiency of investment to the positon represented by the dashed blue curve MEI_2, and the rate of investment would reach I_2, as shown.

As part of a broad attack on poverty, tax credit schemes have been proposed to induce firms to locate in high-unemployment urban areas or to hire and train unskilled workers. Tax credits to businesses have also been suggested for the installation of pollution control devices.

While tax credits are powerful devices for altering economic behavior, there are serious objections to their use. Essentially, a tax credit is a subsidy paid to the business firm by the rest of the taxpayers to induce it to act in a certain way. If such a subsidy were paid outright from the public coffers, it would appear as part of the government budget. Its amount would be clearly specified, its effectiveness could be debated, and it could be weighed against alternative uses of resources as part of the budgetary process.

The subsidy provided by a tax credit does not appear as part of the budget. Since no payments to the firm appear among government outlays, the subsidy appears costless. Moreover, its magnitude is not easily determined and it is difficult to find out how much taxpayers are contributing toward it and whether they are getting their money's worth. The appeal of the tax credit is largely due to the illusion that, since no overt payment is made, it does not cost the taxpayers anything. This, of course, is foolishness. An adequate tax system must impose the full opportunity cost of government on the community, and if the liability of one person is reduced, that of somebody else must be increased. Tax credits only disguise the cost and increase the difficulty of determining who is really bearing the tax burden.

In a private enterprise economy, the most effective way to enlist the cooperation of private business is by paying in cash for what you want done. When government acts like a customer it gets better service than when it relies on tax incentives.

Response of Tax Revenues to Needs

One final aspect of tax systems is worth noting. Since the economy is steadily growing, the need for government service steadily expands. Under these circumstances there is merit in a tax system whose revenues automatically grow in pace with public needs. In this respect, however, the U.S. tax system is rather deficient. The demand for many of the services provided by state and local governments—education is an outstanding example—tends to grow faster than income. As people find their incomes rising, enrollments in state colleges and universities grow disproportionately. More teachers, more classrooms, and more facilities are needed. Community colleges are established, and there is public clamor for better high schools. However, state and local governments derive their tax revenues largely from regressive taxes like specific excises and general sales taxes whose bases rise less than in proportion to income, and from property taxes that in the long run rise only in proportion to income. The results are a constant tendency for expenditure needs to outgrow revenues, recurrent fiscal crises, and a continual need to increase rates on existing taxes and search for new sources of revenue.

The situation of the federal government is quite the reverse. Since the principal object of federal expenditure is the military, demand for services is not; income related, yet most federal revenue is provided by the corporate income tax and the highly progressive personal income tax. The result is a steady tendency for the federal tax system to extract more purchasing power from firms and households than it needs for expenditures. Except for periods of open hostilities, the federal tax system tends to act as a continually tightening brake on aggregate demand. Tax rates must be steadily reduced or expenditures expanded if full use of productive capacity is to be maintained.

As one way out of this dilemma, the federal government has increasingly undertaken transfers of revenue to state and local governments to provide support for education, public health, housing, welfare, and other activities. Such a transfer system has much to commend it. In a close-knit modern nation, the spill-over benefits of education, public health, and similar government services are nationwide. The kind of country we will live in depends increasingly not only on how well fed and well educated our neighbor's children are, but also on how well children are educated and fed everywhere else. This includes poor states as well as rich, and central cities as well as suburbs. The federal government is the only agency that can collect taxes on a nationwide basis of ability to pay and direct the revenues to the localities with the greatest need.

SUMMARY

As the representative of society as a whole, government is responsible for the provision of *collective services* and of those with important *"spill-over"* benefits. In addition, governments often undertake responsibility for services with *high collection costs* and those subject to *natural monopoly* or some kind of *"abuse."* To provide these services, governments purchase almost 25 percent of all goods and services produced in the United States. Governments are also responsible for *transfer payments* that shift income from one group in the population to another.

The *economic cost* of government services, like the cost of anything else, consists of the sacrificed opportunity to produce other things. It follows that the justification for any government program hinges on whether the *benefits* obtained from it exceed those available from the goods and services that must be sacrificed. Such comparisons are necessarily political and decisions about them are reached by political processes. The center of this political decision process is the *government budget,* a systematic array of proposed programs together with the sources of revenue with which they are to be financed.

Government programs are financed largely by taxation, and many different types of taxes are used for the purpose. Since the object of government finance is to apportion cost burdens equitably, *fairness* is an important criterion of taxes. Fairness is partly evaluated by the *benefit principle,* which specifies that individuals should be taxed in proportion to the benefits they receive. But benefits are difficult to evaluate and are often directed toward the people least able to pay. The principle of *ability to pay* is more widely applicable, and it is generally agreed that rich people should pay not only more taxes than poor people, but a larger fraction of their income. That is, fairness requires taxes to be *progressive* rather than *regressive*. The U.S. personal income tax is a progressive tax with rising *marginal tax rates,* but because of a number of *loopholes,* it is not as progressive as it might at first appear.

A second important criterion of taxation is its effect on *economic behavior.* Some taxes are specifically designed to produce certain effects. Excise taxes often serve to encourage people to buy untaxed commodities rather than those taxed, and *tax credits* are sometimes employed to provide incentives for certain kinds of economic behavior. The danger of tax credits is that they function as hidden expenditures that lie outside the budgetary process and are not subject to normal political review. It is difficult to determine what is received for the concession and who is actually financing the cost.

State and local governments depend largely on regressive taxes and others with yields that rise more slowly than the growth in demand for government services, while the federal government, with expenditures relatively insensitive to national income, relies on progressive income taxes. The result is continual financial crisis at the state and local level and revenue that exceeds need at the federal level. Rising use of state and local income taxes is one answer to the needs of state and local governments, *revenue sharing* by the federal government is another.

CHAPTER 13

Money and Banks

Up to this point we have treated money largely as a veil that must be stripped aside when we want to see the operation of the real economy beneath; yet the use of money is essential to a highly specialized, productive society. In addition, money and monetary policy exert a strong influence on aggregate demand, and hence on the level of employment and the use of productive capacity.

In this chapter we will study the nature of money and examine a brief outline of its evolution into modern form. We will see how modern money is created and circulated by banks, and how the creation and circulation of money is controlled by the Federal Reserve System.

THE NATURE AND FUNCTIONS OF MONEY

The use of money is essential to high productivity. Without some kind of money, we could have only the most limited exchange.

We could trade only by bartering the things we have in surplus for those we need. Such a swap is extremely difficult to arrange. To trade a pair of shoes for a shirt, you must find somebody who both has the shirt you want and wants the shoes you have to trade. In a world without money, people would probably spend most of their time looking for somebody to trade with and arranging the terms of deals. Every worker would be paid in the products of the factory, and he and his family would have to hunt for people with other things to trade.

It is easy to see how this system would put severe limits on specialization. It would be better for everybody to make as many things as possible for himself, rather than to specialize in one item and spend time looking for people with the rest of the things he needed.

A Medium of Exchange

The principal function of money is to expedite specialization and trade by serving as a *medium of exchange*. Instead of looking for the rare person who both has what you want and wants what you have, you need only find somebody who wants what you have, and has *money*. You can sell what you have for money, and then use the money to buy what you need from anybody who has it for sale. The money is evidence that you have parted with something valuable and that you are now entitled to receive your choice of an equivalent amount of goods in exchange.

In general, possession of money indicates that the holder has made a contribution to production and is thereby entitled to an equal claim on the products of others. The holder of money need not, of course, exercise the claim himself. He may, if he chooses, give the money to somebody else, thereby transferring his right to the products, or he may lend the money, allowing the borrower to buy products before he has produced any, with the promise that he will ultimately produce something himself and return the money after the item is sold.

Other Functions

In addition to its role as a medium of exchange, money serves as a *standard of value*. Money prices tell us the terms on which products can be exchanged. Two shirts worth $10 each trade equally for 4 books worth $5 each or for a $20 jacket. Even if the deal is a direct swap of the shirts for the jacket, with no money changing hands, the terms of the trade are likely to be set by the amount the respective goods are "worth" in money.

As a third function, money serves as a *store of liquid wealth*. Money need not be spent at once. A person can wait until he finds the kinds of goods he wants, or save for some specific future purpose or even for unforeseen emergencies. As we have

repeatedly emphasized, money is not *real* wealth, but it is a convenient form in which an individual can keep a generalized claim to real wealth. Because of its ready exchangeability for goods, money is often called *liquid wealth*.

FORMS OF MONEY

Older Forms

To perform its important functions, money needs only one property: It must be immediately acceptable in exchange for goods everywhere in the community. A person is willing to take money in payment for his services because he knows that others will accept it from him in exchange for theirs. They take it from him because they know that others, in turn, will accept it, and so on throughout the community.

The entire value of money stems from its universal acceptability, and from nothing else. Any tokens, "chits," or commodities that are received in payment without question are money, regardless of their physical form or legal status. In particular, it is unnecessary for money to be made of material that has value in its own right. We are all familiar with paper money and with coins made of inexpensive metal, while bank credit, which is, as we shall see shortly, the most widely used form of money in a modern society, can hardly be said to have any physical embodiment at all.

The earliest forms of money were usually commodities which had some intrinsic value. Tobacco and whiskey were used in the American colonies, and animal skins played a monetary role among trappers. In many societies, cattle were the first money employed. The patriarchs of the Old Testament reckoned their wealth in flocks and herds, and much of our language still attests to the earlier role of cattle as money. *Pecu-*

nia, the Latin word for money (surviving in modern English words like *pecuniary*), was derived from an older Latin term *pecus,* meaning a herd of cattle. The English word *capital,* applied in finance, is derived from the same medieval Latin root as the word *cattle.*

Cattle are still used for money in Kenya, Uganda, and neighboring parts of Africa, especially as the payment a young man must make to his prospective father-in-law to "purchase" his bride. However, there are obvious problems in the use of cattle as money. For example, agricultural productivity in some parts of Kenya suffers due to soil erosion caused by the overgrazing of land by monetary cattle, and keeping cash on hand is not so easy when it has to be fed, watered, and herded.[1] In any event, cattle are unsuitable for everyday business. What do you do for pocket money? And how do you get change for a cow?

Because metal—especially gold and silver is cheaper, more convenient to store, and divisible into small units, it came to replace cattle as money. This replacement was gradual, and for a long time people continued to think of cattle as "real" money and of gold and silver as merely "representing" cattle. Indeed, for a long time people expressed the value of metal in terms of cattle rather than the other way around. A Homeric *talent* was a weight of gold worth 1 ox, and Homer tells how the Greek warrior Glaukos, in a moment of confusion, traded his gold armor for bronze, "the value of a hundred oxen for the value of ten."[2]

Metal used as money was originally exchanged by weight, and many of our modern currency units were originally units of weight: among them, the *peso,* the *mark,*

and, of course, the *pound.*[3] Weighing metal still left much to be desired in a medium of exchange, because the metal offered had to be weighed before each transaction, and there was no guarantee of its quality. Coins probably originated from the practice of stamping pieces of metal with an official government certification of their weight and fineness.

After the advent of coinage, metal could be exchanged not by weight, but by the number certified on the coin. This number, originally called the *tale* of the coin (compare *teller,* a person who counts money) appears on the reverse side. The use of the term "tail" to distinguish this side of the coin from the one with the portrait or "head" probably derives from this fact.[4]

Paper Money

The rise of paper money represented the next stage in the development of the modern money system. This came about when people with large amounts of coin to store began to entrust it to somebody with a good safe—usually a goldsmith or silversmith—who served as a banker and issued certificates of deposit or "claim checks" for the money and kept the coin and bullion safe until needed. People found that they could avoid the inconvenience of handling large amounts of heavy money by using the paper certificates for payments, rather than

---

[1] "Health Services in Kenya," *World Health Organization Chronicle,* Vol. 15, no. 9. Reprinted in Sripati Chandrasekhar and Charles W. Hultman, *Problems of Economic Development,* Boston, 1967.

[2] *Iliad,* Book 6.

[3] The word *dollar,* incidentally, is derived from the name of the town of Joachimsthal (now Jachymov, Czechoslovakia), famous during the 17th century for minting silver coins that gained wide currency in the New World. Because of their source these became known as *Joachimsthalers,* or *thalers* for short, a term that was anglicised to *dollars.*

[4] The denomination of a coin is always stamped on the "tail" side. The term *tale* is related to the German word *Zahl* (number). When Germans toss coins, they refer to one side as *Kopf* (head) and the other as *Zahl.*

the coins themselves. At first, the paper bills were accepted only because they could be exchanged for coin at any time. Coin was considered the only "real" money, and paper was valid only because it "represented" coin. As time went on, however, people came to accept the paper in its own right and it became true money.

These paper certificates evolved into the *bank notes* in use today. The words "Federal Reserve Note" at the top of the modern U.S. dollar mean that the bill is the liability of one of our Federal Reserve banks. The seal at the left indicates which bank issued the note. Of course, Federal Reserve notes are no longer "certificates," that is, they are not claim checks for gold and silver on deposit, but are issued directly as money, as we will see later.

Bank Deposits and Checks

While paper is vastly more convenient than coin or bullion (not to say cows), it can still be awkward for large transactions. In addition, even paper money requires protection from theft, fire, and loss. The use of *bank drafts* or *checks* has overcome this difficulty. A person depositing coin or bullion with a banker can receive, instead of paper bills, the right to transfer ownership of the deposit by check. Since a check can be drawn for any amount desired, it is a convenient way to make large payments. Moreover, since it is signed by the writer and is payable only to a specified party who must endorse it, a check presents a minimum danger of loss or theft.

A bank deposit subject to transfer by check is called a *demand deposit,* or more commonly, a *checking account.* A check is merely an instrument by which ownership of a demand deposit is transferred from one person to another. It is really a stylized letter to the bank, instructing it to transfer a specified amount from the deposit of the

writer and to place it at the disposal (order) of someone else. Modern check forms often include account numbers and other information that can be read electronically to permit banks to use computers in their accounting, but these are for the convenience of the bank and have no legal status. A perfectly valid check can be drawn on a piece of ordinary note paper, and will be honored by the bank in which the payer has an account, although some banks charge an extra fee for the trouble of processing unusual forms.

So great is the convenience of paying by check that the check-writing privilege itself has become an important medium of exchange. In other words, people no longer want demand deposits in order to claim gold or silver, or even paper money, but because of the check-writing privileges that the deposits confer on them. People accept checks in payment because, when deposited, they transfer check-writing privileges to the depositor. The general acceptability of demand deposits has made them the most important form of money in modern use.[5]

Bank Credit as Modern Money

The emergence of demand deposits as money has altered an important aspect of

[5] Notice, incidentally, that it is the demand deposit—that is, the check-writing privilege—which is the money, not the check. A check is not money, but only a legal instrument by which money is transferred from one person to another. As anyone who has ever tried to cash a check in a strange place is painfully aware, checks do not have the general acceptability that would qualify them as money. There is always the danger that the check may be "bad"—that is, that it may have been written by somebody who did not have a bank account, and who was therefore not entitled to check-writing privileges. Once it has been established that the check is "good"—that is, that it does legally transfer a demand deposit to the receiver—it is accepted without question, anywhere.

our money system. Unlike gold and silver that are available only in limited natural amounts, demand deposits can be created by banks. Moreover, since what people want is check-writing privileges, bankers can create money and lend it at interest by simply granting borrowers the right to draw checks up to the amount of the loan. Checks drawn by borrowers are honored by bankers just like other checks, and check-writing privileges are transferred to the receiver in the same way. The implications of these facts are far-reaching. Every time a bank extends a loan, it actually creates new money in the form of demand deposits, transferable from person to person by check. As shown in Table 1, almost 80 percent of all the money in circulation in the United States today consists of check-writing privileges—demand deposits—created by banks. The remaining 20 percent consists mostly of Federal Reserve notes—themselves a form of created bank credit. The small remainder is composed of the coins we use for small change.

The shift from gold and silver to bank deposits as a medium of exchange was gradual, of course, and involved a long history of experimentation with financial institutions. Moreover, just as some people of an earlier period probably continued to think that gold and silver served as money only because they were "backed" by cows, so some people continued for years to believe that demand deposits and bank notes were not "real" money, but only valuable because they were "backed" by gold

or silver. The fact remains that, except for an occasional vestige (for example, the use of gold in certain international transactions to be examined later) the monetary system of the United States, like that of all other advanced industrial nations, is a system of bank credit, independent of cows, bullion, or any other natural material.

THE BANKING SYSTEM

Commercial Banks

To understand the mechanics of deposit creation and circulation, it is necessary to examine the organization and function of the modern banking system. The basic unit of the American banking system is the *commercial bank.* This is the bank that people and business firms deal with every day. It receives deposits and makes its profit by extending loans at interest. There are 2 types of deposits in a commercial bank. The most important are, as we have seen, demand deposits that can be transferred from person to person by check, but the deposits that most of us first become familiar with as children are savings deposits. *Savings deposits* are actually loans extended to the bank by the depositor, who receives interest in return for the use of his money. Ownership of a savings account cannot be transferred by check; money can be obtained only upon presentation of a passbook. Strictly speaking, since savings deposits are loans to the bank, funds can be withdrawn only on notice of 30 days or more. However, banks seldom invoke this provision except for a special class of savings deposits called *certificates of deposit* which must normally remain with the bank for a designated period of time.

Savings deposits are also received by savings and loan associations, mutual savings banks, credit unions, and other kinds

TABLE 1	UNITED STATES MONEY SUPPLY, JANUARY 1, 1968 (billions of dollars)		
Demand deposits			141.5
Currency outside banks			40.5
Paper currency		$36.8	
Fractional coin		3.7	
Total			$182.0

SOURCE: *Federal Reserve Bulletin,* January, 1968.

of banking institutions. However, only commercial banks receive demand deposits.

The Mechanics of Demand Deposit Creation

There are 2 ways that demand deposits come into existence. The first and most familiar is when people bring currency to the bank and deposit it. When you deposit $100 cash in your checking account, your bank's financial position is affected as shown by the changes in the balance sheet of Figure 1. Receipt of your currency raises the bank's cash assets by $100 and increases its demand deposit liability to you by the same amount. Notice that the total amount of money in circulation (that is, in the hands of the public and available for spending) is not altered by this transaction. You have taken currency out of circulation and "buried" it in the bank's vault, but you have received in exchange a demand deposit of equal value that you can spend by writing checks.

The second way in which deposits come into existence is through bank loans. Suppose you go to the bank and borrow $1,000 to buy a new car. The loan affects the bank's position as shown in Figure 2. Your note, probably secured by a lien on your car, increases the bank's assets by $1,000. In return, the bank increases its demand deposit liability to you by the same amount. The demand deposit, moreover, represents

FIGURE 2

YOUR BANK
Balance Sheet

SELECTED ASSETS	SELECTED LIABILITIES
Your note.......+ $1,000	Your demand deposit........+ $1,000

an increase in the amount of money in circulation. You have exchanged your note —which was not money, and which you could not have spent—for a demand deposit that you can spend by writing checks.

Circulation of Demand Deposits

Whether they originate from the deposit of cash or from loans, all demand deposits circulate in the same way. The essence of the matter is shown by following the arrows around Figure 3. When you write a check to pay for your new car, the automobile

FIGURE 3

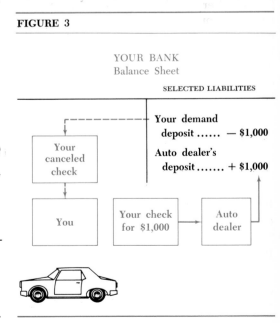

YOUR BANK
Balance Sheet

SELECTED LIABILITIES

Your demand deposit ...... — $1,000

Auto dealer's deposit .... + $1,000

FIGURE 1

YOUR BANK
Balance Sheet

SELECTED ASSETS	SELECTED LIABILITIES
Cash .... + $100	Your demand deposit .... + $100

dealer deposits it in the bank. The bank subtracts the amount of the check from your account, and adds it to the dealer's account. The canceled check is returned to you at the end of the month. You now have the car and the automobile dealer has been paid in full, receiving a demand deposit that he can spend by writing his own checks.

Once created, demand deposits remain in circulation until they are wiped out either by withdrawal of the currency or repayment of the loan that created them. To illustrate, suppose that by the time your loan is due you have accumulated $1,000 in your checking account. The position would again be as shown in Figure 2: The bank holds your note for $1,000, and you have $1,000 in your checking account. When you write a check to the bank to pay off your loan, the bank will return your note and wipe out your demand deposit, reducing the total amount of money in circulation.[6]

The creation and wiping out of deposit money occurs daily as banks extend loans and accept repayment. When banks extend loans faster than they are repaid, the volume of outstanding loans rises, and with it the amount of money in circulation. When banks extend loans more slowly than they are repaid, the volume of outstanding loans declines, and the amount of money in circulation contracts.

THE FEDERAL RESERVE SYSTEM

In one respect the preceding example of deposit circulation was rather special: Both you and the automobile dealer happened to patronize the same bank. What would hap-

pen if you dealt with different banks? How are check-writing privileges transferred from one bank to another? This process involves the Federal Reserve System.

For banking purposes, the United States is divided into 12 *Federal Reserve districts,* and a *Federal Reserve bank* is located in the major financial center of each district.[7] The policies of the 12 Federal Reserve banks are coordinated and centrally controlled by the *Federal Reserve Board.* Located in Washington, D.C., the Federal Reserve Board consists of 7 members, each appointed for a 14-year term of office by the President of the United States with the advice and consent of the Senate.

Federal Reserve banks create demand deposits and issue loans, but they differ from commercial banks in several important ways. First of all, unlike commercial banks, Federal Reserve banks are not private profit-making institutions. Instead, their task is to regulate the supply of money in the best interest of the economy. All the earnings of Federal Reserve banks above the minimum necessary for their continued operation are sent directly to the U.S. Treasury.

Secondly, Federal Reserve banks are the only banks permitted to issue notes for hand-to-hand circulation. As we noticed earlier, Federal Reserve notes make up all the paper money currently in use in the United States.

Third, and most important, a Federal Reserve bank is a banker's bank, its customers are commercial bankers, not the public. A Federal Reserve bank bears the same relationship to the commercial banks of its district that your commercial bank bears to you. Just as you make deposits in your bank, so your bank makes deposits in

---

[6] To keep things simple, we are ignoring interest and other charges, as well as the fact that automobile loans are usually paid off in installments.

[7] The Federal Reserve banks are located in Boston, New York, Philadelphia, Cleveland, Richmond, Atlanta, Chicago, St. Louis, Minneapolis, Kansas City, Dallas, and San Francisco. In addition, there are Federal Reserve branch banks in 24 other cities.

its Federal Reserve bank. Federal Reserve banks create deposits by expanding their loans, but these deposits are owned by commercial banks, and are transferred from one commercial bank to another.

Member Banks

Not all commercial banks can deal with Federal Reserve banks. This privilege is restricted to *member banks,* that is, to commercial banks that have become members of the Federal Reserve System. Although only about half of all commercial banks are member banks, these include most of the large important ones. Over 80 percent of the public's demand and savings deposits are in banks that are members of the Fed-

eral Reserve System. Because of their great importance, we shall restrict our discussion to member banks from this point on.

Bank Reserves and the Circulation of Deposits

The amount a member bank has on deposit with its Federal Reserve bank plus the currency in its own vaults is the bank's *reserves.* For example, a bank with $1 million cash in its own vaults and $3 million on deposit with its Federal Reserve bank, has $4 million in reserves. Bank reserves are the mechanism by which demand deposits circulate from one commercial bank to another. The operation is shown by the arrows in Figure 4.

FIGURE 4   INTERBANK CIRCULATION OF A DEMAND DEPOSIT

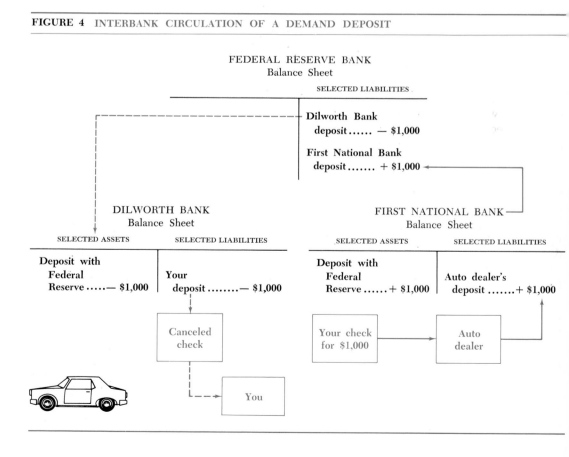

Suppose your account is with the Dilworth Bank, while your automobile dealer banks at the First National. When you pay for your new car, the dealer deposits your $1,000 check in his own account. The First National, in turn, deposits the check in its Federal Reserve bank, where reserves are transferred into the First National's account from the account of the Dilworth Bank. The Dilworth Bank learns of its loss of reserves when it receives your check from the Federal Reserve bank, deducts the $1,000 from your account, and sends you the canceled check.

The end result of the process is just as before. You have transferred $1,000 worth of check-writing privileges to the automobile dealer in exchange for your new car. In the process, however, the Dilworth Bank has lost reserves to the First National.

Bank Lending and Clearing Balances

Checks written in the ordinary course of business flow in large numbers in both directions and tend to cancel out. A business that writes checks to pay its bills normally receives checks from its customers at about the same rate. As some people are writing checks to pay their bills, others are having their accounts replenished by paychecks, and so on. The only reserves actually transferred in the normal course of business are the amounts needed to clear up the net amounts due at the end of the day, known as *clearing balances*.

On the other hand, when a person or firm borrows money, he writes a check to make payment that will *not* be offset by receipts until some time later. Indeed, the very cause of borrowing is the unavailability of receipts to cover expenditures to be made. For this reason, when a bank extends a loan, it can expect a clearing balance that will lose reserves equal to the deposit created and loaned. When a bank contracts its loans by lending less than it

receives in repayments, the reverse is true. The bank wipes out demand deposits and expects to gain reserves equal to the deposits wiped out.

Notice that we say that the bank *expects* to lose or gain reserves, but the expectation is not necessarily fulfilled. For one thing, there is a natural random variation in ordinary day-to-day clearing that may make the clearing balance on any given day exceed or fall short of expectations. More important, a bank's clearing balances are affected not only by its own lending, but by that of all other commercial banks as well. Since expanding banks lose reserves, a bank tends to gain reserves from others when they are expanding, and to lose reserves to them when they are contracting. By the same token, an expanding bank loses fewer reserves than expected when other banks are also expanding, and a bank whose deposits are expanding more slowly than others may even find itself gaining rather than losing reserves. A bank will gain fewer reserves if it is contracting its loans when others are also contracting, and may even lose reserves if it is contracting more slowly than the others.

Reserve Requirements and Short-Run Limits To Deposit Creation

Inability to cover clearing losses would be a serious matter. Prudent banking practice, therefore, demands that a bank regulate the amount it lends with an eye to the gains and losses in reserves to be expected. Even in the absence of any legal requirement, a bank would need to protect a minimum level of reserves to cover random day-to-day variation in clearing balances. In fact, however, a member bank is legally forbidden to allow its reserves to fall below a specified minimum fraction of its deposit liabilities. This fraction is the *required reserve ratio*, which is set by the Federal Reserve Board, and can be varied between limits that depend on the size and location of the bank and on the type of deposits involved.

For purposes of regulating reserves, member banks are divided into 2 classes. The few largest banks in the principal financial centers of the country are called *reserve city banks*. Smaller banks and banks outside the financial centers are called *country banks*. The limits to the Federal Reserve Board's power over required reserve ratios are shown in Table 2.

The required reserve ratio on the demand deposits of reserve city banks can be set anywhere between 10 and 22 percent, and on the demand deposits of country banks, anywhere between 7 and 14 percent. The reserve ratio on savings deposits of banks of either class must be set between 3 and 10 percent.

The amount of reserves required of any member bank is found by multiplying its deposits by the appropriate reserve ratio. When the required reserve ratios are 15 percent on demand deposits and 3 percent on savings deposits, a member bank with $2 million in demand deposit liability and $1 million in savings deposit liability must keep on hand reserves of not less than .15 × $2 million + .03 × $1 million, or $330,000. The higher the required reserve ratio, of course, the more reserves are required for the same deposits. For example, if requirements are raised to 20 percent for demand and 6 percent for savings deposits, the same bank would be required to keep reserves of .20 × $2 million + .06 × $1 million, or $460,000.

Since a bank expects to lose reserves when new demand deposits are created and loaned, it can safely expand its loans only by the amount by which its reserves exceed legal requirements. The bank above, for example, can prudently expand its loans only if its reserves are in excess of $460,000. When it has reserves of $600,000, the bank has excess reserves of $600,000 − $460,000, or $140,000, and can prudently expand its loans by this amount. The bank can sustain the expected clearing loss of $140,000 in reserves and still have the $460,000 legally required. If the bank should expand its loans by more than its excess reserves, it would run a serious risk of a clearing balance that would reduce its reserves below the legal minimum. For example, if the bank above, with reserves of $600,000 and required reserves of $460,000, should increase its loans by $200,000, the expected clearing loss would leave it with reserves of only $600,000 − 200,000, or $400,000, an amount $60,000, shy of legal requirements.

In effect, then, prudent banking practice restricts the deposit-expansion power and lending ability of each bank on any given day to the amount of excess reserves it holds on that day.

Long-Run Limits To Demand Deposit Creation

In contrast to the situation of individual banks on any given day, however, all commerical banks working collectively over a period of time can multiply their initial holdings of excessive reserves into a much larger amount of newly created deposits. For example, starting with an initial $100 million excess reserves on Monday, a banking system subject to a 20 percent reserve ratio can create a total of over $330 million in new deposits by Friday night, and when the process is continued during the following weeks a total of $500 million in new deposits can be created before the long-run limits to deposit expansion are reached.

There is no mystery to this, for bank

TABLE 2   LEGAL LIMITS TO REQUIRED
RESERVE RATIOS
(percent of deposits)

| | DEMAND DEPOSITS | | SAVINGS DEPOSITS |
	RESERVE CITY BANKS	COUNTRY BANKS	BOTH CLASSES OF BANKS
Maximum	22	14	10
Minimum	10	7	3

clearings do not change the total amount of bank reserves but merely shuffle them around from one bank to another. After expanding demand deposits by $100 million on Monday, bankers find total reserves unaltered when they look at their accounts Tuesday morning, for each dollar of reserves lost by one bank has been a dollar gained by another. When bankers add up their *excess* reserves, however, they find *less* than they had Monday morning because each new dollar created as a deposit on Monday added 20 cents to the amount of required reserves, leaving that much less in excess reserves. All told, $100 million in new deposits created on Monday would raise required reserves (and reduce excess reserves) by .20 × $100 million, or $20 million. But after subtracting this amount from Monday's excess reserves, bankers would discover that they still had $80 million in excess reserves on Tuesday morning, and could create more new deposits during Tuesday's business.

By the same logic, when banks create and lend another $80 million in new deposits on Tuesday, required reserves rise and excess reserves decline by another $16 million, and on Wednesday morning bankers find they still have $64 million in excess reserves. In short, each day banks can create new deposits to the amount of their excess reserves, only to find on the following morning that they still have excess reserves equal to 80 percent of the amount they held the day before. As a result, the new deposits that can be created and loaned beginning with initial excess reserves of $100 million on Monday is represented by an infinite series:
$100 million + 80 million + 64 million + . . .
Since each term in the series is 80 percent of its predecessor, the total of the series is given by $100 million/(1 − .80), or $500 million.

The Deposit Expansion Formula   In general, starting with excess reserves of X and a required reserve ratio of r, the new de-

posits, D, that can be created form an infinite series:

$$D = X[1 + (1 - r) + (1 - r)^2 + (1 - r)^3 + . . .]$$

Applying the usual formula for the sum of infinite series we arrive at the *deposit expansion formula: $D = X/r$*.

In other words, starting from a position of $100 million in reserves and a required reserve ratio of 20 percent on demand deposit liabilities, the banking system can create and lend new demand deposits to a limit of $$D = $100 million/.20, or $500 million, provided, of course, that the banking system neither gains nor loses reserves in the meantime.

The bank expansion formula has several important aspects. Banks create money in the process of expanding their loans, but their power to do so is limited by the amount of reserves in the banking system and by the required reserve ratio. The more excess reserves the banking system has at any time, the greater its potential to expand the amount of money in circulation. The higher the required reserve ratio, on the other hand, the smaller the potential bank expansion. If the required reserve ratio were 22 percent in the example above, the limit to the money-creating power of the banking system would be $100 million/.22, or $455 million. Both reserves and the required reserve ratio are under the control of the Federal Reserve Board, which therefore exercises close control over bank lending and over the quantity of money in circulation. This control is an important tool of Federal Reserve policy in stabilizing the economy.

FEDERAL RESERVE CONTROL OVER BANK LENDING

The Federal Reserve Board has 3 main tools to control bank expansion. These are: (1) buying and selling government bonds on the open market, (2) varying the required reserve ratio, and (3) altering the interest rate charged to member banks when they borrow from Federal Reserve banks.

Open-Market Operations

The most powerful and most frequently used tool of Federal Reserve control is the purchase and sale of U.S. government securities on the open market. When the Federal Reserve Board wants to increase member bank reserves, it instructs the Federal Reserve banks to enter the stock exchange and buy government bonds. The seller of the bond receives a check from the purchasing Federal Reserve bank. When he deposits the check, his own bank forwards it to the Federal Reserve bank and acquires a corresponding addition to its reserves. The effect is shown by following the arrows in Figure 5.

By increasing excess reserves, Federal Reserve purchase of government bonds raises the expansion power of the banking system by the multiple given in the deposit expansion formula on p. 237. Federal Reserve sale of government bonds reduces the excess reserves of the banking system and lowers its expansion power by a multiple factor. If the Federal Reserve sold bonds when the banking system was completely without excess reserves, it could actually force banks to lend money more slowly than it was repaid, thus reducing the amount of money in circulation.

The government bonds that are bought and sold in these open-market operations are already outstanding securities. That is, they make up part of the already existing

FIGURE 5   FEDERAL RESERVE BANKS INCREASE MEMBER BANK RESERVES BY BUYING BONDS ON THE OPEN MARKET

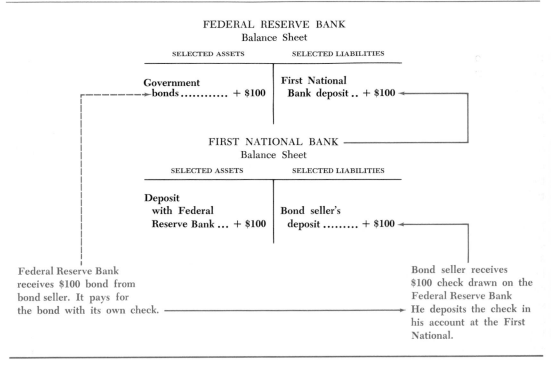

national debt. In fact, one of the important functions served by an outstanding national debt is to provide ammunition for the Federal Reserve open-market weapon. With our present-day national debt of over $350 billion, there is no shortage of marketable government bonds, but the smaller national debt of earlier periods—the barely $16 billion of the 1930s for example—gave little scope for open-market action.

The Variable Reserve Ratio

When the Federal Reserve System was established in 1914, required reserve ratios were fixed by law, but because of the small national debt and the large excess reserves of the period, the banking reform legislation of the 1930s gave the Federal Reserve Board the power to vary required reserve ratios to supplement its open-market operations. The limits to the Board's power to alter reserve ratios have already been indicated in Table 2.

The effect of changing required reserve ratios is easily traced. In the first place, with given bank reserves and deposit liabilities, reduction of the required ratio increases excess reserves. At the same time, the lower reserve ratio increases the amount of new deposits that can be created per dollar of initial excess reserves. In terms of the bank expansion formula, reduction of the required reserve ratio simultaneously increases the numerator (X), and diminishes the denominator (r), both of which contribute to higher expansion power.

For example, suppose member banks have total reserves of $22 billion, and have demand deposit liabilities of $100 billion and savings deposit liabilities of $120 billion. If required reserve ratios are 15 percent for demand deposits and 5 percent for savings accounts, legally required reserves amount to .15 × $100 + .05 × $120, or $21 billion. This leaves excess reserves of $22 − $21, or $1 billion, and the banking system can create and lend an amount of new deposits equal to $1 billion/.15, or $6.67 billion. If the Federal Reserve Board lowers the reserve ratio required on demand deposits to 10 percent, required reserves decline to .10 × $100 + .05 × $120, or $16 billion, and excess reserves rise to $22 − $16, or $5 billion. The reduction in the reserve ratio raises the amount of new deposits that the banking system can create and lend to $5 billion/.10, or $50 billion.

On the other hand, when the required reserve ratio is raised, banks need more reserves to satisfy legal requirements, leaving fewer excess reserves. At the same time the higher reserve ratio also means that each dollar of any excess reserves left will permit fewer dollars of expansion. The effect can be seen by reversing the previous illustration. When the required reserve ratio is raised from 10 percent to 15 percent, the expansion power of the banking system is reduced from $50 billion to $6.67 billion.

The Discount Rate

One of the advantages to membership in the Federal Reserve System is that member banks can borrow additional reserves from Federal Reserve banks. This means that even a bank without excess reserves can make loans by borrowing enough to cover the expected unfavorable clearing balance. When a Federal Reserve bank extends such a loan, it acquires the member bank's IOU as an asset, and increases its deposit liability to the member bank by an equal amount, as shown in Figure 6. Borrowed reserves circulate in the usual way and increase the expansion power of the banking system like any other reserves.

The interest rate charged on loans to member banks is called the *discount rate*. By raising and lowering the discount rate, the Federal Reserve bank can vary the profitability of member banks' lending with borrowed reserves. When the discount rate

FIGURE 6   A FEDERAL RESERVE BANK LENDS
$100 TO A MEMBER BANK

FEDERAL RESERVE BANK
Balance Sheet

SELECTED ASSETS	SELECTED LIABILITIES
Loans to member banks...+ $100	Member bank deposits....... + $100

MEMBER BANK
Balance Sheet

SELECTED ASSETS	SELECTED LIABILITIES
Deposit with Federal Reserve Bank ....+ $100	Loan payable to Federal Reserve Bank.... + $100

is low, say 1 percent or below as it was from 1942 to 1948, member banks can profitably borrow reserves to make loans at very low rates to their customers. When the discount rate is high, say 4.5 percent as it was during 1966, banks cannot afford to borrow reserves unless they can find customers for loans at much higher rates.

When the Federal Reserve System was established, the discount rate was expected to be an important control over bank lending. In fact, however, the discount rate is a relatively ineffective tool. Most member banks dislike to borrow from the Federal Reserve, preferring to stay out of debt even when it would be profitable to lend on the basis of borrowed reserves. In practice, therefore, lowering discount rates rarely induces member banks to borrow additional reserves. Member banks do borrow, but generally only when unexpected clearing losses leave them with reserves insufficient to cover their legal requirements, or when an old and valued customer needs a loan while excess reserves are inadequate to accommodate him. Such emergency borrowing is relatively unresponsive to interest costs, and raising the discount rate does

little to discourage it. The discount rate thus has little if any effectiveness as a regulatory tool.

Limitations to Federal Reserve Power

It is important to recognize the distinction between the ability to limit bank expansion and the ability to control the money supply itself. Federal Reserve controls operate in a one-sided fashion. Open-market operations, variable reserve ratios, and the discount rate give close control over the *limits* to expansion, but do not confer power over the degree to which banks approach the limit. By lowering the limit the Federal Reserve can hold the money supply in check, or even compel the banking system to contract, but when the Federal Reserve relaxes credit and raises the limit to expansion, banks do not necessarily increase their lending, nor does the money supply automatically rise. To increase the money supply, not only must the limit be raised, but banks must be willing to lend, and, in addition, able to find customers who want to borrow.

The effectiveness of curtailing bank lending power by withholding reserves from banks was well illustrated by the tight-money experience of 1966. Bank reserves, which had been expanding along with economic activity for several years, suddenly began to grow more slowly when open-market purchases were reduced and the discount rate raised in the fall of 1965. The results were higher interest rates and reduced bank lending throughout 1966. The impact on residential building was especially severe, as eager builders and would-be home-buyers found themselves unable to borrow mortgage money to finance construction.

An outstanding example of the negative side of the picture was the experience of the Depression of the 1930s. Although bank reserves were maintained while the decline in output from 1929 to 1933 cut GNP in half, commercial banks could find few borrowers even at sharply reduced interest rates. By 1935 total member bank reserves had doubled, but despite further reduction in interest rates, most of the increase merely served to swell excess reserves and had little effect on total demand.

CURRENCY

Although demand deposits constitute by far the greatest proportion of the total amount of money in circulation, paper bills and coins are more familiar to most people. To distinguish them from demand deposits, bills and coins are called *currency,* or sometimes, in order to emphasize their character, *hand-to-hand money.* Paper currency circulates from wallet to till, from till to purse, and from purse to cash register. In slower streams, coins flow from pocket and purse to vending machines, parking meters, pay telephones, and even to piggy banks, and back.

The paper currency in use in the United States today consists entirely of notes issued by Federal Reserve banks. Each Federal Reserve note is the liability of an individual Federal Reserve bank. Like a Federal Reserve deposit, Federal Reserve notes constitute reserves to member banks, but unlike reserve deposits, which circulate only among commercial banks, Federal Reserve notes circulate directly from person to person as money.

The quantity of notes in circulation is governed by the public's need for till and pocket money to carry on the daily business of small purchases and payments. When people need currency, they cash checks at the bank. This does not alter the total supply of money in circulation, but merely changes it to a different form. The Federal Reserve System provides great flexibility in the composition of the money supply, for in cashing checks, banks are not limited to

FIGURE 7 THE FIRST NATIONAL CASHES A CHECK AT THE FEDERAL RESERVE BANK TO REPLENISH ITS VAULT CASH

FEDERAL RESERVE BANK Balance Sheet	FIRST NATIONAL BANK Balance Sheet
SELECTED LIABILITIES	SELECTED ASSETS
Federal Reserve notes .... + $100,000 ———→	Vault cash ... + $100,000
Member bank deposit, First National Bank ... — $100,000 ←———	Deposit with Federal Reserve Bank .. — $100,000

the currency on hand. When banks run low on currency, they can get more by cashing checks on their Federal Reserve accounts. On the books of the Federal Reserve bank the transaction merely increases liabilities for Federal Reserve notes and wipes out an equivalent amount of member bank deposits, as shown in Figure 7.

The reverse process takes currency out of circulation. When people have more currency than they need for daily business, they bring the notes to the bank for deposit. In turn, when member banks accumulate more currency than necessary for their normal operations, they deposit the extra notes in the Federal Reserve bank. On the books of the Federal Reserve bank, member bank deposits are increased and an equal amount of the Federal Reserve notes is wiped out.

Coins circulate in much the same way as Federal Reserve notes, except that coins are minted by the U.S. Treasury. When additional coins are needed, the Treasury deposits them in its account at the Federal Reserve bank.[8] This increases the Federal

[8] In addition to their other functions, Federal Reserve banks furnish banking service to the U.S. government.

Reserve bank's assets and raises its deposit liability to the U.S. government. Coins are withdrawn by member banks and put into circulation as needed by the public.

The Ratio of Currency to Total Money Supply

At the present time, about 22 percent of the total money supply circulates as Federal Reserve notes and coin, but this percentage is subject to considerable variation, depending on habits, payment institutions, and the particular needs of the time. In the early days of deposit banking, few but the wealthiest, most sophisticated merchants understood the use of checks, and currency constituted the overwhelming part of the total supply of money. As shown in Figure 8, even as late as 100 years ago, the value of currency in circulation made up nearly half of the money supply.

By 1890 currency was only about 25 percent of the total, and by the end of the 1920s it had fallen to 13 percent. The declining percentage of currency was sharply reversed by the widespread distrust of banks accompanying the rash of bank failures in the 1930s. The ratio then declined again, only to rise during World War II, reaching nearly 28 percent in 1945. The reason for this wartime rise in the use of currency has never been established, but it was probably related to the use of currency for black-market purchases and other illegal transactions made in violation of wartime price control and rationing laws.

Although today currency is only 22 percent of the money supply, the proportion has been rising in recent years, probably because of the rising use of coin-operated vending machines, parking meters, and other machines. It is indicative that between 1950 and 1967 the volume of paper money grew slightly less than 50 percent from $26.2 billion to $39.1 billion. During the same period the amount of coins in

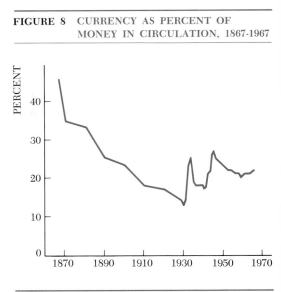

FIGURE 8   CURRENCY AS PERCENT OF MONEY IN CIRCULATION, 1867-1967

SOURCE: 1867–1957 calculated from money supply data in *Historical Statistics of the United States, Colonial Times to 1957*. After 1957 calculated from data from appropriate issues of the *Federal Reserve Bulletin*.

circulation nearly tripled, growing from $1.55 billion to $4.52 billion.

Whatever the cause of the recent rise in the use of currency, it is likely to be temporary. With the steadily growing popularity of credit cards, fewer and fewer transactions require currency, and there is every reason to expect a substantial future decline in the use of cash. Some bankers are already looking forward to a "cashless" society in which all payments will be made by the transfer of demand deposits via a nationwide network of computers, activated by credit cards.

Currency and Bank Expansion

The need for currency as part of the money supply suggests a modification of the bank expansion formula developed above. As we saw, the limit to the new money that could be created by the banking system beginning with excess reserves of X was given by $D = X/r$, provided the banking system lost no reserves in the process. Since currency is a form of bank reserves as well as a form of money, however, any increase of currency in circulation represents an automatic loss of reserves to the banking system as it expands.

To see the effect of these automatic reserve losses, suppose that a bank expands its loans, creating $100 of new deposits. When the borrower spends the money, not all of the checks will be redeposited in bank accounts; a certain percentage will be cashed to provide additional currency. When the public keeps 25 percent of its money in the form of currency, we can expect only about $75 of the newly created money to circulate as demand deposits. The other $25 will be cashed into currency.

As far as the public is concerned, the increase in money supply is still $100: $25 in currency and $75 in deposits. But to the banking system, the $25 currency represents a direct loss of excess reserves. In addition, of course, the banking system has lost excess reserves because the $75 of new deposits remaining in existence means an increase in required reserves. If the reserve ratio is 20 percent, this further reduces excess reserves by .20 × $75, or $15. Taking the new currency and the new deposits together, we see that in the creation of $100 of new money, the banking system has lost excess reserves of $25 + 15, or $40, 40 cents for every new dollar in circulation. On this basis, a banking system starting with excess reserves of $100 million could expand the money supply by a maximum of $100 million/.40, or $250 million. This limit is only half that given by the earlier formula.

This modified bank expansion formula can be generalized. When the required reserve ratio is r, and the public tends to keep a proportion of its money supply k in the form of currency, the banking system, starting with initial excess reserves of X and expanding the money supply by M, will still have remaining excess reserves of $X - M[k + r(1 - k)]$. The limit of bank expansion is reached when remaining ex-

cess reserves have been reduced to 0, at which time

$$0 = \$X - M[k + r(1 - k)]$$

and

$$M = \$X/[k + r(1 - k)]$$

In the example above, $X = \$100$ million, $k = .25$, $r = .20$. Thus,

$$M = \frac{\$100 \text{ million}}{.25 + .20(.75)} = \frac{\$100 \text{ million}}{.40}$$
$$= \$250 \text{ million}$$

Although the modified formula for bank expansion gives a lower and more realistic limit than the earlier one, the importance of the difference between them should not be exaggerated. Both show that potential bank expansion rises with increases in excess reserves and declines with increases in the required reserve ratio. The modified formula merely shows that potential bank expansion also declines when the public decides to keep a larger proportion of its money in the form of currency. The principal determinants of bank lending potential are still under the control of the Federal Reserve Board. When public use of currency (k) varies, the Federal Reserve can offset the effect by appropriate action to alter member bank reserves or to change required reserve ratios.

Bank Failures and Bank Runs

Demand deposits have not always been as fully acceptable as they are today. Commercial banks are, after all, private firms in business to make a profit. Demand deposits are the current liabilities of the firm, and like the liabilities of any other business, their security depends on the solvency of the concern.

A bank is in the business of lending money. The interest it collects provides the revenue to meet its cost, but even the most careful banker sometimes extends loans to businesses that fail and are unable to keep up interest payments. All banks allow for a certain proportion of bad-debt losses in their calculations, but occasionally a bank with poor judgment or bad luck acquires so many defaulted loans that interest collections are inadequate to cover operating costs. Such a bank must suspend operations. Its depositors are in the position of the creditors of a failed business and can expect to lose part of their funds.

The financial position of banks is especially delicate because their depositor-creditors can demand currency at any time, and since deposits are a multiple of reserves, if an unusual number of depositors should all demand payment at once, the bank would have insufficient cash to meet its immediate obligations. The sudden clamoring of a large number of depositors for withdrawal of their funds could force even the best bank to close its doors.

This phenomenon, called a *bank run,* was not uncommon prior to the banking reforms of the 1930s, and contributed greatly to the instability of the banking system. The failure of one bank could touch off runs at several others, as fearful depositors scrambled to withdraw their money. These banks would close their doors, encouraging runs on others, and trouble would spread in a chain reaction.

The danger was especially great during times of economic depression when unusual numbers of business failures left the banking system particularly vulnerable to panic. The climax came during the Great Depression when the number of banks suspended, which had averaged over 500 per year throughout the 1920s, rose to 1,350 in 1930, to 2,293 in 1931, and reached 4,000 in 1933. The federal government ended the disaster by closing all remaining banks simultaneously for systematic reorganization.

Many important changes in banking legislation resulted from this experience. Bank lending standards were raised. Bank inspection standards were made more stringent to protect depositors by earlier detection of trouble. One of the most important reforms was the establishment of the Federal Deposit Insurance Corporation (FDIC). This agency, operated by the U.S. government, insures each deposit made in subscribing banks up to the amount of $15,000. An insured deposit is perfectly secure, regardless of the soundness of the bank itself, making bank runs virtually a thing of the past.

MONEY AND AGGREGATE DEMAND

Although the primary emphasis in this chapter has been on the function of money as a medium of exchange and on the performance of the banking system as an institution, money and banks play a key part in influencing the total level of spending. In our study of the dynamics of price levels, we saw how rising prices coupled with fixed bank reserves reduced the real volume of purchases that could be financed by bank loans and hence limited the amount of real output. In the study of investment demand we noted the important influence of interest rates on investment spending for plant and equipment, inventory, and housing.

In the next chapter we will complete our study of the effect of money on total spending and show how the regulatory power of the Federal Reserve Board, integrated with the government's power to tax and spend, can be combined in an effective stabilization policy to contribute to continued growth at high levels of employment and output.

SUMMARY

The use of *money* as a *medium of exchange* is essential to high productivity in an economic system. In addition, money serves as a *measure of value* and as a *store of liquid wealth*. To perform these functions money must be *generally acceptable* in the community. Anything acceptable in this sense is money.

Originally, money often consisted of cattle, metal, or other commodities of value in their own right, but aside from a few token coins, modern money is exclusively *bank credit,* most of which is in the form of *demand deposits* circulated through *commercial banks* and created by bank lending.

The most important commercial banks are members of the *Federal Reserve System* and maintain reserves in the form of deposits at Federal Reserve banks. Circulation of demand deposits from one commercial bank to another involves the transfer of *bank reserves* through the Federal Reserve System. Member banks are legally required to maintain reserves in currency or on deposit with the Federal Reserve bank in a specified ratio to their deposits. The need to maintain these *legally required reserves* forces bankers to limit the amount of deposits created during any given banking day to the amount of *excess reserves* on hand, but the long-run *deposit-creating power* of the banking system as a whole is a multiple of its initial excess reserves. This long-run limit to bank expansion is defined by the *deposit expansion formula:* $D = X/r$.

The lending power of the banking system is controlled by the Federal Reserve Board, primarily through its power to alter bank reserves by purchases and sales of government securities on the *open market.* The Board can also control lending power by altering the legally required reserve ratio and by changing the *discount rate* at which member banks are permitted to borrow reserves from Federal Reserve banks. Although these controls give the Federal Reserve System complete control over potential bank lending, they do not bestow power over the extent to which the power is actually used.

While most money circulates in the form of demand deposits, about one-fifth is in the form of *currency* used for hand-to-hand transactions. Public need for currency imposes an additional limitation to potential bank lending power. *Bank runs*—a rush of depositors to secure currency in exchange for their deposits—were a common phenomenon that contributed greatly to economic instability 40 years ago. But since the FDIC and the banking reforms of the 1930s, bank runs are a thing of the past.

The next chapter will complete our examination of the effect of money on total demand and show how monetary policy fits into a general program of economic stabilization.

CHAPTER 14

Public Policy for Stable
Economic Growth

Contrary to what many people believed even as recently as 30 years ago, an economic system is not a completely self-regulating mechanism. Without a central agency to help balance aggregate spending against productive capacity, unemployment tends to be chronic, and severe depressions are frequent. In the U.S., the primary responsibility for maintaining economic stability is lodged with the federal government and the Federal Reserve Board. The body of actions by which they influence aggregate demand is referred to as *stabilization policy*. There are 2 broad subclasses of stabilization policy: (1) *Fiscal policy* involves the use of government spending and taxation to influence aggregate demand. (2) *Monetary policy* involves the use of controls over bank lending power, the money supply, and interest rates.

In this chapter we will study the nature and operation of these policy tools in some depth. We will first look at fiscal policy to see exactly how government spending and taxation affect the economy. We will then turn to monetary policy, develop some important elements of monetary theory, and examine their implications for the use of Federal Reserve controls. Finally, we will study the broader problem of coordinating monetary and fiscal tools into a single coherent stabilization policy.

FISCAL POLICY

Deliberate action by the government to use its spending or tax rates to influence GNP is *fiscal policy*. Since government spending forms an important part of the net stimulus acting on the economy during any given year, any change in it exerts a multiplied effect on total output. Changes in tax rates, by altering the amount of disposable income available to households or by changing the profitability of business investment, generate initial changes in expenditures which likewise become part of the net stimulus.

In broad terms, we can think of these tools as a "gas pedal" and a "brake" that government can use to speed up or slow down the economy. Increased government spending represents pushing on the economic throttle to speed up the flow of output, while reduced spending represents easing off on the gas to slow the economy down. With the other foot, so to speak, the government controls the tax "brake." Raising tax rates withdraws buying power from private households and business firms, cutting their spending and slowing down the rate of output, while tax reduction releases the brakes and permits demand to expand. The total effect of fiscal policy depends on how the government combines these tools, but it is more systematic to trace out their influence separately. In what follows, whenever we speak of the effect of an increase in spending, we will refer only to the contribution of the spending part of the government policy, regardless of where the funds originate, and when we speak of the effect of changes in tax rates, we will deal only with the contribution of the tax part of the policy, regardless of what the government does with the money it raises. Once they are understood separately, spending and taxation are easily brought together and their combined effect explored.

Government Spending

The Effect of Government Spending on the Level of GNP   Government spending consists of 2 broad classes of transactions. About two-thirds of all outlays are made for the purchase of goods and services for government use. The remaining one-third consists of transfer payments, mostly payments of pensions to persons. The 2 types have the same multiplier impact on the level of GNP. Government purchase of

goods and services provides a direct stimulus to the economy in the form of increased sales to government, while most transfer payments are received by low-income families who usually spend them dollar for dollar. Since the impact multiplier is 2, each $1 billion change in either government purchases or transfers contributes a $2 billion change to the level of GNP.

The Effect of Government Spending on the Kinds of Goods Produced   The fact that outright government purchase of goods and services has the same total impact on GNP as transfer payments to persons does not make the 2 types of expenditures equivalent. Obviously, the kinds of goods and services produced depend a great deal on what kinds of goods the government buys when it spends its money, and on whether the government spends for itself or transfers money to others to spend. Increased government spending for the military means that more labor and resources are used for missiles and military hardware, spending for schools means more teachers and school buildings, while the transfer of income to poor people means more food, clothing, and better living standards in the slums.

Because of these important differences, the effect of government spending on the size of GNP is inevitably entangled with the effect on the composition of that GNP. A proposal to spend more is inevitably a proposal to increase the output of goods and services in some particular way, and a proposal to cut spending is a proposal to cut particular programs or particular items. As we have seen, decisions about government expenditure on particular items should depend on the benefits to be expected compared to costs. It would be poor policy indeed to cut back urgently needed programs merely to retard the growth of GNP, and it would seriously waste resources to devote them to trivial uses merely to stimulate demand. For this reason, the gas pedal of government spending is a poor tool for stabilizing the economy. It is better to establish the government's expenditure budget by carefully weighing social needs against opportunity costs, and to rely on the tax brake as the principal instrument for adjusting the level of total output.

Taxation

Tax laws affect the stability of the economy in 2 ways. On one hand, the *level* of tax rates in force at any particular time affects the size of the multiplier. On the other hand, *changes* in tax rates produce changes in spending that alter total output. The distinction between these effects is elementary, but failure to recognize it is frequently a source of misunderstanding.

Tax Rates and the Size of the Multiplier

The size of the respending ratio partly depends on how much of any given increase in GNP people are allowed to keep as disposable income. For example, when tax rates extract 20 cents of each additional dollar of earnings, a family whose taxable income rises by $100 adds only $80 to its disposable income. If the family's marginal propensity to consume is typical of that of the U.S. as a whole, $60 out of the added $80 will be spent for increased consumer goods. If the tax rate were as high as 50 percent, $100 additional earnings would mean only $50 of disposable income and the purchase of $37.50 in consumer goods, while if the tax rate were as low as 5 percent, the same additional earnings would result in an addition of $71.25 to consumer spending. Rates of indirect business taxes and the tax rate on corporate profits likewise affect the multiplier. High rates on these taxes limit the fraction of GNP that becomes part of personal income, and make the respending ratio corresponding smaller.

Revenue from U.S. personal and corporate income taxes rises more than 18

cents with each dollar of GNP, and when federal payroll, excise, and other taxes are included, the rise is more nearly 30 cents. Between 1965 and 1967, for example, growth of U.S. GNP of $91.2 billion was accompanied by an increase of $26.7 billion in federal tax receipts. The solid line of Figure 1 shows the approximate relationship of U.S. tax receipts to GNP.

The impact multiplier of 2, characteristic of the U.S. economy in recent years, results partly from high corporate profit and other business taxes that, together with depreciation charges, absorb 30 percent of any increase in gross national income before it reaches households as taxable income, and partly from the high personal tax rates that extract 20 percent of the remainder before it can be spent. During the low-tax era of the 1920s and early 1930s, 80 percent of any change in GNP flowed into people's hands as personal income, and the effective marginal personal tax rate was only about 3 percent. Because of these differences, the U.S. multiplier at that time was very nearly 3! This high multiplier was one of the important causes contributing to the extent and rapidity of the collapse during the Great Depression. When residential construction and investment spending de-

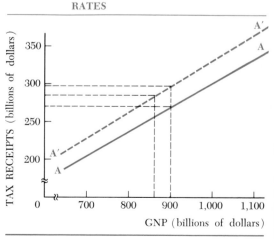

FIGURE 1   AN EXAMPLE OF CHANGING TAX
RATES

TAX RECEIPTS (billions of dollars)

GNP (billions of dollars)

clined, the resulting negative stimulus was subject to a much greater impact multiplier than would be true today with our system of higher tax rates.

Changes in Tax Rates as Economic Stimuli

Taxes become an active stimulus for economic change only when the tax rate itself is altered to increase or decrease the number of dollars collected from firms and households at each given level of income. The consequent change in the amount of disposable income leads people to change their spending, which initiates a multiplied change in output. When tax rates are raised, loss of income leads to reduced spending and GNP falls; when tax rates are cut, people find themselves with more income to spend and the GNP rises.[1]

The point is illustrated by Figure 1. A 10 percent increase in tax rates would be represented by a shift of the line from AA to the dashed line A'A' to indicate that tax collections at any given level of income would be 10 percent higher than before. If the tax increase occurred while GNP was at the $900 billion level, households and business firms would be forced to pay $27 billion more taxes and would have that much less to spend. The resulting reduction of spending would initiate a multiplied reduction in GNP. As GNP declines, of course, so do tax receipts, and the final result might be that shown by the broken line: GNP has been reduced to $860 billion, and actual tax receipts have risen by $14 billion.

In one respect the example of Figure 1 is unrealistic, for no allowance has been made for the contribution of other stimuli to the change in GNP. It is more realistic to say tax increases are used to offset some of the other autonomous increases in spending in order to slow the growth of total spending, not to force an actual decrease. Thus tax increases are not expected to result in a decline in GNP, but merely to reduce the rate of increase as a check to inflation. By the same token, tax reduction is usually intended as an addition to other sources of autonomous spending to speed up the growth of GNP in order to reduce the level of unemployment.

The stimulating effect of a change in tax rates depends on whether the change is made in personal or in business taxes. An increase in personal tax rates leaves households with less disposable income and induces them to cut their consumption spending. Since the marginal propensity to consume is .75, households tend to reduce consumer outlays by 75 cents for every dollar of added tax liability. The reduction in household consumption spending then initiates a multiplied reduction in GNP.

For example, if personal income tax rates were raised by 10 percent at a time when annual personal tax liabilities were already $80 billion, households would be deprived of an additional $8 billion of purchasing power, and would tend to reduce consumption expenditure by .75 × $8 billion, or $6 billion. This initial reduction in spending would, in turn, tend to check the growth in GNP by 2 × $6 billion, or $12 billion.[2] If personal tax rates had been reduced instead of increased, the result would have been the opposite. An $8 billion tax cut would tend to raise household spending by $6 billion, and would contribute $12 billion to the growth of GNP.

A change in business taxes—for example, a rise in corporate profits tax rates—has a double effect. In the first place, higher business tax rates leave less profit after

---

[1] Since an increase in tax rates reduces the multiplier, its total impact depends on the *new* multiplier. In most practical cases, however, year-to-year changes in tax rates have only a negligible effect on the multiplier, and in what follows changes in the multiplier have been ignored.

[2] A more complete analysis would take account of the change produced in this ratio by the alteration of the tax rate itself, but this change is small enough to neglect in most practical cases. (See the preceding footnote.)

taxes to be paid out in dividends, which reduces personal income and means less consumer buying. But since many corporations tend to keep dividend payments stable even in the face of fluctuating profits, the direct effect of business tax rates on consumer spending is small.

The important effect of business taxes is exerted through changes in the marginal efficiency of investment. For instance, a project which, in the absence of a profits tax, would be profitable at an interest rate of 10 percent, would be worthwhile only at 9 percent if one-tenth of the net income were withdrawn in taxes, and only at 5 percent if the tax rate were raised to 50 percent. At given interest rates, therefore, an increase in business tax rates reduces the number of profitable projects, and business investment spending declines. By the same token, a reduction in business tax rates increases the number of profitable projects and contributes to an increase in business investment spending.

This theory is illustrated in Figure 2, in which the solid line, MEI_0, represents the marginal efficiency of investment before a rise in corporate profits tax rates. At the going interest rate r_0, business firms would tend to spend I_0 dollars for new plant and equipment. A rise in corporate profits tax rates would lower the marginal efficiency of investment to the position represented by the dashed curve MEI_1. Given the same interest rate, investment spending would be reduced from I_0 to I_1, which would initiate a multiplied impact on GNP.

FIGURE 2 THE EFFECT OF AN INCREASE IN BUSINESS TAXES ON INVESTMENT SPENDING

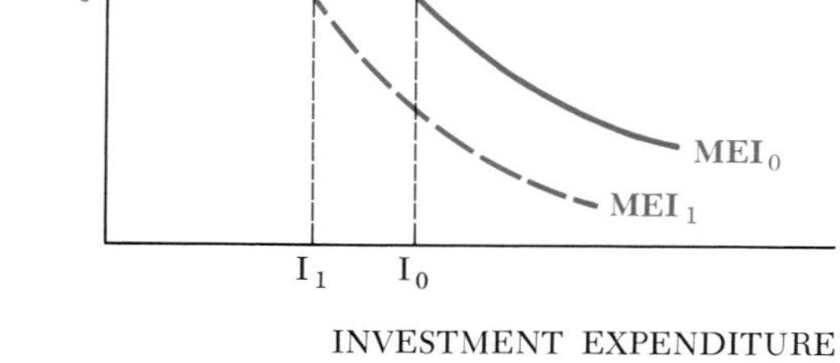

Recent History of Federal Tax Rates At the beginning of the Korean War, federal government spending grew from $18.4 billion in 1950 to $37.7 billion in 1951. Without other offset, this $19.3 billion additional spending would have contributed nearly $40 billion to the gross national product. At the same time, however, a $3.3 billion increase in income taxes cut consumer spending by an initial $2.5 billion. When the impact multiplier is taken into account, the increased tax rates provided an offset of 2 × $2.5 billion, or $5 billion to the rising GNP. With the termination of hostilities in Korea, war expenditures declined, and economic growth slowed sharply. Reduction in personal income tax rates lowered income tax liabilities by $3 billion in 1954, contributing an initial $2.2 billion to household expenditures for consumer goods and almost $4.5 billion to the GNP. Since this was not nearly enough to balance the impact of a $7 billion reduction in government purchases, real GNP declined, and unemployment soared to almost 7 percent of the labor force. Cuts in business taxes initiated at the same time, after the usual lag, stimulated business spending for new plant and equipment, which rose $4.5 billion in 1955, contributing nearly a third of the $33 billion rise to the GNP.

The federal tax cut of 1964–1965 was also deliberately engineered to stimulate the economy. The Revenue Act of 1964 provided for a 2-stage reduction in tax rates. The first stage, effective in 1964, involved a cut of about $6 billion in tax liability. That is, even if production had

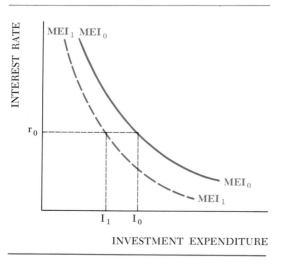

remained unchanged from 1963 to 1964, disposable personal income would have risen $6 billion, generating an initial increase of .75 × $6 billion, or $4.5 billion in consumer spending. Including its multiplied influence, the tax cut added $9 billion to the rise in gross national product in 1964. The second stage of the cut lowered 1965 tax liabilities another $3 billion, of which consumers spent three-quarters, or $2.3 billion. This stimulus contributed $4.6 billion to the rise in GNP in 1965.

With the expansion of the war in Vietnam, government military spending rose from $50 billion in 1965 to almost $80 billion in 1968, an average increase of nearly $10 billion a year for 3 years, contributing $20 billion a year to the growth of GNP. Under this extraordinary stimulus, the unemployment rate, which had averaged 4.5 percent of the labor force in 1965, was reduced to 3.8 percent in 1966 and reached 3.6 percent in 1968.

In keeping with the Phillips curve, this tightening of the labor market was accompanied by increasingly rapid price increases, and by early 1968 the implicit deflator of the GNP was rising at 4 percent per year. In mid-1968 Congress passed a temporary surcharge to increase personal and corporate profits tax liabilities by a uniform 10 percent for all taxpayers. Since the law was made effective only for three-quarters of 1968, however, the effective increase in the tax rate was only 7.5 percent. This increased 1968 personal income tax liabilities by an initial $5.6 billion and checked the growth in GNP by about $11.2 billion. However, since tax rates were raised late in the year, a substantial part of the impact fell in 1969 rather than 1968.

Budgetary Deficits

While it is plain that increased spending stimulates the economy and increased taxation puts on the brakes, the net effect of a given combination of the 2 is not always obvious. One might think that if the government increased expenditures by $1 billion while simultaneously extracting an additional $1 billion in tax revenue, the actions would cancel each other out, leaving the gross national product unaffected. Such a balanced budget, it might be supposed, would reduce private purchases by exactly the amount of the increase in government spending and leave the total unaffected. This is not the case. An additional $1 billion dollars in tax revenue does not cut consumer expenditures equally, but only by about $.75 billion. If the added tax were accompanied by an additional $1 billion dollars in government spending, therefore, the net stimulation would be $1 billion − $.75 billion, or $.25 billion, which would be expanded to a $.5 billion increase in GNP under the impact multiplier.[3] If the process were reversed and spending and taxes were cut by equal amounts, the spending reduction would not be balanced by rising consumer outlays and GNP would decline.

Because of the passive response of tax revenues to changes in aggregate demand, government action to balance the budget is often exactly the opposite of what is needed to stabilize the economy. When private demand begins to decline, government tax receipts automatically shrink as incomes fall. If the government attempts to balance its budget by raising tax rates enough to cover expenditures or by cutting expenditures to match lower tax yields, it subtracts even further from total demand and

[3] As a matter of fact, the process as described would not only result in an expansion of total output, it would even result in an *excess* of tax revenue over outlays. A rate increase that would collect an additional $1 billion of taxes at *existing* levels of income would collect even more when income rises under the impact multiplier. If tax rates were increased just enough to yield an additional $1 billion of revenue, *including* what would be added by the expansion of income itself, the increase in GNP would be about $.8 billion, almost as large as the increase in expenditure itself!

adds to the amount of unemployment. An upsurge of private demand brings an automatic rise in tax receipts, yet corresponding increases in government spending or reductions in tax rates only add fuel to the inflationary pressure on the economy. Proper fiscal policy, then, often requires the government to increase spending and cut taxes at the very time its tax revenues are declining and to decrease spending and raise tax rates when tax revenues are already rising.

An important element in the collapse of the American economy in the 1930s was the frantic reduction of expenditure by all levels of government in an effort to balance their budgets in the face of falling revenues. Total expenditures by federal, state and local governments declined by $2 billion from $12.7 billion in 1931 to $10.7 billion in 1932. Since the multiplier was 3, this contributed $6 billion to the decline in GNP between these years. This was more than a third of the total fall of $17.8 billion!

The National Debt

When government outlays exceed budgetary receipts, the government borrows the difference by issuing government bonds. The sum total of outstanding government bonds is the *national debt*. In other words, whenever the governmental budget shows a deficit, the national debt increases.

There are a few people, even today, to whom the idea of a national debt is highly threatening. For some reason they see it as a tremendous weight bearing down on society, threatening national bankruptcy, passing on a future burden to our grandchildren, and otherwise weakening the national fiber.

This fear has many roots. Debt and money lending have long been associated in people's minds with the idea of exploitation of the helpless. During the Middle Ages money lending was termed usury, and

the practice was forbidden to Christians. Later on debtors unable to repay what they owed were thrown into prison. In the U.S., the image is strong of the farmer, laboring honestly to earn his bread by the sweat of his brow, losing his farm to the money lender from the city. The prototype villain in the 19th-century melodrama was the banker who threatened to foreclose on the old homestead unless the daughter would consent to marry him. A modern wage earner who cannot keep up the payments finds his car and furniture repossessed and his wages garnisheed. The essence of middle-class respectability is to live within your means and to be able to pay what you owe. The threat of the "disgrace" of financial failure is combined with the idea that there is something profligate and characterless in spending more than you earn. The feeling is that somehow the results are bound to catch up with you and present pleasures will be paid for in future misery.

As far as the individual family is concerned, of course, many of these fears are entirely rational. A family *can* get into debt beyond its means, and the result *is* trouble and loss. The error lies in identifying what is true of a family with what is true of a national government. The government of the United States is not a household, and what applies to household debts has no relevance to the government. Congress has the power both to levy taxes and to coin money. Given those powers, what possible danger is there that the government could not meet its obligations? Rising household debt constitutes a serious problem to a family on a fixed income, but the tax receipts of the United States rise steadily with the GNP. If this increase is not enough, it can be augmented by raising tax rates or simply by printing money. No family can do this. Household debt is owed by one household to another. To pay it or to pay the interest on it, money or assets must be transferred from one household to another. But government debt is not owed by one government to another, but by firms and households collectively as taxpayers to particular households and firms who own government bonds.

There is, of course, an economic problem associated with the national debt, but it is peculiar to a *national* debt and cannot be understood in terms of vague fears or mistaken identification with household debt. This is the transfer problem. Payment of interest on the national debt requires that some of the taxes paid by taxpaying firms and households be transferred as interest payments to the bond-owning households and firms. To see the extent of this problem, we must look at the size of the debt and the distribution of ownership of government securities.

Size of the National Debt At the beginning of 1969, the national debt amounted to nearly $358 billion. As shown in Figure 3, most of the debt was accumulated as part of the financing of World War II, when the debt grew from $50 billion in 1940 to almost $260 billion by 1946. In 1946 the national debt exceeded the GNP, which was approximately $200 billion at the time. Although the debt rose another $90 billion

during the following 20 years, this was much slower than the growth in total output, and by 1969 the debt amounted to less than half the GNP. The steady decline of the relative size of the debt reduces the transfer problem in a growing economy, since interest payments involve the redistribution of a smaller and smaller portion of national income.

As we saw in the budget, the interest paid on this debt was the third largest item of federal expenditure, and amounted to 1.6 percent of the GNP. Even so, government interest payments ranked far below social security, medicare, and other social insurance payments, which amounted to nearly 3 times as much.

Government Ownership of Government Securities Actually, the transfer problem is even smaller than the $358 billion debt or the $12.5 billion interest bill suggests, because, as shown in Table 1, a substantial

FIGURE 3 U.S. NATIONAL DEBT, 1929-1968

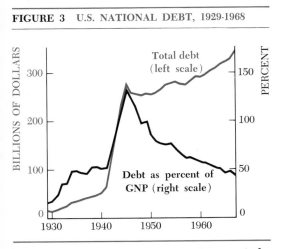

SOURCE: Data given in *Economic Report of the President, 1969.*

TABLE 1 ESTIMATED OWNERSHIP OF U.S. GOVERNMENT OBLIGATIONS, JANUARY 1, 1969

	BILLIONS OF DOLLARS	PERCENT OF TOTAL
Held by governments and governmental agencies	156.3	43.5
U.S. Government trust funds	$76.5	21.3
Federal Reserve banks	52.9	14.7
State and local governments	26.9	7.5
Held by banks and insurance companies	76.9	21.4
Commercial banks	$65.4	18.2
Mutual savings banks and insurance companies	11.5	3.2
Held by individuals	75.1	21.1
Held by nonfinancial corporations	14.6	4.2
Held by other investors	35.1	9.8
Total	$358.0	100.0

SOURCE: *Economic Report of the President, 1969.*

part of the securities represented by that debt are owned by agencies of U.S. federal, state, and local governments. Surprising as it may seem, the U.S. government is, itself, one of the biggest owners of government bonds! When collections of social security taxes exceed the amounts paid out in pensions and for medicare, and when collections of unemployment taxes exceed benefits paid out, the balances are placed in trust funds invested in government bonds. These government trust funds own over $76 billion, or nearly a quarter of the total national debt. Interest payments on this "self-owned" debt amount to bookkeeping transactions within the federal government, and involve no external transfers at all, but appear in the budget as interest received by trust funds.

A second important group of holders of government bonds are the 12 Federal Reserve banks, whose nearly $53 billion in securities, acquired in the course of their open-market operations, constituted another 14.7 percent of the total national debt at the beginning of 1969. By law, all revenue of Federal Reserve banks beyond operating costs and a 6 percent return on the capital invested in them by member banks is paid directly into the U.S. Treasury. Therefore, most of the interest paid on securities owned by the Federal Reserve flows directly back to the Treasury and involves no transfer of funds among private firms or households.

Many state and local governments with budgetary surpluses accumulate funds for future capital expenditure, or build up sinking funds to repay their own securities when due. These funds are often invested in U.S. government bonds. Likewise, some state and local governments that collect taxes only once or twice a year invest substantial amounts in government bonds and other government securities until the funds are needed to meet expenses. Their total holding of nearly $27 billion amounted to

another 7.5 percent of the national debt in 1969. Interest payments by the federal government to state and local governments represent transfers from one public pocket to another, from the people organized as a national government to the same people organized as state governments, city governments, school boards, and so on. Again this process does not involve a transfer from one private firm or household to another.

All told, federal trust funds, Federal Reserve banks, and state and local governments own $156.3 billion, or over 43 percent of the total debt, none of which involves any important transfer problem.

Other Owners of the National Debt The remaining 56.5 percent of the national debt is held outside governments and governmental agencies and does involve income transfers among firms and housholds. Some of these transfers, however, merely finance activities that would have to be supported in some other way. Some proportion of the national debt—the exact amount is unknown, but it is probably a little less than 10 percent—is owned by nonprofit institutions like colleges, universities and schools, hospitals, museums, and research and educational foundations. These institutions provide services that are generally in the public interest and are normally accorded public support. If bond interest were not available, other tax money would probably be used for these purposes. The situation of many household owners of government bonds is much the same. Individuals own $75.1 billion in government securities, constituting over 20 percent of the total national debt. In 1969, $51 billion of these individual holdings were in the form of nonmarketable Savings Bonds, many involving family savings accumulated to help finance education or training or for similar purposes for which scholarship assistance might otherwise have been required.

Of the outstanding government securities

21 percent were held by financial institutions—commercial banks, mutual savings banks, and insurance companies. The transfers involved in interest payment on this part of the debt are widely distributed, since a substantial portion of the interest received by financial institutions is immediately paid out to households and firms as interest on savings and time deposits, or accumulated to increase the value of their insurance policies. The remainder of the debt is held by nonfinancial corporations and by international institutions and foreigners.

Looked at directly as a social institution rather than as an object of vague and undefined fears, the national debt can be seen to involve a problem of transferring purchasing power among income receivers. At its largest, the total amount of these transfers is only about a third the size of those involved in our social insurance programs. Moreover, many of the transfers amount to nothing more than bookkeeping transactions within the federal government, or among different governments representing the same people. Some of the remaining interest payments are used to finance activities that would be otherwise supported anyhow, and most of the rest are widely spread among firms and households. Since these firms and households are themselves taxpayers, it is impossible to say how much net transfer of income results from the process. It is clear, however, that among the difficulties encountered in applying tax and expenditure policy to stabilize the economic system, its effect on the national debt is a low-priority problem.

Legal Responsibility for Fiscal Policy

A glance at economic history reveals that the American record of output and employment leaves much to be desired. As far back as the data can be interpreted, they show periodic surges of demand followed by periods of severe unemployment. There were many reasons for the continuation of this situation, but the predominant one was widespread failure to understand the mechanisms that linked demand for one product to demand for others, and a mistaken belief in a natural tendency for the economic system to balance itself automatically at a position of high employment with stable prices. Since the economic system was supposed to be self-regulating, neither the government nor anybody else took any responsibility for it. In fact, attempts to adjust or regulate the economy were often seen as dangerous interference, and as likely to make matters worse instead of better. The proper role of government was supposed to be to minimize expenditures, balance its budget, and generally to keep out of the way.

The belief in a naturally balanced economy persisted despite almost regularly recurring periods of severe depression and unemployment until the general collapse of the world economy in the early 1930s. The search for the causes of this catastrophe greatly improved our scientific understanding of the nature of aggregate demand, and particularly of its important relationship to government action. Economists, businessmen, and people in government began to realize that a fiscal policy that prescribed cuts in government spending or higher tax rates as a response to declining tax receipts contributed additional impetus to the decline of employment. When U.S. war production converted the 15 percent unemployment of 1940 into a serious labor shortage in 1942, the point became clear to everybody.

As World War II drew to a close, the new understanding of the nature of aggregate demand became coupled with a strong resolution to enlist the power of the federal government to preserve prosperity and to prevent recurrences of widespread and prolonged unemployment. This intention was embodied in the Employment Act of 1946, in which the United States government was assigned the responsibility to use all practicable means "(1) for the purpose of creating and maintaining, in a manner calculated to foster and promote free competitive enterprise in the general welfare, conditions under which there will be afforded useful employment opportunities, including self-employment, for those able, willing, and seeking work, and (2) to promote maximum employment, production, and purchasing power." The Act also established the Council of Economic Advisers, a 3-man team of economists appointed by the President with the advice and consent of the Senate to assist in carrying out the objectives of the Act. With the help of the Council, the President is required to present an annual Economic Report to Congress, giving an analysis of the position of the economy and of steps needed to improve it. The report is received by the Joint Economic Committee, a standing committee of the Congress established by the Act, which holds hearings on it and on the current economic outlook and the relevance of the proposed economic policy to it.

Much remains to be learned about the operation of the economic system and about proper methods of regulation, but since the passage of the Employment Act aggregate demand and employment have experienced steadier growth and greater stability than during any period of the same length in our history. Of course, some of this improvement has been due to changes in economic institutions. The introduction of unemployment insurance, social security, and a highly progressive income tax have lowered the multiplier and reduced the sensitivity of the economic system to initial changes in demand. Some of the improvement is also the result of better understanding on the part of businessmen and others of the way the economic system functions,

but the most important factor is the assumption by the federal government of the formal legal responsibility to maintain an overall balance between productive capacity and aggregate demand.

MONETARY THEORY AND MONETARY POLICY

In its widest sense, monetary policy involves the entire spectrum of financial matters, but from the point of view of stabilization policy it concerns the control over bank reserves and bank lending power exercised by the Federal Reserve to help avoid high unemployment or severe inflation. During periods of high unemployment the Federal Reserve Board can purchase securities on the open-market to swell bank reserves, reduce legal reserve requirements, and lower discount rates to expand bank lending power. The resulting expansion of the money supply provides investment funds to business at lower interest rates, makes mortgage funds available to homebuilders, and allows consumers more favorable terms for installment buying. During inflationary periods when prices are rising too rapidly, the Federal Reserve Board can reduce its open-market purchases or even sell securities to soak up bank reserves, increase legal reserve requirements, and institute higher discount rates to cut down bank lending power and contract the money supply.

The mechanics of monetary policy have already been implied in our earlier discussions. They are reviewed in Figure 4. The curve MEI represents the marginal efficiency of investment at any given time. At the interest rate r_0, business firms tend to spend I_0 on investment projects. If there is severe unemployment under these circumstances, the Federal Reserve Board can take steps to increase the availability of credit and bring down interest rates, say to r_1.

FIGURE 4   CONTROL OF INVESTMENT
           SPENDING BY MEANS OF THE
           INTEREST RATE

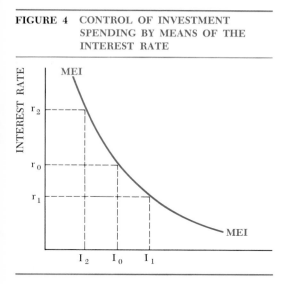

stand how it is exerted, we must first examine some fundamentals of monetary theory.

Idle Money Balances: the Source of Borrowed Money

As everyone knows, interest is the "price" paid by borrowers to induce owners of money to lend it in exchange for a bond, mortgage, or other security. However, not all firms or households have money to spare from their daily needs. Many households, particularly those with low incomes, can barely manage to get through the month on their current receipts. Before anybody can consider whether to lend money or not, he must have more than enough to last until the next payday.

Money balances owned by households or businesses can be divided into 2 parts. One part, consisting of the money that is used for the day-to-day business of earning and spending, is the *active balance*. The other part, held against emergencies or future needs as a generalized store of wealth, is the *idle balance*. These idle balances form the principal source for borrowed funds.

Of course, since a dollar is a dollar, nobody can tell by looking at a family's pocketbook or bank account how much it has in each type of balance. If we watch the ebb and flow of a family's money over several months, however, we can perceive a fairly clear pattern. Some families keep all their money active. They receive their income on the first, spend it all during the course of the month, and wind up just before payday with nothing left. All the money they happen to hold on any given day is in their active balance, is merely being held pending its normal use as a medium of exchange, and will soon be spent. Other families, however, begin and end the month with money on hand, and the minimum kept unspent constitutes an

Business firms would thereby be encouraged to increase their investment spending to I_1, with the attendant multiplied impact on total output and employment. If the period is already one of labor shortage and inflation, the Board can restrict credit availability and force interest rates up to r_2. This would lead business firms to contract their outlays on new investment projects to I_2 and would reduce total demand accordingly.

Although the effectiveness of monetary policy hinges on the rate of interest, direct control over interest rates is not included among the powers of the Federal Reserve Board. The Federal Reserve can control only member bank reserves, legal reserve ratios, and the discount rate. The use of these controls influences the lending power of the banking system, but bank loans are only one—and by no means the largest—source of business financing. In fact, about two-thirds of all business investment funds are obtained internally from retained earnings and depreciation allowances, and a substantial part of the remainder is obtained from the sale of securities to the public.

The power of the Federal Reserve Board over interest rates, in short, is indirect and roundabout. If we are to under-

idle balance, held as liquid wealth. A family that maintains an idle balance of $200, for example, has this amount on hand when it receives its income on the first. It spends its income during the month and winds up just before payday with its original $200 left. Unlike active money that comes and goes, idle money stays.

The division between active and idle money balances applies equally to business firms. Firms receive money during the month for products sold and spend it as they pay their bills. The funds that turn over are in their active balances. Their idle balances consist of any minimum they keep on hand.

Figure 5 represents an overall view of the division of money between active and idle balances. The total vertical distance between lines BB and HH represents the total amount of money in existence, while the passage of time is represented by movement to the right. On any given date, the division of money balances between business and households is represented by a point like X_1, located between the 2 lines. The distance B_1X_1 represents the amount of money held by business firms, while the remaining dis-

tance X_1H_1 represents the amount of money held by households. The day before payday the business community has B_1X_1 dollars on hand, while households have only H_1X_1. On payday, wage and salary checks transfer money from business firms to households. Business firms are left with B_2X_2 dollars; households now have H_2X_2. As households spend their earnings during the month, their balances decline while business balances rise back to the original level, and another payday begins the cycle over again. As we can see, the active money in the economy is the amount, CD, that circulates regularly from account to account, held by business one day and by households the next. The remainder of the money is held in idle balances, BC being held by business and HD by households.

Shifts Between Active and Idle Balances

The division of the total amount of money between active and idle balances is not fixed. Since the amount of money needed for transaction purposes depends on the total amount of spending, the larger the gross national product, the more money is required in active balances. Unless the total

FIGURE 5 THE CIRCULATION OF MONEY

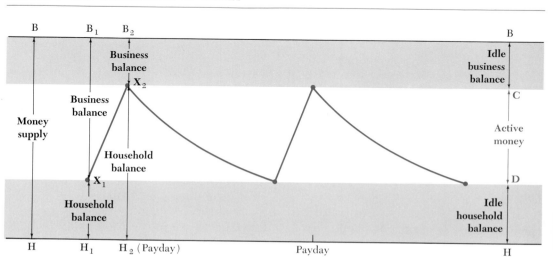

quantity of money is expanded, therefore, a rise in GNP is accompanied by an expansion in the proportion of total money held in active balances and a contraction in the proportion held idle.

How this change in proportion might come about is shown in Figure 6. Up to the date represented by point A, the money supply has been divided between idle balances and active money circulating as shown. After time A, business investment spending increases—perhaps in response to a new invention—and gross national product rises under the impact multiplier. The larger income payments and expenditures associated with increased output require additional active money in circulation. Figure 6 illustrates a typical case, in which business firms get part of the additional funds from their own idle balances and raise part by selling securities to households. The money obtained from households is added to business balances on date A as shown. The new funds, combined with those taken from business idle balances, are paid out on date B in higher gross national income, and remain in circulation thereafter. The total amount of active money has been increased

by reducing the amount of money kept in idle balances.

Idle Balances as Liquid Assets There remains an interesting question. If money can be put to work to earn interest, why does anybody want to keep it idle? If the funds are not needed, why not lend them out? An important part of the answer is that idle balances *are* needed. Money is a *perfectly liquid* asset. That is, it can be spent immediately to meet necessary payments without any other preliminary transaction. If, instead of money, a person's wealth is in bonds, stocks, building lots, or some other form, he can exchange it for something else only by first selling it for money, and then applying the money to his purchase. This means 2 transactions instead of 1, extra time and trouble, and in the event that the money is needed in a hurry, it can also mean serious loss.

This is why many households and firms prefer to keep a portion of their wealth in perfectly liquid form as idle balances despite the sacrifice in earnings. The proportion held varies widely among different families and firms, and from time to time

FIGURE 6 HOW A RISE IN GROSS NATIONAL PRODUCT REDUCES IDLE BALANCES WHEN THE TOTAL MONEY SUPPLY IS GIVEN

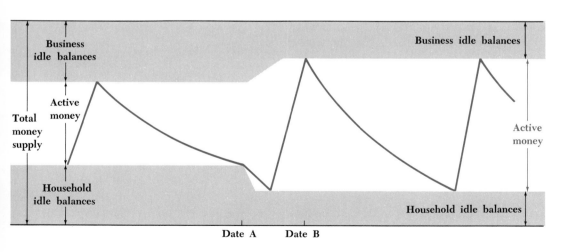

for the same family or firm depending on the economic outlook, individual psychology and a number of other circumstances. More important is the fact that idle balances tend to vary with the amount of business normally conducted. To keep a balance of $100,000 idle cash on hand would be an absurd precaution for a family with normal income of $600 a month, but the same balance would be entirely inadequate for a firm whose receipts and payments averaged over a $1 million a day. Accordingly, the amount of money held in idle balances by all firms and households combined tends to vary with the gross national product.

Idle Balances and Interest Rates   Another determinant of the size of idle balances is the interest rate. When interest rates are low, households and business firms earn relatively little by sacrificing liquidity and generally prefer to keep larger idle balances for any given GNP. When interest rates rise, firms and families are willing to reduce the ratio of idle money to GNP, sacrificing liquidity in order to lend the funds at the higher rate.

The important relationship that emerges is shown by curve LL in Figure 7. The interest rate is measured vertically and the ratio of total idle balances to GNP is measured horizontally. The downward slope of the curve reflects the increasing preference for liquidity at low interest rates. Points near the origin at the left represent small holdings of idle balances compared to GNP and correspondingly high interest rates. Points farther to the right represent larger holdings of idle balances in proportion to GNP accompanied by correspondingly lower interest rates.

The position of the curve LL—the *liquidity-preference* curve—is not fixed, but depends on such things as the expectations of firms and households about their potential need for funds and their uncertainty about the future. An *increase* in liquidity prefer-

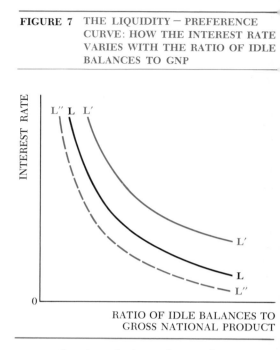

FIGURE 7   THE LIQUIDITY − PREFERENCE CURVE: HOW THE INTEREST RATE VARIES WITH THE RATIO OF IDLE BALANCES TO GNP

RATIO OF IDLE BALANCES TO GROSS NATIONAL PRODUCT

ence—that is, a desire to keep a larger ratio of idle balances to GNP at any given interest rate—would be represented by an upward shift in the curve as shown by the solid blue curve L'L'. Willingness to hold a smaller ratio of idle balances to GNP would be represented by a downward shift in the curve as shown by the dashed blue line L"L".

Interest Rates as Determined by the Ratio of Money Supply to GNP

For purposes of analysis, Figures 6 and 7 can be combined into a single important relationship. In Figure 6 we saw that the smaller the total money supply in relation to GNP, the less money remains in idle balances. It follows that unless the total money supply is expanded in proportion to rising GNP, investment can be financed only if households and business firms are willing to squeeze additional funds out of their declining idle balances. When we turn to Figure 7, however, we learn that the smaller idle balances are, in proportion to GNP, the higher the interest rate needed to pry further investment funds out of households and business firms. When the 2 figures are combined, it follows that low ratios of money supply to GNP tend to be accompanied by high interest rates, while high ratios of money supply to GNP tend to bring interest rates down.

This important relationship is borne out by Figure 8. The interest rate and the ratio of total U.S. money supply to GNP during each of 20 recent years have been plotted as a point, interest rate measured vertically and the ratio of money supply to GNP measured horizontally. The points are closely approximated by the smooth curve drawn through the midst of the scatter. The shape of the curve follows from the liquidity preferences of households and business firms, with low ratios of money supply to GNP at the left accompanied by high interest rates, and high ratios at the right accompanied by low interest rates.

FIGURE 8 OBSERVED RELATIONSHIP OF U.S. INTEREST RATE TO THE RATIO OF MONEY SUPPLY TO GROSS NATIONAL PRODUCT, 1950-1968

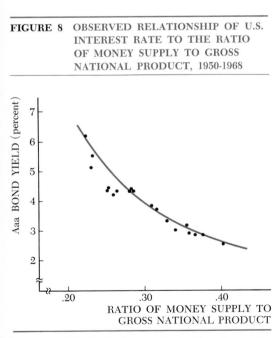

SOURCE: Calculated from data in the *Economic Report of the President, 1969.*

The Influence of the Money Supply on GNP

We have now completed the links in the chain connecting the money supply to the GNP: (1) An increase in money supply adds to the idle balances of households and business firms, increasing their willingness to lend. (2) Increased willingness to lend starts interest rates declining. (3) Lower interest rates permit business firms to spend more on investment. (4) As investment rises, it increases the GNP by a multiplied amount.

The chain of events is illustrated in Figure 9. The liquidity-preference curve *LL* is shown at the left, while the marginal efficiency of investment *MEI* appears at the right. The position of the economic system before the money supply expands is represented by the black lines. To use specific figures for the example, let us imagine that the total money supply was $250 billion and GNP was $1 trillion, making the ratio of money supply to GNP equal to .25 as shown. The corresponding interest rate is shown to be 5 percent. The *MEI* curve at the right indicates that business firms would invest $150 billion per year at the 5 percent interest rate. This amount of investment spending, together with other autonomous expenditures, would maintain the GNP at its $1 trillion level.

The blue lines represent what would happen after $50 billion had been added to the money supply by expansion of bank loans. As the new money began to swell idle balances, households and business firms would become more willing to lend, and the interest rate would start to decline. As lower rates made more investment profitable, investment spending would rise, causing a multiplied increase in GNP. If investment increased by $30 billion as shown, the GNP would rise by $60 billion to $1.06 trillion. Since $50 billion had been added to money supply, the new ratio of money supply to GNP would be .283, bringing the interest rate down to 4 percent as

FIGURE 9   RESPONSE OF THE ECONOMY TO A CHANGE IN MONEY SUPPLY

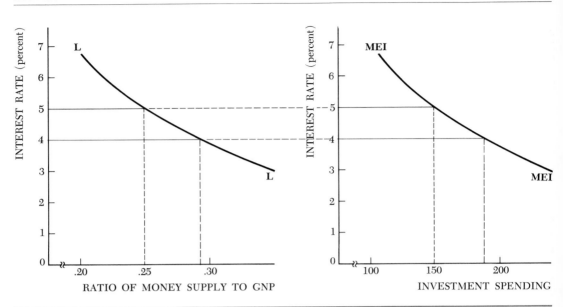

shown. At this point the expansion would stop, for the new interest rate would be just sufficient to maintain the $180 billion investment spending shown.

A contraction of the money supply has just the opposite effect. If we begin with the economy in the position represented by the blue lines, a contraction of money supply by $50 billion would raise interest rates, reduce investment spending, and contract GNP. The contraction would stop when the interest rate again reached 5 percent, permitting only $150 billion of investment spending. GNP would have fallen to $1 trillion, and the ratio of money supply to GNP would have been reduced to its initial level of .25

Realistically, of course, the interest rate is only one influence on investment spending. As we know, the marginal efficiency of investment is not fixed, but shifts widely with changing technology and tax laws. The changes actually observed in investment and GNP depend not only on what happens to the money supply but on how the marginal efficiency of investment shifts

as well. Figure 10 is a more realistic illustration of how changes in both money supply and the marginal efficiency of investment affected the U.S. economic system between 1953 and 1965. Despite the addition of $40 billion to the money supply over this period, the ratio of money supply to GNP declined and interest rates rose. The reason was the strong rise in the marginal efficiency of investment that occurred at the same time. The shift in the marginal efficiency of investment from its low level in 1953, as represented by the black curve MEI_{53} to the high level of 1965 as represented by the blue curve MEI_{65} permitted investment spending to expand to $100 billion, and to raise the GNP to $685 billion.

How Monetary Policy Works

As we know, money is created when the volume of outstanding bank loans rises, and money is destroyed when the volume of outstanding bank loans declines. Thus, while the Federal Reserve Board has **no**

FIGURE 10 THE CHANGES IN INTEREST RATE, INVESTMENT SPENDING, AND RATIO OF MONEY SUPPLY TO GNP BETWEEN 1953 AND 1965

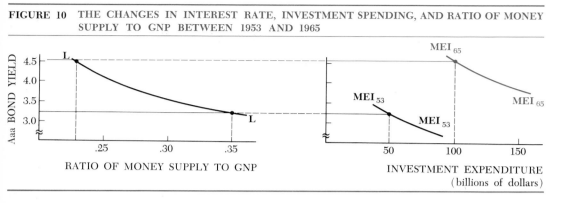

RATIO OF MONEY SUPPLY TO GNP

INVESTMENT EXPENDITURE
(billions of dollars)

direct control over the total money supply, it can powerfully influence it by its power over bank reserves, reserve ratios, and the discount rate. In a period of heavy unemployment, the Federal Reserve can provide commercial banks with greater lending potential, and permit the money supply to expand, reducing interest rates and encouraging investment spending in order to increase the growth of GNP.

During periods of rapidly rising prices, on the other hand, the Federal Reserve can reduce the lending power of the banking system and hold the money supply in check. The resulting rise in interest rates tends to check investment spending and retard the growth of GNP.

As we noted earlier, the Federal Reserve Board's power over the money supply is not symmetrical. In a period of depression the Board can expand bank lending power, but it cannot force up the marginal efficiency of investment nor compel firms to borrow. If there are few profitable projects to finance, augmented lending power is largely used to swell excess bank reserves, contributes little to reduction of interest rates, and provides little stimulation to the GNP. This was the experience during much of the 1930s. On the other hand, the Federal Reserve has considerable power during periods of inflation. When business is clamoring for funds, restriction of bank reserves is an effective way to drive up interest rates and help curtail investment spending.

In fact, the Federal Reserve Board can contribute to checking economic expansion merely by not permitting bank reserves to expand in proportion to the rise in total spending. Under these circumstances economic expansion chokes itself off by driving down the ratio of money supply to GNP until the interest rate reaches levels at which continued expansion is no longer possible.

The Effect of Monetary Policy on the Kinds of Goods Produced The immediate effect of monetary policy is on investment expenditure. Household spending for consumer goods is largely affected only by the subsequent change in income, although interest rates also affect installment credit terms and may influence the buying of automobiles and other durable consumer goods.

Among investors, 2 groups appear to be more heavily affected than others. As we noted earlier, home-buyers are clearly more sensitive to interest rates than other investors. The first major effect of a policy to ease interest rates and increase employment is to increase the number of new houses built, while the effect of credit restrictions is to reduce construction. The other group heavily affected by monetary policy consists of small businesses who have neither the reputation to enable them to compete in the open market for scarce funds nor the internal sources of funds from which to finance themselves.

Finally, high interest rates often prohibit borrowing by state and local governments. Sometimes this is merely because governments prefer to postpone borrowing until they can do so on more favorable terms. In other cases, there are legal limitations to the maximum rates at which governments can borrow for certain purposes, and when this maximum is exceeded by market rates, they are unable to issue their bonds.

COORDINATION OF MONETARY AND FISCAL POLICY

The important fact is that monetary policy, like government spending and taxation, exerts its primary impact on specific uses of resources. For this reason, monetary and fiscal policy are not *alternatives* for economic stabilization, but represent different tools whose initial impacts affect different people and work at different points in the economic system. The proper question is not *which* of the 2 should be employed, but *what mixture* is appropriate in a given situation.

Even the most elementary example of economic control illustrates how the final result depends on the way in which the controls are combined. For example, when personal taxes are reduced to stimulate increased output during a period of low employment, the size of the increase in GNP depends partly on whether the money supply is increased at the same time. As sales and production begin to expand, money is drawn into circulation out of idle balances. The interest rate is pushed up, and the stimulating effect of the tax cut is partly offset by declining business outlays for investment. The opposite occurs during a period of excessive demand when higher tax rates deprive consumers of buying power. If the money supply is not forced to contract as the GNP declines, falling interest rates encourage investment spending and cancel part of the effect of the rise in taxes. It

should be emphasized that this does *not* mean that fiscal policy cannot work without corresponding adjustments in the money supply. But when personal taxes are partly offset by changing interest rates, taxes must be altered *more* than would otherwise be necessary to obtain the desired amount of restraint.

The difference is not only in the size of the overall effect, but in who bears the burden of the adjustment. When tax increases are partly offset by lower interest rates, consumers are forced to give up buying power, some of which is then turned over to business for increased investment. When tax cuts are partly offset by higher interest rates, resources to provide increased consumer goods for households are partly obtained by depriving business firms of resources for investment.

This situation is not necessarily bad. When aggregate demand is running ahead of productive capacity, there is some point to policies that force consumers to cut back on their buying on the one hand, while encouraging business firms to increase capacity on the other. In a period in which aggregate demand does not require full use of the productive capacity already on hand, it might be wise to encourage households to buy more consumer goods and at the same time discourage firms from adding to already excessive capacity. The point is that there is more to stabilization than the mere size of the total effect. Proper stabilization policy necessarily involves the choice of the mixture of fiscal and monetary policy that will provide an adjustment not only of the desired magnitude, but of the desired composition.

An Overview of the Theory of Policy Coordination

For purposes of analysis it is useful to think of policy coordination as involving 2 general questions: (1) What proportion of our total capacity do we want to devote to government rather than private purposes? (2) How do we want to divide the privately used portion of our resources between consumer goods and investment? Both these questions are political. The first involves the expenditures of the government budget. The prospective benefit from each program or project must be carefully weighed against the lost opportunity to use the same resources for private purposes.

The economics of the problem are shown in Figure 11. The production-possibilities curve *ABC* at the top of the figure shows the possible combinations of private and public goods available from existing productive capacity. The curves in the lower part of the figure represent production-pos-

FIGURE 11   THE GENERAL PROBLEM OF
STABILIZATION POLICY

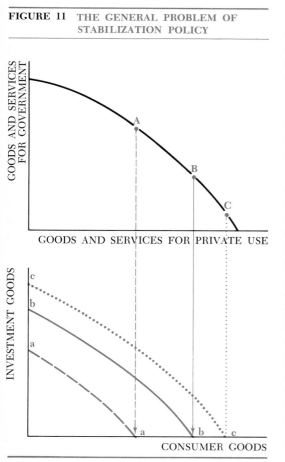

sibilities curves involving consumer goods and investment, showing alternative possibilities for the use of the resources remaining after the government budget has been chosen. Accordingly, each *point* on the curve of the upper figure corresponds to a *curve* in the lower figure. During the 1920s, government purchases of goods and services absorbed only about 8 percent of total capacity, leaving 92 percent to divide between consumption and investment. This would be represented by a point like *C* in the upper figure and would correspond to a curve like *cc* below. At the height of World War II in 1943 and 1944, half of all U.S. productive capacity was devoted to government goods and services, leaving the other half to be divided between consumption and investment. This can be represented by a point like *A* in the upper figure corresponding to the curve *aa* below. In recent years government has absorbed roughly a quarter of total output, a situation that is represented by point *B* and the corresponding curve *bb*.

Once the budgetary choice has been arrived at, the task of stabilization policy is to encourage the fullest private use of the remaining productive capacity and to guide the apportionment of that use between consumer goods and investment. The task is represented in Figure 12. The curve represents the private production possibilities that remain after the government budget has been established. Suppose, however, that private demand is inadequate to employ everybody who wants a job, and the private use of capacity is represented by a point like *X*, corresponding to investment spending of *I* and consumption of *C*. To overcome this unemployment, aggregate demand must be increased. Consumption and investment spending must expand until they correspond to a point on the production-possibilities curve. The policy question then becomes, *which* point? This is no idle question, for whether we recognize it or not, the final allocation of our productive capacity

FIGURE 12   REPRESENTATION OF THE
                POLICY TARGET

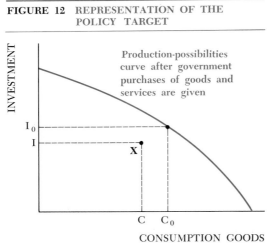

CONSUMPTION GOODS

between consumption and investment is largely determined by the mixture of policy we use to get there. For example, a reduction of personal taxes provides most of the additional output in the form of consumer goods. A reduction in business taxes will raise the marginal efficiency of capital and stimulate investment spending—more or less, depending on the money supply—and the multiplier impact will also provide additional consumption expenditure depending on the size of the multiplier. Expansion of the money supply will lower the interest rate and stimulate investment spending—more or less, depending on business taxes—and responding will contribute to consumption goods—more or less depending on the size of the multiplier. Stabilization therefore involves the choice of an annual "target" amount of investment spending, say I_0, and a consumption "target," say C_0, and the selection of a coordinated policy to get to the target and stay there.

Steering Toward the Target

The problem is illustrated in Table 2. The stimuli that can be identified after the government expenditure budget has been set but *before* any tax or monetary policy has

been applied, are listed at the left. The impact of the $22 billion net stimulus would tend to raise GNP by $44 billion. Since, according to the example, the GNP of the preceding year had been $900 billion, the level to be forecast in the absence of any adjustment of policy would be $944 billion, an amount that is $36 billion short of the output that would represent a satisfactory use of available capacity.

Policy to Stimulate Demand   Under these circumstances, the task of monetary and fiscal policy is to provide additional stimulus to raise aggregate demand by $36 billion. There are many ways this could be done, but suppose that our social targets require that $12 billion be added to investment spending and $24 billion to consumption and other induced expenditures. The column at the right of the table shows how policy adjustments might be made to push the economy to the desired position. An $8 billion cut in personal taxes would add .75 × $8, or $6 billion to initial consumer spending, while a combination of lower business taxes and reduced interest rates would provide for $12 billion of additional investment. The resulting $18 billion additional stimulus would contribute $36 billion to aggregate demand in the proportions desired, bringing it into line with the established target.

The problem of fiscal and monetary coordination to reach the investment target is shown in Figure 13. The investment target I_0 is indicated on the right-hand portion of the figure. The marginal efficiency of investment, as determined by the economic outlook of businessmen, by the rate at which new discoveries and inventions are becoming available, and by the business tax laws in force, is represented by the curve *MEI*. Given the liquidity preferences of lenders represented by the curve *LL* at the left, the ratio of money supply to GNP establishes the interest rate at r, and holds investment to I, the value seen earlier in

TABLE 2   APPLICATION OF STABILIZATION POLICY TO RAISE AGGREGATE DEMAND UP TO DESIGNATED TARGET LEVELS
(billions of dollars)

FORECAST *before* POLICY ADJUSTMENTS			POLICY	
Identifiable stimuli:				
Consumer spending		$ 11.0		
Annual trend	$5.0			
Rising transfer payments	6.0		$8 personal tax cut	$ 6.0
Business investment in new plant and			Lower business taxes and	
equipment		1.0	reduced interest rates	12.0
Residential construction		2.0		
Inventory investment (allowance for				
termination of last year's inventory				
buying)		−10.0		
Exports		3.0		
Government purchases of goods				
and services		15.0		
Projected net stimulus		$ 22.0	Added stimulus	$18.0
Forecast increase in GNP = 2 × $22.0		44.0	Impact = 2 × 18	36.0
GNP, preceding year		900.0	Of which:	
Forecast GNP		$944.0	Consumption and induced spending	$24.0
Target capacity		980.0	Fixed investment	12.0
Demand deficiency		36.0		
Of which:				
Consumption target		$ 24.0		
Investment target		12.0		

FIGURE 13 POLICIES TO EXPAND INVESTMENT   SPENDING

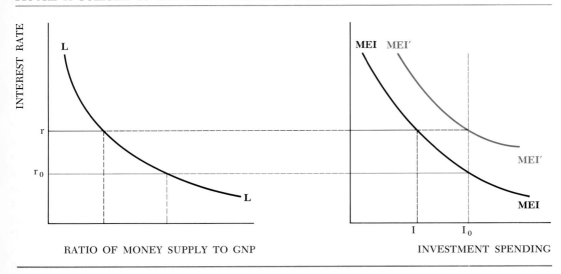

RATIO OF MONEY SUPPLY TO GNP   INVESTMENT SPENDING

Figure 12. The job for the monetary authorities is then to adjust the money supply to a point at which firms will find it profitable to invest the target amount, I_0.

The monetary authority can do this by expanding the money supply enough to bring the interest rate down to r_0. Since the marginal efficiency of investment depends on business taxes, however, business tax reduction permits investment to expand even at high interest rates. If tax concessions shifted the marginal efficiency of investment up to MEI', for example, the target rate of investment could be achieved without reduction in interest rates. But even this requires the cooperation of monetary policy, for as GNP begins to rise under the investment stimulus, additions to the money supply would be required to prevent the interest rate from rising.

By the use of different mixtures of money supply and taxation, the interest rate consistent with target investment can be varied over a considerable range, but while the total amount of investment spending would be the same under each combination, its composition would not. In particular, residential construction is sensitive to interest rates but is virtually unaffected by business taxes. When low taxes are applied to expand investment at high interest rates, most of the expansion occurs in business spending for new plant and equipment. When high business taxes are combined with low interest rates, more of the expansion takes the form of new houses. Thus the choice of policy mixture depends not only on the total amount of investment but also on the kinds of investments we want to encourage.[4]

Policy to Check Inflation   In the preceding example the policy task was to stimulate the economy to bring aggregate demand up to target levels, but sometimes—usually during

[4] The question of interest rates and their effects on the allocation of investment will be examined again in greater detail in Chapter 24.

periods of rapidly rising military spending —it is necessary to apply policies to hold down aggregate demand to prevent target levels from being exceeded. The problem is illustrated in Table 3 where, in the absence of stabilizing action, the forecast level of GNP would exceed target capacity by $36 billion. The policy target calls for a cut of $24 billion in consumer outlays and a reduction of $12 billion in expenditure for fixed investment. The policy prescription at the right is an $8 billion increase in personal taxes and enough increase in business taxes and interest rates to reduce investment spending by $12 billion. Again, the composition of the cut in investment spending will be strongly influenced by the combination of the tax policy and interest rate increase applied.

LIMITATIONS TO STABILIZATION POLICY

Nothing in the foregoing is intended to make the problem of stabilization policy appear simpler than it is. It is a political process, which means that not only is it subject to normal human error, but it frequently becomes stalled in the pulling and tugging among people with different views and objectives. Moreover, since the Federal Reserve Board is independent of Congress and the administration, they are occasionally found working at cross-purposes.

Part of the difficulty lies in the nature of the alternatives themselves. As we saw at the outset of Part Two, unemployment and inflation are matters of degree. As aggregate demand increases, a larger proportion of productive capacity is used. Fewer people are left jobless, but costs and prices rise more rapidly. As aggregate demand decreases, a smaller proportion of productive capacity is used. More people are left jobless while costs and prices rise more slowly. People naturally differ in their views of

TABLE 3   APPLICATION OF STABILIZATION POLICY TO CUT AGGREGATE DEMAND TO DESIGNATED TARGET LEVELS
(billions of dollars)

FORECAST *before* POLICY ADJUSTMENTS			POLICY	
Identifiable stimuli:				
Consumer spending		$ 11.0		
Annual trend	$5.0			
Rising transfer payments	6.0		$8 personal tax increase	−$ 6.0
Business investment in new plant and			Higher business taxes and	
equipment		1.0	increased interest rates	− 12.0
Residential construction		2.0		
Inventory investment (allowance for				
termination of last year's inventory				
buying)		−10.0		
Exports		3.0		
Government purchases of goods				
and services		30.0		
Projected net stimulus		$ 37.0	Added stimulus	−$18.0
Forecast increase in GNP = 2 × $37		74.0	Impact = 2 × 18	− 36.0
GNP, preceding year		980.0		
Forecast GNP		1,054.0	Of which:	
Target capacity		1,018.0	Consumption and induced spending	−$24.0
Excess demand		36.0	Investment	− 12.0
Of which:				
Consumption target		$ −24.0		
Investment target		−12.0		

how much unemployment should be traded for how much inflation, and consequent political conflicts are inevitable.

Another important limitation to stabilization policy is that its actions do not take effect immediately. In general, there is a lag between the time that the need for action is recognized and the time that action can be taken, and, once started, still more time must elapse before the action has the desired effect. The first of these lags is the "reaction time," the second is the "effect lag." Much the same pattern of delay is encountered in any kind of control. The driver of an automobile, for example, experiences a reaction time between the appearance of a red light ahead and the time he can apply the brakes, and still more time must elapse as an effect lag before the brakes take hold and stop the car.

Fiscal policy is subject to a particularly long reaction lag. Government budgets are

submitted 6 months before the beginning of the fiscal year, and all proposals for changes in government spending and tax rates must pass through a long process of hearings, debate, and political maneuvering before they can be enacted and signed into law. Monetary policy has a much shorter reaction time. Monetary decisions are purely administrative and can be put into effect almost immediately upon the recognition of a need. Reserve ratios and discount rates can be altered after a few days' debate, and a change in open-market purchases need not even be announced, but is merely put into effect through normal commercial channels.

Effect lags, on the other hand, are generally shorter for fiscal policy. Government spending has the shortest effect lag, for once government spending begins to change, it institutes the multiplier process with an immediate effect on production and income.

Changes in personal tax rates have a longer effect lag, for consumers are unlikely to modify long-standing plans, and are more likely to make temporary adjustments in the amount of income they save, delaying the effect of tax changes until they can adjust their spending patterns. The long-term planning required for business investment spending makes the effect lag longest for changes in business tax rates.

Monetary policy has very long effect lags. Federal Reserve action to increase the lending power of the banking system, for example, has no effect until banks respond by altering their loans. More time must elapse before the change in money supply can bring down interest rates to make increased investment spending profitable. But it is only still later, when new investment plans can be formulated and construction can actually begin that changes in business spending initiate the multiplier process.

Because of the long lags, policy action must be planned and started well in advance of the time the stimulus is needed. Policy action is therefore necessarily based on forecasts of economic conditions. While we know much more about economic forecasting today than we did even a few years ago, forecasts are still subject to consider-

able error, and stabilization policy can be no more successful than forecasting accuracy permits. Since forecasts are sufficiently precise to furnish clear advance warning of serious trouble, policy actions can stave off severe depression or inflation, but the little "wiggles" in the predicted economic outlook are often forecasting errors and provide no useful guide to policy action. We now know enough about how the economic system functions and how to forecast its behavior accurately enough to avoid repeating calamities like the great depressions of the past. Nevertheless, we are a long way from the ability to steer a perfectly smooth course.

Finally, in much of our discussion it has been convenient to talk as if consumers and businessmen always responded in a regular and predictable manner. Yet nothing is farther from the truth. Stabilization policy does not work in a world of clearly seen relationships and neat formulas, but in a world in which relationships are continually shifting and the immediate response to a policy measure is often at odds with what is expected. In view of the immense difficulties, the American economy has accumulated a remarkable record of stable growth during the last 20 years.

SUMMARY

An economic system is not entirely self-regulating. In the absence of central policy, total spending can fall far short of productive capacity and leave many workers and resources unemployed, or it can greatly exceed productive capacity and result in severe inflation. In the United States, the task of steering the economy is divided between *fiscal policy,* the government's control over spending and taxation, and *monetary policy,* which involves Federal Reserve controls over the banking system.

Government spending has a powerful effect on total demand, but because individual government projects should be evaluated on their own merits, government spending is a poor tool for overall economic control and the major weapon of fiscal policy is taxation. The *level of tax rates* helps to determine the size of the multiplier, while *changes in tax rates* initiate changes in spending, with a resulting multiplied impact on total output. The *size of the impact* obtained from a change in tax rates depends on whether the change is made in personal taxes or in business taxes.

Fiscal policy to stabilize the economy generally requires that tax rates be raised at the very time that tax receipts are already rising, and that rates be lowered just when tax receipts are already declining. In other words, a fiscal policy designed to balance the economy is unlikely to balance the government's budget, and proper fiscal policy often leads to a *budgetary deficit* and increasing *national debt*. Although the idea of the national debt is still traumatic to a few people, the transfers of purchasing power that are involved constitute a relatively minor problem.

Monetary policy functions through the Federal Reserve control over bank lending power. Open-market purchases, reduced reserve ratios, and lower discount rates expand bank lending power, add to *idle balances*, reduce interest rates, and stimulate the economy through increased investment spending. Contraction of bank lending power has the opposite effect.

Since monetary and fiscal controls have different effects on the kinds of goods produced, they are not substitutes for each other, but should be carefully *coordinated* to achieve not only a high level of employment, but an appropriate *composition of output*. In broad terms, proper policy selection consists of an initial choice of government expenditures to meet collective social needs, followed by a choice of tax rates and a level of money supply that will steer the economy toward a desirable combination of consumption goods and investment.

In practice, however, the effectiveness of stabilization policy is limited by *political considerations*, by the *long lags* between the need for action and the time an effect can be felt in the economy, by *forecasting errors*, and by the fact that households and business firms do not always respond as expected. Because of these limitations, stabilization policy will not permit us to steer a perfectly smooth course, but we need never repeat the experience of a great depression.

PART THREE
Prices and Markets

Every year American firms turn out millions of different products, most of them in many different styles and qualities. The mixture of these products, styles, and qualities, however, is constantly changing. The output of automobiles rises and falls from year to year, onions grow this year on farms that produced carrots last year, and so on, while in the long run we find wide changes in the types and qualities of products available. In addition, many products have several alternative uses— vegetables can be frozen, canned, or eaten fresh; leather can become furniture, shoes, or jackets; while corn can be made into margarine, breakfast cereal, or hog feed. The fraction of the product that goes into each use varies widely with the quantity available and with the pattern of consumer demand.

In the United States and other private enterprise economic systems, the quantities of different products turned out and the amount of each product that enters each specific use is largely determined by the decisions of millions of households each trying to get the most for its money, and by millions of private business firms, each trying to find the amount and type of output that will bring in the largest profit. Part Three is devoted to the study of how the preferences and buying habits of consumers, expressed as demand, are brought together with the production costs of business firms searching for profit to determine both the composition of total output and the uses to which individual goods are put. In addition, we will see how business firms are encouraged to find cheaper ways to produce, to bring out new products, and to improve the quality of old products.

The study opens with Chapter 15, "Consumer Demand," which deals with the relationship of prices to consumer buying. We will explore the differences in consumer response to changes in prices of different commodities, and examine the causes of shifts in demand. Chapter 16, "Pricing and the Allocation of Basic Commodities," shows how consumer demand contributes to price determination on an auction market, and how the resulting prices help divide available quantities among competing uses. Although relatively few commodities are sold on auction markets, the principles by which commodities are allocated to different uses are quite general, and the techniques of analysis developed have wide application throughout the economy.

Chapter 17, "Prices Established by Business Firms" deals with the much more common situation in which prices are fixed by sellers on the basis of production cost and expected demand and buyers take them or leave them. Business firms are, of course, generally free to charge any prices they choose, but the profit to be expected from any given price depends heavily on how much other firms are charging for similar products. As a result, the pricing behavior of each individual firm is severely limited by the competitive conditions in the industry.

These competitive conditions and their influence on the performance of the firm are examined in two chapters. Chapter 18, "The Performance of Competitive Industry," deals with the prices, costs, quality, and quantity of output in industries in which production is spread over a large number of relatively small firms. Chapter 19, "Industrial Concentration and Oligopoly," extends the analysis of behavior to industries in which output is heavily concentrated in the hands of a few large firms. We will find that competition forces business firms to turn out better products at lower prices and to keep up a continual search for more productive methods of operation. Unfortunately, the same competitive forces underlie many of our rapidly increasing problems of air and water pollution and contribute to a countryside littered with waste and rubbish. This side of the competitive market is dealt with in Chapter 20, "Environmental Pollution."

Since markets are international in scope, Part Three concludes with Chapter 21, "International Trade and International Payments," in which we will study trade among different nations and how international payments are made.

CHAPTER 15

Consumer Demand

The most important influence over how much of any commodity people buy is its price. Although price is only 1 consideration among many to the buyer, its key role in determining the profitability of production makes it the center of interest in the study of consumer demand. The sensitivity of buyers to prices, the *elasticity* of demand, is affected by such factors as the nature of the good and the need it fills, whether substitutes are available, and whether it is used alone or in conjunction with other products. Elasticity is often different in the long run from what it is immediately after a change in price.

Changes in buying patterns are represented by *shifts* in demand, occurring in response to such factors as variations in income, changes in the prices of other goods, variation in the number and composition of the population, product innovation, consumer psychology, and advertising. Demand elasticity and shifts in demand are fundamental determinants of the way a market economy allocates the use of available productive capacity.

DEMAND

Demand Curves

The *demand* for a good represents the average relationship between the quantity that buyers tend to buy and the price. Buyer response can be seen when prices are plotted on a chart together with quantities purchased. In Figure 1, for example, the annual price of sweet potatoes is plotted on the vertical axis, and the total quantity of sweet potatoes purchased per year is plotted horizontally. The points scatter in a narrow band from upper left to lower right, revealing the normal tendency for people to buy more when prices are low and to reduce their purchases when prices rise.

FIGURE 1   PRICE OF SWEET POTATOES AND
ANNUAL QUANTITY SOLD, 1958-1966

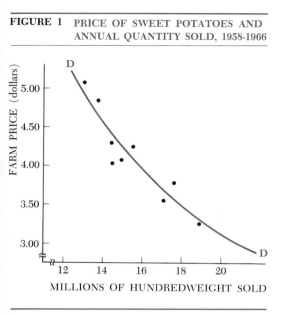

MILLIONS OF HUNDREDWEIGHT SOLD

SOURCE: Plotted from data given in U.S. Department of Agriculture, *Agricultural Statistics, 1967.*

A curve like *DD*, showing the average quantities people tend to buy at each price, is called the *demand curve* for the product, or often simply the *demand*. According to the demand curve *DD*, housewives tend to buy about 18 million hundredweight of sweet potatoes during the course of a year in which they sell for $3.50. During a year in which the price is $4, they tend to reduce their purchases to about 15.8 million, and at $5 they tend to buy only about 12.8 million. The term "demand" should always be restricted to mean an *entire* curve like *DD*, taken as a whole; "demand" is never used to denote a particular quantity of product sold, but always a *relationship* between the quantities people tend to buy and the prices they pay.

The use of the terms "average" and "tend" should be carefully noted. If prices were the only influence on the housewife's decision to purchase, the points of Figure 1 would all lie on a smooth curve, but because of year-to-year variation in family incomes, habits, and tastes, and because of changes

in the prices of white potatoes and other commodities that might be consumed in place of sweet potatoes, the total amount bought at any given price varies from year to year. A curve like *DD* is an attempt to isolate the effect of price by adjusting for other influences. Many statistical problems arise in connection with estimating demand curves, but a practical method is explained in the appendix to this chapter.

Demand Schedules

For many purposes it is useful to represent demand by a table or *schedule* listing prices and, opposite each, the average annual amount that consumers tend to buy at that price. Table 1, which corresponds to Figure 1, was compiled by selecting a convenient schedule of prices and carefully recording the quantity on curve *DD* that corresponds to each. The table shows that an average of about 12.8 million hundredweight of sweet potatoes can be sold during a year when the price is $5. As the price declines, consumers tend to buy more, and the quantity that can be sold tends to rise to about 20.8 million hundredweight at $3.

Such a table is usually called a *demand schedule*. Demand schedules and demand

TABLE 1   DEMAND SCHEDULE FOR SWEET POTATOES

PRICE PER 100 POUNDS	AVERAGE QUANTITY BOUGHT (MILLIONS OF HUNDREDWEIGHT)
$5.00	12.8
4.75	13.5
4.50	14.2
4.25	15.0
4.00	15.8
3.75	16.8
3.50	18.0
3.25	19.2
3.00	20.8

SOURCE: Average quantities read from curve *DD*, Figure 1 of this chapter.

curves are interchangeable ways of representing the same consumer behavior. Which is used in any particular case depends on the purpose at hand: A demand curve furnishes a complete and quickly grasped picture of the relationship between prices and quantities purchased when specific detail is unimportant; a demand schedule presents specific prices and amounts when these are required.

DEMAND ELASTICITY

Measuring Buyer Sensitivity to Prices

Demand curves and demand schedules show the tendency of buyers to respond to price changes by altering the quantities of the things they buy, but the magnitude of this response varies markedly from commodity to commodity. Buyers are quite insensitive to the prices of some commodities—tobacco is a good example—and tend to buy only slightly less at high prices than they do when prices are low. For other commodities, prices are a primary consideration, and small price changes can make the difference between a flood of customers and no sales at all.

Measurement of buyer sensitivity to price requires considerable care. In the first place, how large a price change are we to consider? A rise of $1 in the price of a luxury sports car or a mink coat would not even be noticed, while a $1 increase in the price of a folder of matches or in the charge for a local telephone call would be enormous. To maintain an accurate perspective, it is necessary to measure price changes as percentages of the prices in question. To compare consumer sensitivity to different prices, we must compare their reactions to equal *percentage* increases. For example, we might see what would happen to the number of local phone calls made if the charge were increased from $.10 to $.15,

and compare this with what would happen to the number of sports cars bought if the price were increased from $3,000 to $4,500. Each of these would represent consumer response to a 50 percent rise in price.

But how can we compare the responses, even if the percentage price increases are equal? Suppose people responded to the increase in telephone rates by reducing their local calls from 90 billion to 81 billion per year, while their reaction to the rise in sports car prices were to buy only 800,000 a year, rather than their former purchases of 1 million. Which is the larger response, a 9 billion reduction in number of phone calls, or a 200,000 cut in car buying? Again, the natural procedure is to express each as a percentage change in amount purchased. In our hypothetical case, the same percentage price increase that induced people to reduce phone calls by 9/90, or 10 percent, led them to reduce the number of sports cars bought by 200,000/1 million, or 20 percent. Since the percentage reduction in sports car buying is larger than the one for phone calls, people are apparently more sensitive to automobile prices than they are to telephone rates.

In general, the sensitivity of buyers to change in any price is measured by the elasticity of demand. *Elasticity* is the ratio of the percentage reduction in quantity purchased to the percentage price increase that induced it. In our hypothetical example, since people cut their telephoning 10 percent when the charge was raised 50 percent, the elasticity of demand for local phone calls is 10/50, or .2. The elasticity of demand for sports cars, on the other hand, is 20/50, or .4. These figures provide a concise indication of the responsiveness of consumers to price increases in the 2 hypothetical cases.

Once a demand curve for a commodity has been estimated, it is easy to calculate the elasticity of demand by selecting 2 points on the curve a convenient distance apart and reading off the corresponding prices and quantities. The percentage changes in price and quantity are calculated and their ratio is the elasticity of demand. For example, according to the demand curve of Figure 1, a rise in the price of sweet potatoes from $4 to $4.25 typically induces consumers to reduce their purchases from 15.8 million hundredweight per year to 15.0 million. The 25 cent price increase is .25/4.00, or 6.25 percent. The .8 million reduction in quantity purchased is .8/15.8, or 5.03 percent. This makes the elasticity of demand equal to 5.03/6.25, or .8, approximately.

If we represent the initial price and quantity by P and Q, and their respective changes by ΔP and ΔQ, the percentage change in price is equal to $\Delta P/P$, and in quantity equal to $\Delta Q/Q$. Then the definition of the elasticity of demand, e, is given by the formula[1] $e = -(\Delta Q/Q)/(\Delta P/P)$. In the sweet potato example, $P = \$4$, $\Delta P = \$.25$, $Q = 15.8$, $\Delta Q = -0.8$; therefore, $e = -(-0.8/15.8)/(.25/4.00)$, or 0.8, approximately.

The meaning of differences in elasticity is illustrated in Figure 2. At the initial price of $80, buyers are taking 60 million per year. Elasticity depends on how buyers respond to an increase in price. Suppose the price rises 10 percent to $88. If purchases are reduced by 30 percent to 44 million, elasticity is 3. If purchases are reduced 10 percent to 54 million, elasticity of demand is 1. If purchases are cut only 5 percent to 57 million, demand elasticity is only .5. Curves corresponding to these 3 elasticities are shown in the figure.

Elasticity of demand is the most generally useful characterization of buyer sensitivity to prices, and has many technical applications in the discussion that follows. Moreover, it corresponds to daily business usage, for although businessmen rarely use

[1] Since a rise in price reduces the average quantity purchased, ΔQ is negative. Affixing a negative sign to the formula makes the elasticity a positive number, in keeping with usage.

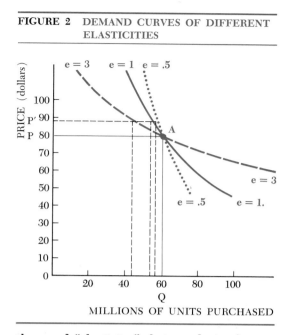

FIGURE 2   DEMAND CURVES OF DIFFERENT ELASTICITIES

MILLIONS OF UNITS PURCHASED

the word "elasticity," their analysis of markets is focused on the same "percentage-wise" comparison of buyer response to price changes.

Relationship of Elasticity to Sales Revenue

Figure 2 also illustrates the important relationship of elasticity to total sales revenue. At the initial price, $P = \$80$, consumers bought $Q = 60$ million per year. The total revenue derived from these sales was $PQ = \$80 \times 60$ million, or $4,800 million. As price rises, the quantity bought falls; total sales revenue is therefore subject to 2 opposite influences. The higher price means that sellers get more for each unit they sell, but the smaller quantity means fewer units are sold. Whether total sales revenue rises or falls therefore depends on which of these influences is the larger.

If the elasticity of demand is 1, each percentage increase in price is matched by an equal percentage reduction in quantity sold, leaving total sales revenue unaffected. If the elasticity of demand is greater than

1, any increase in prices is overbalanced by a larger percentage reduction in purchases, and total sales revenue falls, while if the elasticity of demand is less than 1, the percentage reduction in quantity sold is smaller than the increase in price, and total sales revenue rises. These results can be checked against those of Figure 2. When price rose from $80 to $88, the total expenditures of buyers whose demand elasticity was 3 fell from $4,800 million to $88 × 44 million, or $3,900 million, approximately. Buyers whose demand elasticity was 1 spent approximately $88 × 54 million, or $4,800 million, the same amount as before, while buyers whose demand elasticity was .5 increased their total spending to $88 × 57 million, or $5,000 million.

The nature of this proposition can be seen geometrically. Total sales revenue, PQ, is the area of a rectangle $OQAP$, whose base OQ is the quantity sold, and whose height is OP, the price. Any rise in price increases the height of the rectangle, but the attendant reduction in quantity purchased reduces the base. The new sales revenue is represented by the area of a new rectangle made from the other by adding area to the top and cutting area off the side. The elasticity of demand expresses the amount cut off the side as a proportion of the addition to the top. When the elasticity of demand is greater than 1, the area cut off the side exceeds that added to the top, and the total area is reduced. When demand elasticity is 1, the area added at the top equals that subtracted from the side, and price has no influence on total dollar expenditure. When demand elasticity is less than 1, the area added to the rectangle as price rises exceeds that subtracted from the side, and higher prices produce greater dollar expenditures on the commodity.

Demand elasticity equal to 1, often called *unit* elasticity, forms a dividing point between the elasticities that result in greater, and those that result in smaller total expenditures as prices rise. When demand has any elasticity less than 1, increasing prices always mean larger total sales revenue. When elasticity is greater than 1, increasing prices always mean smaller total sales revenue. It is convenient to refer to all demand curves with elasticity greater than 1 as *relatively elastic* demands, and to those with elasticity less than 1 as *relatively inelastic* demands. Since the demand for sweet potatoes has elasticity about .8, it is classed as a relatively inelastic demand. The elasticity of demand for restaurant meals has been estimated to be 2.3, and is classified as a relatively elastic demand.[2]

As we shall see when we reach the discussion of pricing, its relationship to sales revenue makes demand elasticity a key business consideration in setting pricing margins. Firms whose products have highly elastic demands gain by keeping prices down, since they more than make up in volume for the lower unit price. Firms whose products have lower demand elasticity tend to keep prices high, since they gain more from the higher unit price than they lose from reduction in volume.

Elasticity and the Shape
of the Demand Curve

The demand for sweet potatoes shown in Figure 1 has elasticity of about .8, but all curves of constant elasticity have the same general appearance, forming a smooth arc that is convex when viewed from the origin. The curve is steepest at high prices and becomes flatter and flatter as prices decline. As shown in Figure 3, if a curve of constant elasticity is extended far enough, it approaches the 2 axes as asymptotes. This characteristic shape follows from the way elasticity is measured. Elasticity of demand equal to e means that with each 1 percent

[2] H. S. Houthakker and Lester D. Taylor, *Consumer Demand in the United States, 1929–1970*, Cambridge, Mass., Harvard University Press, 1966, p. 62.

FIGURE 3 DEMAND CURVE WITH CONSTANT
ELASTICITY OF 2

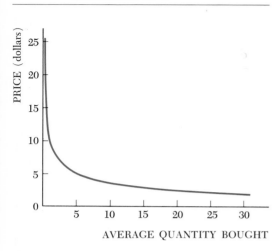

AVERAGE QUANTITY BOUGHT

reduction in price buyers purchase e percent more. As prices fall, however, each
successive 1 percent reduction is a smaller
number of dollars than the preceding one,
while each successive e percent increase in
purchases is a larger quantity than the
preceding one. As smaller and smaller price
reductions produce larger and larger quantity responses, the curve is steep when
prices are high and flattens out as prices
fall.

There are 2 important exceptions to this
general rule. When buyers are completely
insensitive to prices, and buy the same
amount at high as at low prices, demand
elasticity is 0. A demand curve with elasticity everywhere equal to 0 is represented by
a straight line parallel to the price axis as in
Figure 4(a). To see why the demand is
said to have 0 elasticity, choose any 2
nearby points on the curve, say A and B.
From A to B the price rises from its initial
value $P = 6$ by the amount $\Delta P = 2$, while
Q does not change from its initial value of
$Q = 7$. Thus $\Delta Q = 0$. Inserting these values
in the elasticity formula, we get $e =
-(\Delta Q/Q)/(\Delta P/P) = -(0/7)/(2/6) =
-0/.33$, or 0.

The other exception is the situation in

which buyers will take everything offered
at a specified price, but will stop buying
entirely at any higher price. In this event,
demand is said to have *infinite* elasticity. As
shown in Figure 4(b), a demand curve that
is everywhere infinitely elastic is a straight
line parallel to the quantity axis. To see why
the demand is said to have infinite elasticity,
pick any 2 nearby points on the curve, say
A and B. The initial value of P at point A is
$P = 8$. Moreover, since P has the same value
at point B, $\Delta P = 0$. Since Q has the initial
value $Q = 7$, and rises to $Q = 10$ at point B,
$\Delta Q = 3$. Inserting these values in the elasticity formula, we get $e = -(\Delta Q/Q)/(\Delta P/
P) = -(3/7)/(0/8) = -.43/0$, or infinity.

Elasticities of 0 and infinity form special
limiting cases marking the extremes of
buyer sensitivity to prices. All other demand
curves with constant elasticity correspond
to buyer responses between these limits and
have the curvature previously described.

In general, of course, there is no reason
to suppose that buyers have the same sensitivity to prices at all levels. It is unrealistic,
for example, to suppose that people would
continue indefinitely to buy more and more
sweet potatoes, or anything else, as they got
cheaper. Sooner or later a price is reached
that is low enough so that all desire for the
product is satisfied and further price reductions have no effect—people would not use
any more even if the product were free. As
the price approaches that level, demand becomes less and less elastic until people stop

FIGURE 4   DEMAND CURVES

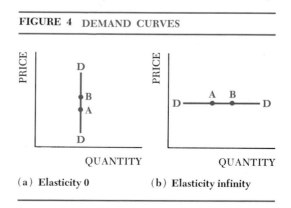

(a) Elasticity 0   (b) Elasticity infinity

responding to prices, and the elasticity becomes 0. At the other extreme, it is unrealistic to suppose that sweet potatoes or anything else could continue to sell regardless of how high the price went. As the price rises, sooner or later a level is reached at which buyers will do without the commodity entirely rather than pay it. As the price nears this level, people become more and more sensitive to further increases. The elasticity of their demand rises higher and higher and ultimately approaches infinity as people stop using the commodity altogether.

If we could observe consumer responses to the entire possible range of prices for any commodity, demand curves might typically look like the one in Figure 5. Such a demand curve varies in elasticity over the entire range becoming 0 at the lower end, where people use all they want of the product, and rising continuously as the price increases, passing unity somewhere near the middle, and reaching infinity at the upper end where buying is completely choked off. It is important to remember, however, that the full range of possible prices for any commodity is rarely, if ever, observed, and that in any practical situation

we find only prices and quantities in the central portion of the curve. For most purposes, demand curves fitted to points in this middle range of prices can be treated as curves with approximately constant elasticity.

Why Demand Is Elastic

Leaving aside for the moment the question of why people appear to be more sensitive to the prices of some things than they are to the prices of others, let us explore a more fundamental question. Why is demand elastic at all? Why, virtually without exception, does a reduction in the price of a commodity lead people to buy more of it?

If we ask a housewife why she buys more at lower than at high prices, she is likely to say that she can "afford" more at the lower price. But what, exactly, does this mean? How is it that a family with a $15,000 income can "afford" a new car when it costs $2,000, but not when it costs $3,000? The answer is, of course, that the family has many claims on its income. In addition to a car, it needs food, clothes, books, medicine, insurance, and so on indefinitely. Spending money on one of these things necessarily means *not* spending the same money on something else. The true cost of a purchase is not the actual dollars given up for it, but the opportunity cost represented by the sacrificed power to buy something else instead. To say we can "afford" something means only that we would rather have that particular thing than any of the other things that the same money could buy.

Effective expenditure of income requires some kind of budgeting. Some families draw up formal budgets, detailing the monthly expenditure pattern that will make the most of their incomes. Other families budget by an informal process based on experience in managing the family's pur-

FIGURE 5   DEMAND CURVE WITH ELASTICITY
RANGING FROM 0 TO INFINITY

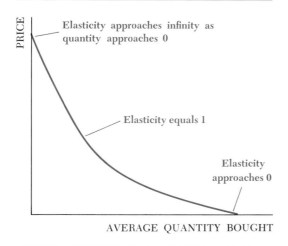

Elasticity approaches infinity as quantity approaches 0

Elasticity equals 1

Elasticity approaches 0

AVERAGE QUANTITY BOUGHT

chases. In either case, proper budgeting means seeing to it that each purchase is worth its opportunity cost; that no trivial desires are satisfied at the cost of failure to satisfy a more serious need.

The Margins of Consumption   One reason that demands are elastic is that choices reflected in family budgets are not, in general, between having something or doing without it altogether. We do not choose food *instead* of clothing. Rather we must choose whether we want a *little more* food instead of a *little more* clothing, or we must choose whether we want a little better quality of food instead of a little better quality of clothing, and so on. The question is not whether the family is going to buy steaks or shirts, but whether the family is going to buy a few more steaks or another shirt. The steaks, shirts, and other goods that enter this comparison are not those in the "center" of the family budget, so to speak, but those on its "edges" or "margins," where small amounts can be shaved off or small additions can be made. The quantities involved in these small changes are referred to as *marginal quantities* of the goods in question. If a family is buying 6 new shirts a year, the budgetary question is whether a seventh shirt would be worth the extra steaks that could be bought instead. The seventh shirt and the extra steaks are marginal quantities.

In these terms, the opportunity cost of acquiring the marginal quantity of one good is the marginal quantities of other goods that must be foregone. We do not compare the usefulness of shirts in general with steaks as a whole. We compare the *marginal* shirt with the *marginal* steaks. Proper budgeting then means that all marginal expenditures must be worth their opportunity costs.

A change in the price of a commodity changes its opportunity cost. For example, at a price of $10, an extra shirt requires the sacrifice of $10 worth of extra steaks, books, neckties, or other things. At a lower price

the purchaser can have the extra shirt and still have some of the extra steaks, books, or whatever he wants. The opportunities sacrificed to the shirt are less valuable than before. Some purchasers who did without the extra shirt at $10 because the opportunity cost was too high will buy when the cost is reduced.

Diminishing Marginal Utility Another reason that people tend to buy more of a commodity as its price declines is that, in general, the more of any good a family consumes, the less importance is attached to increasing its consumption. Expensive goods are reserved for high-priority uses. As their prices come down they are applied to uses of less and less importance. For example, in some parts of the world, poor mountain villages are 2 or 3 miles from the nearest water, and all water must be carried in small quantities by donkey. Because of its high cost, water is reserved for important purposes: cooking, drinking, essential washing. If additional water were available, people could wash clothes more frequently, bathe occasionally, and shave more than once a month. In a modern American city, in contrast, water is freely used for cooking, drinking, washing, sanitation, and even for lawn sprinklers, decorative fountains, swimming pools, and drinking fountains, where it often runs all day.

What is true of water applies generally to all goods and can be expressed in several ways. As the consumption of a good increases, marginal quantities are employed for less and less "valuable" purposes. The marginal units are put to "lower-priority" or "less essential" uses, or used to satisfy less "intense" wants. In economic analysis, concepts like the "value" or "priority" of the use, the "essentiality" or 'intensity" of the want satisfied by marginal quantities of a good are summarized in the term *marginal utility*. Thus situations like water consumption are described as exhibiting *diminishing marginal utility*.

Because marginal utility diminishes, that is, because additional quantities must be put to lower-priority uses, unless their opportunity cost is lowered by price reductions families will not be willing to purchase them. If the price rises, the good is forced out of low-priority uses. The rate of consumption declines and marginal utility rises.

Differences in Tastes and Incomes   A third important reason that demands are elastic is that families differ in income and in their preferences for different goods. One family attaches great importance to having a new car every year. Another keeps the car 10 years, preferring to spend their income on more expensive vacations or a better house. When the price of the car falls, however, the latter family may replace the car every 5 years, doubling their annual rate of purchase. Differences in income are probably even more important. At very high prices, the opportunity cost of a new car to even a modest-income family is inadequate housing, poor diet, and lack of medical care. When the price is lowered, the sacrifice becomes correspondingly smaller and permits the family to buy. Each reduction in the price of cars puts new cars within the reach of families with lower incomes, and increases the annual quantity purchased.

Elasticity of Demand for Different Types of Goods

The elasticity of demand for particular items depends on the nature of the consumer needs they satisfy. Necessities have inelastic demands because most people resist cutting their purchases when prices rise, and they often have little use for more when prices decline. The demand for luxuries, on the other hand, tends to be more elastic. Luxury items disappear from the budgets of many families when their prices rise, and price reduction puts them within reach of more people who are eager to have them.

The Substitution Effect of Price Changes   It is rare that a good provides a unique service or satisfaction. Most often there are large groups of goods, all of which serve much the same purpose. Such goods are "substitutes" because they can replace each other in the family budget. Fountain pens, ball-point pens, and fiber-tipped pens, pens with cartridge refills, plastic pens, and metal pens are all interchangeable for most purposes, and can be used to serve the same, or very similar ends. Slacks and sports coats are substitutes for suits, and a jacket can substitute for an overcoat. Iron, steel, aluminum, and glass cooking utensils are substitutes for each other, and stainless steel can be used instead of silverware on the table. There are, of course, all degrees of substitution. A fiber-point pen, for example, is not a perfect substitute for a ball-point when carbon copies are wanted, but for most purposes one will do as well as the other. Differing brands of the same commodity probably represent the closest substitutes, but commodities as different as air travel and season tickets to local football games are substitutes insofar as both are recreation.

Lowering the price of a commodity tends to increase its use at the expense of its substitutes. This is known as the *substitution effect* of the price change. The strength of the substitution effect depends on how easily a commodity can be substituted for others. Since altering the price of a commodity with close substitutes exerts a strong substitution effect, such goods tend to have highly elastic demands. A reduction in the price of one attracts a large proportion of customers away from the other, now more expensive substitutes, while an increase in its price easily drives customers away. Altering the prices of commodities that have no close substitutes exerts only a weak substitution effect, and such commodities tend to have inelastic demands.

The demand for commercial laundry service is relatively elastic. As a substitute, many housewives do their own washing at home if they have the equipment or employ the services of coin-operated machines if they do not. The resulting demand elasticity has been estimated to be 1.02.[3] In contrast, dry cleaning done at home is not a close substitute for commercial service, and the elasticity of demand has been estimated to be only 0.45.[4]

Aggregation and the Substitution Effect

An important aspect of the substitution effect is that the elasticity of demand depends on how broadly commodities are defined. When we deal with great aggregates like "food" or "clothing," we expect relatively inelastic demands. Buyers have few substitutes to turn to when food or clothing prices rise and often have little use for extra consumption when prices fall. The more narrowly a commodity is defined, the more close substitutes it will have for most of its uses. If instead of food in general, we confine our analysis to meat, we expect to find a more elastic demand because of the available substitute sources of protein. The elasticity of the demand for beef is even higher, since pork, lamb, or poultry can be easily eaten instead. Sirloin steak has even more substitutes and is even more elastic in demand.

The most narrowly defined commodities are different brands or makes of products that are in essence almost identical. The demand for toothpaste may be relatively inelastic, but a particular brand of toothpaste, sold in competition with a large number of substitute brands, will have highly elastic demand. The elasticity of demand for automobiles has been estimated to lie somewhere between .6 and 1, but the evidence suggests that the elasticity of demand for any particular make of car is close to 4.[5] In

other words, if the average price of all new cars declines by 10 percent, the total number of new cars sold tends to rise by something between 6 and 10 percent, but if one manufacturer, say Ford, should reduce the price of its cars by 10 percent, while the prices of the substitutes produced by American Motors, Chrysler, and General Motors remained unchanged, Ford's sales would rise by about 40 percent at the expense of its competitors. As we shall see, high elasticity of the demand for the products of individual business firms is of key importance in industrial pricing and competition.

Complementary Goods and Elasticity

Some commodities are not used alone, but as part of a total package in which they are combined with others in more or less fixed proportions. Gasoline, for example, is rarely used by itself, but is consumed in combination with motor oil, tires, and other items essential to the operation of an automobile. Commodities that are used together in this way are called "complements."

In a sense, complements are the opposite of substitutes. When consumers buy more of one substitute, they usually buy less of another, but when they buy more of one complement, they usually buy more of the others to go with it. For this reason the demand for any one commodity in a group of complements tends to be relatively inelastic. The important thing to the buyer is not the price of the individual commodity, but the price of the entire package. The elasticity of demand for the complete package of complements might be 2, but if the price of one component makes up only 25 percent of the total, a 1 percent reduction in its price lowers the price of the total package only .25 percent, and increases the quantity purchased by only 2 × .25, or .5 percent. In other words, the elasticity of demand for one component member of a group of complements is equal to the elasticity of demand for the total package multiplied by the proportion of the price of the component to the total cost.

[3] Houthakker and Taylor, *op. cit.,* p. 71.

[4] *Ibid.,* p. 70.

[5] Houthakker and Taylor, *op. cit.,* p. 112. Daniel B. Suits, "The Demand for New Automobiles in the United States, 1929–1958," *Review of Economics and Statistics,* no. 40, August, 1958, pp. 273–280.

Gasoline, motor oil, and tires are 3 components in a package required to operate a car. If the price per mile driven is $.015 for gasoline, $.015 for oil, and $.010 for tires, the cost of gasoline is only 37 percent of the 4 cent-per-mile operating cost. Even if people responded to a reduction in the cost per mile with a demand elasticity of 1, the elasticity of demand for gasoline would be only .37 × 1, or 0.37.

Short-Run and Long-Run Elasticity

Like other economic reactions, a buyer's initial response to a change in price often differs from what he does after a period of time. Sometimes people have long been accustomed to using the product and their inertia keeps them buying at the old rate for a while even after its price rises. As time passes, however, buyers may drift away as they discover acceptable substitutes, or find that they can get along with less, after all. The reverse occurs when prices are reduced. It takes time to overcome the inertia of buyers accustomed to purchasing other, now higher-priced, substitutes. This appears to be the case with jewelry and watches. It has been estimated that during the first year following a change in price demand exhibits an elasticity of 0.43. As time passes and buyers adjust their buying habits to the new price, the elasticity approaches .72. Another example is airline travel, which has demand elasticity of only .06 in the short run, but elasticity of 2.36 when people are given time to adjust their travel habits.[6]

Consumers often need time to adjust their buying to prices of goods whose use requires special complementary facilities or equipment that must be acquired first. Reduction in the price of electricity, for example, has little short-run influence on the number of kilowatt-hours consumed, but as increasing numbers of homes acquire freezers, air conditioners, baseboard heat-

[6] Houthakker and Taylor, *op. cit.*, p. 124.

ing, and other electrical facilities, consumption expands in the long run. The demand for gasoline also has this property to some degree. It has been estimated that in the short run, the elasticity of demand is only .15, but that it rises to .46 in the long run as consumers respond to prices by changing the size and style of the cars which they drive.[7]

Sometimes the relationship is reversed, and the short-run elasticity of demand is higher than the long-run elasticity. Buyer response to lower prices is sometimes a substantial initial increase in buying followed by a slow drift back toward the original level. This is true of the demand for many durable goods. A lower price means that more people can own the item, and their initial rush to acquire ownership causes a short-run jump in sales. In the long run, however, annual sales remain higher only to the extent required for extra replacement sales to a larger number of owners than before. The demand for new automobiles is an example of this type. Lower prices mean more new-car owners and a large rise in sales as they buy, giving the demand for new cars a short-run elasticity of between 0.6 and 1.0. The long-run elasticity of demand, however, has been estimated to be only 0.15.[8]

Comparison of Elasticities

Differences in elasticity of demand for different types of commodities can be seen in Table 2. Large aggregates like "home consumption of food" have such low demand elasticities that often no significant buyer response to prices can be detected. After all what can you substitute for food? But demands for individual vegetables, even for staples like potatoes, are sufficiently elastic to permit measurement. Those like potatoes and onions that comprise a regular part of the standard American diet tend to have

[7] *Ibid.*, p. 116.
[8] *Ibid.*, p. 112.

TABLE 2   ELASTICITY OF DEMAND FOR SELECTED GOODS

	ESTIMATED ELASTICITY	SOURCE OF ESTIMATE		ESTIMATED ELASTICITY	SOURCE OF ESTIMATE
FOOD ITEMS			**DURABLE GOODS**		
Home consumption of food	n.s.	H	Household furniture	n.s.	H
Selected vegetables			Kitchen appliances	0.6	H
Cabbage	0.4	USDA	China and tableware	1.1	H
Onions	0.4	S(1)	Jewelry and watches	0.4	H
White pototoes	0.3	USDA	Automobiles, Short-run	0.6	S(4)
Sweet potatoes	0.8	S(2)	Long-run	0.2	H
Green peas, fresh	2.8	USDA	Tires, Short-run	0.6	H
Green peas, canned	1.6	USDA	Long-run	0.4	H
Tomatoes, fresh	4.6	USDA	Radio and television receivers	1.2	H
Tomatoes, canned	2.5	USDA	Sports equipment, boat, pleasure		
Watermelons	1.5	S(3)	aircraft, Short-run	0.6	H
			Long-run	1.3	H
OTHER NONDURABLE GOODS					
			SERVICES		
Tobacco products	n.s.	H			
Clothing	n.s.	H	Physicians' services	0.6	H
Shoes	0.4	H	Legal services	0.5	H
Stationery	0.5	H	Taxi	0.4	H
Newspapers and magazines	0.1	H	Rail commuting	0.7	H
Gasoline and oil, Short-run	0.2	H	Airline travel, Short-run	0.06	H
Long-run	0.5	H	Long-run	2.4	H
			Foreign travel, Short-run	0.7	H
			Long-run	4.0	H

n.s. = no significant buyer reaction to price was detected.

SOURCES: H: H. S. Houthakker and Lester D. Taylor, *Consumer Demand in the United States, 1929–1970,* Cambridge, Mass., Harvard University Press, 1966. USDA: D. Milton Shuffett, *The Demand and Price Structure for Selected Vegetables,* Technical Bulletin no. 1105, U.S. Department of Agriculture, 1954. S(1): Daniel B. Suits and Susumu Koizumi, "The Dynamics of the Onion Market," *Journal of Farm Economics,* no. 38, May, 1956, pp. 475–484. S(2): Calculated from Figure 1, above. S(3): Daniel B. Suits, "An Econometric Model of the Watermelon Market," *Journal of Farm Economics,* no. 37, May, 1955, pp. 237–251. S(4): Daniel B. Suits, "The Demand for New Automobiles in the United States," *Review of Economics and Statistics,* no. 40, 1958.

relatively inelastic demands, while items like green peas and tomatoes that can be more freely substituted tend to have relatively elastic demands. Moreover, demand for fresh produce appears to be more elastic than demand for canned goods.

Many of the entries of nonfood commodities in the table likewise cover wide aggregates, and estimated demand elasticities tend to be low for that reason. Even so, differences between "necessities" like shoes and medical service and "luxuries" like tableware and television sets show up in differences in the elasticity of demand. Demand for services like foreign travel that

require advance planning, or like air transportation that involve habit patterns are more elastic in the long run than they are in the short run. The demands for many durable goods like automobiles and tires are more elastic in the short run than they are in the long run.

SHIFTS IN DEMAND

As we noted at the outset, people vary the quantities they buy for many reasons other than price. The influence of these results in *shifts* in demand. When families decide to buy more of a commodity at given prices than they did before, their demand is said to have *increased*. On a chart, an increase in demand is represented by shifting the demand curve bodily to the right. When buyers tend to take less than they formerly did at given prices, demand is said to *decrease*, and is represented by shifting the demand curve to the left.

In Figure 6, the original curve is represented by the solid line *DD*. The dashed line *dd* repesents the situation after buyers have increased their demand so as to buy more—in this case 50 percent more—at any given price than before. Each point on *dd* represents a quantity 50 percent larger than that at the corresponding price on the original curve *DD*. A 50 percent reduction in demand is represented by shifting the curve from *DD* to a position like *d'd'*, on which each point represents a quantity 50 percent smaller than that at the corresponding price on *DD*.

As an actual example, a substantial increase in demand for lemons is shown in Figure 7. Quantities bought at prices prevailing during the 7-year period 1954–1961 lie close to the solid line. During the next 4 years, the quantities taken by buyers considerably exceeded what would have been expected on the basis of the old demand curve.

Actual year-to-year changes in quantities bought are the result of the combination of demand elasticity and demand shifts acting together. Demand elasticity means that people tend to buy less at higher prices, but if the demand for the product is increasing, the effect of elasticity is partly or entirely offset. In fact, when demand is increasing rapidly enough, families can be observed to buy more rather than less at the higher price. This was the case when residential consumption of natural gas more than tripled between 1950 and 1963, despite a 50 percent rise in price. As shown in Figure 8, price and quantity of gas consumed

are represented by points on successively higher demand curves.

Income Elasticity of Demand

One of the most important causes of shifting demand is changing income. As families earn more, they tend to buy more, but the composition of their expenditure changes. Demand for luxury goods rises more rapidly than the demand for staple necessities, and the demand for goods of inferior quality declines as they are replaced by better-grade items.

The *income elasticity of demand* for an item is the ratio of the percentage shift in demand to the percentage increase in income that caused it. When a 10 percent rise in disposable personal income leads families to buy 30 percent more than they used to at corresponding prices, the income elasticity of demand is 30/10, or 3. When the rise in income shifts demand only 5 percent, the income elasticity is 5/10, or .5. When buyers take less of the product as their incomes rise, the income elasticity of demand for it is negative.

The effect of variation in family income on the consumption of several commodities is shown in Table 3. Since the survey figures were obtained in one year, little of the variation can be ascribed to price, and one can assume that it represents shifts in demand from group to group. Income elasticities can be roughly estimated by comparing consumption by families in the $2,000–$2,999 bracket with consumption of families in the $8,000–$9,999 bracket, representing an increase in income of 250 percent. Since coffee consumption in the higher-income bracket was only about 30 percent above that in the lower, the income elasticity of the demand for coffee can be estimated at about 30/250, or .12. The income elasticity of the demand for soft drinks is about 60/250, or .24, while the shift in demand for alcoholic beverages demon-

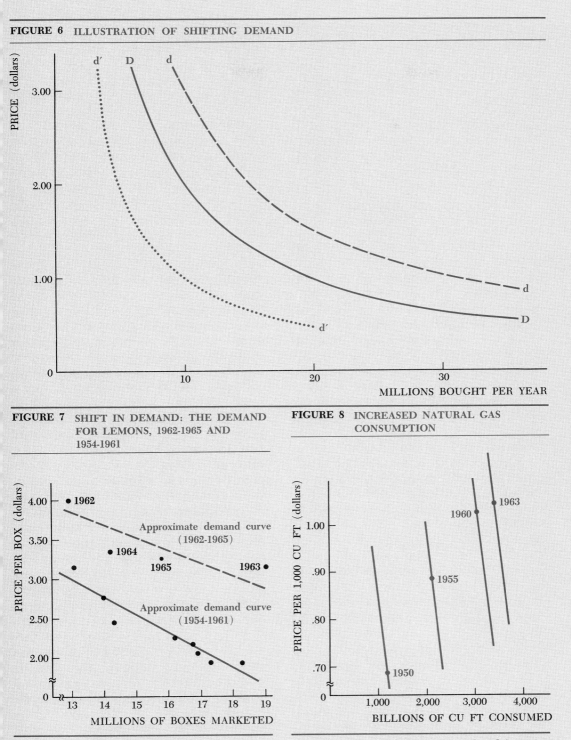

FIGURE 6 ILLUSTRATION OF SHIFTING DEMAND

PRICE (dollars)

3.00

2.00

1.00

0

10   20   30

MILLIONS BOUGHT PER YEAR

FIGURE 7 SHIFT IN DEMAND: THE DEMAND
FOR LEMONS, 1962-1965 AND
1954-1961

PRICE PER BOX (dollars)

4.00 • 1962

3.50   Approximate demand curve
                              (1962-1965)

• 1964

• 1965   1963 •

3.00

Approximate demand curve
(1954-1961)

2.50

2.00

0

13   14   15   16   17   18   19

MILLIONS OF BOXES MARKETED

FIGURE 8 INCREASED NATURAL GAS
CONSUMPTION

PRICE PER 1,000 CU FT (dollars)

1963

1960

1.00

.90   1955

.80

.70   1950

0

1,000   2,000   3,000   4,000

BILLIONS OF CU FT CONSUMED

SOURCE FOR FIGURE 7: Plotted from data given in U.S. Department of Agriculture, *Agricultural Statistics,*
1967.

TABLE 3 WEEKLY PURCHASE OF SELECTED ITEMS, BY FAMILY INCOME BRACKET

FAMILY INCOME	COFFEE (LBS)	SOFT DRINKS (NUMBER)	ALCOHOLIC BEVERAGES ($)	CLOTHING		DRIED BEANS (LBS)
				MEN'S	WOMEN'S	
				($ PER PERSON)		
Under $2,000	.67	1.67	$ .06	$1.25	$ 1.42	1.00
2,000–2,999	.74	2.64	.12	1.55	2.10	.69
3,000–3,999	.82	3.19	.12	2.13	3.00	.62
4,000–4,999	.88	3.23	.23	2.68	3.20	.52
5,000–5,999	.89	3.49	.39	2.72	3.27	.72
6,000–7,999	.94	3.58	.42	3.21	4.05	.61
8,000–9,999	.97	4.23	.60	4.38	5.15	.11
10,000 and over	1.02	5.17	1.83	6.70	11.00	.43

SOURCES: Data on foods and beverages from U.S. Department of Agriculture, *Household Food Consumption Survey*, 1955. Clothing data adapted from U.S. Bureau of Labor Statistics, *Clothing the Urban American Family: How Much for Whom?*, BLS Report 238–16, January, 1968.

strates an income elasticity of about 400/ 250, or 1.60.

Although families at all income levels spend more on women's clothes than on men's, the income elasticity of demand for the 2 are nearly equal. Consumption of a food like dried beans that is cheap but that requires some time and trouble is reduced as incomes rise, and is replaced by canned beans, or by other foods that are easier to prepare. The demand for dried beans therefore has negative income elasticity.

As total disposable income rises we may expect the shifts in the demand for the various goods to correspond to their income elasticities. This is illustrated in Figure 9. A typical demand as of 1965 is represented by the position of the curve *DD*. The 15 percent increase in disposable personal income between 1965 and 1967 increased demand and shifted the curve. Demand for products that had income elasticity of 1.6—approximately the demand for alcoholic beverages—was shifted 1.6 × 15, or 24 percent to the position *dd*. The demand for products whose income elasticity of demand was .3—roughly the demand for soft drinks—rose .3 × 15, or 4.5 percent, as represented by the shift to position *d'd'*, while the demand for products with negative income elasticity declined to a position like *d"d"*.

Cross-Elasticity of Demand

The decision to buy is influenced by the prices of other items as well as by the price of the commodity in question. The demand for an item declines when the prices of its substitutes decline, and rises when their prices rise. When the price of chicken is reduced, families eat more chicken and, at given beef prices, consume less beef than before. When the price of chicken rises, beef is a better buy than before and families consume more of it at any given price in place of the now more expensive chicken.

The extent of the shift in the demand for one thing (beef) in response to changes in the price of another (chicken) is the *cross-elasticity of demand*, and is measured by the percentage shift in demand for one item per percentage change in the price of the other. If a 3 percent rise in the price of chicken causes the demand for beef to increase 2 percent, the cross-elasticity of the demand for beef to the price of chicken would be 2/3, or .67. When people buy *more* of one thing when the price of something else rises, the cross-elasticity of demand is *positive*. When they buy *less*, the cross-elasticity of demand is *negative*. Substitutes, like beef and chicken, have positive cross-elasticities of demand, and the more closely the items can substitute for

FIGURE 9   CONSUMER RESPONSES TO A 15 PERCENT INCREASE IN INCOME

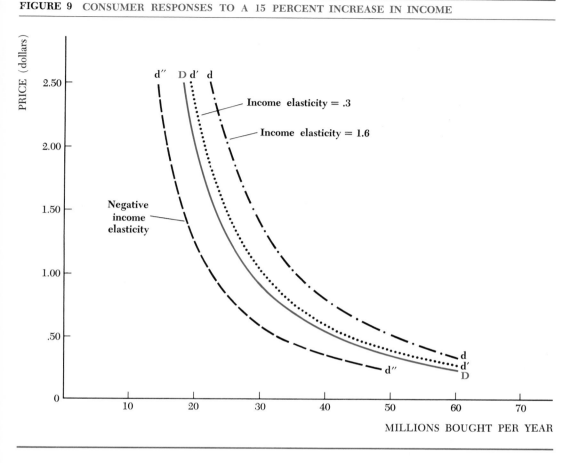

each other, the higher the cross-elasticity will be. The very high cross-elasticity of products that differ only in brand name or make is an important aspect of competitive pricing.

The cross-elasticity of demand between complementary goods like gasoline and motor oil is negative. A rise in the price of one of the items induces buyers not only to use less of it, but also to use less of the complementary items that go with it.

Other Factors in Shifting Demand

Family Composition The kinds and amounts of things a family buys vary with the number, ages, and sexes of family members. Obviously a larger family consumes more of most things than a smaller family. Expenditures also vary by age. A young couple usually makes substantial purchases of furniture, household appliances, and other durable goods as they set up housekeeping. Once acquired, these items need only be replaced when they wear out or are made obsolete by improvements or style changes.

Figure 10 demonstrates the familiar proposition that women spend more on their clothes than do men of the same age. It also shows that expenditure per person rises with age to a peak at about 23 and declines thereafter. Although not shown in the fig-

FIGURE 10   CLOTHING EXPENDITURES VARY
BY AGE AND SEX

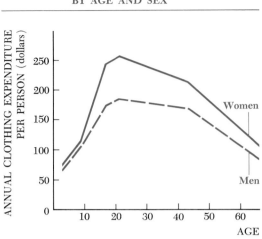

SOURCE: Plotted from data given in U.S. Bureau of Labor Statistics, *Clothing the American Family: How Much for Whom?*, BLS Report no. 238–316, January, 1968.

ure, the ages at which peak expenditures occur vary by type of clothing. Among men and boys, outlays for nightwear are highest at ages 2 to 5; the peak spending for chinos and bluejeans occurs between 6 and 11; the highest shoe bills are for the 12-to-15-year-olds; while spending for jackets, sweaters, and sports clothes reaches its maximum between 16 and 17. Men aged 18 to 24 spend more than others on sport coats, shirts, and jewelry, while older men spend the most for suits, hats, and accessories like belts and wallets.

Education   Better-educated parents tend to attach more importance to such expenditures as periodic medical examinations, personal hygiene, education, and books than to items for personal display or immediate gratification.

The effects on dental care of family income, age and education can be seen in Table 4. Each figure in the table shows the percentage of individuals in each age, education, and income bracket who visited a

dentist at least once during the 12-month period July, 1958–June, 1959. For example, the upper left-hand figure in the table means that of all children under 4 years old whose fathers had less than 9 years' education and whose family income was under $4,000 per year, 3.1 percent visited a dentist during the period. The lower right-hand figure means that of all the people 65 years of age or over in families whose head had 9 years or more education, with annual family income over $4,000, 28.2 percent visited a dentist. Reading down any column, we see the effect of age alone: Dental care rises to a peak during ages 15–24 (a little earlier in the highest education and income group) and tapers off thereafter. Comparing neighboring figures under the same education heading indicates that dental care rises with income regardless of age level, for both high- and low-education groups. Finally, comparing figures at the same age level and in the same income column but in different education columns we see the effect of education. Clearly at all

TABLE 4   PERCENT OF PEOPLE OF
GIVEN AGE, FAMILY INCOME,
AND EDUCATION OF HEAD
OF THE FAMILY, WHO
VISITED A DENTIST, JULY,
1958–JUNE, 1959

	HEAD OF FAMILY HAS LESS THAN 9 YEARS OF SCHOOL		HEAD OF FAMILY HAS 9 OR MORE YEARS OF SCHOOL	
AGE	INCOME UNDER $4,000	INCOME $4,000 OR MORE	INCOME UNDER $4,000	INCOME $4,000 OR MORE
0– 4	3.1	7.7	5.2	13.4
5–14	23.9	45.5	43.0	68.2
15–24	32.4	51.4	52.4	64.8
25–44	26.7	40.7	41.9	58.1
45–64	21.8	31.7	33.7	51.0
65 and over	13.9	18.8	23.2	28.2

SOURCE: *Dental Care, Interval and Frequency of Visits,* Health Statistics from the U.S. National Health Survey, Series B–no. 14., U.S. Public Health Service, Washington, D.C., March, 1960.

age levels and for both income brackets, more dental care is found among families whose head has higher education.

Preferences and Tastes The use of many products varies with the preferences of the family as these are in turn affected by such factors as religious beliefs, ethnic background, experience, region of residence and social status. Table 5 shows the regional variation in annual clothing expenditure. Highest outlays are made by families living in the Northeast. The least is spent by families in the South. While much of this difference is attributable to temperature and weather conditions, it also reflects the lower average incomes of southern families.

Health The use of goods varies with the health of family members. Invalids need special care and corrective devices. Diabetes, allergies, and similar problems required special diets. Sickness results in medical bills; an active, healthy family buys sportswear and vacations.

Innovation In a dynamic modern economy, some of the most important demand shifts result from product improvement or from the appearance of new products on the market. For example, the introduction of plastics reduced the demand for metal in many uses, and the demand for conventional

FIGURE 11 SHIFT OF PASSENGER TRAFFIC FROM RAIL TO AIR

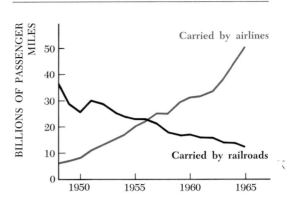

SOURCE: Data from *Historical Statistics of the United States* and from *Statistical Abstract of the United States, 1968.* Rail passenger miles exclude commutation traffic.

soap has declined in favor of detergents. As shown in Figure 11, the appearance of air service has virtually eliminated the demand for long-distance rail passenger service. Television altered the demand for radios, and so on. Some of these demand shifts, like those that followed the introduction of the automobile, reflect a revolution in living habits. Others, like the shift in demand for conventional leather shoes that followed the introduction of pigskin for casual wear, merely alter the composition of demand for particular items.

Psychology and Advertising Demand shifts often reflect changes in consumer psychology. As a human activity, buying is subject to all the vagaries of tastes, attitudes, expectations, and purely human impulses and whims. Demands shift almost continuously for these reasons, and the object of most competitive advertising is to manipulate this psychology so as to persuade consumers to want things they otherwise might not want, or to buy one product instead of another, or to buy more than they otherwise would, or otherwise to shift their demands.

TABLE 5	REGIONAL DIFFERENCES IN FAMILY CLOTHING EXPENDITURE
REGION	EXPENDITURE PER YEAR
U.S.	$639.73
Northeast	719.56
North Central	602.51
South	569.77
West	671.11

SOURCE: Calculated for a family consisting of father, mother, son aged 13, daughter aged 8, from data given in *Clothing the Urban American Family, How Much for Whom?*

THE IMPORTANCE OF DEMAND

Consumer demand, demand elasticity, and demand shifts form the key to the analysis in the chapters that follow. Consumer demand is the ultimate control over how much of each type of product is turned out. When consumers reduce their demand for one product and increase demand for another, producers of the less desirable product find production less profitable and are forced to reduce output, while makers of more desirable products take advantage of expanded demand to increase production. In turn, the actions of these business firms create jobs, tend to raise wages, to attract labor to the production of more desirable goods, and tend to reduce wages of workers engaged in the production of less desirable goods.

Demand elasticity exerts an important influence over prices. Producers of goods with few close substitutes can take advantage of low demand elasticity to raise prices without reducing sales to an unprofitable level. Producers of keenly competitive goods with many close substitutes are forced to price close to cost. Producers who can be first in the market with successful product innovations are rewarded with increased demand and higher profits. The consequent high rate of product improvement is one of the most obvious features of a private enterprise system.

SUMMARY

Buyer response to price is represented by a *demand curve* or *demand schedule* that indicates the total quantity buyers tend to purchase at each price. Buyer sensitivity to prices is measured by the *elasticity of demand,* the ratio of a percentage change in quantity bought to the percentage change in price that induced it.

Demand curves with elasticity greater than 1 are *relatively elastic,* while those with elasticity below 1 are *relatively inelastic.* The total sales revenue received by all sellers of a commodity with relatively elastic demand falls as price rises. When demand is relatively inelastic, sales revenue rises as price rises.

In general, buyers are responsive to changes in prices for 3 related reasons: (1) Lower prices reduce the opportunity cost of an item, permitting the family to buy it with a smaller sacrifice of other purchases. (2) Lower prices permit families to use the item for lower-priority purposes. (3) Lower prices bring the item within the grasp of lower-income families.

The elasticity of demand for individual items depends on the nature of the commodity and on its relationship to other goods. The demand for luxuries tends to be elastic, but the demand for necessities tends to be inelastic. Items with good *substitutes* have elastic demands while items with *complements* have inelastic demands. Moreover, the demand elasticity for some items is different in the long run than in the short run.

Families vary the quantities they buy for many reasons besides price. Demand curves *shift* with changes in income, with changes in the prices of substitute or complementary goods, as well as with education, advertising, and a number of other factors.

Consumer demand is an important key to prices and the behavior of markets, and is the basis on which productive capacity is allocated among different products.

APPENDIX   ESTIMATION OF DEMAND CURVES

Refinement of the Calculation of Elasticity

Ordinarily elasticity is measured as the ratio of a change in the average quantity bought (expressed as a percentage of the initial amount purchased) to a change in price (expressed as a percentage of the initial price). But for technical work, elasticity is more accurately measured when changes are expressed as percentages of the *average* of initial and final values. Percentages based on initial values of price and quantity give higher calculated elasticities when prices are falling than when they are rising.

For example, suppose a price increase from $10 to $11 would reduce the quantity bought from 100 to 80. On the basis of initial values, the price increase of 1/10, or 10 percent would result in a reduction in quantity of 20/200, or 20 percent, to yield a calculated elasticity of 20/100, or 2. Now, if the price fell from $11 back to its original level of $10, the amount bought would rise from 80 back to 100. The price reduction would be 1/11, or 9 percent, and the increase in quantity would be 20/80, or 25 percent, to yield a calculated elasticity of 25/9, or 2.8, approximately. Thus the price reduction gives a higher calculated elasticity than the price increase.

Use of average price and quantity as the base of the percentages gives the same calculated elasticity regardless of whether the price rose from the lower to the higher value or fell from the higher to the lower. That is, when a price changes by $1 between $10 and $11, it is expressed as a change of 1/10.50, or 9.5 percent, regard-less of whether the change is up or down. Likewise, a change in quantity between 80 and 100 is expressed as a change of 20/90, or 22.2 percent. The result is a calculated elasticity of 22.2/9.5, or 2.34, regardless of the direction of the price change.

This method of calculating elasticity has been employed throughout the remainder of this book whenever technical accuracy is required. The same method is applied to the calculation of income elasticity and cross-elasticity of demand.

Estimation of Demand Elasticity from Observed Prices and Sales

All demand curves shift somewhat from period to period, with the result that when prices are observed over a span of time, the accompanying quantities do not lie on the same demand curve, but on curves that shift back and forth in response to changes in income and other economic factors. If the shifts are not too large it is easy to draw a smooth freehand curve through the midst of the points to indicate a representative position of the demand curve. Once this representative curve has been drawn, elasticity can be calculated from any 2 conveniently located points on it. This was the method used to draw the demand curve for sweet potatoes in Figure 1 of this chapter.

When the demand curve shifts widely from point to point, however, this method is inadequate. Substantial shifts in demand spread the points over a wide scatter like that of Figure 12, making it difficult or impossible to locate a smooth curve that would correspond to a meaningful representative position. In order to estimate demand from such data, we must allow for the shifts in the curve. Although there are elaborate statistical procedures for doing this, the following graphical method is simple to use and is sufficiently accurate for many purposes. It is a method of successive approximations in which we guess at a representative position of the demand curve as a first approximation and then use this initial guess to obtain a first approximation to the income elasticity of demand. The estimated income elasticity enables us to "correct" the original observations of quantity for shifts in demand and to fit a more accurate second approximation to the representative position of the demand curve. The new curve enables us to improve the estimated income elasticity, from which a more accurate correction is obtained, yielding a third approximation to the representative position of the demand curve, and so on.

The procedure is best explained by example, using the data of Table 6(a):

1. Plot price and quantity as points in Figure 12. Note that the points do not lie along a well-defined curve, but are widely scattered, giving little indication as to the shape of the demand curve. Any number of curves, none fitting the data with any precision, could be drawn through the scatter.

2. As a first approximation, draw a tentative demand curve like dd through the points. The curve should be fitted so that about as many points fall on one side as on the other, and so that the total deviations on the 2 sides of the curve are about equal. Sometimes some judgment can be formed as to probable demand elasticity, and in such cases the curve should be drawn to conform to this judgment.

3. From curve dd, read the estimated quantity corresponding to each observed price and record it as shown in Table 6(b). For example, at the price of $18, curve dd

shows that about 65 units would be bought; 65 is therefore recorded opposite the price.

4. Subtract each estimated quantity from the corresponding observed quantity and record the deviations in Table 6(c). For example, the deviation of the quantity observed the first year (50) from the quantity estimated on dd (65) was 50 − 65, or −15. The deviation −15 is recorded in Table 6(c) opposite the first year's income.

Since dd is a first approximation to a representative position of the demand curve, the deviations represent first approximations to demand shifts in response to differences in income.

5. In a second chart like Figure 13, plot the estimated demand shifts against income. Draw a smooth curve like yy through the points to approximate the income elasticity of demand. Again, when we know the commodity under consideration, we can often form some judgment as to its probable income elasticity and draw the yy curve accordingly.

6. From curve yy read the estimated shift corresponding to the income level of each year. Record these estimated shifts in Table 6(c) as shown, to be used as "corrections" to the observed quantities. For example, the recorded deviation corresponding to $300 income was −15. The figure estimated from yy was −40, and this has been recorded as the "first correction" to the position of the demand curve in year 1. This means that, as we have approximated it so far, the low income of year 1 was responsible for a shift in the demand curve 40 units below its representative position.

7. Correct each observed quantity in Table 6(b) by subtracting the corresponding first correction from it. For example, one reason the quantity observed the first year was so low (50) was that the low income of that year had shifted the demand curve to the left by about 40. To correct for this shift, the correction is subtracted from the observed quantity: 50 − (−40),

TABLE 6(a)   DATA FOR ESTIMATION OF DEMAND

YEAR	PRICE	QUANTITY	DISPOSABLE PERSONAL INCOME
1	$18	50	$300
2	14	70	350
3	20	78	440
4	16	104	500

FIGURE 12   FIRST APPROXIMATION TO DEMAND

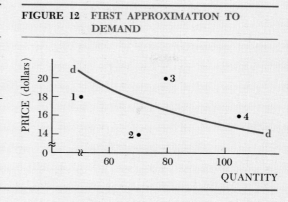

TABLE 6(b)

YEAR	PRICE	QUANTITY	QUANTITY FROM dd	FIRST CORRECTED QUANTITY	QUANTITY FROM d'd'	SECOND CORRECTED QUANTITY
1	$18	50	65	90	78	80
2	14	70	117	95	92	90
3	20	78	52	73	72	74
4	16	104	85	79	88	84

TABLE 6(c)

YEAR	INCOME	DEVIATION FROM dd	FIRST CORRECTION	DEVIATION FROM d'd'	SECOND CORRECTION
1	$300	−15	−40	−28	−30
2	350	−47	−25	−22	−20
3	440	26	5	6	4
4	500	19	25	16	20

FIGURE 13   FIRST APPROXIMATION TO INCOME ELASTICITY

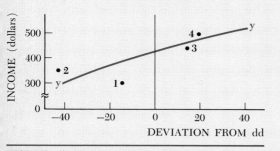

FIGURE 14   SECOND APPROXIMATION TO DEMAND

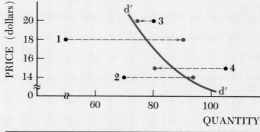

FIGURE 15   SECOND APPROXIMATION TO INCOME ELASTICITY

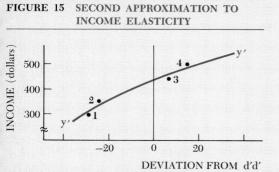

FIGURE 16   THIRD APPROXIMATION TO DEMAND

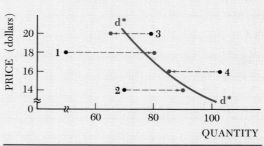

TABLE 7(a)   DATA FOR ESTIMATING APPLE DEMAND

YEAR	PRICE (CENTS PER LB)	QUANTITY (BILLIONS OF LBS)	DISPOSABLE PERSONAL INCOME (BILLIONS OF $)
1959	$.03.79	5.67	$337
1961	.04.15	5.64	364
1962	.04.32	5.69	385
1963	04.21	5.72	405
1964	.04.00	6.24	438
1965	.04.35	5.99	472
1966	.04.64	5.65	509

TABLE 7(b)   ESTIMATING APPLE DEMAND

QUANTITY FROM dd (BILLIONS OF LBS)	FIRST CORRECTED QUANTITY (BILLIONS OF LBS)	QUANTITY FROM d'd' (BILLIONS OF LBS)	SECOND CORRECTED QUANTITY (BILLIONS OF LBS)
6.25	6.25	6.25	6.25
5.35	5.69	5.72	5.72
5.25	5.57	5.46	5.64
5.82	5.47	5.60	5.55
5.98	5.82	5.92	5.88
5.23	5.39	5.40	5.44
5.05	4.90	5.00	4.93

TABLE 7(c)   ESTIMATING APPLE DEMAND

YEAR	INCOME (BILLIONS OF $)	DEVIATION FROM dd (BILLIONS OF LBS)	FIRST CORRECTION (BILLIONS OF LBS)	DEVIATION FROM d'd' (BILLIONS OF LBS)	SECOND CORRECTION (BILLIONS OF LBS)
1959	$337	−.58	−.58	−.58	−.58
1961	364	.29	−.05	−.08	−.08
1962	385	.44	.12	.23	.05
1963	405	−.10	.25	.12	.15
1964	438	.26	.42	.26	.36
1965	472	.76	.60	.65	.72
1966	509	.60	.75	.65	.72

SOURCE: Department of Agriculture, *Agricultural Statistics, 1967*. Data for 1960 have been omitted to improve the demonstration. Apple prices were so high in that year that the small quantity sold provides a strong indication of where the demand curve lies, and removes most of the challenge from the problem.

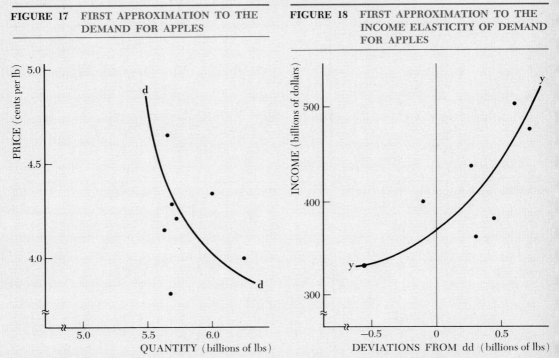

FIGURE 17   FIRST APPROXIMATION TO THE DEMAND FOR APPLES

FIGURE 18   FIRST APPROXIMATION TO THE INCOME ELASTICITY OF DEMAND FOR APPLES

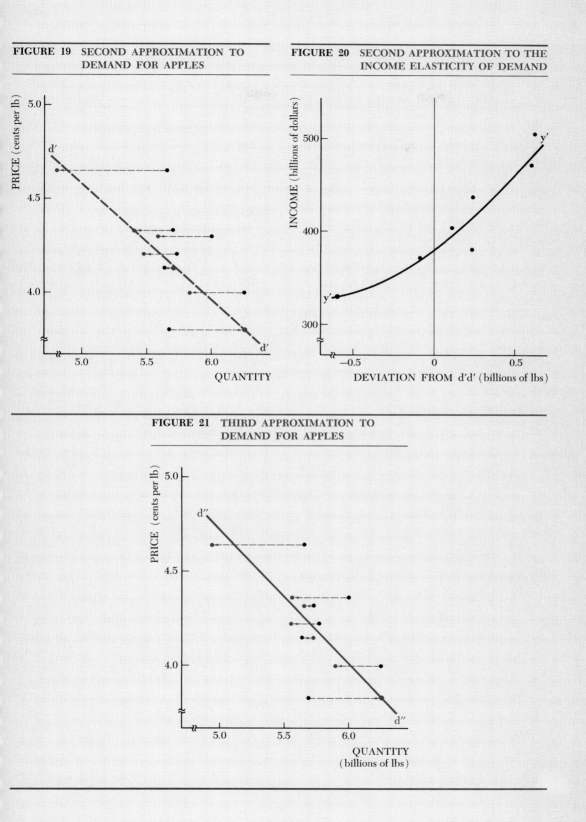

FIGURE 19 SECOND APPROXIMATION TO
DEMAND FOR APPLES

FIGURE 20 SECOND APPROXIMATION TO THE
INCOME ELASTICITY OF DEMAND

FIGURE 21 THIRD APPROXIMATION TO
DEMAND FOR APPLES

or 90, and this is recorded in Table 6(b) as the "first corrected quantity" corresponding to the price of $18. The first correction of the quantity observed during year 4 was 25. That is, because of the high income of year 4, the demand curve was shifted to the right by 25. To correct for this shift, we have calculated 104 − 25, or 79, which is recorded in the proper place in Table 6(b).

8. Plot the corrected quantities against the corresponding prices, as shown by the blue dots of Figure 14. The direction and amount of the correction is represented by a dotted line extending from the initial position as represented by the black points. Since the corrections compensate for shifting demand, the blue points follow the representative position of the demand curve more closely than did the original points. This permits us to draw the improved curve d'd' as a second approximation to the demand.

9. From curve d'd', estimate the quantity corresponding to each price, and record as shown in Table 6(b). Calculate deviations of the original quantities from curve d'd', and record them in Table 6(c), as shown.

10. Plot the deviations from d'd' against the corresponding income, as in Figure 15. Draw y'y', a second approximation to income elasticity. Estimate second corrections from y'y', and record in Table 6(c).

11. Subtract the second corrections from the corresponding observed quantities and record as second corrected quantities in Table 6(b). Plot the second corrected quantities against prices as in Figure 16. Draw d"d" as a third approximation to the representative position of the demand curve. If the relationship appears to be closely approximated, the process can be terminated at this point. In actual practice, the procedure is sometimes repeated 2 or 3 more times in an effort to improve the estimate, and is terminated only when no further improvement is obtained.

12. When a final demand curve has been arrived at, choose 2 convenient points and calculate the elasticity as described above. For example, according to curve d"d", when price = $20, quantity = 70. When price is $16, quantity = 84. This gives a calculated elasticity of approximately $e = (14/77)/(4/18)$ or .9.

Estimating the Elasticity of Demand for Apples

As an example, the procedure described above has been applied to estimate the demand for apples. The data and successive steps are shown in Table 7.

Data for price and quantity were plotted as points in Figure 17, and the curve dd was drawn as a first approximation to the demand for apples. Deviations from dd were then plotted against income in Figure 18 to obtain yy, the first approximation to the income elasticity of demand. When yy was used to "correct" the original observations for shifts in demand due to income, the result was the second approximation to the demand for apples as plotted in Figure 19. Deviations of the points from d'd' provided a second approximation to income elasticity as shown in Figure 20. Finally, "correcting" the original observations for the effect of income as estimated from y'y' permitted a still more accurate third approximation to the demand for apples, represented by d"d" in Figure 21.

The elasticity of demand for apples can be calculated from d"d" as follows: At a price of $.04 per pound, d"d" shows total consumption of 5.95 billion pounds. At a price of $.044 per pound, consumption would be 5.42 billion pounds. The increase in price from $.04 to $.044 is 9.5 percent of the midpoint price, while the decline in quantity bought from 5.95 to 5.42 is 9.35 percent of the midpoint quantity of 5.68 billion pounds. It follows that the estimated demand elasticity is $e = 9.35/9.5$, or about .98.

CHAPTER 16

Pricing and the Allocation of Basic Commodities

Prices are arrived at in a number of different ways, but the one most easily understood is the establishment of prices in a continuous auction market. Prices of agricultural commodities and other basic products are commonly set in this way, and this is the method employed in trading corporate securities.[1] Unlike prices established by business firms—to be studied in the next chapter—prices established in auction markets fluctuate constantly, and daily quotations of them are found in the financial pages of the newspaper.

The interaction of supply and demand not only sets market prices but at the same time performs the important function of *allocation,* that is, of apportioning whatever total amount of each commodity is available among all the potential buyers who want it for alternative uses. Although only basic commodities are sold through auction markets, the allocation of manufactured goods and even the assignment of the services of labor and natural resources among different jobs occur on the basis of the same principles. Indeed, the simple examples to be given in this chapter are only special cases of the powerful general process by which the use of resources is made to conform to consumer desires in a private enterprise economy.

PRICE DETERMINATION

Bargaining

The most direct kind of price-making occurs when a single seller and a single buyer bargain over the purchase of a single specified item. In the Middle East, much of the Orient, and parts of South America, this is the customary method of transacting business. In the United States it is common in buying and selling houses and other real estate, and is found to some extent in the market for new and used automobiles. Col-

[1] The reader may find it useful to review the appendix to Chapter 5 at this point.

lective bargaining between employers and unions also has many of the attributes of this method of price-making, although once a settlement is agreed on, the employer is usually free to vary the number of workers he hires.

Prices set by bargaining are not easily predictable and can usually fall anywhere in a wide range. In a typical case the seller of the item, a house, for instance, has a minimum or "floor" price he will accept. Of course, he would rather get a price higher than the floor—the higher the better as far as he is concerned—but he would accept this lowest price rather than keep the house. The prospective buyer has a maximum limit or "ceiling" price he will pay. Of course, he would rather pay less than the ceiling—the lower the better—but if worse comes to worst, he would rather pay this much than not buy the house.

Ceiling and floor prices depend on many factors. In bargaining over the sale of the house, for example, the seller may want to move, but needs a certain minimum price for his old house to finance the new one, or perhaps his floor price in bargaining with one prospective buyer is the least he thinks he could get from another. In bargaining over a service to be performed—for example the construction of a house—the prospective cost helps set a floor to the price. A buyer's ceiling is affected by such things as the price he thinks he would have to pay for an alternative. If he is bargaining for a house or other large item, financing costs and the availability of credit may affect what he can afford to pay, or he may consider the cost of building or renting rather than buying. When a man intends to resell an item, his ceiling as a buyer depends on what he thinks he can get for it as a seller.

Problems in Bargaining   A typical bargaining situation is represented schematically in Figure 1. The item under discussion is a house for which the buyer is willing to pay no more than $30,000 and for which the

seller is willing to accept no less than $10,000. The range of prices between the seller's floor and the buyer's ceiling is the bargaining range. No price outside this range can be mutually agreeable to buyer and seller, while any price within the range can result in a deal, provided that buyer and seller can agree on which price it is to be.

Reaching an agreement is more difficult than it might at first seem to be. The trouble is that neither party will agree to a price as long as he thinks he can get a better one by holding out a little longer. Not only does this fact tend to make bargaining a time-consuming process, but when unskilled bargainers are unable to read one another's intentions, deals sometimes fall through despite a wide range of mutually agreeable prices. In some cultures, bargaining is reduced to a series of conventionalized steps to minimize the chances of such failure. For example, it may be customary for only the seller to suggest prices, and for the buyer merely to accept or reject the offers. In such a society a counteroffer by a prospective buyer would be considered very bad form. According to another convention, when one party says his offer is "final," it really represents an invitation to split the difference between the "final" figure named and the previous figure named by the other side. Conventions of this sort facilitate bargaining for those who understand the rules and know their proper roles in the game, but the outsider sometimes finds himself in trouble. American travelers who wander away from the usual tourist paths sometimes have trouble getting somebody to deal with them, because their ignorance of the rules is embarrassing to the natives.[2]

[2] Another source of difficulty is that in many societies, bargaining in the marketplace is an important form of social interaction, quite independent of the business transacted. There are many stories of the refusal of natives to sell, at any price, an entire day's stock in one big transaction because they would be left out of things for the rest of the day.

Another way to expedite bargaining is to employ the services of skillful professionals who understand each other and are unlikely to let a feasible settlement escape. This is one reason that houses are sold through real estate agents and that local unions often employ negotiators from the national office to bargain for them. The professional agent or negotiator is not only accustomed to the business and familiar with the rules and conventions, but he is likely to be much more realistic than his clients in his appraisal of the possible terms of agreement.

In collective bargaining between labor unions and management, the seller's floor can be interpreted as the lowest settlement the union will accept rather than strike, while the buyer's ceiling is the highest settlement management will concede to avoid a strike. It is clear that unskillful collective bargaining can fail to find mutually acceptable terms even when they exist, and result in an avoidable strike to the disadvantage of both parties.[3] When union and management have unusual difficulty in arriving at a settlement, they sometimes enlist the services of a labor mediator, who, as a disinterested third party trusted by each of the others, acts to assist the 2 sides to understand each other and to help them find mutually agreeable terms for the contract.

Auction Prices

When there are many active would-be buyers for the same item, its price can be set by auction. The seller meets with all the buyers, who bid competitively for the item, the highest bid setting the price. Figure 2

[3] Once a strike is under way, ceilings and floors can be interpreted with respect to its continuation. In the extreme, unskillful collective bargaining can result in a strike so prolonged that the firm is forced out of business and the workers are compelled to find other jobs, despite the existence of mutually acceptable terms of settlement.

shows the working of an auction market. The seller's floor, or *reservation price*, and the ceiling prices of the different bidders are shown. Obviously, except through misunderstanding or other error, the item will be bought by the bidder with the highest ceiling price, at a price slightly above the next highest ceiling.

In important markets for basic commodities like rubber, tin, sugar, wheat, and cattle, a flow of goods is submitted daily by a large number of sellers to the bidding of a large number of would-be buyers. The price-making mechanism in these markets is illustrated in Figure 3. The bidders are arrayed along the quantity axis in descending order of their ceiling prices. If only 1 item per day were auctioned off, the bidder with the highest ceiling would buy it at a price slightly above the next highest ceiling. If 2 items were sold, they would go to the 2 bidders with the highest ceilings, at a price somewhere above the third ceiling, and so on. Of course, this is a general tendency rather than an exact law. Shipments are auctioned off one at a time and the first lot may be bid up too high by the failure of the bidders to recognize the situation. Or a lot may be sold at too low a price because bidders with higher ceilings misread the state of the market. On the average during the day, however, the price should settle about where expected.

Supply, Demand, and Price

In general, since there are a large number of individual bidders in the market each day, and since each bidder may bid on more or fewer lots depending on how high the prices are going, it is more realistic to neglect the small jumps and discontinuities in their ceilings and to represent the array of bidders by a continuous demand curve like DD in Figure 4. When a fixed quantity per day is to be sold on such a market, the average daily price tends to settle near the

FIGURE 1 BARGAINING

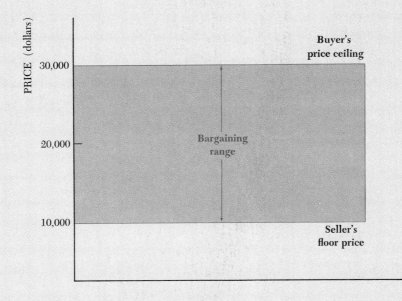

PRICE (dollars)

30,000

Buyer's
price ceiling

20,000

Bargaining
range

10,000

Seller's
floor price

FIGURE 2 AN AUCTION MARKET

FIGURE 3 A CONTINUOUS MARKET

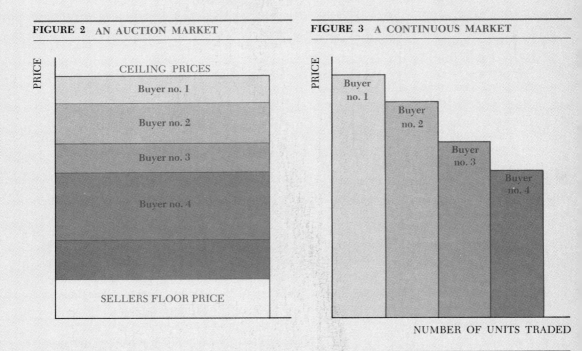

PRICE

CEILING PRICES

Buyer no. 1

Buyer no. 2

Buyer no. 3

Buyer no. 4

SELLERS FLOOR PRICE

PRICE

Buyer
no. 1

Buyer
no. 2

Buyer
no. 3

Buyer
no. 4

NUMBER OF UNITS TRADED

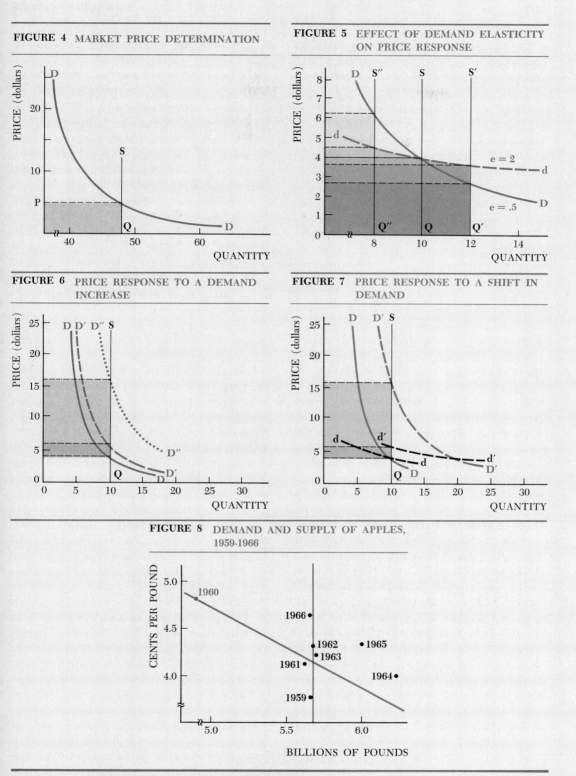

FIGURE 4 MARKET PRICE DETERMINATION

FIGURE 5 EFFECT OF DEMAND ELASTICITY ON PRICE RESPONSE

FIGURE 6 PRICE RESPONSE TO A DEMAND INCREASE

FIGURE 7 PRICE RESPONSE TO A SHIFT IN DEMAND

FIGURE 8 DEMAND AND SUPPLY OF APPLES, 1959-1966

SOURCE FOR FIGURE 8: Data from *Agricultural Statistics, 1967.*

level indicated by the intersection of the demand curve with SQ, the line indicating the quantity coming on the market. When Q per day is being sold, the price tends to settle at P. Any price above P would be temporary, since buyers would quickly discover that they were overbidding, paying more than necessary for what they bought, and leaving shipments for somebody else to pick up later much more cheaply. Any price below P would permit bidders with low ceilings to acquire commodities at bargain prices, leaving bidders with higher ceilings empty-handed. The competition of the latter would soon drive the price back up.

Demand Elasticity and Price Fluctuations
When an increased quantity comes on the market, the price must fall if it is to be sold. How far the price is depressed depends on the elasticity of demand. If demand is highly elastic, only a small decline is needed to bring in enough new bidders to take the increased quantity off the market. If demand is relatively inelastic, price must fall proportionally farther before enough new buyers are induced to buy. When the quantity shrinks, price rises as buyers compete for the limited supply. If demand is elastic, price will not be forced up far, but if demand is inelastic, some of the unsatisfied buyers will continue to bid despite the rise, and a proportionally greater increase in price will result.

Figure 5 illustrates the price response to changes in supply. On a day when the quantity coming on the market is 10, indicated by the line SQ, the average price is 4, as indicated by the middle solid horizontal line. When supply is increased to 12, indicated by the vertical line S'Q', price falls to about 2.75 if the demand has elasticity of 0.5, but only to 3.60 if demand has elasticity of 2. When supply is reduced to 8, as indicated by line S"Q", price rises to 6.25 if demand has elasticity of 0.5, but only to 4.45 if demand has elasticity of 2.

The percentage change in price to be expected in response to a small percentage change in quantity supplied can easily be estimated from the formula for the elasticity of demand. Since elasticity, e, is given by e = percentage change in quantity/percentage change in price, the percentage change in price = percentage change in quantity divided by e. This calculation is exact only for very small percentage changes, but does very well as an estimate even for rather large changes. In Figure 5, the 20 percent increase in quantity would be expected to reduce the price by 20/.5, or 40 percent if elasticity were 0.5, and by only 20/2, or 10 percent if elasticity were 2. As calculations will show, these are close to the results given in the figure.

Effects of Shifts in Demand Given the supply coming on the market, a shift in demand will affect the market price. A rise in demand represents a systematic rise in the quantity buyers try to purchase at the going market price. With only a given quantity available, competition among buyers for the limited supply forces up the price. A fall in demand represents reduced desire for the commodity at market prices. The consequent reduced competition among buyers allows the price to fall.

Given the elasticity of demand, the percentage increase in price depends on the size of the shift in demand, as can be seen in Figure 6. In this example, 10 units per day are supplied to the market, as indicated by the line SQ. When demand is represented by DD, this quantity is sold at an average daily price of 4. When the demand rises to D'D', price rises to 6, but when demand rises to D"D", the competition for the limited supply drives the price to 16.

Given the shift in demand, the influence on price depends on the elasticity of demand. The more elastic the demand, the smaller the price adjustment, as shown in Figure 7. Demand curve DD has elasticity 0.5, while dd has elasticity 2. When 10 units are supplied to the market, as indicated by the line SQ, the market price is 4. If the demands should both double, price in the market with the more elastic demand would rise to only about 5.75, while buyers with the less elastic demand would drive the price to about 16.

The Apple Market: an Example   The combined effects of shifts in demand and changes in the quantity supplied on the price of apples can be seen in Figure 8. The demand curve, shown in the approximate position it occupied during 1960, has an elasticity of about 1. The influence of changes in supply can be seen by comparing the points representing 1960 and 1961. When 4.91 billion pounds were marketed during 1960, the price of apples was 4.84 cents per pound. When the quantity marketed increased 15 percent to the 5.63 billion pounds of 1961, the price of apples declined approximately 15 percent to 4.15 cents. The unit elasticity of demand is also reflected in the almost equal sales revenue received by sellers in the 2 years. Marketing 4.91 billion pounds of apples in 1960 at a price of 4.84 cents, sellers received $.0484 × 4.91 billion, or $237 million. Marketing 5.63 billion pounds in 1961 at a price of 4.15 cents, they received $.0415 × 5.63 billion, or $234 million.

The effect of shifting demand can be seen by the points in the center of the chart. Although virtually equal quantities were marketed in 1959, 1961, 1962, 1963, and 1966, the price rose steadily as demand increased, largely in response to rising consumer incomes during the period. The 4.64 cents a pound paid for the crop of 1966 was over 22 percent higher than the 3.79 cents paid in 1959 for a crop almost exactly the same size. The effect of a combination of demand shift and increase in supply can be seen in the points for 1964 and 1965. Despite the continuing increase in demand, the record crop of 1964 brought the lowest prices since 1959.

ALLOCATING BASIC COMMODITIES

Competitive bidding by different types of buyers allows the desires of final consumers to dictate the use of productive resources. Commodities coming on the market must be divided among all the uses to which they could be put. Which use is to get more, which is to get less, which is to get none at all depends on the demands of consumers as they are felt by business firms and translated into a willingness to bid for commodities.

As the quantity on the market fluctuates, most of the variation occurs in those uses with the highest elasticity of demand. This is as it should be. Elastic demands mean postponable uses, uses in which the commodity can be most easily dispensed with, either because it satisfies a low-priority need or because it has many substitutes that can do the job almost as well. Inelastic demands represent high-priority uses, uses for which there are only poor substitutes, or in which the commodity is an important ingredient in a package of complementary goods. When consumption of the commodity is to be reduced, it should be withdrawn from its least important uses, or from uses that can be postponed or in which it is easily replaced. When consumption of the commodity is to be increased, we can afford to put it in less important uses and to employ it as a substitute for other things.

Composite Demands

The way available supplies are allocated among different groups of bidders is clearly demonstrated when different demands for the product are represented in a single composite diagram. The upper panel of Figure 9 depicts the demand curves of 2 groups of bidders. In part (a), group A, with relatively elastic demand, might represent a group of processors while group B, with re-

FIGURE 9   DEMAND CURVES OF 2 GROUPS OF BIDDERS

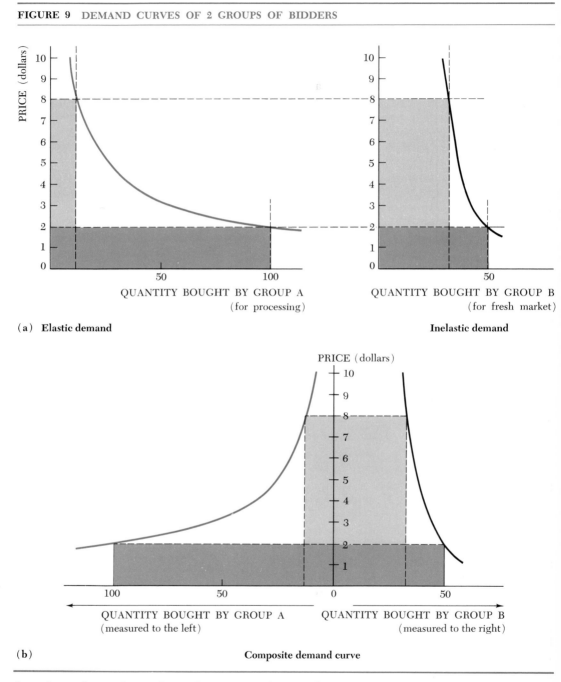

(a)   **Elastic demand**   **Inelastic demand**

(b)   **Composite demand curve**

latively inelastic demand, might consist of a number of buyers for retail outlets. Or the groups might represent firms in 2 different industries bidding for the same indus-

trial raw material. In any case, when the 2 demands are plotted in adjacent charts, the response of each group to a change in price is easily observed. For example, according to the figure, when price rises from $2 to $8, the quantity bought by group A, with the more elastic demand, declines from 100 to 12.5, while bidders in group B reduce their purchases from 50 only to 33.

The same response is more graphically shown when the 2 demand curves are aligned, not as in part (a) of Figure 9, but "back to back" in a single composite picture as in part (b). The figure representing the demand of group A has been reversed and pushed up against the chart of group B. The quantity bought by group B is measured to the right as usual, but the quantity bought by group A is now measured from the origin to the *left*. The demand curve for group A slopes downward to the left, indicating the usual disposition to buy more at low than at high prices.

The total amount taken by the 2 groups together at any price is represented by the distance between the 2 demand curves. As shown, at a price of $2, the 50 units that group B buys is measured to the right, the 100 units bought by group A is measured to the left. The 150 units bought by the 2 groups together is represented by the total distance between the 2 curves.

Allocation Between 2 Groups of Bidders
The allocation of available quantities between the 2 groups of bidders can now be followed graphically. Competitive bidding will force the price to the level at which the quantity coming onto the market is just divided between the 2 groups. The smaller the quantity, the higher the bidding will go and the smaller will be the proportion of the total going to bidders with elastic demand. The larger the quantity coming into the market, the lower the price, and the larger the proportion going to the group with elastic demand. When 150 units are auctioned off, the price is bid up to $2, and 100 units are purchased by members of group A and only 50 by group B. When available supply shrinks to 45.5, as shown by the dotted line, price is bid up to $8.

Bidders with elastic demands are outbid, and get only 12.5 units, while the members of group B take the remaining 33.[4]

Derived Demands

Bidders in a central commodity market are generally buying, not for their own personal uses, but to get goods for resale to consumers through retail stores, or to obtain materials to be processed or manufactured into something else for sale. In either case, the demand on the commodity market is *derived* from the demand of prospective future customers of the purchasing firms, and the firms' willingness to buy is heavily influenced by the quantities it expects to be able to sell at profitable prices to its own customers.

Shifts in derived demand naturally reflect shifts in demand by the customers of the bidders. When housewives come into stores looking for more apples, retailers are going to bid for more at the city produce market. When millers discover that flour sales are slowing down, they cut back their buying on the Chicago wheat market, and so on.

The Elasticity of Derived Demands   Since the willingness of bidders to buy is influenced by the prices they expect to get from their own customers, the elasticity of a derived demand depends on the elasticity

---

[4] The price and allocation of any other quantity coming on the market can easily be determined from the composite demand figure. On the edge of a piece of scrap paper make 2 marks whose distance apart corresponds to the quantity in question as measured by the scale on the horizontal axis. Keeping the paper parallel to the horizontal axis with the left-hand mark on the left hand demand curve, slide it upward until the right-hand mark coincides with the demand curve on the right. The position of the paper on the vertical axis indicates the price such a quantity would bring, while the allocation between the 2 groups of bidders can be read off the 2 demand curves at that price.

of the final consumers' demand for the product. Buyers tend to have elastic demands when they are reselling to consumers with elastic demands. They must drop out of the bidding as prices rise or run the risk of losses on resale. On the other hand, they can buy large amounts when prices decline, secure in the knowledge that they can easily increase their sales when the price savings are passed on. Buyers who are selling to customers with relatively inelastic demands tend to have inelastic demands themselves. They can bid high when necessary, knowing that the high price will have little effect when passed on to their consumers, but they have little use for extra quantities when prices fall, since their own customers are unresponsive to lower prices.

The elasticity of derived demand also depends on the amount of processing that is needed to convert the commodity into its final form. Bidders for commodities like fresh fruits and vegetables that are to be resold in the same form tend to have the same demand elasticity as the housewives to whom they will sell at retail. Buyers of commodities to be manufactured, however, sometimes have demands of lower elasticity than those of their customers because they cannot use the commodity alone, but only as part of a package of complementary goods. A manufacturer of tin cans, for example, must buy fuel, transportation, power, and labor roughly in proportion to the quantity of tin plate he buys. The original price of the tin plate is therefore a small percentage of the final price of the can, and when the changes in price are passed on, they exert a correspondingly small influence on the volume of final sales. When tin plate is only 10 percent of the cost of the finished product, for example, a 1 percent change in its price alters the cost of the can by only one-tenth of 1 percent. Even if the elasticity of demand for tin cans were as high as 4 or 5, a .1 percent change in the price of cans, even when fully passed

on, would alter the number of cans bought —and hence the quantity of tin plate needed—by only 0.4 or 0.5 percent.

On the other hand, many buyers of commodities for industrial use have highly elastic demands because of the wide range of substitutes available for their purposes. Industrial alcohol, for example, can be made from corn, wheat, rice, potatoes, or anything else that will ferment. A slight rise in the price of one of these sends the industrial buyer to a cheaper substitute. Canners and other food processors bidding competitively for a crop to use as raw material, often exhibit demands that are more elastic than those of competing merchants buying fresh vegetables for retail. Unlike the raw material which is highly perishable, the canned product can be kept for a year or more before being consumed. When prices fall, processors increase their purchases of the commodity and process as much as they can. When prices rise, they are in a position to meet part of their demand by drawing on their inventory of canned goods.

A good example of this tendency is shown in Figure 10. The total volume of potatoes delivered to market is divided between those bought by grocers for resale as fresh potatoes, and those bought by processors to make potato chips, frozen french fries, dehydrated mashed potatoes, and so on. Estimated on the basis of a recent 5-year period, the demand for potatoes for table use has elasticity of less than 0.2 compared to approximately 0.8 for potatoes to be processed. In 1961 the average price on the auction market was $2.34 per 100 pounds. At this price, bidders who resold the potatoes to households and restaurants for use fresh bought 154 million hundredweight, while processors took about 140 million. The increase in price to $4.91 in 1964 cut purchases for fresh use by 16 percent, and reduced the amount bought by processors (after "correction" for

FIGURE 10   ESTIMATED MARKET DEMAND FOR WHITE POTATOES

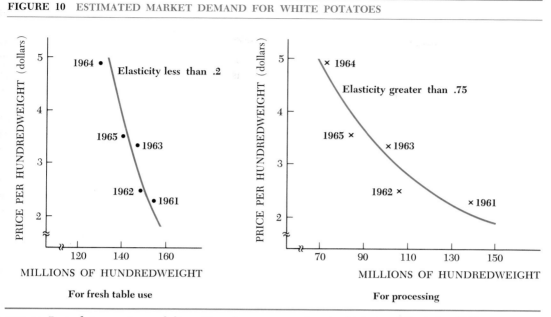

SOURCE: Basic data on prices and disposition of crops are as given in *Agricultural Statistics, 1967.*

the shift in demand that had occurred) by almost 50 percent.

Reallocation in Response to Shifts in Demand

When consumers increase their demand for a product, firms respond by increasing their bidding for the commodities needed for its production. The effect on market prices and on the allocation of the commodity between competing uses is shown by the composite demand curve of Figure 11. The quantity on the market is initially being sold at price P, and is allocated between the 2 uses as shown by the solid line. Group A buys Q_A, group B gets only Q_B. When the members of group B increase their demand to $D'D'$, their increased bidding drives the price up to P'. Some of the other buyers are outbid, and purchases by group A are reduced to Q'_A. Quantities are diverted to the members of group B who buy Q'_B to satisfy

the increased demand of their consumers.

The effect of a reduction in demand is just the opposite. When demand by group B declines from $D'D'$ to DD, their reduced bidding permits the price to fall from P' to P. Members of group A can acquire additional amounts of the commodity for resale to their customers when the lower price is passed on.

In general, of course, year-to-year variation in the prices and allocation of commodities derives from shifts in demand combined with changes in the quantity for sale. The reallocation of white potatoes between processors and buyers for the fresh market is shown in Figure 12. The 1961 crop was divided between demand for the fresh market (dd), and the processors' demand (DD) as shown. The smaller 1965 supply reduced purchases by both groups. Had processors' demand remained unchanged, price would have risen only to about $3.50, and most of the reduction in supply would have been matched by reduc-

FIGURE 11   EFFECTS OF SHIFTING DEMAND

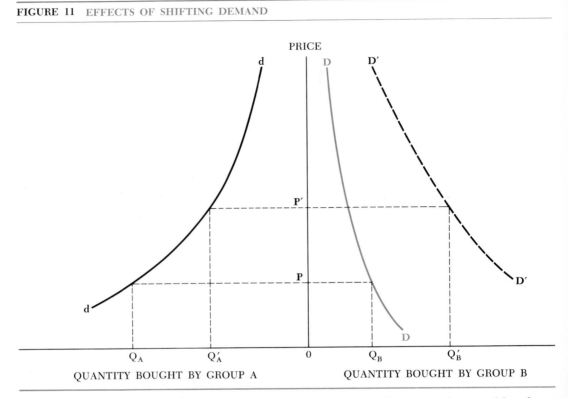

QUANTITY BOUGHT BY GROUP A   QUANTITY BOUGHT BY GROUP B

tion in purchases by processors. In the meantime, however, income had risen, and housewives and restaurants decided that they preferred the convenience of frozen french fries and packaged mashed potatoes to the trouble of cooking their own. The additional demand for their products enabled the processors to bid the price of potatoes up to $4.90, and the reduction in purchases was about equally divided between processors and buyers for retail outlets, despite the inelastic demand of the latter.

The introduction of frozen foods and the general improvement in food-processing technology during the last 30 years has vastly increased the demand for processed vegetables. At the same time, the rising cost of restaurant help and the increased disposition of housewives to work outside the home has reduced the demand for fresh vegetables. The result has been the massive

shift in the allocation of vegetables from the fresh market to processors shown in Table 1.

FIGURE 12   ALLOCATION OF WHITE POTATOES, 1961, 1965

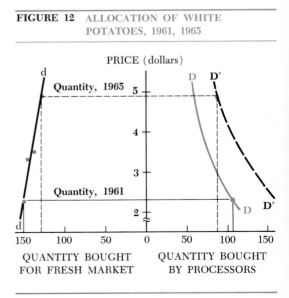

QUANTITY BOUGHT   QUANTITY BOUGHT
FOR FRESH MARKET   BY PROCESSORS

TABLE 1 REALLOCATION OF SELECTED VEGETABLE CROPS

(figures, except percentages, are tons, selected years)

	SOLD FOR FRESH MARKET	SOLD FOR PROCESSING	PERCENT PROCESSED
BEETS			
1939	59,900	44,600	42
1949	45,700	154,000	77
1959	21,900	146,700	87
1966	16,300	193,900	96
GREEN PEAS			
1939	147,500	195,300	57
1949	45,100	347,390	89
1959	13,700	473,200	97
1966	6,100	509,000	99
LIMA BEANS			
1939	35,300	30,560	45
1949	33,500	95,000	75
1959	18,700	82,600	79
1966	12,900	104,500	89
SPINACH			
1939	151,300	54,200	26
1949	133,300	117,100	47
1959	77,500	147,800	66
1966	43,800	145,900	77

SOURCE: U.S. Department of Agriculture, *Agricultural Statistics, 1966.*

Allocation of Commodities Among Different Places

Commodities must not only be divided among various uses; they must also be distributed among buyers in different locations. The process of allocation among markets is similar to allocation among different groups of buyers in the same market, except that commodities usually have different prices in different cities. When they have a choice, suppliers naturally tend to ship their products to the markets where they can get the most from their sale, but since they must pay shipping charges, they will ship to more distant markets only if they expect to find prices there sufficiently higher to cover the added transportation cost.

The process by which shipments are divided between 2 markets is illustrated in Figures 13(a) and (b), where a comparison of demand in St. Louis and Chicago is shown. In (a), too much of the available output is being shipped to Chicago and too little to St. Louis resulting in a substantial price differential. St. Louis prices are so much higher than those in Chicago that it would pay shippers to divert loads headed for Chicago and reroute them to St. Louis for resale at a profit. The diversion of commodities from Chicago to St. Louis would continue until, as shown in (b), prices in the 2 markets differed by no more than the cost of transportation between them.

Buying commodities in one market for resale in another is known as *arbitrage,* and in many markets this procedure is carried on by a group of specialized professionals who maintain constant contact with demand and prices in many cities. By rapid response to price differences, professional arbitrage quickly and smoothly adjusts the flow of commodities to varying conditions. The close relationship maintained among prices in a number of cities is shown in Figure 14.

Speculation in Commodity Markets

If the only price-making force in the market were the demands of bidders who want to buy the commodity for immediate use, prices would decline sharply on days when an unusually large quantity arrived on the market, or when demand was temporarily small, and shoot up on days when an unusually small quantity was delivered or when demand was temporarily greater than usual. There are, of course, daily price fluctuations, but they are not nearly as large as might be expected from the size

FIGURE 13   ALLOCATION OF DELIVERIES BETWEEN CITIES

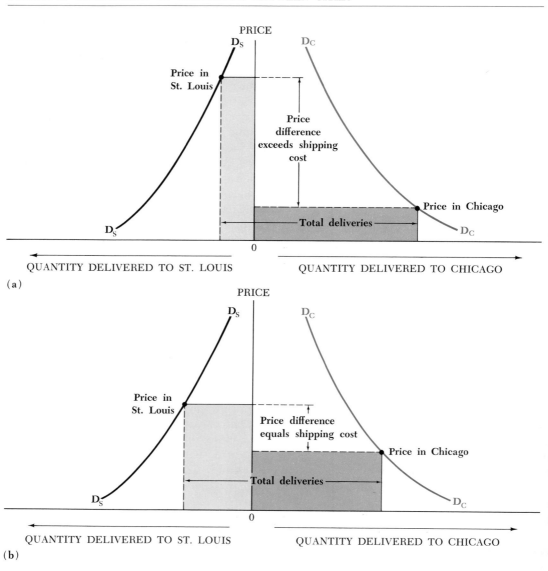

(a)

(b)

of daily variations in deliveries and demand.

This price stability is the work of a special class of bidders called *speculators* who buy commodities for the sole purpose of reselling them on the same market at a later time. This action, known as *speculation,* is often misunderstood. Since specula-

tors do nothing to the goods they handle, their ability to profit from buying cheap and selling dear is frequently interpreted as some kind of parasitic action, yet without speculators the orderly function of many markets would be impossible. The economic role of the professional speculator is to stabilize prices by offsetting day-to-day

FIGURE 14 CORN PRICES IN 5 MAJOR MARKETS, 1955-1965

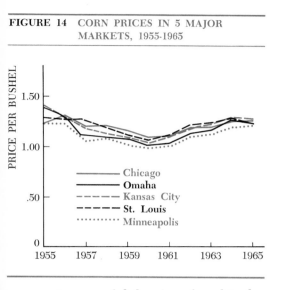

SOURCE: Averages of daily prices of car lot sales, no. 3 yellow corn as reported in *Agricultural Statistics, 1967*.

fluctuations in demand and quantities supplied. When an unusually large quantity arrives on the market, or when there is an unusual reduction in demand, prices begin to fall. Speculators, who keep careful watch over conditions in the market, realize that this is a temporary situation and buy the momentarily cheap commodity in order to profit from resale at a higher price later on. Ceiling prices placed on the commodity by speculative bidders are determined by their expectations of future prices, and when a large number of speculators compete in the market, their bidding will set the price only enough below the expected future price to cover the costs of speculation. The resale of the commodity at a later time when less is coming into the market or when demand is unusually heavy helps to hold prices down.

The price stability contributed by speculation permits suppliers to bring their products to market when they are ready. It also permits buyers to bid on the basis of their needs of the moment with minimum regard for day-to-day timing. Because of

speculation, suppliers will receive and buyers will pay prices reasonably commensurate with the average rate at which commodities are being supplied and demanded, regardless of the particular day on which they conclude their own individual transactions.

Speculation also serves to spread the use of products over time. The entire year's supply of many commodities, including most farm products, is delivered to market during a period lasting only a few weeks. Without the intervention of speculators to hold back output for future use, the flood of deliveries, creating a temporary glut on the market, would drive prices to levels that would permit the year's supply to be used for all sorts of trivial purposes. The short delivery period would then be followed by a long period of shortage and high prices when the commodity would be unavailable for many essential uses. The alternation of glut and famine is prevented by speculators who buy the commodity while it is cheap and store it for resale when prices rise. The speculative demand supports the market when the harvest arrives and the later resale holds prices down and provides a source of the commodity during the long period between harvests.

Storage for resale involves certain costs. Goods must be insured, warehouse or other storage space must be paid for, interest on funds tied up in the operation must be allowed for, and there is a certain amount of inevitable spoilage and loss. In addition, there is the ever-present possibility that the venture may not pay off, and the speculator's compensation for risk should be included as an element of cost. The limit to speculative buying is reached when the difference between the current market price and the expected future price is just equal to the cost of owning and storing the commodities.

The way speculation divides market deliveries between quantities entering current consumption and those held for future re-

sale is shown in Figure 15. Speculators
(group A) base their demand on expected
future demand and storage costs. When deliveries are low (solid lines) prices are
high and most of the commodity goes into
current use. When deliveries increase
(dashed lines) prices decline. If it were not
for speculative demand, price would fall to
0 and the commodity could be used for all
kinds of purposes. But since speculators buy
most of the extra quantities to hold for
future resale, the current price is supported
and the commodity is held back for future
consumption in higher-priority uses.

SUPPLY

Up to this point we have treated the quantity coming on the market as fixed regardless of price. This is a reasonable view of
the behavior of agricultural markets during any particular growing season, for
farmers must plant crops in the spring before they know what prices will be, and
once the crop is grown and harvested, it is

FIGURE 15   HOW SPECULATION HOLDS BACK
COMMODITIES FOR FUTURE USE

PRICE

Expected
future demand

Demand for
immediate use

Storage
cost

Speculators' demand

0

QUANTITY BOUGHT
BY GROUP A
(speculative purchases
for later resale)

QUANTITY BOUGHT
BY GROUP B
(for immediate
consumption)

FIGURE 16   THE DYNAMICS OF LONG-RUN
PRICE ADJUSTMENT

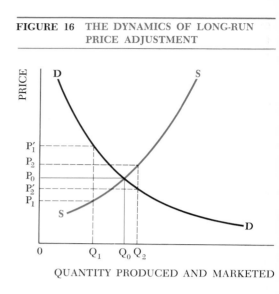

QUANTITY PRODUCED AND MARKETED

too late to do much about it. But while
producers have no advance *knowledge* of
prices, they could hardly stay in business if
they had no reasonable *expectations* based
on their experience with past prices. The
amounts they tend to produce and bring to
market depend on these expected prices,
particularly as they are influenced by prices
during the past year.

Supply Curves

The relationship between expected price
and quantity produced is depicted by the
blue *supply curve* SS of Figure 16. A supply
curve is analogous to a demand curve, but
applies to producers instead of consumers,
showing the amount of the commodity that
firms tend to produce and place on the market at each of a series of expected prices.
The curve slopes upward, in keeping with
the fact that higher expected prices generally lead producers to increase output,
while low prices tend to discourage production. The response of producers to changes
in expected prices can be measured by the
elasticity of supply which, again analo-
gously to demand, is calculated as the ratio

of a percentage increase in quantity to the percentage increase in price that induced it.

The Dynamics of Price Adjustment

When the supply and demand curves are combined, we can see not only the forces setting the price during a particular season, but also the dynamics of adjustment over time. Suppose that during the first season, producers expected a price of P_1. In keeping with the supply curve, this would lead them to plant and produce a total quantity Q_1. When this small quantity emerged on the market, however, buyers would bid the price up to P'_1, in keeping with the demand curve DD.

Pleasantly surprised to find prices higher than they had expected, producers would raise price expectations for the next year, say to P_2, which would lead them to turn out a total of Q_2. The larger quantity coming on the market would push the price down to P'_2, slightly below expectations, causing producers to revise their price expectations again. As this adjustment process continues season after season, the price tends to approach the level P_0, identified by the intersection of the demand and supply curves. This is the *equilibrium price,* the level that just induces firms to produce and market the quantity Q_0 which, when sold, brings the price P_0. Put in another way, price is at equilibrium when the price producers receive when they market their products is just what they expected when they planned the output.

Supply and Allocation

A rise in demand raises the price of the product on the market, but we can now see that it does a great deal more than this, for it also raises the equilibrium price and encourages producers to expand output to a new equilibrium level. Thus, while the short-run effect of an increase in demand is merely to raise the price of the product and to squeeze it out of less essential uses, the long-run effect is to induce an increase in production. Similarly, while the short-run effect of a reduction in demand is merely to lower price, permitting buyers to put the commodity to lower-priority uses, the long-run effect is to discourage output of the commodity because it is no longer desired in such a large volume.

These changes in the volume of output are accompanied by shifts in resource allocation. When consumers place a higher priority on a particular product, their increased demand induces producers to attract labor and other resources from lower-priority uses. When consumers reduce the priority they place on the final product, their reduction in demand has the opposite effect of forcing producers to cut production and release resources for other, now higher-priority, uses.

Shifts in Supply

Markets also alter the allocation of output and resource use in response to changes in production techniques and resource availability. When producers discover a way to get more output from the same amount of labor and resources, their supply curve shifts to the right, indicating that a greater volume of output will come on the market at corresponding prices. The reduction in equilibrium price encourages buyers to employ more of the product. An increase in production cost has the opposite effect, shifting the supply curve to the left as producers put a smaller volume on the market at corresponding prices. The result is a higher equilibrium price that forces buyers to cut back on their use of the product.

The interaction between consumer desires as expressed in the demand curve and production cost as expressed in supply is the key to resource allocation in a private enterprise economic system. The supply and demand of most goods, however, do not interact in an auction market, but through prices established directly by business firms for their own products. This kind of pricing is the subject of the next chapter.

SUMMARY

Although the most primitive pricing mechanism is person-to-person *bargaining*, many basic commodities, including most agricultural products, are initially sold on *auction markets*. Prices set by competitive bidding depend on demand in relation to the quantity delivered to the market. Given demand, prices vary with quantity delivered. A reduction in quantity raises prices, but the higher the elasticity of demand, the smaller the price increase will be. An increase in quantity lowers price, but the higher the demand elasticity, the smaller the price reduction will be. Given a quantity to be sold, price varies with demand, rising when demand increases and falling when demand decreases.

Bidders in basic commodity markets buy commodities for resale through retail outlets, or for use as raw materials in manufacturing processes. In either case, their demand for the commodity is *derived* from the demands of their own customers, the ultimate consumers of the product. Prices set by competitive bidding divide available quantities among different uses in accordance with consumer wishes, as is easily seen when demand is examined as a *composite* of a number of different demand curves, each representing a different group of bidders. When small quantities are delivered for sale, high prices reserve them for the groups with the least elastic demands. When large quantities appear on the market, low prices permit increasing amounts to enter uses with more elastic demands.

Auction markets also serve to regulate the flow of output among markets in different cities. The action of *speculators* helps to stabilize prices and to spread consumption of commodities with seasonal deliveries evenly over the entire year.

The quantities brought to market each year are dependent on the prices expected by producers, and can be represented by a *supply curve*. The result of the interaction of supply and demand is a dynamic adjustment by which price and output tend to approach *equilibrium* values. A shift in demand not only produces an immediate change in price, but also changes the equilibrium price which induces a long-run change in output and a shift in resource allocation. This is the important mechanism by which consumers guide resources into their highest-priority uses.

CHAPTER 17

Prices Established by Business Firms

Most of the prices encountered in daily life are set by business firms on their own products. The customer does not bargain or bid, but buys or refuses to buy at the price marked on the article. This chapter is devoted to the study of how firms set these prices.

MARGINS AND MARKUPS

Everybody knows that prices are related to cost. When it costs $20,000 to build a house but only $10 to make a pair of shoes, it comes as no surprise that houses sell for higher prices than shoes. Closer inspection reveals, however, that the problem of pricing is more complicated than this, for while higher-cost items usually carry higher prices, the *ratio* of price to cost varies widely from product to product. The interesting and important question is what determines this *ratio*. Why is the price of

one item double its cost of production while the price of another is only 10 percent more? Why is the same item priced 50 percent higher than cost at one time, but only 25 percent higher at another?

The relationship of price to cost can be described in a number of ways. Some businessmen, especially retailers and wholesalers, refer to their "gross margins." A *gross margin* is the difference between the selling price and the invoice cost of an item, usually expressed as a percentage of selling price. A clothing store that buys men's shirts for $6 and retails them for $8 obtains a gross margin of ($8 − 6)/$8, or 33 percent of retail price. A store that buys a chair for $27 and prices it at $54 obtains a gross margin of 50 percent.

Among manufacturing firms, it is more common to express the ratio of price to cost as a "markup" rather than a gross margin. A *markup* is the ratio of the firm's selling price to the direct cost per unit of manufacturing the product, as measured by the unit cost of labor, materials, power, containers, and other costs. An item selling for $4 for which the direct cost of manufacture is $3 represents a markup of $4/3, or 1.33.

The Search for the Most Profitable Price

Some business firms actually set prices by using standard markups. For example, a manufacturer of men's suits may set prices by applying a standard markup of 1.3 to the cost of the labor and materials that went into the garment. When the suit costs $60 to manufacture, the price is 1.3 × $60, or $78. More frequently, however, standard markups provide only a starting point in pricing, and the actual price set in any given case is adjusted upward or downward from the calculated level, according to conditions in the market. A chemical manufacturer put it this way: ". . . the simplest technique, and one too often used is the 'cost-plus' method of establishing prices. In the cost-plus-margin version this method makes price calculations easy. The only fault is that the answers are usually wrong. . . .

". . . Cost-plus approaches can easily result in prices higher than the market will permit, or lower than the market is willing to accept in relation to the value offered. Fortunately, market considerations usually take over at this point, and appropriate adjustments are made in the calculated price so the product can be sold. . . ."[1]

In other words, margins and markups are really the *result* of pricing, not its cause. What is important is not the particular steps or calculations by which one or another business firm arrives at its prices, but rather the differences in demand conditions that result in higher margins or markups in one case than in another. A thorough examination of this matter will involve careful study

of the behavior of costs and revenues, but before we plunge into details, let us state the most important results.

1. Total profit depends on profit per unit and the number of units sold. A high price means high profit per unit, but if too few units are sold, total profit will be small. A low price means larger sales volume, but if profit per unit is too low, total profit will again be small. The most profitable markup is one at which the combination of profit per unit and sales volume brings in the greatest total profit.

2. It follows that *the most profitable markup depends on the elasticity of demand.* Firms whose products have very elastic demands find that they must keep prices close to cost and make their profit from large sales volume. If they raise prices, they get a higher margin on each unit sold, but they lose so many customers that total profit falls. Firms whose products have less elastic demands find that they must keep prices farther above cost. If they reduce prices they gain too few customers to make up for the reduction in markup on each unit sold. The remainder of this chapter is a technical exploration of this important result.

COSTS

The costs incurred by a firm during a year can be divided into 2 classes.

Fixed Costs

Fixed costs are those whose yearly magnitudes are independent of the rate of output. For example, buildings and similar facilities deteriorate more or less steadily as time passes, and their annual loss in value, *depreciation*, is a fixed cost to the business whether the facilities are used or not, and regardless of the rate of use. Machinery and equipment also loses value as it becomes

---

[1] W. F. Christopher, as quoted by Jules Backman, *Chemical Prices, Productivity, Wages and Profits*, Washington, D.C., The Manufacturing Chemists' Association, 1964, p. 12.

obsolete with the appearance of technical improvements, changes in product design, or shifts in consumer preferences. Annual cost allowances in anticipation of obsolescence are clearly fixed costs. Since property taxes are proportional to the value of property owned by the firm regardless of the rate of production, they are also fixed costs. Rental of leased property, interest on bonded debt, salaries of officers and other overhead personnel, insurance, and many advertising costs are also fixed.

Thus fixed costs are the annual costs associated with owning and maintaining a fixed productive capacity. When a firm expands capacity by investing in additional plant, its annual bill for fixed costs rises. When the firm reduces capacity by selling equipment or by allowing it to wear out without replacement, its annual fixed cost declines. As long as productive capacity is maintained intact, however, variation in fixed cost results from causes outside the direct control of the firm, as when property tax bills rise and fall with changing tax rates, or when the salaries of managers or other key employees must be raised to retain their services.

Fixed costs must be distinguished from cash outlays. Maintenance cost represents the *average* outlay necessary to maintain equipment in efficient operating condition, but maintenance can often be postponed when sales are slack and made up later when revenues are more adequate. Depreciation cost is not an outlay, but represents the amount that must be earned over the life of a piece of equipment to recover the funds initially invested in it.

It is also useful to distinguish between costs recognized and accounted for in the company's books and costs that, even though not explicitly recognized, must be met if the firm is to stay in business. In a corporation, management salaries appear as explicit costs on the income statement, but the compensation of the sole proprietor of an unincorporated business is likely to appear as part of the residual "profit." Yet unless this residual is at least equal to the amount the proprietor could earn in an equally attractive alternative occupation, he is unlikely to continue to operate the business in the long run. For this reason, wages of the owner-manager, interest on his invested capital, and a minimum return for the risks of doing business are properly included among the economic costs of the business, whether they are explicitly recognized on the firm's books or not. In what follows when we speak of a firm "breaking even," we mean that its revenues just cover all costs, including all such implied costs.

Variable Costs

Variable costs are those costs whose annual magnitudes vary with the rate of production. Since it takes more or fewer manhours of production labor to produce a greater or lesser number of units, the annual wage bill is a variable cost. The amounts of materials, parts, and power purchased each year rises and falls with the rate of output, as does the amount laid out for freight, shipping charges, and similar services. Thus these are also variable costs. Some products (tobacco, alcohol, and so on) are subject to excise taxes, requiring payment of a specified amount per unit of output, and these are clearly variable costs.

Total Cost

The *total cost* of operating at any given annual rate is the sum of the variable cost incurred by that rate of output plus the fixed cost that is incurred regardless of operations.

Marginal Cost

The amount by which total cost increases per additional unit of output is *marginal cost*. If it takes a total cost of $25,000 to produce 160,000 units per year, and a total cost of $25,017 to produce 160,100 units, the additional 100 units of product adds $17 to cost. This would be described as a marginal cost of $17/100, or $.17 per additional unit. Conversely, if total cost of production at a rate of 200,000 is $80,000 and marginal cost is $5, the total cost of operating at an annual rate of 200,100 would be $80,500. Note that marginal cost is not a new "source" of cost to be added to fixed and variable costs, but is a way of characterizing how rapidly total cost rises as output is stepped up.

In most industries marginal cost is roughly constant over a wide range of operating rates. That is, each unit of product requires about the same amounts of additional materials, power, labor, and other inputs as the previous one. For example, each ton of product might require 1 hour of labor at $2.50 per hour, $.85 worth of materials, and $.15 worth of other variable costs. As long as these figures were unchanged, marginal cost would be constant at $3.50, and variable cost would rise in direct proportion to the quantity of output. At a production rate of 1,000 tons, variable cost would be $3,500 per year. At a production rate of 2,000 tons, variable cost would be $7,000 per year, and so on.

At high rates of output, however, this proportionality ceases to hold. The marginal cost of increasing output beyond a certain level is no longer constant, but rises. Marginal cost might remain at $3.50 per unit up to an output of 2,000 tons per year, for example, but a production rate of 2,100 tons might require overtime operation. At time-and-a-half overtime rates, each additional hour of labor would cost $3.75 per ton, raising to $4.75 the marginal cost of each ton in excess of 2,000. Further increases in production rates might require not only overtime labor, but the use of inefficient standby machinery that would raise marginal cost again. The rush to get out still more work might involve spoilage and wasted materials, again pushing up mar-

ginal cost. As the absolute physical limit to plant capacity is approached, increasing inefficiencies are encountered, and marginal costs rise more and more.

The effect of rising marginal cost can be seen in the following simplified example. Suppose a firm has fixed costs of $10 and marginal costs of $2 up to an annual rate of production of 3 units. Beyond that output, however, the marginal cost of each unit produced is $1 higher than the preceding one. The relationship of cost to operating rate would be as shown in Table 1. If nothing is produced, the total cost consists entirely of fixed elements. To produce 1 unit requires an outlay of $2 in variable cost, bringing total cost to $12. A second unit adds another $2 to total cost as does the third. Beyond this, however, total cost rises more rapidly as output expands.

Example: Costs of a Glass Bottle Manufacturing Plant

The costs of a $5,500,000 plant, consisting of bottle molding machines and related facilities with a capacity of 1 million gross of 12-ounce glass beverage bottles, have been estimated as follows:

FIXED COSTS

Depreciation	$550,000
Maintenance and repair	550,000
Taxes, insurance, and other costs	110,000
Fixed salaries and overhead labor	290,000
Annual fixed cost	$1,500,000

VARIABLE COST, PER GROSS, PACKED
(at outputs up to 1 million gross per year)

Sand, lime, chemicals	$ .95
Power	.45
Cartons	1.00
Labor	1.50
Marginal cost	$3.90

At rates of operation above 1 million gross per year, marginal cost rises $.01 per

TABLE 1   RELATIONSHIP OF OPERATING RATE TO RISING MARGINAL COST

OPERATING RATE	FIXED COST	VARIABLE COST	TOTAL COST	MARGINAL COST
0	$10	$ 0	$10	$2
1	10	2	12	2
2	10	4	14	2
3	10	6	16	3
4	10	9	19	4
5	10	13	23	5
6	10	18	28	

gross for each 500 gross above capacity.

According to these estimates, the cost of producing 100,000 gross a year would be:

Fixed cost	$1,500,000
Variable cost	
(100,000 × $3.90)	390,000
Total cost per year	$1,890,000

When the operating rate is raised to 900,000 per year, costs become:

Fixed cost	$1,500,000
Variable cost	
(900,000 × $3.90)	3,510,000
Total cost per year	$5,010,000

The total cost of operating at any other rate within the firm's capacity can be estimated in similar fashion. When operations exceed the rate of 1 million bottles per year, however, higher marginal costs must be considered. The total cost of producing 1,002,000 per year would be:

Fixed cost		$1,500,000
Variable cost		
a. First million	(1 million × 3.90)	3,900,000
b. Next 500	(500 × 3.91)	1,955
c. Next 500	(500 × 3.92)	1,960
d. Next 500	(500 × 3.93)	1,965
e. Next 500	(500 × 3.94)	1,970
Total cost		$5,407,850

The annual costs of operation at selected rates are given in Table 2. As the operating rate (first column) rises, fixed cost (second column) remains at $1,500,000 per year, but variable cost (fourth column) rises proportionally. Marginal cost (last column) is constant at $3.90 until the operating rate reaches 1 million per year. Higher operating rates can be attained, but only by resorting to methods that push up marginal cost. At outputs beyond 1 million per year, therefore, variable cost rises more than in

TABLE 2   COSTS OF A BOTTLE MANUFACTURING PLANT AT SELECTED OPERATING RATES

OPERATING RATE	FIXED COST ANNUAL	FIXED COST PER UNIT	VARIABLE COST ANNUAL	VARIABLE COST PER UNIT	TOTAL COST ANNUAL	TOTAL COST PER UNIT	MARGINAL COST PER UNIT
$ 0	$1,500,000	—	$ 0	—	$1,500,000	—	$, 3.90
100,000	1,500,000	$15.00	390,000	$3.90	1,809,000	$18.90	3.90
200,000	1,500,000	7.50	780,000	3.90	2,280,000	11.40	3.90
300,000	1,500,000	5.00	1,170,000	3.90	2,670,000	8.90	3.90
400,000	1,500,000	3.75	1,560,000	3.90	3,060,000	7.65	3.90
500,000	1,500,000	3.00	1,950,000	3.90	3,450,000	6.90	3.90
600,000	1,500,000	2.50	2,340,000	3.90	3,840,000	6.40	3.90
700,000	1,500,000	2.14	2,730,000	3.90	4,230,000	6.04	3.90
800,000	1,500,000	1.88	3,120,000	3.90	4,620,000	5.78	3.90
900,000	1,500,000	1.67	3,510,000	3.90	5,010,000	5.57	3.90
1,000,000	1,500,000	1.50	3,900,000	3.90	5,400,000	5.40	3.90
1,100,000	1,500,000	1.36	4,390,000	3.99	5,890,000	5.35	5.90
1,200,000	1,500,000	1.25	5,080,000	4.23	6,580,000	5.48	7.90
1,300,000	1,500,000	1.15	5,970,000	4.60	7,470,000	5.75	9.90
1,400,000	1,500,000	1.07	7,060,000	5.05	8,560,000	6.12	11.90

proportion to output. Total cost (the sixth column) is the sum of fixed and variable costs.

Costs in a Multiproduct Firm

Since most firms produce more than one product, the proper assignment of costs to individual products is often a complicated matter for cost accounting. Variable costs, by their nature, are directly assignable to individual products. Even some fixed costs are easily assigned. If one product takes a particular machine, jig, tool, or other fixture, or if it occupies an entire building, these costs are clearly assignable to that product. However, other fixed costs must be prorated on some reasonable basis. Depreciation, heat, light, insurance, and similar costs are frequently assigned to products on the basis of the number of feet of floor space occupied by the respective operations.

As an example, in grocery retailing the variable costs of selling frozen foods include the invoice cost of the food; labor cost per case of unpacking, marking, and setting out in the freezer; and the cost of bags. The assignable fixed costs include depreciation, maintenance and repairs, and the power cost of the freezer, as well as interest on the funds invested in it. In addition, utilities, depreciation on the store and its overhead facilities, rent, taxes, and so on are assigned on the basis of space occupied. The costs of frozen-food retailing with a freezer capacity of about 8,000 cases per year are approximately as follows:

FIXED COSTS, PER YEAR
Assignable costs	$2,000
Prorated costs	5,000
Fixed cost	$7,000

VARIABLE COST, PER CASE
Invoice cost of merchandise	$ 9.75
Labor and other direct costs	.50
Marginal cost	$10.25

According to these estimates, the total cost of frozen-food operations would be $17,250 if 1,000 cases per year were sold, $27,500 if 2,000 cases were sold, and so on.

As will be seen later, the most profitable price is independent of fixed costs. Thus the fact that some fixed costs are arbitrarily prorated to particular products does not directly affect the decision concerning their prices.

Representing Costs by a Break-Even Chart

The relationship of total cost to the rate of operation is conveniently represented by a chart, often called—for reasons that will appear later—a "break-even chart." In Figure 1, costs are plotted on the vertical and annual production rates on the horizontal axis. The chart is drawn to represent the bottle manufacturing firm with fixed costs of $1.5 million per year and marginal cost of $3.90 up to capacity.

Fixed cost is represented by the solid line FF. The fact that it is parallel to and $1.5 million above the quantity axis indi-

FIGURE 1   BREAK-EVEN CHART OF A BOTTLE MANUFACTURING PLANT

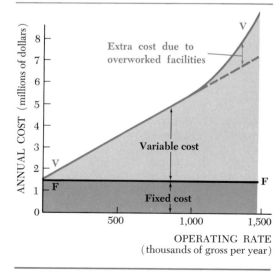

cates that the cost of $1.5 million is incurred annually regardless of the rate of operations. The addition of variable cost to this fixed cost is represented by the line *VV*, which meets the fixed cost line at 0 output, indicating that no variable costs are incurred until production is undertaken. The *slope* of *VV* is marginal cost. *VV* rises $3.90 per unit as output increases up to an operating rate of 1 million per year, in keeping with the $3.90 marginal cost. As output rises beyond the 1 million level, the variable cost curve rises more and more steeply, corresponding to the steady rise in marginal cost as higher operating rates become increasingly expensive.

Average Costs

In analyzing the relationship of price to cost, it is often useful to consider *average cost* per unit, rather than annual cost. As the term implies, average cost per unit is obtained by dividing annual cost by the operating rate. When it costs a total of $2,000 per year to produce 1,000 units, average total cost is $2,000/1,000, or $2. If the $2,000 operating cost consisted of $500 of fixed cost and $1,500 of variable cost, the $2 average total cost would consist of an average fixed cost of $500/1,000, or $.50, and an average variable cost of $1,500/1,000, or $1.50.

Average costs of the bottle manufacturing plant appear in columns 3, 5, and 7 of Table 2. Since fixed cost does not change as operating rates increase, average fixed cost per unit declines steadily as fixed cost is spread over more units. In the operating range in which marginal cost is constant, average variable cost per unit is likewise constant and is equal to marginal cost. As marginal cost rises at operating rates in excess of 1 million gross per year, it pulls up the average variable cost.

As long as average variable cost is constant, falling average fixed cost means that average total cost is reduced as output expands. Even in the early stages of rising average variable cost, the continued decline in average fixed cost more than compensates for higher marginal cost, and average total cost continues to fall. (In Table 2, average total cost is lower at 1.1 million gross per year than at 1 million, in spite of rising marginal cost.) Ultimately, however, rising marginal cost more than offsets the continued decline in average fixed cost, and average total cost rises.

The relationship of average and marginal costs at different levels of output is shown in Figure 2. Average variable and average total costs are plotted separately in the figure. Average variable cost, represented by the curve *AVC*, is a straight line parallel to the horizontal axis up to an operating rate of 1 million gross per year, corresponding to the constant marginal cost in this range. As marginal cost, *MC*, rises beyond this point, it pulls up average variable cost, as indicated by the rising level of *AVC* at higher operating rates.

Average total cost per unit is represented by the curve *ATC*, while average fixed cost is represented by the difference between average variable and average total cost. The gap between the 2 curves di-

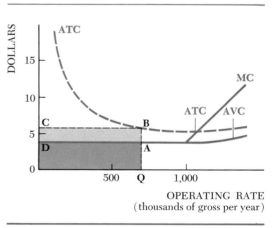

FIGURE 2   AVERAGE AND MARGINAL COSTS
OF A BOTTLE MANUFACTURING
PLANT

minishes as the operating rate rises, corresponding to the decline in average fixed cost.

Since annual costs are the product of average cost and operating rate, they are represented in the average cost chart by areas, as shown. An operating rate of Q units per year corresponds to the length OQ, while average total cost per unit is represented by the height QB. Annual total cost, their product, is represented by the total shaded area $OQBC$. In similar fashion, annual variable cost corresponds to the area $OQAD$, and fixed cost to the area $ABCD$. Total cost is the sum of fixed and variable costs as shown.

PRICING FOR MAXIMUM PROFIT

Profit is the difference between the number of dollars the firm receives for goods sold and the total cost of producing the goods. Given the demand for the product, therefore, the price chosen by the firm determines the quantity it can sell and, with it, both sales revenue and total cost. The task of pricing is to locate the price that will maximize the difference between revenue and cost, leaving the firm the largest possible profit.

The nature of this pricing decision is shown in Table 3. The first 2 columns contain selected prices and quantities from the demand schedule for the firm's product. The other columns show the total sales revenue the firm could expect at each price, the total cost of production, and the resulting profit. As the table indicates, high prices are not always profitable. In fact, at $12 the firm would be unable to sell enough to cover the cost of production and would sustain a loss of $100,718 per year. If price were set at $10, the firm would sell more bottles, and although the extra output would add to cost it would add still more to revenue, and a small profit would be realized. A price of $7 would be more profitable, and as we look down the schedule, we see that profit would rise with each successive price reduction until $6.50 was reached. At this price, the firm could expect to sell 800,000 gross per year, receiving $5,200,000 in sales revenue. After paying the total cost of $4,620,000, the firm would be left with a profit of $580,000 per year. No other price would be quite as profitable as $6.50. If the price were raised or lowered by even as little as a penny, profit would be reduced.

Marginal Revenue

Having located the most profitable price, our task is now to show how it is related to cost and how the most profitable markup

---

TABLE 3   THE PROFITABILITY OF SELECTED BOTTLE PRICES

PRICE	QUANTITY	SALES REVENUE	TOTAL COST	PROFIT
$12.00	172,800	$2,073,600	$2,173,920	−$100,718
10.00	272,500	2,725,000	2,562,750	162,250
7.00	664,700	4,652,900	4,092,330	560,570
6.80	714,700	4,859,960	4,287,330	572,630
6.55	784,800	5,140,440	4,560,720	579,720
6.51	796,931	5,188,021	4,608,031	579,990
6.50	800,000	5,200,000	4,620,000	580,000
6.49	803,085	5,212,023	4,632,032	579,992
6.45	815,500	5,259,975	4,680,450	579,525
6.20	900,300	5,581,860	5,011,170	570,690
6.00	977,200	5,863,200	5,311,080	552,120
5.50	1,214,700	6,680,850	6,237,303	443,547

depends on the elasticity of demand. For this purpose, it is useful to look at the process of finding the most profitable price in a slightly different way. Imagine beginning at the top of Table 3 and searching for the most profitable price by making a series of price reductions, trying each price in turn.

Each successive price reduction would expand the firm's sales, and would influence profit in 2 ways. On the one hand, the larger quantity sold would bring in more revenue. On the other hand, production of the larger quantity would add to total cost. Whether a given price cut could raise or lower profit obviously depends on which of these influences is the larger. When a price reduction would add more to revenue than to cost, it would increase profits; when it would add less to revenue than to cost, it would reduce profit.

The amount that would be added to revenue by each successive price cut is shown in Table 4. For example, the $2 reduction from $12 to $10 would increase sales by 99,700 gross and would add another $651,500 to sales revenue. In order to compare the revenue gain to the corresponding increase in cost, however, it is convenient to express the revenue gain in terms of marginal revenue. *Marginal revenue* from a price reduction is the ratio of the number of dollars gained in revenue to the number of additional units sold. For example, since the price reduction from $12 to $10 would add $651,500 to total revenue through an increase of 99,700 in quantity sold, the marginal revenue would be $651,500/99,700, or $6.53. The reduction from $10 to $7 would jump quantity sold by another 392,200 units and add $1,927,900 to sales revenue for a marginal revenue of $1,927,900/392,200, or $4.92.

Locating the Most Profitable Price by Marginal Revenue and Marginal Cost The point to expressing revenue gains in terms of marginal revenue is that marginal revenue is directly comparable to marginal cost.

Since marginal cost is the additional cost incurred per additional unit produced, the difference between marginal revenue and marginal cost immediately shows the profitability of price reduction. When marginal revenue exceeds marginal cost, the reduction would make profit greater, but if marginal revenue were smaller than marginal cost, the price reduction would add less to revenue than to cost and would actually result in lower profits.

We can now proceed down the series of prices in Table 4 and ask at each point whether profit would be raised or lowered by the next price reduction. At a price of $12, the next reduction would bring in marginal revenue of $6.53, while marginal cost would be only $3.90. Each of the additional units sold would add more to revenue than to cost, and the price reduction to $10 would increase profit. Since the cut from $7 to $6.80 would yield marginal revenue of $4.14 and marginal cost of $3.90, it would also add to total profit. In fact, as we can see by looking down the table, each price cut adds at least as much to revenue as it does to cost until we consider cutting the price from $6.50 to $6.49. This cut would yield marginal revenue of only $3.89, but each additional unit produced would cost $3.90, reducing total profit. It follows that *the most profitable price is the one at which marginal revenue just equals marginal cost.*

This proposition is borne out by Table 4. At high prices, marginal revenue exceeded marginal cost and profit grew with each successive price reduction. As price declined, however, so did marginal revenue, and the cut from $6.51 to $6.50 milked the last dollar of profit out of the demand for bottles. At this price, marginal revenue just equals marginal cost. Cutting below $6.50 would reduce profit because it would yield less marginal revenue than would be added in marginal cost.

Marginal Revenue and Demand Elasticity The marginal revenue that results from any

TABLE 4   MARGINAL REVENUE AND MARGINAL COST AT SELECTED BOTTLE PRICES

PRICE	REDUCTION FROM PRECEDING PRICE	INCREASE IN QUANTITY	INCREASE IN REVENUE	MARGINAL REVENUE	MARGINAL COST
$12.00	—	—	—	—	—
10.00	$2.00	99,700	$ 651,500	$6.53	$3.90
7.00	3.00	392,200	1,927,900	4.92	3.90
6.80	.20	50,000	207,060	4.14	3.90
6.55	.25	70,100	280,480	4.00	3.90
6.51	.04	12,131	47,761	3.94	3.90
6.50	.01	3,069	11,979	3.90	3.90
6.49	.01	3,085	12,023	3.89	3.90
6.45	.04	12,415	47,952	3.86	3.90
6.20	.25	84,800	321,885	3.80	3.90
6.00	.20	76,900	281,340	3.66	3.90
5.50	.50	237,500	817,650	3.44	8.20

SOURCE: Calculated from the data of Table 3.

given price reduction depends on the level of the price being cut, but for any given price, marginal revenue depends on the elasticity of demand. Higher elasticity makes marginal revenue higher, lower elasticity makes marginal revenue lower. This is easily demonstrated by an example. Suppose a firm were selling 20 units of product yearly at a price of $8, for a total revenue of $160. What marginal revenue would it receive if it were to cut its price to $7.50? Clearly this depends on how much more it can sell at the lower price. If demand were not very elastic, the firm might increase its sales to only 22 units at the lower price, raising its revenue to $165. Since the price reduction would add 2 units to output and $5 to revenue, marginal revenue at the low elasticity would be only $5/2, or $2.50.

Suppose, on the other hand, that the demand were so elastic that sales at the lower price expanded to 30, raising revenue to $225. Since the price reduction would add 10 to the quantity sold, and $65 to total revenue, marginal revenue with the more elastic demand would be $65/10, or $6.50, much larger than in the other case.

The relationship of marginal revenue to elasticity can be expressed by an exact formula. When price is reduced by a small percentage, marginal revenue is found by multiplying price by $(e - 1)/e$. For example, when demand elasticity is 3, a small percentage reduction in price from $8 would result in marginal revenue of $(3 - 1)/3 \times \$8$, or $2/3 \times \$8$, or $5.33. When demand elasticity is 4, the small reduction of price from $8 would bring in marginal revenue of $(4 - 1)/4 \times \$8$, or $6, and so on. A firm whose demand has elasticity of 6, and whose product is priced at $18, could obtain marginal revenue of $(6 - 1)/ 6 \times \$18$, or $15 by means of a small price reduction.

To demonstrate the relationship of marginal revenue to elasticity, imagine a firm reducing price just enough to sell 1 more unit. The effect on revenue would be twofold. On the one hand, the firm would collect the lower price for the additional unit sold. On the other hand, the firm would also get less for each of the units it had originally sold at the higher price. Marginal revenue would be the difference between the 2. Suppose the firm were initially selling 100 units at $100 each. If demand elasticity were 5, it would take a cut of 1/5 of 1 percent ($.20) to sell 1 more unit.

This additional unit would sell for $99.80, but after the $.20 price cut the initial 100 units would bring in $20 less than before. Marginal revenue would be the $79.80 difference.

Table 5 applies this principle for a range of elasticities shown in the first column. The second and third indicate the price cut from $100 required to increase sales 1 unit. The fourth column shows the price collected for the extra unit sold, while the fifth column shows the loss of revenue from cutting the price on the 100 units initially sold. The last column shows marginal revenue as the difference between the gain and the loss.

Careful inspection of the table reveals the simple systematic relationship. Regardless of demand elasticity, only a small price reduction is needed to sell the additional unit, and the revenue from its sale can be closely approximated by the initial price. The main cause of differences in marginal revenue comes from reducing the price on the 100 units that were already being sold at the higher price. This revenue loss varies exactly as the reciprocal of the elasticity of demand. When elasticity is 5, the revenue loss is 1/5 of the initial price. When elasticity is 4, the loss is 1/4 of the initial price. In general, when elasticity of demand is e, this revenue loss amounts to $1/e$ of the price.

Representing price by P and demand elasticity by e, the formula for marginal revenue becomes, to a very close approximation,

$$MR = P - \frac{P}{e} = P\left(1 - \frac{1}{e}\right) = P\left(\frac{e-1}{e}\right)$$

The marginal revenues given in the table can be compared with the results given by the formula. For $P = \$100$ and elasticity of 5, the formula gives marginal revenue = $P(5-1)/5 = .8P$, or $80, compared to the tabulated value of $79.80. Similarly, when elasticity is 4, the formula gives marginal revenue of $75, compared to $74.75 in the table. The differences are negligible.

The relationship can be applied to the marginal revenue for beverage bottles. Measurement reveals that the demand for bottles in Table 3 has elasticity of 2.5. For small reductions in price, therefore, the ratio of marginal revenue to price should be 1.5/2.5 or .6. This is in close agreement with the results found for the small price reductions in the middle of the table. For example, at a price of $6.50, marginal revenue was $3.90, making a ratio of $3.90/$6.50 = .6 exactly.

Marginal Revenue Curves A graphical representation of marginal revenue and its relationship to demand is provided by a marginal revenue curve like the blue line in Figure 3. The demand curve DD represents, as usual, the quantity that buyers tend to purchase at the indicated prices. Each point

TABLE 5 RELATIONSHIP OF MARGINAL REVENUE TO DEMAND ELASTICITY

| | PRICE REDUCTION NEEDED | | PRICE RECEIVED | REDUCED REVENUE ON | MARGINAL |
ELASTICITY	PERCENT	DOLLARS	FOR ADDED UNIT	100 UNITS	REVENUE
10	1/10	$.10	$99.90	$10.00	$89.90
9	1/9	.11	99.89	11.00	88.89
8	1/8	.125	99.875	12.50	87.375
7	1/7	.143	99.857	14.30	85.557
6	1/6	.167	99.933	16.70	83.063
5	1/5	.20	99.80	20.00	79.80
4	1/4	.25	99.75	25.00	74.75
3	1/3	.333	99.667	33.333	66.667
2	1/2	.50	99.50	50.00	49.50

FIGURE 3   DEMAND AND MARGINAL
           REVENUE CURVES

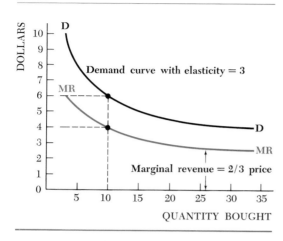

FIGURE 4   DEMAND AND MARGINAL REVENUE
           WITH DIFFERENT DEMAND
           ELASTICITIES

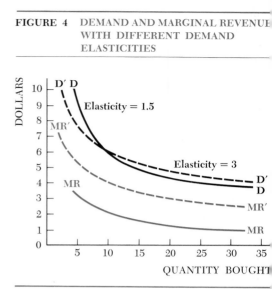

on the blue *MR* curve shows the marginal revenue corresponding to the price on the demand curve directly above it. For example, the point marked on the demand curve in the figure indicates that people tend to buy 10 units when the price is $6. The level of the blue line directly below that point indicates that if the price were reduced slightly from $6, the firm would gain marginal revenue of $4. Since the demand curve has elasticity of 3, each point on the marginal revenue curve is 2/3 of the corresponding price, in keeping with the formula.

When demand elasticity is lower, the marginal revenue curve falls correspondingly farther below the demand curve. The solid black line of Figure 4 represents a demand curve with elasticity of only 1.5. Each point of the corresponding marginal revenue curve, represented by the solid blue line, is only one-third the height of the demand curve. The demand with elasticity of 3 and its marginal revenue curve are shown as dashed lines for comparison. Note that when price is $6, although both demand curves indicate that quantity bought tends to be about 10, the corresponding marginal revenues are widely different.

The Most Profitable Markup

The relationships involving price, elasticity, and marginal revenue provides the final link in the investigation of the most profitable markup. We have now established that: (1) at the most profitable price **P**, marginal revenue *MR* equals marginal cost *MC*. Moreover, (2) marginal revenue is proportional to price by a factor that depends on demand elasticity *e*,

$$MR = P\left(\frac{e-1}{e}\right)$$

It immediately follows that the most profitable price results when

$$MC = MR = P\left(\frac{e-1}{e}\right)$$

or

$$P = MC\left(\frac{e}{e-1}\right)$$

In words, the most profitable price results when the ratio of price to marginal cost is a markup equal to $e/(e-1)$. When demand elasticity is 3, the most profitable markup is $3/(3 − 1) = 3/2 = 1.5$. When elasticity is 4, the most profitable markup is $4/(4 − 1) = 4/3$, or 1.33, and so on.

Since the elasticity of demand for bottles was assumed to be 2.5, the corresponding most profitable markup would be $2.5/1.5 = 1.67$. In the operating range in which marginal cost is $3.90, the most profitable price would be $1.67 × \$3.90$, or $6.50, in exact agreement with the results of Table 3.

Some Implications of the Markup Formula
According to the formula, the more elastic the demand for a product, the smaller the markup becomes. A firm whose products have demand elasticity of 1.5 would find its most profitable markup to be $1.5/(1.5 − 1) = 3$, but a firm with demand elasticity of 11 would make the most profit at a markup of only $11/(11 − 1) = 1.1$. This relationship between demand elasticity and markup is directly in line with what would be expected. The more sensitive customers are to prices, the closer prices must be kept to cost. When a modest price increase would send customers searching for a better buy somewhere else, prices are kept down. When customers are less sensitive to prices, firms find it profitable to raise them.

Every-day examples of the operation of this principle are the prices of hot dogs and cold drinks at baseball parks and football games, which are substantially higher inside the stands than they are outside. The demand for the products of the stadium vendor has low elasticity partly because the refreshments are complementary to watching the game itself and partly because there are no substitutes available inside the stands.

It is important to note that the elasticity in the formula is the elasticity of demand for the firm's own product, not the elasticity of demand for such products in general. The demand for paper is probably relatively inelastic, but the demand for any particular brand or make of paper is more elastic because of the large number of substitute brands among which the buyer can choose. It is the elasticity of demand for its own brand that determines the profitability of the firm's markup. This is why products that must compete with a large number of good substitutes are priced close to cost. The more competitive an industry becomes—that is, the more substitutes are available for the products of any one firm—the closer prices come to cost.

The demand for groceries in general has very low elasticity, but the demand for the items carried in any particular store is highly elastic because customers can go elsewhere if they are dissatisfied with prices. The resulting competition keeps grocery margins low. At the same time, prices are often higher at small neighborhood stores than they are at large supermarkets. One reason is that much neighborhood business consists of small "emergency" purchases by housewives who suddenly need a loaf of bread or a can of fruit. Housewives shopping under these circumstances are less sensitive to price differences and the lower demand elasticity tends to make markups higher. The effect on prices is also reinforced by the higher marginal costs of the small volume of business in the neighborhood store.

A special case of the neighborhood store phenomenon is the question of whether "the poor pay more." Poor people in slum areas not only buy in small quantities with resulting high marginal cost, but without automobiles or other convenient transportation, they are rarely able to compare prices in a number of competing stores. The resulting lower elasticity of demand in slum areas tends to produce higher markups than in suburban areas where housewives have time and transportation to compare values among many stores in a wider area. It has also been alleged that stores in some slum areas regularly raise prices on the day that welfare checks are received. If this is true, it reflects a reduced price sensitivity on the part of hungry families making their purchases.

Prices tend to respond to changes in cost. The introduction of methods that save labor or use cheaper materials reduces marginal cost. Cost reduction makes the operation more profitable than it was before, even at the old prices. But as the markup formula shows, it is even more profitable for the firm to pass on some of these cost savings in lower prices. On the other hand, when wage rates rise more rapidly than labor productivity or when material costs rise, the higher cost reduces profits, but the formula shows that the profit reduction is smaller when the rise in marginal cost is passed on in higher prices.

Further important implications of the relationship of prices to cost will be developed in the study of industrial behavior in the following chapters.

Graphical Analysis of the Pricing Process

Graphical representation of the pricing process not only affords additional insight into the relationship between prices and costs, but provides important tools for the study of pricing behavior under different competitive circumstances.

Pricing with Break-Even Chart   One view of the pricing process is provided in Figure 5. Part (a) contains DD, the demand curve for the firm's product. Part (b) contains the break-even chart representing the firm's costs. Points a, b, c, and so on, indicated on the demand curve, are analogous to the price steps shown earlier in Table 3. The revenue received from the sale of each quantity at the indicated price is plotted as a corresponding point a', b', c', and so on in part (b). Thus the revenue from the quantity that could be sold at price P_a is plotted at a', the revenue from the quantity that could be sold at price P_b is plotted at b', and

so on. If the revenue corresponding to every possible point on the demand curve were plotted, the result would be the blue curve in the lower sector, which shows the total revenue the firm could expect at each possible price on the demand curve.

The gap in part (b) between revenue and total cost represents profit or loss. At the high price P_a, not enough can be sold to cover cost, and point a' below the cost line represents operation at a loss. At price P_b, sales revenue just covers total cost and the firm breaks even. As price is reduced further, revenue rises more rapidly than cost, resulting in profit. Profit reaches a maximum at some most profitable price P_d. Although sales revenue would continue to rise if price were reduced below P_d, marginal revenue is below marginal cost and profit would decline. If price were reduced far enough, the firm would again break even and would incur losses at still lower prices.

Marginal revenue is represented by the slope of the blue curve. At the left end, where prices are high, the steep slope represents high marginal revenue. The reduction in slope as the curve proceeds to the right represents the decline in marginal revenue as price is reduced. The slope of the variable cost line VV represents marginal cost. The most profitable price P_d corresponds to the output at which the slopes of the 2 curves are equal, that is, the point at which marginal revenue equals marginal cost.

Pricing with Average and Marginal Cost Curves   Another view of the pricing process is provided by Figure 6. The black curves represent marginal cost (MC) and average total cost (ATC). The colored curves represent demand (DD) and the marginal revenue curve (MR). The most profitable price is readily identified as P, the price at which the firm sells the total quantity Q that just brings marginal revenue into equality with marginal cost. At prices higher than *P*, marginal revenue would exceed marginal cost, and price reduction would increase profit. At prices below *P* marginal revenue would be smaller than marginal cost, showing price had been reduced too far. The ratio of price to marginal cost is the most profitable markup and corresponds to the formula $e/(e-1)$. The demand curve shown has elasticity of 2, and the price is, accordingly, double marginal cost.

Total cost, revenue, and profit are shown by areas. To produce *Q* units a year involves an average cost of *QB* dollars per unit, or a total cost equal to the area *OQBA*. The sale of *Q* units at price *P* yields revenue equal to the area *OQCP*. The difference be-

FIGURE 6   PRICING FOR MAXIMUM PROFIT SHOWN BY AVERAGE AND MARGINAL COST CURVES

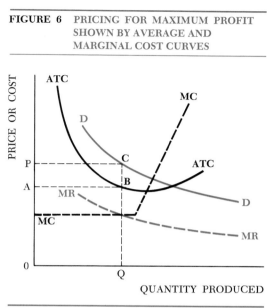

QUANTITY PRODUCED

tween total revenue and total cost is profit, represented by the area *ABCP*.

How Level of Demand Affects Profit   The price that corresponds to the most profitable markup yields more profit (or less loss) than any other price the firm could charge. But the fact that profits are at a *maximum* does not mean that they are necessarily *large*. Indeed, a firm faced with low demand frequently finds that the most profitable price is the one that keeps losses to a minimum. In other words, the actual amount of profit that the firm earns, even at the most profitable price, depends on the level of demand.

The effect of shifts in demand on the profits of our bottle manufacturer can be seen in Figure 7. The black lines form the break-even chart. The blue line shows how much revenue the firm would earn from the sale of bottles *at the most profitable price* of $6.50 per gross. The line emanates from the origin to indicate that no revenue is realized until something is sold and rises $6.50 per gross as it proceeds to the right, in keeping with the most profitable price.

Since profit is the difference between

FIGURE 5   PRICING FOR MAXIMUM PROFIT AS SHOWN BY A BREAK-EVEN CHART

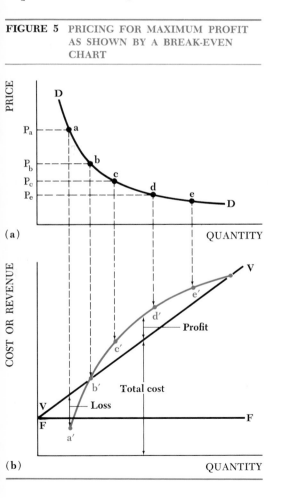

FIGURE 7　THE EFFECT OF DEMAND
　　　　　　　　ON PROFIT

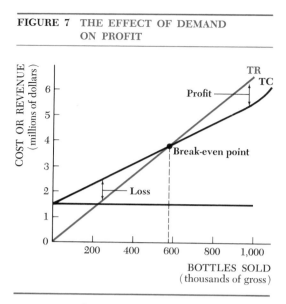

BOTTLES SOLD
(thousands of gross)

revenue and cost, the profit the firm can expect from any given level of demand can be
recognized in the chart as the difference
between the revenue line and the total cost
line. At the level of demand where the 2
lines cross, the firm would experience
neither profit nor loss, but would just break
even, and this level of operations is the
break-even point. The term "break-even
chart" derives from the fact that such charts
facilitate the location and analysis of break-
even points. As we will see in the next
chapter, the effect of fixed costs and demand elasticity on break-even points is an
important factor in the amount of excess
productive capacity that characterizes certain industries.

The break-even point in Figure 7 is
about 576,000 gross per year. When demand
falls below this level, sales revenue declines more rapidly than cost, and the firm
experiences losses. Since the firm is already
charging the most profitable price, price
cuts will not improve the situation, but only
make the losses larger. If the firm is to re-
gain a profitable level of operations, it must
increase the demand for its product by improving its quality or by advertising. The
relationship of product quality and adver-

tising to profits will be explored more fully
when we examine the competitive behavior
of industries in the next chapter.

At levels of demand above the break-
even point the firm makes profits, and the
greater the demand, the higher profit becomes. Even so, until output reaches the
level at which marginal cost begins to rise,
increasing demand is unaccompanied by
rising prices. Since the firm is already
charging the most profitable price, any
price increase would reduce, rather than
increase, the profitability of operations.

There is a limit to the productive capacity of the firm, however, and when demand
begins to approach this limit marginal cost
begins to rise. In the case of the bottle
manufacturer, for example, marginal cost
was $3.90 per gross only up to outputs of
1 million gross per year. At higher operating
rates, the pressure on equipment, overtime
operation, and other extra costs raised the
marginal cost of bottles by $.01 a gross for
every additional 500 gross produced. When
demand reaches these levels, the old $6.50
price no longer corresponds to the most
profitable markup, and the price must be
raised to protect the firm's profit position.
Since the most profitable markup for the
bottle manufacturer was 1.67, the most
profitable price at a marginal cost of $4
becomes 1.67 × $4, or $6.70. When marginal
cost reaches $4.20, the most profitable price
rises to $7, and so on. Very high levels of
demand mean very high profits, but only
if the firm maintains the most profitable
markup of price over rising marginal cost.

RATIOS OF PRICE TO
MARGINAL COST IN U.S.
MANUFACTURING INDUSTRIES

The costs and markups represented by
prices of individual firms are closely
guarded business secrets, but the U.S. Bureau of the Census periodically surveys

manufacturing establishments and collects data on the value of products shipped and on such variable costs as production worker wages, purchased raw materials and parts, containers, fuel, and so on. Although the law forbids disclosure of the operations of individual establishments or firms, the data are regularly compiled and published for each industry. The ratio of the total value of output of all establishments in the industry to their total variable cost provides us with an estimate of the ratio of price to unit variable cost, at least on the average over all products and establishments in the industry. During 1965, for example, the entire U.S. shoe industry produced and shipped $2,466,343,000 worth of shoes. To manufacture these products the industry paid $640,668,000 in wages to production workers, and spent $1,127,447,000 for materials, power, etc., making a total variable cost of $1,768,115,000. On the average over the entire industry, then, the ratio of price to unit variable cost must have been $2,466,343,000/$1,768,115,000, or 1.40. In view of the wide range of constant marginal cost typical of manufacturing, this ratio can be taken as an estimate of the average markup characteristic of the industry during that year.

This method was employed to estimate markups from the cost and sales figures given in the Census of Manufactures for each of 419 industries. The results are summarized in Table 6 and Figure 8. As shown, the median markup was estimated to be about 1.45. That is, half of the value of all manufacturing shipments were made by industries characterized by estimated markups below 1.45, the other half by industries with markups of 1.45 or more. The heaviest concentration of markups occurred in the neighborhood of 1.35. Markups below 1.2 were rare, and accounted for less than 5 percent of all shipments. Likewise, markups of more than 2.5 represented only 2 percent of all shipments.

When markups are estimated over a

TABLE 6   DISTRIBUTION OF ESTIMATED MANUFACTURING MARKUPS

MARKUP	COMBINED SALES OF INDUSTRIES WITH THE INDICATED MARKUP	
	BILLIONS OF DOLLARS	PERCENT OF TOTAL SALES
Under 1.10	$5.01	1.4
1.10 to 1.19	10.38	2.9
1.20 to 1.29	55.73	15.3
1.30 to 1.39	69.77	19.2
1.40 to 1.49	64.46	17.7
1.50 to 1.74	93.16	25.6
1.75 to 1.99	43.02	11.8
2.00 to 2.49	14.79	4.1
2.50 to 2.99	3.86	1.1
3.00 or more	3.31	0.9
Total	$363.49	100.0

SOURCE: Estimated from data in U.S. Census Bureau, *Annual Survey of Manufactures, 1965.*

period of years for the same industry, year-to-year variations in their magnitudes are inevitable, if only because of shifting pro-

FIGURE 8   DISTRIBUTION OF MARKUPS IN U.S. MANUFACTURING

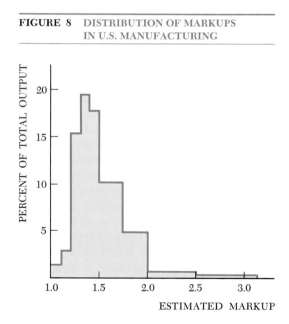

SOURCE: Calculated from data given in U.S. Bureau of the Census, *Annual Survey of Manufactures, 1965.*

portions among many different products each with its own characteristic markup. Nevertheless, estimated markups show surprising stability over time compared to the wide differences observed among industries. This can be seen when a representative sample of industries is compared in Table 7. The largest variation shown is the increase in the average markup in the pharmaceuticals industry from an estimated 2.5 in 1954 to an estimated 3.4 in 1965, a relatively small change in comparison to the difference between the pharmaceuticals industry and all the others in any given year.

It is clear that the variation in markup from one industry to another is not the temporary result of accidental conditions, but is an expression of more permanent differences in competitive conditions. We will explore these differences in the next 2 chapters.

TABLE 7   ESTIMATED MARKUPS FOR SELECTED INDUSTRIES

INDUSTRY	ESTIMATED MARKUP				
	1954	1956	1958	1962	1965
Meat packing	1.08	1.12	1.09	1.10	1.09
Motorcycles, bicycles, and parts	1.26	1.26	1.30	1.27	1.29
Men's and boy's suits and coats	1.26	1.26	1.33	1.28	1.38
Wood furniture	1.34	1.37	1.35	1.38	1.40
Footwear	1.34	1.33	1.36	1.36	1.39
Silverware and silverplate	1.36	1.44	1.48	1.44	1.47
Glass containers	1.49	1.55	1.56	1.52	1.51
Chewing gum	1.97	2.04	2.01	2.12	2.07
Pharmaceuticals	2.5	2.9	2.9	3.2	3.4

SOURCE: Calculated from data in the *Compendium of Manufacturing Statistics for the United States, 1947–1965*, Washington, D.C., Georgetown Economic Data Library, 1967.

SUMMARY

The important question about pricing is what determines the *markup*, which is the ratio of price to cost in any particular case. The profitability of a particular markup partly depends on the behavior of cost at different volumes of output.

Total cost is the sum of *fixed costs*, which are independent of output, and *variable costs*, which depend on the level of production. The behavior of cost as output changes is conveniently described by *marginal cost*, the increase in cost per additional unit produced. For most products, marginal cost is constant over a wide range of output, but rises as the capacity of the firm is approached.

Given demand for the product, price determines the quantity sold and hence sales revenue, total cost, and profit. The task of price-setting is to locate the price that will maximize profit, the difference between revenue and cost. This price can be located by the direct comparison of revenues and costs at different prices, but the relationship of price to cost is better seen when the most profitable price is considered as that at which marginal revenue equals marginal cost.

Marginal revenue is the addition to total revenue per unit of additional quantity sold and is, therefore, directly comparable to marginal cost. Marginal revenue is higher at higher prices, and for any given price, is higher for more elastic demands. The ratio of marginal revenue to price can be expressed by an exact formula: $MR/P = (e-1)/e$.

Since the most profitable price is the one at which marginal revenue and marginal cost are equal, it follows that the most profitable markup depends only on demand elasticity and can be expressed by the *markup formula $e/(e-1)$*. The formula shows that firms with highly elastic demand must keep prices close to cost, while those with less elastic demands can apply larger markups. Graphical representation affords additional insight into the pricing process and provides an important tool for the exploration of industrial behavior.

Markups for individual firms are closely guarded secrets, but averages for entire industries can be calculated from Census data. These show wide dispersion among industries, and it is clear that differences in markup correspond to basic differences in competitive conditions that will be explored in the following chapters.

CHAPTER 18

The Performance
of Competitive Industry

THE INDUSTRIAL ENVIRONMENT AND BUSINESS BEHAVIOR

Individual businessmen must make many decisions. They must decide what products to produce, what production method to employ, what prices to set, how much to produce, and how much to advertise. They must also decide when to improve the quality, design, or style of products, when to invest in additional capacity, and when to introduce cost-saving methods. Since the sales a firm can expect depend not only on the price and quality of its own product, but also on the prices and qualities of competing products, the actions of each businessman is limited by those of other firms in the industry. Whether there is any particular urgency to lowering price or improving product performance often depends on the behavior of business rivals. As a consequence, the decisions businessmen reach and the response of their firms to changes in

conditions depend heavily on the industrial environment in which they operate.

Definition of an Industry

The term "industry" is used in everyday speech to denote a group of producers of the same or closely similar products. It is clear, however, that boundaries between industries are inexact. Whether the products of 2 establishments are "close" substitutes or not is, after all, a matter of degree. The most clearly defined industries are those in which products are *homogeneous*. A perfectly homogeneous product is one like corn of a given grade, steel nails of a given size, or sulphuric acid. Samples of a homogeneous product obtained from different producers, if they are distinguishable at all, are completely interchangeable as far as the buyer is concerned. Many intermediate industrial materials like steel bars, aluminum sheets, chemicals, and paper are homogeneous products, as are most farm commodities. Industrial buyers shop to meet required specifications at minimum cost, with little or no regard to which firm produced the particular batch they buy. Indeed, if bulk purchases are made through a wholesaler or other commercial middleman, the buyer may not even know the source of the products.

Products that are not homogeneous are *differentiated*. It is more or less easy for buyers of such products to distinguish the output of different producers by its style, performance, color, taste, or some other quality. Many final consumer goods are highly differentiated. Anybody who is interested can easily tell the difference between different makes of automobiles or between packages of breakfast cereal made by different firms. The distinguishing features may involve the product itself or merely differences in packaging. Even consumers who are unable to taste the difference between one brand of cola drink and another can distinguish them from across the room by the shapes of the bottles.

When products are differentiated, it is difficult to define exact industrial boundaries. In a real sense, each brand of any product is unique. No other firm can produce exactly the same thing, if for no other reason than that the brand name is copyrighted, and that it is illegal to duplicate the packaging and appearance of another firm's output. Despite the unique qualities of different brands, however, it is clearly useful to speak of, for instance, a "toothpaste" industry because of the high cross-elasticity of demand representing the willingness of consumers to substitute one brand for another in response to price differentials. The question then arises whether manufacturers of powdered dentifrice should be included in the same industry, or whether "toothpaste" and "tooth powder" are really 2 distinct industries. Again, the question is resolved by the cross-elasticity of demand. If the sales of given brands of

toothpaste are highly sensitive to changes in the prices of tooth powders and conversely, both should be classed as members of a single "dentifrice products" industry. If cross-elasticity of demand between toothpaste and tooth powder is low, the 2 should be classed in separate industries.

Similar problems apply to the definition of any other industry. Since aluminum wire is a well-defined homogeneous product, all producers of aluminum wire belong to the "aluminum-wire" industry. By the same logic, all copper-wire producers are members of the "copper-wire" industry, but the question is whether the 2 types of wire are sufficiently different to warrant assigning the establishments making them to 2 distinct industries, or whether they belong to a single "electrical-wire" industry.

Standard Industrial Classification

Since industrial boundaries are not clearly defined, and since industrial classifications that make sense for one application are useless for another, the U.S. Bureau of the Census has established several different "levels" of industrial classifications. Each establishment in the United States is assigned a 5-digit Standard Industrial Classification (SIC) number on the basis of its products. Establishments manufacturing closely related products are given numbers that differ only in the final digit. Manufacturers whose output is one or another form of electrical wire, for example, are assigned 1 of 9 numbers, as shown on the next page.

Since establishments with the same number are more closely related to each other than to those with other numbers, they are treated as members of the same industry, and the finest industrial classification generally employed is the so called "5-digit" industry, consisting of all establishments with the same SIC 5-digit designation. Often, however, the cross-elasticity of demand among closely related 5-digit in-

PRINCIPAL PRODUCTS	SIC NUMBER
Aluminum and aluminum-base alloy wire and cable	33571
Copper and copper-base alloy wire, bare and tinned, for electrical transmission	33572
Other bare nonferrous wire	33573
Communication wire and cable	33574
Nonferrous wire and other woven wire products	33575
Appliance wire and cord, and flexible cord sets	33576
Magnet wire	33577
Power wire and cable	33578
Other insulated wire and cable, n.e.c.	33579

dustries is so high that it is useful to consider them all as part of a larger "4-digit" industry. This classification is obtained by classifying together all establishments whose SIC numbers have the first 4 digits in common. In the example above, all establishments combined form the 4-digit industry 3357, Nonferrous Wire Drawing. For some purposes even this classification is too narrow, and establishments are further combined into 3-digit and 2-digit industrial groups.

Much of the discussion that follows is sufficiently general to make the precise definition of industrial boundaries immaterial. Actual measurement of industrial sales, markups, concentration ratios, or other characteristics, however, can be made only in terms of data from clearly defined industries, and for these purposes, 4-digit Standard Industrial Classifications will be employed.

Market Structure and Competition

Industries differ widely in the performance they impose on their member firms. We have already seen the wide industry-to-industry variation in pricing behavior, with markups ranging from very close to 1 in some industries to values well above 3 in others, but industries differ widely in a number of other aspects of operation. There are differences in the rapidity with which firms adjust to changes in cost, in the rate at which new or improved products are introduced, in the degree to which available plant capacity is normally utilized, and in a number of other respects.

The economically significant features of the environment which contribute to differences in industrial behavior are called the *structure* of the market. Among the most important elements of market structure are:

1. The nature of the demand for the product, particularly its long- and short-run elasticity, and the direction and rate at which it tends to shift over time.

2. The nature of production costs in the industry, particularly the relationship of fixed to variable costs at normal operating rates.

3. The nature of the product, particularly the ease with which the output of one firm can be substituted for that of another.

4. The number and size distribution of firms in the industry, particularly whether output is concentrated in a few large firms or widely spread over many small firms.

5. The ease with which new firms can enter the industry to compete with those already there.

One of the important consequences of the market structure within which a given industry operates is the type of competition to which the firms in the industry are subject. Competitive conditions depend on 2 important factors: the degree to which products of various producers are differentiated, and the degree to which the total output of the industry is concentrated in the hands of a few large firms.

Since each of these aspects of competition is a matter of degree, the number of possible combinations of competitive conditions is infinite, but for analytical purposes we will limit ourselves to 3 broad categories. *Pure competition* is the condition in an industry in which the output of a homogeneous product is spread over a large number of producers, with no individual firm or small group of producers possessing a significant proportion of the total market. *Monopolistic competition* prevails in a market in which the production of a differentiated product is similarly spread over a large number of producers with no firm or group of firms controlling a significant share of the total market. *Oligopoly* (a term derived from Greek roots meaning "few sellers") describes conditions in the market for either a homogeneous or a differentiated product when a significant share of total output is concentrated in the hands of a few large firms. The extreme case of oligopoly, when the entire market is concentrated in a single seller, is called *monopoly*. The remainder of this chapter is devoted to a discussion of pure and monopolistic competition. Oligopoly and monopoly will be treated in Chapter 19.

PURE COMPETITION

Although the best examples of products produced under pure competition are agricultural commodities, many manufactured products like cotton textiles, leather, and work clothing are marketed under conditions that are close enough to pure competition to allow the theory to provide a useful approximation to industrial behavior.

The most significant aspect of pure competition is the inability of the individual producer to control his own prices. In fact, most commodities produced under pure competition are sold at auction markets, where the producer does not know what price he will get until after the product is sold. Powerless to set price, he can only estimate what the future price will be, and plan his output accordingly. Moreover, each producer is such a small part of the total industry that his own production plans

exert no perceptible influence on the ultimate price. When a vegetable grower expects high prices, he plans to increase his output, perhaps by planting more acreage or by using more fertilizer per acre planted. In working out the most profitable plan, he need not worry that his own action might so swell the total output of vegetables that the price will be held down contrary to his expectations. His share of the total output of vegetables is so small that whether he doubles production on the one hand, or goes out of business entirely on the other, will have no measurable influence on price. As far as he is concerned, the price depends on how much all the *other* farmers grow.

Production Planning
on the Basis of Expected Price

The planning of purely competitive producers is illustrated in Figure 1. The average, total, and marginal cost curves shown are typical of agriculture. Fixed cost—land, interest, taxes, equipment, the farmer's own labor, and so on—are high, but once the

FIGURE 1   MOST PROFITABLE OUTPUT PLAN
OF A PURE COMPETITOR

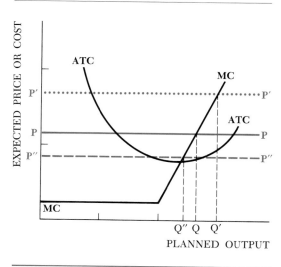

farm is in operation, marginal cost is low. Until all acreage is under cultivation, output can be expanded with little increase in cost beyond extra seed and materials. When all land is in use, however, further expansion of output can be obtained only by more intensive cultivation, heavier fertilizer application, and other expensive methods that cause marginal cost to rise as shown. The expected price is represented by the blue line P. Since it is unaffected by the production plan, the producer can expect to receive this same price for each extra ton of output. That is, as far as the pure competitor is concerned, price and marginal revenue are the same thing. It follows that the most profitable plan is to produce the output Q, at which marginal cost is brought into equality with marginal revenue—that is, with expected price.

If the expected price were higher, corresponding to the dotted line P', the producer would find it profitable to plan more expenditure on fertilizer and more intensive cultivation to raise the output to Q'. The marginal cost needed to increase the output to this level would have been unprofitable at lower expected prices. When expected price falls to P'', corresponding to the dashed blue line, extra yields are no longer expected to pay for the extra fertilizer and cultivation necessary to extract them, and the farmer finds it more profitable to plan to cultivate less intensively and to accept the smaller crop Q''.

Ratio of Price to Cost
Under Pure Competition

Although purely competitive products are usually sold on auction markets, if producers succeed in planning the most profitable output the resulting ratio of price to marginal cost follows the usual markup formula. That is, since the demand for the individual seller's output has infinite elasticity, the most profitable ratio of price to

marginal cost, $e/(e-1)$, becomes equal to unity, and the most profitable output plan results in price equal to marginal cost.

The theory of pure competition is a close approximation to the behavior of several manufacturing industries in which the production of a homogeneous product is widely spread over a large number of firms. Table 1 contains estimated markups for a number of such industries. All fall below the 1.45 median value discovered for manufacturing markups, and many are among the rare instances of markups below 1.2. A long history of the prices of cottonseed oil and of the resulting markups for cottonseed oil mills is given in Table 2. Over the past 60 years, yearly average prices have varied from a low of $.045 to a high of $.269 per pound, but most of these prices have represented markups to producers well below 1.15.

Other Aspects of Performance
of Purely Competitive Industry

The relationship of price to cost is only one aspect of industrial performance. Another

TABLE 1   ESTIMATED MARKUPS IN SELECTED HIGHLY COMPETITIVE INDUSTRIES

INDUSTRY	ESTIMATED MARKUP
Fresh beef	1.08
Grocers' bags	1.11
Wheat flour	1.12
Cottonseed oil	1.13
Wool Yarn	1.17
Cotton sheeting	1.18
Finished cattle hide	1.23
Dressed lumber	1.26
Work clothing	1.26
Wooden boxes	1.28
Men's shirts	1.29
Brooms	1.30
Men's work shoes	1.32

SOURCE: Estimated from data given in the *Census of Manufactures, 1963.*

TABLE 2   CALCULATED MARKUP AT
COTTONSEED OIL MILLS AND
MARKET PRICE OF
COTTONSEED OIL, 1899–1965
(money figures are millions of dollars)

YEAR	COST OF PRODUCTION WORKER WAGES	PURCHASED MATERIALS	TOTAL SALES	ESTIMATED MARKUP	MARKET PRICE (CENTS PER LB)
1899	3.1	45.2	$ 58.7	1.22	n.a.
1904	4.8	80.0	96.4	1.14	n.a.
1909	5.8	119.8	147.9	1.18	10.8
1914	8.5	180.9	212.1	1.10	6.6
1919	20.6	495.2	581.2	1.12	23.9
1921	12.3	194.9	21.72	1.05	7.9
1923	7.9	197.5	226.4	1.10	11.3
1925	11.4	244.3	295.7	1.15	10.8
1927	14.3	220.0	276.3	1.18	9.7
1929	11.2	249.0	298.4	1.14	9.7
1931	8.3	147.2	181.3	1.17	6.0
1933	5.4	78.2	104.2	1.25	4.5
1935	5.9	160.6	187.9	1.13	10.4
1937	8.6	195.7	242.0	1.18	9.2
1939	8.9	138.8	171.5	1.16	6.6
1947	22.6	413.5	518.1	1.19	26.9
1949	27.8	378.1	463.0	1.14	18.1
1950	28.7	361.0	471.4	1.21	22.3
1951	27.5	460.3	575.8	1.18	26.4
1952	30.0	485.4	580.5	1.19	19.5
1953	30.8	534.3	655.6	1.12	21.4
1954	29.8	487.7	592.3	1.14	21.0
1955	24.4	375.0	456.4	1.14	20.1
1956	25.4	380.3	472.4	1.16	20.5
1957	24.1	396.5	489.4	1.16	19.8
1958	20.0	348.6	420.6	1.14	19.4
1959	22.1	360.7	429.3	1.12	15.1
1960	21.8	360.4	443.3	1.15	15.1
1961	22.4	398.8	478.4	1.18	18.6
1962	23.5	415.2	511.7	1.17	16.7
1963	26.0	464.7	555.2	1.13	15.3
1964	26.5	434.5	526.6	1.15	13.7
1965	25.7	460.6	549.4	1.13	14.9

SOURCE: Data for markups from *Census of Manufactures, 1963.* Later years from *Compendium of Manufacturing Production Statistics for the United States, 1947–1965.* Georgetown Economic Data Library, 1967. Cottonseed oil prices are for prime summer yellow oil, New York tank car price, from U.S. Department of Commerce, *Business Statistics,* 1967 and earlier issues.

important aspect is how economically the industry applies the resources at its disposal. Does competition in the industry force costs to a minimum? Or does it encourage wasteful methods and higher costs than necessary? How does the industry respond to shifts in consumer desires? Can facilities expand when consumers want increased production? Does the industry tend to encourage the development and application of cost-reducing techniques? Does the industry tend to develop and bring out new or improved products?

In some of these respects the behavior of purely competitive industry leaves much to be desired, but in several others it is something of an economic ideal. Its long-run dynamics act to force each firm to operate at its most efficient rate. Powerful forces act to compel it to reallocate resources in response to shifts in consumer demand, and to adopt cost-saving technology as fast as it appears.

The Dynamics of Adjustment Under Pure Competition   When the price of a purely competitive product is above the minimum average total cost of production that would be attained by the most efficient operating rates, 2 things can be observed. In the first place, firms in the industry find it profitable to operate at rates beyond capacity, for which average total costs are higher. Secondly, despite these higher costs, firms in the industry enjoy profits in excess of the normal minimum needed to keep them in business. The situation is depicted in Figure 2. The left side of the figure shows conditions in the auction market. As shown by the black lines, when a total of Q tons is delivered to market, demand DD establishes the price at P. The right side of the figure represents the condition of a typical firm in the industry.[1] As shown by the ATC

[1] Note that the vertical price scale is the same on both sides of the figure, but the quantity scales are different because of the small size of the firm compared to the industry.

FIGURE 2 LONG-RUN EXPANSION OF A PURELY COMPETITIVE INDUSTRY

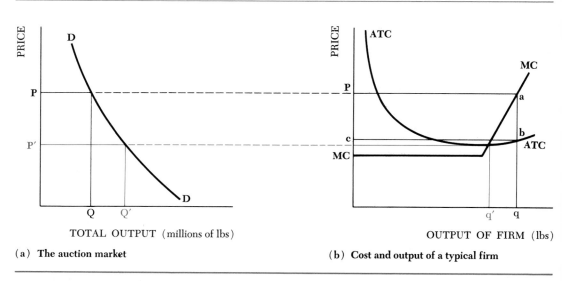

(a) **The auction market**

(b) **Cost and output of a typical firm**

line, the minimum average total cost would be attained at the operating rate q', but since the market price P is higher than this minimum, the most profitable production plan for the firm is the operating rate q that just brings marginal cost up to the expected auction price. Under these circumstances, the actual average total cost would be higher than minimum, as shown, and the firm would earn excess profits equal to the area of the rectangle $abcP$.

Unless there are barriers to the entry of new capital into the industry, this situation cannot persist. The extra profit to be gained acts as a powerful attraction to new firms to enter the industry and encourages those already there to invest in expanded facilities. As capacity expands, increased output depresses market prices. Falling prices induce individual firms to reduce operating rates, but as long as profits remain above normal, the expansion of capacity continues. When price has been driven down to P', the lowest possible break-even point, each firm in the industry is operating at its most efficient rate, all capacity is fully utilized, and excess profits

have been eliminated. With the disappearance of excess profits, the expansion of capacity is ended.

Adjustment of Capacity to Shifts in Demand An important aspect of the long-run dynamics of pure competition is the way industrial capacity is adjusted to the shifting desires of consumers. The process is illustrated in Figure 3, which shows the position of a purely competitive industry that has completed its long-run adjustment to demand DD. As shown by the black lines, the total quantity Q is delivered to market to bring the price P, just enough to enable each firm to break even at its most efficient operating rate. Now, when buyers increase their demand to $D'D'$, industrial capacity is adequate to meet only part of the additional output desired. The increase of price to P' makes it profitable for firms already in the industry to increase their operating rates from q to q', but the resulting excess profits attract additional investment to the industry and set in motion the long-run adjustment process.

As new firms enter the industry and old

FIGURE 3   COMPETITIVE RESPONSE TO A RISE IN DEMAND

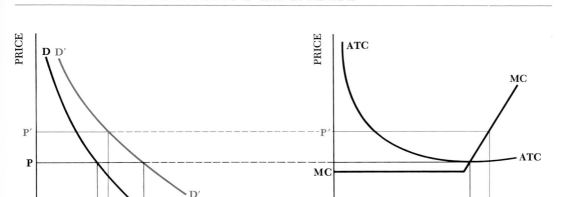

(a) The auction market   (b) Cost and output of a typical firm

firms expand, growing output brings prices down and lowers operating rates to more economical levels. Expansion continues until enough new capacity has been added to the industry to expand total output to Q''. This reduces price back to P and removes excess profits, bringing the expansion to an end. Enough capacity has been created to yield the output Q'' while permitting all firms to operate at their most economical rate.

Response to a reduction in demand acts in just the reverse manner. As consumers reduce their demand for the product, market prices fall. Firms in the industry are compelled to operate below the most economical rates, and suffer losses which set in motion the dynamics of contraction. The poor profit prospects keep other firms out of the industry, while losses ultimately induce some of those present to leave. When enough producers have been driven out of the industry to permit those remaining to operate efficiently, normal profits are restored, and the contraction is brought to an end.

Response to New Production Methods Under Pure Competition Competition provides a powerful incentive for the adoption of cost-saving techniques as fast as they become available. The first firms to introduce the new methods can continue to sell at the old price, but can produce at the new lower costs. The resulting profits attract other producers to the new lower-cost technique, and bring new firms into the industry. As the expanding output begins to force prices down, firms that lag behind the rest of the industry are faced with losses, and unless they shift over to the cheaper method, they are ultimately forced out of business. The process is illustrated schematically in Figure 4. Initially the industry is delivering a total output Q to market, bringing a price P at which producers just manage to break even. When some firms introduce new methods, lowering their costs to ATC' as shown by the blue line, they also increase their operating rates to q'. As long as there are only a few such firms, market price declines only slightly to P', and the innovating firms make high

FIGURE 4   COMPETITIVE RESPONSE TO TECHNICAL CHANGE

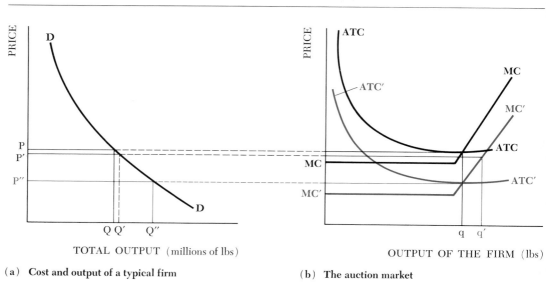

(a)   **Cost and output of a typical firm**   (b)   **The auction market**

profit. As more firms follow suit, expanded production drives prices down until, at *P″*, the low-cost firms can just break even at capacity operation. Any high-cost firms still in the industry are operating at a loss and will ultimately be forced out of business.

Although pure competition is effective in applying pressure to producers to introduce new methods as fast as they appear, it provides little incentive for individual producers to invest in research and development of technical improvements of their own. Not only is the individual firm too small to command the resources necessary for effective research, but the rapidity with which any initial advantage is wiped out by imitation greatly reduces the potential profit to the discoverer. A similar limitation is imposed by the absence of product differentiation. When products of different producers are indistinguishable, there is little incentive for product improvement. It is noteworthy that most agricultural improvements in both products and production methods have resulted from research done in colleges, universities, and agricul-

tural experiment stations, rather than on individual farms.

MONOPOLISTIC COMPETITION

Because of the pejorative overtones of the word "monopoly," the term "monopolistic competition" is unfortunate. Actually, the most important difference between pure and monopolistic competition is the addition of competition in product quality as an important aspect of industrial behavior. The "monopolistic" aspect of monopolistic competition arises from the fact that no producer of typewriters, breakfast cereal, cola drinks, or any other differentiated product can quite duplicate the design, performance, flavor, or appearance of any other. Each producer has, to that extent, a "monopoly" over his own brand. On the other hand, when products of different producers satisfy identical consumer needs, they are clearly in direct competition with each other. The term "monopolistic competition" is intended to represent this competition among producers of different brands or types of goods, each of which represents a private "monopoly" to its own producer.

Ratio of Price to Cost
Under Monopolistic Competition

There is no hard fixed line to divide monopolistic from pure competition. The ease with which consumers switch between the products of different firms is a matter of degree, and monopolistic competition varies from an extreme in which each firm's product is almost unique (a situation more "monopolistic" than "competitive," so to speak) to one in which products are almost literally homogeneous. Unlike pure competitors, however, producers of differentiated products almost invariably set their own prices, and their pricing behavior closely follows the pricing theory developed in the preceding chapter. The most profitable price represents a markup over marginal cost whose magnitude, $e/(e-1)$, depends on the elasticity of demand. In industries with only slight product differentiation, buyers switch freely from firm to firm, giving high elasticity to the demand for the products of any particular producer and keeping markups low. In industries with highly differentiated products, quality differences tend to reduce the disposition of buyers to switch brands in response to price changes. The demands for the output of individual firms have low elasticity, and profitable markups are correspondingly high.

Estimated markups for selected industries with highly differentiated products are compared with those of industries with more homogeneous products in Table 3. Markups on the more highly differentiated products are well above the median value found for all manufacturing, and a few are among the rare cases that exceed 2.5.

TABLE 3   RELATIONSHIP OF MANUFACTURING MARKUP TO HOMOGENEITY OF PRODUCT

	ESTIMATED MARKUP
RELATIVELY HOMOGENEOUS PRODUCTS	
Meat packing	1.09
Flour mills	1.17
Wool yarn mills	1.20
Work clothing	1.25
Leather gloves	1.25
Corrugated shipping containers	1.27
Leather tanning and finishing	1.27
Sawmills and planing mills	1.28
Wooden boxes	1.28
Metal foil and leaf	1.28
Cotton weaving mills	1.32
HIGHLY DIFFERENTIATED PRODUCTS	
Pharmaceutical preparations	3.37
Toilet preparations	2.75
Periodicals	2.41
Book publishing and printing	2.41
Newspapers	2.10
Cereal preparations	1.97
Optical instruments	1.90
Bottled soft drinks	1.89
Greeting cards	1.86
Wallpaper	1.75
Malt liquors	1.73
Metal office furniture	1.67

SOURCE: Calculated from data in U.S. Bureau of the Census, *Annual Survey of Manufactures, 1965.*

The Dynamics of Adjustment
Under Monopolistic Competition

Except for the modifications required to allow for product differentiation, the long-run dynamics of price, cost, and output in monopolistic competition are similar to those in a purely competitive industry. When only a few firms are producing a highly popular product, their abnormally high profits tend to attract new firms and additional investment. Although new firms cannot duplicate exactly the products of the old, the appearance of new substitutes on the market tends to draw customers away from the older firms and probably also raises the elasticity of demand for their products.

The consequences are represented in Figure 5. We first find a typical firm with demand *DD*, selling output *Q* at price *P* and enjoying high profits. As new firms are attracted into the industry and put substitutes on the market, they deprive the old firm of some of its customers. This is represented by a reduction of the demand for the old firm's products and an increase in its elasticity. New firms continue to enter the industry until the typical firm finds its demand has fallen to a level like *D'D'*, and the best it can do is just break even by selling output *Q'* at price *P'*. The disappear-

ance of excess profits puts an end to the expansion.

Product Differentiation and Excess Capacity

As Figure 5 also illustrates, one of the important aspects of the behavior of monopolistically competitive industries is that in the long run producers tend to break even at operating rates below capacity. This tendency means that monopolistic competition is characterized by a strong tendency to excess capacity that is greatest in industries with the most highly differentiated products.

As illustrated in Figure 6, when products are highly differentiated and demands

FIGURE 5   LONG-RUN EXPANSION UNDER MONOPOLISTIC COMPETITION

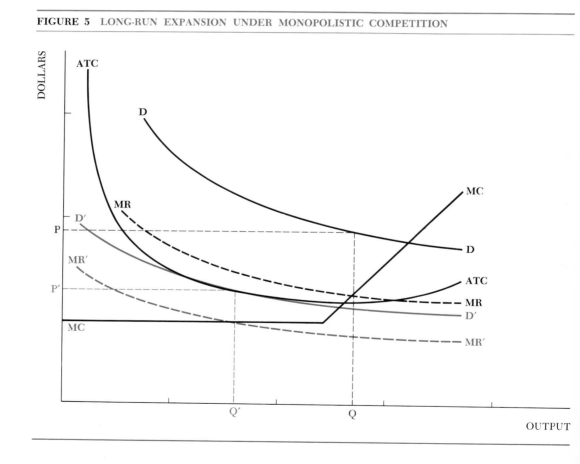

FIGURE 6 BREAK-EVEN POINT DEPENDS ON
DEMAND ELASTICITY

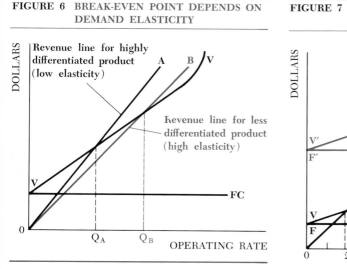

FIGURE 7 INFLUENCE OF FIXED COST ON
BREAK-EVEN POINT

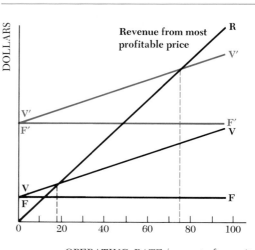

OPERATING RATE (percent of capacity)

are less elastic, the steep black revenue line *OA* (corresponding to the higher price) permits breaking even at output *QA*, well below capacity. In the long run this permits the desired total output of the industry to be divided among more firms, each operating at only a fraction of its most economical rate. When demands are more elastic, lower markups and lower prices involve the less steep blue revenue line *OB* that leads to higher break-even points. In the long run, this forces firms to break even at outputs closer to capacity, and the desired output of the industry is supplied by fewer firms each with less excess capacity.

Excess Capacity and Fixed Cost Given demand elasticities, a second important determinant of the amount of excess capacity is the ratio of fixed to total cost. When the total cost of operating at capacity consists mostly of variable cost as shown by the black line *VV* in Figure 7, the break-even point tends to occur at a lower operating rate than it does when fixed cost is a greater proportion of total as shown by the blue line *V'V'*.[2]

[2] Notice that the 2 firms depicted in the figure have equal marginal costs—the lines *VV* and *V'V'* are parallel. Moreover, the elasticity of demand is

The composition of cost varies widely among industries. Since wholesale and retail firms require little in the way of machinery or production facilities, the greatest part of their total cost is the invoice cost of goods sold. In wholesale operations, fixed costs represent warehouse space with minimum customer facilities. At normal operating rates only about 15 percent of total wholesaling costs are fixed costs. Retail firms must put up a better front. Their need for more careful merchandise display, more expensive fixtures, and more space per item sold all add to fixed costs, bringing them up to an average of about 20 percent of total cost.

There is wide variation among firms in different retail lines. Fixed costs of grocery stores amount to only about 12 percent of total. Among clothing stores fixed costs are about 25 percent, and in furniture stores they are close to 30 percent of total costs. Fixed costs of restaurants and other eating places amount to almost 40 percent of total cost. This high percentage is partly because

the same for both firms, thus they are charging equal prices—they have the same revenue line (*R*).

of the furniture and fixtures needed for restaurant operation, but a more important reason is the heavy concentration of business at particular hours. A successful restaurant must have sufficient capacity to meet peak mealtime demand with minimum waiting and customer inconvenience. This leaves expensive facilities idle most of the time, placing a correspondingly higher burden of fixed cost on output.

Fixed costs of manufacturing firms average about 25 percent of total cost, varying from about 15 percent in food processing—where raw materials, containers, and labor are important cost elements—to 35 percent or more in chemical production involving heavy investments in automatic equipment. In industries like railroads and public utilities with lines, stations, switching facilities, and other extensive plant, fixed costs rise to about 60 percent of total at normal operating rates. Break-even charts of firms in selected industries are shown in Figure 8.

Probably the most obvious everyday example of excess capacity is found in gasoline retailing. In common with other retail activity, the invoice cost of the goods sold—a variable cost—is the most important part of total cost. Moreover, gasoline is a highly differentiated product, although the differentiation is probably less a matter of quality and performance than of advertising and other merchandising techniques. Oil companies discourage consumers from substituting among brands not only by extensive advertising campaigns, but possibly more by issuing credit cards good only at their own stations, by encouraging consumers to collect trading stamps, and in recent years, by instituting "games" for customers to "play" in an effort to win prizes. The result of the low fixed cost and the high product differentiation is the familiar sight of several filling stations in an area—often on the same corner—serving a flow of customers that could be handled by any one of them alone.

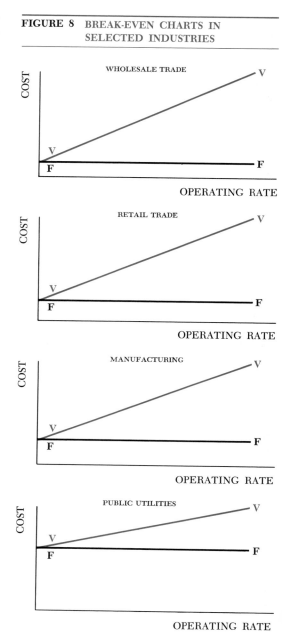

FIGURE 8   BREAK-EVEN CHARTS IN SELECTED INDUSTRIES

Excess Capacity and Price   The existence of excess capacity makes the cost, and hence the long-run price, of differentiated products higher than they might otherwise be, but great care must be exercised in evaluating this fact. In the first place, the extra cost is the normal price consumers must pay for variety of style, quality, performance, or service. If there were only one kind of refrigerator, automobile, electric iron, or typewriter, that kind could be produced more cheaply per unit than the present wide variety, but the person who wanted something a little different would be out of luck. Product differentiation is a market response to the buyer's desire for choice, and when buyers are more sensitive to differences in the product than they are to differences in price, the market responds by providing a greater assortment spread among more establishments, even if each firm ends up operating at higher cost.

The cost of product differentiation, moreover, depends on the size of fixed costs. If fixed cost is a small proportion of total, the difference in average total cost between operating at capacity and at lower rates is small, and the price of variety is correspondingly low. When fixed cost bulks large in the total, operation at rates much below capacity involves correspondingly severe cost penalties, and consumers are likely to opt for fewer choices spread among fewer firms, each operating close to its optimum rate.

Monopolistic Competition and Product Improvement

More important than the alternatives available to buyers at any given time is the dynamic pressure on each firm to improve its products. Profits wiped out by the normal long-run encroachment of substitutes can be regained by improving the product to further differentiate it from those of other firms. A producer who can offer a better product or service can capture the sales volume that will form the difference between making substantial profits and breaking even. In addition, successful product

improvement tends to lower the elasticity of demand for the innovator's goods, raising the most profitable markup he is permitted to take.

The competition in product quality is an extra dimension supplied by monopolistic competition that is absent when firms produce only homogeneous products, and as with other kinds of competition, the attractiveness of the possible profit to be made from a successful product improvement is coupled with the alternative prospect of losses to firms whose products do not improve as rapidly as others in the industry. A producer who fails to improve his product is not left as he is. The additional sales gained by firms making successful product improvements may come partly by attracting new users to the product, but in the nature of things they come mostly from customers lured from the firms lagging behind.

The competitive struggle for high volume at low cost is the economic force responsible for the continual product innovation and improvement that is one of the most striking features of modern economic life. It is this force more than anything else that has brought the country from a horse-and-buggy society into the space age, with all that implies, during the lifetime of many people still alive.

The important point here is not that such product development occurs—it can hardly be overlooked—but that it occurs as the result of the normal drive of producers of differentiated products to stay in business, and if possible, to operate at a profit. The economics of product improvement are illustrated in the 3 parts of Figure 9. In part (a), a firm that has been just breaking even with demand DD introduces a new improved product, increasing its demand to $D'D'$ and generating profits, as shown.[3]

[3] Product improvements often, but not always, involve higher costs, a fact that has been ignored here to simplify the analysis.

FIGURE 9 THE DYNAMICS OF PRODUCT
IMPROVEMENT

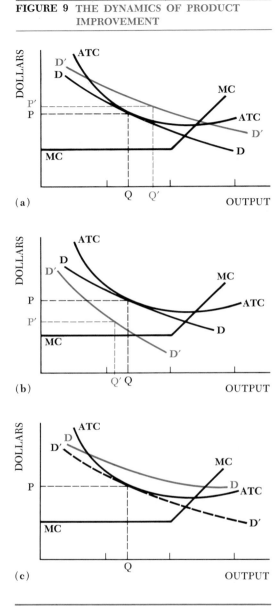

(a)

(b)

(c)

As the innovation meets with customer approval, other firms imitate it to capture extra profit for themselves. Expanding demand for the improved product, however, is partly composed of customers diverted from firms still producing the old type of item. Their loss of customers is represented by the decline in demand for their products

from *DD* to *D'D'* in part (b) of the figure. As the losses force widespread adoption of the new product by other firms in the industry, customers are recaptured from the initiating firms whose demands decline from *DD* to *D'D'*, eliminating extra profits as shown in part (c). In the long run, the profits that were the incentive for and the immediate result of the product improvement tend to be wiped out as the idea is generally adopted, but the improvement itself remains as a permanent feature of the product.

Competition and Advertising

Advertising plays a double role in monopolistic competition. In the first place, before product improvement or price reduction can stimulate sales, people have to learn about it. One important function of advertising is, thus, to provide potential buyers with information about products and their uses, their prices, where they can be bought, and other facts relevant to their purchase.

Informative advertising of this kind is a necessary part of getting the product into the hands of the consumer, and any additional cost it may involve is as much a part of the cost of the final product as shipping charges or retailing margins. On the other hand, sales volume can be stimulated by attracting buyers even in the absence of any special merit in the product. Sometimes this is done by advertising which is worded and presented to give the impression of merit where none exists; for example, by combining a strong invitation to purchase with an elaborate description of unique but irrelevant features of the product. At other times it is done by showing the product being used by people who are admired, or under circumstances that are desired by the potential buyer.

The effects of competitive advertising is shown in the average cost charts of Figure

10. With minimal advertising consistent with consumer information, a typical firm is just breaking even with demand *DD*. An increase in its advertising budget can be expected to accomplish several things. By adding to fixed cost, it raises average total cost. In addition, however, it increases the demand for the firm's product, and, by increasing its differentiation from competing products, decreases its elasticity, permitting the firm a larger markup.

If the process ended here, advertising outlays would be immensely profitable, but part (b) shows the customers gained by the advertising firm are attracted from other producers, and when competitors increase their own advertising budgets in self-defense, the initial gain from advertising is offset. In the long run the industry approaches position (c) in which profits are again held to the normal return on investment. Although advertising outlays are largely mutually offsetting, no firm can reduce its own budget without serious risk of losing out on sales.[4] The consumer is left with no better product than before, but with higher costs and higher prices.

FIGURE 10   THE DYNAMICS OF COMPETITIVE ADVERTISING

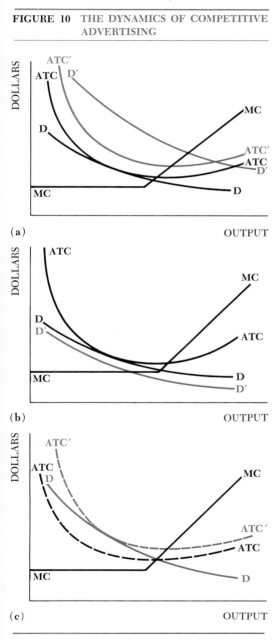

(a)

(b)

(c)

PUBLIC POLICY TO INCREASE THE EFFECTIVENESS OF COMPETITION

Maintaining Fair and Honest Practices

If competition is to be an effective regulator of industrial behavior, it is necessary that firms not only compete, but compete in the right way. Unless there are rules that forbid lying, cheating, and other unethical practices, competition can drag everybody down to the lowest level of behavior. Instead of the service the firm renders, the criterion of success can become which firm can get away with the most underhanded dealing. To increase the effectiveness of competition, the consumer must be protected from adulterated food and drugs and

[4] It has been suggested that the alacrity with which cigarette manufacturers agreed in 1969 to drop all television advertising by 1971 was partly because they realized that their expensive advertising campaigns were merely canceling each other out.

from other products damaging to his health and safety. He must also be assured that labels are honest and convey the information he needs for intelligent buying, that advertising claims are reasonably accurate, that goods are what they claim to be, and that he will get what he pays for.

At the most elementary level this means protecting buyers against short weight or deficient measure. Governments have a long-standing tradition of establishing standards of weight and measure and enforcing their honest application. Beyond this, it is necessary to enforce minimum standards of quality and to prevent the adulteration of food, use of unsafe ingredients, and like practices. In the United States, standards of sanitation in food preparation are enforced by local inspection, while meat and poultry in interstate commerce are federally inspected.

Drugs, cosmetics, chemical food additives, pesticides, and similar products must be approved as safe by the U.S. Food and Drug Administration (FDA) before they can be marketed. The FDA is also authorized to establish minimum standards of quality and condition for canned goods.

A kindred public policy is aimed at forcing sellers to label goods so that would-be buyers receive the information they need to make reasonable purchases. Goods must be properly branded, and labels and advertising must disclose all relevant information about the contents or nature of the product. The buyer must be warned of any danger or ill effects that might follow from use, and he should not be misled in any material respect. Federal legislation for this purpose began with the Food and Drug Act of 1906, which forbade misbranding of foods and drugs in interstate commerce. The law was later strengthened and widely extended to other types of goods by a series of acts. The Wool Products Labeling Act of 1939 requires that woolens bear a label specifying the percentage of new and re-used wool and other fibers in the material. With the growing importance of synthetics, a similar requirement was extended to other natural and artificial fibers by the Textile Fiber Products Identification Act of 1958, and a similar law applies to fur goods. Certain information about the price of a new automobile must be pasted on the car under the Automobile Information Disclosure Act passed the same year. Still more recently, cigarette manufacturers have been required to specify on the label that smoking may be injurious to health.

More general protection against misrepresentation, false advertising, and other deceptive practices was provided in the Federal Trade Commission Act of 1914, which outlawed "unfair methods of competition" and established the Federal Trade Commission (FTC) to oversee the enforcement of its provisions. As amended by the Wheeler-Lea Act of 1936, the law forbids false advertising claims, misbranding, mislabeling, and a wide range of deceptive practices. Offenses under the Act include "passing off" one good as another (for example, selling mahogany veneer furniture as solid mahogany), misrepresenting the geographical origin of goods (selling "French" wine made in California), falsely claiming or implying that goods have been examined and endorsed by an authoritative agency (selling a dictionary or reference book "approved" by the National Education Association when it has given no special endorsement), misrepresenting the performance or results of a product (selling a useless battery additive under the claim that it will enhance performance or prolong the life of the battery), and misrepresenting the prices of goods (suggesting that a special discount is being allowed when, in fact, the goods are being sold at the regular price).

The staff of the Federal Trade Commission maintains continual surveillance over newspaper and magazine advertising, and monitors radio and television commercials. The FTC can prosecute violators for misleading advertising claims, although cases rarely go to court when the offending firm agrees to desist from the questionable practice or claim.

Public Policy To Limit Competition

There are a few industries in which unbridled competition results in severe human suffering, waste of scarce resources, or other serious social problems. In these cases public policy is directed toward preventing too much competition. Unlimited competitive extraction of petroleum and natural gas is an extremely wasteful process. An oil pool normally underlies a wide area. If landowners had unrestricted rights to drill and extract oil from the same limited pool, the man who could draw it out fastest would get the biggest share. Left to itself, the competitive scramble would quickly empty the well regardless of present demand, leaving nothing for the future. In addition, unless oil fields are carefully and systematically exploited, declining well pressures leave significant quantities of oil that can be pumped only by expensive methods, or that are completely uncapturable.

The only rational way to exploit oil or natural gas deposits is to provide overall control of the number, type, and location of wells that can be drilled and the rates at which they can be operated. In the United States, oil extraction is supervised by state regulatory commissions, among which are the Texas Railroad Commission, the California Division of Oil and Gas, the Louisiana Commissioner of Conservation, and the Corporation Commission of Oklahoma. These commissions control such matters as the spacing of wells, the method of drilling, and the method and rate of extraction. If many different owners have claims to the area in which a single well is to be drilled, they may be compelled to pool their interests.

The work of the state commissions in allocating production is coordinated by the U.S. Bureau of Mines, which makes monthly forecasts of the demand for oil products, determines a recommended total output for the month, and allocates this production to the individual states. Although these recommendations have no legal status, the federal government can prevent interstate shipment of oil in excess of state quotas, and in practice, all state commissions follow the allocation as recommended, and assign appropriate shares to the producers within their states.

Similar need to control competition is found in whaling and in ocean and freshwater fishing. Agricultural policy, with its price supports and acreage allotments, and labor law, guaranteeing to workers the right to organize and bargain collectively in unions of their own choosing, represent other aspects of this problem that we will examine at a later point.

Public Policy To Enforce Competition

The most serious policy problem, however, is neither that competition takes antisocial forms nor that it sometimes leads to excesses. Quite the contrary, in many industries it is easy for business firms to suppress effective competition and behave in ways better suited to their own advantage than to the service of the consumer. The biggest problem of public policy is not to curb competition, but to foster it. Effective competition is particularly difficult to maintain in oligopolistic industries in which production is heavily concentrated in the hands of a small number of firms, and this is the problem to which we will turn in the next chapter.

SUMMARY

The behavior of each business firm is limited by what its competitors are doing. Thus firms do not function in isolation, but as members of an *industry* consisting of businesses whose products are close substitutes for one another. Since "substitution" is a matter of degree, industrial boundaries are often arbitrary. The *Standard Industrial Classification* employed by the U.S. Census Bureau classifies establishments into industries of several different levels, partly on the basis of how readily products of different establishments can be substituted.

The performance of an industry depends on the *market structure* within which it operates. The most important consequence of market structure is the type of competition in the industry, of which 3 important types are distinguished: *Pure competition* occurs in industries in which the production of *homogeneous products* is widely spread over a large number of small producers with no firm or small group of firms producing a significant share of total output. *Monopolistic competition* occurs when the production of a *differentiated product* is similarly spread over a number of small producers. *Oligopoly*, the subject of the next chapter, is the condition in an industry in which a significant share of total output is concentrated in the hands of a few firms.

In many respects, pure competition is something of an economic ideal. Firms cannot set their own prices, but must plan production on the basis of expected prices. Under these circumstances, price and marginal revenue are identical, and the ratio of the most profitable price to marginal cost is unity. When consumer demand rises, pure competitors find it profitable to operate beyond the normal capacity of their plants and reap extra profits. The profit attracts new capital to the industry, however, and in the long run purely competitive firms are forced to operate near their most economical rate of output. Pure competitors are also forced to adopt cost-saving methods as they appear. On the other hand, pure competition offers little consumer choice, and provides little incentive for firms to improve products.

Monopolistic competition makes product quality an added dimension of competition. Since differentiated products are imperfect substitutes for each other, however, demand for each firm's product is less elastic than under pure competition, and the most profitable ratio of price to marginal cost tends to be higher. The dynamics of adjustment of a monopolistically competitive industry are similar to those of pure competition, except that the industry tends to generate excess capacity. The amount of excess capacity depends on how highly products are differentiated, and on the level of fixed compared to variable costs. Excess capacity means higher costs, but to some extent the added cost is merely the price of choice. Monopolistic competition provides a powerful incentive for firms to improve their products and to differentiate them from those of other firms by packaging, appearance, and advertising.

To prevent competition from degenerating to the lowest common denominator of behavior, government policy is directed toward maintaining honest and fair competitive practices. An effort is made to see that the prospective buyer is provided with the information he needs for intelligent decisions, and that he is provided with some assurance that products will perform as they are supposed to. There can also be "too much" competition, and certain public policies are designed to confine competitive behavior to socially useful limits. The most serious policy problem, however, is to maintain the effectiveness of competition, and to this problem we turn next.

CHAPTER 19

Industrial Concentration and Oligopoly

CONCENTRATION OF PRODUCTION

About half of U.S. manufacturing sales are made by industries in which the 4 largest firms produce 30 percent or more of the total output, and more than 10 percent of all sales involve industries in which the 4 largest firms are responsible for more than 70 percent of production. High industrial concentration creates a special situation known as *oligopoly*. Firms in an oligopolistic industry can no longer view the competitive environment as outside their own control, but must recognize that it is the result of their own actions. The purely competitive behavior in which each firm acts for itself regardless of the effect on others is replaced by the recognition that when each firm attempts to undersell the others, all make lower profits.

Measuring Concentration

Like product differentiation, concentration is a matter of degree, varying smoothly from practically 0 in the highly competitive industries, to 100 percent in a monopoly. Concentration of production can be measured in many ways, but one of the most useful is by the *4-firm concentration ratio*. This ratio is the percentage of total industry shipments that are made by establishments belonging to the 4 largest firms producing in the industry. As part of the Census of Manufactures, 4-firm concentration ratios are regularly compiled for 4-digit manufacturing industries. For example, the Census of Manufactures of 1963 reported that the $2,251,132,000 annual sales of the U.S. shoe industry were distributed among 785 different shoe companies. When all the firms were ranked in order of total sales

TABLE 1   DISTRIBUTION OF MANUFACTURING SALES BY 4-FIRM CONCENTRATION RATIOS

	INDUSTRY SALES		
CONCENTRATION RATIO	NUMBER OF INDUSTRIES	BILLIONS OF DOLLARS	PERCENT OF TOTAL
Under 20 percent	84	$ 81.7	22.3
20–29.9	73	92.6	25.2
30–39.9	63	59.6	16.3
40–49.9	43	31.8	8.7
50–59.9	37	43.2	11.8
60–69.9	27	17.9	4.9
70–79.9	20	27.1	7.4
80–89.9	9	5.9	1.6
90 percent or more	13	6.5	1.8
Total	369	$366.3	100.0

SOURCE: Concentration ratios from *Census of Manufactures, 1963.* Sales from *Survey of Manufactures,* 1965. In compiling the table, "catch-all" industries (for example, "Textile goods, not elsewhere classified") have been omitted as irrelevant.

FIGURE 1   DISTRIBUTION OF U.S. MANUFACTURING SALES BY 4-FIRM CONCENTRATION RATIO

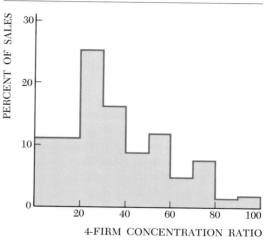

SOURCE: Table 1.

volume, it was found that the value of shoes sold by the 4 largest firms totaled about $562 million, or 25 percent of the sales of the entire industry. This was reported as a 4-firm concentration ratio of 25 percent.

Distribution of Concentration Ratios

The distribution of 4-firm concentration ratios as estimated from the Census of Manufactures of 1963 is shown in Table 1 and Figure 1. The median ratio was about 31.5 percent. That is, about half of total U.S. manufacturing sales were from industries with 4-firm concentration ratios below 31.5 percent, and the other half were from industries in which ratios were 31.5 or higher. Concentration ratios below 20 were common (over 22 percent of total manufacturing sales) but ratios above 70 were relatively rare (10 percent), and only 3.4 percent were 80 or over. The lowest ratios were found in the industries manufacturing wood partitions and ready-mixed concrete, in each of which the 4 largest firms shipped only 4 percent of the industrial total. The

highest ratios were found in industries manufacturing locomotives and parts (97 percent), flat glass (94 percent), and non-cellulosic organic fiber, which is chiefly nylon (94 percent). Exact information for some of the most concentrated industries is unavailable, however, presumably because publication of the 4-firm ratio would enable an interested party to figure out something about the operations of one of the firms. This is apparently the situation in several industries, among them safes and vaults, aircraft propellers, and primary aluminum.

Limitations to Concentration Ratios

Since the industrial boundaries established by the Census represent compromises among a number of conflicting purposes, concentration ratios derived from Census data must be evaluated with care. This is particularly true when establishments producing the same product are assigned to different industries on the basis of the technology employed. Establishments producing cane sugar are in one industry (Cane sugar refining, SIC number 2062), while those producing beet sugar are in another (Beet sugar refining, SIC number 2063). Since refined sugar is virtually homogeneous regardless of source, the 4-firm concentration ratio of either industry alone may give a false impression of the degree of concentration. A similar problem arises when multiproduct establishments using similar technology to produce a range of products are placed in different industries on the basis of which product happens to predominate in their sales. Establishments assigned to an industry because a particular product predominates in their own production may actually produce less of that specific product than those assigned to other industries. For example, only 30 percent of all steel nails and spikes are produced in the establishments that make up the "steel wire drawing and nails and spikes" industry (3315). The great bulk of them are manufactured as secondary products of establishments in "the steel works and rolling mills" industry (3312). Only 31 percent of all men's and boys' underwear is made in the "men's and boys' underwear" industry (2322), the bulk being manufactured by "knitting mills." Similarly, establishments in the industries named for the products produce only 33 percent of all lubricating oil and greases, and only 37 percent of all steel pipe and tube.

Other Census industries are too broadly defined to yield a precise estimate of the degree of concentration. For example, Census concentration ratios on the basis of total nationwide sales are a poor representation of conditions in industries like newspaper publishing in which establishments sell in essentially local markets, with minimum competition between those in different localities.

Concentration and Estimated Markups

Despite the imperfections in Census concentration ratios, there is a striking ten-

dency for industries with the highest concentration ratios to exhibit the highest estimated markups. Table 2 and Figure 2 compare the distribution of estimated markups for all 4-digit industries with 4-firm concentration ratios below 20 percent with that of industries with ratios of 80 percent or more. The average markup in the least concentrated group was 1.48. Less than 10 percent of all shipments were made by industries with markups of 1.75 or higher, and no industries were found with markups as high as 2.5. In contrast, the average markup among the most concentrated industries was 1.77. Of all shipments, 63 percent came from industries in which the estimated markup was 1.75 or more, and 11 percent of all shipments were characterized by markups of 2.5 or above.

Table 3 contains individual comparisons of the markups of the 26 industries with the lowest 4-firm concentration ratios (11 percent or below) with those of the 22 industries with the highest concentration (80

TABLE 2　COMPARISON OF MARKUPS IN INDUSTRIES WITH LOW CONCENTRATION WITH THOSE IN INDUSTRIES HAVING HIGH CONCENTRATION

| | SALES OF INDUSTRIES WITH 4-FIRM CONCENTRATION OF: | | | |
| | BELOW 20% | | 80% OR OVER | |
MARKUP	BILLIONS OF DOLLARS	PERCENT	BILLIONS OF DOLLARS	PERCENT
Under 1.20	$ 3.23	4.0	$0.02	0.2
1.20–1.29	11.34	13.9	0.11	0.8
1.30–1.39	14.55	17.9	0.61	4.9
1.40–1.49	23.74	28.2	0.67	5.4
1.50–1.74	20.76	25.5	3.27	26.3
1.75–1.99	3.28	4.0	5.92	47.7
2.00–2.49	4.48	5.5	0.42	3.4
2.5 or over	—	—	1.40	11.3
Total	$81.38	100.0	$12.42	100.0
Average Markup	1.48		1.77	

SOURCE: Compiled from data in the *Census of Manufactures, 1963.*

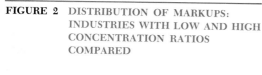

FIGURE 2 DISTRIBUTION OF MARKUPS: INDUSTRIES WITH LOW AND HIGH CONCENTRATION RATIOS COMPARED

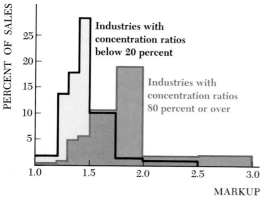

percent or more). Although markups differ widely from industry to industry within each group, the differences between the 2 groups are remarkable. No industry in the least concentrated group had an estimated markup as high as 1.7, and only 3 were higher than 1.55. Although the lowest markup estimated among the most highly concentrated industries was lower than most of those in the least concentrated group, only 4 were below 1.55. Most were over 1.7, and several exceeded 2.0.[1]

OLIGOPOLY PRICING

Regardless of the number of firms in an industry, each firm can clearly perceive the demand for its own products in 2 different ways. As illustrated in Figure 3, the demand curve *dd* represents the demand for the

---

[1] The interested reader is referred to a careful and detailed study of the relationship of margins to concentration: Norman R. Collins and Lee E. Preston, *Concentration and Price-Cost Margins in Manufacturing Industries*, Berkeley, Calif., University of California Press, 1968.

firm's products when it varies its own prices, the prices of all other firms being unaffected by its behavior. If the firm should cut its own price from *P* to *P'*, while other firms continued to charge the same price, *P*, as before, its sales would rise from *Q* to *q'*. If the firm increased its prices to *P''* while other firms kept theirs fixed, its sales would decline to *q''*. At the same time, every producer also recognizes a second demand curve *DD*, representing what would happen to his sales if all the other firms in the industry changed their prices with his. If his price cut to *P'* were matched by all the other firms, his sales would expand only to *Q'*. On the other hand, if all the other firms in the industry joined in the price increase to *P''*, his sales would fall only to *Q''* instead of to *q''*.

The demand curve *DD* represents the individual firm's fixed share of the variation in total industry sales that occurs when all firms in the industry change prices together, while *dd* represents the sales of the individual firm as an increasing and decreasing share of the total market when it varies its own price away from the prices other firms are charging. Clearly the elasticity of *dd* is substantially greater than that of *DD*, since the former involves large shifts of customers among firms in the industry, while the latter represents the individual firm's share of the total gain or loss of customers for the industry as a whole. If all firms in the industry set prices on the basis of the demand curve *DD*, each firm would get larger profits than it would if all firms set prices on the basis of demand curves like *dd*.

Since this is true even in purely competitive industries, and since all firms in the industry can recognize the truth, why don't they hold their prices up in keeping with the lower elasticity of *DD*? Why do they set lower prices on the basis of *dd*? Essentially, the answer is that when each firm is an insignificant part of the total industry, it always appears most profitable to set its prices on the assumption that they will not

TABLE 3 MARKUPS IN LEAST CONCENTRATED AND MOST CONCENTRATED MANUFAC-
TURING INDUSTRIES

LEAST CONCENTRATED INDUSTRIES	4-FIRM CONCEN- TRATION RATIO	ESTIMATED MARKUP	MOST CONCENTRATED INDUSTRIES	4-FIRM CONCEN- TRATION RATIO	ESTIMATED MARKUP
Wood partitions and fixtures	4	1.38	Locomotives and parts	97	1.39
Ready-mixed concrete	4	1.46	Flat glass	94	1.75
Signs and advertising			Organic fiber, noncellulosic	94	2.08
displays	5	1.54	Reclaimed rubber	93	1.49
Screw machine products	5	1.47	Steam engines and turbines	93	1.49
Concrete blocks	5	1.52	Electric lamps	92	1.92
Plating and polishing	5	1.69	Telephone, telegraph		
Dresses	5	1.34	apparatus	92	1.59
Typesetting	6	1.61	Cathode-ray picture tubes	91	1.85
Special dies and tools	6	1.53	Safes and vaults	90+	2.12
Fur goods	7	1.24	Aircraft propellers	90+	1.80
Millwork plants	7	1.29	Primary aluminum	90+	1.64
Women's suits	8	1.33	Cyclic (coal tar) crudes	90+	1.23
Photoengraving	8	1.68	Chewing gum	90	2.08
Metal doors, sash,			Electron tubes,		
and trim	8	1.42	receiving type	87	1.89
Industrial patterns	9	1.53	Hard-surface floor		
Pleating and stitching	9	1.62	covering	87	1.88
Millinery	9	1.40	Cereal preparations	86	1.97
Creamery butter	11	1.11	Gypsum products	84	1.76
Knit outerwear mills	11	1.29	Carbon and graphite		
Blouses	11	1.36	products	84	1.76
Women's and children's			Household vacuum		
underwear	11	1.30	cleaners	81	1.94
Logging camps and			Primary batteries	81	1.81
contractors	11	1.32	Sewing machines	80+	2.02
Sawmills and planing mills	11	1.29	Cigarettes	80	1.78
Wood furniture, not					
upholstered	11	1.40			
Handbags and purses	11	1.34			
Sheet metal work	11	1.46			

SOURCE: Concentration ratios from *Census of Manufactures, 1963*. Markups calculated from data in *Survey of Manufactures, 1965*.

influence anybody else. After all, even if it undercuts everybody else, the firm's capacity is so small that when it draws customers from the industry at large, nobody else loses a noticeable number. On the other hand, if the firm altruistically held its own prices high in keeping with the lower elasticity of *DD*, it would lose most of its customers, but each of its many competitors would pick up only a few. In other words, no matter what a single small firm does

about its prices, it has no significant influence on the sales or earnings of any other firm. Indeed, the other firms are hardly aware of its existence at all, and it is perfectly reasonable for each to price on the basis that—whatever else may happen—the other firms in the industry will not respond to its action.

The situation in a concentrated industry is entirely different. When an oligopolist reduces prices, any important increase in

FIGURE 3   TWO CONCEPTS OF A SINGLE FIRM'S DEMAND CURVE

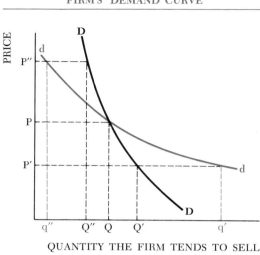

QUANTITY THE FIRM TENDS TO SELL

his customers becomes a significant loss of customers to his rivals in the industry. It is idle to assume that his competitors would stand by and allow their business to disappear. It is much more likely that they would protect their positions by matching his price cut. In other words, the individual firm in an oligopolistic industry is wise to set prices on the basis that other firms *will* respond to his action. The "every-man-for-himself" behavior of the highly competitive industry is replaced by a "live-and-let-live" attitude whereby each firm in the industry sets its prices on the basis of the less elastic demand curve *DD*, secure in the knowledge that all other firms understand the obvious advantages of doing the same. The resulting prices tend to maximize the total profits of the entire industry, which, when shared among the firms, leave each with a larger profit than could be earned by self-defeating price cuts.

In terms of our analysis of markups, the resulting price should tend to be

$$P = MC(e/e - 1)$$

where e represents the elasticity of market demand for the output of the industry as a whole. The fact that this demand is less elastic than the demand for the output of any individual firm acting alone explains the strong tendency for markups in highly concentrated industries to exceed those in less concentrated industries.

Conflicts in Pricing

When production is confined to a few large firms of roughly equal size, all sharing a common view of demand conditions and all having similar costs, oligopolistic pricing behavior arises naturally from the obvious identity of interest among the competitors. Under other circumstances, however, important conflicts arise that make it difficult for the industry to maintain a common pricing policy. One of the most obvious sources of conflicting interests is differences in costs. When the industry's product has demand elasticity of about 1.5, the most profitable price should represent a markup of about $1.5/(1.5 - 1)$, or 3. If all firms have the same marginal cost, say $1, each of the firms arrives at the same $3 price as most profitable for the industry, but when marginal costs range from a low of 80 cents in one firm to a high of $1.20 in another, a conflict arises. The low-cost firm would find an industry price of $2.40 to be most profitable, the high-cost firm would prefer a price of $3.60, while the other members of the industry would be spread out in between. Nobody in the industry would want a price above $3.60 nor a price below $2.40, but within this range any price move that would make one firm more profitable would reduce the profit of others.

A second important source of conflict arises from differences in the perception of demand. A firm that believes that the elasticity of demand is high wants to set lower prices than a firm that thinks demand is less elastic. Differences of opinion about short-run elasticity can work themselves out without much difficulty. A firm that really believes that lower prices will bring a substantial increase in profits for the industry as a whole can reduce prices. If other firms fail to follow suit, it gains customers at their expense. If other firms match its cuts, they will presumably discover that their profits have risen and they will become converted to the low-price view of demand. Of course, if the firm is wrong in its belief about consumer response, everybody will make *lower* profits than before, the firm will learn its lesson, and prices will be restored to their higher level.

More serious conflicts arise from different views of the long-run elasticity of demand. A businessman who is convinced that, despite the low elasticity of short-run buyer response to prices, the long-run elasticity of demand is high, naturally believes that although lower prices would mean temporarily lower profits, they would pay off with higher profits over the long run. Unless this view is widely shared in the industry, however, he finds himself in direct conflict with others who view long-run demand as less elastic. Moreover, even when businessmen agree on long-run demand elasticity, conflicts arise over what to do about it. Some firms may be concerned with immediate high returns and place a heavy discount on the future of the industry. This "bird-in-the-hand" attitude leads them to prefer higher prices now, even at the possible sacrifice of greater future sales and profits. Forward-looking firms, on the other hand, are more concerned about the long pull and are anxious to encourage the growth of future sales by keeping prices low. In addition, as we shall see below, such firms are often concerned about keeping prices below levels that might be too attractive to new firms and encourage entry into the industry.

Resolving Pricing Conflicts

Whenever a number of people hold conflicting views on an important matter of mutual concern, they must be discussed and somehow reconciled before common action can be undertaken. Since outright collusion on prices is illegal, most discussions of this sort are carried on through speeches made by industry leaders, in releases to the financial press, and in other indirect ways. A statement by the president of one company that "the future of the industry lies in larger volume at lower prices that will bring new customers to the product" represents an invitation to other firms to consider price reductions. If the sentiment is echoed in other speeches, interviews, and comment in the trade press, the stage is set for lower prices. Finally, one firm will lower its prices and the others will quickly follow suit.

Price Leadership In some industries the exchange of opinion in the public and trade press is supplemented by the institution of *price leadership*. A *price leader* is a firm—usually, but not always, the largest in the industry—whose announcements or published prices are adopted by other firms in the industry. In many industries the price leader is the first to announce price changes. When new cost or demand conditions appear, other firms wait for the price leader to change its prices first and then speedily match its action. In other industries prices may not be initiated by the price leader, but they are treated as tentative until "ratified" by that firm. In such cases, one or more other firms may announce price changes first. The price leader then either matches these or announces different prices of its own. In the latter case, the other firms readjust their prices to those of the price leader. For example, a nonleader firm is sometimes the first to announce a price increase during a period of rising costs. This represents both an invitation to the price leader to raise prices and a suggestion of how large a price rise would be agreeable. If the price leader considers a price increase inappropriate, it fails to respond, and after a reasonable waiting period, the initiating firm rescinds its action. When the price leader agrees with the need for higher prices, but disagrees about the desirable amount, it raises its own prices to what it considers an appropriate figure, and other firms follow suit.

Something of this sort seems to happen when the automobile industry announces the prices of forthcoming models. General Motors appears to play the role of price leader, but does not necessarily announce its prices first. For example, in 1966, 1967, and 1968 the first announcements of prices for the coming model year were made by the Chrysler Corporation. In each case, the Chrysler announcement was followed a few days later by General Motors, which posted price increases smaller than those proposed by Chrysler. Ford followed with prices close to those of General Motors, and the earlier Chrysler increases were rolled back to the General Motors level. Since Chrysler is the high-cost producer in the industry, its initial announcement can be interpreted as a strong vote for prices higher than those preferred by the others. The General Motors response was that of a low-cost producer, and one concerned about the growing encroachment of imported cars on the demand for domestic models.

In industries in which no individual firm predominates, price leadership has no power behind it except the enlightened self-interest of the competitors. When one firm is significantly larger than the others, however, its price leadership can often be enforced. Figure 4 represents the 2 demand curves seen by one of the smaller firms in the industry after the price leader has established price *P*. As before, *DD* represents the response of the firm's sales when all firms in the industry change prices together, while *dd* represents what the firm could expect to sell at various prices if it were permitted to go it alone. When the price leader is a predominant firm, however, the small follower's view of price increases and decreases is not symmetrical.

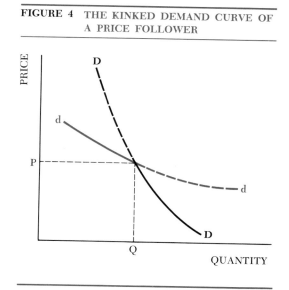

FIGURE 4 THE KINKED DEMAND CURVE OF A PRICE FOLLOWER

If he were to raise his price above the leader's, he is pretty sure the leader would leave him high and dry with few customers, in keeping with the upper branch of *dd*. If he should cut prices below the leader, however, the leader would merely match the cut, and the small firm would gain few customers and lose profits in keeping with the lower branch of the less elastic curve *DD*. Realistically, in other words, the follower firm is faced, not with 2 separate demand curves, but with a single "kinked" curve as represented by the solid line in the figure. At prices above those set by the leader, the firm's demand follows the more elastic *dd*, and at prices below the leader's price it follows the less elastic *DD*. Any departure in either direction from the established price is penalized by lower profits.

Price Warfare People who cannot resolve conflicting interests by peaceful discussion sometimes resort to force, and businessmen are no exception. A firm unable to convince others to go along with its view of the market will sometimes signal its displeasure by deliberately undercutting the prices of other firms. It is willing to accept temporarily lower profits or even losses in order to inflict them on other firms, in the hope that they can be forced to adopt its point of view. When other firms retaliate by undercutting in turn, a series of price cuts and countercuts sometimes ensues during which prices are forced to unprofitable levels, if not actually below cost. This situation is a *price war.*

Most price wars are confined to local markets for milk, bread, gasoline, and similar consumer goods, but they occasionally occur on a national scale. A price war involving the producers of metal cans is an excellent illustration. In the late 1950s, metal can producers faced the possibility that some of their important food-packing customers might begin to manufacture their own cans. Since this possibility could be headed off by lower prices, it amounted to an increase in the elasticity of demand for cans, particularly in the long run. The higher elasticity led low-cost can manufacturers, particularly those that placed a premium on the long-term future of the industry, to prefer lower prices. But this view was not universally shared, as indicated by the statement of an executive of one of the can producers that "it's a cold economic fact that the all-season packers can produce [cans] more cheaply than we can sell to them. . . . I say, let them go. Don't wreck the whole industry by trying to hold onto them."[2]

The adverse view of price reduction was bolstered in the fall of 1958 when U.S. Steel —a traditional price leader in the steel industry—announced an increase in the price of tin plate, to be effective November 1. Shortly after this announcement, the American Can Corporation, long the price leader in the metal can industry, announced a 6 percent increase in all can prices. Instead of following this increase, however, Con-

tinental Can, a producer of approximately the same size as American, announced an increase of only 3 percent. American Can immediately retaliated by rescinding its announced price increase and instituting price cuts of 3 to 5 percent depending on the size and price of the can. These reductions were promptly matched by Continental, who made the lower prices effective 2 weeks earlier than the American reduction.

American matched Continental's date, and a number of other reductions followed, not always announced in the trade press. According to one report, the price of beer cans was cut 6 times in a period of a few months. In April, 1959 American Can announced 4 to 10 percent reductions in the price of packers' cans and was immediately followed by Continental and the other firms in the industry.

Prices remained low for more than a year, as profits in the industry declined. Finally, in late 1960, American Can announced price increases that would remain firmly in force except for any necessary adjustments for changing material costs. This was, in effect, an announcement of a desire for an end to hostilities, and when the other firms followed suit, the price war was over. Subsequent price increases not only restored markups but by 1964 had pushed them above their "prewar" levels. The effect of the price war is clearly observable in the estimated markups calculated from Census data for the metal can manufacturing industry shown in Figure 5. Before the outbreak of the price war, can prices represented an average markup of 1.30 above marginal cost. At the height of hostilities in 1960, this declined to an average of 1.25, but rose to 1.35 following the settlement of the disagreement.

Collusion The risks of price warfare and other painful misunderstandings provide a constant temptation to members of oligopolistic industries to go beyond indirect

[2] Quoted in Charles H. Hession, "The Metal Container Industry," in Walter Adams, ed., *The Structure of American Industry*, 3rd edition, New York, Macmillan, 1961, pp. 430–467.

FIGURE 5   ESTIMATED MARKUPS IN METAL
CAN MANUFACTURING, 1956-1965

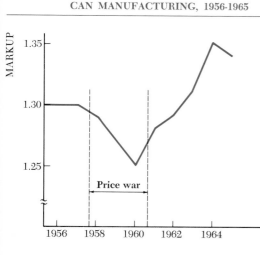

SOURCE: Markups from Census data as compiled
in the *Compendium of Manufacturing Production Statistics for the United States, 1947–1965*,
Washington, D.C., Georgetown Economic Data Library, 1967.

communication to arrive at explicit agreements about prices, terms, and other competitive matters. As the early economist
Adam Smith wrote almost 200 years ago,
"people of the same trade rarely meet together, even for merriment and diversion,
but the conversation ends in conspiracy
against the public or some contrivance to
raise prices." Collusive arrangements vary
in complexity from simple agreements about
prices to complex arrangements involving
territorial divisions and who is to be the
low bidder on contracts. The difficulty of
collusion is increased by its illegality, since
to escape detection the agreed prices or
bids must bear an outward resemblance to
results that might have been independently
reached. The lengths to which producers
have been known to go in their efforts to
avoid detection make some cases read more
like spy fiction than economics. To cite an
example uncovered about 10 years ago, U.S.
firms manufacturing electrical equipment

had not only agreed on the prices to be
charged, but had also established a method
for bidding on government contracts
whereby the firm that was to submit the
lowest bid was identified by the phase of
the moon at the time bids were submitted.
The favored firm submitted the agreed industry price as its bid, while the other firms
added random amounts to the agreed price
to make their bids higher.[3]

The Corporation as an Instrument
To Concentrate Control

Illegal in themselves, collusive agreements
are naturally legally unenforceable, depending only on mutual trust. At the same time,
they present a powerful temptation to each
firm to double-cross the rest of the industry
by secretly shading its own prices below the
agreed level whenever it appears profitable
to do so. Under the circumstances, it is
hardly surprising that collusive agreements
tend to be unstable and short-lived unless
bolstered by stronger controls. Several arrangements to establish such controls, many
of them based on the legal characteristics of
the corporation, were common during the
19th century before they were legislated
out of existence. A *trust* was a device
whereby owners of the controlling interest
in competing firms deposited their shares
with a single group of trustees in exchange
for trust certificates that entitled them to a
share in the total profits of the trust operation. This placed legal control over all the
affairs of the "competing" firms in the hands
of the trustees, who proceeded to operate
all the firms as a single unit. The wide
popularity of this device before 1890 was
the source of the term "trust-busting," used

[3] See "Collusion Among Electrical Equipment
Manufacturers," *Wall Street Journal*, January 10,
12, 1962, as reprinted in Edwin Mansfield, ed.,
Monopoly Power and Economic Performance,
New York, W. W. Norton, 1964.

to describe government action to dissolve large industrial combinations, and gave the name "antitrust" to legislation and policy designed to foster competition.

The institution of *interlocking directors* was another method of enforcing agreements among firms. An interlocking director is a man elected to serve on the board of directors of 2 or more competing firms. An extensive system of interlocking directors could effectively tie together the policies of a number of firms and ensure conformity of behavior.

Mergers and Holding Companies By far the tightest control over a number of producers is obtained by combining them into a single firm. An outright *merger* occurs when 2 firms are combined into 1, usually by one firm absorbing the other. When the stockholders of the 2 firms agree to merge, the holders of the stock in the firm to be absorbed exchange their shares in an agreed ratio for the shares of the other firm, and the absorbed firm ceases to exist as an independent entity.

Another way to merge control over separate firms is by the use of a *holding company*. A holding company is a firm whose primary purpose is not production, but the acquisition and ownership of the securities of other corporations. When a group of investors wants to gain control of a number of companies, they set up a corporation with enough capital to buy controlling interests in each of the desired companies. When the securities of the operating companies are widely held, the investment needed for control is, of course, only a fraction of the outstanding securities. Moreover, by *pyramiding*—that is, setting up holding companies to control other holding companies —and by the judicious use of preferred stock, a modest investment can be used to control a vast industrial empire.

The nature of a holding company pyramid is illustrated in Figure 6. In the lowest tier are 4 operating companies, A, B, C,

FIGURE 6   CONSOLIDATION OF CONTROL BY HOLDING COMPANIES

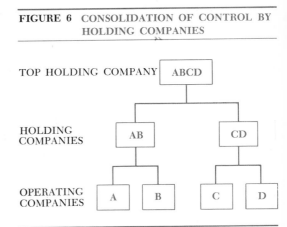

and D, each with assets of $250 million and common stock equity of $160 million. The next tier of the structure consists of 2 holding companies, AB and CD, each owning a controlling interest in 2 of the operating companies. Since the common stocks of the latter are widely held, probably less than a third is needed for control. Each holding company therefore represents an investment of $100 million, 40 percent of which is financed by nonvoting preferred stock, and 60 percent by common stock. Airtight majority control of the voting shares is held by the top holding company ABCD, with an investment of $60 million, entirely financed by common stock. The controlling group, however, owns only the 50 percent of the shares needed to retain control over ABCD. As a result, their investment of $30 million in the top holding company enables them to exercise full authority over a billion-dollar operation at the bottom. It is clear that by further pyramiding, the control leverage could be increased to the point at which the $1 billion of operating assets could be controlled by the investment of only a few dollars at the top.

Holding company control may merely coordinate the activities and policies of the member firms, leaving them as apparently distinct, or it may be the prelude to outright merger. From the standpoint of both economic effect and relevant antitrust law, there is little difference between the 2 methods of control, and they are both usually designated as "mergers" without distinction.

Types of Mergers The effect of mergers on competition depends on the relationship between the firms being merged. There are 3 distinguishable types of mergers. A *horizontal* merger results from the combination of 2 or more firms that sell in the same market. The recent merger of the New York Central and Pennsylvania railroads to form the Penn Central was a horizontal merger, and many of our largest manufacturing firms originated as horizontal mergers, usually via holding companies. Since horizontal mergers combine erstwhile competitors, they increase the degree of industrial concentration and tend to contribute to a reduction of competition in the industry.

A *vertical* merger results when one of the firms in the combination supplies the other with an important service or intermediate product. The merger of a bottle manufacturer with a soft drink producer, or of a paper mill with a newspaper would be a vertical merger. Although the firms involved are not direct competitors, vertical mergers sometimes result in a considerable reduction of competition by providing a way for a firm holding substantial control in one market to spread its control to another. When control of the output of a key intermediate product or raw material is already concentrated, a large producer's vertical integration into the market for products made from the material can leave independent firms without a source of supply. Conversely, when firms that control a substantial share of the sale of final products extend their power into the intermediate-product market by vertical integration, independent suppliers may find themselves without customers for their output.

A *conglomerate* merger is one in which the firms involved are in distinct, often unrelated, industries. The merger of a cotton textile firm with a steel manufacturer would be a conglomerate merger. Although conglomerate mergers are less likely to influence competitive conditions than either horizontal or vertical mergers, they can have an effect when the 2 firms merged are strong potential competitors. Buying up a firm that is contemplating entering your industry and that is clearly equipped to be an efficient competitor is one way to keep control. Conglomerate mergers can also reduce the scope of competition when the 2 firms involved are important customers of each other.

BARRIERS TO ENTRY AND THE PERSISTENCE OF OLIGOPOLY

Any unusual profits from oligopoly pricing provide strong incentives for investors to enter the industry. Since the entry of new firms into the industry would reduce concentration and force prices and profits to a competitive level, oligopoly can persist in the long run only if some important barrier prevents new firms from gaining a foothold. There are 4 general types of barriers to entry: key resources, cost differentials, product differentiation, and predatory action.

Key Resources

Concentration of production is found in many industries because only a limited number of firms have access to some "resource" that is essential to the product. Sometimes this "resource" is literally a natural resource like an essential ore, mineral, or other material. When all natural sources of supply are in the hands of existing producers, there is clearly no way for rival firms to break into the industry. Close holding of the available high-quality bauxite deposits is an important factor restricting entry into the aluminum industry, and the predominant position of the International Nickel Corporation as the producer of a large fraction of the world's nickel arises from its ownership of most of the world's known nickel reserves, concentrated in a small area around Sudbury, Ontario.

In other instances the "resource" is a patented process that permits the holder to control the number of firms in the industry. Key patents were an important element in restricting entry into the production of business machines, shoe machinery, certain plastics, light bulbs, and other products. In some industries closely guarded trade secrets substitute for patents.

Cost

One of the most important barriers to entry into many industries is the cost advantage held by firms already in operation. The established, experienced firm has had time to learn how to keep costs down. Its buyers are familiar with the cheapest sources of materials and how to obtain the highest quality for the lowest cost. Managers know how to train workers to do their jobs effectively and how to coordinate production for minimum cost. If a labor union is involved, the experienced management is likely to be a tougher and more effective collective bargainer, able to extract concessions that less experienced negotiators fail to obtain.

Given time, of course, the new firm could probably learn to operate just as economically as those already established, but in the meanwhile it would be faced with the prospect of a long period of losses. If they are sufficiently large, these act as an effective deterrent to entry.

Scale of Production

An important special aspect of cost is the scale of operations. There is more than one way to produce most products. Which method is cheapest depends not only on the price of parts, materials, and so on, but on the volume to be turned out. The cheapest way to produce in small quantities is to keep fixed cost down, even at the expense of high variable cost. When only 2 or 3 special racing cars are to be produced, for example, they are largely handmade. Parts are individually produced or machined from stock parts and assembled by highly skilled mechanics using general-purpose metalworking machinery. When output was small in the early days of the automobile industry, the same hand methods were the cheapest way to produce ordinary passenger cars. In modern high-volume automobile manufacturing, however, cars are mass-produced with the aid of highly specialized equipment, production lines, and expensive automatic machinery. The fixed cost is vastly higher than that of a hand-operated shop, but when spread over the large volume of output, the average total cost is much lower.

Relationships among different production methods is illustrated in Figure 7(a). Costs of using 3 alternative techniques are shown. Despite its high variable cost, small-scale technique with low fixed cost is the cheapest method of producing when output does not exceed the low level Q_s per year. When output falls in the medium range between Q_s and Q_m per year, the use of certain specialized labor-saving equipments pays off. As long as enough can be sold, the reduction in variable cost more than makes up for the higher fixed cost of the machinery. Large-scale production involves a more fully automated production technique. Because of its high fixed costs, the total cost of producing less than Q_s by automated methods would be double or triple that of hand operations, but when these fixed costs can be spread over a total output in excess of Q_m, this is the cheapest method of operation. The dashed blue curve in Figure 7(a) indicates the lowest cost for producing any given volume.

FIGURE 7   BREAK-EVEN CHARTS AND
AVERAGE TOTAL COST CURVES OF
FIRMS OPERATING ON DIFFERENT
SCALES

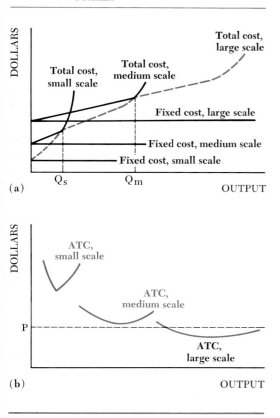

(a)

(b)

to a minimum a manufacturer should be able to turn out 8 to 15 percent of all soap used.[4]

Whenever large-scale operations permit substantial cost saving, prices that would yield good profits to larger producers would be ruinous to firms operating on a smaller scale, making it difficult or impossible for a new firm to contemplate starting out on a small scale and gradually growing larger. It would require a heavy initial commitment to a risky proposition to break into the market at all, a fact that represents a serious barrier to entry.

The effectiveness of cost barriers to entry is often enhanced by the price policies of firms already in the industry. If cost is the principal barrier to entry, it is to the long-run advantage of producers to hold prices below what would appear to be the most profitable short-run level. The higher prices that would temporarily increase the profitability of operations would also increase the rewards to successful entry and provide a greater temptation to new firms to come into the field.

Product Differentiation

When oligopoly is coupled with high product differentiation, as among soft drinks, television sets, washing machines, and similar consumer products, an additional barrier to entry is posed. The new firm must attract customers to its unknown product, away from firms with widespread reputations and consumer goodwill. This frequently requires massive initial investments in advertising and selling costs, with limited probability of success. The chances are especially poor in breaking into a market for high-priced household equipment. The possibility of making a large outlay for a

Another view of the same comparison is shown by the average cost curves of Figure 7(b). As shown by the dotted line, a price at which the large plant could reap profits if its output could be sold would involve losses for any smaller plant.

The technology of some industries makes the most economical scale of operation so large that the most efficient firm becomes an important fraction of the entire industry. It has been estimated that the most economical production of typewriters requires a firm capable of supplying 10 to 30 percent of the total U.S. market. The most efficient cigarette producer should be large enough to supply 15 to 20 percent of all U.S. smokers, while to keep production costs of soap

[4] Figures are from Joe Bain, *Barriers to New Competition: Their Character and Consequences in Manufacturing Industries,* Cambridge, Mass., Harvard University Press, pp. 80–86.

machine that may not perform up to expectations tends to lead consumers to established makes. The chances of breaking in are better in markets for inexpensive, frequently purchased items which consumers might be convinced to try once or twice by a massive selling campaign.

Predatory Action

In the past, natural and legal barriers have often been supplemented by deliberate actions taken by one or more producers in an industry to prevent new firms from entering or to squeeze out firms already in. This has sometimes involved such overtly criminal action as hijacking shipments, sabotaging equipment, and threatening rivals' customers. Firms have been known to bribe retailers and servicemen to recommend and push their products while spreading false reports of defects in rival products. Firms have even been known to bribe competitors' employees to produce defective products.

More subtle predatory methods are extensions of ordinary business relationships. When a large firm is an important customer, suppliers are often willing to offer especially favorable prices to keep its business. This sometimes enables a large firm to force its suppliers to maintain a substantial spread between the prices it pays and those charged to its competitors. One of the most notorious instances of this type of concession occurred more than a century ago in the agreement between the railroads and the Standard Oil Company, whereby the railroads rebated to the oil company 50 percent of the freight rate charged per barrel of crude oil shipped. At a time when competing oil companies were charged 80 cents per barrel on crude oil shipped from the Pennsylvania oil fields to Cleveland, the Standard Oil Corporation got back 40 cents per barrel, not only on its *own* oil shipments, but on the shipments of all competing oil as well!

Another form of predatory behavior is the *exclusive dealership,* whereby a large producer of a popular item insists that retailers or agents who want to sell it must agree not to carry competing products, making it difficult for competitors to gain access to the market. A related device is the *tying contract,* under which a dealer who wants to carry certain very popular items is forced to purchase other parts of the firm's line in order to obtain the desired articles. This practice enables a firm with a decided advantage in one of the products of an industry to spread its power to other items. Another version of the tying contract applies directly to customers. In a classical example, the United Shoe Machinery Corporation forced shoe manufacturers who wanted to obtain essential machinery of which it was the sole producer, to employ only United Shoe supplementary equipment. This shut out other manufacturers of supplementary equipment, regardless of the cost or the quality of their products.

Finally, of course, there is predatory pricing, whereby a large firm drives smaller competitors out of business by price warfare, maintaining prices on a ruinous level until they fail. Small independent local operators are especially vulnerable, since they can be picked off one by one by a national firm that makes up for local losses by higher profits elsewhere.

PUBLIC POLICY TOWARD OLIGOPOLY

Industrial concentration and collusion result in prices higher in relation to cost than those of competitive industries. These higher prices restrict consumer purchase of the products and force labor and other resources into more competitive industries where they expand the production of less desirable, low-markup products. If we are to rely on competition to allocate productive resources according to consumer desires, we must prevent firms from adopting noncompetitive behavior. For this reason the main approach of public policy to oligopoly has been antitrust legislation to enforce competition. Some industries, however, are natural monopolies in which competition is not a viable arrangement. Public policy toward such industries is to constitute them "public utilities" and to regulate their behavior administratively.

Antitrust Legislation

Racketeering and related predatory tactics have always been criminal, and there is a strong common-law tradition against conspiracy. As big business emerged during the 19th century, however, a pressing need developed for new legislation to curb collusive behavior and growing economic concentration.

The Sherman Act The first federal antitrust law was the Sherman Act of 1890, whose substantive provisions can be quoted in full:

> Section 1. Every contract, combination in the form of a trust or otherwise, or conspiracy, in restraint of trade or commerce among the several states, or with foreign nations, is hereby declared to be illegal. Every person who shall make any such contract or engage in any such combination or conspiracy, shall be deemed guilty of a misdemeanor. . . .
>
> Section 2. Every person who shall monopolize, or attempt to monopolize, or combine or conspire with any other person or persons, to monopolize any part of the trade or commerce among the several states, or with foreign nations, shall be deemed guilty of a misdemeanor. . . .

The earliest results of the Sherman Act were considerably less than what its proponents had hoped. In fact, its passage was followed by one of the most active merger periods in American history. The years between 1890 and 1902 were marked by the formation—usually via the holding company device—of more than 200 new nationwide firms, including such giants as American Tobacco, American Sugar Refining, National Lead, General Electric, U.S. Rubber, and U.S. Steel.

One reason for this result was the Court's fumbling initial interpretation of the meaning of the Sherman Act. The first Sherman Act case to reach the Supreme Court in 1895 involved an attempt by the government to prevent the American Sugar Refining Company from acquiring stock in several firms that would have brought it control over 98 percent of all U.S. sugar refining capacity. Although the Court acknowledged that this constituted monopoly, it attempted to draw a distinction between "trade or commerce" on the one hand, and "manufacturing" on the other. By this distinction, sugar refining—as manufacturing— was not "trade or commerce." This removed it from the coverage of the Sherman Act, and the stock purchase was allowed to stand.[5] This extremely limiting interpretation of the law was short-lived. The Court applied the Sherman Act to a combination effected by a holding company 9 years later and declared its applicability to industrial enterprises selling in interstate markets.[6] The Standard Oil Company and the American Tobacco Company were convicted under the Sherman Act 2 years later and ordered broken into smaller firms.[7] Even this application of the law, however, illustrated its inadequacy, for every shareholder in the parent company received an allotment of the stocks of each of the smaller

[5] U.S. v. E. C. Knight Co., 156 U.S. 1.

[6] Northern Securities Co. v. U.S., 193 U.S. 197 (1904).

[7] Standard Oil Co. v. U.S., 221 U.S. 1 (1911) and U.S. v. American Tobacco Co., 221 U.S. 106 (1911).

constituent companies in proportion to his holding of the parent stock. As a result, the very same group of owners that had originally controlled the parent company ended up controlling all of the individual smaller companies.

A contributing cause of the disappointment in the Sherman Act was that while it declared certain end results to be illegal, it did not attack the specific actions or means by which these results might be attained. For example, although "attempts to monopolize" were outlawed, nothing was said about acquisition of stocks by holding companies, employment of interlocking directors, or any of the other specific devices by which power over markets could be consolidated. The result was something like having a law against traffic accidents, but no law to prevent driving at excessive speed or on the wrong side of the street.

The Clayton Act and the Federal Trade Commission The Clayton Act and the Federal Trade Commission Act, both enacted in 1914, represented efforts to repair the deficiency in the Sherman Act. The important provisions of the Clayton Act forbade price discrimination (section 2), tying contracts (section 3), the acquisition by one corporation of shares in a competitor (section 7), and interlocking directors (section 8). In each case, however, the prohibition was not outright, but applicable only "where the effect may be to substantially lessen competition or tend to create a monopoly." The Federal Trade Commission Act was an antitrust law insofar as certain predatory practices were proscribed as "unfair methods of competition." In addition, the Federal Trade Commission was established and given the power to supervise the enforcement of the antitrust laws by investigating corporations, requiring them to file reports and special information about their activities, examining corporate practices or arrangements not in conformity

with the antitrust acts, and recommending readjustments to secure conformity.

Since 1914, several additional laws have been enacted to supplement antitrust legislation. The price discrimination provisions of section 2 of the Clayton Act were strengthened in 1936 by the Robinson-Patman Act. The Celler Antimerger Act of 1950 amended section 7 of the Clayton Act to forbid, in addition to the *acquisition* of stock of one competitor by another, the *use* of such stock by voting, granting proxies or otherwise, and the acquisition of the *assets* of competitors as well.

Enforcement of Antitrust Laws Section 2 of the Sherman Act declares that "every person who shall monopolize, or attempt to monopolize . . . any part of . . . trade or commerce . . . shall be deemed guilty of a misdemeanor. . . ." Strictly interpreted, this means that merely *having* a monopoly is illegal, regardless of how it was acquired, or whether the monopoly position was exploited once attained. By this strict interpretation, a firm could monopolize a part of trade or commerce without any intention of so doing, merely by the exercise of business acumen, foresight, and competitive enterprise. Courts have been reluctant to enforce this strict interpretation of the law, and with good reason. A society that depends on the acumen, foresight, and enterprise of its businessmen to guide production according to consumer wishes, to find and bring out new products, and to raise the productivity of its members, can ill afford to turn around and prosecute them for performing too well.

For this reason antitrust laws have always been most effectively enforced against restriction of competition by overt collusion, conspiracy, or predatory action. Such behavior as collusive agreements on prices or actions to drive a competitor out of business are necessarily undertaken with willful intent. One cannot "accidentally," or "unknowingly," or otherwise "innocently" do these things in the course of ordinary business, and the existence of intent greatly simplifies the prosecution of the case. It is noteworthy that in ordering the dissolution of the old Standard Oil and American Tobacco companies in 1911, the Court's decision was heavily influenced by evidence that both firms owed their existence in some part to long histories of deliberate predatory behavior in the form of price discrimination, coercion of suppliers, price warfare, and similar practices.[8] When the United States Steel Corporation was prosecuted just a few years later, however, the Court pointed to the absence of evidence of such practices and acquitted the company of attempting to monopolize the steel industry. The firm controlled 50 percent of all steel production in the United States, but, said the Court, "The law does not make mere size an offense . . . but . . . requires overt acts."[9] Although U.S. Steel was large, it did not "secure freight rebates . . . it did not undersell its competitors in some localities by reducing its prices there below those maintained elsewhere . . . there was no evidence that it attempted to crush its competitors or drive them from the market."[10]

More recently, however, both prosecution and the courts have moved toward the strict interpretation of the law. In 1945 the Aluminum Company of America (ALCOA) was found guilty of violating section 2 of the Sherman Act merely on the grounds that it manufactured more than 90 percent of the virgin aluminum used in the United States. Although the company was also found guilty of predatory use of its position as a vertically integrated firm, the Court

explicitly held that ALCOA would be guilty of monopolization even in the absence of these practices.[11] Although ALCOA was convicted, it was not broken up into smaller firms. It was, however, required to license competitors under its patents and to sever its connection with Aluminium Limited of Canada. Moreover, government-owned aluminum plants that had been constructed during World War II were sold to competing firms.

A similar decision was reached in the United Shoe Machinery case, when the company was found guilty under section 2 of the Sherman Act because its business practices—entirely legal in themselves—had excluded competitors from the field. The Court concluded that monopoly power is unlawful "if that power is . . . the result of barriers erected by its own business methods (even though not predatory, immoral, or restraining trade under section 1 of the Sherman Act) unless the enterprise shows that the barriers are exclusively the result of superior skill, superior products, natural advantages, technological or economic efficiency, scientific research, low margins of profit maintained permanently without discrimination, legal licenses, or the like."[12] In other words, this decision appears to put the business community on notice that when firms find themselves in the process of acquiring a monopoly, they must be prepared to show that the monopoly is the result of the kind of advantages that characterize successful competition at its best, rather than other actions or accidents.

Antitrust and Mergers   In enforcing the antitrust laws applied to mergers, cases are usually brought under section 7 of the Clay-

---

[8] Standard Oil Co. v. United States, 221 U.S. 75–77 (1911). United States v. American Tobacco Co., 221 U.S. 181–183 (1911).

[9] U.S. v. U.S. Steel Corporation, 251 U.S. 451 (1920).

[10] *Ibid.*, p. 441.

[11] U.S. v. Aluminum Co. of America, 148 F 2nd 416.

[12] U.S. v. United Shoe Machinery Corporation, 110 F. Supp. 296–97.

ton Act, as amended by the Celler Act, which forbids a corporation to acquire the stocks or assets of another and prohibits the combination of two or more corporations through stock ownership where the effect "may be substantially to lessen competition . . . or tend to create a monopoly." Whether a given proposed merger will contravene this law or not is, of course, a specific question to be determined in court, but the Antitrust Division of the U.S. Department of Justice has established certain guidelines to explain its normal policy in deciding whether to bring a case against a merger. The Division's general enforcement procedure is "directed primarily toward the identification and prevention of those mergers which alter the market structure in ways likely . . . to encourage or permit noncompetitive conduct."[13] Whether the Division will challenge a given merger depends on the type of merger, on the degree of concentration already existing in the markets that would be affected, and on the size of the firms involved.

The guidelines on horizontal mergers are set forth in Table 4. In the view of the Division, whether a merger of 2 firms in the same market will "substantially" lessen competition or "tend to create a monopoly" depends on how concentrated the industry already is. If the 4-firm concentration ratio in the appropriate market is already 75 percent or more, the merger of 2 firms, each with only 4 percent of the market, will be challenged. In industries with lower initial concentration, mergers of slightly larger firms will be allowed to pass unchallenged unless market concentration has been growing rapidly. If concentration is on the increase, the Antitrust Division is prepared to challenge any mergers regardless of market shares. Moreover, it will invariably challenge any merger that involves the acquisition of a firm that has been particularly "disturbing" or otherwise unusually competitive, or of a firm with unusual competitive potential, for example one holding a patent on a significant new improvement. This last provision is designed to prevent a large firm from perpetuating its position by grabbing every innovation that might provide competitors with a chance to upset its dominance.

[13] U.S. Department of Justice, *Merger Guidelines* (mimeo) May 30, 1968.

TABLE 4   U.S. DEPARTMENT OF JUSTICE ANNOUNCED MERGER GUIDELINES

HORIZONTAL MERGERS WILL ORDINARILY BE CHALLENGED WHEN:

A. The 4-firm concentration ratio in the appropriate market is approximately 75 percent or more, and the firms involved in the merger account for the following percentages of the market:

Larger or Acquiring Firm	Smaller or Acquired Firm
4%	4% or more
10%	2% or more
15% or more	1% or more

B. The 4-firm concentration ratio is less than approximately 75 percent, and the firms involved in the merger account for the following percentages of the market:

Larger or Acquiring Firm	Smaller or Acquired Firm
5%	5% or more
10%	4% or more
15%	3% or more
20%	2% or more
25%	1% or more

(Under both A and B, percentages not shown in the table should be interpolated between those given.)

C. In industries in which the concentration ratio for any group of firms from the 2 largest to the 8 largest has increased 7 percent or more in the last 5 to 10 years, the Department will challenge any merger involving a firm whose market share is roughly 2 percent or more.

SOURCE: U.S. Department of Justice, *Merger Guidelines* (mimeo) issued May 30, 1968.

The Antitrust Division's attitude toward

vertical mergers is to prevent raising barriers to entry by closing off access to customers or supplies or by imposing on newcomers the burden of entering the industry on an integrated basis or not at all. Here again, the Division's policy is to challenge mergers on the basis of the shares of the 2 firms in their respective markets. In general, any vertical merger between a supplier firm and a consumer firm will be challenged if it involves a supplier firm whose share of the supplier market is 10 percent or more and a user firm whose share of the market for its own products is 6 percent or more. In addition, however, it is the Division's announced policy to challenge any vertical merger if the supplier has some special advantage, such as possessing a scarce resource or a new product innovation, that would provide a competitive advantage to any consumer firm that could capture it for its own use.

Regulation of Natural Monopolies

The philosophy of antitrust legislation is that competition can be enforced in most industries, and, when enforced, will sucessfully regulate prices, output, and industrial behavior. There are, however, a few industries in which, for purely technical reasons, competition cannot survive, cannot be enforced, and would be highly wasteful. These are industries, often called *natural monopolies,* in which, to be most economical, a firm must be large enough to occupy the entire market.

Electric power is a clear example of a natural monopoly. The heavy fixed costs of electricity production include not only expensive generating facilities, but also the cost of poles, lines, cables, transformers, and other distribution equipment that extend the physical plant to the point of use. Once this fixed plant is in place, the marginal cost of fuel and labor to operate the establishment is very low. If 2 power companies were to compete in the same territory, most of these fixed costs would be duplicated. To enable consumers to choose which firm's service they wanted, both firms would need lines running in front of every house, complete duplication of all transforming and switching facilities, and duplication of generating plant. Furthermore, since laying lines, repairing cables, and other maintenance activities often require blocking traffic or tearing up streets, there would be twice as much disruption of daily life.

In addition, electricity is a completely homogeneous product, and the ease with which a user could substitute power produced by one firm for that of another would give very high elasticity to the demand for the service of each individual competitor, despite the low elasticity of demand for electric power in general. As we noted earlier, the combination of high fixed cost, low marginal cost, and product homogeneity, creates a strong pressure toward full plant utilization and tends to prevent excess capacity in the industry. This would suggest that electric power production has a natural tendency toward a single firm in each market.

We can see how the process would work if we imagine 2 seriously competing power producers serving the same area. Since each would be large enough to supply the entire market, both would operate below capacity. The low marginal cost and high demand elasticity would offer each the temptation to undercut the other to capture its customers. Since the market demand for electricity is inelastic, however, successively lower rates would do little to expand total use of power, and the main result would be lower and lower revenues, forcing losses on both competitors. Left to itself, the situation would be resolved in one of 2 ways. Either the firms would get together and agree to eliminate competition, or one firm would go out of business leaving the other as sole survivor. Either way, the result would be monopoly.

Public Utilities   When the service rendered by a natural monopolist is considered sufficiently important to be affected with the public interest, the firm supplying it is granted a franchise to operate as a monopoly and in exchange for this monopoly franchise, the government retains the right to regulate its rates, to specify the quantity and quality of service it renders, and to supervise many other aspects of its behavior.

Firms operating under these regulations are *public utilities*. The term "public utility" is popularly confined to suppliers of electric power, water, and gas, but is used here in its wider sense to encompass telephone, telegraph, radio, and television communication; railroad, streetcar, bus, truck, air, and pipeline transportation; and so on. Most of these industries share with electric power, water, and gas the characteristic high fixed and low marginal costs that arise from the need to extend the physical plant (pipe, rail, phone line, etc.) to the point of use. Exceptions like highway trucking are industries that could, themselves, probably function effectively as unregulated competitive industries, but which are important competitors of other industries—railroads, in the case of trucking firms—that could not.

The objective of public utility regulation is to use the government's regulatory power to maintain good service and low prices in imitation of the results of competition, while gaining the economic advantages of monopoly operation. If this goal is to be attained, even approximately, regulation must be sufficiently flexible to permit rates and service to respond to changes in cost and market demand. It would hardly do to require a new charter or a special act of the legislature every time new prices or a change in the quality of service was called for, and the regulation of public utilities is ordinarily vested in a special regulating commission established for the purpose. On the federal level, interstate railroads, trucks, buses, and barge lines are regulated by the Interstate Commerce Commission (ICC). Electric power and natural gas distribution is regulated by the Federal Power Commission (FPC), airlines by the Civil Aeronautics Board (CAB), while interstate telephone and telegraph communication and radio and television broadcasting are regulated by the Federal Communications Commission (FCC). Intrastate services are regulated by various public utility commissions, railroad commissions, and so on, established by the several states.

Rather than prices that would maximize monopoly profits, utility commissions attempt to set rates that are just adequate to cover costs and still leave a high enough return to enable utilities to attract the capital necessary for their operations. In the absence of competitive discipline, commissions must also maintain surveillance over expenditures and costs to minimize wasteful outlays and avoid unnecessary service costs. Commissions also regulate the type and quality of service to be rendered. Utilities must expand into new areas as required, and cannot abandon services or parts of the market without commission approval. There are, understandably, many serious problems connected with public utility regulation, but the important objective is to employ administrative regulation in an effort to elicit from a natural monopoly the same performance that is imposed on other industries by the forces of competition.

SUMMARY

Oligopoly characterizes an industry in which a significant share of total output is concentrated in the hands of a small number of firms. Since concentration can cover a wide range, oligopoly, like monopolistic competition, is a matter of degree. One useful index of the degree of oligopoly in an industry is the *4-firm concentration ratio,* the percentage of total industry sales in the hands of the 4 largest firms. In U.S. manufacturing industries, the bulk of output comes from industries in which the 4-firm concentration ratio is no more than 31.5 percent, but ratios can be observed as high as nearly 100 percent.

High concentration creates a special pricing situation in which firms can no longer take the competitive environment as given, but must recognize that their own actions affect those of other firms. The competitive behavior in which each firm acts for itself regardless of the effect on others is replaced by recognition that when each firm attempts to undersell others, all make lower profits. In consequence, oligopoly prices tend to represent higher markups over marginal cost than those of competitive industries.

At the same time, the profitability of high markups provides a strong temptation to individual firms to shade prices just enough to capture some of their neighbor's business. This tends to make oligopoly prices unstable, particularly when firms have different costs, different views of demand elasticity, or otherwise fail to see eye to eye about the most profitable level of prices. In an effort to stabilize prices and permit exploitation of their oligopolistic position, firms in concentrated industries have resorted to *price leadership, collusion,* and a number of other devices designed to maintain closer control over competition. Many of these devices involve capitalizing on the legal characteristics of the modern corporation, and corporate *mergers* have been an important means of concentrating control over markets. In the long run, however, oligopoly depends on the existence of one or more *barriers to the entry* of new firms into the industry.

Public policy toward concentration takes 2 general forms. *Antitrust legislation* like the Sherman Act, the Clayton Act, and the Federal Trade Commission Act is designed to forestall the growth of concentration and to prevent firms from resorting to collusion or predatory behavior to maintain industrial discipline. *Public utility regulation* imposes administrative control over *natural monopolies* in an effort to elicit performance like that encouraged in other industries by the force of competition.

CHAPTER 20

Environmental Pollution

POLLUTION AS A SOCIAL PROBLEM

In recent years people the world over have become more and more concerned about increasing environmental pollution. In the midst of improvements in products, rapidly rising productivity, and steadily growing output per capita, it becomes increasingly difficult to find fresh air, clean water, and quiet. The abandoned automobile and the junk heap are a common sight, and litter, broken bottles, and beer cans flattened on the street have become a normal part of the urban scene. Contamination of our rivers and lakes has converted valuable recreation resources for fishing, swimming, and boating into ugly, fetid, and often dangerous sewers and commercial drains. Runoff of DDT has made Lake Michigan salmon unacceptable for commercial fishing, and DDT absorbed by fish in the Mississippi Valley has had such far-reaching effects as to threaten the survival of the bald eagle in America. City dwellers are surrounded by noise from air hammers, industrial equipment, traffic, fans, blowers, and air conditioning equipment, while the countryside is exposed to the roar of expressway traffic. Helicopters and other aircraft are noisy, while jet aircraft taking off can make life miserable for those living near airports. Even as far as 20 miles down the flight path, jet noise will drown out a radio set at normal volume across the room.

Probably the greatest concern is air pollution. Particularly around our cities, air is increasingly loaded with dust, smoke, and other particulate matter from such sources as incomplete combustion. The atmosphere is increasingly burdened by chemical pollution in the form of carbon monoxide, sulfur dioxide, and other chemicals. The automobile is the greatest single source of chemical pollution. Every gallon of gasoline burned yields 3 pounds of carbon monoxide, a quarter to a half pound of hydrocarbons, and about an ounce of nitrogen oxides. The daily carbon monoxide output of American traffic exceeds a quarter of a million tons.

Effects of Pollution

The detrimental effects of air pollution on health are increasingly clear. When death rates during a period of severe contamination are compared with those normally expected, "epidemic" effects can be shown. During a "pea souper" in London in 1952, excess deaths were estimated at 4,000 in a 5-day period. In New York City, during a week of severe smog 200 extra deaths were estimated, not counting an equal number who died in a plane crash partly attributed to low visibility, and a similar finding was made in London in 1962.

Comparisons of death rates in different places reveal continuing "endemic" effects of air pollution. Common colds are found to occur more frequently in polluted areas. Chronic bronchial conditions are correlated with pollution. As shown in Figure 1, deaths from lung cancer vary from locality to locality with the concentration of particulate matter. In recent years a higher gen-

eral death rate has been observed along a section of Staten Island exposed to wind from the industrial section of New Jersey. In addition chemical pollution has been a serious factor in damage to livestock and crops, and has caused damage to paint, materials, and machinery. Ozone from automobile exhaust contributes to the deterioration of rubber. In one estimate, total property damage from air pollution has been set at more than $15 billion a year.

Growth of the Problem

Although many forms of environmental pollution have long been known, it is only in recent years that it has been recognized as an urgent problem, and many people, even today, fail to grasp its full magnitude.

During the last 20 years U.S. GNP has risen an average of nearly 4 percent per year. Water use has risen at roughly the same rate, while annual consumption of automobile gasoline has been rising at 5 percent and aviation fuel twice as fast. This means that the output of pollutants into the limited environment has been doubling once every 7–17 years. This rising volume must remain suspended in the environment until it can be reabsorbed or recycled through natural processes, and since the carrying power of the environment is finite, it becomes increasingly contaminated. The earth's atmosphere, for example, is only about 12 miles deep. If we imagine the earth as a good-sized apple, the atmosphere would be about as thick as the outside skin. Pollutants put into it must be naturally or artificially removed or they remain. Surprising as some people find the idea, pollution cannot "blow away," or "float away." It can, of course, be diluted to the point at which it is no longer a problem, but only as long as the volume is small compared to the carrying power of the environment.

The way the problem of pollution grows is represented in Figure 2. The limited

FIGURE 1   DEATH RATE FROM LUNG CANCER IN RELATION TO CONCENTRATION OF PARTICULAR MATTER

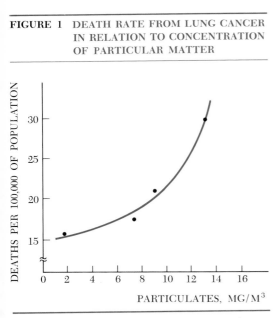

SOURCE: *Air Pollution Control:* Hearings Before a Special Subcommittee on Air and Water Pollution of the Committee on Public Works, U.S. Senate, September 9, 10, and 11, 1963, Appendix.

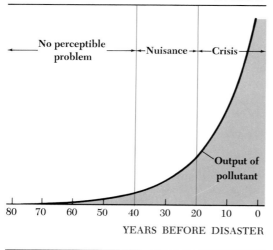

FIGURE 2   GROWTH OF A POLLUTION
                        PROBLEM AT 7 PERCENT PER YEAR

CARRYING CAPACITY OF THE ENVIRONMENT

YEARS BEFORE DISASTER

incidents. Somebody makes a mistake and acid, poison, or another pollutant goes down a drain and scours out the environment. An accident of this kind occurred in the summer of 1969 near Bingen in West Germany. About 200 pounds of endosulfan, an insecticide, accidentally entered the Rhine River and in a few days covered the river with a carpet of 40 million dead fish. In the U.S. in 1967 the Department of the Interior listed a total of 375 reports of fish kill attributable to specific incidents. An estimated total of over 11 million fish were killed, 80 percent as a consequence of industrial operations, most of the remainder as a consequence of agricultural practices.[1]

Bad as these accidents are, however, they are responsible for a relatively minor part of environmental pollution, for the overwhelming bulk of pollution is the result not of accident or neglect, but of the very same market mechanisms that drive business firms to turn out more and better goods at increasingly lower costs. Pollution is not a casual accompaniment of economic progress. It is created along with progress by the competitive process itself. To understand the problems of pollution and its control, we must first understand how pollution arises in the competitive process.

capacity of the environment to carry and reabsorb pollutants is represented by the ceiling on the chart. The compound interest growth curve represents the output of pollutants growing at 7 percent per year—a rough average of the rates mentioned above. At this rate, output doubles every 10 years, but the rate at which the carrying capacity of the environment is exhausted becomes frightening. Pollution is only a mild nuisance 40 years before real disaster, and it is only a severe nuisance just 20 years before it becomes absolutely intolerable. When the present generation of college students was born, pollution output was only about a quarter of what it is today, and when their children reach college age, it will be 8 times greater than it now is unless we recognize it as a critical problem and take massive steps to correct it.

BOTTLES AND BEER CANS: AN EXAMPLE

Although in terms of its present magnitude and current level of damage, litter is one of the less urgent pollution problems, we can begin our analysis with the familiar broken bottle and the flattened beverage can. Once this relatively simple case has been explored, we can return to the more critical problems of air and water pollution.

Causes of Pollution

A certain amount of pollution is pure accident. This is often true of the fish-kill

[1] U.S. Department of the Interior, Federal Water Pollution Control Administration, *Pollution-Caused Fish Kills, Annual Report, 1967.*

A Nickel Back on the Bottle

Beverages were sold in expensive, heavy bottles 30 or 40 years ago. Since the customer wanted the contents, not the expensive bottle, and since the beverage manufacturer wanted to reuse the bottles, it was the practice to require the buyer to leave a cash deposit with the merchant which was returned to him when he brought the empties back. From the standpoint of environmental pollution, this was an admirable system, since it provided a strong incentive to the customer not to abandon the bottle, but to keep it and return it. We can get a good idea of the magnitude of this incentive if we remember that a typical deposit was 5 cents at a time when factory workers averaged only about 40 cents an hour and many people worked for half that amount. A corresponding deposit today, when average hourly earnings in factories exceed $3, would be nearly 40 cents a bottle! A deposit of this size encouraged customers to bring their empties back, but even when they did not, anybody else who found them lying around had a strong incentive to pick them up.[2]

It is useful to pause to contemplate this system.

1. If the environment was not to be cluttered up with abandoned bottles and broken glass, somebody had to pick the bottles up.

2. The system imposed the cost of picking up the bottles on the consumer of the product himself. He could pick the bottle up himself; if not, he relinquished his deposit to pay somebody else to do it for him.

3. People who were unwilling to pay this cost, either in terms of their own efforts or by the sacrifice of their deposit, could not buy the product.

Essentially, this system treated environmental cleanup as a cost of production

along with the cost of labor and materials. The user of the product paid the full cost for using the product, including the cost of cleaning up the environment.

This system dealt effectively with the bulk of the problem, until the product was "improved." Soft drinks and beer are highly differentiated products, and manufacturers are constantly alert to new ways to attract customers. If a producer could devise a way to package the product that would relieve the customer of the inconvenience of cleaning up—say by putting it in "convenient" *throw-away* cans and bottles—he could save trouble for his customers and increase his own sales and profits. So great would be the competitive advantage of this type of packaging that it provided a powerful incentive to can manufacturers to develop a method of canning carbonated beverages. Once this was found, no beverage manufacturer could avoid adopting it, even if—as was not, in fact the case—he had foreseen all its consequences for the environment. A producer of canned drinks had a competitive advantage over his rivals, and had they not followed his lead, they would have been driven out of business.

The shift to cans also had a competitive impact on the bottle-manufacturing industry. The declining market for old-style reusable bottles produced a powerful incentive to invest in the development of a cheaper, lighter, disposable bottle to recapture the market from can makers, and the reusable bottle disappeared from the scene.

But the cost of cleanup did *not* disappear. Bottles and cans taken on a picnic must still be cleaned up, or they remain to spoil the park. Either we pay the cost by devoting time and trouble (our own or somebody else's) to picking them up and taking them away, or we pay the cost in unsightly parks and beaches and badly littered streets. In fact, if anything, the disposable container has *increased* the cost. The old-fashioned beer bottle, once pro-

[2] As a matter of fact careless picnickers sometimes found that their empty bottles disappeared while they were not watching.

duced, remained in circulation from bottler to retailer to household and back again. The disposable container travels in one direction, from bottler to retailer to household, and even if its ultimate destination is the city dump instead of the beach or park, some provision must be made to handle it.

No Deposit, No Return

But who pays this cost? Notice how the new system works. The user of the product no longer has any economic incentive to clean up after using the product. If he picks up his own cans and bottles, it is because of his thoughtfulness, or because he does not want to be a "litterbug." Out of 10 people, 9 may respond to this incentive, but 10 percent of the litter still remains in the environment. Not only is there no incentive for the customer to clean up his own litter, but he is no longer forced to pay somebody else to do it for him. The empty can or bottle is valueless. Picnickers no longer find that their empties have mysteriously disappeared. They are more likely to discover that they have been mysteriously multiplied by the donations of others.

Competition as a Pollution-Producer

The final result is the broken bottle and the empty beer can as common features of the environment, not by accident or bad luck, but as a direct result of the way the competitive system is allowed to operate. To make sure that this point is understood, let us first review the competitive aspects of cost saving in general, as illustrated in Figure 3. The average total cost of production of some product, say shoes, is shown for each of 2 firms in the industry. At the outset they have identical total costs represented by the black curves C_aC_a and C_bC_b. If the firms are to remain in business, prices must at least cover total costs, a

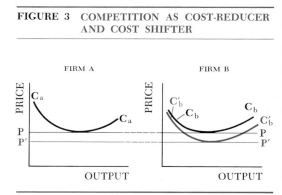

FIGURE 3   COMPETITION AS COST-REDUCER AND COST SHIFTER

situation represented by the height of the black price line PP.

Now suppose firm B, on the right, discovers and introduces a way to eliminate certain operations and reduce average cost as shown by the blue curve $C'_bC'_b$. It is at once apparent that firm B can now earn extra profits, even while selling at the old price in competition with the rest of the industry. The prospect of similar profits provides a powerful incentive to other producers to do the same thing, and as firms shift to the cheaper process and new firms enter, prices are driven down toward the lower cost level represented by the line $P'P'$. We see that a firm like A which would be unable or unwilling to adopt the new method could no longer cover costs and would be forced out of business.

When competition works this way, the result is better and cheaper products, but the very same powerful system can create pollution. This can be represented in the same figure. Again we have 2 representative firms, this time beverage manufacturers. The industry is operating with returnable bottles, and 2 types of cost have been distinguished. The height of the lower curve $C'_bC'_b$ represents all production cost except the cost of environmental cleanup. To this production cost we have added the average cost of cleaning up and returning the bottle, bringing the average total cost up to the level C_bC_b. Presumably this average cost of cleanup is embodied in the deposit made on the bottle and is paid to whoever brings the bottle back. If the customer returns his own bottles, he receives the deposit as payment for his trouble. If somebody else does the cleaning up instead, he presents the empty bottle and receives the deposit as payment for his services. Either way, the cost of maintaining an environment free of discarded bottles is actually incorporated in the cost of doing business and is passed on to the consumer as part of the competitive price *PP*.

When beverage manufacturer B adopts cans and disposable bottles, however, he need no longer pay the cost of environmental cleanup, and as far as he is concerned, costs have fallen to $C'_b C'_b$.[3] This cost "saving" is passed on to consumers by eliminating the deposit, bringing the price down to *P'P'*. This removes the incentive to the customer to clean up the environment and eliminates the payment to anyone else for doing so.

The effect on competition is like the cost saving in the first example, and those who fail to follow are forced out. But notice the important difference between the 2 cases. The disposable container does not reduce the *true* economic cost of the beverage. Somebody must still bear the cost of environmental cleanup, either by picking up bottles and cans or by living with the added litter. Indeed, as we noted above, if the disposable container has had any effect, it has increased the real cost of cleanup. Rather than reducing cost, the innovation has enabled the firm (and hence its customers) to shift part of the cost onto somebody else.

Left to itself, the competitive process does not distinguish between true cost reduction and cost shifting. If a method is found by which competitive firms can avoid paying a cost, whether by actually eliminat-

[3] Adoption of the new method would doubtless alter costs in other ways as well. The analysis could be made more complicated to allow for these changes, but the point would be the same.

ing it or merely by passing it on to somebody else, competition forces its adoption. The first firms to adopt it make profits for themselves, while those that cannot or will not adopt it are ultimately forced out. If the new discovery is a true cost reduction, the result is greater productivity and higher living standards. If the new discovery is a way of shifting the cost of environmental cleanup, either the job is assumed by somebody else, or the environment is polluted.

Removing the Incentive To Pollute

In other words, an important cause of environmental pollution is the same incentive system that, working positively, drove real U.S. gross national product from $400 to $4,000 per capita in only a century. If pollution is to be controlled, the economic incentive to pollute must be removed and economic incentives to control or clean up pollution must be made effective. There are several ways this can be done in the case of cars and bottles, and it is instructive to examine some that have been suggested.

1. One way to deal with the problem is to make it illegal to sell beverages in nonreturnable containers. Such a law might also stipulate a deposit sufficiently high to maintain the desired level of incentive. A law of this sort has been proposed in the Province of Ontario.

2. Nonreturnable containers could be permitted—they might be cheaper, more sanitary, or have other advantages—but under a tax sufficiently high to finance a bounty payable to persons returning containers to designated collection points. A plan of this kind must be applied on a national level. If a single state paid a bounty high enough to be effective, it might also make it profitable for people to "import" used containers from other places, forcing the state to assume the added costs of cleaning up its neighbors' environment as well as its own.

3. One might merely tax the sale of beverages at a rate sufficiently high to defray the cost of collection and cleanup by public agencies. This would be feasible on a local level without national legislation but would provide no incentive to the consumer to help. Widespread litter is expensive to hunt down and clean up, and it is cheapest to enlist the help of the consumer, who is, after all, right on the spot at the time.

4. One suggestion sometimes heard is that government should ignore all pollution problems in the hope that private business will find a use for the offending pollutant. There have been important examples in which changing technology has converted an erstwhile pollutant into a valuable resource. Probably the best example is gasoline, which in the early days of the petroleum industry was a dangerous and unwanted byproduct remaining after the heavier illuminating oil had been removed. With the advent of the automobile the hitherto unwanted byproduct became the most valuable part of crude oil.

In the case of beverage cans, it has been suggested that with proper organization, the aluminum in used beer cans could be recovered and "recycled" through the aluminum industry. One can always hope, but any economic incentive for this procedure has been present all along, yet so far the aluminum industry has found it cheaper to exploit virgin sources. Once a "bounty" system had been established, however, "recycling" might be a constructive answer to the question of what to do with scrap cans after they had been collected. Moreover, whatever value the scrap has would help defray the cleanup cost.

The important point to remember, however, is that since private industry had a strong incentive to pollute the environment in the first place, the problem will continue unless the system of incentives is altered. This can be accomplished deliberately by legislation. In the absence of such action,

we must rely on luck, a notably undependable instrument of control.

THE GENERAL PROBLEM OF POLLUTION CONTROL

Although different physical and chemical mechanisms are responsible for air, water, and other kinds of environmental pollution, the economic mechanism is essentially the same for all. The operation of the competitive system literally forces producers who can shift part of the cost of waste disposal onto the community to do so. Pollution is not the work of men who are exceptionally greedy or even particularly insensitive. (Although they *are* likely to live upwind from their own factories, if they live near them at all, and to vacation far away from polluted lakes and streams.) The major cause of pollution is that industry is trapped in a competitive system that applies the same severe sanctions to firms whose operating costs are high because they refuse to pollute the environment that it does to those whose costs are high because they cling to obsolete or inefficient production methods. A competitive producer who can shift the cost of disposal onto the community by pouring industrial wastes into rivers or by blowing them into the atmosphere has no more choice in whether to do so than he has in whether to adopt the new labor-saving device that enables his competitors to undersell him.

Costs of Control Equipment

Some pollution-control equipment is only a small addition to the cost of the basic production unit itself. For example, a recent study of costs of pollution-control equipment showed that a crude-oil distillation unit of 37,000 barrels per hour capacity required an investment of over $3 million.

A vapor-control system to go with it would add only $10,000.[4] A unit to manufacture 30 tons of liquid hydrogen a year costs over $8 million, while an air-pollution control flare adds only $17,700. In such cases a small incentive would be adequate to encourage the installation, but in other cases the pollution-control equipment is a significant part of the total cost. A unit to manufacture 30,000 tons of synthetic rubber per year costs $1,600,000, while the accompanying vapor manifold and flare cost $250,000. An open-hearth furnace of 60 tons heat could be built for $200,000, but an electric precipitator to use with it costs $150,000. In some cases the cost of the pollution-control devices even exceeds the investment in the basic equipment. Equipment for coating pipe, including spinning, wrapping, and dipping 4 to 10 lengths per hour costs $23,500, while the scrubbers to control its exhaust cost $32,000. An insulation production unit, including cupola, blow chamber, and curing oven with 5,000 lbs. per hour capacity comes to only $13,000 while the baghouse, scrubber, and afterburner to control pollution add another $30,000!

Can We Afford the Cost?

Nobody is in favor of pollution, and everybody approves control when the cost is not too much, but what do we do about industries in which pollution control costs as much or more than the product itself? Is it possible for the industry to bear this burden? Is pollution control economically feasible under these circumstances? As we have already seen, what is at stake is not always a question of true cost, but sometimes of who is to bear the cost. Environmental pollution is *itself* a cost, borne by all of us in terms of less pleasant surroundings, more expensive living costs, bigger medical bills, and higher death rates. If the industry cannot afford to cover these costs, is there any reason for the population to bear them instead?

The great power of the private competitive system is precisely that an industry that can produce the product for the least cost deprives less efficient industries of resources and forces them out of business, yet applying this same idea to pollution costs sometimes bring anguished cries of unfair competition! Thus, a group of private utilities joined with representatives of the United Mine Workers recently in demonstrating the "unfairness" of a proposal to compel electric utilities to burn only coal that had been processed to reduce its sulphur content. The idea of the proposal was to reduce air pollution from sulphur dioxide, but the demonstration of "unfairness" was to show that sulfur treatment by known methods would make the cost of coal-generated electricity too high to compete with that generated by nuclear reactors. In other words, if these figures were correct, the only reason coal generation can continue is that coal-burning utilities can shift part of the cost onto the public. When the true costs are correctly calculated, coal is already a more expensive fuel. Is it "fair" to ask the public to bear the difference in cost so that coal burners can stay in business?

In the case of electrical generation there is at least a reasonably inexpensive alternative. In many cases, however, we are told that pollution-control costs are "prohibitive" and out of the question until more "economical" control methods can be found. In evaluating this argument it is useful to reflect on what it is that "prohibitive" costs usually prohibit. Ordinarily when costs are "prohibitive," the necessity to pass them along to consumers in high

[4] These and following figures are costs of actual installation in the Los Angeles area, given in *Air Pollution Control*: Hearings Before a Special Subcommittee on Air and Water Pollution of the Committee on Public Works, U.S. Senate. September 9, 10, and 11, 1963.

prices prohibits purchase of the product and prohibits the firm or industry from producing it. Is there any reason pollution costs are any different? If the customer will buy the product only if somebody else will bear part of the cost, he is clearly unwilling to pay the opportunity cost involved. This merely means that he does not want the product as much as he wants the other things that could be produced with the same resources.

Incentives for Developing New Control Technology

There is a second important aspect to the problem of pollution control. Permitting firms to shift heavy costs onto the public seriously reduces the incentive for equipment manufacturers to devise better control methods or to develop more effective equipment. Equipment manufacturers are, after all, business firms, too, and will develop those aspects of their products that will have the greatest customer appeal. There is a severe limit to the demand for devices to reduce costs that are already shifted onto somebody else, and therefore relatively little private research and development effort goes into pollution-control items.

The automobile is an excellent example of this proposition. Although automobile exhaust is one of the most important sources of air pollution, the driver is not held accountable. Instead of paying to clean up his mess, he merely pushes the cost onto society. Since he, himself, is a negligible part of the total problem, the individual driver has no incentive to control his own exhaust, nor even to reduce his own driving. The automobile manufacturer who added any pollution-control device to the car, would therefore get no return for his pains, for he would have added a feature that was not desirable to the consumer. Manufacturers, therefore, have had no incentive to add pollution-control equipment

to their cars, nor even an incentive to finance research in this direction. While immense research has gone into making cars faster, easier to drive, more economical, and more stylish, virtually no research has gone into pollution control until the rather mild government requirements were recently imposed.

Altering Incentives for Control

The most important key to pollution control is to change the system of incentives to bring the powerful apparatus of competition to bear on eliminating the problem rather than adding to it. One perfectly straightforward method would be simply to apply a special tax to people and business firms in proportion to the severity of the pollution for which they were responsible. The tax should be high enough to make a substantial difference in the total cost of production—doubling or tripling it in many cases and making it prohibitively high at severe levels of pollution. This would radically change the incentives for the installation of known control devices and would be a powerful stimulant to their improvement and the development of new technology.

In the cases of automobiles, trucks, aircraft, and similar equipment, when systematic monitoring of the individual vehicle is not feasible, strict requirements must be legislated for the installation of control devices as standard equipment. A start has already been made in this direction. The 1965 Amendments to the Clean Air Act authorized the Secretary of Health, Education, and Welfare to set standards for automobile emissions. Standards established effective with 1968 models required 100 percent control of crankcase emissions and will make a significant reduction in total pollution. Higher standards are badly needed for exhaust emission, but adequate controls are expensive. Note, however, that the fact that such control methods might double or triple the price of gasoline-powered cars and the cost of driving are not a reason to reject them. True, they could quite conceivably shift the market to electrical vehicles, or to those powered by external combustion steam engines, but if this proved to be the case, it would merely indicate the degree to which the "low-cost" gasoline automobile owes its competitive position to shifting operating costs onto somebody else.

Indeed, a careful evaluation of costs would probably reveal that private automobile transportation is one of the most inefficient, most heavily subsidized activities in the world. Not only is the driver permitted to blow his exhaust into the air, but he is provided with streets and expressways at no direct cost to his driving. In addition, the subsidy provided to the petroleum industry by the oil-depletion allowance results in a larger output of gasoline at lower prices than would be possible under competitive circumstances. Nor is the unsightly clutter of oil rigs nor the pollution of the shore by leaking wells and wrecked tankers included as any part of the cost of production. The result is gasoline so cheap that most of the cars in any stream of city traffic carry only 1 person. If American gasoline prices reflected the full cost of production and their contribution to pollution, the demand for adequate public transportation systems would be greatly strengthened.[5]

Tax Credits

One recent pollution-control proposal that has been widely discussed is to amend the corporate profits tax to provide tax credits to firms that install pollution-control equipment. Although this appears superficially much the same as a tax imposed on pollu-

tion, there are important differences both in the size and kind of incentive provided and in the fairness of the system.

In the first place, it might be difficult to make the size of the tax credit depend on actual accomplishment in pollution reduction. The credit is much more likely to be defined by the cost of the equipment itself, which would provide quite a different kind of incentive. Secondly, a tax credit is limited by the existing tax rate. A firm can only be forgiven all its taxes, which is an insufficient incentive if equipment is so expensive that its installation could involve losses.

Thirdly, even to the extent that the tax credit succeeded in reducing pollution, it would still fail to require firms to assume the full burden of their own costs. Firms that did not pollute in the first place, and hence needed no pollution control equipment, would pay the usual profits tax rate, while those who did pollute could recover part of the cost of control from the public in lower taxes. The public would still pay, not the firm and its customers.

Finally, tax credits are probably poor psychology. They make the public appear to be coming hat in hand to plead with the producer. The producers' natural reaction is to treat the matter as a special favor to the community rather than a matter of competitive urgency, and to respond accordingly.

The Need for Federal Action

Not only does control of pollution require public action, but in most cases the action must be nationwide, and in some, even international. Many problems occur not in the neighborhood of the source, but some distance away. The community at the source has no problem and no motive to act, and the community with the problem and motive is powerless. This separation of source and problem usually arises when afflicted communities are downwind or

[5] Even beyond this, there is much to be said for the outright exclusion of private passenger automobiles from dense downtown areas.

downstream from pollution sources. One of the most serious air-pollution problems in Canada is found in Windsor, Ontario, which lies downwind from the industrial exhaust of Detroit, just across the river. The situation is reversed a few miles north, where Sarnia, Ontario contributes to the problems of Port Huron, Michigan.

Stream pollution is almost universally of this character. The river carries the waste away from the source to create problems for people living farther downstream. No community can protect itself; all it can do is to protect others, which it has a much weaker motive to do. Each community is faced with the necessity of cleaning up the problem created by somebody else over whom it has no control, but it has no reason to pass clean water on to its neighbors.

Even when the problem is inflicted by the locality on itself, however, it is not locally controllable if the offender is in close competition with firms in other areas. Regulation to prevent the local firm from shifting part of its costs onto the community would merely raise its costs above those imposed on its competitors, located elsewhere and not subject to the regulation. A competitive firm cannot survive under these circumstances and would be forced either to move or to shut down. In either case, jobs and business would disappear from the community along with pollution, and the threat of such loss is usually sufficient to forestall local action. The only hope in these circumstances is to apply controls to all competitors. For most purposes this means nationwide regulation.

NONINDUSTRIAL SOURCES OF POLLUTION

Pollution is by no means limited to industrial processes and consumer products Some of it is created by the public for itself by the way it deals with sewage, garbage and refuse, trash incineration, chemical weed controls, and insecticides. Some of this pollution is attributable to the separation of the source from the problem as noted above, and some is a consequence of divided administrative responsibility, but probably the greatest cause is the simple failure of people to recognize that a critical problem exists, or that anything can be done about it. We seem to continue to hope that the problems will go away, yet left to themselves such problems inexorably double about once every decade. Not only will they not go away, but it will take a massive program of research and development merely to slow down their rate of increase.

Control of pollution is a serious problem, and it can be solved only by devoting large quantities of effort and resources to its solution. We know how to build nuclear reactors, hydrogen bombs, supersonic aircraft, and space vehicles because we spent immense sums to find out. If we are to find out how to handle the problems of sewage and garbage disposal, we must go about it in the same way. A number of years ago an American novelist remarked that we would land a man on the moon before we solved New York City's refuse problem. She was right, not because the world necessarily works that way, but because we only solve the problems we are willing to attack. We spent $5 billion a year to solve some of the problems of space flight. If we do not start thinking in the same terms about pollution control, space flight may be the only way out.

POLLUTION AND CONSERVATION

Pollution is only one aspect of the broader question of preserving the integrity of the environment around us. Many related problems arise because we ignore substantial costs of production. Part of the competitive advantage of strip and open-pit mining compared to other methods arises because mining firms are not held responsible for the resulting soil erosion, nor even required to refill the holes they dig. More broadly still, cost calculations often omit any account of the destruction of scenery, woodland, wild-life habitat, beaches, and countryside. These are often of great value not only for human recreation and as productive resources, but as crucial links in vital cycles of air and water. The use of streams to dispose of sewage and industrial waste is not cheap when account is taken of the loss of commercial fishing and seafood production, contamination of beaches and recreation areas, and the added cost of water purification.

Not only do we fail to include the additional pollution output as part of the cost of highway extentions, but neither do we allow for the destruction of woodlands and the consequent reduced environmental capacity to absorb the pollutant. Nor is the disruption of neighborhood structure reckoned as part of the price of an urban expressway. Yet if these costs are not included, the use of our resources is just as wasteful as if labor costs had been somehow forgotten when prices were set.

Until very recently, it was the practice in the U.S.S.R. to construct new factories by providing the industrial planning commission with a fixed total budget which was to cover all construction costs. The commission was then expected to build the best possible factory within their budgetary limits. The budget did not, however, include any allowance for the purchase of land. This was in keeping with the Marxian labor theory of value by which only the products of labor were deemed to have worth.[6] In place of a budgetary allowance to buy land, the planning commission was given the right to commandeer whatever land they wanted for the factory site. The natural result was that, given a choice

[6] The labor theory of value is discussed in Chapter 24.

between an uncleared, rocky, bumpy field which it would be difficult to farm and a highly productive, smooth, level field already cleared and under cultivation, the commission almost invariably chose the valuable farm land for the factory site and left the poorer land for cultivation! The reason was that since the good land was already cleared and level, the cost of site preparation was kept at a minimum, permitting the planning agency to apply more of its budget to construction and equipment of the factory itself.

It finally occurred to the Soviet authorities that there might be a connection between their difficulties in raising farm productivity and the fact that the best agricultural land was going for factory sites, leaving poorer land for crops. In more recent years, Soviet planning commissions are required to buy their land out of their budget at prices based on agricultural productivity.

We in the U.S. sometimes make exactly the same mistake in our approach to the recreational and aesthetic value of unspoiled countryside. Redwood timber is of great commercial value, but redwood forests are also of great value as a unique part of the world in which we live. Any decision about their consumption through lumbering should take into account the great cost of lost recreational value. It is often difficult to place a value on this aspect of the world, but it should certainly be reckoned somewhat higher than the value implied by the remark, attributed to one government official, that "if you've seen one tree, you've seen them all." It is a commentary on our economic system that a proposal to dam the Colorado River and flood the Grand Canyon in the interest of irrigation and power production could actually reach Congress with the cost arising from the destruction of this wonder of nature completely ignored. If we are to protect ourselves from making a polluted junkpile of the world, we must insist that every such project be reckoned at its full cost, and that these costs contain full recognition of lost opportunities, not only to use these resources for other industrial purposes, but to leave them in their unspoiled condition.

SUMMARY

Pollution is emerging as a widespread social problem, with detrimental effects on personal health and safety and damage to crops, land, and other property. The problem not only is serious today, but is growing at a rate of 4 to 10 percent annually. At these rates of growth, the margin of time that separates a nuisance and a disaster is only 7–17 years.

A certain amount of pollution is due to accident, but the overwhelming bulk is created by the same forces of competition that bring us better products at lower costs, for the incentive to minimize cost also forces competitive firms to shift costs onto somebody else if they can. The most important step in pollution control is to replace the competitive incentive to pollute by positive incentives to clean up pollution, to install control devices, and to invest in the development of improved control techniques.

The cost of pollution-control devices is often large compared to the investment in other facilities, but shifting the cost onto the public does not make it smaller. Nor is there any validity to the argument that firms cannot "afford" the equipment, for this is merely a confession that the industry's products are not worth what they really cost and should not be produced in the first place. Regulation is only feasible, however, if it is uniformly applied over the entire market. Locally regulated firms that compete in a national or international market are merely driven out of business or forced to move.

A significant volume of pollution is nonindustrial and results from the behavior of governments and people in their handling of such things as refuse disposal, sewage, and insecticides. To control this kind of pollution we must be prepared to invest resources on the same massive scale as we do in military procurement and space research. The problem of pollution is only one facet of the broader problem of maintaining the integrity of the environment. We must learn to account for the effects on environment as an important part of all cost calculations.

CHAPTER 21

International Trade and International Payments

If each family had to supply all its own needs, we would all be reduced to bare subsistence living. When each worker can specialize at the job he does best and exchange his products with others, everybody lives better. Much the same is true of regions. When workers in each region specialize in the production of items which are best suited to their own climate and resources and exchange their specialties for those of other areas, people in all regions end up with more than they could produce at home for themselves. In the U.S., automobiles made in the Midwest are exchanged for wheat grown on the plains, fruit from the West, oil from the Southwest, and clothing manufactured in the East from cotton grown in the South. Although some of these products are also produced in the Midwest, the people there can get much more and better food, clothing, and other things in exchange for their automobiles than they could possibly produce entirely from their own resources.

As a matter of fact, they get more and better automobiles as well. If each area were self-contained, the need to employ labor in occupations of low productivity, unsuited to the resources of the region, would hold real incomes to a low level. The production of necessities would absorb so much of the area's manpower and resources that few people, even in the automobile-producing region, would be able to afford cars. Moreover, the cost per car would be immensely higher because an automobile industry limited to a total market of only a few million low-income people could not exploit the mass production methods permitted by a market of more than 200 million high-income consumers. By the same token, specialization and exchange also improve the lot of families in all the other regions, giving them higher incomes and cheaper products than would be possible if they tried to be self-sufficient.

INTERNATIONAL TRADE

International specialization and exchange is only a variation of regional specialization. Although international trade crosses national boundaries, the gains are exactly the same as those reaped from regional trade. The existence of the political boundary, however, introduces some special aspects that tend to disguise the precise nature of these gains, and people sometimes forget that the gains are there. For this reason it is worth taking a closer look at international trade itself.

It is easy to understand how Americans gain by exchanging manufactured goods for South American coffee. Labor productivity in manufacturing is much higher here than in South America, while the climate makes coffee growing highly productive in South America and virtually impossible in most of the U.S. As long as we exchange our own products for coffee, tea, bananas, or other items that American workers cannot produce, everybody can understand the gains from trade. But when we import steel, textiles, and other things that American workers can and do produce, some people get confused. If we can produce these things ourselves, how do we gain in buying them from abroad? The confusion is enhanced by the fact that American workers are frequently more productive and better paid than those in the countries from which we buy.

Comparative Advantage

The riddle is most easily explored by example. The hypothetical productivities of U.S. and Japanese workers in coal mines and in motorcycle manufacturing plants are shown in Table 1. According to the table, the average output per manhour of labor applied to coal mining is 1 ton in the United States, but only .2 tons in Japan.[1]

[1] The productivity figures allow not only for the number of manhours employed directly in the

TABLE 1   ILLUSTRATION OF COMPARATIVE ADVANTAGE

	U.S.	JAPAN
Output per manhour in:		
Coal mining	1.0 ton	.2 ton
Motorcycle manufacturing	.020 vehicles	.015 vehicles
Opportunity cost of:		
Coal	.020 motorcycles	.075 motorcycles
Motorcycles	50 tons of coal	13.3 tons of coal
Wage rate	$3.00	¥300
Money prices before trade:		
Coal	$4.50 per ton	¥2,250 per ton
Motorcycles	$225 each	¥30,000 each
Equilibrium prices after trade:		
Coal	$4.90	¥1,820
Motorcycles	$114.00	¥40,000

Put the other way around, it takes only an average of 1 manhour of labor to produce a ton of coal in the U.S., while 5 manhours are needed in Japan.

Although the difference is smaller, the table also supposes greater productivity of American workers in the production of motorcycles. With a motorcycle of a given standard quality as a measure, U.S. labor productivity is .02 vehicles per manhour, while in Japan it is only .015. That is, it takes 50 manhours on the average to produce a motorcycle in the U.S., but 67 in Japan.

Now, since American workers are more effective than the Japanese in the production of both coal and motorcycles, why should we buy either from Japan? Would we not be better off to produce them at home with our own efficient labor? An easy

mines, but also for the labor needed to produce materials, supplies, and other purchased inputs, and for the workers employed in producing replacements for the mining machinery used. The figures in the table are hypothetical, but are reasonably realistic.

way to see why we would not is to calculate the opportunity cost of the products in each country. In the United States when the 1 manhour of labor required to produce a ton of coal is withheld from the motorcycle industry, we forego .020 vehicles that could otherwise be produced. Thus, the opportunity cost of a ton of coal is .020 motorcycles. In Japan, on the other hand, 5 manhours must be withheld from motorcycle production to produce a ton of coal. Since this involves the sacrifice of 5 × .015, or .075 vehicles, the opportunity cost of Japanese coal is .075 motorcycles.

Now compare the costs of motorcycles. In the U.S., 50 manhours are needed to produce a motorcycle. Had they been employed in coal production, they could have produced 50 tons of coal. In Japan, 67 manhours are needed to produce a motorcycle. Although this is more manhours than in the U.S., the productivity of labor in Japanese coal mining is so low that 67 manhours would have produced only 13.3 tons of coal.

When we look at the results of these calculations as recorded in Table 1, we see that the real opportunity cost of coal is lower in the U.S. than in Japan, while the real opportunity cost of motorcycles is higher in the U.S. than in Japan. A U.S.-produced motorcycle costs the equivalent of 50 tons of coal. If, instead of producing the motorcycle, we use the same amount of labor to turn out coal, we can trade the 50 tons of coal to the Japanese for 2 or 3 motorcycles. The Japanese are happy to cooperate. The best way for them to get coal is not to produce it themselves at a cost of .075 motorcycles per ton, but to produce .075 motorcycles and trade them for 2 or 3 tons of coal.

This situation is described in terms of *comparative advantage.* If we take Japanese productivity in each industry as an index of 100, the comparative productivity of U.S. workers is 500 in coal mining, but only 133 in motorcycle manufacture. The average index of the 2 U.S. industries together, 316, measures the average productivity advantage of American industry over the Japanese. The U.S. has a *comparative advantage* over Japan in those industries in which the U.S. productivity advantage is above average. It has a *comparative disadvantage* in industries in which the U.S. productivity advantage is below average. The U.S. has a comparative advantage over Japan in coal mining, where the productivity advantage is 500 compared to the 316 average. The U.S. has a comparative disadvantage in motorcycles, where the productive advantage of 133 is below the average.

The Japanese position is examined by using U.S. productivity as the basis of the comparison. On the basis of U.S. = 100, the comparative productivity of Japanese workers is 20 in coal mining and 75 in motorcycle manufacture, giving an average of about 47. The Japanese have a comparative advantage over the U.S. in motorcycles, where the index is above average, but a comparative disadvantage in coal mining.

Products in which a nation has a comparative advantage cost less to make at home than abroad. They use labor and resources on those jobs where productive advantage is highest. The cost of products with a comparative disadvantage is higher at home than abroad. Their production would take labor and resources away from jobs in which productive advantage is above average and put them on jobs of below average advantage. It follows that all countries are materially better off when each specializes in the products in which it has comparative advantage, and trades for the other things it needs.

The Terms of Trade

If Americans had only 100 manhours of labor available, they could produce 50 tons of coal and only 1 motorcycle. If, however, they used the labor to turn out 100 tons of coal, they could keep 50 and trade the other 50 for 2 or 3 motorcycles. In other words, as long as the U.S. can get a motorcycle in trade for anything less than 50 tons of coal, it will do better to specialize in coal and buy motorcycles from Japan. By the same token, as long as the Japanese can get more than 13.3 tons of coal for a motorcycle, they will do better to specialize in motorcycles and buy their coal from the U.S.

The terms on which coal and motorcycles exchange are the *terms of trade*. Limits to the terms of trade are set by comparative advantage. Figure 1 illustrates the situation that might arise if an American company were to bargain with a Japanese firm to trade coal for motorcycles. Since Americans can make their own motorcycles for 50 tons of coal, they are unwilling to pay more than this for imported models. Since the motorcycles cost the Japanese 13.3 tons of coal to produce, they will not sell them for less than this amount. Bargaining between the 2 companies would fix the terms of trade somewhere between the maximum price the Americans will pay and the minimum price the Japanese will accept.

Figure 2 depicts the situation that

FIGURE 1 BARGAINING JAPANESE
MOTORCYCLES FOR U.S. COAL

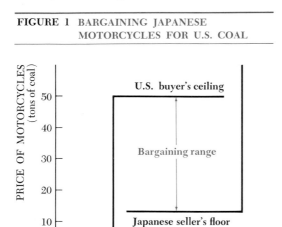

FIGURE 2 "BARGAINING" U.S. MOTORCYCLES
FOR JAPANESE COAL

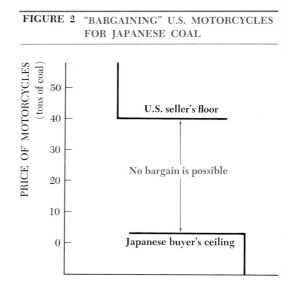

would occur if an American company wanted to bargain U.S. motorcycles for Japanese coal. Since the U.S. seller could get 50 tons of coal for each motorcycle, he would accept nothing less. The Japanese buyer could get Japanese motorcycles for only 13.3 tons of coal, and would pay no more. The would-be buyer's ceiling price is below the would-be seller's floor price, and no mutually satisfactory bargain is possible.

Wages, Prices, and Trade

To demonstrate the profitability of trade and to understand how terms of trade are fixed within their possible limits, we must first determine the prices of the respective products in the 2 countries. For this purpose, suppose that the U.S. wage rate is $3 per hour, while the average Japanese worker earns ¥300 per hour. Since labor is about two-thirds of total unit cost, prices (covering average total cost) would tend to be as shown in Table 1. In the U.S., coal would tend to sell for $4.50 a ton and motorcycles for $225 each, while in Japan, coal would sell for ¥2,250 a ton and motorcycles for ¥30,000 each.

Now imagine an American trading firm investing $450,000 in 100,000 tons of coal. The coal is shipped to Japan and sold for ¥225,000,000. The firm then invests the proceeds in 7,500 motorcycles to be shipped back to the U.S. and sold for $225 each for a total of almost $1,875,000. Even allowing for shipping, insurance, and other costs, this represents a handsome profit. Japanese companies could, of course, play the same game. An investment of ¥30,000,-000 in 1,000 motorcycles would bring $225,000 in the American market. The proceeds could buy 50,000 tons of U.S. coal to sell in Japan for ¥112,500,000; again a handsome profit.

As such profitable trade attracted more investors, prices would begin to adjust. The flood of coal into Japan would push prices down to levels that would force the unproductive Japanese mines out of business. The motorcycles coming into the U.S. market would push prices down and force high-cost U.S. manufacturers out of business. At the same time, expansion of U.S. coal production would tend to raise marginal costs as mines were worked more intensively. Expansion of Japanese motorcycle production might, likewise, be accompanied by rising costs and prices.

The situation might reach an equilibrium like that shown in Table 1. The price of coal has risen to $4.90 in the U.S. and fallen to ¥1,820 in Japan. The price of motorcycles has fallen to $114 in the U.S. and risen to ¥40,000 in Japan. At these prices, the producers of coal and motorcycles and the trading companies can just cover total costs, including a normal profit on operations. The equilibrium prices determine where, within the original bargaining range, the terms of trade are finally set. When calculated in U.S. prices, the terms of trade are about 29 tons of coal for 1 motorcycle. The prices of Japan imply 22 tons of coal for 1 motorcycle. The difference in the terms of trade in the 2 sets of prices represents the cost of transportation and exchange.

The final prices also imply an exchange rate between dollars and yen. In terms of coal-purchasing power, $4.90 = ¥1,820, or $1 = ¥370. In motorcycle-purchasing power, $114 = ¥40,000, or $1 = ¥350, approximately. Using $1 = ¥360 as an average, we can compare U.S. and Japanese wage rates. In terms of dollars, if the American worker receives $3 per hour, the Japanese worker's ¥300 represents about 300/360, or 83 cents. In terms of yen, if the Japanese worker receives ¥300 per hour, the American worker's $3 represents 3 × 360, or ¥1,080. This confirms what we already knew: The less productive Japanese worker earns lower real wages than his more productive American counterpart.

It is comparative advantage that makes trade mutually beneficial. Moreover, comparative advantage determines those products in which each country can profitably specialize and sets the limits to the terms of trade that will be mutually agreeable. In particular, note that the import of motorcycles into the United States does *not* depend on the pay scale of Japanese workers. Although from the comparison above it is apparent that the greater productivity of U.S. labor results in higher real earnings and living standards in the U.S. than in Japan, this fact is quite independent of the advantages of trade between the 2 countries. As a matter of fact, since trade must go both ways, it should be quite clear that imports must depend on something more than whose wages are lowest. If low Japanese wage rates were what allowed Americans to buy Japanese motorcycles, then what would allow the Japanese to buy American coal?

The Pattern of U.S. Trade

The United States with its continent-wide economy is less dependent on foreign trade than most other nations. As shown in Table 2, U.S. exports amount to only about 5 percent of GNP, one of the smallest ratios among the important trading nations of the world. Nations with less variety in their resources and with domestic markets too small to permit full specialization must trade on a wider scale to maintain their living standards. In most important nations the proportion of total output that enters foreign trade is 3 or 4 times that of the U.S., while a small but rich country like the Netherlands exports nearly half of its gross national product in exchange for specialized products of other nations. Among the nations shown in Table 2, only the U.S.S.R. (another continent-wide economy) shows a ratio of exports to GNP below that of the United States.

Nevertheless, American life would be vastly different without the many things in our daily life that come from abroad. Imports supply virtually all of our bananas, coffee, tea, cocoa, copra, silk, carpet wool, and crude rubber. We import 97 percent of the manganese used in our steel and 87 percent of the bauxite we refine into aluminum, as well as 60 percent of our apparel wool, 43 percent of our sugar, 42 percent of our bicycles and motorcycles, and 34 percent of our chinaware. Imported cameras, radios, binoculars, and automobiles are common.

TABLE 2 THE WORLD'S LARGEST EXPORTERS

	TOTAL EXPORTS	
	MILLIONS OF DOLLARS	PERCENT OF GNP
United States	30,013	5
West Germany	20,134	21
United Kingdom	14,132	18
France	10,889	15
Japan	9,777	11
Canada	9,551	22
U.S.S.R.	8,841	4
Italy	8,032	18
Belgium-Luxembourg	6,829	36
Netherlands	6,750	44
Sweden	4,264	25
Australia	3,074	16

SOURCE: United Nations, *Statistical Yearbook, 1967.*

A significant part of the output of many of our important industries is traded in payment. Of our milled rice 55 percent is sold abroad, along with 44 percent of our sulfur, 27 percent of cash grain production, and one-fifth of our cotton crop. Among manufactured goods, firms in other countries buy 25 to 30 percent of our total output of mining and oil field machinery, sewing machines, and certain types of office machines. Exports also include 15 to 25 percent of our output of metal-working equipment and machinery for the textile, woodworking, food products, and paper industries. We export 21 percent of our X-ray apparatus, along with 17 percent of our aircraft and 15 percent of our scientific instruments.

Although small in relation to U.S. gross national product, the total value of U.S. trade is by far the largest in the world. U.S. exports of recent years have amounted to 15 percent of world trade and have nearly equaled the combined exports of West Germany and the United Kingdom, the next 2 ranking countries.

The pattern of U.S. trade is shown in Table 3. Western Europe took a third of our exports and was our best customer for most individual products. Notable exceptions were grain, most of which went to India, cotton sent to Japan, and automobiles delivered to Canada. We also bought more from Western Europe than from any other area, but by a narrower margin. In individual products, European nations were our most important sources for imported machinery, alcoholic beverages, and iron and steel products, although the Japanese were an important runner-up in the latter. We spent only slightly less on European automobiles than on cars and components imported from Canada—the latter being largely the products of Canadian branches of American firms. Canada was our main source of wood pulp and of nonferrous metals, while Latin America was our most important outside supplier of

TABLE 3   VALUE OF U.S. TRADE IN LEADING COMMODITIES, BY AREAS
(millions of dollars)

	TOTAL	CANADA	AMERICAN REPUBLICS	WESTERN EUROPE	ASIA AND NEAR EAST	OTHER AREAS
EXPORTS						
Total	31,534	7,173	4,126	10,099	6,252	3,884
Agricultural commodities						
Grains and preparations	2,681	102	235	781	1,242	321
Fruit, nuts, vegetables	492	196	41	178	48	29
Tobacco, unmfg.	498	4	8	371	77	38
Soybeans	772	63	4	458	217	30
Cotton	464	33	1	113	296	21
Nonagricultural commodities						
Ores and scrap	520	78	31	116	291	4
Coal, coke, briquettes	501	144	34	189	132	2
Petroleum products	447	61	69	129	111	77
Chemicals	2,803	421	527	928	580	347
Machinery	8,251	2,211	1,309	2,486	1,097	1,148
Agricultural	844	352	141	138	82	131
Other nonelectrical	5,311	1,338	872	1,629	714	758
Electrical	2,097	520	296	719	302	260
Road motor vehicles	2,448	1,504	402	164	114	264
Aircraft, civilian	1,213	170	119	600	144	180
Pulp, paper, and mfgs.	726	98	129	281	126	92
Metals and mfgs.	1,734	526	265	456	301	186
Textile products	531	134	75	150	56	116
Other products and "Special category" exports[a]	7,453	1,428	877	2,699	1,420	1,029
IMPORTS						
Total	26,732	7,099	3,825	7,985	5,062	2,761
Agricultural commodities						
Meat and preparations	645	39	117	177	3	309
Fruit, nuts, vegetables	556	27	292	107	105	25
Coffee	964	—	670	—	41	253
Sugar	588	—	334	1	178	75
Nonagricultural commodities						
Alcoholic beverages	528	138	3	382	2	3
Pulp, paper, mfgs.	1,381	1,256	2	100	13	10
Ores and scrap	974	409	231	19	38	277
Petroleum and products	2,088	391	967	42	43	645
Chemicals	963	270	84	416	80	113
Machinery	3,103	72	20	1,471	811	19
Automobiles and trans. equipment	2,688	1,476	—	1,033	175	4
Iron and steel products	1,289	102	30	606	532	19
Nonferrous base metals	1,477	534	299	352	199	93
Textile products	812	17	38	248	481	28
Fish and shellfish	522	136	118	55	111	102
Other products	8,238	1,522	648	3,046	2,247	775

[a] "Special category exports" include military and strategic materials and other exports not classified by kind for reasons of security.

SOURCE: *Statistical Abstract of the United States, 1968.*

TABLE 4 THE PATTERN OF WORLD TRADE (millions of dollars)

IMPORTED BY

EXPORTED BY	WORLD[a]	U.S.	CANADA	U.K.	JAPAN	EEC	OTHER WEST. EUROPE
World	$164,700	$20,772	$7,894	$13,398	$6,356	$44,974	$22,096
U.S.	27,400	—	5,602	1,592	2,061	4,974	2,193
Canada	8,534	4,671	—	1,097	293	588	235
U.K.	13,710	1,455	582	—	149	2,744	2,927
Japan	8,452	2,517	214	205	—	484	407
EEC	47,916	3,425	480	2,368	342	20,836	10,079
Other Western Europe	17,894	1,402	166	2,671	141	5,662	3,408
Australia, New Zealand, and Union of S. Africa	5,470	683	81	1,535	668	905	166
Latin America	10,400	3,618	362	658	432	2,164	717
Other Western Hemisphere	1,700	571	128	269	23	208	127
Middle East	7,100	334	86	849	962	2,165	562
Other African countries	7,200	592	47	1,251	165	3,365	492
U.S.S.R.	8,164	43	9	300	216	632	566
People's Republic of China	n.a.	—	13	75	202	175	48
Other Eastern Europe, N. Korea, N. Vietnam, and Cuba	11,325	96	407	62	63	883	1,065
Other Asia	8,600	1,493	141	847	1,105	828	268

[a] Detail does not add to total due to errors and omissions in underlying data.

fruit, nuts, coffee, sugar, and petroleum. Asia sent over half of our imported fabrics, while most meat products came from the remaining areas of the world.

The Pattern of World Trade

The overall pattern of world trade, derived from a study made in 1965, is represented in Table 4. Important individual countries or trading regions are listed down the left side as exporters, and across the top of the table as importers. The total exports of each country on the left are divided up according to import area. That is, each entry in the table shows the dollar volume of exports from the country at the left delivered as imports to the country listed at the top. For example, of the $27,400 million total exports of the U.S., Canada bought $5,602, the U.K. took $1,592, $2,061 went to Japan, and so on. Missing items and a number of inconsistencies leave much to be desired in the figures, but they are sufficiently accurate to show several important characteristics of world trade patterns.

1. Developed industrial countries tend

				IMPORTED BY					
AUSTRALIA, NEW ZEALAND, UNION OF S. AFRICA	LATIN AMERICA	OTHER WESTERN HEMISPHERE	MIDDLE EAST	OTHER AFRICAN COUNTRIES	U.S.S.R.	PEOPLE'S REPUBLIC OF CHINA	EASTERN EUROPE, N. KOREA, N. VIET-NAM AND CUBA	OTHER ASIA	OTHER
$6,113	$8,286	$2,120	$4,453	$6,360	$2,228	$1,210	$3,318	$10,200	$2,467
1,263	3,751	486	910	608	44	—	95	2,690	1,131
240	249	92	28	38	183	97	149	143	5
1,895	410	275	687	941	128	72	236	1,133	76
518	405	92	296	649	168	245	68	2,191	40
911	1,603	262	1,326	2,730	368	231	1,361	1,447	433
309	555	78	445	467	643	51	985	387	75
299	38	25	67	109	96	19	190	356	208
30	1,016	671	55	34	116	96	187	59	157
5	70	84	3	31	—	—	2	18	82
247	80	72	327	119	168	62	211	319	48
81	20	4	80	412	69	66	95	115	104
2	49	1	100	62	—	n.a.	n.a.	197	n.a.
27	1	1	34	75	n.a.	—	n.a.	459	b
276	350	b	307	93	n.a.	n.a.	n.a.	174	b
273	88	21	229	218	243	116	164	1,343	89

b Less than $1 million.

SOURCE: International Monetary Fund, *Direction of Trade Annual, 1961–1965.*

to trade more with each other than they do with less developed countries, while less developed countries trade more with developed countries than they do with each other. Over 60 percent of total U.S. exports go to Canada, Britain, Western Europe, Japan, and other highly industrialized areas. Of the total exports from members of the European Economic Community 80 percent go to Europe, the U.K., the U.S., and Canada. In contrast, 65 percent of exports from Latin America go to the U.S. and Western Europe; less than 10 percent go to other Latin American nations, and only about 1 percent goes to Africa. Less than 5 percent of all African exports go to other African nations and only 1/2 of 1 percent to South America.

This pattern, which is clearly apparent in Table 5, follows from the nature of output and demand in the different countries. In rich, highly industrialized countries, output and demand run heavily to goods for high-income customers, while countries of lower productivity concentrate on agriculture and raw materials. As exporters of raw materials and importers of manufactured products, undeveloped coun-

TABLE 5 PATTERNS OF TRADE AMONG DEVELOPED AND LESS DEVELOPED ECONOMIES

| EXPORTED BY | WORLD[a] | IMPORTING AREA | | |
		DEVELOPED ECONOMIES	LESS DEVELOPED ECONOMIES	UNCLASSIFIED
World				
Millions of $	164,700	121,576	32,000	8,641
Percent	100	73	20	5
Developed economies				
Millions of $	129,380	95,906	26,394	6,658
Percent	100	74	20	5
Less developed economies				
Millions of $	35,300	25,670	5,606	1,982
Percent	100	72	15	5

[a] Details do not add to total due to errors and omissions in underlying information.

SOURCE: Adapted from data in International Monetary Fund, *Direction of Trade Annual, 1961–1965.*

tries have little to gain from trade with each other but must export their materials to industrial nations who can furnish manufactures in exchange. This is, however, only a small part of the trade of rich, industrialized countries, most of whose commerce involves exchanging specialized industrial products that people in less productive economies cannot afford.

2. There is a strong tendency for nations to trade with their neighbors. Of all U.S. trade 40 percent is in the Western Hemisphere. Half of Canadian trade is with the U.S. EEC members do 40 percent of their trading with each other, and Japan sells about as much to Asia as to the U.S. Costs of trade between neighbors are generally lower, partly because of shorter transportation distances, partly because of greater convenience and familiarity.

3. Trade tends to be mutual. The value of exports from one country to another tends to equal the value of imports coming back. The nations of the European Economic Community exported $2,280 million to the U.K. and bought back $2,520 million. Latin America exported $320 million to Canada and bought back $310 million. Considering the reciprocal nature of exchange, this tendency is hardly surprising.

Notice, however, that trade between each pair of nations does not exactly balance. There are several reasons for this fact. In the first place, trade is multilateral. Exports sold to the rest of the world provide firms and households with money claims on the rest of the world that enable them to buy the things they need. However, they need not limit their purchases to their own customers. A second reason for the absence of equality between exports and imports is international borrowing, lending, grants, and gifts. Europeans, for example, can acquire American goods without selling to Americans, provided the U.S. is willing to lend or give them the money to buy its products.

Restrictions on Trade

Since international trade crosses political boundaries, it is often subject to special controls and taxation. *Tariffs* or *duties* levied on the international movement of goods have long been important forms of taxation. In the U.S., for example, the original constitutional restrictions placed on the taxing power of the federal government left import duties as virtually the sole taxing mechanism. As late as 1862, 95 percent of total federal revenue came from tariffs on imports. With the rising importance of the federal government, however, greater dependence was placed on internal revenue. By 1910 customs made up only one-half of the federal revenue, and today it is less than 1 percent.

As we saw in our study of taxation, however, the role of many tariffs is not to raise revenue, but to discourage imports. Duties used for this purpose are called *protective tariffs* because they protect domestic producers from the competition of foreign firms. The same kind of protection can be obtained without the use of tariffs by the application of import quotas. A *quota* establishes a legal limit to the physical amount of a specified commodity that can be imported. The United States applies quotas to a number of important imports including petroleum and sugar.

From our study of market structure, it should be apparent that proponents of quotas and protective tariffs are generally up to no good. An industry that can be undersold by imports is producing products at a higher cost than necessary, which is precisely why it cannot survive competition from abroad. When protection restricts competition in the industry, the resulting higher prices enable the firms to attract workers and resources away from more productive jobs in other industries, and holds down the standard of living in the community accordingly.

In view of this obvious fact, it is remarkable that the most common argument advanced in favor of tariffs is that they "protect the high wages and living standards of American workers against competition with cheap foreign labor." The argument clearly implies that if Japanese firms had to pay wages as high as ours, they could not sell in our market. However, as we have seen, the direction of trade and its terms depend on comparative advantage, not on real wages. Real wages are determined by labor productivity. They are higher in the U.S. because American labor is more productive than Japanese labor. When each nation specializes in producing those things for which its own opportunity costs are lower and imports those whose costs are higher, real wages and living standards are raised in both nations.

Toward Greater Freedom of Trade

The last 40 years have seen slow but steady progress toward lower tariffs and fewer trade restrictions. One important early effort in this direction was the U.S. policy of negotiating bilateral trade agreements under the Trade Agreements Program initiated in 1934 during the Roosevelt administration. As shown in Figure 3, the course of U.S. tariffs since that time has been generally downward.[2]

[2] Part of the apparent rate reduction shown in the figure is the result of rising prices rather than lower tariff rates. Many tariffs are specific excises, and when the price of the imported product rises, the fixed tax per unit becomes a smaller percentage of the value.

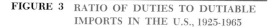

FIGURE 3 RATIO OF DUTIES TO DUTIABLE IMPORTS IN THE U.S., 1925-1965

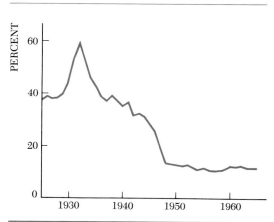

SOURCE: *Historical Statistics of the United States.* Data since 1960 from *Statistical Absract of the United States, 1968.*

In 1947, the important western commercial nations established the General Agreement on Tariffs and Trade (GATT) by which to work for tariff reduction and the elimination of quotas. The signatories agreed not to apply discriminatory tariffs, but to give the imports of all members the most favorable treatment accorded any one member. They further agreed not to impose import quotas except in cases in which similar restrictions were applied to domestic production (as is true of agriculture in the U.S. and in many other parts of the world) or in which the nation was suffering from balance of payments difficulties.[3]

A series of negotiations through GATT has contributed to the mutual scaling down of trade barriers. Tariff bargaining is, however, a slow and painful process. Firms that owe their existence to protection rather than to economic efficiency are understandably reluctant to see that protection reduced, and can often rally the support of labor and members of the communities in which they are located to oppose any alteration of their status.

Another important recent development in international trade was the formation in 1957 of the European Economic Community (EEC). Usually called the Common Market, the EEC consists of Belgium, France, Italy, Luxembourg, the Netherlands, and West Germany.[4] The nations of the EEC agreed to eliminate all tariff barriers in trading with each other, but to provide a common tariff against the rest of the world. The participants hope that the resulting expansion of the market will provide gains from increased specialization and exchange. The free-trade aspects of the EEC are, however, largely limited to its members, and have produced problems for other countries. For example, before the formation of the Common Market, U.S. and Italian manufacturers of sewing

machines competed on equal tariff terms in France. Now the EEC common external tariff applies to French imports from the U.S., while those from Italy are all duty free.

One consequence of this aspect of the European Economic Community was the formation, under British initiative, of the European Free Trade Association (EFTA), now including Austria, Denmark, Finland, Norway, Portugal, Sweden, and Switzerland in addition to the United Kingdom. EFTA forms a free-trade area in manufactured goods and provides for bilateral agreements on trade in agricultural products. Other common market arrangements have been formed in Central America and in East Africa.

EXCHANGE RATES

Suppose you want to buy something from a British firm. You have dollars to spend, but the British firm needs pounds to pay its bills. If you are to make the purchase, dollars must somehow be exchanged for pounds. There are 2 ways in which this can be done. You can pay with your own personal check, traveler's check, or money order. The British firm, upon receiving your dollar check, takes it to a foreign exchange dealer in London who buys it for pounds. The foreign exchange dealer—generally a London bank—then deposits your check in his own account at one of the large New York banks, and the check is cleared back to you in the usual way. Later the foreign exchange dealer will sell a check on his New York account to a British importer who needs dollars to pay for American goods. The dealer is a "retailer" of dollars and other foreign currencies who realizes a profit by maintaining a margin between his buying and selling prices.

The other way for you to pay is to go to an American foreign exchange dealer (or

---

[3] See below, p. 414 ff.

[4] Greece became an associate member in 1963 and is to assume full responsibilities at a later time.

arrange for your bank to handle the transaction for you) and buy a check for the required number of pounds drawn by the American dealer on his deposit in a London bank. The American dealer previously bought the pounds from an American exporter who accepted them from a British firm in payment for goods or services.

Aside from dealers' margins and service charges, the dollar price at which a foreign currency is bought or sold is the *exchange rate* for the currency, and it varies continuously under the forces of supply and demand. The clipping from the financial pages of the *New York Times* in Table 6 shows New York selling prices for various currencies during a typical trading day. During the day reported, prices paid in New York for the British pound, sterling, varied from a high of $2.3925 to a low of $2.3918. The final sale of the day was at $2.3923, slightly higher than the final price of $2.3920 on the day before. The same day, the Canadian dollar varied between a high of $.9280 and a low of $.9271, with a final price of $.9278. For less active currencies, only the closing or final quotation is shown. For example, on the Thursday shown, the Japanese yen closed at .2795½ cents, slightly above the .2794¼ cents of the day before.

TABLE 6

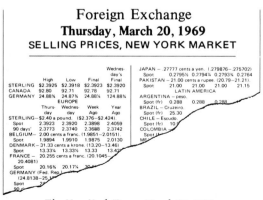

Foreign Exchange
Thursday, March 20, 1969
SELLING PRICES, NEW YORK MARKET

SOURCE: *The New York Times*, March 20, 1969.

FIGURE 4 THE WORLD MARKET FOR BRITISH POUNDS

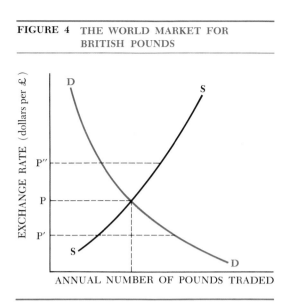

Market Determination of Exchange Rates

The exchange rates for foreign currencies fluctuate under the forces of supply and demand as shown in Figure 4. The dollar price at which exchange dealers sell the pound is plotted vertically, while the annual number of pounds traded is plotted horizontally. The world demand for pounds—that is, the demand by all firms and households outside Britain—is represented by the demand curve *DD*. The shape and position of this curve depends on the need for people in the rest of the world to make payments to British firms. Given the pound prices of goods in Britain, their prices to people in the rest of the world depend on the exchange rate for the pound. An English bicycle selling in Britain for £30 costs American purchasers $84 when the exchange rate for the pound is $2.80, but only $72 when the exchange rate is $2.40. As the exchange rate for the pound declines, then, British goods become cheaper. People in the rest of the world tend to buy more of them, and to purchase more pounds for the purpose. When the exchange rate for the pound is high, British

FIGURE 5   MARKET RESPONSE TO SHIFTING
DEMAND FOR POUNDS

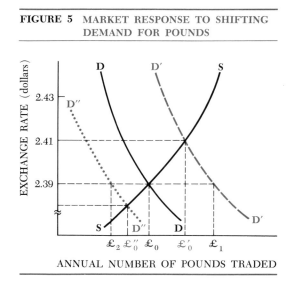

ANNUAL NUMBER OF POUNDS TRADED

ing into the market. Competition for the scarce pounds would drive the price back up to P. If dealers should set too high a price, say P'', the British would want to sell more pounds than buyers wanted, and the price would be competed back down to P.

Determinants of Supply and Demand for Currencies

The supply of a nation's currency on the world exchange market depends on the needs of its households, firms, and government to make payments to the rest of the world. Since most payments involve the purchase of goods and services, anything that encourages people to import tends to increase the supply of their currency on the world market. For this reason, the supply of pounds to the world foreign exchange market tends to rise and fall with the British GNP. Rising output and personal incomes involve increased purchase of imported raw materials and more consumer buying of imported foreign products. Payment for them tends to increase the supply of pounds. Increasing prosperity likewise means more foreign travel and an increased flow of pounds abroad in payment for tourist services. Contraction of output, higher unemployment, and lower income, on the other hand, result in reduced payments for imported goods and services and a correspondingly reduced supply of pounds.

Import buying also depends on relative prices. When the prices of British goods rise compared to foreign products, the supply of pounds to the rest of the world increases as the import of cheaper foreign goods rises. When foreign prices rise relative to local products, the flow of pounds abroad declines as imports are priced out of the market.

Not all payments involve purchases of goods and services. Some are connected with gifts, grants, military aid, and other

goods become correspondingly more expensive to the rest of the world. Fewer British goods and a correspondingly smaller number of pounds are purchased, giving the world demand for pounds its downward slope.

The curve SS represents the supply of pounds coming on the market as people in Britain make payments to the rest of the world. When the exchange rate for the pound is high, British families can get more dollars, marks, francs, or other currencies for their pounds. Foreign goods and services are therefore cheaper for them, and they tend to buy more, spending more pounds for the purpose. Conversely, when the exchange rate for the pound is low, people in Britain find foreign goods relatively more expensive to import and spend fewer pounds to get them. The supply of pounds to the rest of the world slopes upward to represent the greater number of pounds the British tend to offer for imports when the exchange rate rises.

The demand and supply shown in Figure 4 would tend to set the exchange rate for the pound at P. If foreign exchange dealers should set any lower price, say P', people in the rest of the world would want more pounds than the British were bring-

unilateral transfers. When retired British workers living abroad receive larger pension checks, the supply of pounds to the world exchange market increases. The British also supply pounds by sending money to friends, relatives, and organizations abroad. Other transactions involve lending and borrowing. When the English invest abroad—for example, by buying stocks and bonds of American corporations, by purchasing U.S. government bonds, or even by buying back foreign-owned securities of British firms—pounds are supplied to the rest of the world. Since money lenders tend to seek out the highest return for their funds, the supply of pounds depends on how interest rates in London compare with those elsewhere. Higher interest rates abroad tend to increase the supply of pounds to the rest of the world, while higher interest rates at home reduce it.

Figure 5 shows how the exchange rate for the pound responds to shifts in demand. The initial exchange rate of $2.39 is determined by demand DD and supply SS as shown, and $£_0$ are traded. When Americans and others want to increase their payments to Britain, demand rises to $D'D'$. At the old exchange rate, people in the rest of the world would want to buy $£_1$, but only

$£_0$ are available. The shortage $£_1 - £_0$ forces the rate up to $2.41 at which price $£_0'$ are traded. When demand declines to $D''D''$, the reverse result occurs. At the old rate, people in the rest of the world would tend to buy only $£_2$, but since $£_0$ are coming on the market, the surplus $£_0 - £_2$ would force the exchange rate down and $£_0''$ would be traded.

Adjustments to changes in supply can be depicted in similar fashion. As shown in Figure 6, an increase in the supply of pounds to S'S' forces down the exchange rate, while a reduction to S''S'' forces it up.

Competitive Devaluation

There is an important difference between markets for currency and those for real goods and services. The supply of goods and services is limited by real opportunity cost, but the supply of currency is not. Since currency consists of bank deposits created by banks, the central bank or other monetary authority of each nation has the power to expand the supply of its own currency on the world exchange market to an unlimited extent. It can do this by creating its own currency in the usual way and using it to purchase foreign currencies on the open market. For example, when the Bank of England wants to expand the supply of pounds, it enters the foreign exchange market and buys dollars, francs, marks, and other currencies with its own pound deposits created for the purpose. When the Federal Reserve Board wants to increase the supply of dollars on the world market, it instructs the Federal Reserve Bank of New York to buy foreign currencies, paying with checks drawn on itself.

But why would monetary authorities want to do such a thing? To understand, we must leave the relatively prosperous world of the last 25 years and look back to the period of the Great Depression of the 1930s. Faced with severe unemployment,

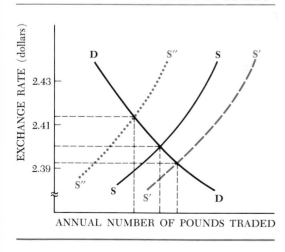

FIGURE 6   THE RESPONSE OF THE MARKET
TO SHIFTING SUPPLY OF POUNDS

ANNUAL NUMBER OF POUNDS TRADED

each nation desperately sought ways to stimulate aggregate demand for its products. One way was to encourage exports by making them cheaper to the rest of the world, and one quick way to make exports cheaper was to *devalue* the currency; that is, to increase its supply on the world market and drive its exchange rate down.

The idea was clear enough. Foreigners were supposed to buy the now cheaper exports. The resulting stimulus to the domestic economy was supposed to produce a multiplied expansion of output, create more jobs, and reduce unemployment. The flaw in the argument was that while exports would mean more jobs in one country, the competition of exported goods with domestic products would mean fewer jobs and more unemployment in the importing country. The overall effect of devaluation would have been to export not only goods and services, but unemployment as well. It might have benefited one country, but only at a neighbor's expense.

Of course, other countries would not stand for that. To protect themselves, and if possible to turn the tables and benefit at the exporter's expense, his neighbors also devalued. Everybody began to play the devaluation game, trying to push his unemployment problems onto somebody else. In the ensuing chaos, international trade nearly vanished.

COORDINATING WORLD EXCHANGE RATES

The International Monetary Fund (IMF)

The International Monetary Fund, which was established in 1944 and began operation in 1946, is an agency to help ensure a smoothly functioning, worldwide monetary system with stable exchange rates. The Fund now has over 100 members and includes most of the important countries out-

side the Communist group.[5] In order to keep nations from manipulating their exchange rates in a futile effort to export their domestic difficulties, each member country has agreed with the Fund on a *par value* for its currency, defined in terms of the U.S. dollar. The par value is to represent a realistic exchange rate in view of the underlying forces of supply and demand for the currency on the world market. Although the U.S. dollar has no par, the U.S. government agreed to maintain free exchange of the dollar for gold at a fixed price of $35 per ounce.

Each member of the Fund has further agreed to maintain the actual exchange rates at which its currency is bought and sold on the world exchange market within limits set 1 percent above and below the par value. As this is written, the par value of the British pound, for example, is fixed at $2.40, and the U.K. has agreed not to permit the value to rise above $2.424 nor to fall below $2.376. Within these fixed limits, the forces of supply and demand are allowed to work, but when the supply of the currency or the demand for it shifts to such an extent that the rate would be driven beyond either limit, the monetary authorities of the U.K. are committed to take steps to hold it within bounds.

Limiting Exchange Fluctuations

The process as it might apply to the British pound is illustrated in Figure 7. Initially, demand DD and supply SS determine the exchange rate for the pound at $2.41, well within the limits. Now suppose that with increased demand for British goods, the demand for pounds rises to D'D'. Left to itself, competition would drive the exchange rate up to $2.45, but as the upper

[5] Yugoslavia is the only Eastern Europe country with membership in the Fund. Switzerland is the most important western country that is not a member.

FIGURE 7   ACTION TO HOLD THE EXCHANGE
RATE WITHIN THE UPPER LIMIT

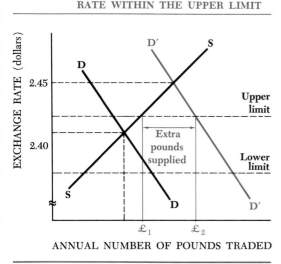

ANNUAL NUMBER OF POUNDS TRADED

Holding the pound above the lower limit is another matter. Figure 8 illustrates how the exchange rate for the pound is supported and kept from falling below its lower limit. Beginning again with a rate well within the limits, suppose foreign buyers find British goods less attractive, perhaps because of lower prices in other countries, and the world demand for pounds declines to $D'D'$. Left to itself, the exchange rate for the pound would fall below the lower limit. To prevent this, the British monetary authorities must enter the exchange market with foreign currencies and augment the demand for pounds enough to prevent the rate from falling further. At the lower limit, foreigners with payments to make in Britain tend to buy only $£_2$ while British importers supply $£_1$. The British monetary authorities must purchase $£_1 - £_2$ with foreign currencies to make up the deficiency in demand.

To support the exchange rate above its lower limit, British monetary authorities must buy pounds with dollars or other

limit is approached, the British monetary authorities intervene by entering the foreign exchange market and purchasing dollars and other foreign currencies for pounds. This action adds enough pounds to the supply to keep the rate from rising further. As the figure shows, foreigners tend to buy $£_2$ at the ceiling exchange rate, while British importers supply only $£_1$ to the world market. The government's use of pounds to purchase foreign currency makes up the supply deficiency, $£_2 - £_1$. Holding the pound down against upward pressure on its international value seldom occasions major difficulty for a nation. Since British banks can create pounds in any desired quantity, the British can never run out, but can continue to supply any amount foreigners are willing to buy.[6]

[6] Purchase of foreign currency by the monetary authority does, however, expand the reserves of commercial banks and augments their lending power. The central bank can wipe out these additional reserves by selling government securities in the open market, but if the national debt is small, it may run out of ammunition. Countries in this situation sometimes prefer to raise the par value of their currencies to a level more in keeping with supply and demand rather than to permit continual

expansion of the lending power of the banking system.

FIGURE 8   ACTION TO HOLD THE EXCHANGE
RATE ABOVE THE LOWER LIMIT

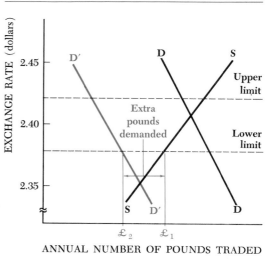

ANNUAL NUMBER OF POUNDS TRADED

foreign currencies. Since these cannot be created by British banks, either they must be already acquired and held in reserve for the purpose, or they must be bought by selling gold or other assets, or borrowed. The gold and foreign currencies held by the monetary authorities of a nation and available to support its currency constitute its *monetary reserve*. Since every nation's monetary reserves are limited, so is its ability to support the international exchange value of its own currency.

IMF Drawing Rights

The International Monetary Fund gives extra assistance to nations that need to support their currencies by providing a source from which they can supplement their own reserves. Each member of the Fund is assigned a *quota* set by a complicated formula involving its GNP and the size and variability of its foreign trade. The U.S. quota, exceeding $5 billion, is the largest, followed by that of the U.K., which is about half as large. Each country is required to deposit with the Fund an amount equal to its quota. Three-quarters of the subscription is in the member's own currency, but one-quarter must be in gold valued at $35 an ounce.[7]

In exchange for its subscription each member is accorded *drawing rights*. These permit it to supplement its own reserves with foreign currency drawn from the Fund in exchange for additional deposits of its own. Drawing rights are designed to provide temporary short-term assistance to countries whose currencies are pushing toward the lower limit, permitting them to weather a temporary rush of speculation,

and providing them a breathing space within which to make more fundamental readjustments of the economy. In keeping with the temporary nature of drawing rights, countries are expected to replace all foreign currency drawn within 3 to 5 years.

In addition, drawing rights are conditional on the member's efforts to remedy the underlying imbalance between the supply and demand for its currency. In general, the more a member draws from the Fund, the greater the degree of assurance it must provide that it is taking appropriate steps to protect its reserve position. For this purpose, each member's drawing rights are divided into a number of portions called *tranches*. The first portion, or tranche, is equal to one-quarter of the member's quota. Since this tranche is equal to the member's gold subscription to the Fund, it is usually referred to as the *gold tranche*. Members are permitted to draw foreign currencies up to the limit of their gold tranche virtually at will, and the amount of unused gold-tranche drawing rights are normally counted among the member's own monetary reserves.

The next tranche of drawing rights, equal to another quarter of the member's quota and often called the *first credit tranche*, can be withdrawn only after formal consultation with the Fund, but the Fund rarely raises any barrier. Applications for drawing *higher tranches*—portions beyond the first credit tranche—must be accompanied by stronger evidence of effort to adjust underlying conditions. Such evidence usually involves a carefully worked out fiscal and monetary program, or an agreement to comply with suggestions made by the Fund as to the appropriate measures to be taken.

[7] The gold portion of the subscription must be in the form of 400-ounce bars deposited at either the Federal Reserve Bank of New York, the Bank of England, the Bank of France, or the Reserve Bank of India. The currency portion consists of a deposit to the Fund's account in the member's central bank or other designated depository.

Policy Steps To Adjust Supply and Demand

IMF drawing rights do nothing to alter the underlying gap between the supply of currency to the world market and the demand for it. Even with IMF assistance, a nation cannot continue to support the exchange rate for its currency for an indefinite period, but must take steps to close the gap between supply and demand.

Among the measures to be taken in such a case are the institution of higher tax rates and reduced government spending to check the growth of income. Such measures will reduce expenditures for imported consumer goods and raw materials. In addition, the check they provide to domestic output and employment helps to reduce the prices of domestic products compared to those made abroad. Not only does this reduction encourage substitution of domestic products for higher-priced imported goods, but it also improves the competitive position of domestically produced goods in foreign markets.

Monetary policy to restrict bank lending not only adds to the general economic slowdown, but also results in high interest rates which help to attract loan funds from abroad. Restrictive fiscal and monetary policy is often supplemented by special direct steps to reduce the supply of and increase the demand for the currency. For example, during the prolonged period of support for the pound from 1964 to 1966, the British government not only raised tax rates, cut government spending, and curtailed bank lending, but also imposed a special 15 percent tax surcharge on all imported manufactured and semimanufactured goods, established a system of tax rebates on exports, reduced the number of pounds a British traveler could take out of the country, and applied direct government controls to wages and prices in an effort to improve the competitive position of British exports in foreign markets.

sive to support the exchange rate often result in severe unemployment. Under these circumstances, the currency may be *devalued*. That is, its par value may be reduced to a level more in keeping with the realities of supply and demand. Members of the IMF are free to change the par value of their own currencies by no more than 10 percent without consulting the Fund. Larger changes can be made only after appropriate consultation and agreement.

When the Fund began operations in 1946, the par value of the pound was set at $4.03. This price was so unfavorable to British exports, however, that in 1949 the British proposed a reduction in their par, and in September of that year the pound was devalued to $2.80. Even at that level it required continual support, and measures to hold the British economy in check became highly painful. The pound was devalued again in 1967 to a new par of $2.40. The Canadian dollar, after being allowed to fluctuate freely for a period, was devalued in 1962. The French franc was devalued by 17 percent in 1958 and for 10 years was one of the strongest currencies in Europe. Following the wage and price adjustments that grew out of the strikes and civil disorders of 1968, however, the franc became overvalued, and after the end of the de Gaulle government the franc was devalued by an additional 12.5 percent in 1969. Currencies are also occasionally revalued upward. In 1961, for example, West Germany and the Netherlands both increased the par value of their currencies by 5 percent.

In the fall of 1969 the West German government again raised the parity of the mark after a temporary period during which it was allowed to sell freely above its old par.

Changes in Par

When the gap between supply and demand for the currency is large, however, fiscal and monetary measures sufficiently repres-

Speculation in Currencies

Speculators play the same important role in international exchange markets that they do in markets for grain and other commodities: Their arbitrage operations help maintain uniform prices in all financial centers. If pounds are selling higher in Paris than in New York, for example, exchange dealers will profitably buy them in New York and sell in Paris until the rates differ by no more than transaction costs.

In addition, speculation helps to smooth out the use of foreign currencies over time, just as grain speculators help spread the use of the wheat harvest over the year. If every pound supplied to the market had to be sold immediately to a prospective importer of British goods, the exchange rate on the pound would oscillate wildly between its limits. On the day a large number of pounds arrived, the price would fall to the lower limit and British monetary authorities would be forced to buy them up. A surge in demand for pounds the next day would drive the rate to the upper limit, and the monetary authorities would have to intervene again to hold it down. Speculators smooth out these variations. When pounds come onto the market in unusual quantities, speculative purchases keep the price from falling too far. When an unusual demand for pounds appears, speculative sales keep the price from rising too far. As long as it is clear that the authorities have adequate monetary reserves to support the currency, the actions of speculators contribute to the stability of exchange rates and reduce the need for intervention by governments. In fact, when exchange rates approach the lower limit, speculators are presented with a one-sided bet. Speculators who buy the currency are betting that the exchange rate will rise. If it does, they can sell at a substantial profit. If it does not, they will not lose much, since the monetary authorities will support the exchange rate at the lower limit.

Speculation as a Destabilizing Influence
When a long period of support at the lower limit has drained a country's monetary reserves, the effect of speculation suddenly

turns around. Instead of helping to support the currency, the actions of speculators increase the difficulty of maintaining the lower limit and add to the likelihood of devaluation. The reason is that severe loss of reserves turns the one-sided bet around. In such a situation, the monetary authorities are unlikely to *raise* the exchange rate. If they do anything, they will devalue. Thus, a speculator who sells has a great deal to gain if the currency is devalued, but little or nothing to lose if it is not. Sales by speculators who suspect that the monetary authorities are nearing the end of their reserves swell the supply of the currency. Instead of helping, this action increases the need for support. Not only do speculators rid themselves of their own currency holdings, but they also borrow more from banks to sell on the international market, swelling the supply even further. The position of the pound in 1967 is shown in Figure 9. Left to themselves, demand DD and supply SS would have resulted in an exchange rate below the \$2.772 minimum. This required the British monetary authorities to dip into their monetary reserves to buy the extra $\pounds_2 - \pounds_1$ off the market. As support continued, the suspicion grew that the British were exhausting their reserves and would

FIGURE 9   DEVALUATION OF THE POUND

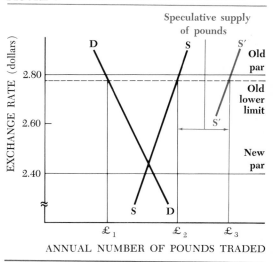

ANNUAL NUMBER OF POUNDS TRADED

be unable to continue to support the pound at this level. Speculators, dumping their own holdings on the market and borrowing still more from British banks, pushed the supply out to $S'S'$. This action increased the drain on monetary reserves to $£_3 - £_1$. As the drain grew, the speculators' bet became increasingly one-sided, and the supply of pounds grew faster. It was impossible to stem the tide, and the pound was devalued.

After the devaluation, speculators who had borrowed pounds and sold them for $2.772 repaid the loans with pounds bought back at nearly $2.40, making a speculative profit in excess of 10 percent. If the currency had not been devalued, speculators could still have repurchased pounds at prices only slightly above the price for which they had originally sold them, avoiding substantial losses in any case.

Alternatives to Devaluation

There are several reasons why nations sometimes go to considerable lengths to avoid devaluation of the currency. For one thing, speculation remains a stabilizing force only as long as speculators believe in the government's commitment to the existing exchange parity. When that belief is shaken, speculative action becomes destabilizing. A country that can convince speculators that it will never devalue has much less trouble supporting its currency. But this conviction cannot be maintained if the currency is, in fact, frequently devalued. Each devaluation undermines the credibility of the government's commitment to parity, and reinforces the speculators' willingness to bet against the currency the next time it needs support.

Sometimes even devaluation cannot restore equilibrium to the supply and demand for the currency. Firms sometimes borrow from people in other countries on terms that require interest and principal to be paid in the lender's currency. For ex-

ample, a British manufacturer may sell bonds in the U.S. with interest and principal to be repaid in dollars. This fixes the number of dollars needed annually to service the debt, regardless of the exchange rate for the pound. Devaluation cannot reduce the firm's need for dollars, but merely increases the number of pounds it must supply to the world exchange market to obtain them. Under these circumstances, the supply of pounds becomes *perversely elastic*. That is, more pounds come on the market at low than at high exchange rates. In such a case, devaluation may make the situation worse rather than better.

There are several alternatives to devaluation. One of these is to increase tariffs, a measure which constitutes a kind of disguised devaluation. The value of the currency is reduced, not in terms of foreign currency, but in terms of its ability to buy foreign goods, which has the same effect. The effect is the same when legal restrictions are imposed on imports by means of quotas. Unable to buy imports, households and firms cut back their supply of currency to the world market.

More thorough control over the use of foreign currency is obtained through complete exchange control. Under this system, all households and firms are required to turn over any foreign currency they own to the central bank and are forbidden to buy, sell, or even to own foreign currency themselves. All incoming exchange must be sold to the central bank at the fixed exchange rate, and foreign currency may be legally purchased only from the bank, and only under license for specified uses. Travelers are restricted in the amount of the currency they can take out of the country with them, and foreign lending or other capital transactions can be made only under special permit.

Countries under exchange control sometimes adopt a multiprice system under which the price paid by the bank to a seller of foreign exchange depends on how he got it: Coffee exporters may be paid one price, oil exporters another. In turn, users of foreign exchange are charged different prices depending on what they want it for: Food importers and importers of materials needed to make products for export pay a lower price than importers of luxury goods for domestic consumption.

Far-reaching exchange control of this kind is not only inconvenient—involving priorities, import licenses, applications, standing in line, and bureaucracy—but it also sacrifices the power of the open market to guide foreign exchange into the highest-priority uses. Moreover, the ease with which money can be concealed and manipulated causes serious enforcement problems.

THE BALANCE OF PAYMENTS

Before a country can propose steps to protect its reserves and to restore the international position of its currency, it needs to know how big the monetary problem is and where it comes from. The *international balance of payments* is an important device in this analysis. To compile a balance of payments, every transaction is classified according to whether it represents a *source* of monetary reserves (a *credit* or *plus item*) or a *use* of monetary reserves (a *debit* or *minus item*). In addition, a distinction is made between *current* transactions—involving the purchase and sale of goods and services, gifts, transfer payments, and other day-to-day business—and *capital* transactions that involve investing, lending, or borrowing funds on a long-term basis.

Balance of Payments of a Family

Although balance-of-payments accounting is applied primarily to the international payments of a country, the same system can describe the transactions of a business firm or household. Before we venture on to the international level, let us look at a balance of payments for the Jay family.

Last month, as shown in Table 7, the Jay family sold its old car for $300. This was recorded as a credit (plus) because it was the source of cash (monetary reserves) to the family. Since this was a sale of goods to people outside the family (the rest of the world) it was entered under current items as an "export." The work Mr. Jay did on the job (an export of services) was likewise a plus item in the current account. Service rendered during the month by the family's capital was the source of a $50 dividend, another current plus item as shown.

During the same month the Jay family acquired goods and services from others. "Imports" in the form of groceries and clothing involved the use of $200 of cash reserves and were recorded as a minus item

TABLE 7 JAY FAMILY BALANCE OF PAYMENTS

Current items	
Exports of goods and services	
Sold old car	+$ 300
Labor	+ 1,000
Dividends	+ 50
Imports of goods and services	
Groceries and clothing	−$ 200
New car	− 3,000
Interest on car loan	− 10
Net exports	−$1,860
Unilateral transfers	
Contributed to church	−$ 50
Present from Uncle George	+ 70
Net unilateral remittances	+$ 20
Balance on current account	−$1,840
Capital items	
Purchased U.S. Savings Bond	+$ 100
Loan on new car	+ 1,500
First payment on new car	− 40
Balance on capital account	+$1,360
Balance of payments	−$ 480
Increase in charge accounts payable	$ 60
Decrease in cash reserves	420
	$ 480

in the current account, as was the newly acquired car, the service of their rented house, and the service rendered them by the bank on their auto loan. The family donated $50 to the church (a minus item, or use of funds) and received a $70 check from Uncle George as an anniversary present (a plus item). Since there was no *quid pro quo* for either of these latter transactions, they were recorded as unilateral ("one-way") transfers.

The sum of all the current items, added up with due regard to sign, is the *balance on current account*. For the Jay family, this was −$1,840. That is, the month's current transactions, taken as a whole, involved the use of $1,230 more cash than was made available by current credit items.

The month's business was not restricted to current transactions, however. The family also extended a loan and borrowed on a long-term basis. The "foreign loan" was the purchase of a $100 U.S. Savings Bond. Since this capital outlay drew down cash reserves, it was entered as a debit in the capital account. To help finance the new car, the family floated an automobile loan of $1,500 at the local bank. Since this was a source of cash to help pay for the car, it was recorded as a plus item. During the month, the $40 first payment on the car came due and was recorded as a minus item. The sum of the capital items with due regard for signs is the *balance on capital account*. Capital transactions made available to the Jay family $1,360 more cash than it paid out.

The combined sum of the balance on current account and the balance on capital account is called the *balance of payments* and indicates the amount by which the family's cash reserves grew (+) or declined (−) during the month. A positive balance of payments is called a *surplus*, a negative balance is called a *deficit*. For the month, the balance of payments for the Jay family showed a deficit of $450. Actually, however, the family did not draw down its

cash balance by this amount. The balance was partly financed by adding $60 to the amount due on family charge accounts. This was an increase in liquid liabilities to "foreigners," and since it had to be paid shortly, was accorded the same accounting status as an outright loss of cash reserves. The rest of the balance of payments was financed by drawing down cash reserves by $420.

U.S. Balance of Payments

The items of the U.S. balance of payments in Table 8 are analogous to those of the Jay family. During the year 1968, American firms exported $33,598 million in merchandise, the U.S. government sold $1,427 million in military equipment to foreign

TABLE 8 U.S. BALANCE OF PAYMENTS, 1968 (millions of dollars)

Current account	
Exports of goods and services	$50,594
Merchandise	$33,598
Military sales	1,427
Income on investments	7,699
Other services	7,870
Imports of goods and services	− 48,078
Merchandise	− 32,972
Military expenditures	− 4,530
Other services	− 10,576
Unilateral transfers to foreigners	− 2,865
Balance on current account	− 349
Capital account	
U.S. government loans and grants	− 2,240
U.S. private capital, net	− 5,157
Long-term foreign capital, net	8,565
Balance on capital account	1,159
Errors and unrecorded items	− 717
Balance of payments	$ 93
Increase in liquid liabilities for foreigners	$ 787
Decrease (+) or increase (−) in U.S. holdings of gold and convertible currencies, including IMF gold tranche position	− 880
	− 93

SOURCE: *Survey of Current Business*, June, 1969.

governments, while services of capital and other services rendered to the rest of the world by U.S. firms came to $15,569 million more. At the same time, U.S. firms and households imported $32,972 million in merchandise, and $10,576 million in other services, while the U.S. government spent $4,530 million overseas to obtain food, supplies, and services for the military. The difference between export and import items was the $2.5 billion net exports figure in the 1968 national accounts. When the $2,865 million debit representing net remittances was added to net exports, the total was the −$349 million balance on current account.

On capital account, the U.S. government loaned and granted $2,240 million to people in the rest of the world; U.S. private investment, loans, and other capital involved a $5,157 million net debit, while net long-term loans and investments in the U.S. by people in the rest of the world represented a credit of $8,565 million. The total was a net credit on capital account of $1,159 million.

In the case of the Jay family, the balance of payments obtained as the sum of the balance on current and capital account exactly equaled the increase in current liabilities plus the decrease in cash reserves. Since entries in the U.S. balance of payments accounts are estimated from a variety of sources that suffer from omissions and other errors, it is necessary to include a net "fudge factor" to bring the estimated balance of payments into agreement with independently estimated changes in liquid liabilities and monetary reserves. This appears as the "errors and unrecorded transactions" item of −$717 million. The resulting 1968 balance of payments was the $93 million shown.[8] Below the line we see that

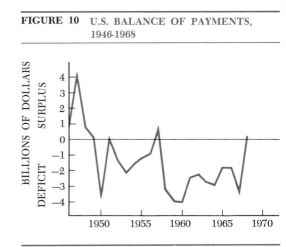

FIGURE 10   U.S. BALANCE OF PAYMENTS, 1946-1968

SOURCE: *Survey of Current Business*, June, 1969.

the U.S. acquired $880 million in gold, foreign currencies, and other reserves, but at the same time liquid liabilities of foreigners increased by $787 million. The difference represents the net addition of $93 million to the total monetary reserves of the country.

The Deficit in the U.S. Balance of Payments

The balance of payments for 1968 was the first surplus in the payments position of the United States in more than a decade. Although the U.S. balance of payments showed strong surpluses from the end of World War II until 1949, beginning in 1950, in 18 out of the following 19 years, the balance of payments showed deficits ranging between about $1 billion and $4 billion annually. As shown in Figure 10, the

8 This balance of payments is measured on a "liquidity" basis to emphasize the net change in monetary reserves and liquid liabilities to all foreigners, regardless of their status. An alternative method of accounting yields the "official reserves transactions balance" that focuses on monetary

reserves and on changes in liabilities (liquid or not) to foreign central banks and other "official" monetary authorities alone. Under this latter system of accounting, changes in liquid liabilities to "unofficial" foreigners are included as an item in the capital account, but changes in nonliquid liabilities to official monetary authorities are not.

only exception was a small surplus (about half a billion dollars) in the year 1957. U.S. monetary reserves, which had reached a peak of $26 billion in 1949, were steadily drawn down, until by early 1968 only $15 billion remained.

There were several obvious factors contributing to these deficits. In the first place, the relationship between merchandise exports and imports underwent a decided change. During the years immediately following World War II, output in Europe and Asia was limited. Exports from the U.S., liberally financed by the Marshall Plan and other foreign aid, were essential to survival abroad, while products for import into the U.S. market were scarce and high priced. As European and Asian factories were rebuilt and modernized, products abroad became cheaper in comparison to those from America, and U.S. merchandise imports grew more rapidly than exports.

U.S. military expenditure abroad was an even greater influence on the balance of payments. Little more than $500 million in 1950, it grew to $4.5 billion by 1968. This single minus item alone exceeded the total payments deficit during 16 out of the 18 years from 1951 to 1968. During the 2 exceptional years—1959 and 1960—U.S. military expenditure abroad came to $3.1 billion compared to a balance of payments deficit of $3.9 billion.

The third major source of the U.S. deficit was composed of transfers abroad in the form of U.S. foreign aid and other government grants, which averaged about $3 billion per year over the period.

Gold and the U.S. Payments Deficit

Since all other par values are defined in its terms, the dollar is placed in a special position. It has no explicit par, but only an implicit par defined by the entire system of the par values of other currencies. Moreover, since a change in this implicit par would require proportional changes in the par values of all other currencies, the U.S. is powerless to change it even within narrow limits without the help of the Fund.

Nevertheless, U.S. monetary authorities have an important stake in keeping the world supply of dollars balanced against demand. A large supply of dollars appears to all other nations as a large demand for their own currencies. If the imbalance is sufficiently large, it requires monetary intervention to hold exchange rates within the upper limits. Since the limiting operation requires the monetary authorities to buy dollars with their own currencies, they acquire more and more dollars to add to their foreign exchange reserves. This process creates a problem because many monetary authorities prefer to keep part of their exchange reserves in gold. Some are subject to legal requirements that a specified proportion of their monetary reserves be held in gold. Others hold gold as a reserve from longstanding tradition. For these reasons, as the world supply of dollars begins to exceed the current need for them, some of the excess is used to purchase gold. As its part of the IMF agreement, the U.S. agreed to sell gold in unlimited amounts at a fixed price of $35 an ounce. That is, foreigners could "cash in" extra dollars for gold at the U.S. Treasury. Thus, when the supply of dollars to the rest of the world is excessive, the U.S. tends to lose monetary reserves just as others do.

As a result of the continuing U.S. payments deficits U.S. current liabilities to other countries grew from $12 billion in 1950 to $30 billion by 1968. At the same time, dollars were steadily being cashed in for gold, and the U.S. gold stock declined to $10 billion, less than half its 1950 level of $22 billion. With the rise in liabilities and the decline in gold stock, speculators began to feel that they were confronted by a one-sided bet that the U.S. would raise the price of gold to protect its reserves. The steady cashing of dollars for gold grew into a speculative torrent and with $30 billion current liabilities clamoring for $10 billion in gold, the U.S. was unable to continue to sell gold at the official price.

However, the speculators' one-sided bet did not pay off. Rather than raise the price of gold, the U.S. agreed with monetary authorities in other countries to stop selling gold on the open market. The reason for this move is clear when we realize that the price of gold is not an exchange rate. A rise in the price of gold would make South African gold mines more profitable and would also reward speculators for their destabilizing behavior, but it would not change the terms on which dollars sell for pounds, francs, or other currencies. Since foreign exchange parities of all IMF member currencies are set in terms of the dollar, they are unaffected by the price of gold.

The refusal of central banks to sell gold on the open market has resulted in a "2-tier" gold system. Private individuals buy and sell gold on the London gold market at prices of $35 per ounce and upward, as determined by supply and demand. Central banks, however, have agreed to sell gold privately no longer, and gold held as part of monetary reserves is not sold on the market, but traded only from bank to bank at the official price of $35 an ounce.

PROPOSALS FOR IMPROVING THE INTERNATIONAL MONETARY SYSTEM

Although the International Monetary Fund and the system of parity exchange rates have constituted a marked improvement over previous monetary arrangements, the recurrent crises that have beset the Fund in recent years have given rise to a number of suggestions for modification. The most modest of these has been merely to widen the range within which exchange rates should be allowed to fluctuate without intervention. If, instead of 1 percent, currencies were allowed to fluctuate within 3 percent from par, 2 nondollar currencies could differ with respect to each other by as much as 6 percent without calling support action into play. Since this margin would accommodate a wider range of economic conditions before requiring intervention, its proponents believe that it would materially reduce the frequency of crises. Moreover, they argue that the wider band would tend to increase the possible penalty attached to speculating against a currency that is near its lower limit. With more room for the currency to rise, speculators would face the possibility of greater losses if they guessed wrong about devaluation, and the potentially greater loss should, it is claimed, reduce the one-sidedness of destabilizing speculative bets and render speculators more cautious about making them.

Probably the most radical suggestion for reform is to extend the "wider band" idea to its logical conclusion and abolish all parities and support limits, allowing each exchange rate to be entirely free to find its natural level under the forces of supply and demand. Proponents argue that this is the way most prices are set, and that such a system would bring powerful market forces fully into play in allocating foreign currencies among different uses and users. The unhappy experience of the 1930s, however, presents a cogent objection to returning to a system that leaves governments completely free to manipulate exchange rates.

There are 2 other proposals that have been directed toward retaining exchange parities but modifying the rules for their adjustment to provide greater flexibility. Both suggestions embody a mechanism for replacing large, once-and-for-all changes in parity by a prolonged series of small adjustments. According to one idea, a nation in balance-of-payments difficulties should announce a percentage rate per year at which the par value of its currency would creep upward or downward until the necessary adjustment had been made. Advocates claim that the present system allows maladjustments to accumulate until they build up to crisis proportions. If small readjustments could be made smoothly over a long period, they feel that perhaps serious maladjustments could be forestalled.[9]

An alternative suggestion has been made to permit each currency's parity to vary slowly but *automatically* in response to market demand and supply. For example, a new parity could be defined each day, equal to the average of actual exchange rates over the past 12 months or a similar period. This system would force currencies continually selling below par to devalue slowly, and those continually selling above par to revalue slowly, without requiring formal action by the monetary authorities. Since no limit would be set to the level such parities might reach, all exchange rates would adjust completely to

supply and demand in the long run, but would still be limited in the short run to variation within established limits.[10]

Finally, in a different vein, it has also been proposed that the world move in the direction of a genuine international monetary system. No currency in the world is related in any effective fashion to gold, yet gold retains an important role as an international monetary asset, even under the present "2-tier" price system. This vestige of an earlier age still leaves the liquidity of the world monetary system subject to the limited supply of a particular commodity. It has therefore been proposed that, as a supplement to or ultimate replacement for monetary gold, the IMF create and distribute among its members a new paper monetary reserve asset. Member nations would hold this asset and transfer it among their central banks in a fashion roughly comparable to the way that members of the U.S. Federal Reserve System hold and transfer among themselves deposits with Federal Reserve banks. Provision for the creation and distribution of these paper monetary assets, called *Special Drawing Rights* (SDRs), has been embodied in an amendment to the Articles of the International Monetary Fund and submitted to the membership. As this is written, the new arrangement has been approved, and is in process of implementation.

[9] Once such a creeping parity had been announced, of course, speculators would know which way the exchange rate was going to move and how fast. This would present them with a sure bet. For example, if a downward trend for the pound were announced, speculators could borrow pounds from British banks and sell them on the world market for dollars at today's high rate, secure in the knowledge that they could buy them back and repay the loan when the pound was cheaper. However, since the parity would creep slowly, the speculator would have to pay interest on his borrowed pounds for some time before he could complete the transaction. If British monetary authorities were to raise interest rates, they would make such "speculation" unprofitable.

[10] Again, to the extent that such automatic movements in parity are predictable, interest rates would have to be adjusted to remove the profit from "speculation" in a sure thing.

SUMMARY

Differences in the endowment of natural resources and in the skill and productivity of workers cause wide variations in productivity in different nations, but international productivity differences are not uniform in all occupations. For example, although U.S. workers are, on the average, about 3 times as productive as the Japanese, they are 5 times as productive in coal mining, but only 33 percent more productive in manufacturing motorcycles. A region has a *comparative advantage* in those items for which its productivity advantage is above average, and all regions gain when each specializes in those things for which it has the greatest comparative advantage and gets the others it needs by trade with other regions.

There are special aspects to international trade which arise from the fact that political boundaries are crossed. The advantages of trade are often disguised, and nations have traditionally resorted to *protective tariffs, quotas,* and other measures to limit or to control it. During the last 40 years, however, there has been a slow but fairly steady liberalization of international trade restrictions. A number of new international institutions have been established, including the *European Economic Community,* usually known as the Common Market.

Another problem caused by political boundaries is that different countries use different currency systems. International payment requires the exchange of one country's money for that of another. This exchange takes place on a world market at *exchange rates* subject to the forces of supply and demand. In addition, however, many of the important commercial nations of the world have agreed through the *International Monetary Fund* to maintain the exchange rates for their currencies within narrowly defined limits. Occasionally, this commitment involves a serious loss of *monetary reserves* for individual countries required to support the exchange rates for their currencies. The loss of reserves, intensified by speculative activity, may require *devaluation* of the currency, or a resort to *exchange controls.*

The *balance of payments* is an accounting device for keeping track of the magnitude and causes of changes in monetary reserves. After 18 years of balance of payments *deficits,* reserve losses by the United States generated a crisis which altered the role of gold in the international reserve system.

Although the present international monetary system works smoothly most of the time, recurrent crises have given rise to a number of recommendations for improvement.

PART FOUR

The Distribution of Income

The final step in the process of production is the payment of incomes to the individuals who have contributed to the output. These incomes provide each person with a claim to a share of the goods and services produced, and no matter how great the total output, the material welfare of each individual family depends on its own income share. Wide income differences among families is a familiar fact of life everywhere in the world, including countries like the U.S.S.R. In the United States, where the average income makes most families rich almost beyond belief in terms of the standards by which most of the world's people live, family incomes range from those of multimillionaires to some as low as can be found anywhere on earth.

Since the basic distribution of income occurs through the sale of productive services on markets at prices established by supply and demand, Part Four begins with an analysis of these prices and their role in the allocation of productive services among competing uses. Chapter 22, "Wages," deals with wage rates as the price of labor. We will see how the demand for particular types of labor derives from the demand for the products of labor and how differences in wage rates tend to guide workers into those jobs in which their services are the most valuable. In Chapter 23, "Rent," we will see how payment for the services of land arises out of its scarcity, and how the owners' efforts to get the highest rents influence the crop that is planted or the industrial use to which the land is put. Chapter 24, "Interest and Profits," examines 2 closely related types of income that involve investment and economic growth. We will see how interest rates allocate investable resources among competing projects and how profit derives from the enterpriser's effort to increase the productivity of resources. We will also examine the Marxian theory of profit as surplus value.

Chapter 25, "Incomes of Families and Individuals," deals with the overall pattern of income distribution that emerges from the operation of the markets for productive services. We will examine the range of incomes among families at a given time, and also over the life cycle of the individual family. We will also explore the racial distribution of income. The inequality of the present-day U.S. income distribution will be compared with that of the U.S. of 40 years ago and that existing in other nations of the world today. Chapter 26, "Poverty in America," takes up the important questions of how many Americans are poor, who and where the poor families are, and what can be done to abolish poverty from the United States.

Chapter 27, "The Economy as a Control System," serves as a final general overview of the operation of economic systems, setting our entire study in a general theoretical context which relates the economic system to a broader complex of social systems that regulate the behavior of mankind.

CHAPTER 22

Wages

The largest single share in our gross national income goes to people as payment for the contribution of their own personal effort to production. Of the 1968 gross national income of $860 billion, nearly 60 percent consisted of wages, salaries, and other labor income paid to employees. Not all work, however, is done by people employed by somebody else. The owner of a small business who works alongside his employees in production or waiting on customers is performing the same functions they do. The manager of a factory has to do much the same job, whether he is hired by somebody else or owns the plant himself. By any reasonable reckoning, small businessmen and farmers derive more of their income from work as managers, buyers, accountants, and ordinary laborers in their own firms than they do from profits or interest on invested capital. Doctors, lawyers, engineers, and other professionals are often self-employed but draw their incomes from the service they render, not as the profit of a business.

When the incomes of professionals, proprietors, and farmers are combined with employee compensation, the total share remains remarkably stable at about two-thirds of gross national product. As shown in Table 1, the steadily growing share earned by wage and salary workers over

TABLE 1 PERCENT OF U.S. GNP OF EMPLOYEE COMPENSATION, BUSINESS AND PROFESSIONAL INCOME, AND INCOME OF FARM PROPRIETORS, 1929–1968

	EMPLOYEE COMPEN- SATION	BUSINESS AND PRO- FESSIONAL INCOME	INCOME OF FARM PROPRI- ETORS	TOTAL
1929	49.5	8.7	6.1	65.3
1939	53.1	8.1	4.8	66.0
1949	54.6	8.8	4.9	68.3
1959	57.6	7.2	2.6	67.4
1968	59.6	5.5	1.8	66.9

SOURCE: Calculated from data in *The National Income and Product Accounts of the United States, 1929–1965.* Data for later years from appropriate issues of the *Survey of Current Business.*

the past 40 years has mostly represented the decline of the independent farmer and the displacement of small proprietors and merchants by corporate enterprise. Jobs that were once performed by self-employed proprietors are now done by hired accountants, managers, and other employees. Since nearly 90 percent of the total compensation is paid to employees, it is convenient to speak of wage rates and of workers hired and laid off, but it should be thoroughly understood that we are concerned with the compensation for labor effort in general, whether of hired or self-employed people.

Wages have two important aspects: First, as the price of an hour's work, a wage rate helps to allocate labor among different uses much as market prices allocate commodities among different buyers. That is, differences in wage rates provide a powerful incentive for workers to move into those industries, occupations, and regions where consumers put the highest priority on their services. Second, as the worker's return for effort, wage rates constitute income by which he can acquire a share of the goods and services society has produced. These two aspects of wages are closely interconnected, and it is impossible to deal with either one without involving the other. However, the first part of this chapter places its main emphasis on the allocation of labor, while the second part deals primarily with wages as income. Because of the importance of collective bargaining in the determination of many wage rates, the chapter will conclude with a brief discussion of the economic role of unions and of public policy toward organized labor.

WAGES AND THE ALLOCATION OF LABOR

The number of employees a given firm tends to hire and the number of hours they work depend on the wage rate the firm

must pay for their services. Payrolls are an important element of variable cost. Higher wages mean higher costs which, when passed on to customers in higher prices, lead them to purchase less than before. Production cutbacks follow reduced sales, and workers are laid off. Conversely, when wages are low, the firm can pass on lower costs in the form of lower prices to its customers. Stepped-up production follows expanded sales, and the firm hires additional workers.

The Demand for Labor by an Individual Employer

The way an employer adjusts his work force to changing hourly wage rates is shown in Figure 1. The wage rate—the "price" of labor—is measured vertically, and the number of people the firm tends to employ—the "quantity" of labor—is measured horizontally. The curve DD represents the firm's demand for labor. At a low wage rate like W_0, low costs and prices are accompanied by high sales, and E_0 em-

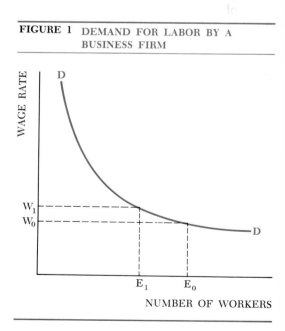

FIGURE 1   DEMAND FOR LABOR BY A BUSINESS FIRM

ployees are needed. At a higher wage rate like W_1, high costs and prices are accompanied by lower sales and only E_1 workers are employed.

The response of the employer is described by the elasticity of his demand for labor, calculated as the ratio of the percentage reduction in number of workers employed to the percentage increase in wage rate that occasioned it. It would appear from the figure that the rise from W_0 to W_1 represented a wage increase of about 20 percent, while the consequent reduction in employment from E_0 to E_1 was about 40 percent. Accordingly, this particular employer's demand for labor would appear to have elasticity of 40/20 or 2, approximately.

A Derived Demand   The demand for labor is a *derived demand* because its properties all derive from the series of links between wage rates, costs, prices, sales, and employment. The series can be represented as a chain of causal links: Wage rate → Marginal cost → Price → Sales → Output → Employment. That is, the reason an employer varies the number of workers on the job when wage rates change is that wage rates affect marginal cost which determines the most profitable price for the product. In response to price changes, customers alter their purchases according to the elasticity of their demand for the product, and employment must be varied to match output to sales.

Elasticity of Demand   The elasticity of an employer's demand for labor depends on two key links that vary widely from industry to industry. One of these is the percentage of labor as an element of marginal cost. In industries in which a large fraction of marginal cost consists of wages, changes in wage rates cause substantial changes in prices and tend to exert correspondingly large influences on employment. In industries in which only a small fraction of mar-

ginal cost derives from wages, the same alteration of wage rates results in a much smaller percentage change in costs and prices, and correspondingly smaller percentage changes are observed in employment. For example, since wages amount to nearly 40 percent of the marginal cost of manufacturing felt hats, an increase in wage rates paid by a hat maker has a substantial effect on his marginal cost; his prices must be raised, and the firm's work force tends to decline as customers buy fewer hats or turn to those made by competitors. In contrast, wages amount to only about one-half of 1 percent of the marginal cost of operating a flour mill. Wage rates can rise substantially but still have only a negligible effect on marginal cost and price, with a correspondingly small influence over the number of mill hands hired. Other things being equal, we would expect the hat manufacturer's demand for labor to be more elastic than that of the flour mill.

The second important link in the chain is the elasticity of demand for the firm's product. Prices tend to rise by the same percentage as marginal cost. Therefore, given the proportion of labor in marginal cost, the effect of a rise in wages on sales, output, and employment depends mainly on customer response to price increases. If customers have elastic demands and make large cuts in their buying, employment will have to be cut correspondingly, and the employer's demand for labor will likewise be elastic. If customers have inelastic demand, on the other hand, their small reduction in the quantity bought will lead to an inelastic demand for labor. Since the demand for highly differentiated products tends to have lower elasticity than the demand for homogeneous products, monopolistic competitors tend to have a less elastic demand for labor than pure competitors, given the same proportion of labor in marginal cost. Likewise, individual firms in oligopolistic industries tend to have less elastic demand for labor than firms with similar cost structures in less concentrated industries.

These two important links combine into a single simple relationship. The elasticity of an employer's demand for labor is the product of the proportion of labor in his marginal cost multiplied by the elasticity of the demand for his output. For example, a hat manufacturer whose marginal cost, as we noted, consists of 40 percent labor, sells a product for which the elasticity of demand is typically about 3. This means that his demand for labor has elasticity of .40 × 3, or 1.2. In the absence of any increase in demand for hats, a 10 percent wage increase would lead him to reduce the number of employees about 12 percent. In contrast, the flour miller, whose payroll is only one-half of 1 percent of his marginal cost, sells a homogeneous product for which demand elasticity is typically about 10. As a result, his demand for labor has elasticity of only .005 × 10, or .05. A 10 percent wage increase would lead him to reduce his work force only one-half of 1 percent.

The Demand for Labor: an Example As an example, consider the demand for labor by a bottle-manufacturing firm like the one discussed in Chapter 17. The hypothetical cost structure of the firm is shown in Table 2. Depreciation, taxes, and other fixed costs are $1,500,000 per year. In addition, the operation of the firm entails variable costs of which $2.40 per gross is the marginal

nonlabor cost of materials, power, and cartons. Since the production of bottles requires one-half manhour per gross, marginal labor cost depends on the wage rate. At the rate of $3 per hour shown, marginal labor cost is $1.50, and together with the nonlabor cost of $2.40, gives the firm a marginal cost of $3.90 per gross of bottles produced.

Given these costs, the manufacturer's most profitable price depends on the elasticity of demand for his bottles. The hypothetical demand for the firm's product is given in Table 3. Since this schedule has an elasticity of about 2.5, the firm would find its most profitable markup to be $e/(e-1) =$ 2.5/1.5, or 1.67. Under these circumstances, the most profitable price to set would be 1.67 × $3.90, or $6.50. According to the demand schedule, customers would be expected to purchase 600,000 gross per year at $6.50 per gross. The cost figures show that the firm needs an average of one-half manhour for each gross of bottles turned out. At that rate, the firm would have to employ 1/2 × 600,000, or 300,000 manhours per year. At 2,000 hours per full-time employee, this would be equivalent to a work force of 150 full-time people.

We have derived 1 point on the curve representing the firm's demand for labor. At a wage rate of $3 per hour, the firm tends to hire 300,000 manhours per year, or about 150 full-time people. To see how many people the firm would hire at some other wage rate, we need merely repeat all the calculations, using the new wage rate in place of the old. These calculations are

---

TABLE 2   PRODUCTION COSTS OF A BEVERAGE BOTTLE MANUFACTURER

Fixed cost		$1,500,000 per year
Variable cost per gross of bottles, packed		
Nonlabor cost		$2.40
Sand, lime, chemicals	$.95	
Power	.45	
Cartons	1.00	
Labor cost (1/2 manhour at $3.00)		1.50
Marginal cost		$3.90

TABLE 3   DEMAND FOR MANUFACTURER'S BEVERAGE BOTTLES

PRICE	SOLD PER YEAR GROSS OF BOTTLES
$8.18	338,000
7.35	440,000
6.50	600,000
6.10	696,000

TABLE 4 DERIVATION OF DEMAND FOR LABOR OF A BEVERAGE BOTTLE
MANUFACTURER

HOURLY WAGE	MARGINAL COST			PRICE (MARKUP = 1.67)	ANNUAL SALES	MANHOURS (1/2 HR/ GROSS)	NUMBER OF FULL-TIME EMPLOYEES
	LABOR (1/2 HR)	NONLABOR	TOTAL				
$5.00	$2.50	$2.40	$4.90	$8.18	338,000	169,000	84.5
4.00	2.00	2.40	4.40	7.35	440,000	220,000	110
3.00	1.50	2.40	3.90	6.50	600,000	300,000	150
2.50	1.25	2.40	3.65	6.10	696,000	348,000	174

summarized in Table 4. When the wage rate is $5 an hour, the labor part of marginal cost is $2.50 per unit. Combined with nonlabor cost, this makes a marginal cost of $4.90 which is marked up to a price of $8.18 per gross. According to the demand schedule, this price will lead customers to buy 338,000 gross, the manufacture of which involves 169,000 manhours or the equivalent of 84.5 full-time employees. As the wage rate declines, so does cost and price, and the number of employees expands. The completed demand for production workers is plotted through these points in Figure 2.

FIGURE 2 DEMAND FOR LABOR BY A
BEVERAGE BOTTLE
MANUFACTURER

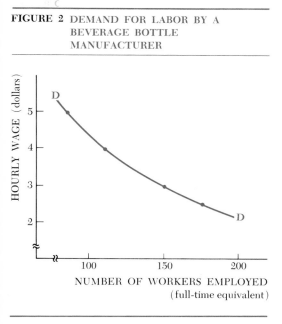

NUMBER OF WORKERS EMPLOYED
(full-time equivalent)

To check these results against the relationship developed above, the elasticity of the bottle manufacturer's demand for production labor can be estimated from Figure 2 in the usual way. The increase in wage rate from $2.50 to $3 is about 18 percent and is accompanied by about a 15 percent decline in the number of workers as the work force is cut from 174 to 150.[1] This yields an estimated elasticity of 15/18, or 0.83. The demand for the firm's bottles has elasticity of 2.5 and at a wage of $2.50, labor is about 34 percent of marginal cost. These figures imply the firm's demand for labor should have elasticity of about .34 × 2.5, or 0.85, in almost exact agreement with the estimate.

Elasticity of Demand for Labor by an Entire Industry

The demand for labor by an entire industry tends to be less elastic than that of any individual firm. When only one employer must pay higher wages, his prices are forced up in comparison to those of his competitors, and heavy loss of sales gives high elasticity to his demand for labor. When all producers in the industry must pay the same higher wages, however, costs and prices of all competitors rise together. Firms tend to lose sales only to substitute products made in other industries. The re-

[1] For technical accuracy, changes have been expressed as percentages of midpoint values. See Appendix to Chapter 15.

sulting elasticity of demand for labor depends on the less elastic industry-wide demand for the product, rather than on the more highly elastic demand for the output of an individual firm.

The demand for labor by the bottle manufacturer had elasticity of .8 because, under the conditions assumed, it was the only firm in the industry whose wage rates were varying. Wage rates of all other bottle manufacturers were presumably held fixed during the calculations, and the employment responses were determined by the elasticity of demand for the bottles of this particular manufacturer, selling in competition with those of other makers. If the wages and prices of all bottle manufacturers rose together, the elasticity of the industry-wide demand for bottles would depend only on how many customers were lost to producers of beverage cans and would be considerably below the 2.5 elasticity characteristic of an individual firm.

For the sake of the example, suppose that a 1 percent industry-wide increase in bottle prices would reduce total industry sales by .9 percent. If marginal costs of bottle manufacturers were typically 34 percent labor costs, as in the example, the industry's demand for labor would have elasticity of .34 × 0.9, or 0.3, approximately. Unless offset by an increase in the demand for bottles, the response of manufacturers to a 10 percent industry-wide wage hike would be to lay off about 3 percent of their workers.

One consequence of the difference between these elasticities is important for collective bargaining. A union that has organized only a few firms in an industry is severely limited in the wages it can demand. A few cents an hour often make the difference between normal profits and going out of business, and the power of the union to bargain under these circumstances is sharply curtailed by the prospect of a heavy loss of jobs as a probable consequence of higher wages. When all em-

ployers in the industry are subject to the same demands, the prospective loss of jobs is a much smaller percentage of employment.

Demand for a Specialized Type of Labor

It is also important to distinguish between the demand of an industry for production labor as a whole and its demand for workers with a particular skill. The cost of a few key workers with unique experience, skill, training, or other qualifications is often a small part of the total labor cost of production. A rise in the rate commanded by such specialists causes only a small percentage increase in marginal cost, and the demand for such labor is correspondingly inelastic.

American trade unionism had its first strong start among such skilled workers as carpenters, masons, machinists, and locomotive engineers, rather than among the mass of unskilled or semiskilled workers. All workers of a given skill or craft were organized into a single union, regardless of the firm or industry for which they worked. Unions of this kind, called *craft unions*, predominated in the early days of the American Federation of Labor. Since such skilled workers constituted only a small part of the total wage cost of the products they produced, the demand for their services was inelastic. Once organized, the skilled workers were in a position to increase their wage rates with little risk of a reduction in the amount they could work. Since this advantage would disappear if the unskilled or semiskilled workers were to share in the increases, there was little incentive to include them in the organization.

Long-Run Elasticity of Demand

The demand for labor by an industry tends to be more elastic in the long run than in the short run. Given time, there are a number of ways a firm can adjust to wage changes other than merely changing prices. One of the most important of these is the installation of labor-saving machinery. Whether it is profitable for employers to install a machine to replace workers on a given job depends on the cost of the machine compared to the cost of the labor that it can save. When wages are low compared to the price of the machine, hand methods will persist. When wages rise, however, installation of the machine may quickly pay for itself.

Since prices of machines depend partly on wage rates in the machinery-manufacturing industry, the critical element in mechanization is not the absolute level of wages, but how wage rates in the potential machine-using industry compare to those in the machine-producing industry. As Figure 3 suggests, the relatively high wages of coal miners have been an important pressure toward the mechanization of U.S. coal mining during the past 60 years.

FIGURE 3   AVERAGE HOURLY EARNINGS,
            COAL MINING AS PERCENT OF
            MANUFACTURING, AND
            MECHANICALLY CUT COAL AS A
            PERCENT OF UNDERGROUND
            PRODUCTION, 1909-1955

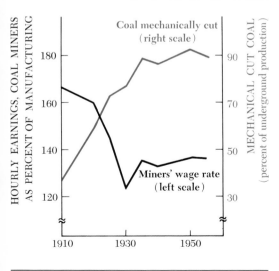

SOURCE: Calculated from data in *Historical Statistics of the United States.*

Higher long-run elasticity of labor demand also results when firms can redesign products or services to reduce the amount of labor required. This can be done by reducing tolerances, lowering inspection standards, and accepting greater losses from customers' rejection of defective items; by eliminating parts that have to be worked by hand; or even—as the supermarket has done so effectively—by substituting the consumers' own labor for that of hired employees.

Some industries respond to higher wage rates in one region by moving to another. This was an important factor in the shift of the textile industry from New England to the South.

Allocation of Labor Among Industries

How demand for labor assigns each industry its proper share of workers is shown in Figure 4, where demand curves for two industries are plotted on the same chart. Wage rates are plotted on the vertical axis, employment is plotted horizontally. The demand for workers by one industry—hat manufacturers—is represented by curve D_hD_h, with the number of hat workers measured to the right. Curve D_hD_h slopes downward to the right in keeping with the fact that hat manufacturers tend to hire more workers at low than at high wage rates. The demand for labor by the other industry, flour milling, is represented by the curve D_mD_m, with the number of flour-mill employees measured from the origin to the *left.* The tendency of flour mills to hire more workers at low wages causes D_mD_m to slope downward to the left.[2] When the total number of workers available to the two industries corresponds to the length of *MOH*, the equilibrium wage rate tends to be $W per hour. At that wage, *OH* workers

[2] This is the same scheme that was employed earlier to represent the allocation of commodities among different uses. See Chapter 16.

FIGURE 4 ALLOCATION OF EMPLOYMENT
BETWEEN 2 INDUSTRIES

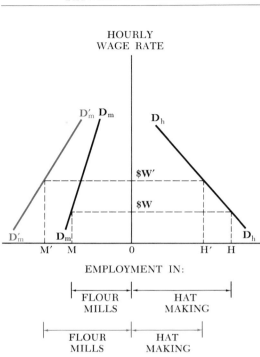

FIGURE 4 ALLOCATION OF EMPLOYMENT
BETWEEN 2 INDUSTRIES

are employed by hat firms and *OM* by flour mills.

Reallocation of Labor in Response to Shifts in Demand A change in the demand for labor by one of the industries would set forces in motion to alter the allocation of workers. Suppose there were an increase in the demand for flour by housewives and bakeries. This would be reflected in a rise in the demand for flour-mill workers from $D_m D_m$ to $D'_m D'_m$. In an effort to attract the extra workers they need, flour mills would ultimately be forced to offer higher wages. As the wage rate were competed up to W', costs of hat manufacturing would be increased. Higher prices would cut back hat sales, and employment would decline in keeping with the elasticity of demand for labor by hat makers. The workers laid off from hat manufacturing ($H'H$) would be

hired by flour mills to satisfy the added demand for flour.

Although only a schematic device, Figure 4 is a good representation of the powerful forces that operate on the pattern of wage rates and the allocation of labor. The pay offered a given kind of worker depends on the demands of all industries competing for his services in relation to the number of similar workers available for employment. When consumers want more of a product, their increased demand provides its manufacturer with the power to pay higher wages and attract a greater number of workers from the competing demands of other industries.

The Dynamics of Wage Patterns

A more realistic understanding of how labor markets work requires some examination of their dynamics. In the first place, a realistic approach to the pattern of wages and the allocation of labor must recognize that neither the demand for labor nor the number of workers wanting jobs remains constant. In an expanding economy, demands for labor tend to rise steadily as a growing population with increasing income demands more of most products. At the same time, a growing labor force sends a constantly increasing number of workers out looking for jobs. Figure 4, therefore, should be interpreted as showing the effect of a *relative* shift in demand for the two products on the *proportion* of workers employed in the respective industries. The rise in demand from $D_m D_m$ to $D'_m D'_m$ designates a demand for labor by flour mills that has been growing compared to that by hat manufacturers. As a result of this growth, a larger proportion of new workers tend to find jobs in flour mills. There need be no actual net layoff of workers by hat manufacturers.

Wage adjustments likewise tend to be

dynamic. Flour mills trying to increase their work force find it necessary to offer the more attractive wage, W'. Since this is not matched by simultaneous increases by hat manufacturers, a wage differential is created. The higher wage rates at flour mills steadily attract workers away from other jobs, however, and other employers ultimately find it necessary to match the increase in order to fill their own employment needs. The wage differential is ironed out as the allocation of labor approaches the new equilibrium position of Figure 4.

Short-Run Shifts in Employment In the short run, movement of workers in response to wage differences is largely limited to going from one firm to another, or to leaving one occupation for another that requires similar skill, training, and experience. Even so, a surprising number of workers make such changes every year. A survey by the U.S. Census Bureau revealed that more than 8 million out of a total experienced male labor force of 48 million changed jobs during the year 1955. Some of these changes resulted from layoffs, illness, and other causes, but nearly 40 percent were motivated by a desire for higher earnings. Moreover, while many of these men stayed in the same occupation—merely moving to a similar but better-paying job in another firm or location—over half of them actually changed their occupational classification.[3]

Long-Run Shifts Among Occupations The same market forces that allocate workers among industries guide people into occupations in which their talents are most in demand. In Figure 5, the demand for insurance agents is plotted to the right, and the demand for lawyers is plotted to the left. When there are I insurance agents

[3] U.S. Bureau of the Census, *Job Mobility of Workers in 1955*, Current Population Reports Series P–50, February, 1957.

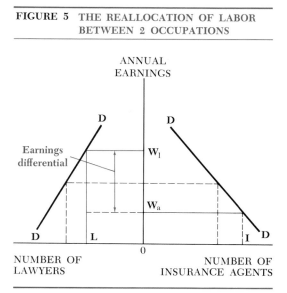

FIGURE 5   THE REALLOCATION OF LABOR
BETWEEN 2 OCCUPATIONS

but only L lawyers, the shortage of lawyers gives them earnings of W_1 compared to only W_a for insurance men. The resulting earnings differential attracts people to the legal profession. The number of lawyers grows relative to the number of insurance agents, and their earnings tend to equalize, as shown.

The main reallocation of the labor force occurs as a result of the choices of training and occupation made by young people and must be studied over a period of years. The flow of labor toward higher income is dramatically demonstrated by comparing the long-run rates of growth in the number of persons in various occupations. The censuses of 1950 and 1960 gave information on the number of persons engaged in each occupation and on their median earnings. According to the theory of allocation, we should expect those occupations with higher earnings in 1950 to show more rapid growth over the following decade than those with lower earnings, and this expectation is confirmed (see Figure 6). The number of doctors, dentists, architects, managers of manufacturing firms, lawyers, engineers, and others in the highest-paid

FIGURE 6   INCREASE IN EMPLOYMENT BY OCCUPATIONS IN RELATION TO MEDIAN INCOME

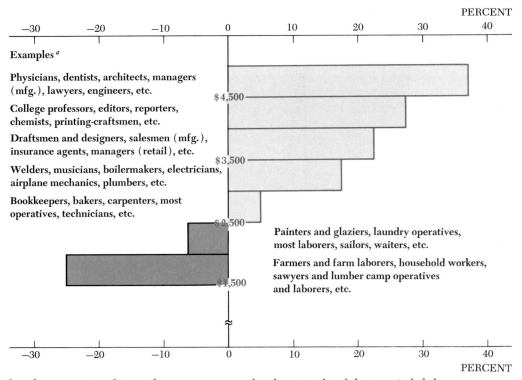

Examples^a

Physicians, dentists, architects, managers (mfg.), lawyers, engineers, etc.

College professors, editors, reporters, chemists, printing-craftsmen, etc.

Draftsmen and designers, salesmen (mfg.), insurance agents, managers (retail), etc.

Welders, musicians, boilermakers, electricians, airplane mechanics, plumbers, etc.

Bookkeepers, bakers, carpenters, most operatives, technicians, etc.

Painters and glaziers, laundry operatives, most laborers, sailors, waiters, etc.

Farmers and farm laborers, household workers, sawyers and lumber camp operatives and laborers, etc.

^aOnly a few occupations from each income group are listed as examples of the types included.

SOURCE: Median Earnings from U.S. Bureau of the Census, *U.S. Census of Population, 1950, Characteristics of the Population, United States Summary.* Percentage increases from U.S. Bureau of the Census, *U.S. Census of Population, 1960, Detailed Characteristics, United States Summary,* Final Report PC (1)–ID.

occupations increased nearly 40 percent. In contrast, the number of farmers, household workers, lumber-camp laborers, and others in the lowest-paid occupations declined about 25 percent. Growth rates of other occupations varied between these extremes in relation to their earnings.

The Allocation of Labor Among Regions
The forces of supply and demand not only guide workers into the right industry and occupation; they also encourage people to move to locations where their talents are most needed. People living in areas with a large population relative to the demand for labor tend to have incomes below the national average, while those in areas of higher labor demand and fewer residents tend to have incomes above the national average. Although climate, regional customs, type of work available, and many other factors influence where people choose to live, there is a steady drift out of low-income regions and into regions of greater economic opportunity. The dynamics of the process are similar to those that shift workers among occupations. With a large population relative to the demand for

labor, a state like Mississippi has a low per capita income. The population of California is smaller relative to the demand for labor, and the resultant higher per capita income represents an inducement to people to move to California. The income differential between the states tends to disappear as populations come into equilibrium with demand.

The actual effect of income differences on migration is shown in Figure 7. The per capita income of each state in 1950, expressed as a percentage of the U.S. average, is plotted vertically, and net migration into or out of the state during the following decade is plotted horizontally. Each point represents a state. The general upward drift of the points, represented by the line drawn through their midst, represents the powerful attraction of higher incomes. However, income is not the only factor at work. The net migration into Florida and

Arizona, the outstanding exceptions, consisted largely of older people in search of warm climate, while Nevada—not quite so much of an exception—offered other attractions.

Productivity and Labor Allocation

The discovery and introduction of automatic machinery, automated controls, and other devices to raise labor productivity reduce the amount of labor required per unit of output in the industries in which they are adopted and lower the cost and price of the products. The strong tendency of prices to move with labor productivity is readily observable when trends of the 2 are plotted for a number of industries, as in Figure 8.[4]

Given the effect of productivity on prices, the response of consumers will bring about a new allocation of labor. If consumers have little use for additional quantities of the product in question, the demand for it will be inelastic. Consumers will purchase little more of it at the lower prices and production will not expand enough to offset the labor saved per unit. The demand for labor will decline and workers will be forced out of the industry. On the other hand, if the product is something for which consumers have a highly elastic demand, they may buy so much more at the lower price that more workers will be needed despite higher productivity; the industry will show an increased demand for labor, and workers will be attracted away from other jobs.

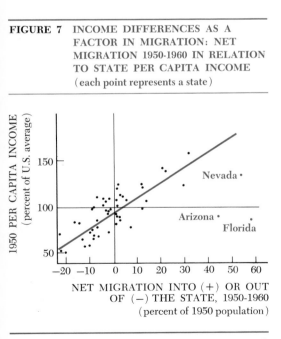

FIGURE 7   INCOME DIFFERENCES AS A FACTOR IN MIGRATION: NET MIGRATION 1950-1960 IN RELATION TO STATE PER CAPITA INCOME
(each point represents a state)

[4] One important reason the relationship shown in the figure is not exact is that labor is not the only element of marginal cost. A given rise in labor productivity tends to reduce prices more in industries in which wages are a substantial part of marginal cost than in those in which labor costs are only a small fraction of marginal cost. A second reason, of course, is that wage rates did not behave identically in all industries.

SOURCE: State per capita incomes from *Survey of Current Business,* August, 1968. Net migration from U.S. Bureau of the Census, *Current Population Reports* Series P–20, no. 124.

FIGURE 8   PRICE AND PRODUCTIVITY TRENDS
                19 MANUFACTURING INDUSTRIES

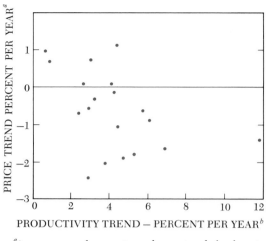

PRODUCTIVITY TREND — PERCENT PER YEAR[b]

[a]Average annual percentage change in wholesale price index, 1959-1964.

[b]Average annual percentage change in output per employee manhour, 1959-1964.

SOURCE: *Economic Report of the President, 1965*, p. 58.

The automobile industry provides 2 good examples of how labor demand responds to technical change. The introduction of labor-saving, assembly-line methods by the Ford Motor Company 60 years ago raised the demand for labor. Unit labor requirements, which had exceeded 421 manhours per vehicle as late as 1909, were forced down to about 112 by 1916. Since wages were a substantial portion of marginal cost, the saving permitted the Model T touring car, priced at $950 in 1909, to sell for $360. High elasticity of demand expanded annual sales from 10,607 to over 730,000 units, and employment rose from 1,655 to 32,701 workers.[5]

In contrast, production-worker wages today represent only about 12 percent of

[5] Figures are based on data given by Allen Nevins, *Ford: The Times, the Man, the Company,* New York, Charles Scribner's Sons, 1954, Appendixes III (p. 644), V (p. 646), and VII (p. 648).

the variable cost of automobile production, while demand for new cars has an elasticity estimated to lie somewhere between 1.2 and .6. It follows that the technical improvements now being introduced by automobile manufacturers lower their demand for labor. Automobile employment declined from over 800,000 in 1950 to 753,000 in 1963, despite an increase in automobile production.

The implications of labor-saving technology extend far beyond the industry that adopts the new method. When lower labor costs permit reduction in the price of a product, expanded output raises demand for power, fuel, and purchased materials, and hence the demand for labor to produce them. Moreover, if the innovating industry is itself a supplier of materials for further processing, its lower prices stimulate the output, and hence the demand for labor, of its customers. At the same time, if the cheaper materials replace more expensive substitutes, the demand for labor declines in industries producing the latter.

Finally, it should be remembered that the labor-saving machinery installed by one industry is, in turn, the product of labor in other industries. The automatic-packaging equipment that lowers the labor demand of makers of glass containers raises employment in the industrial-machinery industry. The process-control computer that permits higher-quality cement at lower unit labor cost raises labor demand in the electronics industry. The electrification of industry during the last 70 years has reduced the demand for labor to produce steam engines and steam power transmission equipment and for the engineers, firemen, and maintenance men needed to operate them and has increased the demand for labor to produce electrical machinery and electrical control apparatus and to generate electricity.

Changes in the Type of Labor Demanded
Technical change not only shifts the demand for labor, it alters the type of worker

used. In the earliest period of industrialization, mechanized processes replaced skilled artisans. Semiskilled machine operators took over the jobs of the weaver, cobbler, wheelwright, and cabinetmaker as production moved from shop to factory. The modern trend is in the reverse direction. The increasing use of automated equipment and computerized control is replacing unskilled and semiskilled machine operators by scientists, engineers, mathematicians, and skilled technical maintenance men.

The consequence of the shift of demand from unskilled to skilled labor was apparent in Figure 6, above. The high-paid, growing occupations involve highly skilled technical work. Growth in the number of engineers and chemists has been especially rapid. The low-paid, declining occupations are those requiring little skill or training.

The change in the type of labor used is the most painful aspect of technical innovation. It often displaces mature workers whose specialized skills, developed by a lifetime of training and experience, are no longer needed. The resistance of such workers to the installation of the new method is readily understandable. A recent example has been the strong resistance of typesetters and linotype operators to the use of computerized typesetting equipment by newspapers. To cushion the shock, businesses often undertake to keep all those whose skills are made obsolete by the technical change, allowing their employment to shrink only as they retire or quit. In highly competitive industries, this is possible only on the basis of an industry-wide agreement, usually with a labor union.

WAGES AS LABOR INCOME

Differences in Equilibrium Earnings

If jobs were all alike and people were perfectly interchangeable, long-run shifts in labor allocation would continue until all wages were equal. Since jobs and people are not all the same, however, differences in earnings persist, even in the long run. There are 3 reasons why earnings on some jobs are permanently higher than on others: (1) Some jobs require a special ability that is rare among workers and this forms a natural barrier, keeping those without the ability out of the occupation. (2) There are institutional barriers to entry into some occupations. (3) Some occupations are more satisfying than others, and people are willing to enter them despite lower earnings.

Differing Job Requirements Any healthy male with a strong back can be a baggage porter, sweeper, ditch digger or car washer, but a high order of intelligence, memory, and personality is needed to become a successful trial lawyer. Earnings in occupations for which almost everybody is qualified cannot exceed those in occupations with special requirements, for any differential would be promptly eliminated by people with higher qualifications moving into the less restricted jobs. The reverse is not true. If income incentives were adequate, lawyers could work as filing clerks or salesmen, but regardless of how high lawyers' incomes rise, people without the necessary personal equipment and training cannot become lawyers. The nature of the resulting "one-way" competition is illustrated by the black lines in Figure 9. In Figure 9(a), the small number of skilled workers compared to demand creates a wage differential in their favor, but unskilled workers cannot respond to it by taking skilled jobs. On the other hand, as shown in Figure 9(b), a "shortage" of unskilled workers could not maintain a differential in wage rates because skilled workers could always leave their more highly skilled jobs and take the better-paying unskilled work. One-way competition of this kind shows up not only in pay differentials based on skill, but in lifetime earnings

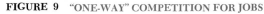

FIGURE 9   "ONE-WAY" COMPETITION FOR JOBS

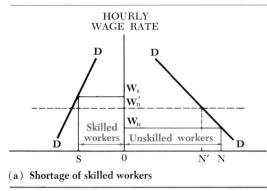

(a) Shortage of skilled workers

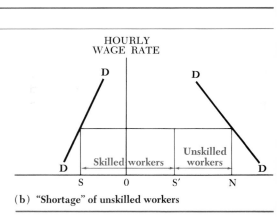

(b) "Shortage" of unskilled workers

differentials in favor of people with higher education, as shown in Figure 10.

One-way competition among groups with different skills also places severe limits to efforts to raise the wages of unskilled workers by minimum-wage laws. As the name implies, minimum-wage laws establish a legal minimum money wage that must be paid by employers regardless of

FIGURE 10   LIFETIME EARNINGS OF U.S. MALES IN RELATION TO EDUCATION

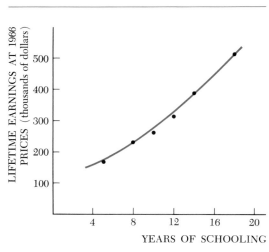

SOURCE: *Statistical Abstract of the United States, 1968.* Data are estimates compiled by the Bureau of the Census on the basis of a cross-section of the population.

conditions in the labor market or of the qualifications of the individual worker. The intent of such a law is presumably to permit any worker on any job to earn a wage consistent with some minimum standard of decency, but its effect is often to increase the unskilled worker's difficulty in finding a job. Forcing employers to pay higher wages to workers of low productivity makes the latter's services too expensive compared to those of more skilled labor or of machinery.

The situation is schematically illustrated in Figure 9. Without the legal minimum wage, one-way competition maintains a differential between the wage rate W_s, earned by the more skilled group, and the rate W_n earned by less skilled. Establishment of W'_n as a legal minimum wage has little effect on the employment of the skilled workers, but while the change provides some low-skilled workers with higher wages, others are no longer able to find work, and employment declines to N'. It has been suggested that the increased unemployment among inexperienced black teenagers observed in recent years is partly due to higher minimum wage rates, but in general the effect of minimum-wage legislation is short lived. If the minimum wage is not set too high above the wage rates that low-skilled workers would earn in any case, the general upward drift of money wages soon makes the minimum level purely academic until it is again raised by the legislature.

Institutional Barriers to Occupations
Some workers who are otherwise entirely qualified are barred from a job by institutional arrangements. One common barrier is "closed" union membership. Some unions, including many of the skilled trades, are exclusive and admit only a narrowly restricted, carefully selected number of new members. An otherwise qualified young man can rarely enter one of the skilled trades without a relative or some other "contact" to get him into the union. It should be immediately added that most unions are "open," admitting anybody who will pay dues, and that these open unions do not form artificial barriers to unionized occupations.

Discrimination on the basis of sex, race, religion, or ethnic group likewise works to prevent equalization of earnings. Discrimination bars access to the training required for skilled occupations, or excludes otherwise qualified persons from them. It sometimes takes the form of different pay scales for employees doing the same jobs. Table 5 shows pay differentials between men and women in the same city, the same industry, and identical occupational classifications.

The effects of racial discrimination are reflected in the fact that a smaller percentage of nonwhites than whites have jobs in the better-paid occupations and that, within each occupation, nonwhite workers are, on the average, paid less than white workers. Although more recent information is unavailable, the situation has improved little from that shown by the Census data given in Table 6.

In addition to its injustice and attendant deprivation, frustration, and suffering, discrimination is an expensive practice. When potentially valuable people are unable to make their best contribution to society, the quantity and quality of output is held down. Labor is our greatest economic resource, and its misallocation reduces the living standards not only of those discriminated against, but of everyone else as well.

Satisfaction from Different Occupations
The attractiveness of occupations is a matter of taste. Science appeals to one person, teaching to another, a third likes the competitiveness and independence of running a business. Some occupations like acting or entrepreneurship, which promise immense returns to the successful few but little to the majority, attract the venturesome. Other occupations like school teaching and civil service, which promise smaller, more certain incomes, attract workers who value security. The attractiveness of occupations also varies with the extent to which one meets and deals with people, with the amount of responsibility, the freedom to exercise initiative, the discipline demanded, the hours required, the amount of physical effort involved, and with the time, money, and effort necessary for training.

People who put primary emphasis on the social nature of work rather than on income are attracted to certain occupations

TABLE 5 AVERAGE STRAIGHT-TIME WEEKLY EARNINGS OF MEN AND WOMEN IN SELECTED OFFICE OCCUPATIONS IN MANUFACTURING FIRMS, BOSTON, MASS.

OCCUPATION	EARNINGS	
	MEN	WOMEN
Accounting clerk, Class A	$126.00	$107.00
Class B	95.00	89.00
Tabulating machine operator,		
Class A	126.00	115.50
Class B	107.50	96.50
Order clerk	124.00	90.00
Payroll clerk	117.50	95.50

SOURCE: *Occupational Wage Survey: Boston, September, 1968,* Bureau of Labor Statistics Bulletin 1625–15, January, 1969.

TABLE 6   OCCUPATIONAL DISTRIBUTION AND EARNINGS, ALL U.S. MALES
AND NONWHITE ONLY, 1960

| | TOTAL U.S. | | NONWHITE ONLY | |
OCCUPATION	MEDIAN EARNINGS	PERCENT ENGAGED	MEDIAN EARNINGS	PERCENT ENGAGED
Managers, officials, and proprietors, except farmers	$6,664	10.4	$3,869	2.2
Professional, technical, and kindred workers	6,619	10.1	4,563	3.7
Craftsmen, foremen, and kindred workers	5,240	20.0	3,480	10.4
Sales workers	4,987	6.7	2,809	1.4
Clerical and kindred workers	4,785	6.9	4,072	5.0
Operatives	4,299	20.4	3,040	23.8
Service workers (including household)	3,310	6.1	2,529	14.3
Laborers and others	2,948	11.9	2,394	28.7
Farmers and farm managers	2,169	5.0	788	3.8
Farm laborers and foremen	1,066	2.5	816	6.7
Total	4,621	100.0	2,703	100.0

SOURCE: U.S. Bureau of the Census, *U.S. Census of Population: 1960. Detailed Characteristics, United States Summary,* Final Report PC(1)–ID., Washington, D.C., U.S. Government Printing Office, 1963, Table 208.

despite lower earnings. For example, although men in teaching and social work belonged to an income class that grew only about 17 percent in the period shown in Figure 6, during the decade shown the number of men teaching school increased 90 percent, while the number in social work rose by 55 percent. Although the earnings of clergymen put them in a class of occupations that, as a whole, had declined by more than 6 percent, the number of clergymen increased by 22 percent during the decade. In the equilibrium, the extra attractiveness of such occupations tends to keep the earnings of workers below those of similarly qualified people in other jobs.

Average Earnings of All Labor

Thus far we have dealt with the causes and consequences of differences in wages of workers in different industries, in different occupations, or with different qualifications. What about the average wage rate for all labor taken together? Why is the average wage rate higher at one time than at another? Before the question can be answered, it must be properly asked. There are two quite different meanings to the term "average wage rate." The *money wage* is the average number of dollars received per hour of work, regardless of how much those dollars can buy. The *real wage* is the buying power of an hour's work and is measured by adjusting money wages for changing prices. Even when money wages decline, workers receive higher real wages if the prices of the things they buy fall faster than money wages. Even when money wage rates rise, real wages decline if the prices of the things workers buy rise faster than the money wage.

The Dynamics of the Average Money Wage Rate

In our earlier examination of price levels, we found that the rate of increase in money

FIGURE 11   DYNAMICS OF THE MONEY WAGE

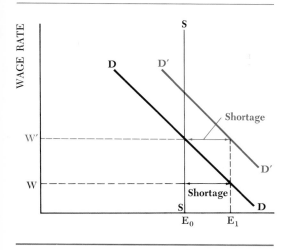

wages depends on the unemployment rate. The relationship between unemployment and rising wages—earlier expressed in the Phillips curve—can be represented in terms of the supply and demand for labor.[6] In Figure 11, the existing average level of money wage rates is represented by W, the total demand for labor by all industries combined by DD, and the number of workers available by SS. As the figure is drawn, business firms want to employ E_1 workers at existing wage rates, but only E_0 workers are available, leaving a labor shortage. The competition for the available workers tends to drive the wage rate upward.

Careless interpretation of Figure 11 would lead us to think that when the average wage rate had reached W', the shortage of labor would be eliminated by higher labor costs and wage rates would level off. But this will not occur, because rising wage rates with the attendant rising prices put additional purchasing power into the hands of households, and the additional household income expands the demand for prod-

[6] The reader might well refresh his memory at this point by reviewing the discussion of Phillips curves in Chapter 8.

ucts. Since the demand for labor derives from household demand for products, expanded household demand means equal expansion of the demand for labor. Each rise in the money wage rate is accompanied by an equal expansion of the demand for labor, and by the time the money wage rate reaches W', demand for labor has shifted to $D'D'$. The labor shortage at the higher wage rate is just as large as before! The money wage rate continues to rise, but it cannot bring the market into equilibrium because each upward movement of wages and prices expands demand in proportion, leaving employers still scrambling to out-compete one another for the labor available.

When employers want to hire more labor than is available at the going wage rate, money wages are driven up and *continue* to rise until some change in underlying demand conditions—a decline in private investment, perhaps, or higher tax rates—reduces the demand for labor.

The wider the gap between the number of workers that employers need and the number available, the faster wage rates tend to rise. The size of this gap is related to the unemployment rate. Because much unemployment is frictional and structural, there is often some shortage of certain types of labor even when unemployment is as high as 6 or 8 percent of the labor force, but these small shortages produce only slowly rising wage rates. As unemployment declines, however, labor shortages grow larger and spread to more different types of labor. Accordingly, wage rates tend to rise faster, in keeping with the Phillips curve.

Productivity and Real Wages

The important thing to a worker is not how many dollars he earns, but how much his income will buy. Even if he gets no more money, he is better off when the prices of the things he uses are lowered. The buying power of the worker's wage is called his *real wage* and is represented as the ratio of his money wage rate to the average price of final products. If we represent the average money wage rate by W and the average price of final products as P, the average real wage rate, W^*, is expressed by $W^* = W/P$.

When money wages rise faster or decline slower than prices, real wages rise. When money wages rise slower or decline faster than prices, real wages decline. But since prices depend on costs—an important element of which are wages—money wages and prices are bound together and cannot vary independently. At wage rate W, the marginal labor cost of products in an industry with labor productivity π is expressed by the ratio W/π. For example, if production workers are paid $3 per hour and produce an average of 5 tons per manhour, marginal labor cost would be $3/5, or $.60 per additional ton produced. Of course, labor is not the only marginal cost, and we also need to take the cost of materials into account. Materials are the output of an earlier stage of production, whose costs are also partly labor and partly materials. The cost of these materials, in turn, depends on labor cost and materials from yet an earlier stage of production. If we consider the economy as a whole and consolidate all the stages of production, marginal cost is seen to consist almost entirely of labor cost.

This proposition can be most readily seen by tracing cost backward through a number of stages. To keep things simple, suppose that marginal cost at each stage was one-half labor cost and one-half cost of materials purchased from an earlier stage. Of the marginal cost of $100 at the first or final stage, $50 is marginal labor cost, and the remainder consists of materials bought from the preceding (second) stage. The cost of these materials resolves into $25 of labor cost and $25 materials from the third stage. On a consolidated basis, then, the marginal costs of stages 1 and 2 together consists of $75 of labor and $25 of materials

from stage 3. When stage 3 is incorporated in the consolidation, marginal cost resolves into $87.5 labor and $12.5 materials from stage 4, and so on. When 5 stages are all viewed on a consolidated basis, we find that marginal cost consists of $96.875 labor and only $3.125 materials from still earlier stages.

In other words, when all the stages of production are considered on a consolidated basis, labor is virtually the only marginal cost. If labor productivity at the various stages averages π per manhour, the consolidated marginal cost becomes W/π. Prices at each stage of production depend on the most profitable markup on the products of that particular stage. As we trace back through the stages, these markups compound into some average markup m, and we can represent the price of the final product as, $P = m (W/\pi)$. When this analysis is repeated, a similar result emerges for each final product. Averaging all these results then gives us P, the average price of final products as, $P = m (W/\pi)$. Where m is the average markup of all firms in the economy, W is the average money wage rate, and π is the average output per manhour of production labor.

When the relationship between wages and prices is incorporated in the definition of the real wage rate, we find, $W^* = W/P = W/m(W/\pi)$, or $W^* = \pi/m$. In words, the real wage rate, to a very close approximation, depends on only 2 factors: the productivity of labor (π) and the average markup of price over marginal cost (m). Moreover, markups depend on market structure and competitive conditions in all the different industries in the economy. Since these tend to be stable over time, the sole important determinant of the buying power of an hour's work is the average productivity of labor. When the average productivity rises 10 percent with no change in the average markup, the real wages of labor tend to rise 10 percent. That is, workers will be able to buy an average of 10 percent more final goods and services with the money they get for an hour's labor.

The average real wage is determined by productivity of labor and is unaffected by changes in money wage rates. In the absence of rising productivity, higher money wages merely tend to increase prices in proportion, leaving the average hour's work with the same buying power it had before. But higher labor productivity tends to appear in higher real wages, regardless of what happens to money wage rates.

It should be noted that the productivity involved here is that of the production workers whose wages enter marginal cost. This is the *marginal productivity* of labor, and the relationship developed above is expressed by the proposition that the real wage rate is proportional to the marginal productivity of labor. Evidence indicates, however, that the proposition holds very closely for the average productivity of all labor.

In Figure 12, the real hourly earnings of U.S. manufacturing workers—taken as representative of labor as a whole—are compared to the average output per manhour of U.S. workers in private employment. The closely parallel trends of the 2 series over the past 40 years show clearly the extent to which real wage rates vary with labor productivity.

LABOR UNIONS

Real Wages and Collective Bargaining

The fact that real wages depend virtually entirely on labor productivity means that collective bargaining over money wage rates cannot raise the average real wages of labor. If this is so, then what are labor unions all about?

There are 2 answers. In the first place, the exclusive dependence of real wages on

FIGURE 12   AVERAGE HOURLY REAL EARNINGS IN MANUFACTURING AND AVERAGE U.S. LABOR PRODUCTIVITY, 1929-1968

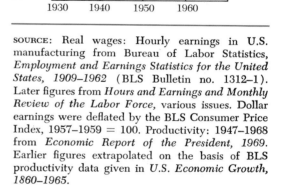

SOURCE: Real wages: Hourly earnings in U.S. manufacturing from Bureau of Labor Statistics, *Employment and Earnings Statistics for the United States, 1909–1962* (BLS Bulletin no. 1312–1). Later figures from *Hours and Earnings and Monthly Review of the Labor Force,* various issues. Dollar earnings were deflated by the BLS Consumer Price Index, 1957–1959 = 100. Productivity: 1947–1968 from *Economic Report of the President, 1969.* Earlier figures extrapolated on the basis of BLS productivity data given in U.S. *Economic Growth, 1860–1965.*

labor productivity holds only on the average, over all industries in the economy. When the money wage rate in one industry is raised by collective bargaining, it tends to raise that particular industry's prices in proportion. But since this industry is only a small part of the total, the average level of prices in the economy rises much less. This means that real wages of workers in the affected industry have increased because their money wages have risen in comparison to the average price level. Workers in all other industries, by the same token, have received a slight reduction in their real wage rates because they must pay slightly higher prices although they earn the same money wages as before. To the extent that collective bargaining can force up wages in one industry faster than they rise in others, therefore, it benefits the workers in that industry at the cost of lower real wages elsewhere.

It follows that unions and collective bargaining cannot raise the real wages of labor as a whole, but they can and do change the pattern of wages and raise the real wage rates of organized workers above those of the unorganized. The power of unions is severely limited, however, because when union wage rates are raised, employment in organized industries is reduced compared to that in others. The wider the wage differential maintained by the union, the fewer jobs there will be for union members. If the union pressed too far, it could bargain itself completely out of existence.

The effect of this limitation can be seen when wage rates bargained by different locals of the same national union are compared from place to place. A good illustration is the hourly union scale for local-transit bus drivers, shown in Table 7. Money wage rates that unions can obtain in high-wage areas like San Francisco and Boston are impossible in cities like Topeka and Knoxville. A similar limitation applies to union power over the wage rates of organized labor as a whole. Although difficult to measure with precision, careful empirical studies suggest that the average power of all American unions over their members' wages is limited to a differential over unorganized workers of somewhere between 10 and 15 percent.[7]

Unions and Working Conditions

The second part of the answer to the question of what unions are all about is that unions provide a means for workers to ex-

---

[7] See Albert Rees, *The Economics of Trade Unions,* Chicago, Ill., University of Chicago Press, 1962, Chapter IV, "The Influence of Unions on Relative Wages," and the studies there cited.

TABLE 7   UNION HOURLY SCALE, LOCAL-TRANSIT BUS DRIVERS IN SELECTED CITIES, JULY 1, 1968

CITY	HOURLY RATE
San Francisco, Calif.	$3.91
Boston, Mass	3.89
Chicago, Ill.	3.70
Cleveland, Ohio	3.38
New Orleans, La.	3.09
Indianapolis, Ind.	2.95
Madison, Wisc.	2.93
Portland, Ore.	2.85
Atlanta, Ga.	2.84
Richmond, Va.	2.62
Jackson, Miss.	2.40
Oklahoma City, Okla.	2.29
Charlotte, N.C.	2.20
Knoxville, Tenn.	2.13
Topeka, Kan.	2.07

SOURCE: *Union Wages and Hours: Local-Transit Operating Employees, July 1, 1968,* Bureau of Labor Statistics Bulletin no. 1620, April, 1969. Rates are for drivers after 1 year's experience, and apply on the day shift.

press themselves concerning, and play some part in deciding the millions of questions that affect their daily lives. Before the days of unions, workers generally held their jobs at the pleasure of an employer who could fire them at will. When the work force was to be reduced, workers had no control over who was to be laid off and who was to be retained. Older workers who had devoted their lives to the firm and who would have the hardest time finding new jobs had only the employer's goodwill to save their jobs and were often the first laid off, while younger workers were given preference in being recalled. Work speeds and performance standards could be established and altered without consulting the workers affected. Few workers had vacation rights or sick leave, and if they left their jobs for any reason, they had to take their chances when they returned. Control over lighting, ventilation, safety conditions, lunch periods, hours of work, shift assignments, and even the number of minutes a day a worker could stop work to smoke or visit the toilet was the exclusive province of the employer. Even the right to considerate treatment from foremen and supervisors was beyond the worker's reach.

With the advent of unions, these matters became negotiable. Collective-bargaining contracts provide seniority for older workers and designate the order in which employees are laid off and recalled and their rights to promotion, transfer, and retirement. Workers receive rights to vacation and sick leave, and the contract specifies work standards, rules, and working conditions. In addition to its substantive provisions, a collective-bargaining agreement also provides for grievance machinery and procedures by which workers who believe that they are unfairly or improperly treated can have the merits of their case examined. It is in this wider role of providing workers with an effective voice in matters that intimately affect their day-to-day working lives that unions make their most important contribution to labor.

Public Policy Toward Labor Unions

Today, labor unions are viewed as an important aspect of the organization of production, and it is recognized that the public has the same kind of stake in their function that it does in other economic organizations like banks and business firms. However, this public stake has not always been recognized, and the earliest efforts of workers to organize were often viewed with suspicion and legal disfavor. Courts frequently treated unions as combinations in restraint of trade or as outright criminal conspiracies. Employers were able to obtain *labor injunctions* in the form of court orders forbidding workers to organize, strike, picket, or even publicize their demands on pain of jail sentences. Employers could compel workers to sign so-called "yellow dog" contracts by which the worker agreed, as a

condition of employment with the firm, not to join a union. Such contracts were enforceable at law, and anyone attempting to organize workers employed under yellow dog contracts could be sent to jail for inducing breach of contract.

The Wagner Labor Relations Act Increasingly during the 1930s, the public came to recognize that the right of workers to join unions affected the welfare of a large segment of society and deserved encouragement and protection. The labor injunction was abolished and the yellow dog contract was made unenforceable. The most important step, however, was the passage of the Wagner Labor Relations Act of 1935, which provided general legal protection to the worker's right to join a union and bargain collectively. The Act established the National Labor Relations Board (NLRB) to administer the provisions of the law and provided that when a minimum of 30 percent of the workers in a plant had formed a union, they could petition the NLRB for an election. If a majority of the workers voted for the union, it was certified as the official bargaining agent for all the workers in the plant, and the employer was required to accord it recognition and to bargain in good faith with its representatives. The Act also forbade employers to engage in specified unfair labor practices such as discrimination against union members, interference with union elections, and similar techniques that an employer might use to weaken or break up a union.

The Taft-Hartley Act Under the protection of the Wagner Act, the membership of labor unions grew from less than 4 million in 1935 to over 15 million by 1947. At the same time, to an increasing extent, strikes and other aspects of collective bargaining involved injury to the public and to other "neutral third parties." The Taft-Hartley Act of 1947 sought to increase public protection against failure of the collective-bargaining process. For this purpose, the Act established an independent Federal Mediation Service to provide a staff of experienced professional labor mediators who could step in when negotiations stalled and help the parties find grounds for a mutually agreeable settlement.

The Act also provided increased protection to the public against strikes in which public health and safety were involved. When the President determines that an actual or threatened work stoppage will "imperil the national health and safety," he can appoint a "fact-finding" committee to investigate and report on the case. Upon receipt of the report, the President can instruct the Attorney General to obtain a court injunction forbidding any work stoppage for a maximum period of 80 days, during which further mediation effort can be made to head off the strike. The Act does not, of course, prevent the work stoppage if the 2 parties are unable to reach an agreement at the end of the period. Its sole purpose is to provide additional time for the parties to reach a settlement without action harmful to the public.

The Landrum-Griffin Act   The most recent important step in labor legislation, embodied in the Landrum-Griffin Act of 1959, expresses the public interest in protecting the rights of individual union members from exploitation by entrenched officials. Like corporations, unions are frequently run by a small controlling group that is in a strong position to divert union funds to its own advantage and otherwise to abuse its power. The Landrum-Griffin Act contains a "bill of rights" for labor that guarantees every union member equal rights to attend meetings, to participate in union elections, to discuss union affairs with other members, and to register opposition to union officials and their policies. The Act also deals specifically with union elections, requiring that election of officers be held by secret ballot and specifying the minimum permissible period between elections. Union members must be given reasonable opportunity to make nominations, to campaign, and to present their views to the rest of the membership. Another section of the law requires the bonding of officials who handle union funds and restricts the financial relationship between unions and union officials.

Like the corporation, the labor union evolved in response to the emergence of a social need. The corporation was needed to accommodate the accumulation of large quantities of capital; the union evolved in response to the rising need of workers to share in decisions that intimately affect their everyday lives. Public recognition of this important need has been accompanied by legal support of unions and protection of their right to exist and function. But, again very much as in the case of the corporation, the proper relationship of unions to other organizations and to their own members has required frequent redefinition in the public interest, and new legislation will be needed as conditions change.

SUMMARY

Labor is allocated among different occupations by the pattern of demand *derived* from buyers' demands for labor's products. The elasticity of the demand for labor can be expressed as the product of the fraction of labor in marginal cost and the elasticity of demand for the output. Since the demand for the output of the industry as a whole is less elastic than the demand for the output of any particular firm, the *industry-wide* demand for labor is less elastic than the demand by any particular employer. Moreover, since the wages of highly skilled key workers are a small part of labor cost, demand for them tends to be inelastic, permitting them to extract higher wages without substantial loss of employment. In the long run, the elasticity of demand for labor also depends on the ability of employers to substitute machinery for workers or to make other adjustments to avoid high labor costs.

Differences in wage rates that emerge from differences in the supply and demand for labor in different occupations or industries provide powerful *incentives* for workers to move. Although in the short run labor mobility is restricted, in the long run differences in earnings encourage workers to train for and to enter occupations where the highest priority is placed on their services. Changes in *labor productivity* likewise cause labor to move into or out of the industry, depending on the *desires of consumers* as expressed in the elasticity of demand for the product. When consumers are eager to have more of the product, their elastic demand encourages more workers to enter the industry; when consumers have little use for more of the product, their inelastic demand forces the labor saved by higher productivity to find employment in some other industry.

If jobs were equally attractive, if people were interchangeable, and if all could move freely into any job, wage rates in all jobs would approach equality in equilibrium. *Differences* persist, however, because people differ in their *skills* and other qualifications. In addition, some people are *barred from entry* to or training for certain occupations by law, custom, union policy, or outright discrimination. Moreover, some jobs make up for lower earnings by greater *attractiveness*.

Considering all industries taken together, the *total demand* for labor influences the direction and speed of money wage adjustments, but because the demand for labor is heavily influenced by the wage level itself, there is no equilibrium money wage rate. Instead, money wages tend to rise as long as the demand for labor exceeds the available number of workers. Each increase in wage rates is accompanied by a corresponding increase in demand which leaves the shortage as severe as before. In similar fashion, massive unemployment drives money wage rates down, but the demand for labor declines in proportion, leaving unemployment just as severe at low wages as at high. This is the mechanism that underlies the *Phillips curve*.

When we look behind the money veil, however, we find that the relationship between prices and marginal cost fixes the *real buying power* of the average hour's work in proportion to the *marginal productivity* of labor. Given the average markup as determined by the market structure of the economy, the buying power of labor as a whole cannot be altered merely by changing money wage rates, for prices rise in proportion. On the other hand, rising productivity tends to be accompanied by proportionally higher real wages regardless of money wages.

The dependence of average real wages on productivity means that while collective bargaining over money wages can, to a limited extent, improve the real earnings of *union labor* at the expense of unorganized workers, it cannot improve the real earning power of labor as a whole. In fact, however, the important task of unions is to provide workers with a strong voice in the decisions that affect their daily working lives. As such, unions are an indispensable part of the organization of production and there has been increasing recognition of the public's interest in their rights, power, and conduct.

CHAPTER 23

Rent

THE SOURCE OF RENT

Rent as a Component of Income

Like so many words, the term "rent" has several different meanings. In ordinary popular usage, it means payment for the temporary use of anything that one does not own himself. A family "rents" an apartment, a vacationer "rents" an automobile, a farmer "rents" a field. In technical economics, the term is narrower in one sense and broader in another. Economic usage is narrower in that the term "rent" is restricted to income derived from the services of land and other natural resources whose supply is naturally fixed. In this sense, the farmer's payment for a field is an example of economic rent. The land was put there by nature and will remain, regardless of human needs. It will not increase or decrease in response to demand for it. The economic question is purely how to use it. We can

plant it, erect a building on it, build a road over it, or even leave it idle, but we have no control over how much there is of it.

Payment for the use of houses is rent only to the extent that it covers the services of the lots they stand on. No economic rent at all is involved in hiring an automobile. Houses and automobiles are not fixed in amount. The economic question is not only who will get the use of the existing units, but how many new units to make and how large a stock to maintain.[1]

Rent appears as an explicit payment when a landowner rents or leases the services of his land to somebody else, but since most land is used by the owner in his own business, most rent is received as an

---

[1] Since it takes time to alter the stocks of buildings or durable equipment, these are virtually fixed within any short period. For this reason, the short-run behavior of returns for their services has many of the properties of economic rent, and is often called "quasi rent."

implicit part of the owner's residual income.[2] For example, part of the income of a farmer who cultivates his own land is attributable to rent. Likewise the "profits" of an oil or coal producer consist very largely of rent from the ownership of wells or mines. Under these circumstances the rent of a piece of land is defined as the annual amount that a would-be user would pay for its services on a competitive market. In other words, the part of a farmer's income that can be attributed to rent is the amount his own land would cost him annually if he rented or leased it from somebody else at competitive prices.

The Farmer's Residual Income

Since most land is used by owners, it is easier to analyze the return to land if we momentarily ignore rent as a separate element and examine the behavior of a land-owning firm. A farmer has at his disposal a certain tract of land, located in a particular place. He owns buildings and equipment. He has technical knowledge, experience, and information about the cultivation and marketing of different crops. He has money in the bank or access to credit to buy supplies, seeds, and so on. The basic decision for the farmer is how to use these resources. What crops should he grow and how much of each? The alternatives among which he can choose are limited by his situation. The type of soil and the climate of his region lend themselves better to some crops than to others. Transportation cost is sometimes an important limitation; for example, milk production requires locations close to market, while tomatoes for

2 The item "rental income of persons" reported in the national accounts as part of national income consists mostly of the imputed value of the services of owner-occupied dwellings. As such, it includes not only the true site rent for the house, but the quasi rent from the building as well.

processing must be grown near the cannery and, since they require considerable labor, where farm workers are available. Even weather conditions at planting time are a factor in the farmer's decision.

Choosing among the feasible alternatives is a complex process, but the overwhelming tendency is for farmers to cultivate those crops that, in view of expected prices, will bring in the highest residual income. The farmer's sales receipts will constitute the total market value of the crops he grows and sells, but to calculate income he must deduct all production costs, including not only seed, fertilizer, hired labor, and other out-of-pocket expenses, but also allowances for depreciation of machinery and buildings and for interest on his own invested capital.

The farmer is likely to refer to any income that remains as his "profit," although as we already know, most of it is not profit at all, but wages for his own labor. In addition, some part of it is rent on the land he owns and uses. The important thing, however, is that it is this total residual income that the farmer generally tries to maximize. When he is wise in his choice of crops, accurate in his guess about high future market prices, and lucky enough to get good weather, the residual is large and he prospers. When he plants the wrong crops, misjudges prices, or has a poor growing season, the residual is small or even negative, and he suffers.

Acreage Planted and Income per Acre

Since net income is the difference between cost and sales revenue, it varies with crop prices. When it costs $20 to plant, cultivate, and harvest an acre yielding 70 bushels of corn, the residual income is only $70 − 20, or $50 per acre when corn is $1. But it rises to $105 − 20, or $85 per acre when corn sells for $1.50. The price of corn or any other crop depends on demand and supply, and given the demand, the more acreage farmers plant to a crop, the lower its price tends to fall. It follows that the net revenue a farmer derives from any particular acre planted to a crop depends on how many acres are planted to that same crop by all farmers together. Given demand, low total acreage planted means small output, high prices, and correspondingly high farm income per acre. Increased total acreage expands output, drives prices down, and reduces net income per acre.

The straightforward relationship of net income per acre to total acreage planted is most easily demonstrated by example. Table 1 contains a demand schedule for onions. According to the schedule, an annual total output of 23,750,000 hundredweight of onions tends to bring a price of about $5 per hundredweight. As total output expands, price falls sharply in keeping with the inelastic demand and reaches $1.50 per hundredweight at an annual output of 38,700,000. Table 2 shows the resulting relationship connecting price and income to the total acreage planted. At the assumed yield of 250 hundredweight per acre, 95,000 acres yields an output of 23,-750,000. Since, in keeping with the demand schedule, this crop would tend to bring a price of about $5 per hundredweight, the revenue from 250 hundredweight would be $1,250 per acre. Deducting the assumed cost of $500 per acre, we have a net income of $750 for each acre planted to onions.

When farmers increase onion planting to 100,000 acres, total output expands to 25 million, dropping the price to $4.50. This brings revenue per acre down to $1,125 and leaves a net income of $625 per acre.

The relationship is plotted in Figure 1. Revenue per acre is measured vertically, and total acreage planted is measured horizontally. The curve RR represents declining revenue per acre as the total acreage expands. The horizontal blue line represents cost per acre, and the difference between revenue and cost represents the net income per acre that would be expected when farmers plant the total number of acres indicated. When 112,500 acres are planted to onions, as represented by the dashed black line at A, the crop on each acre is worth $830. Deduction of the $500 per acre cost therefore leaves the farmer with net income of $330 for each acre he has planted. If farmers planted a total of 138,000 acres of onions, represented by the solid black line at B, revenue would just cover cost but would leave nothing to pay the farmer for his labor, for the use of his land, or for any-

TABLE 1 HYPOTHETICAL DEMAND SCHEDULE FOR ONIONS

PRICE PER CWT	QUANTITY BOUGHT
$5.00	23,750,000
4.50	25,000,000
4.00	26,200,000
3.50	27,600,000
3.00	29,300,000
2.50	31,630,000
2.00	34,400,000
1.50	38,700,000

FIGURE 1 RENT AS THE NET INCOME ABOVE ALL COSTS, INCLUDING WAGES FOR THE FARMER'S OWN LABOR

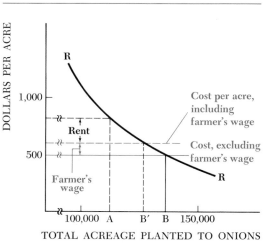

TOTAL ACREAGE PLANTED TO ONIONS

TABLE 2   THE RELATIONSHIP OF ACREAGE PLANTED TO NET INCOME PER ACRE

ACRES PLANTED	TOTAL PRODUCTION (250 CWT PER ACRE)	PRICE (PER CWT)	REVENUE PER ACRE (250 × PRICE)	COST PER ACRE	NET INCOME PER ACRE
95,000	23,750,000	$5.00	$1,250	$500	$750
100,000	25,000,000	4.50	1,125	500	625
105,000	26,200,000	4.00	1,000	500	500
110,000	27,600,000	3.50	875	500	375
117,000	29,300,000	3.00	750	500	250
126,500	31,630,000	2.50	628	500	128
138,000	34,400,000	2.00	500	500	0
155,000	38,700,000	1.50	275	500	− 225

thing else. If planting were expanded beyond 138,000 acres, prices would fall below cost, and the farmer would be unable to recover even depreciation and taxes. If acreage were sufficiently expanded, he could not even get back his outlay for materials.

If onion farmers could have all the land they wanted, free for the taking, they would still tend to plant somewhat less than 138,000 acres, for if more than these were planted, onion prices would fall below the point at which farmers could break even. The resulting losses would force some farmers to stop growing onions and to plant other, more lucrative crops or to stop farming entirely. If exactly 138,000 acres were planted, all onion growers could just cover out-of-pocket costs, depreciation, and interest, but they would still receive no income for themselves, not even a return for their own labor, and they would continue to reduce their acreage until prices reached the point at which they could expect at least an appropriate income from their own labor. If we allow $100 per acre for the farmer's own time and trouble in raising onions, the situation would appear as shown by the dotted blue line in Figure 1. Even if land were free for the taking, farmers would tend to limit onion planting to B', about 127,000 acres, since this is the most that could be planted allowing an adequate compensation for labor.

Rent and the Scarcity of Land

In fact, of course, there is not enough suitable land for onion farmers to have all they want. In general, the amount of usable land is limited, and this fact stops the expansion of acreage long before it reaches the "break-even" point at which farmers would just make wages. If the number of acres available were limited to the total represented by point A in the figure, the net income of onion growers would be *more* than enough to cover costs, even including an appropriate allowance for their own wages. Production could not be further expanded because no more land would be available, and this fact would prevent the net income of farmers from falling to the level of wages.

The excess of net income above total cost, including the farmer's wage, is rent, which arises out of the scarcity of land. This rent can be claimed by the owner of the land, whether he uses the land himself or rents it to somebody else. It is easy to see why. A farmer who could get the free use of an acre of scarce land could earn not only a suitable return for his own labor, but also the extra net income. If the owner of the land offered its services on the competitive market, however, other farmers would be willing to pay for the right to its use. A farmer who could get the acre by paying only half the rent to the owner would still keep the other half as income above any cost to himself. This would lead another farmer to offer an amount equal to, say, three-quarters of the rent, hoping to keep the other quarter for himself. The limit to this bidding is, clearly, an amount equal to the entire rent. Rent is equal to the net income available from the land after *all* production costs have been deducted. It arises because there is not enough land to permit production to expand to the point at which costs could be just covered.

Early Theories of Rent

The fact that agricultural production yields rent while industrial production tends only to cover production cost led François Quesnay (1694–1774) and his followers, a group of French economists known as the *Physiocrats*, into a serious misunderstanding. The Physiocrats attributed rent to the special productive abundance of nature and referred to it as a "net product" (*produit net*). Since no other economic activity returned more than its cost, they thought agriculture was the only source of wealth. Men who cultivated the soil were considered to belong to the "productive" class. Others were designated as "unproductive" or "sterile." The economic policy proposed by the Physiocrats was designed primarily to foster agriculture, for they believed, as Quesnay wrote, that "everything that is disadvantageous to agriculture is harmful to the State and the nation, and everything that favors agriculture is beneficial to the State and the nation."

It was not until the time of the British economist David Ricardo (1772–1823) that the nature of rent was understood. Ricardo showed that rent derived, not from the abundance of nature, but from scarcity. No matter how productive land might be, Ricardo pointed out, if there were enough of it, its use would expand until farmers

would just cover the inclusive cost of production, and no rent would be earned.

RENT AND THE ALLOCATION OF LAND

Scarcity would result in rent even on land that could grow only a single crop. In general, however, each type of land has many uses. The soil in which onions are grown can also be used to grow carrots and celery, or to produce lawn sod. Farmers tend to put each kind of land to the use that earns the highest rent. The choice of crop is depicted by the demand diagram of Figure 2. The curve R_oR_o represents the relationship of revenue per acre of onions as it varies with the number of acres planted, measured to the right. The curve R_cR_c represents the revenue per acre from carrots as it varies with the number of acres planted to carrots, measured to the left. Depending on the cost of seed, fertilizer, cultivation, and so on, the cost per acre of onions is sometimes higher and sometimes

FIGURE 2   RENT AND THE ALLOCATION OF
LAND BETWEEN 2 CROPS

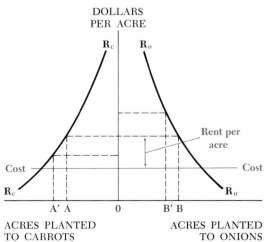

lower than that of carrots. For simplicity, Figure 2 represents a case in which the costs per acre (including the farmer's own wages) are equal. Under these circumstances, farmers tend to allocate the available acreage *AOB*, as shown by the dashed black line, with *AO* acres planted to carrots, and *OB* acres planted to onions. The allocation *A'OB'*, is a misallocation of land. Compared to the demand for the crops, too many acres are planted to carrots and too few to onions. The difference in rent leads some farmers to shift their cultivation from carrots to onions, and the shift continues until rents from the alternatives are equalized.

Response to Changes in Demand

Their search for maximum return leads farmers to change their crops in response to changes in demand. When households and processors increase the demand for carrots, farmers discover that they get greater net income from growing carrots than from growing onions. This leads some onion farmers to plant carrots instead. As land is withdrawn from onions, their price rises, and the rent from onion acreage increases. The increased number of acres devoted to carrots lowers the rent on carrot acreage, and the transfer is complete when rents are again equal for the 2 crops.

The process is shown in Figure 3. Farmers initially plant *AO* acres to carrots and *OB* acres to onions. When the demand for carrots rises, the revenue from carrot acreage likewise rises, as shown by the blue curve $R'_c R'_c$. Growers find that they can receive higher rent from carrots. As onion planting declines and carrot production increases, rent from onions rises and that from carrots falls. Equality is approached at the new division of land between the 2 crops, in which *A'O* acres of carrots are grown together with *OB'* of onions.

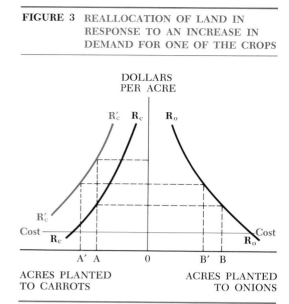

FIGURE 3 REALLOCATION OF LAND IN RESPONSE TO AN INCREASE IN DEMAND FOR ONE OF THE CROPS

Rent on Land of Varying Quality

Land is not homogeneous. One tract of land is better suited than another to a given crop. If a small output is desired, it can be grown at the most suitable locations, but expanded output requires resort to poorer-quality land. Land may be poorer in quality because the climate or soil type is less suited to the crop, because of the costs of irrigation, fertilizer, or treatment needed, or merely because it is located farther from market. In any case, costs per acre are higher on the poorer land. Unless prices rise enough to cover higher costs, the poorer land cannot be brought into production.

Variation in yield per acre and in production cost means that not all acres receive the same rent. Given the price of the crop, tracts with high yield and low cost will tend to yield high rent, while those with low yield and high cost will yield low rent. The relationship can be depicted as in Figure 4. Revenue per acre is measured vertically and the total number of acres is

FIGURE 4   THE VARIATION OF RENT ON
LAND OF DIFFERING YIELD AND
PRODUCTION COST

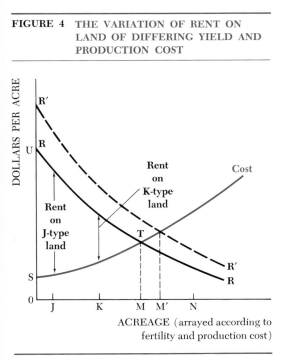

FIGURE 4   THE VARIATION OF RENT ON
LAND OF DIFFERING YIELD AND
PRODUCTION COST

ACREAGE (arrayed according to
fertility and production cost)

the revenue that could be earned from it,
and it tends to remain idle.

The total rent received by all farmers
combined is the sum of all the rent received
on all acreage in use. This is the area of the
sector *STU* lying between the revenue
curve *RR* and the cost curve. When the
demand for farm products rises, prices increase and so does the revenue obtainable
from any given acre. This is represented by
a rise in the curve *RR* to a new position
represented by the dashed line *R'R'*. All
acres formerly in use earn more rent than
before. Some land that had previously been
too poor to cultivate is brought into production, and land of lower fertility at *M'* is
now identified as the margin. The increase
in demand not only shifts the margin onto
less fertile land, but increases the share of
the total product that goes to landowners
in the form of rent.

measured horizontally. In this case, however, the total acreage planted is held fixed,
and we imagine the successive tracts of
planted land "lined up" along the axis. The
highest-yield, lowest-cost acres are placed
nearest the origin, and as we proceed to the
right, the yields on successive tracts decline
and production costs rise. Each point on
the horizontal axis corresponds to a particular acre of land belonging to a particular
farmer. The rent he earns on that particular
acre corresponds to the difference between
revenue and cost as represented on the
chart at that point. Point *J*, near the origin,
represents highly fertile land with low cultivation cost. Point *K*, further to the right,
corresponds to higher-cost, less fertile land
and receives lower rent. Land corresponding to point *M* on the chart is so infertile
that the owner can just cover his production cost, with nothing left over for rent.
Land of this type, which is in use but yields
no rent, is *marginal* land. Land corresponding to a point like *N* lies beyond the margin. The cost of working such land exceeds

Cost and Allocation

Differences in fertility and production cost
are not uniform. Land on which one crop
grows with low yield at high cost sometimes produces another at high yield and
low cost. Clearly, other things being equal,
the highest rent can be obtained by planting individual tracts to the crops for which
they are best suited. As a result, we find
cotton growing in the South, wheat in the
prairies, and pineapples in Hawaii. Sandy
loam is used for potatoes while muck land
is planted to onions.

Often, however, the question of which
crop gives the highest net return on a piece
of land depends on wage rates, prices of
fertilizer and materials, and other costs.
For example, a tract of sandy loam can be
used to grow either potatoes or tomatoes,
but the yields and labor costs are different.
When the farmer plants potatoes, he can
expect a yield of 200 hundredweight at a
cost of 50 manhours of hired labor. When
he plants tomatoes for sale to processors, he

can expect a yield of 15 tons per acre, but he must employ 100 manhours of labor. The decision as to which crop will give the highest net return depends not only on the prices of potatoes and tomatoes, but also on the level of the farm wage rate.

When potatoes bring $2 a hundred-weight while tomatoes sell for $30 a ton, receipts from an acre of potatoes are $400, compared to $450 from tomatoes. Since it takes 50 more manhours to grow the tomatoes, however, the extra revenue would be just enough to make up for the extra labor cost if the wage rate were $1 an hour. At this wage rate, the 2 crops would give equal rent on this acre, and it would be a matter of indifference to the farmer which he planted. If the wage rate were less than $1, the revenue advantage to tomato growing would exceed the cost difference, and the land would afford the highest rent when planted to tomatoes. At any wage rate above $1, on the other hand, the cost difference would exceed the revenue advantage, and potato growing would give the farmer the highest rent.

The relationship is illustrated in Figure 5. Rent per acre is plotted vertically against the farm wage rate, measured horizontally.

FIGURE 5   CROP WHICH GIVES THE HIGHEST RENT DEPENDS ON WAGE RATES

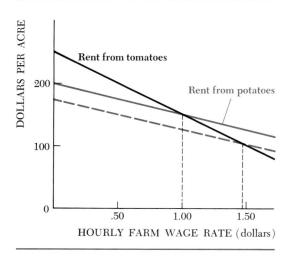

For this purpose all production costs except the wages of hired labor have been taken to be $200 per acre for both crops. If the wage rate were 0, the farmer could net $250 rent from tomatoes, but only $200 from potatoes. At higher wage rates, rents from both crops are lower, but because more labor is required per acre of tomatoes grown, the rent from tomato production, represented by the black line, declines more steeply than rent from potatoes, represented by the blue line. At the $1 per hour wage rents from the crops reach equality, and at higher wages the farmer gets the most rent by planting potatoes. The level of wages that equalizes the rent from the 2 alternate uses depends on the prices of the crops. If the price of potatoes falls to $1.87, corresponding to the dashed blue line, the greatest rent would be earned by planting tomatoes at any wage rate below about $1.48 an hour.

The Location of Economic Activity

The total cost of production includes all outlays necessary to get commodities into the hands of final users. Since this includes transportation cost, one of the important differences in production costs lies in the distances of tracts from the market. If the cost of transportation is a uniform rate per mile, production cost tends to rise and rent to decline linearly with distance from the market.

Since transportation cost per mile is not the same for all crops, the effect of distance on rent depends on which crop is grown. Rent from crops with high cost per mile drops steeply as we move away from the market, while rent from those that cost less to transport declines more slowly. Because they must reach market quickly and require special handling, fresh-cut flowers have a high transportation cost per mile, and rent from land used for greenhouses and flower culture drops steeply as we move away from the city, as represented by the solid black line in Figure 6. Rent from grain and field crops that travel well and can be handled in bulk declines more slowly, as shown by the dotted black line, while fresh vegetables and milk occupy an intermediate position, indicated by the blue line in the figure.

The differences in transportation rates per mile influence the locations of different economic activities. Because of low transportation cost, flower growers can outbid others for the use of land in the zone *OF* lying closest to the city. Beyond *F*, however, it costs too much to ship flowers, and florists cannot bid high enough to keep land away from the vegetable growers and dairy farmers who occupy the zone from *F* to *V*. Beyond point *V*, transportation of vegetables and milk is too expensive to enable growers to bid successfully against grain farmers for the use of land.

Changing production methods and cheaper transportation often result in relocation of activity. The increased consumption of canned and frozen vegetables has reduced the premium on growing vegetables close to cities, and they have tended to move away to concentrate in areas with

processing plants nearby. The automobile and expressway have reduced the cost and time of commuting, increasing the attractiveness of suburban living, and we find the former vegetable fields converted into subdivisions. This development, in turn, leads to the disappearance of the advantage of downtown shopping areas, with the result that retail establishments, doctors' offices, and other services are moving to the perimeter.

THE LONG-RUN SHARE OF RENT IN GROSS NATIONAL INCOME

The nature of rent led early economists to a gloomy view of the long-run future of the world. They thought that continuing population growth, with the attendant increase in the demand for food, would result in a steady extension of the agricultural margin to land of lower and lower quality. The productivity of labor at the margin, on which real wages depend, would steadily decline, while the rent of landowners would steadily and inexorably rise. The passage of time would, the early economists believed, produce increasing misery for the bulk of the population as well as increasing concentration of income in the hands of a few landowners, until the evil day when only enough income was left over from rent to provide a bare subsistence for the rest of the population.

This gloomy prediction—which led people to designate economics as the "dismal science"—has already been represented in Figure 4. The curve *RR* shifts upward in proportion to population, representing the rising demand for food. The rising cost of production on marginal land represents the declining marginal productivity of labor as less fertile soil is worked while rent absorbs an ever-larger share of gross national income.

FIGURE 6   TRANSPORTATION COST AS A FACTOR IN LOCATION

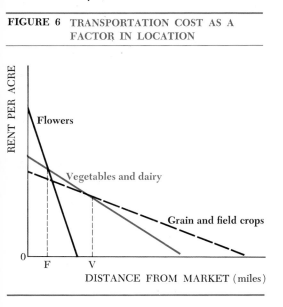

RENT PER ACRE

Flowers

Vegetables and dairy

Grain and field crops

0

F   V

DISTANCE FROM MARKET (miles)

Rent and Technological Change

We need only look around us, however, to see that as far as our own economic system is concerned, the forecasts of these early pessimists were at least premature. After nearly 200 years of growing population and increasing demand, the people of America and Western Europe have vastly higher standards of living than they had in Ricardo's time. Instead of finding most of the gross national income siphoned off in rent to landowners, we find a long history of falling farm incomes and a steady movement of both land and people out of agriculture. The older economists expected wealthy farmers and starving factory workers, but we find prosperous factory workers and farmers unable to pay their taxes.

As is so often true, this striking contradiction resulted less from an incorrect understanding of the phenomenon in question than from incomplete analysis. The long-run consequences were expected because the predictors ignored or underestimated the effect of improvements in farming methods. The introduction of new varieties of crops, better cultivating methods, and cheaper fertilizers regularly increases the number of bushels per acre planted. Higher yields affect rent in 2 opposite ways. On the one hand, a larger number of bushels is obtained from each acre and, for any given price, this increases revenue per acre and hence rent. On the other hand, higher yield also means a larger total output from any given number of acres planted, reducing prices and tending to reduce revenue per acre, and hence rent.

The Role of Demand Elasticity In the end, whether the farmer gets more or fewer dollars per acre depends on which of these effects is stronger. This depends on the elasticity of demand for the crop. If this demand has unit elasticity, the increase in yield per acre is exactly offset by the reduction in price, and the revenue per acre received by farmers for any given total

acreage planted remains the same. When demand for the crop has elasticity greater than unity, prices decline by a smaller proportion than yield rises, and the revenue per acre rises for any given total acreage planted. But when the demand is inelastic, the decline in price more than offsets the greater yield per acre, and the farmer's revenue per acre declines.

This simple relationship of demand elasticity is shown in Table 3, where results are given for 3 crops. Panel (a) shows the effect of technical improvement on the revenue per acre received by farmers planting a crop like watermelons, for which the demand is elastic. Part (b) applies to a crop like apples, for which demand elasticity is unity, while part (c) applies to a crop like potatoes, for which demand is quite inelastic. The total output of each commodity, its price, and the resulting revenue per acre are shown as they would be corresponding to total plantings of 5,000, 10,000, and 20,000 acres. On the left side of each panel, the calculations are made on the basis of a yield of 100 units per acre, while on the right side the yield has been raised to 200. Prices in each case are calculated on the basis of the appropriate elasticity of demand.

Inspection of the results shows that for any given total acreage planted, a rise in yield of the crop with relatively elastic demand increases the revenue per acre that farmers receive. When 10,000 acres are planted, for example, farmers receive $100 per acre at the lower yield but $126 when yield doubles. Farmers planting crops whose demand elasticity is unity receive the same revenue per acre at high and low yields. When 10,000 acres are grown, farmers receive $100 per acre whether the yield is 100 or 200. Part (c) shows that growers of crops with demand elasticity below unity receive smaller revenue per acre when yield rises. When farmers plant a total of 10,000 acres, their crops are worth $100 per acre at a yield of 100, but only $50 when yield doubles.

It follows that whether rising yields at-

TABLE 3   THE EFFECT OF RISING YIELD ON REVENUE PER ACRE FOR
CROPS WITH DIFFERING DEMAND ELASTICITY

(a)   Commodity with relatively elastic demand, like watermelons

TOTAL ACRES PLANTED	QUANTITY @ 100 UNITS PER ACRE	PRICE PER UNIT, $	REVENUE PER ACRE, $	QUANTITY @ 200 UNITS PER ACRE	PRICE PER UNIT, $	REVENUE PER ACRE, $
5,000	50,000	$1.59	$159	100,000	$1.00	$200
10,000	100,000	1.00	100	200,000	.63	126
20,000	200,000	.63	63	400,000	.40	80

(b)   Commodity with unit elastic demand, like apples

TOTAL ACRES PLANTED	QUANTITY @ 100 UNITS PER ACRE	PRICE PER UNIT, $	REVENUE PER ACRE, $	QUANTITY @ 200 UNITS PER ACRE	PRICE PER UNIT, $	REVENUE PER ACRE, $
5,000	50,000	$2.00	$200	100,000	$1.00	$200
10,000	100,000	1.00	100	200,000	.50	100
20,000	200,000	.50	50	400,000	.25	50

(c)   Commodity with relatively inelastic demand, like potatoes

TOTAL ACRES PLANTED	QUANTITY @ 100 UNITS PER ACRE	PRICE PER UNIT, $	REVENUE PER ACRE, $	QUANTITY @ 200 UNITS PER ACRE	PRICE PER UNIT, $	REVENUE PER ACRE, $
5,000	50,000	$4.00	$400	100,000	$1.00	$200
10,000	100,000	1.00	100	200,000	.25	50
20,000	200,000	.25	25	400,000	.0625	12.50

tract more acreage or induce farmers to shift their acreage to some other crop depends on how intensely consumers want more of the crop. When lower prices result in the development of new uses for a commodity, or enable it to replace substitutes on a large scale, demand is elastic and rising yields tend to induce farmers to plant more of the crop than before. When consumers have little use for additional quantities even at low prices, demand is inelastic. When yields rise, less land is needed for production, and land is transferred to other purposes.

The effect of changes in yields on the allocation of land between beans and tomatoes is illustrated in Figure 7. Dollars per acre are plotted vertically against the total number of acres planted, measured horizontally. Land planted to tomatoes is measured from the origin to the right, while planting to beans is measured to the left. The revenue curves R_bR_b and R_tR_t are drawn to be consistent with elastic demand for tomatoes, but inelastic demand for beans. Before any change in yield, farmers equalize rent from the crops by planting BO acres to beans and OT to tomatoes. Figure 7(a) shows the response to a rise in the yield per acre planted to tomatoes. Since the demand for tomatoes is relatively elastic, the higher yield shifts the revenue curve upward, corresponding to the blue curve $R'_tR'_t$. The result is that tomato growers find that they are making higher returns than before. When bean farmers, attracted by the higher income from tomatoes, have transferred BB' acres to tomatoes, rents are again equal.

Figure 7(b) represents the reallocation

that follows a rise in the yield of beans. Since the demand for beans is relatively inelastic, price declines more than output per acre rises, and farmers find that they are earning less per acre than before. This leads bean growers to transfer BB' acres to tomatoes, and again the rents are brought into equality.

In either case, higher yield results in more land planted to the commodity whose demand is elastic and less land planted to the one with inelastic demand. Notice,

---

FIGURE 7   THE EFFECT OF HIGHER YIELD PER ACRE DEPENDS ON DEMAND ELASTICITY

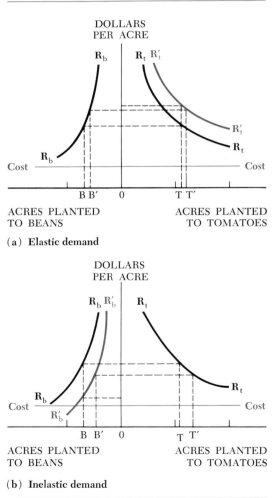

(a) **Elastic demand**

(b) **Inelastic demand**

---

however, that an increasing yield of commodities for which the demand is relatively elastic tends to increase total rent, while a rising yield of commodities for which demand is inelastic tends to reduce total rent.

The Shift of Land from Corn to Soybeans, 1949–1966: an Example Since corn and soybeans thrive on the same soil type and climate, the shift of acreage between them provides an excellent illustration of the effect of rising yields. A virtual revolution in U.S. corn-growing technique since 1949 has more than doubled output per acre. Because the demand for corn has low elasticity, the growth in yield lowered the revenue per acre that growers could extract from any given corn acreage planted and contributed to the shift of acreage from corn to soybeans. As shown in Table 4, when corn yield rose from 38 bushels per acre to over 72, planted corn acreage declined from 77.1 million acres to 56.9 million. The total acreage planted to the 2 crops together was nearly constant throughout the period. The rising price of soybeans suggests, however, that the transfer was supported by rapidly growing demand for soybeans as raw material for plastics, margarine, synthetic dairy products, and other items.

The shift in acreage is shown schematically in Figure 8. Improved corn yields working against inelastic demands for corn lowered the curve of revenue per acre from R_cR_c to $R'_cR'_c$ as shown. At the same time, the rising demand for soybeans increased revenue per acre of soybeans from R_sR_s to $R'_sR'_s$. The result was the shifting of CC' acres from corn to soybeans.

The U.S. Farm Problem

Since the demand for food and farm products as a whole is very inelastic, rising U.S. farm yields have held down farm incomes

TABLE 4   ACREAGE, YIELDS, AND PRICES OF CORN AND SOYBEANS, U.S., 1949–1962

YEAR	CORN			SOYBEANS		
	MILLIONS OF ACRES	BUSHELS PER ACRE	PRICE PER BUSHEL, $	MILLIONS OF ACRES	BUSHELS PER ACRE	PRICE PER BUSHEL, $
1949	77.1	38.2	$1.24	10.8	22.3	$2.16
1951	71.2	36.9	1.66	13.6	20.8	2.73
1954	68.7	39.4	1.43	17.0	20.0	2.46
1957	63.1	48.3	1.11	20.9	23.2	2.07
1960	71.4	54.7	1.00	23.7	23.5	2.13
1963	59.2	67.9	1.11	28.6	24.4	2.51
1966	56.9	72.1	1.29	36.6	25.4	2.77

SOURCE: U.S. Department of Agriculture, *Agricultural Statistics, 1968,* Washington, D.C., U.S. Government Printing Office, 1968.

in the face of a growing population. In the last 30 years, farm output has doubled, while 78 million acres have been taken out of cultivation. Instead of the threatened evil day of wealthy landlords and starving workers, we find American farmers unable to leave the farm fast enough to maintain farm incomes comparable to those in other occupations. The number of Americans living on farms, which had reached 32 million by 1910, had declined to 10 million by 1969, while the total U.S. population more than doubled over the same period.

FIGURE 8   THE SHIFT OF ACREAGE FROM CORN TO SOYBEANS BETWEEN 1949 AND 1966

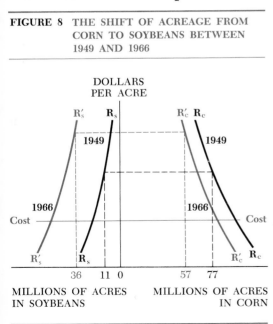

MILLIONS OF ACRES IN SOYBEANS   MILLIONS OF ACRES IN CORN

The technical changes that underlay these increased yields are generally familiar. New varieties were developed that furnished more output per plant. Increased application of commercial fertilizer and new growing methods permitted closer planting and made plants grow larger and stronger. Meat and dairy animals have become larger and more productive. Increased mechanization of production processes has permitted more intensive operations at lower cost per unit. As shown in Table 5, consumption of commercial fertilizer has grown sevenfold since 1910; output per acre has doubled; farm tractors, almost unknown in 1910, have now virtually replaced horses and mules as a source of power. Not only has this change resulted in higher yields per acre of crop land, but in addition, net output per acre has been increased by eliminating the use of crop land for growing horse and mule feed.

U.S. Farm Policy

Governmental attempts during the past 30 years to ease the impact of new technology on farmers resulted in a number of policies designed to maintain farm income in the face of rising output per acre. Most of these policies have been embodied in actions to support farm prices in various ways. The general policy target has been to maintain

TABLE 5   CHANGING U.S. FARMING METHODS, 1910–1965

YEAR	CONSUMPTION OF COMMERCIAL FERTILIZER (MILLION TONS)	NUMBER OF TRACTORS ON FARMS (THOUSANDS)	NUMBER OF HORSES AND MULES ON FARMS (MILLIONS)	PERCENT OF PLANTED ACREAGE USED FOR FEED FOR HORSES AND MULES	YIELD PER ACRE (1957–1959 = 100)
1910	5.5	1	23.3	27	68
1920	7.2	246	25.1	25	74
1930	8.2	920	18.7	18	65
1940	8.3	1,545	13.9	12	76
1950	19.3	3,394	7.6	5	84
1960	25.6	4,685	3.1	2	109
1965	34.5	4,800	n.a.	n.a.	120

SOURCE: *Historical Statistics of the United States* and *Agricultural Statistics, 1967*.

parity between the prices farmers get for their crops and the prices of the things they buy. As originally formulated, the parity price for each farm product was the price that would bear the same relationship to the index of prices paid by farmers, as it had on the average during the 5-year base period 1910–1914. For example, in a year when the prices-paid index stood at 250, a crop that sold for 50 cents a bushel on the average during 1910–1914 (when the index was 100) would have a parity price equal to $.50 × 250/100, or $1.25 per bushel. More recently, parity prices have been calculated by a variety of complicated formulas involving different base periods for different commodities and a number of special adjustments.

Since rising farm productivity forces farm prices to fall when left to the free play of the market, the government has intervened to support them at or near parity levels. This has been accomplished by a variety of programs, variously aimed at controlling output, holding supplies off the market, reducing acreage, and encouraging demand. These programs have been further supplemented by payment of outright subsidies.

The Commodity Credit Corporation (CCC)   The principal instrument for supporting farm prices has been the Commod-

ity Credit Corporation, a government agency that lends money to farmers, accepting their crops as collateral. For the purpose of CCC loans, however, the crop is valued at a special *loan rate* based on its parity price, rather than at market value. When the market price is $1.20 a bushel and the CCC loan rate is $1, farmers sell their crops on the market in the usual way, but when the market price drops below the loan rate, farmers can take the crop to the CCC and "borrow" on it at the loan rate of $1 a bushel. If, later on in the season, the market price rises above the loan rate, farmers can pay off their loans and market the crop, but if the market price remains low, the farmer does not repay the loan, but lets the Commodity Credit Corporation take ownership of the crop.[3] CCC loans are available on "basic" commodities, defined to include corn, cotton, peanuts, rice, tobacco, and wheat. In addition, support is also extended to certain other "nonbasic" commodities. For example during 1966, in addition to "basic" commodities, CCC loans were extended on barley, grain sorghum, honey, oats, rye, tung oil, dried beans, flaxseed, rosin, and soybeans.

[3] CCC loans are made "without recourse." That is, when farmers default on their loans, the corporation takes possession of the collateral used for security—the crop—but the farmer has no further liability for the "debt."

The operation of the CCC as a price-support agency is shown in Figure 9. The loan rate is established at price P_o as indicated. Demand is represented by DD. When the quantity harvested is small, as represented by SS, the market price, P_m, is above the loan rate, and farmers market their crops. When quantity harvested grows to $S'S'$, however, prices tend to fall. Left to itself, the price would decline to P'_m, but farmers are able to obtain the price P_o by borrowing from the CCC and allowing their loans to default. At the price P_o, households and processors buy the quantity Q_o, leaving the amount Q_oS' to be taken by the CCC as collateral of defaulted loans.

Incidentally, Figure 9 shows the true definition of the term "surplus" farm commodities. Buyers would be willing to take the whole output, but only at the low market price P'_m. "Surpluses" arise, not because more is grown than people will buy, but because more is grown than can be sold at the support price. Given output and demand, the higher the support level is fixed, the greater the surplus will be. Some proponents of farm legislation argue that the largest surpluses, in this sense, are not agricultural but are found among the products

of highly concentrated industries in which oligopolistic firms establish their own "support prices" and hold surpluses off the market by operating below capacity. Because agriculture is perfectly competitive when left to itself, it is argued that farm legislation merely makes the government do for the farmer what many other industries already do for themselves.

The loan operations of the Commodity Credit Corporation during 1967 are summarized in Table 6. Farm products acquired by the CCC as collateral for defaulted loans are kept off the domestic market either by storage or by distribution through special channels. During 1967 the CCC disposed of $2.3 billion out of its commodity holdings. Of this about half went to domestic food programs as assistance to low-income families and contributions to school lunch programs. Most of the remainder was exported as part of our food assistance to underdeveloped countries.

Farm Output Limitations   If the government did nothing but support farm prices, continually rising farm yields would force the CCC to acquire and hold ever-increasing surpluses. An effective price-support program is feasible only if accompanied by limitation of output. Over the years, this has been accomplished by a variety of programs whose provisions have been continually changing with shifting political

FIGURE 9   FARM PRICE SUPPORT BY THE COMMODITY CREDIT COPORATION

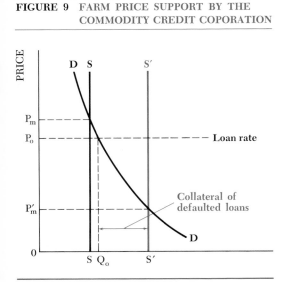

TABLE 6   COMMODITY CREDIT CORPORATION TRANSACTIONS DURING 1967

Loans outstanding, January 1, 1967	$2,101,133,000
Plus: New loans	1,840,938,000
Less: Repayments	1,185,990,000
Collateral acquired in settlement	299,088,000
Loans written off	40,803,000
Loans outstanding, January 1, 1968	$2,416,190,000

SOURCE: *Agricultural Statistics, 1968.*

positions. At times, the law has provided that farmers who agreed to reduce their acreage planted to designated crops be given cash payments in compensation and made eligible to receive higher price supports than were offered other farmers. Under other laws, marketing quotas have been imposed after a vote of the farmers involved, limiting the quantity each could bring to market. Marketing quotas were sometimes accompanied by additional compensation and sometimes not. Under other legislation, farmers have been compensated for taking land out of crop production and applying it to conservation purposes, and so on.

Output limitations, together with foreign assistance and domestic food programs, have limited the growth of CCC inventories. Total holdings since 1949 are shown in Figure 10. Low at first because of World War II and its aftermath, agricultural stocks were further depleted during the conflict in Korea. This drop was followed by a substantial build-up, and holdings reached peak levels in 1955 and 1959 as a consequence of the decline in demand during the recessions of 1954 and 1958. Rapidly rising demand during the period following 1964, however, resulted in another great reduction in holdings.

Agriculture and Rent in the Future

Despite American experience to the contrary, something very like the gloomy

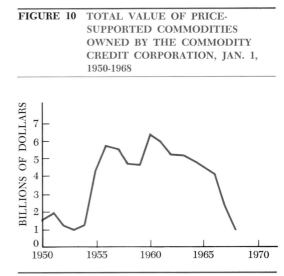

FIGURE 10 TOTAL VALUE OF PRICE-SUPPORTED COMMODITIES OWNED BY THE COMMODITY CREDIT CORPORATION, JAN. 1, 1950-1968

SOURCE: U.S. Department of Agriculture, *Agricultural Statistics, 1968.*

picture painted by the early economists actually characterizes life in many underdeveloped countries today. In some, food is produced by landless workers with low productivity on marginal land, and most income beyond bare subsistence accrues as rent to a few rich landowning families. In addition, world population, now growing at a rate of almost 2 percent per year compounded, doubles nearly every 35 years. Unless this rate of growth can be checked, widespread starvation and overcrowding will soon be serious problems, regardless of land tenure institutions. Perhaps the early prophets were mistaken in the *timing* of their forecast, but it is premature to call them wrong.

SUMMARY

Income derived from the services of land is *economic rent*. It consists of the excess of receipts from production involving land over cost, including appropriate allowances for interest on the owner's invested capital and wages for his own labor. The source of rent is the *scarcity of land*.

If there were enough land, no rent would arise from its use. The Physiocrats, a group of early French economists, mistakenly thought that rent arose from the special abundance of the soil, but David Ricardo (1774–1823) showed that rent resulted not from natural abundance, but from the scarcity of land.

The rent from an acre planted to a given crop depends on the total number of acres planted to that crop by all farmers together. The action of farmers, each seeking to earn the highest rent from his land, tends to *equalize rents* from land of the same quality and to match the acreage planted to the demand for different crops. *Fertility* and *cost differences* play important roles in assigning land to different crops. *Differential rents* on lands at varying distances from the market help establish the location of different activities.

Early economists predicted that a growing population and rising demand for food would require the cultivation of increasingly less fertile land. Real wages would be pushed to subsistence, and the rest of income would become rent, concentrated in the hands of a few landowners. This picture has not materialized in the developed western nations because the demand for farm products is inelastic and because farm yields have risen even faster than demand. In the U.S., yields have risen faster than farmers could leave the farm, resulting in a prolonged period of low farm incomes. A number of *government programs* have been employed to support farm prices in an effort to mitigate the effects of this process on farmers. In some of the less developed nations of the world, however, something like the gloomy long-run forecast is beginning to materialize.

CHAPTER 24

Interest and Profits

Interest and profit are closely related income shares that arise in connection with investment and economic growth. In fact, some early economists often used the terms interchangeably. Neither topic is new, for we have already examined the determination of interest rates in connection with monetary policy, while the nature and behavior of profits have been constantly recurring themes throughout our study.

The purpose of this chapter is to consolidate what we know about interest and profits and to look at them from a fresh point of view. We will examine the structure of interest rates and show how they guide investments into those projects that contribute the most to economic growth. Since profit is the most widely misunderstood form of income, it is useful to deal briefly with the Marxian view of profits at this point, and to review once again the important function of profits in the dynamics of economic growth.

INTEREST

A household, business firm, or government that wants to make payments in excess of its immediate receipts must obtain money from some outside source. When these funds are borrowed, the annual payment for their use, expressed as a percent of the principal, is the *rate of interest*. We have already examined the role of interest in the economic system and the factors that determine the level of interest rates at any given time.[1] At this point we are concerned with differences in interest rates on various kinds of loans, with the way interest rates allocate available investment resources among competing uses, and with interest as an element of income.

As in the case of other income shares it is necessary to distinguish between the

[1] It is suggested that the reader refresh his memory by reviewing the discussion of interest and monetary policy in Chapter 14.

amount of interest explicitly paid from one party to another, and the total amount of interest that should properly be included in income. Once a rate has been established for borrowed funds, even a business firm that uses its own money incurs an implicit interest cost on its investment. If the firm had not used the money for its own purposes, it could have earned interest by lending it to somebody else. Firms receive this implicit interest as part of their residual share of total receipts and report it as part of their "profits." Even banks and other financial institutions whose receipts are predominantly interest report their net earnings as "profits." Therefore, most interest, like rent, appears in the national accounts intermingled with other types of incomes.[2]

The Structure of Interest Rates

Although it is convenient to speak of "the" interest rate, there are in reality a wide range of interest rates in effect at any given time.

Risk   One important cause of the level of the interest rate on any given security is the degree of risk that borrowers will be unable to pay when a payment is due. Lenders naturally prefer safer loans unless higher-risk borrowers pay interest rates that are sufficiently higher to compensate for the added risk.

The risk premium can be clearly seen when securities of 3 different risk classes are compared in Figure 1. Securities of the U.S. government carry the lowest risk and

[2] The item *personal interest income* that appears as part of personal income in the national accounts includes only interest income received by persons either directly as money payment or indirectly in the form of services rendered on their behalf by financial institutions.

FIGURE 1   AVERAGE MARKET YIELDS OF U.S. GOVERNMENT TAXABLE BONDS, Aaa AND Baa CORPORATE BONDS (MOODY'S), 1950-1968

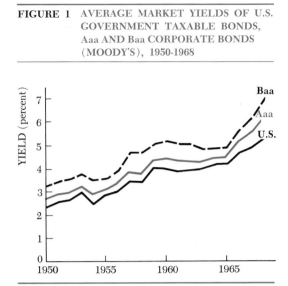

SOURCE: *Economic Report of the President, 1969.*

the lowest interest rates. High-quality (Aaa) corporate bonds pay a higher rate, while rates on lower-quality, higher-risk (Baa) corporate bonds are the highest shown. Consumer loans, with low security and notoriously high risk, often carry rates double those on corporate bonds.

Risk is partly a matter of the uncertainty of the success of the project being financed, and partly a matter of the reputation of the borrower. Because bankers judge many moderate-income families to be uncertain risks, some cannot get conventional mortgage credit on terms they can afford. As part of its program to encourage home ownership, the U.S. government established the Federal Housing Administration (FHA), an agency to insure home-construction mortgages in cases in which certain provisions concerning design, location, and other specifications are met. Since they are guaranteed, such mortgages carry low risk to the bank, and bankers are willing to make them at correspondingly lower interest rates.

The Term Structure Interest rates also differ according to the *term to maturity* of the loan; that is, the length of time until the principal is to be repaid. When interest rates are expected to remain unchanged for an indefinite period, long-term and short-term loans can be obtained for about the same interest rate. Aside from the small difference in convenience, it is immaterial to a lender whether he makes a series of short-term loans, relending his principal each time it is repaid, or makes one single loan for a long period. But when interest rates are expected to rise, the situation changes. Lenders who make a series of short-term loans at successively higher interest rates would expect to earn greater returns than those who contracted a single long-term loan at low current rates. If long-term borrowers are to obtain funds under such circumstances, they must be willing to pay an interest rate sufficiently higher than the short-term rate to compensate lenders for the expected rise.

When rates are expected to decline, the situation is reversed. Lenders who start a series of short-term loans at successively falling interest rates will earn less than those who contract a single long-term loan at current high rates. Competition among lenders for long-term securities drives the long-term rate below those demanded on short-run loans.

The relationship between interest rates on short-term and long-term securities can be illustrated by a comparison of the yields on 3-month U.S. Treasury bills, and those on Treasury Bonds with maturities of about 10 years. During most of the last 30 years, while interest rates rose steadily from the low levels of the Depression of the 1930s, the expectation of continual increases kept short-term interest rates well below those on long-term securities. As interest rates approached record high levels in the late 1960s, shifting expectations about rate movements caused long and short rates to change positions several

times. This vacillation is clearly seen when yields on the two classes of securities are plotted in Figure 2. When interest rates shot up in late 1966, the expectation of an imminent decline held the yield on 3-month bills above the long-term rate. As the long-term rate began to rise early in 1967, the expectation of further increases in rates held the bill rate below the return on longer-run securities. With the passage of the surcharge on the personal and corporate income tax in 1968, a decline in interest rates was once more anticipated, and the bill rate again rose above the long-term rate.

Tax Exemption and Interest Rates By act of Congress, the interest paid by the bonds of state and local governments is exempt from income taxation. This exemption leads investors to prefer state and local bonds to

FIGURE 2   THE DIFFERENCE BETWEEN SHORT-TERM AND LONG-TERM INTEREST RATES: MARKET YIELDS ON 3-MONTH TREASURY BILLS AND LONG-TERM U.S. BONDS

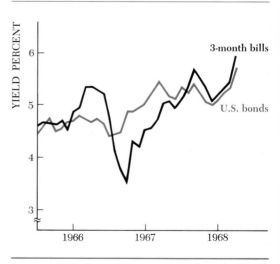

SOURCE: Data from *Economic Report of the President, 1969*. Long-term rates are represented by market yield on "Taxable Treasury Bonds." Since 1953 these have consisted of bonds neither due nor callable before 10 years from date of issue.

other forms of lending of equivalent risk and term to maturity. Competition for these securities by investors in high tax brackets enables state and local governments to obtain credit at lower interest rates than other borrowers must pay. This difference is conveniently expressed as a percentage differential in yields. The higher the differential, the lower the yield of tax-exempt compared to taxable bonds. If the rate on taxable bonds is 8 percent, a 6 percent return on tax-exempt securities would represent a 25 percent yield differential. A 4 percent return on tax-exempts would represent a 50 percent differential, and so on.

The relationship of the differential to an individual investor's tax rate indicates the value of tax exemption. If yields on tax-exempt bonds are 25 percent below those on other securities, they represent a poor investment to families in the 20 percent tax bracket. Such families would earn more by buying the taxable security and paying the tax on the higher yield. Families in the 25 percent tax bracket would earn the same after-tax return whether they owned taxable or tax-exempt securities, but families paying marginal tax rates above 25 percent could save more from tax exemption than they would lose from the lower yield.

The market determination of the percentage differential in yield is illustrated in Figure 3. The volume of tax-exempt securities is plotted horizontally, and the interest differential is measured vertically. The slope of the demand curve *DD* reflects the fact that at high differentials only a few families in the highest tax brackets could gain by owning such securities, but as the differential declines, they become a good investment for families in lower income brackets. The total volume of tax-exempt securities outstanding is represented by SS. Bidding for tax-exempt securities tends to drive up the interest differential until just enough investors profit by holding the total outstanding volume. The differential in the figure is about 25 percent, a realistic

FIGURE 3   DETERMINATION OF YIELD DIFFERENTIAL FOR TAX-EXEMPT BONDS

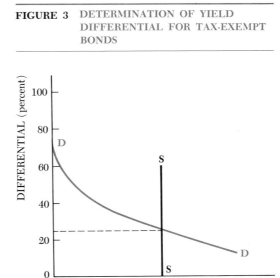

value. At this "price," investors in the 25 percent tax bracket find tax-exempt bonds just as good a buy as taxable securities. Investors in lower tax brackets lose by buying tax-exempts, while to those in higher tax brackets, the tax saving outweighs the loss in yield.

When tax rates rise, or when rising prices and incomes put more families in higher tax brackets, rising demand for tax-exempt securities raises the differential. When tax rates and incomes fall, the differential declines. Yields on high-grade, tax-exempt municipal bonds and on Aaa-grade corporate bonds, taken as representative of taxable securities of comparable risk, are compared for recent years in Figure 4.

Interest Rates and Investment

Total Investment   It is important to recall that the total amount of productive resources available for investment depends on the saving habits of the community, together with tax laws and government spending programs. High taxes, low government expenditure, and a low propensity

FIGURE 4   YIELDS ON TAX-EXEMPT
MUNICIPAL BONDS COMPARED
WITH Aaa CORPORATE BONDS

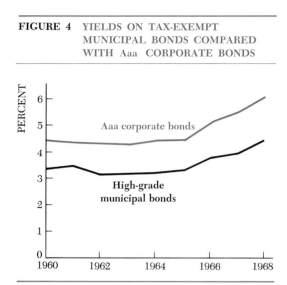

SOURCE: *Economic Report of the President, 1969.*

to consume combine to release a substantial proportion of available productive capacity for investment purposes. Low tax rates, heavy government spending, and a high propensity to consume combine to put most available capacity to work turning out consumer goods and government services, leaving relatively little for investment. A properly functioning monetary policy maintains interest rates at levels that just permit firms with investment projects to mobilize available unused resources.[3] An interest rate which is too high makes investment too costly and leaves labor and other resources unemployed, while one which is too low leads to demand for more output than the system can produce and results in inflation.

Allocation of Investment   Business firms seek investment funds for many different purposes. Some are in the process of introducing new products or new methods of production that will reduce costs. Others find the demand for their products expanding beyond their capacity to produce them efficiently and need additional equipment

[3] See Chapter 14.

to bring their productive facilities into closer conformity with the pattern of consumer desires. Of course, not all these "needs" for investment are equally important. Whether a project is worth undertaking or not depends partly on how much it costs to raise the necessary money.

The interest rate helps to allocate investable resources to those industries in which they will make the greatest contribution to productive capacity. It does so by restricting available investment resources to the most profitable investments—to those that promise the greatest contribution to the total value of output. Less promising projects must be abandoned or postponed until some later time when either more resources are available for investment, or there is less competition from more productive projects.

The allocation of investment between 2 industries is shown in Figure 5. The *CC* curve represents the marginal efficiency of investment of camera manufacturers, indicating the number of dollars, measured to the right, that firms in the industry could profitably invest at each interest rate. The *MM* curve represents the marginal efficiency of investment of outboard motor

FIGURE 5   THE ALLOCATION OF INVESTMENT
BETWEEN 2 INDUSTRIES

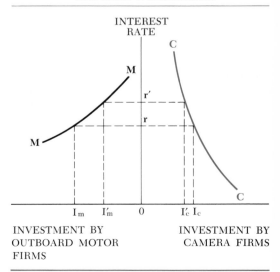

producers, measured to the left. Competition sets the interest rate at *r*, allocating investment funds equal to I_mI_c between the 2 industries as shown. If less money were available for investment, say $I'_mI'_c$, the interest rate would be driven up to *r'*. In the figure, the marginal efficiency of investment in the camera-manufacturing industry is less elastic than that in the outboard motor industry. Therefore, the greatest effect of rising interest rates would be to cut back investment by outboard motor manufacturers. The sensitivity of outboard motor producers to interest rates reflects the fact that they have no important new products to bring out, nor any cost-reduction scheme, nor are they particularly in need of expanded facilities. If only few resources are available for investment, they can be used more productively by camera firms.

Of course, once the camera industry had completed its capital expansion, or if consumer demand for cameras declined, the marginal efficiency of investment in the camera industry would fall. If the same investment resources were available as before, the declining interest rate would release them from the camera industry and permit outboard motor manufacturers to step up their investment projects. The effect of this change is shown in Figure 6. Black lines represent the marginal efficiency of investment in the 2 industries at the beginning of the investment program in the camera industry. As the innovation in camera production methods is completed, the marginal efficiency of investment in the camera industry declines to the position represented by the blue curve, releasing resources for investment in the production of outboard motors.

By the same token, the appearance of an innovation in outboard motor design or an upsurge of demand for outboard motors could change the picture. The marginal efficiency of investment in the outboard motor industry would rise, diverting investment resources to outboard motors and away from cameras.

FIGURE 6   THE REALLOCATION OF INVESTMENT WHEN THE CAPITAL EXPANSION PROGRAM IN 1 INDUSTRY HAS BEEN COMPLETED

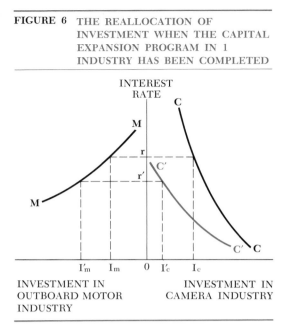

INTEREST RATE

INVESTMENT IN OUTBOARD MOTOR INDUSTRY

INVESTMENT IN CAMERA INDUSTRY

Public Policy and Allocation   Interest rates apportion available investment resources to those investment projects with the highest profitability. Although profitability depends on consumer demand and on the number of new methods and products awaiting introduction, it is also affected by tax laws, government regulations, and other policy measures. For example, unequal tax treatment raises the marginal efficiency of capital in favored industries and encourages them to expand more rapidly than those less favorably treated.

The effect of a policy favoring investment in a particular industry is shown in Figure 7. The black curves represent the hypothetical location of the marginal efficiency of investment in the favored industry (measured to the left) and in other industries (measured to the right) in the absence of special policy treatment. Under these circumstances, *AO* dollars per year would be invested in the favored industry and *OB* per year in the rest of the economy. The blue curve indicates the position of the marginal efficiency of investment in the favored industry after a tax benefit or some other policy to encourage investment has

FIGURE 7   THE EFFECT OF GOVERNMENT
POLICY ON THE ALLOCATION OF
INVESTMENT

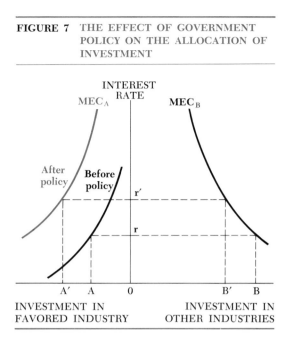

INVESTMENT IN   INVESTMENT IN
FAVORED INDUSTRY   OTHER INDUSTRIES

been instituted. If the same total investment resources were available, interest
rates would tend to be somewhat higher,
and $A'A$ dollars of investment would be
diverted from other industries and invested
in the industry favored by the policy.

A number of examples of such policy
treatment can be cited. The mineral-deple-
tion allowance permitted to petroleum,
natural gas, iron ore, and other extractive
industries has meant greater investment in
wells and mining operations than would
otherwise have occurred. Permitting home-
owners to deduct mortgage interest from
their incomes before computing their income taxes has had the general effect of
reducing their interest costs and, together
with the benefits of the FHA program, has
directed more investment into residential
construction than would otherwise have
taken place. Protective tariffs and import
quotas provide other examples of the use of
public policy to alter the allocation of investment.

The pressing need to expand the use of
pollution-control equipment can also be
seen as a problem in allocation policy. Unless pollution-control devices either contribute directly to the desirability of the
product itself or capture valuable byprod-
ucts (in which cases, pollution control is
only incidental), or induce a valuable improvement in public relations, the marginal
efficiency of investment in them is low and
declines rapidly. This fact leads industry to
neglect this important area and to use investment resources in projects which pay
off more directly.

To encourage the installation of pollution-control equipment, policy steps must
be taken to raise the marginal efficiency of
investment in it. As already shown in Chapter 20, the most straightforward method is
to pass laws that severely limit a firm's
ability to operate without adequate pollution control. Such measures would force
firms with inadequate equipment to curtail
production, just as they would if their facilities were inadequate in any other sense,
and pollution-control devices would become
as necessary to production as any other
piece of equipment. Similar effects would
result from special penalty taxes on firms
responsible for pollution. Another alternative would be to subsidize firms that install
pollution-control equipment either directly
or through special tax concessions.

PROFITS

Owners of businesses are the recipients of
the final residual remaining from the value
of production after all other participants
have been paid shares contracted at going
market prices. While this residual includes
profit, it includes a great deal more. Part of
the residual must cover the depreciation of
the buildings and equipment contributed
by the owners. In addition, to the extent
that owners contribute their own land,
labor, and capital to operations, some of
the residual is properly assignable to rent,
wages, and interest.

In particular, the owner's wages should include any earnings that can be attributed to his managerial skill. A skillful manager who pays close attention to costs, who can anticipate the wants of consumers better than his competitors, and who can keep operations going smoothly earns a larger residual than one who is sloppy about organization, careless about costs, and slow in catering to the whims of his customers. The superiority of their managerial skill permits some businessmen to obtain a substantial residual income under circumstances in which others at best can only cover costs. Earnings attributable to this difference in ability should be considered as the wages of more skillful management, rather than as a part of profit. If the owner were to quit the business and offer these managerial skills for hire, competition for his greater talent would drive his salary well above that offered a man of less ability, and this amount should be deducted from his residual to arrive at profits.

In its strict economic sense, *profit* is that portion of the residual share remaining after the deduction of the market value of all contributions to production by the owners themselves. These contributions specifically include the market value of managerial skill in addition to rent on land and interest on invested capital. Because these deductions are market values, profit can also be defined as any residual share of income that would remain to the owner of the business if he hired all the land, labor, capital, and materials used in production, including the necessary labor of management.

Size and Stability of Profits

Although reported corporate profits include earnings from land and interest on stockholders' capital, they provide the best indication of the general size and behavior of the profit share of income. Before taxes,

corporate profits average about 10 percent of gross national income. Because of fixed costs, however, profits of any given year are sharply affected by the level of aggregate output. As we saw in our study of break-even charts, sales revenues cover total costs and leave a substantial residual for profit only when sales are high. When sales decline, the residual share shrinks, and if sales fall far enough the firm incurs losses.

As a result, profits are the most volatile of all income shares, as is shown when they are compared to wage and salary payments in Figure 8. Between 1945 and 1968, the growth trend of corporate profits was almost identical to that of the wages and salaries paid by private firms, but the year-to-year path of profits was much more irregular than the comparatively smooth growth in wages.

FIGURE 8   CORPORATE PROFITS COMPARED TO PRIVATE WAGES AND SALARIES, U.S., 1945-1968

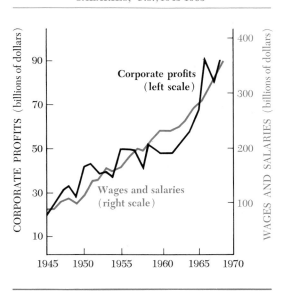

SOURCE: 1945–1962 from Office of Business Economics, *The National Income and Product Accounts of the United States*, Washington, D.C., 1966. Figures for later years from appropriate issues of the *Survey of Current Business*.

Marxian Profit Theory:
Profits as Surplus Value

Since profits are the share of value left over after all productive services have been paid, they consist of the share of output going to business owners *purely by virtue of ownership* for which they, themselves, make no direct current contribution to production. Paradoxical as it seems, although profit is the main driving force in a private enterprise economic system, it is not pay for the current performance of a job. Indeed, it may seem like payment for doing *nothing at all!*

The appearance of being "something for nothing" has made profits one of the most widely misunderstood of all economic phenomena. To many people, profit appears as a payment that has been somehow extorted from productive workers by the power of the property-owning class. In this view, profits represent pure exploitation, and their receipt places business enterprisers in a class with slave-owners, racketeers, and pirates. If anything, such comparisons often favor the latter groups as "honest brigands" in contrast to the businessmen who "craftily hide behind economic institutions that do their dirty work for them."

Karl Marx was the most widely recognized and most effective exponent of this general point of view, and it is interesting to examine his ideas as set forth in *Capital,* a 3-volume work published in 1867.[4] According to Marx, capitalist enterprisers contract for labor at going market-determined wage rates, but the commodities produced by this labor turn out to be worth more than the labor that went into them. Marx called the difference *surplus value,* and Marxian economics is an effort to explain where this

surplus value comes from and how the enterpriser's struggle to maintain and increase it account for the observed behavior of society.

The first step in Marxian analysis was to establish why commodities sell at the prices observed. Marx's conclusion was that what "determines the magnitude of the value of any article is the amount of labor socially necessary, or the labor-time socially necessary for its production. . . . The value of one commodity is to the value of any other, as the labor-time necessary for the production of one is to that necessary for the production of the other."[5] The strange sound of this proposition, usually called the *labor theory of value,* derives from its somewhat cumbersome terminology. If Marx is given the benefit of the doubt, however, a liberal translation of his proposition into modern usage might be that "prices of different products tend to be proportional to marginal labor costs." If this is what Marx meant by his labor theory of value, he was on sound ground. As we have seen, prices of products *do* tend to be proportional to marginal cost, and when materials are traced back, all marginal cost resolves largely into labor cost.

The second step in the Marxian analysis involved the labor market. Marx observed the commonplace fact that most workers in a capitalistic economy cannot produce their own commodities but must sell their labor on the market at a market-determined price. That is, ". . . the owner of money must meet in the market with the free labourer, free in the double sense, that as a free man he can dispose of his labour-power as his own commodity, and that on the other hand, he has no other commodity for sale, is short of everything necessary for the realization of his labor power."[6] The real question, however, was what deter-

---

[4] References, hereafter cited as *Capital,* are to the paperback centennial edition published by International Publishers, New York, 1967.

[5] *Capital,* vol. I, pp. 39–40.
[6] *Ibid.,* p. 169.

mined the wage rate that resulted from this confrontation in the market. As Marx wrote, "We must now examine more closely this particular commodity labour-power. Like all others, it has value. How is that value determined?"[7] Marx answered his own question in the very next sentence: "The value of labour-power is determined as in the case of every other commodity, by the labour-time necessary for the production . . . and consequently also the reproduction of this special article."[8] The wage rate, as the price of labor, was the amount of socially necessary labor time needed to produce labor itself! In other words, according to Marx, the cost of producing a day's work would be the labor time necessary to turn out the minimum amount of food, clothing, shelter, and other products that a worker must consume daily in order to survive. In addition, the cost must include the time needed to produce minimum daily consumption for the worker's family to assure that new workers would be available when they were needed to replace the old.

It is interesting to make a crude estimate of the cost of producing a day's labor in the U.S. in recent years. It has been estimated that at 1967 prices, about $1,200 per year is required to provide a minimum acceptable living standard per person.[9] Since about 40 percent of the population is in the labor force, an average of about 2.5 people must be supported for each 1 on the job. This would make the cost of a year's labor 2.5 × $1,200, or $3,000. If we allow 250 working days per year, we can

<hr>

[7] *Ibid.*, p. 170.

[8] *Ibid.*

[9] Adapted from figures given for a "lower-budget" standard of living as estimated in *3 Standards of Living for an Urban Family of 4 Persons*, BLS Bulletin no. 1570–5, 1967. The figures are probably higher than those that Marx would consider the true cost of labor, but they will serve to illustrate the proposition.

estimate $3,000/250, or $12 per day as the dollar cost of producing and reproducing labor.

To determine the labor time necessary to produce this dollar value, we must take account of the productivity of labor. Adjusted to the same 1967 prices, labor productivity in the U.S. is about $6 per manhour, and at this rate it requires an average of 2 hours per day to produce the $12 worth of commodities necessary to keep a worker on the job. This estimate of the production cost of labor would, according to Marx, be all the laborer would receive. The output of the first 2 hours of each day's work would produce the cost of the labor itself and would be paid out in wages. The rest of the time, Marx said, workers produce surplus value over and above the cost of the labor itself, which accrues to the employer as profit.

If this were the nature of profit, several important consequences would follow.

1. Since surplus value is supposed to equal the total number of manhours worked in excess of the cost of labor itself, the longer the working day, the greater profits should become. If it takes 2 hours a day to maintain the average worker, he would produce surplus value for 6 hours out of an 8-hour day, but for 10 hours out of a 12-hour day. As a result employers would be led to exploit labor by pushing the working day to maximum length.

2. The cost of labor itself (and hence the wage rate) would depend partly on how many nonworkers were to be supported per active worker. If more workers could be squeezed out of a population, the cost of labor would fall, and surplus value would rise. This would lead employers to exploit child labor and to force older people to work until they dropped on the job.

3. The cost of labor itself would also depend on the productivity of labor. The more productive workers became, the

fewer hours they would need each day to produce their own subsistence, and the more hours per day they would produce surplus value. Thus there would be continual pressure on employers to introduce new machinery and other labor-saving devices. As shown in Figure 9, the result would tend to be greater total profits. The real wages of labor would be fixed at subsistence and would not rise.

4. The pressure to increase productivity by mass production methods would cause increasing economic concentration.

5. Finally, the continual pressure for higher productivity would occasionally force wages above the minimum subsistence level as business firms overextended the rate of investment. However, the result would be periodic economic crises and depressions, while the displacement of workers by machinery would give rise to permanent unemployment in the form of an "industrial reserve army."

When Marx wrote more than a century ago, his analysis appeared to explain much that could be observed in daily economic life. In most of the world, wages *were* barely high enough for subsistence. Hours

of work were long, and child labor was common. Moreover, businessmen did press to raise labor productivity, while the following 100 years were characterized by growing economic concentration and by recurrent depressions and unemployment, culminating in the Depression of the 1930s.[10] Yet, impressive as this predictive performance was, when we look at the theory underlying the structure, we find that experience has contradicted the basic premise of Marxian doctrine. The length of the working day has shortened; the number of workdays per year has declined; child labor in the U.S. and most of Europe has almost disappeared, and workers retire at younger ages. The productivity of labor has, it is true, been driven steadily upward, but instead of a growing share of profit in total output, the result has been the steady growth of real wages. In place of the predicted misery of the working class, we find that the majority of modern workers earn incomes undreamed of in Marx's time.

[10] This period corresponds almost exactly to the century of U.S. economic growth discussed in Chapter 4. It would be useful to review that chapter at this point.

FIGURE 9   THE MARXIAN PROFIT THEORY

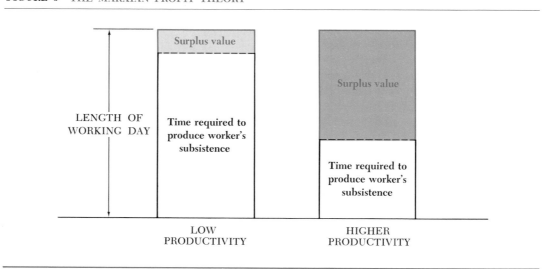

Why Did Real Wages Rise?   Marxian logic had the appearance of a classical syllogism:

1. The value of all commodities is determined by the socially necessary labor time involved in their production.

2. Labor is a commodity.

3. Therefore: The value of labor (the wage rate) is the socially necessary labor time involved in the production of labor.

If we review our "liberal translation" of Marx's labor theory of value, however, the fallacy of the argument is at once apparent. At that point we agreed that the prices of *products* tend to be proportional to their marginal cost, and that marginal cost is largely, if not entirely, labor cost. But we did not agree—and do not agree—that labor is a *product*. Products, as the term implies, are items continually produced for use or sale. Except in a slave society in which the masters breed other humans like cattle, people are not products. The prices of *products* sold on competitive markets tend to be set in proportion to marginal cost by business firms trying to achieve the highest profits, but no similar force operates on the price of human labor.

As we saw, the average real wage of labor as a whole is not determined by the same laws that affect the prices of products.[11] The same competitive business behavior that keeps prices proportional to marginal cost tends, in the long run, to keep the real wage rate proportional to the productivity of labor. Once the validity of this statement is shown, the Marxian surplus value theory collapses as an empty *non sequitur.*

Profit and Innovation

In one important respect, however, Marx was right. Unlike wages, rent, and other payments for present services, profits are

[11] See Chapter 22.

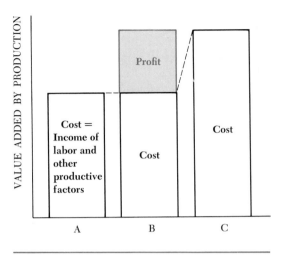

FIGURE 10   THE DYNAMICS OF PROFITS

not received in exchange for services currently being rendered. Where Marx went wrong was in his failure to understand that profits *are* received as a reward for action taken in the past, in particular for having been among the first to introduce a new idea or to respond to a shift in the pattern of consumer wants.

A representation of the nature of profits more in keeping with reality is depicted in Figure 10. We begin with an industry in competitive equilibrium as at *A*, with the costs of production paid in wages and rent equal to the entire value added by production.[12] Profits arise at *B* when one firm successfully introduces a new technique. The innovation may be a way to extract more output from the same input of resources, a way to improve old products, or an entirely new product. The particular

[12] These costs include, of course, the return for the labor services of management by the owner and rent on the land and resources owned by the firm. In addition, the cost includes the labor and resources neeeded to replace depreciating equipment. However, we are ignoring business taxes and similar cost elements to simplify the example.

form is immaterial; the important thing is that the firm can hire workers and purchase materials at prices little, if any, higher than before, and employ them to produce a more valuable product. The increased value of the product is the profit earned by the innovating firm.

The profit is only temporary, however, for once one firm has demonstrated the profitability of the new idea, others follow suit in an effort to capture a share of the profit for themselves. As the new method spreads, expanded production forces down markups and prices, while competition among firms using the new technique forces up wages and other costs. The spread of the new method continues until, with lower prices and higher costs, the entire value of the product is needed to pay for its production, leaving nothing for profit. In the end, the greater productivity that first appeared as a profit to the innovating firm has been transferred to others in the form of higher real earnings as at C.

We have examined this phenomenon from a number of points of view. We first encountered it as part of U.S. economic history in Chapter 6. We met it again in our study of the dynamics of competitive behavior in Chapter 18, where we saw how the first firms to introduce a new method or product receive profits which are eliminated as competitors follow suit. Another aspect of the phenomenon appeared in Chapter 22 as we saw how the competitive fall in prices and the scramble of producers for workers steadily transformed profits into higher real wages.

Why Don't Profits Vanish?

There remains, however, an important question. Why is it that—aside from periods of severe depression—profits appear year after year like a permanent fixture of a private enterprise economy?[13] If real profits tend to be swallowed up by rising real costs, why haven't they disappeared?

There are several reasons for this persistence. In the first place, profit as *reported* represents the entire residual income going to owners, regardless of source. To the extent that it includes the earnings of owners' managerial skills and other returns on owners' resources, it exceeds true profit. A firm would still report earnings from these sources, even if its true profit were, in fact, 0.

In the second place, the forces of competition needed to eliminate profits do not always operate. The disappearance of profits is a feature of competition, and to the extent that the entry of new firms into a market is blocked, continued profits can be expected. If new firms are unable to scramble freely for a share of profit, industrial expansion tends to stop short of the point at which profits are eliminated.

Much more important than either of these reasons, however, is the fact that innovation is a continuous process. Profits from a given innovation tend to disappear as firms rush to adopt the new idea, but if new techniques are introduced in a steady stream, profits from new ones appear as fast as those from the older ones are eroded. If innovation came to an end, real wages and other resource incomes would catch up to productivity, and profits would disappear. But profits persist as long as productivity continues to rise, and the faster enterprisers increase productivity, the larger the profit share of income tends to be. This is the explanation of the paradox of profits. The share of income which, from one point of view, appears to be a return for doing nothing, turns out to be the reward for the most important job of all—reorganiz-

[13] The only instances of negative total profits during the past 40 years were in 1931 (−$0.4 billion) and 1932 (−$2.3 billion).

ing production to increase the productivity of resources and to raise everybody's standard of living.

Profits and the Distribution of Income

The effect of competition is to distribute the productivity gains from innovation over the economy at large. The observed tendency for real wages to rise with labor productivity is familiar evidence of this process. When productivity gains first appear as profits, however, they are heavily concentrated among a relatively small number of people. On the one hand, this concentration is part of the process by which economic growth feeds on itself and contributes to the powerful dynamics of economic development, for it concentrates income in the hands of those people most likely to invest it. At the same time, however, it results in a heavy concentration of income in the hands of a relatively few wealthy families, and has important implications for the pattern of distribution among households that we will examine in the following chapter.

SUMMARY

Interest and *profits* are both closely connected with investment and economic growth. The role of investment is to increase the productivity of labor and other resources by reducing costs, by improving products, and by reallocating productive capacity to correspond more closely to the pattern of consumer demand.

Not all investment projects pay the same *interest rate*. Projects with high *risk* pay higher rates than those with lower risk, and loans of differing *maturity* bear different rates, depending on the expected future movement in rates. In addition, certain rates, like those on state and local bonds, are held down by *special tax treatment*.

The economic function of interest rates is to help *allocate* available investment resources to their most profitable uses. Since firms bid against one another for financing, projects that promise to make the greatest contribution to the economy can outbid less profitable projects. Profitability is, however, affected by public policy actions, and the allocation of investment funds partly depends on taxation and similar laws. For example, if pollution control is to have a serious claim to investable resources, appropriate action must be taken to improve the profitability of control devices compared to alternative investments.

Profits are the final residual remaining after all costs—including the market value of the owner's labor and the services of his property—have been deducted from the value of output. Since many of these costs are fixed, profits are sharply affected by changes in the level of output, and profit is the most volatile of all income shares.

The "something-for-nothing" appearance of profits led Marx to call them *surplus value* and to attempt to explain their behavior by a *labor theory of value*. Although Marxian theory produced an impressive series of predictions, its basic explanation of profits was wrong. Profits arise when a firm finds a way to increase the productivity of labor and other resources. As long as the innovating firm can continue to hire the services of the more productive resources without bidding up their prices, it can earn a profit. But in a competitive economic system the scramble of other firms to imitate the profitable idea drives up costs and reduces prices until the gains in productivity have been converted into higher real wages and rents.

Historically profits do not disappear, partly because of the presence of large elements of rent and other resource income in reported profits, and partly because of the restriction of competition in certain oligopolistic industries. The main reason profits persist, however, is that *innovation* is an ongoing process. Profits are received as a consequence of rising productivity, and as long as productivity continues to be driven up by the introduction of more valuable products or more productive methods, firms will continue to receive profits.

The concentration of profits in the hands of successful enterprisers further contributes to economic growth by placing income in the hands of the very people most likely to invest it. At the same time, however, the resulting concentration has serious implications for the distribution of income.

CHAPTER 25

Incomes of Families and Individuals

Of the total gross national income produced in the United States during recent years, roughly 9 percent went directly to government in indirect business taxes, and another 9 percent represented depreciation of capital equipment. The remainder, about 82 percent of the value of final output, constituted the total compensation received for labor services, for the rent of natural resources, for interest on invested capital, and as profits.

We have already examined the forces that determine the way the total is divided into these major functional shares. Our next step is to investigate the resulting distribution of personal income among families and individuals, and to find out how much of this total income each family receives, and why American families are found in income brackets that range from starvation levels to tens of millions of dollars a year.

CENSUS INCOME DATA

The most complete U.S. data on income distribution are compiled by the Bureau of the Census on the basis of personal money incomes reported by a large sample of families and unrelated individuals. These data have been extensively used in the discussion that follows, but they are subject to several important qualifications.

First, only personal *money* income has been reported in the statistics, excluding any allowance for the services of owner-occupied dwellings or other household capital. Although all money transfers and gifts are included, no recognition is given to the services received from the government in the forms of public education, parks, medical care, or other services. This omission should be particularly borne in mind in making income comparisons among families of different sizes.

A second important qualification arises from the exclusion from personal income of expense-account outlays or the provisions of services in kind by employers. To the extent that meals, clothing, travel, or entertainment provided on expense accounts replace similar outlays the family would otherwise make on its own, personal income understates the share of goods and services received by the family.

A much more important qualification arises from the exclusion of capital gains and retained corporate earnings from the concept of personal income. Only about half of after-tax corporate profits is paid out in dividends. The remainder, retained in the company and generally reinvested, adds to the value of the stockholders' equity but is not recorded as part of their personal incomes. Since retained earnings and gains from the sale of securities or other property are heavily concentrated in high-income brackets, their omission imposes an important qualification on the degree of inequality shown by the data.

As a partial offset to this inaccuracy, however, no deduction from income has been made for personal taxes. Thus, while the data include as part of personal income all social security pensions, unemployment compensations, welfare payments, and even money gifts from other individuals, the redistribution of income effected by somewhat heavier taxation of higher incomes has not been taken into account.

The Income-Receiving Unit

Income distribution can be studied in a number of different ways. Under some circumstances we are concerned with the amounts received by individual income recipients, but for most purposes these are of relatively minor interest. Since most people are organized and supported in family groups of one sort or another, the important question is how much income goes to each group as a whole.

These groups are not homogeneous, however, and before examining their incomes, it is useful to recognize their diversity of organization. According to U.S. Census definitions, a *family* is a group of 2 or more persons related by blood, marriage, or adoption and residing together. One member of the family is designated as the *head*. In all husband-wife families, this is the husband. In other cases it is the person designated as the head by members of the family themselves. About 87 percent of American families are husband-wife families, and about another 2 percent are headed by males with other marital status. The remaining 11 percent are families with female heads.

As can be seen from the definition, not all people are members of families. About 6 percent of Americans are *unrelated individuals* living alone or in groups unrelated by kinship. As would be expected from the relatively greater independence of males, there are more young men than young women classified as unrelated individuals, but the longer life expectancy of women leaves many more widows and single women in the older unrelated group, and when all ages are taken together there are twice as many women as men classed as unrelated individuals.

Although in some income studies each unrelated individual is treated as a "one-person family" and included along with other family groups, the problems of unrelated individuals are sufficiently different to merit separate examination. Most of the analysis that follows is restricted to families and excludes unrelated individuals.

THE PATTERN OF FAMILY INCOME DISTRIBUTION

Tables 1 and 2 show how total U.S. personal income was distributed in 1967. The poorest 2.1 percent of all families—those whose incomes were under $1,000—re-

TABLE 1   U.S. INCOME DISTRIBUTION BY TYPE OF FAMILY AND UNRELATED
INDIVIDUALS, ALL RACES, 1967

		FAMILIES						UNRELATED INDIVIDUALS		
		MALE HEAD								
			MARRIED, WIFE PRESENT							
TOTAL MONEY INCOME	TOTAL	TOTAL	TOTAL	WIFE IN PAID LABOR FORCE	WIFE NOT IN PAID LABOR FORCE	OTHER MARI- TAL STATUS	FE- MALE HEAD	TOTAL	MALE	FE- MALE
Number (Thousands)	49,834	44,501	43,292	15,845	27,447	1,210	5,333	13,114	4,845	8,269
Percent	100.0	100.0	100.0	100.0	100.0	100.0	100.0	100.0	100.0	100.0
Under $1,000	2.1	1.3	1.2	0.5	1.7	4.4	8.4	19.5	12.9	23.4
$1,000–$1,499	1.8	1.4	1.3	0.5	1.8	2.9	5.3	15.1	10.9	17.6
$1,500–$1,999	2.6	2.1	2.1	0.7	2.9	4.2	6.4	9.6	7.9	10.7
$2,000–$2,499	3.3	2.7	2.6	1.0	3.6	4.5	8.0	7.3	7.3	7.4
$2,500–$2,999	2.7	2.3	2.3	1.0	3.0	3.9	6.3	5.4	4.9	5.7
$3,000–$3,499	3.3	2.9	2.8	1.6	3.6	4.2	6.8	5.7	5.8	5.6
$3,500–$3,999	3.0	2.7	2.7	1.7	3.3	2.3	5.8	4.0	3.8	4.2
$4,000–$4,999	6.5	6.0	6.0	4.7	6.8	8.1	10.4	7.6	8.2	7.2
$5,000–$5,999	7.8	7.6	7.6	6.2	8.4	8.3	9.3	7.1	8.4	6.3
$6,000–$6,999	8.3	8.3	8.3	6.8	9.2	8.7	8.4	5.5	7.2	4.4
$7,000–$7,999	8.9	9.1	9.2	8.2	9.7	7.8	6.5	3.9	6.7	2.3
$8,000–$8,999	8.3	8.8	8.8	9.0	8.7	8.9	4.5	2.5	4.3	1.4
$9,000–$9,999	7.1	7.5	7.6	8.5	7.0	6.1	3.3	1.5	2.1	1.2
$10,000–$11,999	11.8	12.7	12.8	16.2	10.9	7.7	4.4	2.0	3.7	1.1
$12,000–$14,999	10.6	11.5	11.6	16.5	8.7	8.0	2.9	1.4	2.8	0.6
$15,000–$24,999	9.6	10.4	10.4	14.5	8.1	8.5	2.9	1.2	2.4	0.6
$25,000–$49,999	2.1	2.3	2.3	2.2	2.4	1.0	0.6	0.4	0.7	0.2
$50,000 and over	0.3	0.4	0.4	0.3	0.4	0.3	0.1	0.1	0.1	0.1
Median income (Dollars)	7,974	8,400	8,441	9,956	7,611	6,814	4,294	2,391	3,544	1,923
Mean income (Dollars)	9,019	9,464	9,508	10,803	8,760	7,899	5,305	3,637	4,740	2,991

SOURCE: U.S. Bureau of the Census, *Income in 1967 of Families in the United States,* Current Population Reports Series P–60 no. 59, April, 1969.

ceived less than one-tenth of 1 percent of all personal income paid out during the year. According to the Bureau of the Census, this averaged only $163 per family, and when account was taken of the number of family members, amounted to only $52 per person, a figure comparable to average incomes in the poorest underdeveloped countries in the world. At the other extreme, a group about the same size—the 2.4 percent of all families with incomes of $25,000 and over—received 10 percent of total personal income and averaged $37,172 per family.

The poorest 25 percent of all families

had incomes below $5,000 and altogether received only 8 percent of total personal income. The richest 25 percent had incomes over $11,000 and received 50 percent of total income. The 50 percent of the families in the middle were those with incomes from $5,000 to $11,000 who received 42 percent of total income.

The highest incomes were received by husband-wife families. The difference was especially noticeable at the extremes of the distribution. While fewer than 7.5 percent of husband-wife families had incomes below $2,500 per year, 16 percent of families with

TABLE 2 U.S. CUMULATIVE PERCENT DISTRIBUTIONS OF SELECTED FAMILY
CHARACTERISTICS BY TOTAL MONEY INCOME, 1967

	ALL FAMILIES	TOTAL PERSONS IN FAMILIES	TOTAL CHILDREN IN FAMILIES	TOTAL AGGREGATE INCOME
Cumulative Percent with Income:				
Under $1,000	2.1	1.8	2.0	*a*
Under $1,500	3.9	3.2	3.2	0.3
Under $2,000	6.5	5.2	4.8	0.8
Under $2,500	9.8	7.8	7.1	1.6
Under $3,000	12.5	10.1	9.2	2.4
Under $3,500	15.8	13.0	12.0	3.6
Under $4,000	18.8	15.7	14.7	4.9
Under $5,000	25.3	21.9	21.0	8.1
Under $6,000	33.1	29.6	29.4	12.8
Under $7,000	41.4	37.9	38.3	18.7
Under $8,000	50.3	47.0	48.1	26.0
Under $9,000	58.6	55.6	57.3	33.7
Under $10,000	65.7	63.0	65.2	41.1
Under $12,000	77.5	75.5	78.1	55.2
Under $15,000	88.1	86.7	88.7	70.7
Under $25,000	97.7	97.2	97.9	90.0

a Rounds to zero.

SOURCE: U.S. Bureau of the Census, *Income in 1967 of Families in the United States,* Current
Population Reports Series P–60 no. 59, April, 1969.

male heads with other status fell in this
class, and nearly 30 percent of all families
headed by women. At the upper end, while
over 13 percent of husband-wife families
had incomes of $15,000 or more, this was
true of less than 10 percent of other families
headed by males, and of only 3.6 percent of
families headed by women.

To some extent these differences were
due to the special limitation of the earning
power of a single adult who must simultaneously be both wage earner and parent.
In part, however, particularly in the case of
families headed by women, they were
ascribable to age and race. Although only
14 percent of all heads of families were 65
or older, this percentage included 20 percent of all female family heads. Moreover,
while only 9 percent of all family heads
were Negroes, this figure included 22 percent of all female family heads.

Unrelated individuals have still lower
incomes, with medians of $3,544 for men

and only $1,923 for women.[1] Since more
than half of all families have 2 or more
wage earners, it is natural to expect lower
incomes for unrelated individuals. Again,
however, the incomes of women are heavily
influenced by age. Of all women classified
as unrelated individuals, 45 percent were
65 or older.

INCOME AND
THE FAMILY LIFE CYCLE

In one important respect the distribution of
income observed during any given year

[1] The *median* is the income that splits the group
in half. Half of all families receive incomes higher
and half lower than the median income. Medians
are usually preferred to ordinary averages (*means*)
for income comparisons because they are less affected by the presence of a few very high incomes,
and hence are more representative of typical families.

exaggerates the extent of economic inequality. Families in the earliest and latest stages of their life cycles commonly have incomes well below those of families in their middle years. Since the families who happen to be the youngest or oldest during each particular year receive lower incomes than others, the annual data contains a source of inequality that would not be present if incomes were measured over the entire lifetime of all families.

Because they lack the skill and judgment that come with experience, the earning power of young workers is typically low. In addition, some young workers are employed only part time while they complete their education or are employed on temporary jobs before settling down to more permanent occupations. The earning power of young families is further held down by the appearance of children and the withdrawal of wives from paid employment.

As the family matures, earnings rise to levels commensurate with the increasing productivity of the experienced worker and the greater job security brought by seniority. The family income is further augmented by the earnings of the wife, who is increasingly likely to work after her children are old enough for school. Further income supplements occur in some families as the children mature and begin work.

As shown in Figure 1, family earnings reach a peak in the 45–54 age bracket, and then begin to decline. To some extent the decline represents merely the departure of young adult earners as they marry and establish families of their own, but it also represents an increasing incidence of illness and disability among wage earners. Finally, income drops sharply as workers retire.

The Effect of Wives' Incomes

Among families in which both husband and wife are present, variation in the wife's

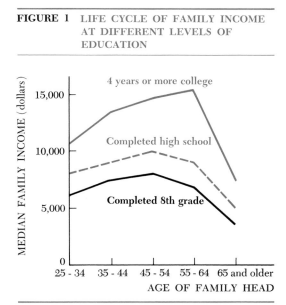

FIGURE 1   LIFE CYCLE OF FAMILY INCOME AT DIFFERENT LEVELS OF EDUCATION

SOURCE: U.S. Bureau of the Census, *Income in 1967 of Families in the United States,* Current Population Reports Series P–60, no. 59, Washington, D.C., 1969.

income contributes to the typical pattern of income over the life cycle of the family. Since many wives in young families are involved with child rearing, a relatively small proportion of them work outside the home. For example, only about a third of wives whose husbands are aged 25 to 34 are in the paid labor force. As the family matures, however, wives increasingly add to the family income, and by the time the husbands reach age 45 to 54 nearly half of all wives are working at paid jobs. From this age on, however, wives' employment again declines; only about a third of wives with husbands aged 55 to 64 work, and only slightly more than a tenth of those whose husbands are 65 or older are job holders.

The Influence of Education

Educational background affects both the level of income and its pattern over the family life cycle. Not only do college graduates start at higher earnings, but their incomes rise more rapidly and continue to rise to a later age, reaching a peak in the 55–64-year range, about 10 years later than others. In contrast, families of high school graduates and those whose heads have only an 8th-grade education start at lower levels, rise more slowly, and begin to decline sooner. These patterns are shown in Figure 1. The steep drop in family incomes of college graduates upon retirement is in keeping with their greater earnings on the job. Despite this sharp decline, median family incomes of older college graduates are only slightly below the income peak reached by typical families of wage earners with 8th-grade education.

Income and Family Size

Age and education combine to produce an interesting relationship between the number of young children and the level of family income. Young families tend to have low earnings and few children, and the number of children and the family's earning power tend to grow simultaneously as the family matures. Among older families, the same process operates in reverse. As children mature and leave home, their numbers decline during the same period that family earnings are falling, until the oldest families are again like the youngest, with no children and low incomes.

As a consequence, families with larger numbers of children tend also to have higher incomes. But this pattern is valid only for families of 3 children or less. Beyond 3, the opposite relationship appears. Parents with lower education not only have lower average incomes, they also tend to have larger families than parents with higher education. Therefore, the average incomes of larger families are found to be lower than those of families with 3 children.

Even among small families, however,

the average income per family member steadily declines as the number of children increases. Among very large families, average income per member declines under the double impact of rising numbers and falling family income.

INCOME AND RACE

Comparison of Incomes of White and Negro Families

All the elements that work to the disadvantage of black Americans culminate in the unequal distribution of income shown in Table 3. Although only 12.5 percent of all U.S. families had incomes below $3,000, this included 28.1 percent of Negro fami-

TABLE 3   FAMILY INCOME BY RACE

	PERCENT OF TOTAL FAMILIES		
		NONWHITE FAMILIES	
TOTAL MONEY INCOME	WHITE FAMILIES	TOTAL	NEGRO FAMILIES
Under $1,000	1.6	4.4	4.7
$1,000–$1,499	1.5	4.5	4.8
$1,500–$1,999	2.3	4.8	5.2
$2,000–$2,499	2.7	7.2	7.6
$2,500–$2,999	2.4	5.5	5.8
$3,000–$3,499	2.8	6.5	6.9
$3,500–$3,999	2.7	5.0	5.0
$4,000–$4,999	5.8	9.9	10.2
$5,000–$5,999	7.1	9.5	10.0
$6,000–$6,999	8.1	8.0	8.0
$7,000–$7,999	8.9	7.1	7.0
$8,000–$8,999	8.6	5.9	5.5
$9,000–$9,999	7.5	4.3	4.0
$10,000–$11,999	12.7	6.7	6.3
$12,000–$14,999	11.7	5.3	4.8
$15,000–$24,999	10.8	4.4	3.7
$25,000–$49,999	2.4	0.8	0.5
$50,000 and over	0.4	0.1	0.2
Total	100.0	100.0	100.0
Median income	$8,471	$5,232	$4,993
Mean income	$9,539	$6,326	$6,025

SOURCE: U.S. Bureau of the Census, *Income in 1967 Families in the United States,* Current Population Reports Series P–60 no. 59, April, 1969.

lies. In fact, although the Negro population made up only 9 percent of the total number of families, it comprised 21 percent of all families with incomes below $3,000. Comparison at the highest income levels shows the same situation. Barely more than 4 percent of all Negro families could claim incomes of $15,000 or more, compared to nearly 13 percent of white families.

The median income of Negro families was only $4,993 compared to $8,471 for whites. On this basis, a middle-income black family had only about 59 percent as much income as a middle-income white family. The graphic comparison of incomes in Figure 2 is even more forceful. Each bar shows the proportion (measured vertically) of families of each race whose incomes fell in each bracket (laid out at the base). The low position of Negro families on the scale is dramatically represented by the high percentages concentrated at the lowest income levels. If, instead of those with median incomes, we accept as typical the families whose incomes correspond to

the greatest percentage concentration, Negro families are found to be even worse off in comparison to whites.[2] Judging by the heights of the bars in Figure 2, the heaviest concentration of Negro family incomes was found in the range from $2,000 to $3,000, compared to the $7,000–$8,000 range for white families. On this basis, incomes of typical Negro families were only about a third as high as those of typical white families.

Changes in the Relative Incomes of Negro Families

Exact information about the incomes of Negro families is unavailable for the years prior to 1964, but data for all nonwhite

[2] The income representing the greatest concentration is called the *mode* of the income distribution. Since the height of the bar represents the percentage concentration of families in each bracket, the mode falls in the income bracket corresponding to the highest bar on the chart.

FIGURE 2   INCOME DISTRIBUTIONS OF NEGRO AND WHITE FAMILIES COMPARED

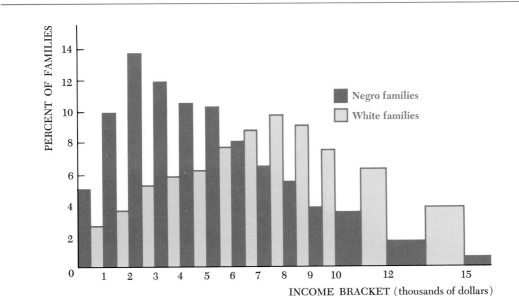

SOURCE: Data from U.S. Bureau of the Census, *Income in 1967 of Families in the United States.*

families can be employed.[3] Although both whites and nonwhites participated in the great growth in income during the past 20 years, incomes of nonwhite families grew slightly faster than those of whites. While in 1947 the level of income of the median nonwhite family was only 51 percent of that for white, the ratio had grown to 62 percent by 1967.

This is slow progress of a kind, but, as Figure 3 demonstrates, the income ratios have exhibited wide fluctuations. Moreover, the entire gain, such as it is, has appeared only since 1964. Growing concern about civil rights and the problem of poverty doubtless contributed to this improvement, but Figure 3 suggests that the level of unemployment has had a much more important effect. The decline in unemployment during the Korean War from 5.9 per-

[3] About 90 percent of nonwhite American families are Negro families. The remainder are American Indians, Chinese, Japanese, East Indians, and other nonwhite families.

cent of the labor force in 1949 to 3 percent and below in 1952–1953 was accompanied by the rise in the median incomes of nonwhite families from 51 percent of the median level of white families to 57 percent. The return of higher unemployment rates was accompanied by a decline in the ratio, which returned to 51 percent as unemployment reached 6.8 percent during the recession of 1958. The ratio was still back at the 1948 figure as late as 1963, but rose to 62 percent with the enlargement of the war in Vietnam and the accompanying decline in unemployment.

Growing out of the insecure employment of the nonwhite worker, this cyclical behavior of the income ratio betrays the same disadvantaged position as does the low general level of income.

CONCENTRATION OF INCOME IN THE UNITED STATES

The Gini Ratio as a Measure of Income Concentration

The overall pattern of income inequality in the United States is represented graphically by the Lorenz curve of Figure 4. It will be recalled that if all families had equal incomes, the Lorenz curve for the distribution would follow the diagonal line *AC*. Concentration of a disproportionate amount of income in the hands of the richest families is represented by the departure of the curve from the diagonal, and the more unequal incomes are, the farther the curve is bowed away from the line. At the extreme limit of inequality where all income would be concentrated in the hands of a single family, the Lorenz curve would follow the right angle *ABC*. The black curve in Figure 4 represents the distribution of 1967 income among all U.S. families.

A useful summary measure of the de-

FIGURE 3   GROWTH IN MEDIAN INCOMES OF WHITE AND NONWHITE FAMILIES, 1947-1967

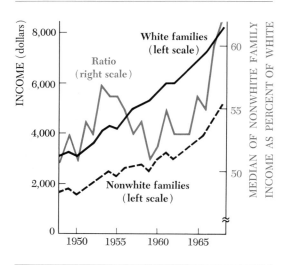

SOURCE: U.S. Bureau of the Census, *Income in 1967 of Families in the United States.*

gree of income concentration is provided by the *Gini ratio of concentration,* which expresses the area of the bow-shaped sector between the Lorenz curve and the diagonal as a percent of the total area of the triangle. The more nearly equal are the incomes of all families, the closer the Lorenz curve lies to the diagonal and the lower the Gini ratio becomes, approaching 0 when all families receive exactly the same income. The more unequal incomes become, the greater the area between the curve and the diagonal, and the larger the Gini ratio. Inspection of Figure 4 suggests that the bow-shaped sector between the black curve and the diagonal occupies about a third of the total area of the triangle. This is confirmed by careful measurement, which reveals a Gini ratio of .35.

Since inequality results partly from income differences among age groups, a Lorenz curve confined to families of a given age should show smaller inequality than one encompassing all ages together. This is borne out by the blue curve of Figure 4, which represents the income distribution among only those families whose heads are aged 45 to 54. Smaller inequality is shown by the smaller bow in the blue curve. The reduced area of the bow-shaped sector corresponds to a Gini ratio of .30, a 14 percent reduction from the .35 calculated for all families together.

Property Ownership and Concentration

Ownership of property is much more highly concentrated than income. Wealth ownership by the small fraction of Americans with estates valued at $60,000 or more is shown in Table 4. Inspection of the table provides some idea of the concentration of property ownership, but exact measurement is difficult. Since some of the estates valued at over $10 million are very large indeed, it is impossible to say what proportion of the total wealth they contain. But

even if the average size of the largest estates is taken to be no more than $15 million, the .05 percent of top wealth-holders would own about 4 percent of the personal wealth shown.

On this basis, the 71,000 families and individuals with estates valued at $1 million or more constituted only 1.7 percent of the number of estates, but owned almost 25 percent of all the wealth. In addition, it should be borne in mind that we are talking here of only the very rich, who include no more than 8 or 10 percent of American families. At the lower end of the scale, 70 percent of U.S. families own less than $10,-000 in financial and income assets, even counting their own homes. This number includes 14 percent at the very bottom with no property at all.

The concentration of wealth is mirrored in the composition of incomes of different sizes. Low incomes consist predominantly of wages, salaries, and other earnings from personal effort. For example, among U.S. personal tax returns with 1966 incomes from $4,000 to $5,000, 87 percent of all income reported consisted of wages and salaries, and most of the rest was business and professional earnings and farm income, while less than 8 percent was property income.[4] In contrast, personal earnings made up less than 10 percent of all income on returns reporting more than $200,000. In this bracket, 24 percent of income came from dividends and 56 percent consisted of capital gains.

Incomes of $200,000 or higher were found on only .08 percent of the 70 million tax returns filed, but this small fraction accounted for 23 percent of all dividends and 37 percent of all capital gains reported. The 644 taxable returns reporting adjusted gross incomes of $1 million or more constituted only .0008 percent (eight ten-thou-

[4] These and the following figures were calculated from data in U.S. Internal Revenue Service, *Statistics of Income, 1966: Individual Income Tax Returns,* Washington, D.C., 1968.

sandths of 1 percent) of all returns, but reported 3.6 percent of all dividends and 7 percent of all capital gains.

The Lorenz curves of Figure 5 indicate the great concentration of property income in the form of dividends and realized capital gains compared to wages and salaries. Gini ratios estimated from the data show concentrations of .75 for dividends and .80 for realized capital gains compared to .40 for reported wages and salaries.[5]

Dynamics of Property Income The immense concentration of property and property income is partly due to the dynamics of earning power. Today's family income depends on the health and education of the wage earners and on the ownership of personal wealth, but families whose incomes are high enough to permit saving can accumulate property. As the family matures, its growing wealth adds further to income and permits even faster accumulation. The result of this reinforcement can be seen when property incomes are compared among families of different ages as in the upper panel of Figure 6. The oldest families receive about 50 times as much income from property as the youngest. Moreover, property income is not only lower among young families, but grows more slowly, in keeping with the low earning power and greater consumption needs of young people. The growth of property ownership—corresponding to the steepness with which property income rises with age—is most rapid during the middle years of peak earnings and then slows again as earning power declines and as retired people cease to accumulate and begin to spend their assets.

The dynamics of wealth accumulation

[5] Comparison with the Gini ratios calculated earlier reveals that wage and salary receipts are somewhat more concentrated than personal income as a whole. This is largely because personal income includes social security, unemployment benefits, welfare, and other transfers, most of which go to low-income families without labor income.

do not terminate with the life of the family, however, for wealth is passed on to children in inherited estates, giving the next generation a head start on the growth of its own income. Some idea of the effect of inherited wealth can be gained by comparing the property incomes of families with the amount of initially inherited wealth, as shown in the lower panel of Figure 6. Property incomes of families that reported no inherited wealth averaged only $551 per year, while those whose inherited estates were initially evaluated at $24,950 or more received an average of $4,224 in property earnings.

The dynamics of income inequality extend beyond property to other forms of inheritance. Higher earning power is also passed on in greater investment in the health and education of children. In addition, the smaller average number of children in better-educated families not only provides more saving from a given income, but permits larger educational investment per child, and leaves fewer children to divide the inherited estate.

To all this must be added the great frequency with which young men and women marry into families with wealth, income, and educational backgrounds similar to their own. This propensity—attested to by common experience and the society pages of any metropolitan newspaper—prevents the equalization of property holdings and perpetuates the inequality of income.

Declining Income Concentration in the U.S.

During the last 40 years, the U.S. personal income distribution has moved in the direction of equality. Although not large, the shift is apparent when a Lorenz curve from a recent year is compared in Figure 7 with one from 1929. The Gini ratio, calculated including unrelated individuals with families to provide comparability with 1929, stood at .40 in 1967 compared to .50 nearly 40 years earlier. A number of important causes contributed to this shift. In part it was a consequence of widening educational opportunity that increased access to higher-paying occupations. It grew partly out of greater mobility that reduced interregional income differences as population migrated to the areas of greatest opportunity. Part of it was certainly the very slow but discernible widening of occupational opportunities to Negro and other nonwhite families.

To a considerable extent, also, the improvement resulted from extensive changes in the system of transfer payments. Where in 1929 and earlier years the man out of a job was virtually an economic nonentity, modern workers eligible for unemployment insurance now receive an average amount that is nearly 40 percent of average weekly earnings on the job. In some industries this amount is further supplemented by special collective-bargaining arrangements with employers. Likewise, before the days of social security, most older workers were left to fend for themselves when they were no longer productive. Today, old-age pensions and disability insurance contribute to the support of over 11 percent of the U.S. population, including retired workers, their wives, husbands, children, and other dependents. Here again, retirement incomes are increasingly supplemented by private pension arrangements provided for in collective—bargaining agreements and other arrangements with employers. Additional transfers to people of low earning power are made in the form of public assistance payments such as aid to the blind, aid to the disabled, aid to families with dependent children, and general assistance. In early 1969 receipts from all government transfer programs combined amounted to over 8 percent of total personal income, and were heavily concentrated at the low end of the income scale.

The final important factor that has worked to reduce the inequality in personal incomes has been taxation. Although personal income is, by definition, measured *before* personal taxes are deducted, its concentration is nevertheless affected by tax laws. Rising tax rates on corporate income leave smaller earnings after taxes and correspondingly smaller dividends. Since stock ownership is concentrated among families in high-income brackets, higher corporate tax rates mean reduced income concentration. The change has been substantial. The corporate income tax rate, which was only 12 percent during World War I, varied between 10 and 13 1/2 percent during the 1920s and stood at 11 percent in 1929.[6] The rate was increased during the 1930s to reach 24 percent in 1940, and since 1951 it has been near 50 percent. The difference the higher rates make can be seen partly in the fact that dividends, which were nearly 60 percent of before-tax corporate profits in 1929, constituted only 25 percent of them in 1968.

Secondly, rising personal income tax rates indirectly affect the distribution of income by reducing the ability of high-income families to save and accumulate property. Except for a brief period during the Civil War, there had been no U.S. income tax until 1913, and most of the high-income families of the 1920s were the beneficiaries of wealth accumulated from tax-free incomes of an earlier period. Although income tax rates were raised during World War I, they declined again during the 1920s, and by 1929 the highest marginal tax rate was 24 percent on all incomes over $100,000. Beginning with the tax legislation of the 1930s, rates were raised substantially. At the peak of wartime tax rates in 1944, the marginal rate on all incomes over

[6] The federal corporate income tax is slightly graduated. For example, the law in effect in 1965 provided a rate of 22 percent on incomes under $25,000 plus 48 percent on all incomes above this amount. Since the first brackets are so low, the rates given here are the marginal rates in the top brackets.

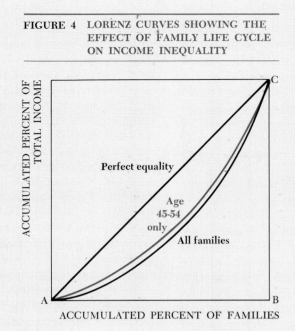

FIGURE 4 LORENZ CURVES SHOWING THE
EFFECT OF FAMILY LIFE CYCLE
ON INCOME INEQUALITY

ACCUMULATED PERCENT OF TOTAL INCOME

Perfect equality

Age
45-54
only

All families

ACCUMULATED PERCENT OF FAMILIES

TABLE 4 DISTRIBUTION OF WEALTH AMONG
TOP U.S. WEALTHHOLDERS

SIZE OF GROSS ESTATE	NUMBER	PERCENT OF TOTAL
$60,000 to $99,999	1,593,000	38.6
$100,000 to $199,999	1,627,000	39.4
$200,000 to $499,999	692,000	16.7
$500,000 to $999,999	149,000	3.6
$1,000,000 to $9,999,999	69,000	1.7
$10,000,000 and over	2,000	a
Total of all estates of $60,000 or more	4,132,000	100

[a] Less than one-half of one percent.

SOURCE: *Statistical Abstract of the United States, 1968.*
Data were estimated by the U.S. Internal Revenue Service from information on tax returns of 1962.

FIGURE 5 LORENZ CURVES COMPARING THE
DISTRIBUTION OF WAGES AND
SALARY INCOMES WITH
DIVIDENDS AND CAPITAL GAINS

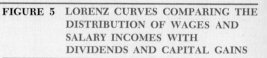

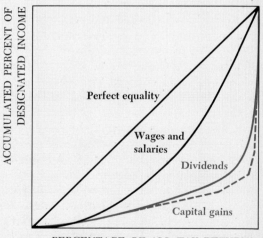

ACCUMULATED PERCENT OF DESIGNATED INCOME

Perfect equality

Wages and
salaries

Dividends

Capital gains

PERCENTAGE OF ALL TAX RETURNS,
ACCUMULATED IN ORDER OF ADJUSTED
GROSS INCOME FROM ALL SOURCES

SOURCE: Data from U.S. Internal Revenue Service,
Statistics of Income, 1966: Individual Tax Returns,
Washington, D.C., 1968.

FIGURE 6   THE DYNAMICS OF PROPERTY INCOME

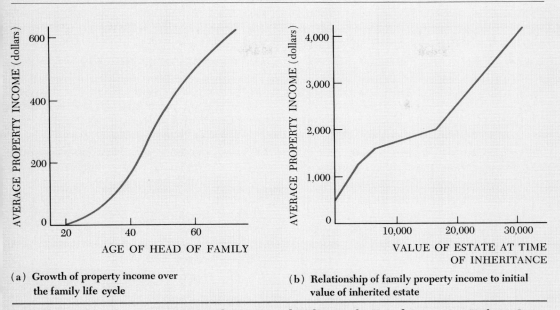

(a) Growth of property income over
the family life cycle

(b) Relationship of family property income to initial
value of inherited estate

SOURCE: Data from James N. Morgan *et al., Income and Welfare in the United States,* New York, McGraw-
Hill Book Company, 1962.

FIGURE 7   LORENZ CURVES OF INCOME
DISTRIBUTION AMONG FAMILIES
AND UNRELATED INDIVIDUALS,
1929 AND 1967

FIGURE 8   LORENZ CURVES SHOWING THE
EFFECT OF THE FEDERAL
INCOME TAX IN REDISTRIBUTION
OF INCOME

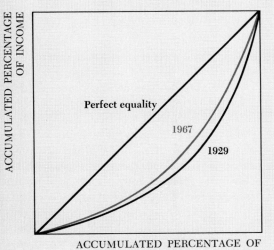

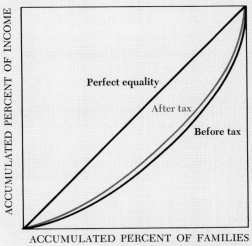

SOURCE: 1929 data from *Historical Statistics of the
United States;* 1967 data from *Incomes in 1967
of Families in the United States.*

SOURCE: Plotted from data given in Joseph A. Pechman and Benjamin A. Okner, "Applications of the
Carter Commission Proposals to the United States:
A Simulation Study," *National Tax Journal,* March,
1969.

$200,000 was set at 94 percent, although with the limitation that the total tax should take no more than 90 percent of the total income of any taxpayer. Although these were wartime rates, they have changed little for 20 years. As this is written, the highest marginal rate is 77 percent for all incomes over $200,000.[7]

These high tax rates make it much more difficult to amass a sizable estate, and it is no accident that the largest fortunes recently accumulated have involved mineral extraction and similar activities given special income-tax treatment.

Finally, inheritance and estate taxes imposed on wealth at the death of the owner have reduced the transmission of property ownership from one generation to the next. Until the federal estate tax was instituted in 1916, wealth could be passed from parents to children virtually intact. The 1916 law subjected estates to a graduated tax schedule with a maximum marginal rate of 10 percent, imposed on the amount by which the value of any estate exceeded $5 million. Much higher rates have been legislated since then, and the 1941 law—still in effect as this is written—applies a maximum marginal rate of 77 percent, reached when the value of an estate exceeds $10 million.

Taxation and the Redistribution of Income

The analysis of income concentration is incomplete until some allowance has been made for the direct effect of taxation itself. What matters to people is not how much personal income they initially receive, but how much disposable income they have left after their taxes have been paid. If families at all income levels paid the same propor-

[7] It should be recalled, however, that people with high incomes have a number of tax loopholes available which enable them to pay rates substantially lower than those indicated. See the discussion in Chapter 12.

tion of their incomes to the government, each would be left with the same share of income after taxes that it had before. A regressive tax system, by taking the largest percentage of income from the lowest-income families, would make the distribution of income more unequal and would be represented by increased bowing of the Lorenz curve away from the line of perfect equality. A progressive tax, on the other hand, takes a smaller percentage from low-income families than from those with high incomes. This reduces the inequality of after-tax incomes and is represented by a reduced bow in the Lorenz curve.

U.S. income distribution before and after taxes have recently been compared by Joseph Pechman and Benjamin Okner, economists at the Brookings Institution, with the result shown in Figure 8. For purposes of this comparison, the researchers first adjusted personal income before taxes to include all corporate earnings, whether paid out in dividends or not, as incomes of shareholder families, and also included such sources of capital income as capital gains and imputed rent on owner-occupied dwellings. The Lorenz curve of the distribution of this pretax income among families and unrelated individuals is shown by the black curve of Figure 8.

The distribution of the corresponding after-tax income is represented by the blue curve. Its slightly flatter bow represents the reduction in inequality to be expected from the progressive tax, but the change is remarkably small. In fact, the change in the Gini ratio involves only about an 8 percent reduction of the area of the bowed sector on the chart. Of course, the total redistribution of income among families depends on the entire system of all taxes combined, rather than on the result from any one tax taken alone, but the federal income tax is the most progressive of the U.S. taxes. Property taxes are much less progressive, while the important payroll taxes, the general sales taxes, and most selective excises are regressive. For this reason, the U.S. tax system taken as a whole is much less progressive than the income tax, and the resulting reduction in income inequality is still smaller than that suggested by Figure 8.

INTERNATIONAL COMPARISON OF INCOME DISTRIBUTION

Despite extremes of affluence and poverty, incomes are actually less highly concentrated in the U.S. than in most other parts of the world. The greatest inequalities in distribution are found in underdeveloped nations rather than in industrialized western societies. The majority of people in underdeveloped nations are extremely poor; a few are extremely rich, but there are few people in the middle. In a recent survey of household incomes in Thailand, for example, it was found that the poorest 50 percent of households received less than 10 percent of total income, while the richest 2.2 percent received a full third! In developed industrial societies, in contrast, a minority are very poor and a few are extremely rich, but the overall concentration of income is lower because of the great majority of modest-income families in between.

These differences are evident when Lorenz curves for different nations are compared in Figure 9. The U.S. income distribution, with a Gini concentration ratio of .35, is represented by the solid black line. The greatest inequality of incomes (Gini concentration ratio of 61) was found in Thailand, the least developed of the 4 economies shown. Ecuador, somewhat more developed, was characterized by less inequality (a Gini ratio of .50). Although most available evidence suggests that income distribution in most European countries differs little from that of the U.S., there is significantly lower concentration in

Sweden, where the Gini ratio is only about .25.[8]

Income data comparable to that of the U.S. are not published by the U.S.S.R. nor by any other Eastern European nation. Tentative figures that can be assembled from fragmentary bits of information suggest that although inequality is probably lower in the Soviet Union than in the U.S., incomes are far from equal. A Lorenz curve fitted to a set of recent income estimates for the U.S.S.R. is plotted in Figure 10. The calculated Gini ratio was only .23, but unfortunately the data cover only the wage and salary incomes of industrial workers. This means not only that bonuses and other elements of high Soviet incomes are missing, but also that collective farmers, with their very low incomes, are entirely unrepresented. The nature of the data necessarily precludes any close comparison with other societies, but it is clear that the U.S.S.R. relies heavily on wage and salary differences to allocate workers among occupations, locations, and industries, just as other economic systems do.

HOW MUCH INEQUALITY SHOULD THERE BE?

If the income distribution in the U.S. shows greater inequality than that of Sweden or the U.S.S.R., it is somewhat less unequal than it has been in the past, and much less unequal than it is today in most other parts of the world. In any case, what of it? How much income inequality is proper for an industrial society? Almost everyone will agree that some inequality is inevitable in a well-run economy. Income differences

[8] On comparison of income inequality between U.S. and European countries, see Robert M. Solow, "Income Inequality Since the War," in Edward C. Budd, ed., *Inequality and Poverty*, New York, W. W. Norton and Company, 1967, pp. 50–64.

FIGURE 9 INTERNATIONAL COMPARISON OF FAMILY INCOME DISTRIBUTIONS

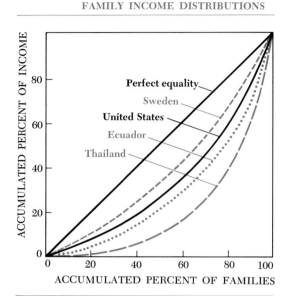

SOURCE: U.S.: U.S. Bureau of the Census, *Income in 1967 of Families in the United States.* Thailand: *Statistical Yearbook of Thailand, 1966.* Ecuador: calculated directly from data from an unpublished survey of household income taken in 1968. Internal evidence suggests that the survey underreports very high incomes, and that the actual distribution is probably more concentrated than that shown. Sweden: adapted from data on distribution of income among individual income receivers given in *Statistical Abstract of Sweden, 1968.*

provide an important incentive to labor and other resources to render their services most effectively, and to enter the industries and occupations that best fit the pattern of demand for their products. Other methods can be used for this purpose—for example, labor can be conscripted—but income differences are so powerful, flexible, and convenient that they are used almost as widely in the U.S.S.R. and other Eastern European countries as they are anywhere else.

Income inequality performs a necessary economic function, but if it is to perform it well, there must be equality of opportunity. People must be able to respond to the chance for greater earnings by changing their jobs, by moving to a new area, or by preparing themselves in school for a profession. If certain individuals or groups are unable to respond to income differences, if they cannot get the better job, if they are kept out of the better-paid occupation, if they are cut off from access to education, or if they are otherwise fenced away from economic opportunity, then income inequality is not only no longer an incentive for constructive behavior, it is a source of bitter frustrations and dangerous social division.

Income inequality in the U.S. is much greater than can be attributed to the economic role of income differences. Moreover, the dynamics of property accumulation act to concentrate incomes and to perpetuate economic inequality from generation to generation. The rich in America do not all

FIGURE 10 LORENZ CURVE OF WAGE AND SALARY INCOMES OF INDUSTRIAL WORKERS IN THE U.S.S.R.

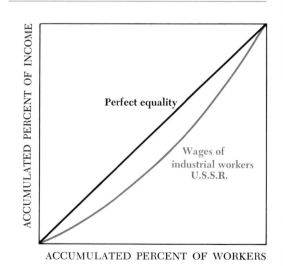

SOURCE: Based on data given in Murray Yanowitch, "The Soviet Income Revolution," in Morris Bornstein and Daniel R. Fusfeld, eds., *The Soviet Economy*, rev. ed., Homewood, Ill., Richard D. Irwin, Inc., 1966. Data include wage and salary income only and exclude all workers on collective farms.

remain rich, nor do the poor all stay poor, but it is much easier for the children of rich parents to remain rich than for those of poor parents to become rich, and it is much more likely that the children of poor parents will remain poor than that those of rich parents will become poor. The most serious manifestation of this grave inequality is the problem of poverty in the midst of plenty, to which we will turn next.

SUMMARY

Most of our knowledge about the distribution of *personal income* derives from Census data, which include only personal money income and exclude capital gains and retained earnings. Since the latter are important sources of high incomes, the resulting figures probably understate the degree of U.S. income concentration.

Although the U.S. median income is the highest in the world, the poorest 2.1 percent of U.S. families receives only one-tenth of 1 percent of total U.S. personal income. The incomes of these families are comparable to those of the poorest families in the world. At the other extreme, the 2.4 richest U.S. families receive 10 percent of U.S. personal income.

Income varies over the *life cycle* of the family, starting low among young families, rising with experience and promotion to a peak in the 45–54 age bracket, and declining thereafter with illness and retirement. Variation in wives' incomes with age reenforces the pattern. Although families with higher education earn higher incomes for a given age, the variation over the life cycle is similar for all. As a special consequence of the life-cycle pattern, family income tends to rise with family size up to 3 children, but because of the correlation between low education and large families, income declines when family size exceeds 3 children.

As a consequence of the *racial differences* in training and occupational opportunities that we have observed throughout our study, Negro families have lower average incomes than white families. Moreover, although there has been steady improvement in the real incomes of families of both races over the last 20 years, there has been little systematic improvement in the relative incomes of nonwhite compared to white families.

Income concentration is graphically depicted by the *Lorenz curve* and is measured by the *Gini coefficient* of concentration, which would be 0 if all families had equal incomes but would be 1 if all income were concentrated in a single family. In the U.S., the Gini ratio is about .35.

A major factor in income concentration is the concentrated ownership of *property*, which is reflected in the Gini ratios of .75 for dividend income and .80 for capital gains. Ownership concentration arises partly from the dynamics of property accumulation by which income from property makes it easier to acquire more property. In addition, rich families can transmit property, together with special educational and social advantages, to their children. The concentration of property is further encouraged by the disposition of rich families to intermarry.

Despite these dynamics, however, there has been a noticeable decline in the concentration of U.S. family incomes during the past 40 years. This decline is partly due to higher taxes and the introduction of social security legislation and partly to increased educational opportunity and to improvement in civil rights.

In the underdeveloped areas of the world, incomes are even more highly concentrated than in the U.S., but in some countries like Sweden, income concentration is significantly lower. Unfortunately, comparable figures are unavailable for the U.S.S.R., but the distribution of Soviet wage income shows the heavy use of wage differences as economic incentives.

Income inequality provides an important *incentive* to guide workers and resources into industries and occupations in which their services are required, but income differences can perform this function only when people can respond to them. Existing inequality in U.S. income distribution exceeds the amount that can be attributed to the economic role of income incentives.

CHAPTER 26

Poverty in America

Even in the richest country in the world, there are people without enough to eat, with inadequate clothes, living crowded together in urban slums or tumbled-down rural shacks. There have always been such people, and even today they constitute the majority of the population in most of the world. Until quite recently poverty had been largely taken for granted. Indeed, some people still think of poverty as a "cause" of human misery. That is, many when asked "why" some people are hungry or live in slums will reply that it is "because" they are poor. Of course, they are begging the question. "Poverty" *means* being hungry, wearing few or ragged clothes, and living in substandard quarters. The question is rather, why are some people so poor? Why are they apparently ignored when the fruits of productive power are passed out?

THE DIMENSIONS OF POVERTY

How Poor Is Poor?

In one sense, almost everybody is "poor." There are few of us, indeed, who cannot think of things we would like to have but cannot afford. It is indicative, for example, that even among families with incomes of $15,000 a year or more, few think of themselves as "rich," although they are among the highest 13 percent of U.S. income receivers. Moreover, while there is a vast difference between being unable to satisfy one's whims and facing the stark inability to get enough to eat or to wear, there is no income level that can be objectively singled out as necessary for the survival of human life. There are, after all, degrees of malnutrition, and even the simple criterion of survival is meaningless unless coupled with such questions as how long, how actively, and in what state of health.

Another difficulty of defining poverty is that the kinds and amounts of goods needed to maintain a given quality of life are not constant over time. In the very early days when the scale of production was small, most people lived in small towns, close enough to walk to work. As society grew larger and the scale of production increased, offices and factories began to draw people from a wide area. Frequent streetcar and bus service made it possible for working people to get to work, but the bus or carfare had to be included as an extra cost in the family budget. At that period of American history an automobile would have been considered a great luxury, but in many U.S. cities today public transportation, if available at all, has become so inconvenient, infrequent, expensive, and slow that a family automobile is a necessity of modern life and must be regarded as part of a minimum survival budget.

A related but more troubling problem is whether the real living standard against which we measure poverty—assuming it can be properly measured—should be uniform over time or should be adjusted to conform with changing views of what is adequate. The living standards of 1800, applied today, would doubtless show that poverty in the U.S. is virtually wiped out. The standards of today, applied to 1800, would probably show that the great majority of the population then living was desperately poor, including many who considered themselves quite comfortably off at the time.

On the other hand, if we allow the definition of poverty to change, we run into the fact that ideas of economic inadequacy are partly influenced by what is actually observed at the low end of the living scale. If poverty is merely the condition of the poorest 10 percent of the population, it can never be eliminated or even reduced, no matter how hard we try.

One widely applied definition of poverty developed for use in the United States by the Social Security Administration is based on a minimum nutritionally sound food plan designed by the U.S. Department of Agriculture for "emergency or temporary use when funds are low." This plan was used to estimate food requirements for each member of the family on the basis of age and sex and these requirements were combined to yield a family total. The cost of the minimum food budget was then multiplied by 3 in line with the observed fact that low-income families must spend a third of their incomes on food. The result was used as a criterion of poverty. Families whose incomes were less than the resulting calculated budget were classified as "poor" or "living below the poverty level."

Poverty criteria for families of different sizes are shown in Table 1, with prices adjusted approximately to the level of early 1969. According to the estimates, an urban family of 4 needed an income of slightly more than $3,500 per year to provide a minimum adequate diet and the accompanying bare necessities. Farm families, with lower food costs, needed only about $2,100.

Although inexact, a definition of poverty based on these minimum standards can hardly be considered generous. At 1969 food prices, the budget allowed an average of $5.35 per person for a week's food. This works out to an average of 27 cents a meal! The cost of a minimum diet for emergency periods defines the minimum a family need spend for food if the housewife knows how to buy, how to get the most for her money, how to prepare it, and how to plan meals to use all leftovers completely. It means not only no impulse buying, but no mistakes, no deception by packaging or advertising, nothing spilled or thrown away. Moreover,

TABLE 1   AVERAGE POVERTY CRITERIA FOR DIFFERENT FAMILIES[a]

| NUMBER OF FAMILY MEMBERS | NONFARM | | FARM | |
	MALE HEAD	FEMALE HEAD	MALE HEAD	FEMALE HEAD
1 (Head under age 65)	$1,860	$1,720	$1,120	$1,040
1 (Head 65 or older)	1,670	1,660	1,010	990
2 (Head under age 65)	2,340	2,230	1,400	1,330
2 (Head 65 or older)	2,100	2,080	1,240	1,260
3	2,760	2,660	1,410	1,580
4	3,540	3,520	2,180	2,100
5	4,160	4,140	2,500	2,500
6	4,660	4,650	2,810	2,860
7 or more	5,760	5,650	3,670	3,480

[a] Figures are dollar incomes required at 1969 prices to furnish estimated minimum requirements to families of indicated types.

SOURCE: Adjusted on the basis of food prices from data for 1964 given in Mollie Orshansky, "Counting the Poor: Another Look at the Poverty Profile," in Louis A. Ferman, Joyce L. Kornbluh, and Alan Haber, eds., *Poverty in America*, Ann Arbor, Mich., The University of Michigan Press, 1968.

there is no extra allowance for meals eaten at school or on the job, which must come out of the minimum food budget regardless of their cost and whether they are purchased or carried.

How Many Americans Are Poor?

Estimates made by the U.S. Department of Commerce in conjunction with the Department of Health, Education and Welfare revealed that the 1968 incomes of more than 10 percent of American households, including a total of nearly 22 million people, failed to exceed the poverty criterion.[1]

Large through the proportion of poor

[1] *Economic Report of the President, 1969.*

Americans is, it is probably lower than ever before in our history. As shown in Figure 1, according to the fixed standard provided by the minimum Social Security Administration budget, the incidence of poverty declined from 30 percent of the population in 1947 to about 12 percent in 1968. This amounted to a decline of 4.3 percent per year in the incidence of poverty, but the rate of decrease varied widely in the population. During the last 7 years of the period, the proportion of Americans living in poverty declined by 30 percent, the decline being 35 percent for whites, but only 25 percent for nonwhites. The proportion of poor among families headed by men declined 38 percent for both races, but the proportion of poor among those headed by women declined only 23 percent for whites and only 15 percent for nonwhites. As a matter of fact, the incidence of poverty among families headed by nonwhite females did not decline fast enough to offset the rising total number of such families: There were actually more poor families of this kind in 1966 than there had been in

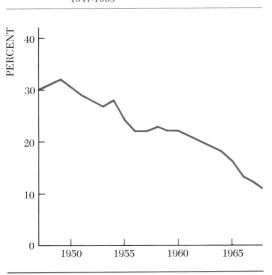

FIGURE 1   POOR PEOPLE AS A PERCENTAGE OF TOTAL U.S. POPULATION, 1947-1968

SOURCE: *Economic Report of the President, 1969.*

1959. Although the proportion of children growing up in poverty declined 31 percent, the decline was only 6 percent for nonwhite children in families headed by women. The incidence of poverty among unrelated individuals declined by 18 percent, but there were more poor unrelated women of both races in 1966 than there had been 7 years earlier.

Who Are the Poor?

In 1968 the U.S. Bureau of the Census published a detailed study of the characteristics of poor American families based on incomes in 1966.[2] The study showed that poverty was not confined to families with any other known set of characteristics but was found among families of all races, in all types and sizes of families, at all ages, at all levels of educational background, and in all broad occupational classes. At the same time, however, larger proportions of poor families were found among those with some characteristics than among those with others.

Table 2 shows the incidence of poverty among U.S. families as revealed by the study. The pattern followed what would be expected from what we already know about family incomes. Families with male heads are largely husband-wife families, and the proportion with incomes below the poverty level was largest for those with only 2 members (consisting disproportionately of the very young and very old) and for large families. Most families with women at the head, however, had only 1 wage earner, and among these the proportion of poor families increased with family size.

About 20 million poor Americans were

[2] U.S. Bureau of the Census, *The Extent of Poverty in the United States, 1959 to 1966,* Current Population Reports Series P–20 no. 54, May, 1968. Most of the following material is drawn from this study.

TABLE 2 PERCENT OF FAMILIES BELOW THE POVERTY LEVEL, BY SIZE OF FAMILY AND SEX AND COLOR OF HEAD, 1966

	MALE HEAD		FEMALE HEAD	
SIZE OF FAMILY	WHITE	NON-WHITE	WHITE	NON-WHITE
2 persons	11.3	21.7	21.2	42.6
3 persons	5.0	18.3	25.2	48.7
4 persons	4.6	19.9	36.6	62.1
5 persons	6.0	26.7	43.9	76.0
6 persons	8.4	34.7	50.9	83.8
7 persons or more	18.3	47.6	62.3	83.9
Total	8.2	27.0	27.7	60.2

SOURCE: U.S. Bureau of the Census, *The Extent of Poverty in the United States 1959 to 1966,* Current Population Reports Series P–60, no. 54, May, 1968.

white; the remaining 10 million poor were nonwhite. Since there are more whites than nonwhites in the United States, it is hardly surprising that they predominate among the poor, but nonwhite people were less of a minority among the poverty-striken than they were in the population at large. While only 1 American out of 12 was nonwhite, 1 out of every 3 poor Americans was nonwhite. The higher incidence of poverty among nonwhite families was partly the result of differences in family size and of the higher proportion headed by women, but even for families headed by men, the incidence of poverty was 2 to 4 times higher among nonwhite families.

Of American children, 12,500,000 under 18 were growing up in families too poor to afford a minimum budget. Here again, white children were only slightly in the majority. Out of every 12 poor children, 5 were nonwhite. In fact, more than half of all nonwhite children were being raised in poor families! This figure included nearly 90 percent of all nonwhite children in families with more than 3 children. Part of the reason for the racial disproportion among poor children is the greater frequency of large families in the nonwhite population, particularly among the poor. Of poor white families, 43 percent were completely child-less, compared to only 20 percent among the nonwhite poor.

When family size, race, and the sex of the family head are considered in combination, the extreme differences in the incidence of poverty are astonishing. The least poverty was found among white families of 4 members with a man at the head. In this group, which contains the stereotype suburban family at whom most television advertising is aimed, less than 1 family in 5 was classed as poor. As almost a mirror image, among nonwhite families with 6 or more members headed by women, less than 1 in 5 was *not* classed as poor.

Why Are They Poor?

In a society in which families without property must depend on the quality of the labor services they can furnish and their ability to market them, the poor are concentrated among those who are unable to work at all, those who can work but who are unable to find or hold jobs, and those who can and do work, but whose earning power is inadequate to support their families. The heads of 39.7 percent of all poor families did not work at all during 1966, and another 27.2 percent worked only part of the year, but 31.9 percent of the heads of all poor families not only could, but did work the entire year at earnings too low to support their families.

Inability To Work   Heads of 14 percent of all U.S. families were unable to work at all during 1966 because of illness, injury, old age, the need to care for other family members, or other reasons. The incidence of poverty found within this group and among its different subgroups is shown in Table 3.

Of families whose heads did not work during 1966, 35.1 percent were classified as poor, compared to an overall incidence of

12.4 percent among all families. Within this group, the incidence of poverty was higher among families headed by females than those headed by males. This was partly because most families headed by men were husband-wife families who still had at least one wage earner other than the husband and partly because some of the men who were not at work were retired persons of some means. (Notice the lower incidence of poverty among families headed by older men, compared to those headed by younger men who did not work.) The incidence of poverty among nonwhite families was uniformly about double that among whites.

Part-Year Employment   Among the 41 million heads of families who worked at some time during 1966, only 80 percent worked the full year. The remaining 7,800,000 did not work a complete year for one reason or another. Heads of two-thirds of these families failed to work a full year because they were ill, injured, retired, or needed at home, or because they stopped work for some other reason. Since these people were either unable or unwilling to work, they were not counted as members of the labor force during the period they were out of work, and hence were never classed as unemployed. The remaining third consisted of the 2,858,000 heads of families who actually experienced unemployment according to the formal definition of the term.

About 20 percent of all families headed by part-year workers were classified as poor, and there was no important difference between those whose partial employment was represented as unemployment and those for whom other factors were responsible. The incidence of poverty among these families, shown in Table 3, follows a pattern similar to that observed when the family head did not work at all. The proportion of poor among families headed by women who worked only part of the year was roughly double that for men

TABLE 3 INCIDENCE OF POVERTY AMONG FAMILIES WITH DIFFERENT CHARACTERISTICS, 1966

	WHITE	NONWHITE	TOTAL
HEAD NOT WORKING DURING 1966			
Male			
24–64	34.1	65.0	38.2
65 or older	26.6	52.5	28.6
Female	37.2	72.1	44.3
Total	30.9	64.8	35.1
HEAD WORKING PART OF 1966			
Male			
25–64	12.6	33.8	15.6
65 or older	18.9	49.3	21.6
Female	35.2	66.9	43.9
Total	19.0	45.0	21.2

SOURCE: U.S. Bureau of the Census, *The Extent of Poverty in the United States, 1959 to 1966,* Current Population Reports Series P–60, no. 54, May, 1968.

of the same race, while the incidence of poverty among nonwhite families was 2.5 to 3 times as high as among whites.

Low-Income Occupation Even among those employed year round, 7.8 percent, or 3 million families, had insufficient income to meet the minimum standard. As shown in Table 4, the incidence of poverty varied widely among occupations. Only 2.4 percent of the families of professional, technical, and kindred workers were poor, and only 4 to 8 percent of nonfarm managers, officials and proprietors, clerical workers, craftsmen, foremen, operatives, and kindred workers. At the same time, almost 20 percent of the families of farmers, domestic servants, and other service workers were poor, and 23 percent of all laborers.

Moreover, within each occupation the difference in incidence between white and nonwhite families is even greater than among those who did not work at all. For

example, of families headed by men, the incidence of poverty among craftsmen, foremen, and kindred workers was 3.6 percent for white families but 17.3 percent for nonwhite families, almost 5 times as high. This is extreme, but in few occupations was the ratio less than 3, and in none at all— even in the most poorly paid occupations with the highest poverty incidence—was the incidence of poverty among nonwhite families less than double that of white families.

Similar results were found for differences in sex, with the incidence of poverty among families headed by females generally 3 or 4 times that among males. The extreme variations in the incidence of poverty resulting from the combination of differences in occupation, race, and sex resulted in a poverty incidence of 2.0 percent of the families of white males in professional and technical work at one extreme, and 59.4 percent among families of nonwhite females in service work at the other.

The Dynamics of Poverty

Since the data employed in the preceding sections were drawn from one particular year, doubtless some of the people classified as poor were only temporarily reduced to straitened circumstances by unusual unemployment, crop failure, or other accident. In fact, since the sole criterion of poverty was income rather than total family resources, perhaps a few people classified as poor were actually rich people with temporary losses, who were living comfortably off bank accounts, the sale of family assets, or borrowed money. Nevertheless, the evidence is that in most cases poverty is a long-term, partly self-reinforcing state.

For example, a careful study of the life histories of each of a large sample of poor families in 1960 revealed few families who could be considered only temporarily poor.

Not only had these families insufficient income to meet their minimum needs in 1960, but in a majority of cases they had *never in their lives* earned an income as high as this minimum.[3]

In many respects, the dynamics of poverty are merely the dynamics of income growth working in reverse. Inadequate education and poor health produce low earning power. Low earnings mean little or no room to maneuver for a better job, no chance to travel in search of a more promising opportunity, no margin on which to take chances. They mean large families of malnourished children, growing up in a world in which they take lack of opportunity and frustration for granted. In need of the best, the children of the poor are often accorded the poorest public education, and leading lives in which ambition is stifled, they are often unable to take advantage of the education that is available.

The transmission of poverty from one generation to the next is evident not only in material facts, but in the attitudes of the poor and in their limited ambition for themselves and their children. The study of poor families cited above indicated that only 31 percent of poor families expect their sons to enter college, compared to 66 percent of all families.[4]

In addition, the study showed that there is more to poverty than these outward symptoms. When the authors attempted to account for the incomes of the poor merely in terms of such factors as race, education, health and physical condition, age, occupation, region and size of city of residence, type of family structure, and a number of other factors affecting earning power, they found that, calculated

purely on the basis of the average earnings of people with similar attributes, heads of poor families would be expected to earn an average of $2,200 per year. Although this figure was already well below the average minimum budget needed for subsistence, it was still more than double the average of only $932 that heads of poor families were actually observed to earn! In other words, poor people are poor not only because of the low earning capacity they have to begin with, but because they cannot effectively employ what capacity they have.

Similar results are obtained when the transmission of education and occupation from one generation to the next is studied. In terms of the education, occupation, income, and social status of their parents, heads of poor families would have been expected to have, on the average, more education and better occupations than they were found to have.

Although these results are hardly surprising, they serve as reminders that poverty is much more than economics and that any program to improve the position of the poor must consider cultural, social, and psychological aspects of their problem.

PUBLIC POLICY TOWARD POVERTY

Public concern with the poor and the problem of poverty is expressed in a wide variety of programs, including some of the most controversial social legislation of recent years. One should distinguish 2 separate types of poverty programs. The first and most traditional are those that provide the poor with direct assistance in one form or another. They are primarily concerned with alleviating the symptoms of poverty rather than with trying to treat the underlying causes. The second and relatively newer type of program consists of efforts

[3] James N. Morgan, Martin H. David, Wilbur J. Cohen, and Harvey E. Brazer, *Income and Welfare in the United States,* New York, McGraw-Hill Book Company, 1962, Chapter 16, "Poverty in the United States."

[4] *Ibid.*

TABLE 4 INCIDENCE OF POVERTY IN U.S. AMONG EMPLOYED FAMILY HEADS, BY MAJOR OCCUPATION GROUP, SEX, AND COLOR, 1966 (numbers in thousands)

SEX AND COLOR OF HEAD OF FAMILY	TOTAL	PROFES- SIONAL, TECHNICAL, AND KINDRED WORKERS	FARMERS AND FARM MANAGERS	
Total	38,885	5,338	1,588	
Below poverty level	3,021	129	315	
Percent of total	7.8	2.4	19.8	
White	35,260	5,082	1,498	
Below poverty level	2,071	112	262	
Percent of total white	5.9	2.2	17.5	
Nonwhite	3,625	256	90	
Below poverty level	950	17	53	
Percent of total nonwhite	26.2	6.6	58.9	
FAMILIES WITH MALE HEAD				
Total	36,292	5,052	1,572	
Below poverty level	2,379	107	309	
Percent of total	6.6	2.1	19.7	
White	33,254	4,834	1,485	
Below poverty level	1,712	95	258	
Percent of total white	5.1	2.0	17.4	
Nonwhite	3,038	218	87	
Below poverty level	667	12	51	
Percent of total nonwhite	22.0	5.5	58.6	
FAMILIES WITH FEMALE HEAD				
Total	2,593	286	16	
Below poverty level	642	22	6	
Percent of total	24.8	7.7	a	
White	2,006	248	13	
Below poverty level	359	17	4	
Percent of total white	17.9	6.9	a	
Nonwhite	587	38	3	
Below poverty level	283	5	2	
Percent of total nonwhite	48.2	a	a	

[a] Base less than 75,000.

that are directed mainly toward improvement of education, training, job opportunities, and civil rights, and toward other means to break into the dynamic cycle of poverty and remove its underlying causes. The 2 types are, however, closely connected. Depending on how they are provided, welfare payments can either reinforce the poverty syndrome or provide incentives and reinforcement for self-improvement. If pay and support conditions are attached to training programs, they add to the family incomes of trainees and provide direct support at the same time that they prepare family heads for more productive jobs.

As a third class of poverty programs, one might include such social insurance programs as unemployment insurance, social security, and workmen's compensation,

MANAGERS, OFFICIALS, AND PROPRIE- TORS, EXC. FARM	CLERICAL AND SALES WORKERS	CRAFTS- MEN FOREMEN, AND KINDRED WORKERS	OPERA- TIVES AND KINDRED WORKERS	LABORERS EXC. MINE	SERVICE WORKERS INCL. PRIVATE HOUSE- HOLD
5,759	5,146	8,050	7,696	2,297	3,011
233	225	353	648	533	585
4.0	4.4	4.4	8.4	23.2	19.4
5,622	4,819	7,583	6,739	1,673	2,244
217	189	272	428	290	301
3.9	3.9	3.6	6.4	17.3	13.4
137	327	467	957	624	767
16	36	81	220	243	284
11.7	11.0	17.3	23.0	38.9	37.0
5,641	4,323	8,014	7,230	2,269	2,191
216	125	350	546	515	211
3.8	2.9	4.4	7.6	22.7	9.6
5,513	4,063	7,551	6,369	1,658	1,781
202	103	270	365	280	139
3.7	2.5	3.6	5.7	16.9	7.8
128	260	463	861	611	410
14	22	80	181	235	72
10.9	8.5	17.3	21.0	38.5	17.6
118	823	36	466	28	820
17	100	3	102	18	374
14.4	12.2	a	21.9	a	45.6
109	756	32	370	15	463
15	86	2	63	10	162
13.8	11.4	a	17.0	a	35.0
9	67	4	96	13	357
2	14	1	39	8	212
a	a	a	40.6	a	59.4

SOURCE: U.S. Bureau of the Census, *The Extent of Poverty in the United States, 1959 to 1966,* Current Population Reports Series P–60, no. 54, May, 1968.

which provide money payments to people meeting certain criteria of eligibility. Although not limited to, or specifically directed at the poor, these transfers make an important contribution to the support of poor people and supplement the incomes of many others who would be poor without such aid. An important characteristic of these programs is that those eligible for compensation receive it as a matter of right, without regard to their other resources. There is no "means test"; that is, one need not show that he "needs" a social security pension or an unemployment insurance check in order to draw one. This aspect, particularly as it applies to unemployment insurance, is not always understood. Articles occasionally appear in the press citing instances of unemployment insurance benefits being paid to movie stars or other high-income (but momentarily unemployed) people, as if these were examples of "abuse" of the system. They are not. A covered person draws a benefit check when he is unemployed with as much right as he receives a check from his insurance company for a crumpled fender on his car.

Assistance in Kind

A broad class of programs provides direct support in kind to people who "need" it. These programs involve a "means test," both to determine eligibility for assistance and, usually, to fix the amount of assistance to be provided. Among the programs that provide direct aid in kind are the food programs, by which surplus commodities are distributed to families on relief through state and local agencies. Although the food is furnished free by the federal government (generally from CCC surpluses), the aid is available only at the request of state authorities and in many states is provided only in severely limited amounts. In the food-stamp program the federal government provides stamps to local agencies for sale to needy families in certain cases and for free distribution in others. The stamps are purchased by families at about two-thirds the value they command when exchanged for food at stores.

Aid to Families with Dependent Children

Programs that provide direct money payments are much more important than those that provide services and goods in kind. During recent years between 9 and 10 million Americans received a total of almost $5 billion per year in assistance from such programs, most of which were financed jointly with the federal government and administered by state and local authorities. By far the single largest welfare program provides aid to families with dependent children (AFDC). In 1968 AFDC pay-

ments totaled over $250 million a month, paid to more than 1.5 million families, including more than 4.5 million children. Each state administers its own program under certain general federal regulations, establishes its own scale of payments, and contributes to their financing. The federal government matches the state's contribution on a sliding scale by which the proportion of federal support declines as the average benefit rises. For example, federal funds supply $15 out of the first $18 of monthly aid per recipient, but decline to $7–$9 of the next $14, depending on the per capita income of the state.

The result is a monthly payment scale that, in early 1969, averaged $43 per recipient over the United States, but which varied from $9.50 in Mississippi and $15.45 in Alabama to $48.40 in California, $64.75 in New York, and over $65 in Massachusetts and Connecticut. The average U.S. payment was $2,016 per year for a family of 4 on relief, barely more than half the $3,520 then estimated as the cost of minimum subsistence. Even in the highest-paying states, allowances fell slightly short of subsistence, although with food stamps or other supplementation, a family might survive.

Even at best, however, welfare programs like AFDC subject many poor people to controls and restrictions that detract greatly from the privacy and dignity of their lives. To determine their eligibility, their affairs must be examined, often by suspicious investigators. To receive benefits they must be under the jurisdiction of a social worker who supervises their cooking, child rearing, and housekeeping. Moreover, as originally formulated, federal regulations withheld support from families with 2 parents. The idea was to encourage fathers to work, but fathers who could not find work or whose earnings were inadequate when they did, found that they were of greater economic assistance in deserting their families than in remaining at home. Although this federal regulation is no

longer in effect, the provision is still retained by almost half the states, and is
sometimes enforced by midnight raids in
search of a man in the house.

In addition, the terms on which aid is
provided discourage the family's efforts to
help itself. The mother of a family receiving
aid to dependent children can earn a maximum of $30 per month to supplement her
welfare payments. Beyond this figure, her
welfare check is reduced 67 cents for every
dollar she earns. As far as she is concerned,
this reduction has the effect of cutting her
hourly earnings to a third. Her job may pay
$1.20 an hour, but by the time the cut is
taken out of her welfare check, she is actually working for only 40 cents. Looked at
in another way, since she gets to keep only
one-third of her earnings, the effect of the
law imposes on indigent mothers a marginal income-tax rate of 67 percent, a rate
that the rest of the population does not
reach until their gross adjusted incomes
exceed $140,000 a year!

The disincentive effect of this provision
was modified by federal legislation passed
in 1967 withholding AFDC payments from
any father, mother, or child of working age
who was found able to work or to benefit
from training but who refused to accept a
job or a training opportunity that was
offered. The legislation further provided
for federal grants to establish training programs and day-care units for children of
parents enrolled in such programs. This
aspect of the law is designed to put pressure on poor families to support themselves, but it would hold a greater promise
of success if it were reinforced rather than
opposed by the effective marginal tax rate
built into the payments system itself.

The Negative Income Tax

Neither the high marginal tax rate applied
to welfare recipients, nor the psychology of
poverty and despair sometimes engendered
by the indignities of their dependent position are calculated to stimulate poor families' efforts to improve their status. Indeed,
in some respects it is difficult to imagine a
program more poorly adapted to this purpose than AFDC, and in recent years a
number of alternatives have been proposed
to avoid its worst features.

The *negative income tax* is a proposal to
supplement or replace welfare assistance
programs by amending the tax law to provide that families with incomes below certain levels automatically become eligible
for direct transfers from the government.
In other words, in such a program, tax
liabilities are to diminish as income declines, but instead of stopping at 0, they are
to become negative when income becomes
sufficiently low, so that families will receive
money from the government as "negative
taxes." One version of this proposal is illustrated in Figure 2. As shown at the far
left, families with incomes below a specified "break-even" amount—set as $4,000 in
the figure—receive an annual payment
equal to half the difference between their
income and the break-even level. This arrangement would set a floor to family income, for if a family had no other source of
funds, they would receive $2,000—half the
difference between 0 and $4,000. At the
same time, the family could always improve its economic position by working for
additional income, since it would always
keep some of its extra earnings. A family
with an income of $1,000 would be eligible
for a transfer of $1,500, bringing its total
disposable income to $2,500. A family that
earned $2,000 would end up with $3,000,
and so on. Families with incomes above the
break-even level would pay "positive"
taxes, as shown by the black portion of the
tax line.

The net amount of income redistribution resulting from a negative income tax of
this sort depends on the break-even point
and on how the negative tax rates are set.
Presumably the break-even level would
vary with family size and composition. The
schedule depicted in the figure might cor-

FIGURE 2   EXAMPLE OF A NEGATIVE INCOME TAX

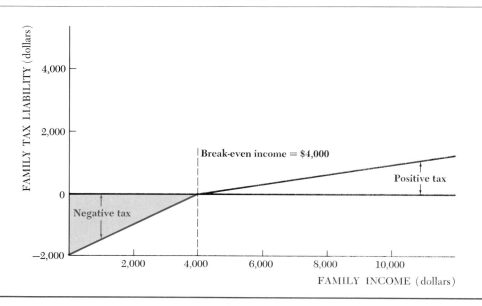

respond to the tax liability of a family of 4 with the break-even level of $1,000 per family member. Rough calculations based on 1968 family incomes indicate that a negative income tax of this sort would have required the transfer of about $25 billion to the poorest families in that year. This was the amount spent that year for the war in Vietnam. A break-even level of $3,000 for a family of 4 would have cost roughly $6 billion—only a little more than the U.S. spent on space exploration.

The proposed negative income tax would represent a substantial improvement over the existing welfare system as it affects the dignity and integrity of the recipient. There would be no special means test other than that universally applied in the community by income tax laws, and the tax returns of the poor would be subject to audit on the same terms as those of the rich. Moreover, the recipients of payments under the negative tax provisions would no longer be second-class members of society.

At the same time, however, the structure of the negative tax plan outlined sub-

jects the poor to an effective marginal tax rate of 50 percent. For example, under the negative tax, a wage earner making $2,000 in wages would have disposable income of $3,000, but if he worked harder, or if his wife went to work to earn an additional $1,000, the family disposable income would rise by only $500 to $3,500. Half of the increase would be removed by the tax law, a percentage that is not reached by a family of 4 on the present "positive" tax scale until their income exceeds $50,000 a year.

The negative income tax proposal also poses certain administrative difficulties. Income taxes are ordinarily filed annually, yet poor people need receipts at least monthly. The obstacle is not insuperable, but arrangements for monthly receipts might involve considerable staff and paperwork.

Other Income Maintenance Proposals

Several alternative proposals have been advanced as improvements on the negative income tax idea, the most important of which lower marginal tax rates on poor families by substituting outright cash payments to all families regardless of income in place of the negative income tax rates applicable only to low-income families. The most far-reaching proposal of this sort, called the "credit income tax," would provide flat-sum, tax-exempt payments to every man, woman, and child in the country, coupled with a proportional general income tax on all other income, with no exceptions.[5] This plan would guarantee each family a minimum income equal to its total credits but would subject all families to the same marginal tax rate, regardless of income. The constant marginal tax rate is not an essential element in the plan, and a graduated tax with very low initial marginal rates could be applied instead.

The *children's allowance* proposal is a modification of the credit income tax in which exemptions for children are abolished from the income tax and instead each family is provided a direct cash payment or allowance based on the number of children. The scale suggested has been $1,400 for the first child, $900 for the second, $600 for the third, and $400 for the fourth and subsequent children.[6] These allowances would be paid to the family in cash but would be subject to a special income tax at a rate that would depend on the number of children in the family and on the level of income from other sources, reaching a maximum of 95 percent of the allowance for families in upper-income brackets. Except for the removal of exemptions for dependent children, income from other sources would be taxed as at present.

Calculations based on the number of

[5] See Earl R. Rolph, "The Negative Income Tax," *National Tax Association Proceedings,* no. 59, p. 147.

[6] See Harvey E. Brazer, "The Federal Income Tax and the Poor," *California Law Review* no. 54, April, 1969, p. 422. This excellent analysis also includes a careful discussion of the negative income tax and related programs.

families of various sizes indicate that payments of such children's allowances would involve a total outlay of about $68.5 billion per year, of which $7 billion would be offset by the elimination of tax exemptions, $52.1 billion would be recovered by the special tax, and $1.8 billion would be recovered by abolishing AFDC.[7] This would leave a net cost of only $7.6 billion to be financed by higher tax rates or by reduced expenditures in other parts of the budget.

Since the children's allowance plan does not apply to the childless poor, it is an incomplete poverty program, but it does provide an effective substitute for AFDC. Moreover, while expanded in scale, it is similar to programs long in effect in Canada and most industrialized countries other than the United States, and its administrative practicability has been adequately demonstrated. Finally, its proponents argue that since it requires no major modification of the existing income tax, the children's allowance plan avoids entanglement with other important tax-reform issues, enhancing its political feasibility.

Attacking the Causes of Poverty

The second broad class of poverty programs has been directed toward attacking the underlying causes of poverty. Several of these are programs of long standing that are primarily directed toward other objectives, but which make important contributions to preventing or curing poverty. These include public education, training of the physically handicapped, and the enforcement of fair-employment practice laws, open housing, and civil rights in general. The attempt to formulate major programs specifically directed toward reducing poverty began on a large scale only very recently with the recognition of govern-

[7] *Ibid.*

ment responsibility in this area, and the experiment is so new that little more than a brief sketch can be provided.

We can distinguish 3 broad programs or groups of programs: area redevelopment, manpower development and training, and the highly controversial Office of Economic Opportunity (OEO).

1. *Area redevelopment* embodies efforts to improve employment opportunities in areas that have been left behind in the course of economic development. These programs include the Area Redevelopment Act of 1961, the Appalachian Regional Commission, and the Economic Development Administration set up in the U.S. Department of Commerce in 1965. They are intended to extend federal aid, largely in the form of grants to local governments and low-interest loans to private business firms, to projects that will increase employment and incomes in areas with higher unemployment and lower average incomes than the U.S. as a whole. Projects have included extensive highway construction to integrate isolated regions with the rest of the economy and encourage relocation of industry, water and sewer systems, vocational training centers, and long-range loans at low interest rates to firms in depressed areas unable to obtain financing from other sources.

2. *Manpower development and training*, originally established to raise the skill level of experienced adults, now emphasizes training jobless young people and those with little education. State employment offices, which have been broadened from their original function of administering unemployment insurance to undertake a wider manpower role, select the trainees for the program. The training program is administered by state vocational education authorities, but training costs are met entirely by the federal government.

About half of all trainees are trained on the job at roughly 6,000 participating busi-ness firms and are paid for the work they do. Employers are reimbursed by the government for the training costs, and experience has shown that the chances are 9 out of 10 that the trainee will be kept on the job after his training is complete. Although experience with the program is limited, it has been estimated that the government recovers its investment in training several times over in reduced unemployment compensation, lower relief payments, and higher tax collections, while benefit to the worker in higher lifetime earnings may be as high as 5 times the training cost.[8]

3. *The Office of Economic Opportunity* (OEO) was established by the Economic Opportunity Act of 1964 as an agency in the Executive Office of the President. It has general responsibility and serves as the coordinating agency for the government antipoverty program as a whole; in addition, it has a wide variety of programs of its own. Among these is the Job Corps, a program for remedial education and training of young people gathered together in centers roughly akin to those of the Civilian Conservation Corps during the 1930s. The Neighborhood Youth Corps provides part-time jobs to students to permit them to stay in school; summer jobs, especially in urban areas; and full-time jobs for new entrants to the labor force to help them learn work habits. The OEO has also been responsible for Volunteers in Service to America (VISTA), a "domestic peace corps." Headstart was designed to help ready under-privileged preschool children for school experience, while Upward Bound was directed toward helping prepare high school students for college. OEO also helps to set up and carry out community-action programs originated by local groups. These have included health, recreation, and legal

[8] Garth L. Mangum, *Contributions and Costs of Manpower Development and Training*, Institute of Labor and Industrial Relations, Ann Arbor, Mich., The University of Michigan, 1967.

centers, credit unions, day-care centers for children of working mothers, and a wide variety of other projects.

Can We Afford the Cost of Antipoverty Programs?

An analysis of the incomes of the poor indicates that to provide every single American with at least enough income to buy the minimum emergency budget, leaving nobody poor in the sense that we have used the term, would require the annual transfer to the poor of between $6 and $7 billion. While this is a great deal by some standards, it is only slightly larger than the $5.4 billion agricultural program provided in the 1969 federal budget, almost all of which went directly to farmers as income. To use other standards, it is about the magnitude of our peak annual outlay to date on the manned space program, less than a quarter of the annual cost of the Vietnam War, and less than 10 percent of the U.S. military budget.

If we remember, once more, that the true economic cost of a program is not money, but the alternatives that must be foregone, then to ask whether we can afford to end poverty is really to ask whether ending poverty for everybody in the U.S. is worth giving up a space program or its equivalent. The comparison is apt. We do not yet know what real benefits, if any, we can expect from our space program, but the benefits in terms of increased human welfare and reduced social tension that would accompany a substantial reduction in poverty are obvious. At least, the *initial* benefits are obvious. We do not know what heights might be reached if the dynamics of poverty were replaced by the dynamics of income support. In terms of the potential long-run payoff, the reduction of poverty to this extent is not only something we can afford to do, it is something we can ill afford not to do.

SUMMARY

Poverty means having an income inadequate to meet minimum "needs," but it is virtually impossible to arrive at an objective definition of exactly how high such a minimum should be. For most purposes today, poverty is defined as an income inadequate for a *family budget* calculated on the basis of the size and composition of the family to provide a minimum survival diet "for emergency use when funds are low." On this basis, over 10 percent of American households, containing 22 million people, were poor in the year 1968. When the same standard is applied over time, however, a smaller percentage of American families are poor today than ever before.

Although poverty is found among all kinds of families, families with certain characteristics exhibit a greater incidence of poverty than others. Although most poor families are white, the proportion of the poor is much greater among nonwhite families. Poverty is also concentrated among families headed by women and among large families. To consider the extreme incidence of poverty, 4 out of 5 nonwhite families of 6 or more members headed by women are classed as poor.

Poor people are those who are unable to work at all, those who work but are unable to work a full year, and those employed year-round at a low-income occupation. In 1966, nearly a third of all heads of poor families could and did work a full year at earnings too low to support their families on an adequate level. The incidence of poverty among the fully employed was especially high for laborers and service workers, for nonwhite workers, and for female heads of families.

During any given year some families are classed as poor whose incomes are only temporarily low, but poverty is a *permanent state* for most poor families, and one that tends to be transmitted from one generation to the next, much like the dynamics of wealth working in reverse.

Poor laws and regulations governing the poor have had a long history, but widespread serious concern for the eradication of poverty has only recently materialized. There are in general 2 types of anti-poverty laws: those that *alleviate symptoms* by providing poor families with goods or money, and those that attempt to *attack the causes* of poverty. A possible third class contains social insurance laws which are designed for other purposes but which transfer income to poor people. Programs to alleviate the symptoms of poverty include *surplus-food* and *food-stamp programs* and direct money payments for child support through *Aid to Families with Dependent Children*. Although there is an element of federal financing in all these programs, they vary widely from state to state. Many states make only limited use of food programs, while monthly allowances under AFDC vary from $10 to over $65 per person.

Existing antipoverty programs are clearly inadequate. In the U.S. on the average, AFDC allowances cover only half of the minimum emergency budget used as a poverty criterion. In addition, programs often subject the poor to indignities and interfere with incentives to work. Dissatisfaction with existing welfare programs has given rise to a number of proposals for change, including the *negative income tax* and other *income-maintenance schemes*.

The attack on the causes of poverty has included *area redevelopment, manpower development and training programs*, and the establishment of the *Office of Economic Opportunity*. Like other uses of resources, poverty eradication programs have a cost, but in view of their obvious immediate benefits and their probable long-run contribution to society, we cannot afford not to have them.

CHAPTER 27

The Economy as a Control System

An economy is an intricately interconnected system in which each part influences the behavior of all the others in many complex ways. We recognized this fact at the outset of our study when we said that an effective working understanding of any one aspect of the economy demands some familiarity with the functions of the parts to which it is related. It is difficult to have a complete grasp of any piece of the system without some comprehension of all of it. Now that we have completed our study part by part, a fitting way to review and consolidate what has gone before is to examine the economic mechanism as a complete system whose function is to control the production process.

In the broadest sense, a *control system* is any mechanism or arrangement for regulating and coordinating interrelated operations to attain some specified end result. Control systems are found all around us and include not only a wide variety of mechanical controls, but systems for the regulation of social and biological processes as well. The temperature, heartbeat, and growth of your body, the flight of an interplanetary vehicle, the metamorphosis of a tadpole into a frog are all processes working under the direction of control systems.

CONTROL SYSTEMS

*The Electric Refrigerator
as a Control System: an Example*

Abstracting from differences in goals and in organic or institutional arrangements, all control systems have certain basic elements in common that can be most easily seen in terms of a relatively simple mechanism like a household refrigerator. The essential parts of a refrigerator are represented in Figure 1. At the right is the insulated food chest to be maintained at a specified temperature. This is the task the refrigerator is supposed to accomplish, the job to be done. In general terms, maintaining the temperature in the chest at the proper level is the *target* of the system. In the nature of things, every control system must have a target, although in the case of highly complex operations, the target may be a correspondingly complex set of objectives.

In any case, the problem is not merely to achieve the desired target, but to do so under varying conditions. In the case of the refrigerator, the proper temperature is to be maintained in the box despite varying outside temperatures, differences in the temperatures of food put in the chest, and changes in the frequency with which the door is opened by the housewife. These conditions form the *load* on the system, and the system must be designed to respond to changes in load in a way that will keep it on target.

To respond to changes in the load, a control system needs 2 additional elements. One of these is an *actor* or "doer," an instrument or arrangement that can act to change the operation of the system. In the refrigerator, the actor consists of a pumping mechanism that circulates a refrigerant through cooling coils inside the chest and removes the heat to be dumped outside. The other component of the system is a sensing device that can *monitor* or keep track of the system and *feed back* informa-

tion to tell the actor what to do in order to stay on target. In the refrigerator this function is performed by a thermostat inside the chest which monitors the temperature and compares it with the target. When the temperature in the box is too high, the thermostat feeds back instructions to turn on the pump and cool the box down. As the pump works, the temperature in the box falls and, when the desired level has been reached, the information is fed back and the pump turns off.

Automatic and Administrative Controls

Although control systems differ widely in complexity, all must have at least 1 actor and 1 feedback device. A highly complex system with an elaborate target to be achieved will have many interconnected actors and feedback arrangements to perform a number of tasks simultaneously. The human body is such a highly complex system, with actors in the form of muscles, glands, and organs, and an extremely complex monitoring system feeding back information over a large number of channels. Many of these controls, like those that maintain blood pressure, operate involuntarily without our being consciously aware of them, but other parts of the body are voluntarily controlled. When you set out to accomplish a specific task, you can observe your own feedback mechanisms at work. When you put away a book, for example, your hand and arm muscles are partly guided by the eye that keeps them aimed at the book as you reach out and keeps them informed about how much farther you still have to reach. Feedback from the eye is coordinated with information on muscle tension picked up inside the muscles and with information about touch. When the feedback indicates that the hand is the proper distance from the book, instructions are issued to actor muscles to close the hand hard enough to hold the

FIGURE 1   HOUSEHOLD REFRIGERATOR AS A CONTROL SYSTEM

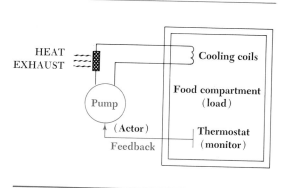

book and to lift. The grasp on the book is monitored by touch and muscle tension, while the lifting is partly monitored by eye to determine when the book reaches the proper level and orientation to slide onto the bookshelf in the desired position.

It requires all parts functioning together to maintain the system on target, but the monitoring and feedback system is the key to control, for a system that has no feedback cannot stay on target under varying load conditions. It is useful to distinguish 2 different types of feedback devices according to whether they are an integral part of the mechanism and operate within it automatically and "involuntarily," so to speak, or depend on the voluntary intervention of an outside agency. Literally speaking, of course, the terms "voluntary" and "involuntary" have no meaning when applied to many mechanical or social systems, but they represent an important distinction between controls that operate automatically and those that depend on the intervention of human action as part of the feedback to the actor. The household refrigerator operates without the intervention of the housewife. She may, of course, change the setting of the cold control knob inside the chest, but this action merely redefines the target. Once the target is specified, she does not participate in its achievement. Many other mechanical systems, however, depend on feedback supplied by a human operator whose eyes, ears, and other sense organs monitor the condition of the system and whose hands and feet control the machine. For example, the human driver is the feedback element in an automobile, and if he goes to sleep at the wheel, the car will probably go into a ditch.

In the discussion that follows we will refer to systems whose controls are built in and operate without the intervention of deliberate human control as *automatic* systems, and to those in which the job of providing feedback is left to deliberate outside action as *administrative control* systems. In this sense, a refrigerator is an automatic system, while an automobile is an administrative control system, but many systems like jet aircraft or electric kitchen ovens involve both kinds of controls. The oven, for example, has a thermostat that monitors the temperature and maintains it at the preset level, but the target of the oven is not merely to maintain a fixed temperature, but to roast the turkey. This may require a series of temperatures maintained for specified times ("Bake at 400° for 20 minutes. Reduce the heat to 350° and roast 20 minutes to the pound."). It is the cook who must administer these adjustments. In general, she also monitors the contents of the oven to see how much more cooking is to be done, regulates the controls accordingly, and terminates the operation at the proper time. Such combined systems cause no theoretical difficulty, however, because it will always be clear from the context which of their aspects is under discussion.

Equilibrium of the System

A control system is said to be *in equilibrium* when it is adjusted to its load and the information fed back by the monitor calls for no change in the adjustment. In practice, equilibrium is an ideal state that is rarely attained, and when reached, is usually maintained only briefly. Every slight change in load alters the position of the system and requires action to get back on target. This fact can readily be observed in drivers, who, even on a perfectly straight road, are continually making small adjustments in steering as the car reacts to slight irregularities in the pavement, cross-winds, internal vibrations, or other small factors that move it off target.

Stability of Equilibrium

What happens when a system is disturbed from its equilibrium depends on what corrective action the feedback triggers and how much. A system with a *stable* equilibrium is one in which a disturbance feeds back corrective action that restores the equilibrium. An *unstable* equilibrium is one in which any disturbance feeds back in such a way that the disturbance is reinforced, and the system is pushed even farther from the target. A *neutral* equilibrium is one in which displacement of the system is not fed back to influence the position either way. A neutral system, in other words, has no feedback and is not a control system. It merely tends to stay wherever it happens to be.

As shown in Figure 2, the 3 types of stability can be represented by the positions of a cone or pyramid. When the cone is resting on its base, it is in a position of stable equilibrium. Any temporary force acting to displace the tip of the cone from its vertical position alters the influence of gravity and restores the cone to its position. When the cone is precisely balanced on its tip, it is in unstable equilibrium, for the slightest tremor will send it toppling over. When the cone is laid on its side, however, it is in neutral equilibrium. It tends to stay in place until something moves it, but when it is moved, it stays in its new location; nothing tends to bring it back.

The example of the cone is revealing in 2 other respects. In the first place, it is clear that the same system can have more than one equilibrium position, and that it may be stable in one equilibrium but not in another. Secondly, whether an equilibrium is stable or not depends partly on how big a displacement the system must endure. The cone standing on its base is not stable under all circumstances. It can recover from a small displacement, but if we push it over far enough, it will be unable to recover and will topple onto its side. An equilibrium that is stable for a small displacement but not for a large one is said to be *locally stable* or *stable in the small*. A system that is stable under any displace-

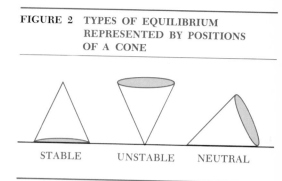

FIGURE 2 TYPES OF EQUILIBRIUM REPRESENTED BY POSITIONS OF A CONE

STABLE   UNSTABLE   NEUTRAL

ment, however large, is said to be *stable in the large*. The cone set on its base is stable in the small, but not in the large. The cone balanced on its tip is not even locally stable, since the slightest displacement sets off feedback that topples it.

Cycles in Adjustment

Control systems also differ in the way they adjust back to equilibrium after being disturbed. Some systems are *cyclical;* that is, adjustment not only carries them back to the equilibrium position, but pushes too far and overshoots in the opposite direction. A cyclical system does not return directly to its equilibrium position, but readjusts in a series of waves or cycles. A stable cyclical system acts like a pendulum that is pushed away from its vertical equilibrium position and swings back and forth, reapproaching the equilibrium only as the swings die out. The recovery path of a cyclical system is represented by the blue curve of Figure 3. When the system is pushed below its equilibrium, the upward pressure carries it beyond the equilibrium. The downward pressure generated by the overshoot carries the system below equilibrium again, and so on.

The *period* of the cycle is the time required for the system to pass through 1 complete oscillation. For example, the period of a pendulum is the number of seconds it takes for the pendulum to swing

FIGURE 3   CYCLICAL AND NONCYCLICAL ADJUSTMENT

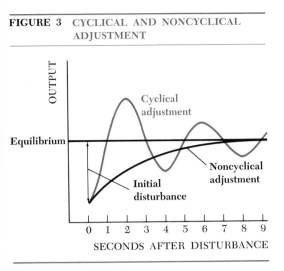

from one extreme to the other and back again. The period of the blue curve in Figure 3 measured from peak to peak is 4 seconds.

A *noncyclical* system is one that readjusts without cycles. A common example of a noncyclical system is a water tank in which the water level is monitored by a float connected to an intake valve. When the water level drops, the float opens the valve. As the water level pushes up the float, however, the valve gradually closes and the flow is shut off as the equilibrium level is reapproached. A noncyclical system does not overshoot equilibrium, but gradually approaches from one direction as shown by the black curve in Figure 3.

CHARACTERISTICS OF ECONOMIC SYSTEMS

Markets as Automatic Control Systems

As seen in Figure 4, commodity markets can be schematically represented as automatic control systems much like household refrigerators. The actor is a collection of firms that delivers a stream of product to the marketplace to satisfy the load imposed by consumer demand. Information about the relationship of deliveries to demand is fed back to the firms in the form of market prices. An increase in demand raises prices. Rising prices, when perceived by producers, induce them to increase output. A reduction in demand lowers prices and the output declines. Realistically, of course, the task of the market system requires monitoring costs as well as prices and involves markets for productive services as well as for products. An illustration of the market as an overall control system is given in Figure 5. The figure shows 2 sets of actors, the business community at the top and consumer households at the bottom. Households deliver productive services to the market on the right, allocating them among uses on the basis of wage rates, rents, and other elements of income. Business firms absorb these services and convert them into products on the basis of their profitability as revealed by comparing costs with prices reported from various product markets. These same product prices, compared with incomes and family needs, provide the basis for purchases by households.

Because competitive market systems perform their functions automatically, it was long thought that the entire economy functioned as an automatic control system and required no substantial intervention by any outside agency. One of the most important economic lessons of the first half of

FIGURE 4   A COMMODITY MARKET AS A CONTROL SYSTEM

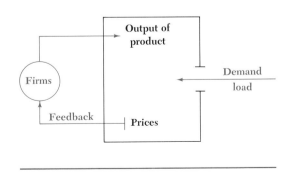

FIGURE 5   MARKET CONTROL SYSTEM

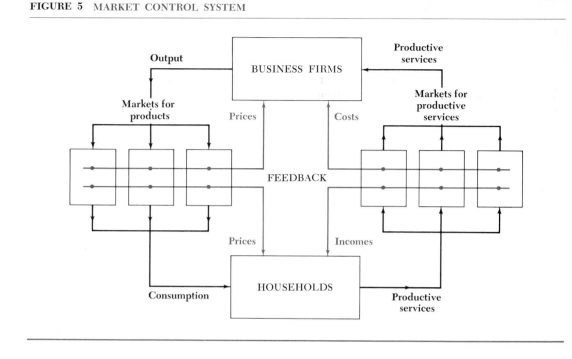

this century, however, was the final realization that despite the delicate and highly automatic control it exercised over allocation, the economic system had no automatic feedback mechanism to control the overall use of productive capacity. On the contrary, the economy was more like an automobile racing down the road with nobody in the driver's seat. In the absence of administrative intervention, it would—and frequently did—go in the ditch. The establishment of the Federal Reserve System in 1914 and the passage of the Employment Act of 1946 represented the acceptance by government of responsibility for monitoring and steering this global aspect of the economy. Through the Federal Reserve Board, the Council of Economic Advisers, the Treasury, the Bureau of the Budget, and other agencies, information about unemployment, inflation, economic growth, and capacity utilization is fed back to alter government budgets, tax rates, bank reserves, and other economic controls.

Stability of Economic Equilibrium

Most familiar examples of economic equilibrium are stable. For example, the allocation of commodities among different demands is a stable equilibrium. As the system drifts away from equilibrium, too little goes to one market and too much to another. Fed back to sellers as price differences, the disturbance leads them to reallocate their use of labor and other resources.

Some markets are only locally stable, a good example being the speculative market for foreign exchange studied in Chapter 21. It will be recalled that as long as a nation's balance-of-payments deficit is small enough to give speculators confidence that the country can maintain the price of its currency within the required limits of its established par, they will buy the currency when its price is near the lower limit and sell it when its price is near the upper limit, thereby pushing the price back toward the par value. Beyond a certain point, however, a balance-of-payments deficit leads speculators to doubt the nation's ability to support the price of its currency, and encourages them to sell when the currency falls toward the lower support limit. These sales contribute to the crisis, attracting more speculators to follow suit and increasing the probability that the currency will have to be devalued—the equivalent of toppling over.

Although unstable economic systems are relatively rare, they are often important. For example, one of the great problems of maintaining mass public transportation systems in modern cities is the fact that they are unstable systems. The nature of this instability can be seen when we look back over the past 50 years of U.S. history. In the early days, city layout was well adapted to the streetcar and commuter train. People tended to live along lines reaching out from the center of the city, served by frequent public transport. With the advent of the automobile, however, people began to drive to work. This change permitted them to locate away from the old traffic patterns and reduced the demand for public transportation. With fewer passengers, public transportation service was curtailed and its quality deteriorated. This occurrence, of course, further encouraged the shift to the automobile, further reduced the demand for public transportation, and contributed to further deterioration in its quantity and quality. Today, few big cities have adequate public transportation and most are choked with traffic. Access to downtown areas has become increasingly difficult, and many of the downtown functions have migrated to the perimeter of the city where they are more readily accessible by car. This shift leaves the public transportation system with little left to do. The system has toppled.

Economic Growth as an Unstable Equilibrium
Not all instability represents a social

problem, however. Some of the most powerful and useful properties of the economy can be represented in terms of an unstable equilibrium. The overall process of economic growth is represented in this way in Figure 6. Productive capacity, measured in terms of potential GNP, is measured along the horizontal axis, and gross capital formation is measured vertically. The blue line represents the disposition of people to invest in productive equipment. As GNP grows to the right, the curve rises to represent the familiar tendency of nations with greater productive capacity to invest more than those with less. The black line represents the effect of gross investment on productive capacity. As gross investment rises up the vertical axis, the black line moves steadily to the right to indicate that a higher gross investment will maintain a larger total productive capacity.

The intersection of the 2 lines represents the equilibrium. At that point productive capacity (GNP) is just adequate to induce the nation to invest enough of its output to maintain its productive capacity. The equilibrium is unstable, however, for any slight increase to GNP' raises gross investment to I'. Since this level of investment raises capacity, GNP begins to rise, but with each increase in GNP, investment rises further, and the 2 reinforcing actions feed back on each other to generate continued expansion as represented by the zigzag system of arrows. Any disturbance in the opposite direction would cause the system to topple over the other way. Initial reduction of GNP to GNP'' would cut investment, lower GNP again, and cut investment even further. The economy would decline as the arrows show until it could no longer survive.

Product Quality and Instability
The dynamics of product quality under competition are similarly represented in Figure 7. The qualities of products of 2 representative firms are measured on the axes, with

FIGURE 6   ECONOMIC GROWTH AS A SYSTEM WITH AN UNSTABLE EQUILIBRIUM

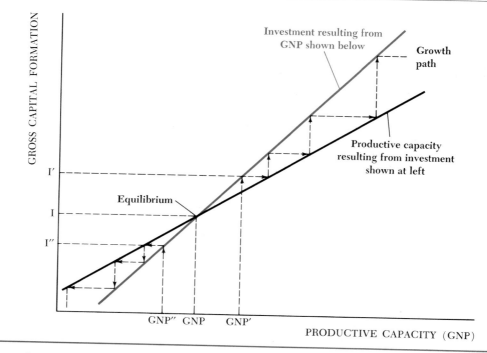

the quality of firm A's product measured horizontally to the right, and that of firm B's product measured vertically. Each point in the plane represents the quality of the products of the respective competitors at a given moment. For example, at point X, the quality of A's product is represented by OA, while B's product has quality OB. The line OK, which makes an angel of 45° with the axis, corresponds to the points that represent equal quality produced by the 2 competitors. A point on this line represents no profit to either producer, for profit accrues only to firms whose products have higher quality than those of competitors. This means that, whatever quality firm A produces, if firm B wants profits, it must produce a product of better quality. That is, it must struggle for a position that would be represented by a point above the 45° line. Likewise, however, firm A's search for profit leads it to try to keep the quality of its product higher than B's, and hence to seek a position represented by a point to the

right of the 45° line. The race between the 2 firms to keep ahead of each other would be represented by a path like the one indicated by the arrows. Each improvement by one competitor must be topped by the

FIGURE 7   THE DYNAMICS OF COMPETITIVE IMPROVEMENT IN PRODUCT QUALITY

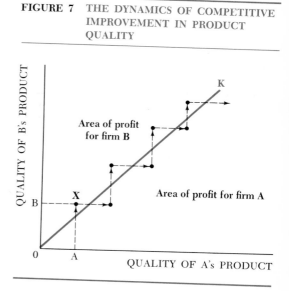

other, and the result is steady improvement in the quality of both products.[1]

Economic Cycles

The American economy contains several cyclical systems, and cycles in economic adjustment are commonplace. There are several causes of cycles, but most are related to lags between the time the system gets out of adjustment and the time that action can be taken to restore equilibrium. As a result of information delay, the actor continues to push the system after the equilibrium has been achieved, causing it to overshoot the mark. Moreover, the longer the lag in the system, the longer the period of the cycle; that is, the longer the time between one peak and the next.

The Potato Cycle Cycles are sometimes observed in markets for seasonal farm products, for, as we saw in Chapter 16, the quantities that farmers produce in the fall depend on their price expectations in the spring. Since the latter are usually based on the prices of the preceding fall, there is a lag of an entire year in the feedback mechanism. The potato market is a well-known example of this kind of cyclical adjustment. When potato production is below equilibrium one season, high prices induce farmers to plant more potatoes the following season. Farmers appear to overrespond to the stimulus, however, and output rises above equilibrium, forcing prices too low. Low prices cause another overreaction in the other direction, and the equilibrium output is approached via a series of diminishing cycles. When the annual potato crop is plotted as in Figure 8, we can see how the continuous displacement of the system by weather and shifting demand results in

[1] Economic systems have no monopoly on unstable equilibrium. If we replace quality of product by military spending, and firms A and B by the U.S. and the U.S.S.R., we have an excellent representation of an arms race.

a series of cycles in which, with only 3 exceptions in the 23 years shown, rising output one year was followed by falling output the next and vice versa. Measured from peak to peak, the period of the potato cycle is 2 years, in keeping with the 1-year lag in price expectations.

The Hog-Corn Cycle A particularly fascinating cyclical adjustment mechanism produces what is called the *hog-corn cycle.* When corn is cheap on the market compared to hogs, it is more valuable when used to feed high-priced pork than it is when sold as low-priced corn. When corn prices are high compared to hogs, corn is worth more sold on the market than when used to produce cheap pork. The relative price of corn is represented by the number of bushels that trade for 100 pounds of hogs at going prices. For example, in 1966 corn averaged $1.23 a bushel at farm-belt farms, while hogs sold for $22.80 per hundred pounds. At these prices it would take $22.80/1.23, or 18.5 bushels of corn to trade for 100 pounds of hogs. In 1964, corn averaged $1.12 a bushel, while hogs were down to $14.80. At these prices it took only $14.80/1.12, or 13.4 bushels of corn to trade

FIGURE 8 CYCLES IN U.S. POTATO PRODUCTION, 1945-1966

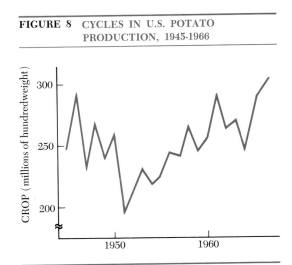

SOURCE: U.S. Department of Agriculture, *Agricultural Statistics, 1967.*

FIGURE 9   THE CORN-HOG CYCLE

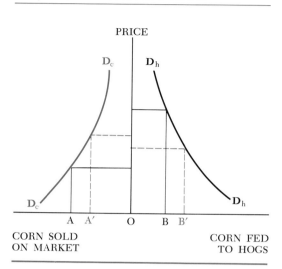

CORN SOLD   CORN FED
ON MARKET   TO HOGS

ratio is charted by the black line, while the blue line represents annual hog production. Notice not only that price and output show pronounced cycles, but that movements in hog production tend to lag behind the hog-corn ratio. The longer lag of the system gives the hog-corn cycle a peak-to-peak period of 4 years. As can be seen in Figure 10, peak hog production occurred in 1951, 1955, 1959, and 1963.

Inventory Cycles   The interaction of the multiplier and accelerator mechanisms is another important source of cyclical adjustment in the economic system. As we noticed in connection with inventory accumulation, a rise in sales induces business firms to step up production not only enough to meet the greater demand, but enough to enable them to build inventory to a level consistent with the higher sales rate. Higher inventory buying, moreover, feeds back through income to push sales and hence production to still higher levels, adding further to the need for inventory and pushing the system above equilibrium. When inventory stocks accumulate to the

for 100 pounds of hogs. A high hog-corn price ratio means that corn is more valuable as hog feed than as marketed corn, while a low ratio means that corn is more valuable when sold on the market than when used for feed and sold later for pork.

In Figure 9, corn sold on the market is measured to the left and corn fed to hogs is measured to the right. The black line represents a situation in which too much corn (*AO*) goes to market and too little (*OB*) into hog feed. This situation, fed back to farmers in the form of a high hog-corn price ratio, leads them to step up hog production. Since it requires time to breed and raise a larger number of pigs, hog production cannot jump immediately in response to the high hog-corn ratio, but takes well over a year to rise. Because of this lag, the system overshoots, as represented by the blue lines. Corn becomes more valuable on the market than as hog feed, and the reverse adjustment begins. By the time hog production reaches its peak, the hog-corn price ratio has already declined and is encouraging farmers to cut back hog production and allocate more corn to the market. The resulting cycle is shown in Figure 10, in which the path of the hog-corn price

FIGURE 10   U.S. CORN-HOG CYCLES, 1946-1966

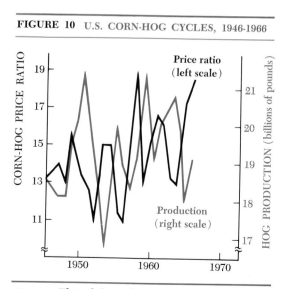

SOURCE: Plotted from data in U.S. Department of Agriculture, *Agricultural Statistics, 1968.*

FIGURE 11 ANNUAL CHANGE IN NONFARM BUSINESS INVENTORIES, 1946-1968

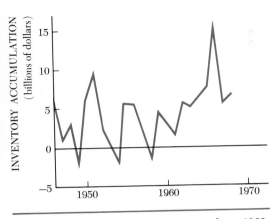

SOURCE: *Economic Report of the President, 1969.*

desired level, however, inventory buying declines. As sales decline under the resulting multiplier impact, firms suddenly discover that they are overstocked, and production rates are cut enough not only to match the lower sales level, but to permit inventory reduction. This process reduces inventory a little too much, and the cycle swings back the other way. The tendency of inventory accumulation to respond cyclically can be clearly seen when data for a long period of years are plotted as in Figure 11. Like the hog-corn cycle, the period of the inventory cycle appears to be about 4 years, with inventory accumulation reaching peak rates in 1951, 1955, 1959, 1962, and 1966.

ECONOMIC CONTROL IN THE U.S. AND U.S.S.R.

In this book, most of our attention has been centered on free enterprise systems like that of the United States, but at a number of points we have examined particular properties of the Communist economic systems of the U.S.S.R. and Eastern Europe.

It is now useful to make some overall comparisons between the 2 systems in terms of their operation as control systems.

Administrative Control

In several respects, the systems are more alike than different. Both use administrative controls at some points and market controls at others. Indeed, at the most general level, both the U.S. and the U.S.S.R. depend on administrative controls exercised by political institutions to maintain a high level of capacity utilization and to apportion the use of capacity among consumer goods, investment, and goods delivered directly to the government. Of course, a political system is, itself, a control mechanism, and the final outcome of the system depends heavily on the amount and type of *political* feedback to the government. In the United States, this feedback occurs in connection with elections, political parties, and other democratic institutions, with the result that an allocation of productive capacity too far out of line with the voters' wishes tends to be corrected by a change in administration. The nature of this political feedback is doubtless one of the important factors behind the heavy allocation of U.S. productive capacity to private goods, particularly consumer goods, rather than to more public goods. In the U.S.S.R. political feedback comes primarily from the Communist Party and its leadership, and only remotely from the people. Partly as a result of this fact, Soviet consumers are accorded a much smaller share of GNP than are those in the U.S., and productive capacity is much more heavily devoted to investment in future economic growth.

Even at the central administrative level, however, the U.S. and Soviet economies differ in the control devices used by their authorities. In both the U.S. and in the U.S.S.R. taxes are employed to restrict consumer buying and interest payments are offered as incentives to save, but in our private enterprise economy, the task of mobilizing the resources thus released is left primarily to private firms whose desire for gain leads them to apportion them to their most profitable uses. In the U.S.S.R. investment resources are assigned directly to each enterprise as they are needed to fulfill the central production plan. A number of criteria of investment "needs" are followed in making this allocation among Soviet enterprises, but profitability is only one among them.

A second important general similarity between the 2 types of economic systems lies in their common use of income differences as the main feedback device for allocating labor. Again, however, there is a difference in the kind of mechanism employed. In the U.S. economy, wage and salary differences largely represent automatic feedback from the market, and a shortage of labor in one industry or occupation automatically raises its wage rates compared to others. In the U.S.S.R., on the other hand, the absence of competitive labor markets requires that wage and salary differentials be set by government action.

Decentralization of Control

We have seen how the search for profit, together with an intricate system of automatic feedback of prices and costs, controls the allocation of productive effort in a free enterprise system among the vast number of products available on the market. In a centrally planned system, in contrast, this detailed allocation is an extension of central administrative control. In the U.S.S.R., for example, enterprises are assigned specific quotas of manpower and resources to employ in fulfilling assigned output targets, and enterprise managers are accorded bonuses based on their success in meeting their planned targets. But no central plan-

ning agency could possibly plan the total output of a large economic system down to the last detail. The most that can be done is to assign broad totals to the individual enterprises, leaving it to their managers to allocate that total among various sizes, qualities, and designs of products. Given no other restriction, the Soviet enterprise manager naturally tends to allocate output in the way that will make it easiest to meet the planned target. If the target established is a total tonnage of output to be turned out, for example, Soviet managers tend to concentrate on turning out those types and sizes that have the greatest weight per unit of labor and input material. When the target is set in terms of number of units, on the other hand, the manager concentrates on those types and sizes that permit him to get the greatest number out of his quota of resources. In neither case does it pay the manager to devote much of his total quota of resources to quality improvement beyond what is already specified in the central plan.

The source of the neglect of profit as part of the planning process was, of course, the Marxian theory of profit as a surplus value with no place in a socialist society. Once an economic system is considered as a control mechanism, however, it becomes clear that profit performs a necessary function as part of the feedback to keep the economy working properly. If this particular type of feedback is abolished, it must be replaced by something else that will accomplish the same end. Under the circumstances, it is not surprising to find that the Soviet attitude toward profit has been undergoing a decided shift, and that profitability is becoming increasingly important as a criterion of management success.

SYSTEMS AND SUBSYSTEMS

A complex system like an economy or a human body contains many interconnected parts, some of which are control systems in their own right. That is, the larger system consists of a network of subsystems, each controlling a particular aspect or operation, all linked together by feedbacks and controls that guide the performance of the whole. The behavior of the larger system depends not only on the characteristics of each of the subsystems of which it is composed, but also on how they are connected with each other. Any attempt to account for or predict the behavior of the complete system without recognizing these interconnections must obviously fail, yet some of the fallacies most frequently encountered in economic reasoning follow from neglect of this fact.

The nature of such errors is easily demonstrated by returning to the example of the household refrigerator. A refrigerator is only one unit in a larger household system that also includes a furnace, hot-water heater, kitchen stove, and other devices to regulate temperatures for special purposes. Considered as a subsystem in the larger household system, the refrigerator can be seen to do more than merely maintain a preset temperature in a food compartment. In particular, the heat extracted from the chest is dumped out in the kitchen and raises the temperature of the room very slightly.

For most purposes the connection between the refrigerator and the temperature of the rest of the room is negligible, at least provided that the unit is located where air can circulate freely around it. But in one instance it becomes of ruling importance. On hot days, poorly informed people have been known to try to cool off the kitchen by leaving the refrigerator door open. When this is done, however, the heat extracted from the chest and dumped out in the room finds its way directly back to the chest again, and the temperature of the room is not lowered. On the contrary, since the refrigerator motor runs all the time, the procedure actually raises the temperature of the room. Before a refrigerator can become

an air-conditioning unit, its connection with the rest of the system must be altered—for example, by putting the heat exhaust outside the house.

An almost exactly analogous mistake in reasoning led people for many years to believe that the proper cure for unemployment was a general reduction in wage rates. The notion was rooted in the observation that when the number of people seeking employment in a given occupation exceeded the number of job openings, a fall in the wage rate increased the number of people who could be hired and simultaneously reduced the attractiveness of the occupation. Under the combined influence of these 2 responses, unemployed labor was eliminated from the occupation.

In addition to restoring equilibrium to the labor market for the particular occupation, however, the declining wage rate also reduced the buying power of the affected workers. As long as we are concerned only with a single market, this income effect is negligible, but when we examine the entire system, it becomes a ruling consideration. A general reduction in wage rates does not eliminate general unemployment because when all wages are reduced together the income effect is no longer negligible. Lower wages mean lower household incomes, lower demand for products, and no more output or employment than before, despite lower prices.

BEYOND THE ECONOMIC SYSTEM

The economy itself is only one subsystem that—along with social, political, moral, religious, ecological, and biological systems—affects human behavior, links man with his environment, and defines his place in the universe. Not only the commercial details of our daily lives, but the quality of life and the very survival of mankind as a species depend on the proper operation of many interconnected systems. What happens in one sphere of life has repercussions everywhere. Imagine the network of profound ramifications resulting from just one initial change, the appearance of the automobile. It has shifted our society from one in which only the very few, very rich kept a carriage to one in which the most universal problem is finding a parking place. The physical appearance of the landscape has been altered not only by cement ribbons of interstate highways and urban expressways, but by oil derricks, refineries, filling stations, drive-in movies, and the rest. The neighborhood that was once a coherent social unit no longer has meaning. Central cities no longer play the roles they once did in economic, social, or cultural life, and the organized downtown district has given way to clutter and urban sprawl. Interpersonal relationships have been radically changed and personal morals have been revolutionized. The air we breathe is polluted by exhaust, beaches are contaminated by oil, the rusting abandoned automobile is an eyesore and a disposal problem, and highway accidents are a common cause of death.

When we add to this list the implications of radio, television, aviation, plastics, chemicals, nuclear energy, drugs, computers, and the thousands of other major changes of recent years, it is immediately apparent that the systems surrounding mankind today differ profoundly from those of even a generation ago. We are all linked together more closely than ever before. Feedbacks are more rapid and work on a wider scale, and the margin of safety has been reduced. Most important, the rapidity of change has greatly outstripped our knowledge of the systems. Our understanding is necessarily rudimentary, partial, and often mistaken. Yet if mankind is to survive, we must learn how these new systems function, what feedback controls are missing, and how they can be supplied by automatic or administrative institutions. We need to recognize environmental pollution, populaton explosion, and arms races for what they are—not intractable laws of nature, but the normal consequences of systems with unstable equilibrium. Left to themselves they can end only in disaster, but they can be controlled.

In this book we have made only a small start on the analysis of one of the important social subsystems. Much that has been covered here should contribute much to the understanding of the practical problems of daily economic life, but beyond this, perhaps the most important thing to learn is to view the economy as part of a larger, overall social control system that requires continual attention and adjustment if we are to survive.

SUMMARY

A *control system* is an arrangement for regulating interrelated operations to attain some specified result or *target* under a varying *load*. The essential parts of the system are an *actor* or "doer" that affects the performance of the system and a *monitor* to keep track of the condition of the system and to *feed back* information to the actor. In a household refrigerator, the target is to maintain the food chest at a specified temperature. The actor consists of the pump and cooling coils, while the thermostat monitors the temperature.

A system may act *automatically*, like a refrigerator, or it may require *administrative control,* like an automobile. Many systems involve a mixture of both types of controls.

A system is *in equilibrium* when it is on target and the monitor calls for no action to change its state. Action is initiated when the system is pushed out of equilibrium by a change in load. If the action tends to restore equilibrium, the system has a *stable* equilibrium, but if the action pushes it even further away from equilibrium, the system has an *unstable* equilibrium. A mechanism that merely remains wherever it happens to be has *neutral* equilibrium and is not a control system.

Some systems are *cyclical;* that is, a push away from equilibrium sets them vibrating or swinging. A *noncyclical* system is one which readjusts along one direction path.

In economic systems, the actors are business firms, consumer households, and similar organizations. Automatic feedback occurs in such forms as prices, costs, and income flows, but important segments of the economy are not automatically governed and require administrative control.

Most individual markets have a stable equilibrium, but many important economic phenomena are characterized by unstable equilibrium. The instability of the public transportation system creates serious economic problems, but economic growth and quality improvement are examples of useful properties of unstable equilibrium.

Cycles in economic adjustment are often the result of *lags* in feedback, and the period of the cycle depends on the length of the lag. The lag between prices and production produces a period of 2 years in the *potato cycle,* and of 4 years in the *hog-corn cycle. Inventory cycles* also have a period of about 4 years.

Economic control in the U.S. and the U.S.S.R. both involve administrative control at the global level. In the U.S., however, prices, profits, and competition decentralize controls, while details of the operation of the Soviet Union are an extension of the centralized control, a fact that interferes with the quality and mix of the Soviet output.

An economic system is a network of *subsystems,* and many lapses of economic reasoning arise out of the failure to recognize the interconnections in the system. The economy in turn is only a subsystem in a larger network of social, political, biological, and other systems that affect man and his environment. These systems are changing rapidly and the survival of mankind depends on our understanding of their operation and our ability to bring them under control.

INDEX

RESERVE

DISCHARGED
DEC 18 1951
DISCHARGED
DEC 2 ... DISCHARGED

DISCHARGED

DISCHARGED